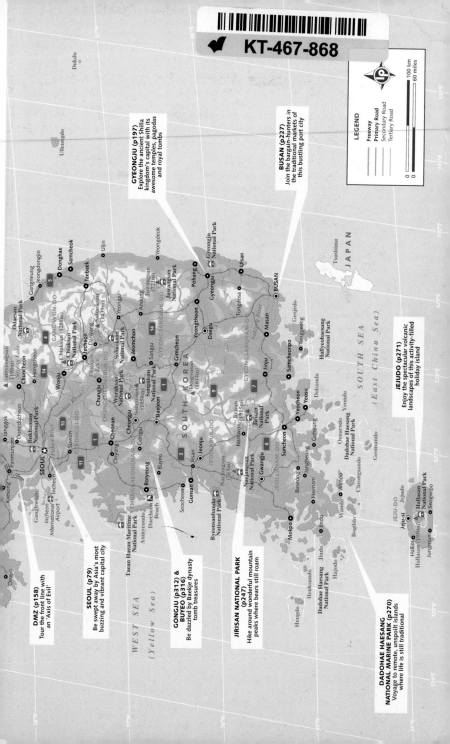

Korea

Asian Tiger, a seriously wired country or the world's most heavily fortified border? All are accurate descriptions of South Korea though none fully captures the essence of this fascinating, complex nation. Social relations may be grounded in ancient Confucianism but South Korea is most decidedly a forward thinking country thanks to its hurry-hurry approach to everything, an insatiable appetite for technological advancement and an indomitable can-do attitude. No one knows where the country is headed, but it's fast-forward all the way. That's what makes South Korea so exiting and at times unnerving; it's a country of endless possibilities with limits imposed only by you.

New York might be the city that never sleeps, but Seoul is the city that never stops. Late night traditional markets, early morning cinemas and 24-hour public baths are all available before and after you've visited the galleries and toured the palaces. There's an infectious energy in Seoul and it's easy to get caught up in the Korean *joie de vivre*, one best experienced with a group over a barbecue dinner and several bottles of *soju* (the local, distilled brew) to bridge cultural gaps, nullify language barriers and build a spirit of conviviality that could last well into the morning, and perhaps a lifetime.

Few international travellers explore the countryside, which is a tragedy and a blessing. Serene temples, picturesque mountains, lush rice paddies, unspoiled fishing villages and endless hiking opportunities are so far off the beaten track, it's unlikely you'll meet any Westerners on the road less travelled. English-language services are rare in the countryside, but that's part of the charm. Come as an explorer, seek out adventure, cut your own trail. Challenge yourself and you may develop an appreciation for South Korea's rich cultural tapestry and a newfound sense of personal freedom, the hallmarks of any truly great journey.

Korea

Martin Robinson
Ray Bartlett, Rob Whyte

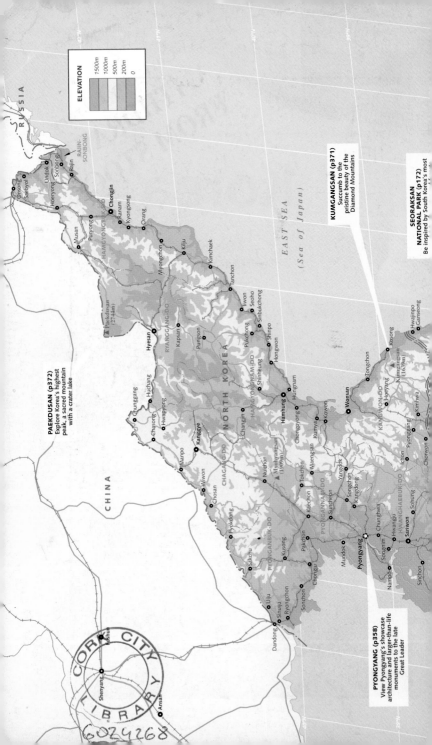

PAEKDUSAN (p372)
Explore Korea's highest peak, a sacred mountain with a crater lake

KUMGANGSAN (p371)
Succumb to the pristine beauty of the Diamond Mountains

SEORAKSAN NATIONAL PARK (p172)
Be inspired by South Korea's most

PYONGYANG (p358)
View Pyongyang's showcase architecture and larger-than-life monuments to the late Great Leader

ELEVATION
1500m
1000m
500m
200m
0

RUSSIA

CHINA

NORTH KOREA

EAST SEA
(Sea of Japan)

Mountains & Temples

JOHN BANAGAN

Admire the Sakyamuni Buddha statue (p203) at Seokguram Grotto

RICHARD I'ANSON

Spend the night at a Buddhist temple (p196) in Haeinsa, Gyeongsangbuk-do

OTHER HIGHLIGHTS

- Scale the rugged rocky peaks of Maisan (Horse Ears Mountain), Maisan Provincial Park (p300)
- Feast your eyes on a 500-year-old camellia forest at Seonunsa (p303), a temple in Seonunsa Provincial Park

JULIET COOMBE

Experience the colour and vibrancy of Buddha's birthday celebrations (p120)

Take a hike in spectacular Wolchulsan National Park (p266), Jeollanam-do

MARTIN MOOS

Sights

Feel the tension in the Demilitarized Zone (DMZ; p158) where soldiers from the North and the South stand only metres apart

OTHER HIGHLIGHTS

- Venture inside a small North Korean submarine (p179) at Unification Park
- Check out the impressive changing of the guard ceremony (p103) at Deoksu-gung, where over 50 guards dress up as Joseon-era soldiers and bandsmen

Soak up the atmosphere of a traditional Korean village (p147)

Explore Seodaemun Prison (p104) for a graphic presentation of Korean history

Savour the serenity of the Secret Garden at Changdeokgung (p101), Seoul

Activities

Join the crowds ice skating (p78) in downtown Seoul

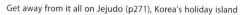

Hire a bicycle and admire the scenery along the Han River cycleway (p114)

Grab a sled at Muju Ski Resort (p301), Deogyusan National Park

Get away from it all on Jejudo (p271), Korea's holiday island

Food & Drink

Indulge in a delicate rice cake at an Insadong eatery (p125)

Get a taste for ginseng at Geumsam (p311), Chungcheongnam-do

Tempt all five senses at the Namdaemun Market (p135), Seoul

OTHER HIGHLIGHTS

- Squeeze yourself into a tiny teashop (p129) in Insadong
- Grill your own food (p63) at a Korean barbecue restaurant

Dine Korean style at one of the many restaurants in Seoul (p124)

Contents

Regional Map Contents

NORTH KOREA
p346

GANG-WON-DO
p162

SEOUL p84
GYEONGGI-DO
p140

CHUNGCHEONGBUK-DO
p324

CHUNGCHEONGNAM-DO
p307

GYEONGSANGBUK-DO
p188

JEOLLABUK-DO
p295

GYEONGSANGNAM-DO
p226

JEOLLANAM-DO
p251

JEJU-DO p273

The Authors

MARTIN ROBINSON
Coordinating Author

This is the second *Korea* guide that Martin has coordinated. He also authored the last two editions of Lonely Planet's *Seoul* guide. Before that Martin lived in South Korea teaching English, working in a provincial governor's office and writing a hiking guide to Jeollabuk-do. Other Asian experiences have included a stint with the British Council in Tokyo and writing travel articles for newspapers. He's married and lives in New Zealand. For this edition, Martin wrote the Getting Started, Itineraries, Environment, Food & Drink, Jeollanam-do, Jeju-do, Jeollabuk-do, Chungcheongnam-do, Chungcheongbuk-do, Directory and Transport chapters, and contributed to Korea Outdoors.

The Coordinating Author's Favourite Trip

Jeju-do (p271) has fantastic volcanic landscapes, tangerine orchards and a laid-back attitude. I hire a scooter in Jeju-si (p275), munch barbecued pheasant for lunch and head east to Manjanggul (p281), the world's largest lava tube. I stay the night in Seongsan-ri with a great view of Ilchulbong (p282), a volcanic crater which I climb up for the sunrise (5.30am) next morning. After that I take a boat trip to Udo Island (p283) for a scoot round its black lava cliffs and white coral-sand beach. I spend the night in Seogwipo (p285) and enjoy a scuba dive, a balloon ride, and an acrobat show at Happy Town the next day. On day four I hike up Hallasan (p292), Korea's highest and prettiest mountain, hoping to spot a cute roe deer.

RAY BARTLETT

Ray Bartlett began travel writing at the age of 18, when he jumped a freight train for 500 miles and sold an article and photos about the journey to a newspaper. More than a decade-and-a-half later, Ray is still wandering the globe with pen and camera in hand. He regularly contributes to *Cape Cod Life* magazine, is a staff author for Lonely Planet specialising in Japan, Korea and Mexico, and his prose and photography has been published in a variety of newspapers, magazines and essay collections including the *Seattle Times, Denver Post, USA Today* and the *Miami Herald*. He lives on Cape Cod, Massachusetts. For this edition Ray wrote the Gyeonggi-do, Gang-won-do and Gyeongsangbuk-do chapters, and contributed to Korea Outdoors.

LONELY PLANET AUTHORS

Why is our travel information the best in the world? It's simple: our authors are independent, dedicated travellers. They don't research using just the internet or phone, and they don't take freebies in exchange for positive coverage. They travel widely, to all the popular spots and off the beaten track. They personally visit thousands of hotels, restaurants, cafés, bars, galleries, palaces, museums and more – and they take pride in getting all the details right, and telling it how it is. For more, see the authors section on www.lonelyplanet.com.

ROB WHYTE

For 11 years Rob has lived in Korea, teaching the past tense to college and university students. A shocking example of someone who never bothered to formulate a life plan, let this be a lesson to anyone with hopes of becoming a teacher in Korea: don't get too comfortable otherwise you may end up staying longer than you ever imagined. A one-time civil servant at Busan City Hall, he and four others were the first foreigners employed by a municipal government in Korea. Rob lives with his family in Busan, where his only regret is the lack of affordable golf. For this edition, Rob wrote the Destination, Snapshot, Culture, Seoul and Gyeongsangnam-do chapters, and contributed to Korea Outdoors.

CONTRIBUTING AUTHORS

North Korea was newly researched for this edition, but we have chosen not to identify our author so as to protect his identity and that of the North Koreans who assisted him on his travels.

Dr Trish Batchelor wrote the Health chapter. She is a general practitioner and travel-medicine specialist who works at the CIWEC Clinic in Kathmandu, Nepal, as well as being a Medical Advisor to the Travel Doctor New Zealand clinics. Trish teaches travel medicine through the University of Otago, and is interested in underwater and high-altitude medicine, and in the impact of tourism on host countries. She has travelled extensively through Southeast and East Asia and particularly loves high-altitude trekking in the Himalayas.

Getting Started

Squashed onto its small patch of hilly peninsula, South Korea is a compact nation, just an hour by plane from north to south, so it's easy to tour around the country's bundle of delights. Hike through green forested mountains and national parks, listen to shaven-headed monks chanting in remote, colourful Buddhist temples, and step ashore onto unspoiled islands populated by bronzed fisher folk who turn into chefs in the evenings. Explore the relics of ancient Korean dynasties, tour round the extraordinary volcanic scenery of its two largest islands, Jejudo and Ulleungdo, and experience the warlike menace of the Demilitarized Zone (DMZ) border with impoverished, dictator-worshipping North Korea.

Discover the country's unique barbecue and seafood cuisine; knock back pine-needle *soju* (Korean vodka) one-shots with new-found friends in convivial bars or on scenic mountainsides; and immerse yourself in boisterous traditional markets or glitzy modern malls. Here, the most wired, busy-busy cities on the planet are straining every sinew to become Asia's IT, cultural, sporting and style leaders, the hub of a global trading empire with a GDP that's already in the world's top 10. Everybody is hard at work, but somehow they find time to befriend foreign visitors and make their visit memorable. Only in Korea do taxi drivers turn down tips, and drivers go out of their way to drop hitchhikers where they want to go.

Transport on planes, buses, trains, subways and taxis is a reasonably priced marvel, while smart new US$35-a-night motels provide clean, facility-filled rooms to stay in all over the country. If no one understands what's coming out of your mouth, simply think back to party charades and use the language of gesture and mime. If you get lost, don't worry as someone is bound to offer to help, especially if you're a solo traveller.

Korea in a word? Dynamic. Korea in two words? Dynamic and conservative. Westerners see this as a (sometimes infuriating) contradiction, but to Koreans its yin and yang, two linked aspects that make up the circle and cycle of life.

WHEN TO GO

Korea has four very distinct seasons, each with its own special characteristics. The best time of year to visit is autumn, from September to November, when skies are blue, the weather is usually sunny and warm and the forested mountainsides are ablaze with astonishing fall colours.

See Climate Charts (p386) for more information.

Spring, from April to June, is another beautiful season, with generally mild temperatures and cherry blossoms spreading north across the country in April. Camellias, azaleas and other plants and trees flower, but as with autumn, some days can be cold, so bring warm clothing.

Winter, from December to March, is dry but often bitterly cold, particularly in northern parts. Siberian winds drag January temperatures in most of the country (except Jejudo) to below zero. This is the time of year when you really appreciate *ondol* (underfloor heating) and *oncheon* (hot-spring spas) as well as the ubiquitous saunas and spicy soups. White snow on *hanok* (traditional house) roofs is very picturesque, and winter is the time for skiers, snowboarders or ice-skaters to visit.

Try to avoid peak summer, from late June to late August, which starts off with the monsoon season, when the country receives some 60% of its annual rainfall, and is followed by unpleasantly hot and humid weather. Although air-conditioning makes summers much more bearable these days, many locals flee the muggy cities for the mountains, beaches and islands, which become crowded, and accommodation prices double. There is also the chance of a typhoon or two.

View www.kma.go.kr for detailed weather forecasts in English.

COSTS & MONEY

Korea is a developed country, but you can get by on a modest budget, although the ever-rising won (appreciating 10% a year against the US dollar) has been making the country more expensive for foreign visitors. Accommodation is always the main travel expense, and comfortable, en suite rooms cost around W30,000 (approximately US$33) in smart new motels or W5000 less in older-style *yeogwan* (motel). Top-end hotels are rare outside major cities, but their rack rates are generally heavily discounted to around W200,000 to W250,000. Midrange hotels are being squeezed by the new high-rise motels, and their normal W150,000 rates are sometimes discounted below W100,000.

Transport, Korean meals, alcohol, saunas and admission prices to sights and national parks are still relatively cheap, so careful-spending duos travelling around Korea can manage on W70,000 a day, while W100,000 a day allows for some luxuries – classier rooms, more taxi rides and *bulgogi* (sliced beef) instead of *samgyeopsal* (sliced fatty pork). The ultra-thrifty could hope to reduce their costs to W50,000 a day by staying in youth-hostel dormitories or rather grotty rooms, taking advantage of hospitable Koreans they meet, and living on a diet of *gimbap* (rice rolled in dried seaweed), *bibimbap* (vegetables, meat and rice) and *ramyeon* (instant noodles). Staying in Seoul is cheaper than touring the country. Splashing out on luxury hotels, top-class meals and duty-free shops ups the budget to W400,000 a day or more.

HOW MUCH?

Local newspaper W700

Food-court lunch W5000

Cinema ticket W7000

Steak dinner W25,000

Motel room W30,000

See also Lonely Planet
Index, inside front cover.

BOOKS & BLOGS

The best-selling *Korea Unmasked* by Rhee Won-bok (2002) takes an illuminating and humorous look at contemporary Korean attitudes in a cartoon format that compares Korea to neighbouring rivals China and Japan.

Korea and Her Neighbours by Isabella Bird (1997) is an insightful account of the intrepid author's travels around Korea in the 1890s.

DON'T LEAVE HOME WITHOUT...

- Studying the food chapter (p62) so you know the difference between *samgyetang* (ginseng chicken soup) and *samgyeopsal*.

- Checking your socks have no holes in them as you must remove your shoes to enter Buddhist shrines, traditional restaurants and private homes.

- Packing your hiking boots, as Korea is stuffed with scenic mountains and well-marked trails.

- Improving your skill at charades and gestures as not many Koreans understand English.

- Learning the 24 *Han·geul* letters (p410) so you can figure out *Han·geul* motel and restaurant names, *Han·geul* menus and *Han·geul* bus destinations.

- Practicing being naked in front of strangers so you can enjoy Korea's many excellent and reasonably priced hot-spring spas (p76).

- Packing a pair of sheets if you're planning to stay in budget accommodation, which often has just quilts.

- Bringing personal hygiene and brand-name medical items that may be difficult to obtain.

TOP TENS

Only in Korea

- Venture inside a **North Korean spy submarine** (p179) near Jeongdongjin on the east coast.
- Peer inside the Korean president's bedroom in **Cheongnamdae** (p327) in Chungcheongbuk-do.
- Hike inside the **world's largest lava tube** (p281) on Jejudo.
- Get up at 3.30am to chant sutras with Buddhist monks on a **temple-stay programme** (p384).
- March along a **North Korean invasion tunnel** under the DMZ (see boxed text, p160) that the North claimed was a coal mine.
- Admire **giant penises** at Haesindang Gong·won (Penis Park; p183) and Totem Pole Park (p316).
- Dive with sharks (and live to tell the tale) in **Busan Aquarium** (p76).
- Sit inside a Buddhist version of paradise in the replica of **King Muryeong's tomb** (p313) in Gongju.
- Squeeze yourself into a goblin-sized t**eashop** (p129) in Insadong, with birds flying around.
- Discover the **Secret Garden** (p101) inside a Seoul palace where kings wrote nature poetry and students sweated over their exam papers.

Cultural Icons

- *banchan* – small side dishes such as *kimchi* that accompany nearly every meal
- ceramics – world class celadon (green-tinged pottery) that was produced during the Goryeo dynasty (918-1392)
- *dancheong* – ornate and multicoloured eaves that adorn Buddhist temples and other buildings
- embroidery – superb craftsmanship is shown in this traditional female art
- *hallyu* – the wave of recent Korean TV dramas, films, fashions and music that has proved popular all over Asia from Mongolia to Malaysia
- *hanbok* – traditional gown-like clothing that is more admired than worn
- *Han·geul* – the Korean writing system that was invented in the 1440s but which took over five centuries to replace Chinese characters
- *hanok* – traditional wooden buildings with a tiled or thatched roof that were grouped around a courtyard and heated with *ondol* (underfloor heating system)
- *samul·nori* – a lively and popular farmer's drum-and-gong dance that is full of colour and rhythm
- taekwondo – Korea's famous martial art with a kick

Natural Wonders

- Hallasan – an extinct 1950m volcano with a crater lake on Jejudo (p292)
- Seongsan Ilchulbong – another spectacular extinct volcanic cone on Jejudo (p282)
- Ullsan Bawi – giant granite cliffs in Seoraksan National Park (p173)
- Gosu Donggul – a huge limestone cave near Danyang (p340)
- Manjanggul – the world's largest lava tube, on Jejudo (p281)
- Maisan – two rocky peaks in Jeollabuk-do that look like a horse's ears (p300)
- Seonyudo – an island jewel off Jeollabuk-do (p305)
- Chungju Lake – Korea's largest and most scenic waterway in Chungcheongbuk-do (p328)
- Ulleungdo – a beautiful, rugged volcanic island in the East Sea with an off-the-beaten-track atmosphere (p212)
- Dokdo – remote, rocky islets in the East Sea that are claimed by Japan (p215)

TOP FORTRESS PICKS

- A World Heritage marvel, **Hwaseong** (p144) was built in the 1790s by King Jeong...... around part of Suwon city for 5.7km.

- South of Seoul, **Namhan Sanseong** (p144) has walls that stretch for nearly 10km and provided a refuge for King Injo in 1636.

- The south coast fortress of **Jinju** (p245) was the scene of carnage when the Japanese attacked it in 1592.

- Near the west coast, **Haemi Fortress** (p322) was where early Catholic converts were imprisoned and executed during the 1860s.

- The walls of the well-preserved, 15th-century **Gochang Fortress** (p304) in Jeollabuk-do are nearly 2km long.

The Koreans by Michael Breen (1999) is an expat but expert analysis of the complex and often baffling Korean psyche.

Palaces of Korea by Kim Dong-uk (2006) covers the unique Confucian palaces in detail with the help of photos and illustrations.

A Walk Through the Land of Miracles by Simon Winchester (1988) describes a classic walk from Jejudo to Seoul that vividly describes encounters with Korean monks, nuns, artists, marriage arrangers and US generals. The highlight is a visit to a barber shop.

To Dream of Pigs by Clive Leatherdale (1994) describes a journalist's jaunt around North and South Korea and the oddball characters he meets.

View http://throughwhiteyseyes.blogspot.com for quirky commentary about life on planet Seoul plus links to other blogs, or go to http://realtravel.com and enter 'South Korea' into 'search' for a bounty of blogs by expat English teachers with time on their hands.

INTERNET RESOURCES

Korean Culture (www.korea.net) A treasure trove of all things Korean, including literature and folk tales.

Korean Films (www.koreanfilm.org) Reviews of the best Korean movies.

Korean History (www.kimsoft.com; www.froginawell.net/korea) Online browsing for history buffs.

Korean Language (www.learnkoreanlanguage.com; www.learnkorean.com) Get the hang of *Han·geul* with some free online help.

Korean Martial Arts (www.koreanmartialarts.com) Covers taekwondo (the one with high kicks and breaking wooden blocks with your bare hand) and *hapkido* (the one that includes a bit of every other martial art).

Korean News (http://times.hankooki.com; www.koreaherald.co.kr; http://english.joins.com) News updated daily, plus classified ads, archive articles and links.

Korean Tourism Organisation (www.tour2korea.com) Tons of useful tourist info.

Living in Korea (www.g4f.go.kr) A new one-stop government website about studying, investing, working and living in Korea.

Lonely Planet (www.lonelyplanet.com) Book Seoul accommodation and read the latest Thorn Tree traveller's tips on Korea.

Itineraries

CLASSIC ROUTES

DISCOVER KOREA   10 days / 750km
This classic route traverses mountains, rice fields and lakes to the sandy beaches and seafood restaurants of the east coast.

Catch a bus or train from Seoul to **Gangchon** (p166) and cycle to the waterfall. Hop on a bus to the lakeside city of **Chuncheon** (p163) and cycle along the lake shore. Head to Soyang Dam, take a boat trip to Yanggu and paddle down an unspoilt river in **Inje** (p167).

Dine on fresh seafood in **Sokcho** (p170) and then hike around the peaks and waterfalls of **Seoraksan National Park** (p172). Next, journey north up the coast to relax on the sandy beach at **Hwajinpo** (p171), home to some historical holiday villas. Head back south to the small seaside resort of **Jeongdongjin** (p179) and venture inside a tiny North Korean spy submarine. At **Samcheok** (p182) explore the huge cave at nearby **Hwanseon Donggul** (p183). South of Samcheok, check out the unforgettable **Haesindang Gong-won** (Penis Park; p183).

Travel back to feudal times at **Hahoe Folk Village** (p220) and don't miss the cultural museums of **Andong** (p217). Then on to the tour highlight – **Gyeongju** (p197), the ancient capital of the Shilla kingdom – for two or more days among the royal tombs and Buddhist treasures.

Board a ferry in Ulsan to rugged, volcanic **Ulleungdo** (p212) for a special off-the-beaten-track experience. Back on the mainland, arrive in **Busan** (p227), a bustling port city with fast ferry connections to Japan.

This route is 750km of shifting countryside, historical sights, succulent seafood and sandy sunrise beaches, with a relaxing hot-spring spa at the end of the road.

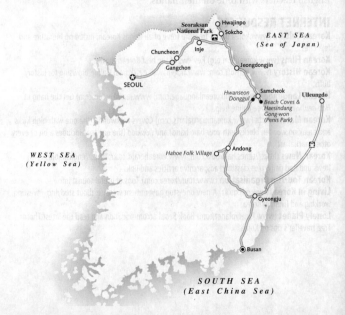

HONEYMOON ISLAND
1 week / 300km

A constant stream of flights and ferries provide speedy and convenient transport to Jeju-si on Jejudo, Korea's holiday and activities island, where palm trees and orange groves add an exotic Mediterranean feel.

The entire island is black volcanic rock which makes for outstanding scenery. Hike up the gentle slopes of **Hallasan** (p292), where gentle roe deer roam; head east from Jeju-si and be awed by the world's longest and largest lava-tube cave, **Manjanggul** (p281), and on the island's eastern tip, climb up 'sunrise peak' **Seongsan Ilchulbong** (p282). Then explore nearby **Udo Island** (p283), which is touristy but still full of rural charms, and one of the places where *haenyeo* (female divers) still gather seafood from the ocean floor.

The island's unique culture and rural past can be experienced at **Seong-eup Folk Village** (p284) and **Jeju Folk Village** (p285) in the south east. Just a generation ago, before the age of tourists and guidebooks, Jejudo was a different place.

In Seogwipo enjoy **waterfalls** (p286), a **submarine tour** (p286) or **scuba diving** (p287) around islands of colourful coral, with fish that look as if they're heading to a fancy-dress party. Honeymooners staying in the luxury southern coast resorts at **Jungmun Beach** (p289) put on identical T-shirts and stroll hand in hand and mouth to mouth under the palm trees at sunset.

Two giant glass buildings near Jungmun Beach are **Yeomiji** (p289), an indoor and outdoor botanical garden, and the **Jeju International Convention Centre** (p289).

On the southwestern coast soak up ancient Zen spirituality in a cave at **Sanbanggulsa** (p290) and take a short hike along the dramatically eroded **Yongmeori Coast** (p290) where the cliffs look like catacombs.

It's impossible to do all the activities and see all the island's gardens, museums, art parks and sights, so pick what appeals most. But don't leave without seeing at least one of the three amazing Chinese acrobat shows at **Green Resort** (p291), **Happy Town** (p291) and **Jeju Magic World** (p291).

Leg it through lava-tube caves, venture up extinct volcanoes, wonder at waterfalls, sup on seafood, scuba at Seogwipo, bask on beaches and be awed by acrobats – you'll soon discover why Jejudo is Korea's favourite holiday island.

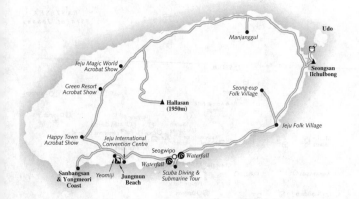

ROADS LESS TRAVELLED

COAST TO COAST   2 weeks / 800km

Journey through glorious mountain scenery, feast on pheasant and unwind on sandy beaches and in hot-spring spas. Along the way visit the presidential summer villa and admire treasures from the Baekje dynasty.

> From the buzzing streets and flashing neon of Seoul to remote fishing villages, from motel castles to mountain fortresses, from lakes to caves and from ancient tomb treasures to a presidential villa: travelling from the sunset coast to the sunrise coast is a great way to experience the variety on offer in Korea.

From Seoul take the subway to **Suwon** (p144), hike around the World Heritage 18th-century fortress, eat the best *galbi* (beef ribs) in the country and lose yourself for hours in the **Korean Folk Village** (p147). Next stop is near Cheonan at the **Independence Hall of Korea** (p322), which charts the history of the epic but unsuccessful Korean struggle against Japanese colonialism before WWII. This is followed by two days of historical sightseeing in the Baekje kingdom's ex-capitals of **Gongju** (p312) and **Buyeo** (p316).

Next, head to **Daecheon Beach** (p319) for the best beach and seafood restaurants on the west coast. Cruise around quiet offshore islands and stay and eat with a fisherman's family on **Sapsido** (p320), before touring pretty **Anmyeondo** (p321) and watching the sunset from **Mallipo Beach** (p322). Travel inland via **Haemi Fortress** (p322) to Daejeon and **Yuseong Hot Springs** (p309).

Buy ginseng products in **Geumsan** (p311) and then stay in a W30,000 (US$30) motel castle in **Cheongju** (p325) and dine on black chicken in a **mountain fortress** (p326). Next day, tour the lakeside presidential villa **Cheongnamdae** (p327) with its own golf course and splendid gardens.

Spot a shy goral antelope in **Woraksan National Park** (p339), rejuvenate tired limbs in **Suanbo Hot Springs** (p338) and feast on pheasant. Take a two-hour scenic ferry trip from Chungju across Chungju Lake to sleepy **Danyang** (p340). From there explore nearby **limestone caves** (p340) and **Gu·insa** (p343), an amazing temple complex. Go bush in remote **Jeongseon** (p184), where you might see an ox-drawn plough. In Taebaeksan Provincial Park visit the mountain-top **Dan·gun altar** (p184), which honours Korea's mythical half-bear founder. Finally dive into the East Sea at a beach near **Samcheok** (p183). See p18 for Samcheok and beyond.

THE GREEN TRAIL
2 weeks / 1200km

The Jeolla provinces have always been the rice bowl of Korea and still retain a semblance of the traditional agrarian lifestyle. The region is famous for its fresh food, traditional crafts like paper making, *pansori* opera, dissident poets, Goryeo-dynasty ceramics and political protest. The south coast is Korea's greenest coastline, where hundreds of rural, relaxing islands and their pristine beaches invite island-hopping jaunts far from the madding crowds.

Jeonju city's fascinating **hanok village** (p297) is crammed with traditional houses and buildings. You must eat Jeonju *bibimbap* (rice topped with egg, meat, vegetables and sauce) and try *moju*, a sweet gingery alcoholic drink. See the rock-pinnacle garden and climb a horse's ear at **Maisan Provincial Park** (p300), then go hiking or skiing in beautiful **Deogyusan National Park** (p301). *Bokbunja* juice (an alcoholic drink made from berries), scenic splendours and an ancient Buddha carved on a cliff await you at **Seonunsan Provincial Park** (p303). Take a ferry from Gunsan to a slice of island paradise called **Seonyudo** (p305) or to rarely visited **Eocheongdo** (p305), which attracts bird enthusiasts.

Further south in Gwangju, visit the **May 18th National Cemetery** (p253), a sombre reminder of the 1980 uprising against the military government of the time. Admire the ceramics in **Gwangju National Museum** (p252), explore more art and craft in **Art Street** (p256), eat in a **duck restaurant** (p256) and don't miss the bamboo town of **Damyang** (p257).

At Mokpo visit the **museums** (p267) before taking a boat to the remote havens of **Heuksando** (p270) and **Hongdo** (p270). Mould your own ceramic pot in **Gangjin Celadon Museum** (p262) and taste food and drinks made from healthy green tea at the beautiful **Boseong Daehan Dawon** (Boseong Tea Plantation; p262). From Yeosu, hike up to **Hyang-iram** (p262), a Buddhist temple perched on a cliff with awesome coastal and island views.

Jinju fortress (p245) has a terrible story to tell, and for a final eco experience don't miss the beautiful hike on the unspoiled **Yeonhwa island** (p243), which is easily reached by ferry from Tong-yeong. Finally, the Green Trail comes to an abrupt end in the bustling port of **Busan** (p227), Korea's second largest city.

Enjoy the green landscapes and healthy food of Korea's least developed region, with hundreds of unspoilt islands, countless seafood restaurants and artistic traditions.

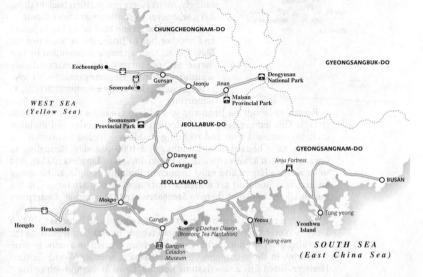

TAILORED TRIPS

KARMA KOREA

Located in beautiful forest-covered mountain areas are some of Asia's most outstanding Buddhist temples, where monks and nuns still live and pursue their dream of enlightenment and freedom from the chains of desire. Their remoteness often makes the pilgrimage by bus difficult and the journey covers around 1500km, but it begins (like all journeys) with a single step. Buses go to all the temples, but often there is a 'mind-washing' walk through the forest before you finally reach the temple buildings. Try to leave the cares of the world behind when you enter the gates of a temple, in order to get the most out of the experience.

Buses from Seoul run to **Gu·insa** (p343), the headquarters of the Cheontae sect and quite different from any other Korean temple, with multistorey modern buildings lining both sides of a steep valley. It has a Utopian atmosphere, and delicious, free vegetarian meals are available. From here take a bus to Danyang and on to Gongju and **Magoksa** (p316), an ancient and traditional temple in a remote spot with a hall of 1000 pint-sized disciples that are all slightly different. Can you find the one that looks most like you?

Journey southeast to Daegu and on to stunning **Haeinsa** (p195), which houses a staggering library of over 80,000 World Heritage 14th-century

NORTH KOREA
○ SEOUL
SOUTH KOREA
🪧 Gu·insa
🪧 Magoksa
Jikjisa 🪧 🪧 Haeinsa
Tapsa 🪧
Seongnamsa 🪧 🪧 Bulguksa
🪧 Tongdosa
🪧 Unjusa

woodblocks. They were carved in an unsuccessful attempt to ward off Mongolian invaders. Back in Daegu, an hour on the bus takes you to Gimcheon, the gateway to **Jikjisa** (p196), a magnificent temple dating back to the 5th century. A soldier monk from here, Sa-myeong, led the fight against Japanese invaders in 1592. Interestingly, monks were not pacifists back in those days, whenever the nation was under threat.

Return to Daegu and then take a bus to Jeonju and another bus to Jinan, the access town for **Tapsa** (p300), a tiny temple surrounded by two 'horse ear' mountains and an extraordinary sculptural garden of 80 stone pinnacles (or towers) that were piled up by a Buddhist mystic, Yi Kapmyong.

Return to Jeonju via Jinan and go south to Gwangju and on to **Unjusa** (p257). This temple has a fine collection of stone pagodas and Buddhas including unusual twin and reclining Buddhas – legend has it that the site originally housed 1000 Buddhas and 1000 pagodas. Returning to Gwangju, catch a bus eastwards to Busan and on to **Tongdosa** (p242), said to be Korea's largest and most important Buddhist temple, and housing an excellent Buddhist art museum containing 30,000 artefacts. Catch a bus to Ulsan and from there to **Seongnamsa** (p242), a visual masterpiece set in a provincial park.

Finally return to Ulsan and press on to Gyeongju and **Bulguksa** (p202), a Unesco World Cultural Heritage–listed temple replica that represents the crowning glory of Shilla architecture and is constructed on a stone terrace.

Nearby, in the mountains above Bulguksa is another World Cultural Heritage–listed site: a superb stone Buddha, hewn in the mid-8th century, that resides in the Seokguram Grotto.

GOURMET GALLOP

Korean cuisine outside Seoul covers such a multitude of flavours and styles that it would take a lifetime to sample everything, but here's a start.

Red-bedecked restaurants in Incheon's **Chinatown** (p152), a subway ride west of Seoul, offer delicious Chinese food including the famous *jajangmyeon,* a Korean/Chinese noodle dish.

Sokcho, a fishing port on the east coast, is noted for squid *sundae* (squid stuffed with all sorts of goodies). Enjoy it in upmarket and green surroundings at the well-known and well-regarded **Jinyang Hoejip** (p170).

In Daegu city, take a break from Korean food at the ultra-romantic **Dijon** (p192) with its high-class euro food, candles and a beautiful rose on every table.

After a hard day touring Shilla relics in Gyeongju, satisfy your appetite with the wholesome fare at **Kuro Ssambap** (p206). Enjoy the folk museum ambience and feast on a banquet of more (refillable) side dishes than even the Joseon monarchs could handle. Wrap side-dish combos in lettuce and other leaves before popping them in your mouth.

Further south in Busan, drop into **Grandmother Lee's Raw Fish House** (p236) near Hae·undae beach for sushi served straight from the tanks outside. The owner speaks English and loves to explain why Koreans adore raw fish.

Head west along the south coast until you reach the beautiful green-tea plantation **Boseong Daehan Dawon** (Boseong Tea Plantation; p262), where you can try shakes, yogurt and ice cream all made with *nokcha* (green tea). Lunch in the restaurant on green-tea flavoured *jajangmyeon* or *bibimbap.*

Then take a bus to Mokpo, where **Igabon·ga** (p269) offers a splendid *tte-okgalbi,* a giant meat patty with seafood, bamboo shoots, salad and side dishes served on leaves and decorated with flower petals.

Head north to the stylish and smart **Bakmulg-wan Apjip** (p257) in Damyang. It specialises in bamboo dishes. Rice topped with nuts and beans are cooked inside a bamboo stem, the *doenjang* (soybean paste) soup is flavoured with bamboo shoots, and bamboo leaf tea is free. Diners can take home their bamboo rice container as a souvenir.

The next stop north is Jeonju in Jeollabuk-do, the birthplace of *bibimbap,* and **Hankookkwan** (p299) is a buzzing restaurant that serves up this classic dish with a bowl of *moju* homebrew. Order *dolsot bibimbap* if you don't want raw meat.

Then head on to Daejeon city, where **Pungnyeon Samgyetang** (p310) is a large, unpretentious restaurant that cooks up an excellent *samgyetang* (ginseng chicken) served with foreigner-friendly lettuce and delicious cucumber side dishes.

From Daejeon take a short, scenic bus ride south to **Geumsan** (p311), known as Ginseng Town, where restaurants and stalls sell *samgyetang, insam twigim* (ginseng in batter) and *insam makgeolli* (ginseng rice wine), and hundreds of shops and stalls sell ginseng tea, liquor, sweets and other ginseng products.

Next up is a detour to Suanbo Hot Springs in Chungcheongbuk-do, where **Satgatchon** (p339) serves up a seven-course pheasant meal that includes pheasant *mandu* (dumplings), mini pheasant kebabs, pheasant steamboat and pheasant soup.

Back in Daejeon, Seoul is less than an hour away on a KTX train.

NORTH KOREA

INTRODUCTION TO DPRK

A standard tour to North Korea lasts roughly a week, but it's amazing the number of sights that can be packed in, with the guides keeping you busy day-in day-out with a seemingly endless stream of revolutionary sights.

On day one, you'll take the short flight from Beijing into another world, landing in **Pyongyang** (p358), where the rigorous pace of North Korean tourism quickly becomes apparent. Spend two full days taking in this unique city with its barrage of monuments, statues, museums and other 'attractions'. From here, head south down the Reunification Highway to the ancient city of **Kaesong** (p368), where you'll be able to visit the country's most atmospheric hotel, the **Kaesong Folk Hotel** (p369), and see what for many is the highlight of their trip: the DMZ at **Panmunjom** (p369). From the tense heart of conflict on the Korean Peninsula, you'll normally be taken to relax in the mountains, North Korean style. Usually this will be in **Myohyangsan** (p370) where, as well as mountain walking along concrete steps embellished with revolutionary slogans, you'll pay a visit to the utterly bizarre **International Friendship Exhibition** (p370), with every gift ever presented to the two Kims displayed in huge vaults built into the side of a mountain. The last day is usually spent in Pyongyang and a visit to the incredible **Mass Games** (p355) between August and October, before boarding the overnight train back to Beijing.

OFF THE BEATEN TRACK

You don't get much more off the beaten track than North Korea itself, but if you're determined to see parts that no one else has seen then there are some options. Of course, you'll still have to be on a tour (or at least with two guides) but you can really get out and see places few others do. While you'll fly or take the train to Pyongyang, there's still a huge amount in the city that isn't usually included on tours: request the zoo, a trip to the shooting gallery, the film studios and the three revolutions exhibit, for example. From Pyongyang, a charter plane can fly you up to **Paekdusan** (Mt Paekdu; p372) for a visit to Korea's holy mountain and the magnificent crater lake Chon, mythically associated with the anti-Japanese struggle and the birth of Kim Jong Il. Returning by plane to Pyongyang, having seen one of the remotest areas of the country, move on to the little visited east coast of the country. Overnight in the major port city of **Wonsan** (p373); from there a trip into the beautiful **Kumgangsan** (p371) is possible. If you really want to go the whole hog, a flying visit (again, by charter plane unless you enter overland from China) to the 'Special Free Trade Zone' of **Rajin-Sonbong** (p375) is about as different as you can get. You're pretty certain not to meet anyone else who has been to this oddest area of an extremely odd country.

Snapshot

Given the country's appetite for change, Korea's evolving outlook on the world is hardly surprising. Increasingly, the American government is perceived as a barrier to a fruitful dialogue with the North. The apex of this sentiment was a fringe-group campaign to raze a statue of General McArthur. The man surely had his faults, but McArthur's legacy includes one significant accomplishment: he saved South Korea's ass. If it weren't for McArthur, South Korea's citizenry could conceivably find themselves bowing to Dear Leader and watching reruns of last year's Mass Games on a black-and-white TV while eating tree-bark soup.

The US is reducing troop strength in Korea by a quarter, or more. Some bases have been closed, like Busan's Camp Hialeah; others will be relocated, such as the Yongsan Garrison near Itaewon. Base closures and relocations are opening up large tracts of land in urban centres, but the future of this real estate is uncertain. Rumours about parks persist though it's difficult to remain optimistic, given the country's tradition of apple boxes filled with 'cash gifts' and penchant for 25-storey residential towers.

Japan and Korea continue to act out their own version of *Mad* magazine's Spy Vs Spy. Much of the wrangling concerns a territorial dispute over Dokdo (p35), a handful of islets 200km off Korea's east coast. The attachment to Dokdo is emotional – the prospect of Japan snagging a piece of territory is gut wrenching for every Korean – and financial: sovereignty over the rocks ensures territorial rights to fertile fishing grounds and a seabed of energy reserves.

Most Koreans are warming to the idea that building ties with North Korea yields benefits, despite the costs. Undeterred by the North's admission of nuclear-weapon capabilities, the government clings to the Sunshine Policy (p42). Aid, coupled with investments in the Kaeseong industrial park, is viewed as a long-term strategy to stabilise the North, build links where none have existed for 50 years (such as rail lines and roads) and make a few bucks for South Korean companies who pay the North Korean government US$60 per month per factory worker to churn out pots, auto parts and electrical components.

Free trade is sharpening Korea's international economic focus. Talks with India, Japan, Canada and the US are at different stages. During preliminary negotiations with the US, Korea argued that goods manufactured in Kaesong should fall within the scope of a free-trade agreement. Only the future will tell if this puzzling idea is a stroke of genius or a sterling example of lateral thinking gone too far. Trade liberalisation is the future, it seems, but it's going to take a wizard to get through Korea's domestic politics, which include a vocal agricultural sector regarded as a loser in any future deal. Most people agree that protecting a national industry is important, but at some point someone has to ask why a small bag of locally grown carrots costs more than a kilogram of imported beef.

FAST FACTS:

The average employee in Korea works 2423 hours per year, the highest level among 30 OECD countries

40,000 women in Korea are registered as *mudang* (female shaman)

78% of Korean homes have a computer

Household savings in Korea as a percentage of disposable income in 1994: 20.7%. In 2004: 5.1%

Average life expectancy in Korea in 1960: 52 years. In 2003: 77 years

Korean–American video artist Baek Nam-june coined the phrase 'electronic superhighway' in 1974

Koreans can earn up to W10 million by snitching on manufacturers or distributors of counterfeit goods

Online commercial transactions in Korea totalled US$10 billion in 2005

History

An Ancient People

Koreans emerged as a people on a mountainous peninsula. Someone once said that if the Korean peninsula were flattened with an iron, it would be as big as China; although Koreans don't try to compare their country to China, they are more than willing to compare it to Japan and to say that theirs is a significant, important and, when prompted, world-beating country. Koreans associate their origins with one of the most beautiful points on the globe, the great mountain on their northern border, Paekdusan (or White-Head Mountain), with a crystal-pure volcanic lake at its summit. (The North Koreans say that Kim Jong Il was born there, even if most historians think he was born along the Sino-Russian border.) Koreans remain today a 'mountain people', who identify with hometowns and home regions that, so they argue, differ greatly from other places in Korea. Koreans are also an ancient people: they are one of the few peoples in the world who can trace a continuous history and presence on the same territory going back thousands of years. Since Korea has had next to no ethnic minorities, Koreans have traditionally thought that they are a homogeneous and unique people – and that they always have been.

The imagined beginning of the Korean nation was the 3rd millennium BC, when a king named Dan·gun founded old Joseon. Joseon (Choson) remains the name of the country in North Korea, but South Koreans use the term Han·guk, a name dating from the 1890s.

The first Korean – Dan·gun – was not just a person but a king, and a continuous presence from his time down to the present, a kingly vessel filled by different people at different times, who drew their legitimacy from this eternal lineage. Under its first president, for example, South Korea used a calendar in which Dan·gun's birth constituted year one – setting the date at 2333 BC. If the two Koreas can't agree on many things, including what to call their country, they can agree on Dan·gun. In 1993 North Korea announced with great fanfare the discovery of Dan·gun's tomb at a site close to Pyongyang: 'The founding of Kojoson (old Joseon) by Dan·gun 5000 years ago marked an epochal occasion in the formation of the Korean nation... The Koreans are a homogeneous nation who inherited the same blood and culture consistently down through history'. All the scribes came forward to proclaim Koreans as the oldest (and therefore finest) people in the world, with one continuous line of history from the 30th-century BC down to the present.

Unfortunately there is no written history of Korea until the centuries just before the birth of Christ, and that history was chronicled by Chinese scribes. But there is archaeological evidence that human beings inhabited this peninsula half a million years ago, and that an advanced people were there seven or eight thousand years ago in the Neolithic period – as revealed by the ground and polished stone tools and pottery they left to posterity. These Neolithic people practiced agriculture in a settled communal life, and are widely supposed to have had consanguineous clans as their basic social grouping. Nationalist historians also trace many Korean

Sourcebook of Korean Civilisation (1993) edited by Peter Lee has a wide selection of original historical documents and materials, in translation and with commentary.

A New History of Korea by Lee Ki-baik (1984) takes a cultural and sociological perspective on the country's history.

2333 BC	668–918
Mythical founding of the Korean nation by Dan-gun and his bear wife	Shilla kingdom rules a Korea unified up to the Taedong River from its capital Gyeongju

social and cultural traits back to these Neolithic peoples, but around the time of Christ three ancient kingdoms emerged that influenced Korean history down to our time.

The first state to emerge in the Three Kingdoms era (57 BC–AD 668) was Baekje (Paekche), which was a centralised, aristocratic state melding Chinese and indigenous influence. By the 3rd century AD, Baekje was strong enough to demolish its rivals and occupy what today is the core area of Korea, around Seoul. The common Korean custom of father-to-son royal succession is said to have begun with Baekje king Geun Chugo. His grandson inaugurated another long tradition by adopting Buddhism as the state religion (in 384). The northern kingdom, Goguryeo (Koguryŏ), conquered a large territory by AD 312 and expanded in all directions, especially toward the Taedong River in the south, which runs through Pyongyang. Peninsular geography shaped the political space of Baekje and Goguryeo and a third kingdom called Shilla (Silla), which fills out the trilogy. Approximately three-quarters of the way down the peninsula, at the 37th parallel, the major mountain range veers to the southwest, dividing the peninsula. This southwest extension of mountains framed Baekje's historic territory, just as it did the Shilla kingdom to the east. Goguryeo, however, ranged over a wild region consisting of northeastern Korea and eastern Manchuria, giving rise to contemporary dreams of a 'greater Korea' in territories that now happen to be part of China and Russia. While South Korea identifies itself with the glories of the Shilla kingdom, which they say unified the peninsula in 668 AD, the North identifies with Goguryeo and says the country wasn't truly unified until the founding of the Goguryeo dynasty. Meanwhile people in the southwestern part of the country felt abused by dictators and left out of the growth of South Korea for decades until one of their own was elected president in 1997 (Kim Dae-jung), and often identified with the Baekje legacy.

Korea by Angus Hamilton (1904) is a rare and lively description of life in Korea under the last dynasty.

Buddhism in Korea

Buddhism came to Korea from China in the latter part of the Three Kingdoms era, establishing itself first in Goguryeo and Baekje in the late 4th century and then in Shilla in the early 6th century. With royal support the faith spread throughout the peninsula and became the official religion in all three states – and remained so until the end of the 14th century. It wasn't quite the familiar Buddhism of ascetic monks, however – some monasteries became wealthy and owned large estates and thousands of slaves, and some monks dressed in silk robes, rode fine horses and indulged in wine, women and song. Korean Buddhism also incorporated indigenous shamanist beliefs; many of the colourful wooden temples you can still visit in the mountain temples have a small hall dedicated to shamanist deities like the mountain gods and have histories that stretch back over a thousand years.

Far from being pacifists, Korean monks often came to the defence of their country. Many mountain fortresses found throughout the Korean peninsula contained temples and were garrisoned by warrior monks. Toughened by their spartan lifestyle and trained in martial arts, monk warriors played a major part in resisting the Japanese invasions in the 1590s – even though Confucianism had become the state doctrine and the

918–1392	1231
Goryeo dynasty rules Korea and produces some of the most exquisite celadon pottery	Mongols sweep through China and invade Korea

new rulers treated them as lowborn and no better than beggars. Monks were not allowed to enter the gates of Seoul, for example, which is why many temples are hidden away on remote mountains. Today Buddhist sects in Seoul sometimes come to blows over their disputes, and some monks even marry and have children; the ascetic Seon (Zen) doctrine is the most common one, but has many rivals. If all this sounds heretical, the Korean approach to religion is often eclectic – the same person might be a Christian, a Buddhist and a Confucianist, depending on the day.

Shilla Ascendancy

Shilla emerged victorious on the peninsula in 668, and it is from this famous date that South Korean historians speak for the first time of a unified Korea. This brought an end to the era of the Three Kingdoms, but not before all of them had come under the long-term sway of Chinese civilisation by introducing Chinese statecraft, Buddhist and Confucian philosophy, Confucian practices of educating the young, and the Chinese written language. Artists from Goguryeo and Baekje also perfected a mural art found on the walls of tombs, and took it to Japan where it deeply influenced Japan's temple and burial art. But it is the blossoming of Shilla that still astounds contemporary visitors to Korea, and makes its ancient capital at Gyeongju (Kyŏngju) one of the most fascinating tourist destinations in East Asia.

Shilla had close relations with the great Tang dynasty in China, sent many students to Tang schools, and had a level of civilisation high enough to merit the Chinese designation 'flourishing land in the East'. Shilla culture melded indigenous and Tang influences: in 682 it set up a national Confucian academy to train high officials, and later instituted a civil-service examination system modelled on that of the Tang. But Shilla had a flourishing indigenous civilisation clearly different from the Tang, one that was among the most advanced in the world. Its capital at Gyeongju was renowned as the 'city of gold', where the aristocracy pursued a high culture and extravagant pleasures. Chinese historians wrote that elite officials possessed thousands of slaves, with like numbers of horses, cattle and pigs. Their wives wore solid-gold tiaras and earrings of delicate and intricate filigree. Scholars studied the Confucian and Buddhist classics and developed advanced methods for astronomy and calendrical science. 'Pure Land' Buddhism, a simple doctrine, united the mass of common people, who like today's Hare Krishnas could become adherents through the repetition of simple chants.

The crowning glory of Gyeongju is the Bulguksa (Pulguksa) temple, which was rebuilt in the 1970s, and the nearby Seokguram Grotto. Both were built around 750 and are home to some of the finest Buddhist sculpture in the world. Buddhists came on pilgrimages to Gyeongju from as far away as India and Arab sojourners sometimes came to the temple to stay.

In spite of Shilla's military strength, broad territories of the old Goguryeo kingdom were not conquered and a section of the Goguryeo elite established a successor state known as Parhae (Balhae), above and below the Amnok and Tuman boundaries that now form the border between China, Russia and Korea. Parhae's continuing strength forced Shilla to

Korea's Place in the Sun: A Modern History by Bruce Cumings (2005) offers an overview of Korean history from year one to the 1860s, followed by a close examination of the modern period.

build a northern wall in 721 and kept Shilla forces permanently below a line running from present-day Pyongyang in the east to the west coast. As one prominent South Korean historian wrote, 'Shilla and Parhae confronted each other hostilely much like southern and northern halves of a partitioned nation'.

Like Shilla, Parhae continued to be influenced deeply by the Chinese civilisation of the Tang, sending students to the capital at Ch'angan, on which it modelled its own capital city. But it was cold in Parhae territory, up to 40°F below zero in winter, and Parhae people bequeathed a lasting invention to the Korean people: sleeping on *ondol* floors, a system that uses flues from a central hearth to heat the floors of each room – still in wide use in contemporary Korea, with the stone flues covered by waxed and polished rice paper. Ice may form in a water jug on the table while a person sleeps comfortably on a toasty warm *ondol*.

Unification under Goryeo

A formidable military leader named Wang Geon had defeated Shilla as well as some Baekje remnants by 930, and established a flourishing dynasty, Goryeo, from whence came the name Korea. Korea was now fully unified with more or less the boundaries that it retains today. Wang was not just a unifier, however, but a magnanimous one. Regarding himself as the proper lineal king of Goguryeo, he embraced that kingdom's survivors, took a Shilla princess as his wife and treated the Shilla aristocracy with unprecedented generosity. His dynasty ruled for nearly a millennium, and in its heyday was among the most advanced civilisations in the world.

'Korea was now fully unified with more or less the boundaries that it retains today'

With its capital at Kaesong, a town north of Seoul bisected by the 38th parallel, the Goryeo dynasty's composite elite also forged a tradition of aristocratic continuity that lasted down to the modern era. By the 13th century there were two government groupings: civil officials and military officials. At that time the military people were stronger, but thereafter both were known as *yangban* (the two orders), which became the Korean term for aristocracy. Below the hereditary aristocracy were common people like peasants and merchants. Below them were outcaste groups of butchers, tanners and entertainers, who were called *cheonmin* and who lived a castelike existence, often in separated and ostracised villages, and whose status fell upon their children as well. Likewise, slavery was hereditary (matrilineally), with slaves making up as much as 30% of Goryeo society.

The elite fused aristocratic privilege and political power through marriage alliances and control of land and central political office, and fortified this class position to the point of impregnability by making status hereditary. Goryeo established a social pattern in which a landed gentry mixed its control of property with a Confucian- or Buddhist-educated stratum of scholar-officials, usually residing in the capital. Often scholars and landlords were one and the same person, but in any case landed wealth and bureaucratic position became powerfully fused. At the centre, a bureaucracy influenced by Confucian statecraft emerged, which thereafter sought to influence local power and which was a contrast with the Japanese or European feudal pattern of castle towns, landed domains and parcellised sovereignty all backed by a strong military class (although Korea came

1592–1598	1801
Japanese invasions devastate Korea	Thousands of Korean Catholics executed

close to the feudal pattern in the 9th and 10th centuries, when strong walled-town lords and military commanders challenged central power).

The large landed families held their land in perpetuity and could bequeath it to their survivors; its produce was at the service of the owner, after taxes were paid. Worked mostly by peasant tenants who paid rent in kind, this land system often produced vast estates of great wealth worked by hundreds of tenants or slaves, and in its essential form persisted through the subsequent Joseon period and the Japanese colonial period. Family landholding became more important than office-holding in perpetuating aristocratic dominance over time. The wealthy, aristocratic landlord became a beneficence or a plague (depending on your point of view) from early Goryeo down to modern times, and an egalitarian redistribution of the land became a focal point of Confucian reformers, capitalist modernisers and communist agitators alike.

The Goryeo aristocracy was by no means a class without merit, however. It admired and interacted with the splendid Chinese civilisation that emerged during the contemporaneous Song dynasty (960–1279). Official delegations and ordinary merchants brought Korean gold, silver and ginseng to China in exchange for silks, porcelains and woodblock books. Finely crafted Song porcelains stimulated Korean artisans to produce an even finer type of inlaid celadon pottery – unmatched in the world before or since for the pristine clarity of its blue-green glaze and the delicate art of its inlaid portraits. Buddhism was the state religion, but it coexisted with Confucianism throughout the Goryeo period. Buddhist priests systematised religious practice by rendering the Korean version of the Buddhist canon into mammoth wood-block print editions, known as the Tripitaka. The first was completed in 1087 after a lifetime of work, but was lost; another, completed in 1251, can still be viewed today at the Haeinsa temple (p195). By 1234, if not earlier, Koreans had also invented movable metal type, two centuries before its inception in Europe.

Hendrick Hamel's fascinating account of his 13 years in Korea, after he and 36 other sailors were shipwrecked on Jeju Island in 1653, is available in Gari Ledyard's *The Dutch Come to Korea*, with full scholarly annotation.

This high point of Goryeo culture coincided with internal disorder and the rise of the Mongols, whose power swept most of the known world during the 13th century. Korea was no exception, as Kublai Khan's forces invaded and demolished Goryeo's army in 1231, forcing the government to retreat to Ganghwado Island, a ploy that exploited the Mongol horsemen's fear of water. But after a more devastating invasion in 1254, in which countless people died and some 200,000 people were made captives, Goryeo succumbed to Mongol domination and its kings came to intermarry with Mongol princesses. The Mongols then enlisted thousands of Koreans in ill-fated invasions of Japan in 1274 and 1281, using craft made by Korea's great shipwrights. The Kamakura Shogunate turned back both invasions with help, as legend has it, from opportune typhoons known as the 'divine wind' or *kamikaze*.

Last Dynasty

The overthrow of the Mongols by the Ming dynasty in China (1316–1644) gave an opportunity to rising groups of Korean military men to contest for power. One of them, Yi Seong-gye, grabbed the bull by the horns and overthrew Goryeo leaders, thus becoming the founder of Korea's longest and last dynasty (1392–1910). The new state was named

1876	1882
Japanese gunboats open Korea's ports to foreign trade	Treaty signed with the US

Joseon, harking back to the old Joseon kingdom 15 centuries earlier, and its capital was built at Seoul. General Yi announced the new dynasty by mobilising 200,000 labourers to surround the new capital with a great wall; it was completed in six months in 1394, and scattered remnants of it still stand today, especially the Great South Gate (Namdaemun) and the Great East Gate (Dongdaemun). He was generous to his defeated Goryeo antagonists, sending them off to comfortable exile. Such magnanimity encouraged one writer to wax poetic about Yi Seong-gye's virtues – a typical example of how Koreans sing the manifold praises of their leaders, especially dynastic founders:

> His presence is the mighty warrior, firm
> He stands, an eagle on a mountain top;
> In wisdom and resource none can compare,
> The dragon of Namyang is he.
> In judgment on the civil bench,
> Or counsel from the warrior's tent, he rules;
> He halts the waves that roll in from the sea,
> And holds the sun back from its heavenly course.

The deep Buddhist influence on the previous dynasty led the literati to urge the king to uproot Buddhist economic and political influence, which led to exile in the mountains for monks and their disciples. Over many decades the literati thus accomplished a deep Confucianisation of Joseon society, which particularly affected the position of women. Where many women were prominent in Goryeo society, they were now relegated to domestic chores of childrearing and housekeeping, as so-called 'inside people'. Up until recent times the woman's role in Korean society seemed to be as old as the bones in ancestral graves: just as central, just as hidden, and just as unchangeable.

Goryeo society had a relatively strong matrilineal system. It was by no means a matriarchy, but it wasn't nearly the patriarchy of later centuries. A new husband was welcomed into the wife's house, where the children and even grandchildren would live. Many men were happy to take this route because women shared rights of inheritance with their male siblings. Women were so valuable that men wanted several; a Chinese envoy in 1123 found a wealthy man in Gaeseong with four. But plural wives were not dependent on one man; often living apart, they had their own economic underpinnings. Detailed ritual did not surround the act of marriage, nor the relations between sexes: 'the general free and easy contact between the sexes amazed…Chinese observers.' There were no restrictions on widows remarrying; women took serial husbands, if not several at the same time.

Influential literati in the Joseon dynasty were ideologues who wanted to restore Korean society to its proper path as they saw it, which meant using the virtues to discipline the passions and the interests. The reforming came in the name of Neo-Confucianism and Chu Hsi, the Chinese progenitor of this doctrine. The result was that much of what we now see as 'Korean culture' or 'tradition' was the result of a major social reorganisation accomplished by self-conscious ideologues in the 15th century. Many foreign observers would declare that Korea was 'more Confucian than China'.

Chihwaseon (2002) directed by Im Kwon-taek is based on the true story of a talented but wayward painter who lived at the end of the Joseon dynasty. The painter's nonconformist life was a series of personal misfortunes that nevertheless inspired his best art. The film won the director's prize at the Cannes Film Festival.

1894	1894
Donghak peasant uprising defeated	Slavery abolished

The unquestionable effect of the new reforms and laws was a slow-moving but ultimately radical change in women's social position and an expropriation of women's property, more or less complete by the late 15th century. From then on, the latticework of Korean society was constituted by patrilineal descent. The nails in the latticework, the proof of its importance and existence over time, were the written genealogies that positioned families in the hierarchy of property and prestige. In succeeding centuries a person's genealogy would be the best predictor of his or her life chances; it became one of Korea's most lasting characteristics. Since only male offspring could prolong the family and clan lines and were the only names registered in the genealogical tables, the birth of a son was greeted with great fanfare.

War Diary of Admiral Yi Sun-sin edited by Sohn Pow-key (1977) is a straightforward and fascinating account by Korea's greatest admiral of the battles, floggings and court intrigues that were his daily preoccupations.

Such historical influences remain strong in both Koreas today, where first sons and their families often live with the male's parents and all stops are pulled out to father a boy. Hereditary aristocratic principles became so ingrained that according to the late Edward Wagner, a relative handful of elite families were responsible for most of the 14,000-odd exam passers of the civil-service examination system in the 500 years of the Joseon, exams being the critical route to official position.

The self-conscious Confucianisation of Korean society had clear deleterious effects for women and common people, but it also reinforced some of modern Korea's most admirable qualities: the deep concern for family; the broad respect for education (scholars and philosophers were at the pinnacle of Confucian reform), more or less automatic admiration for elders (and the elderly); and a belief that ultimately human society should be governed by the virtuous, not the powerful or the wealthy.

Korea & China: An Enduring Relationship

Smack in the middle of the grand boulevard approaching the central government offices in Seoul is a gigantic statue of Admiral Yi Sun-sin, whose artful naval manoeuvres and command of the *geobukseon* (the first metal-clad ship in the world) saved Korea from Japanese conquest in the 1590s. This statue is a nice symbol of the general idea that for most Koreans most of the time, foreigners might be people intent on invading Korea. Japan is the best case, of course, with the warlord Hideyoshi laying waste to the peninsula only to be turned back by Admiral Yi, and with Japan's victories over China in 1895 and Russia in 1905, establishing Japanese colonial rule in Korea. Mongols, Manchus and others usually grouped as 'barbarians' came charging across Korea's northern borders. But the Mongols and Manchus were also conquerors of China, which made them barbarians, too, and led many Koreans to think that China was not just the centre of an admirable civilisation but also a good neighbour, giving to Korea more than it took away.

General Yi Song-gye founded his dynasty when he refused to send his troops into battle against a Chinese army, and instead turned around and used them to overthrow his own government and make himself king. Not surprisingly, he received the blessing and support of the Chinese emperor, and Korea became a 'tributary' country to China – but more than that, it became the ideal tributary state, modelling itself on Chinese culture and statecraft. Most of the time China left Korea alone to run its

1894–1895	1904–1905
Japan defeats China	Japan defeats Russia; Korea becomes a Japanese protectorate

own affairs, and Korea was content to look up to China as the centre of the only world civilisation that mattered. This policy was known as *sadae* (serving the great). Because of this special relationship, when Hideyoshi's forces attacked in the 1590s, Chinese troops were sent to help repel them. In just one battle as many as 30,000 Chinese soldiers died. *Sadae* was in the background during the Korean War as well, when a huge Chinese army intervened in late 1950 and helped rescue the North from certain defeat. Meanwhile, many South Koreans felt that the behaviour of the Chinese troops during the Korean War was superior to that of any other force, including the American troops. Today China is South Korea's largest trading partner, with thousands of Korean students studying there, while China maintains its long-term alliance with North Korea. So, it can be said that Korea's relationship with China is one of the only foreign entanglements that most Koreans seem happy with, and it's likely to grow ever stronger in the 21st century.

Of course, it isn't clear what the common people thought about China until the modern period, nor were they asked; the vast majority were illiterate in a country that marked its elite according to their literacy – in Chinese. The aristocrats were enthusiastic Confucianists, as we have seen, adopting Chinese painting, poetry, music, statecraft and philosophy. The complicated Chinese script was used for virtually all government and cultural activities throughout the Joseon period, even though the native alphabet, *Han·geul,* was an outstanding cultural achievement. Developed under Korea's greatest king, Sejong, in 1443, it was much simpler and easier to learn than Chinese characters. *Han·geul* is a phonetic script: concise, elegant and considered one of the most scientific in the world in rendering sounds. But the Confucian elite opposed its wide use, hoping to keep the government exams as difficult as possible so that only aristocratic children had the time and money to pass. *Han·geul* didn't come

Wearing a topknot was a traditional male custom that went back to antiquity and was particularly widespread during Korea's pleasant relations with the Ming dynasty – and then it became a symbol of 'Ming loyalists' in Korea after that dynasty fell. In 1895 King Gojong had his topknot cut off, but conservatives did not follow his example or share his enthusiasm for reforms.

DONGHAK DEMANDS

The Donghak rebellion, which had been building for decades, erupted in 1893 in Jeolla province, attracting large numbers of peasants and lowborn groups of people. The rebels were only armed with primitive, homemade weapons, but they defeated the government army sent against them. The rebellion then spread to neighbouring provinces, and when King Gojong called in Chinese troops, Japanese troops took advantage of the uproar to march into Seoul. The rebels were defeated and their leaders, including Jeon Bong-jun, who was known as the 'Green Pea General' because of his small size, were executed by Japanese firing squads.

The demands of the rebels reveal their many grievances against the Joseon social system:

- Slaves should be freed.
- The low-born should be treated fairly.
- Land should be redistributed.
- Taxes on fish and salt should be scrapped.
- No unauthorised taxes should be levied and any corrupt *yangban* should be severely punished.

- All debts should be cancelled.
- Regional favouritism and factions should be abolished.
- Widows should be allowed to remarry.
- Traitors who support foreign interference should be punished.

1910	1919
Japan annexes Korea and abolishes the monarchy	Nationwide protests against Japanese rule crushed

into general use until after 1945, and then only in North Korea; South Korea used a Sino-Korean script requiring the mastery of thousands of Chinese characters until the 1990s. Today, though, Chinese characters have mostly disappeared from Korea's public space, to the consternation of Chinese and Japanese travellers who used to be able to read all the street and commercial signs.

Royal Pomp & Ceremony

Many of the premier cultural attractions in Korea today, such as Seoul's Gyeongbokgung (p83), Namdaemun (p103) and Changdeokgung (p101) are imperial relics of the long-lived Joseon dynasty. They are windows into a time in Korea's history when absolute monarchs ruled. Pomp and ritual also became an essential aspect of royal power, with attention to ritual and protocol developed into an art form. Koreans appeared to break sharply with this royal system in the 20th century, but when we look at the ruling system in North Korea, or the families that run most of South Korea's major corporations, we see the family and hereditary principles of the old system continuing in modern form.

It is difficult to imagine the wealth, power and status of Joseon kings in these more democratic times. The main palace, Gyeongbokgung, contained 800 buildings and over 200 gates; in 1900, for example, palace costs accounted for 10% of all government expenditures. In the royal household were 400 eunuchs, 500 ladies-in-waiting, 800 other court ladies and 70 *gisaeng* (female entertainers who were expert singers and dancers). Only women and eunuchs were allowed to live inside the palace – male servants, guards, officials and visitors had to leave at sunset. Most of the women lived like nuns and never left the palace. A *yangban* woman had to be married for years before daring to move in the outer world of society, and then

Soup, fish, quail, pheasant, stuffed and rolled beef, vegetables, creams, glace walnuts, fruits, claret and coffee were on the menu when Isabella Bird Bishop had dinner with King Gojong and Queen Min.

LIVES OF THE EUNUCHS

The eunuchs were the most extraordinary people. They could become as powerful as leading government officials because they were around the king and the royal family 24 hours a day. All access to the king was through them, as they were the royal bodyguards and responsible for the safety of their master. This was an easy way to earn money and they usually exploited it to the full. These bodyguard eunuchs, toughened by a harsh training regime of martial arts, were also personal servants to the king and even nursemaids to the royal children. They played so many roles that life must have been very stressful for them, particularly as any mistake could lead to horrific physical punishments.

Although often illiterate and uneducated, a few became important advisors to the king, attaining high government positions and amassing great wealth. Most were from poor families and their greed for money was a national scandal. Eunuchs were supposed to serve the king with total devotion, like monks serving Buddha, never thinking about mundane matters like money or status.

A surprising aspect is that the eunuchs were usually married and adopted young eunuch boys who they brought up as their sons to follow in their footsteps. The eunuch in charge of the king's health would pass on his medical knowledge to his 'son'. Under the Confucian system not only gays but also eunuchs had to get married. The system continued until 1910 when the country's new Japanese rulers summoned all the eunuchs to Deoksugung and dismissed them from government service.

1945	1948
Korea liberated following the surrender of Japanese forces to the Allies	Republic of Korea and Democratic People's Republic of Korea established

only in a cocoon of clothing inside a cloistered sedan chair, carried by her slaves. In the late 19th century foreigners witnessed these same cloistered upper-class women, clothed and swaddled from head to toe, wearing a green mantle like the Middle Eastern *chador* over their heads and bringing the folds across the face, leaving only the eyes exposed. They would come out after the nightly curfew, after the bells rang and the city gates were closed against tigers, and find a bit of freedom in the darkness.

Isabella Bird Bishop visited the newly restored Gyeongbokgung in 1895 and noted in *Korea and Her Neighbours*: 'What with 800 troops, 1500 attendants and officials of all descriptions, courtiers and ministers and their attendants, secretaries, messengers and hangers-on, the vast enclosure of the palace seemed as crowded and populated as the city itself'.

In James Scarth Gale's *History of the Korean People,* Harriet Heron Gale, a missionary, observed the pampered life of the crown prince: 'An army of attendants and maids in long blue silk shirts and yellow jackets hover about his little kingship all day long, powdering his face, painting his lips and finger tips, shaving the top of his head, pulling out his eyebrows, cutting his food into the daintiest of morsels, fanning him with monstrous long-handled fans, never leaving him alone for a moment…even at night guarding and watching by his bedside, singing him to sleep with a queer little lullaby'.

Because the eunuchs were the only 'male' staff allowed to live inside the palaces, they were privy to all the secrets of the state, and had considerable influence because they waited upon the king.

Eunuch (1968), an artistic film directed by Shin Sang-ok, is based on a story about a lady who is forced by her father to become the king's concubine although she loves someone else. The film depicts the inner sanctum in those now empty and dusty palaces.

Korea & Japan

In 2005 the South Korean president refused to hold a summit meeting with the Japanese prime minister because the latter insisted on visiting the Yasukuni shrine, a memorial to Japan's war dead that happened to include Class A war criminals from WWII, and because all year long both countries squabbled over the ownership of an uninhabited pile of rocks in the East Sea, known as Dokdo (that is, Takeshima). Relations between these two countries have not always been difficult and controversial, but certainly they have been for at least four centuries, since Hideyoshi sought to subdue Korea on the way to conquering China.

In 1592, 150,000 well-armed Japanese troops, divided into nine armies, rampaged throughout Korea looting, raping and killing. Palaces and temples were burnt to the ground and priceless cultural treasures were destroyed or stolen. Entire villages of ceramic potters were shipped back to Japan, along with thousands of ears clipped from dead Koreans, which were piled into a mound in Japan, covered over and retained into modern times as a memorial to this war. Fortunately a series of brilliant naval victories by Admiral Yi Sun-sin, using iron-clad warships called *geobukseon* (turtle ships), helped to turn the tide against the Japanese. Ming troops also arrived from China, and by 1597 the Japanese were forced to withdraw. A year later Hideyoshi died a broken man. Stout resistance on land and sea thwarted Japanese ambitions to dominate Asia, but only at the cost of massive destruction and economic dislocation in Korea.

Japan's ambitions to seize Korea resurfaced 300 years later, at the end of the 19th century, when Japan suddenly rose up as the first modern

Samurai Invasion by Stephen Turnbull (2002) is a detailed account of the Japanese invasions of Korea in the 1590s.

| Korean War | Park Chung-hee seizes power in a military coup |

My Innocent Uncle by Chae Man-shik is a shocking short story, written in a direct, colloquial style, that portrays a pro-Japanese Korean opportunist who refers to Japan as his home country and wants to marry a Japanese girl. His uncle is innocent of such treacherous views but his opposition to Japanese rule is ineffective.

great power in Asia. Seizing on the Donghak peasant rebellion in Korea, Japan instigated war with China, defeating it in 1895. After another decade of imperial rivalry over Korea, Japan smashed Russia in lightning naval and land attacks, stunning the world because a 'yellow' country had defeated a 'white' power. Korea became a Japanese protectorate in 1905 and a colony in 1910, with the acquiescence of all the great powers. It was a strange colony, coming 'late' in world time, after most of the world had been divided up, and after progressive calls had emerged to dismantle the entire colonial system. Furthermore Korea had most of the prerequisites for nationhood long before most other countries: common ethnicity, language and culture, and well-recognised national boundaries since the 10th century. So the Japanese engaged in substitution after 1910: exchanging a Japanese ruling elite for the Korean *yangban* scholar-officials; instituting central coordination for the old government administration; exchanging Japanese modern education for the Confucian classics; building Japanese capital and expertise in place of the Korean versions – Japanese talent for Korean talent; eventually even replacing the Korean language with Japanese.

Koreans never thanked the Japanese for these substitutions and did not credit Japan with creations. Instead they saw Japan as snatching away the *ancien regime,* Korea's sovereignty and independence, its indigenous if incipient modernisation and, above all, its national dignity. Most Koreans never saw Japanese rule as anything but illegitimate and humiliating. Furthermore the very closeness of the two nations – in geography, in common Chinese civilisational influences, and in levels of development until the 19th century – made Japanese dominance all the more galling to Koreans and gave a peculiar intensity to the relationship, a hate/respect dynamic that suggested to Koreans, 'there but for accidents of history go we'.

The result: neither Korea nor Japan has ever gotten over it. In the North countless films and TV programmes still focus on atrocities committed by the Japanese during their rule, and for decades the descendants of Koreans deemed by the government to have collaborated with the Japanese occupation authorities were subject to severe discrimination. South Korea, however, punished very few collaborators, partly because the US Occupation (1945–48) reemployed so many of them, and partly because they were needed in the fight against communism.

At the Court of Korea by William Franklin Sands gives a first-hand account of King Gojong and his government at the turn of the century.

The Independence Hall (p322), in Chungcheongnam-do, is the South Korean shrine commemorating the heroes of the anti-Japanese resistance. March 1 is a huge national holiday, honouring the day in 1919 when the death of ex-king Gojong and the unveiling of a Korean declaration of independence sparked massive pro-independence demonstrations throughout the country. The protests were ruthlessly suppressed, but still lasted for months. When it was over the Japanese claimed that 500 were killed, 1400 injured and 12,000 arrested, but Korean estimates put the casualties at ten times these figures.

A certain amount of Korean collaboration with the Japanese was unavoidable given the ruthless nature of the regime under the Japanese colonialists, and then in the last decade of colonial rule when Japan's expansion across Asia caused a shortage of experts and professionals throughout the empire. Ambitious Koreans found new careers opening to them just at the most oppressive point in this colony's history, as Koreans were commanded to change their names and not speak Korean, and millions of Koreans were used as mobile human fodder by the Japanese. Koreans constituted almost half of the hated National Police, and young Korean officers (including Park Chung-hee, who seized power in 1961), and Kim Jae-gyu (who, as intelligence chief, assassinated Park in 1979) joined the aggressive Japanese army in Manchuria. Pro-Japanese *yangban* were rewarded with special titles, and some of Korea's greatest early nationalists, like Yi Gwang-su, were forced into public support of Japan's empire. Although collaboration was an inevitable result of the repression of the Japanese occupation, it was never punished or fully and frankly debated in South Korea, leaving the problem to fester until 2004, when the government finally launched an official investigation of collaboration – along with estimates that upwards of 90% of the pre-1990 South Korea elite had ties to collaborationist families or individuals.

Under the Black Umbrella: Voices from Colonial Korea by Hildi Kang (2001) is a fascinating and accessible memoir of a Korean woman growing up under Japanese rule.

Westernised Japanese and Korean bureaucrats ran the colonial government. They implemented policies that developed industries and modernised the administration, but always in the interests of Japan. Modern textile, steel and chemical industries emerged along with new railroads, highways and ports. Koreans never thanked Japan for any of this, but it left Korea much more developed in 1945 than, say, Vietnam under the French. Still, the main trauma of the occupation was probably psychological rather than political or economic, because Japan tried to destroy the Korean sense of national identity.

www.twotigers.org has a dozen personal testimonies by Korean 'comfort women' that give a unique insight into their horrifying ordeals.

The burst of consumerism that came to the world in the 1920s meant that Koreans shopped in Japanese department stores, banked at Japanese banks, drank Japanese beer, travelled on the Japanese-run railway and often dreamed of attending a Tokyo university.

By 1940 the Japanese owned 40% of the land and there were 700,000 Japanese living and working in Korea – an enormous number compared to most other countries. But among large landowners, many were as likely to be Korean as Japanese; most peasants were tenant farmers working their land. Upwards of three million Korean men and women were uprooted from their homes and sent to work as miners, farm labourers, factory workers and soldiers abroad, mainly in Japan and Manchukuo, the Japanese colony in northeast China. Over 130,000 Korean miners in Japan – men and women – worked 12-hour days, were paid wages well under what Japanese miners earned, were poorly fed and were subjected to brutal, club-wielding overseers. The worst aspect of this massive

A LONG PROTEST

Since 1992, Hwang Geum-joo and a handful of other Korean 'comfort women', survivors of the WWII camps where they were forced to have sex with Japanese soldiers, have protested outside the Japanese embassy in Seoul every Wednesday at noon. 'Our numbers are dwindling every year and nothing has changed,' she has said. With their young supporters, the old ladies hold up placards demanding an apology and financial compensation. Hwang Geum-joo has taken part in over 554 protests outside the embassy but has refused to give up. 'We are still full of anger and they should apologise for what they did to us!'

1991	1992
Agreement signed between Seoul and Pyongyang to make the Korean peninsula nuclear free	Kim Young-sam elected president, ushering in a more democratic political era

mobilisation, however, came in the form of 'comfort women' – the 100,000 to 200,000 young Korean women who were forced to work as sex slaves for the Japanese armed forces (p37).

It was Korea's darkest hour but Korean guerrilla groups continued to fight Japan in Manchukuo; they were allied with Chinese guerrillas but Koreans still constituted by far the largest ethnic group. This is where we find Kim Il Sung, who began fighting the Japanese around the time they proclaimed the puppet state of Manchukuo in 1932 and continued into the early 1940s. After murderous counter-insurgency campaigns (participated in by many Koreans), the guerrillas numbered only about 200. In 1945 they returned to northern Korea and constituted the ruling elite from that point down to the present.

Japan's surrender to the Allies in 1945 opened a new chapter in the stormy relationship between the two countries. Thanks to a very soft peace and munificent American support, Japan began growing rapidly in the early 1950s. South Korea got going in the mid-1960s, and today companies and workers in both countries battle each other to produce the best ships, cars, steel products, computer chips, mobile phones, flat-screen TVs and other electronic equipment. The new rivalry is a never-ending competition for world markets, just as sports became another modern-day battleground to decide who is top dog.

The Korean War

In the immediate aftermath of the obliteration of Nagasaki, three Americans in the War Department (including Dean Rusk, later Secretary of State) drew a fateful line at the 38th parallel in Korea, dividing this nation that had a unitary integrity going back to antiquity. The line was supposed to demarcate the areas in which American and Soviet forces would receive the Japanese surrender, but Rusk later acknowledged that he did not trust the Russians and wanted to get the nerve centre of the country, Seoul, in the American zone. He consulted no Koreans, no allies and not even the president in making this decision. But it followed on from three years of State Department planning in which an American occupation of part or all of Korea was seen as crucial to the postwar security of Japan and the Pacific. The US then set up a three-year military government in southern Korea that deeply shaped postwar Korean history.

The Soviets came in with fewer concrete plans for Korea and moved more slowly than the Americans in setting up an administration. They thought Kim Il Sung would be good as a defence minister in a new government, but sought to get him and other communists to work together with Christian nationalist figures like Jo Man-sik. Soon, however, the Cold War rivalry overshadowed everything in Korea, as the Americans turned to Syngman Rhee (an elderly patriot who had lived in the US for 35 years) and the Russians to Kim Il Sung. By 1948 Rhee and Kim had both established separate republics and by the end of the year Soviet troops had withdrawn, never to return again. American combat troops departed in June 1949, leaving behind a 500-man military advisory group. For the only time in its history since 1945, South Korea now had operational control of its own military forces. Within a year war had broken out and the US took back that control and has never relinquished it,

The marathon at the 1936 Berlin Olympics was won by Kitei Son of Japan, but his real name was Sohn Kee-chung and he was from Korea.

illustrating that the US has always had a civil war deterrent in Korea: containing the enemy in the North and constraining the ally in the South.

In 1949 both sides sought external support to mount a war against the other side, and the North succeeded where the South failed. Its greatest strength came from tens of thousands of Koreans who had been sent to fight in China's civil war, and who returned to North Korea in 1949 and 1950. Kim Il Sung also played Stalin off against Mao Zedong to get military aid and a critical independent space for himself, so that when he invaded he could count on one or both powers to bail him out if things went badly. After years of guerrilla war in the South (fought almost entirely by southerners) and much border fighting in 1949 (with both sides at fault), Kim launched a surprise invasion on 25 June 1950, when he peeled several divisions off in the midst of summer war games; many high officers were unaware of the war plan. Seoul fell in three days, and soon North Korea was at war with the US. The Americans responded by getting the UN to condemn the attack and gaining commitments from 16 other countries, although Americans almost always bore the brunt of the fighting, and only British and Turkish combat forces had a substantial role. The war went badly for the UN at first, and its troops were soon pushed far back into a small pocket around Busan (Pusan). But following a daring landing at Incheon (Inchon) under the command of General Douglas MacArthur, North Korean forces were pushed back above the 38th parallel.

The question then became, 'was the war over?' South Korea's sovereignty had been restored and UN leaders wanted to call it a victory. But for the previous year, high officials in the Truman administration had been debating a more 'positive' strategy than containment, namely 'rollback' or liberation, and so Truman decided to march north to overthrow Kim's regime. Kim's long-time relations with Chinese communists bailed his chestnuts out of the fire when Mao committed a huge number of soldiers, but now the US was at war with China.

www.kf.or.kr has video lectures on history (though the sound is not very good) and has a link to *Koreana,* a magazine with some history articles.

By New Year's Eve US forces were pushed back below the 38th parallel, and the communists were about to launch an offensive that would soon retake Seoul. This shook America and its allies to the core, Truman declared a national emergency, and WWIII seemed to be at the doorstep. But Mao did not want general war with the US, and did not try to push the UN forces off the peninsula. By spring 1951 the fighting had stabilised roughly along the lines where the war ended. Truce talks began and dragged on for two years, amid massive trench warfare along the lines. These battles created the Demilitarized Zone (DMZ) and the truce talks bequeathed the *quonset* huts at Panmunjom, where both sides have met periodically ever since to exchange heated rhetoric and where millions of tourists have visited.

At the end of the war, Korea lay in ruins. Seoul had changed hands no less than four times and was badly damaged, but many prewar buildings remained sufficiently intact to rebuild them much as they were. The US Air Force pounded the North for three years until all of its cities were destroyed and some were completely demolished, leaving the urban population to live, work and go to school underground, like cavemen. Millions of Koreans died (probably three million, two-thirds of them in the North), millions more were left homeless, industries were destroyed and the entire country was massively demoralised, because the blood-

1997	1998
Kim Dae-jung elected	Kim Jong Il takes full power on the 50th anniversary of the founding of the regime

letting had only restored the status quo. Of the UN troops, 37,000 were killed (about 35,000 of them Americans) and 120,000 wounded.

Post-War Period

The 1950s were a time of depressing stagnation for the South but rapid industrial growth for the North. Then, over the next 30 years, both Koreas underwent rapid industrial growth. However, by the 1990s huge economic disparities had emerged. The North experienced depressing stagnation that led finally to famine and massive death, while the South emerged as an economic power ranked 11th in the world, with roughly the GNP of Spain. The North's industrial growth was as fast as any in the world from the mid-1950s into the mid-1970s, and even in the early 1980s its per capita GNP was about the same as the South's. But then the South began to build an enormous lead that soon became insurmountable.

This great triumph came at enormous cost, as South Koreans worked the longest hours in the industrial world for decades and suffered under one military dictatorship after another. Corrupt, autocratic rulers censored the media, imprisoned and tortured political opponents, manipulated elections and continually changed the country's constitution to suit themselves; meanwhile Washington backed them up (except for a brief moment in the 1960s) and never did more than issue tepid protests at their authoritarian rule. Student protests and less-frequent trade-union street protests were often violent, as were the police or military forces sent to suppress them. But slowly a democratisation movement built strength across the society.

When the Korean War ended in 1953, Syngman Rhee continued his dictatorial rule until 1961, when he and his wife fled to Hawaii following widespread demonstrations against him that included university professors demonstrating in the streets of Seoul. Ordinary people were finally free to take revenge against hated policemen who had served the Japanese. Following a military coup later in 1961, Park Chung-hee ruled with an iron fist until the Kennedy administration demanded that he hold elections; he won three of them in 1963, 1967 and 1971 by spreading enormous amounts of money around (peasants would get white envelopes full of cash for voting). In spite of that, a young man named Kim Dae-jung nearly beat him in 1971, garnering 46% of the vote. That led Park to declare martial law and make himself president for life. Amid massive demonstrations in 1979 his own intelligence chief, Kim Jae-gyu, shot him dead over dinner one night, in an episode never fully explained. This was followed by five months of democratic discussion until Chun Doo-hwan, a protégé of Park, moved to take full power and the citizens of Gwangju rebelled in May 1980. That rebellion was put down by such brute and wanton military force (see p254) that it became a touchstone in Korean life, marking an entire generation of young people in university in the 1970s and 1980s.

Finally in 1992 a civilian, Kim Young-sam, won election and began to build a real democracy. Although he was a charter member of the old ruling groups, he surprised everyone by putting Chun Doo-hwan on trial, where he was convicted of treason and monumental corruption. That was a great victory for the democratic movement. One of the strongest labour

www.kimsoft.com has a wide range of history articles, people profiles and useful links.

2000	2002
Summit between Kim Dae-jung and Kim Jong Il in Pyongyang; Kim Dae-jung wins Nobel Peace Prize	Roh Moo-hyun elected

movements in the world soon emerged, and when former dissident Kim Dae-jung was elected at the end of 1997, all the protests and suffering and killing seemed finally to have been worthwhile. Kim was ideally poised to solve the deep economic downturn that hit Korea in 1997, as part of the Asian financial crisis. The IMF demanded reforms of the conglomerates as the price for its $55 million bailout, and Kim had long called for restructuring the conglomerates and their cronyism with the banks and the government. By 1999 the economy was growing again.

South Korean presidents serve a five-year term and cannot run again, so when President Kim retired his party selected a virtual unknown, Roh Moo-hyun, a self-taught lawyer who had defended many dissidents in the darkest periods of the 1980s. To the surprise of many, including

TRIBUTE TO CHINA

Starting from 1637, three official embassies travelled to China every year, at the New Year, the birthday of the emperor and the birthday of the crown prince. Later they were supplemented with another mission at the winter solstice. A new king in Korea or the death of an emperor in China occasioned special missions, since the Korean kings sought approval of the Chinese Son of Heaven. From 1637 until the end of the practice in 1881, Korea sent a total of 435 special embassies and missions to China. The tribute was a tangible symbol of Korea's formal status, which was subordinate to China's, with Korea's kings needing (and wanting) the legitimacy of investiture by the Chinese emperor. The emperor sent gifts in return, even if they did not match what he received, and the lavish hospitality provided to the Chinese emissaries when they came to Seoul was very expensive and could take up 15% of the government's revenue. But the envoys were not allowed to visit the interior of the country, and had to take a single route from the border through Pyongyang and down to Seoul. The Chinese would arrive at Seodaemun, the West Gate of Seoul (demolished by the Japanese in 1915) and be greeted by the king. In 1898 Koreans erected the Independence Gate (located down the road from where the old West Gate stood), when King Gojong declared Korea to be an empire and himself to be Emperor Gwangmu.

The missions were also covers for a lot of Sino-Korean trade. Goods carried to the Forbidden Palace in Beijing varied, but one agreement listed 100 tael of gold and 1000 tael of silver (a tael weighed about 40g, so that meant 4kg of gold and 40kg of silver). The emperor was also to receive 100 tiger skins, 100 deer skins and 400 other animal skins. Also on the gift list were a thousand packs of green tea, rice, ginseng, pine seeds and other Korean delicacies; not to mention horses, swords and buffalo-horn bows; and large quantities of paper, cotton, ramie cloth (an almost transparent textile made from bark) and floral-patterned straw mats from Ganghwado. Less publicised were the eunuchs and virgins destined for the emperor's vast harem. In return the Chinese emperor would send the best-quality silk, herbal medicines, porcelain pottery and a library of books, amounting to hundreds of volumes. Tribute trade was thus a cultural and economic exchange between the two countries.

The 300-strong tribute party took one to two months to cover the 1200km route to Beijing, and spent the same amount of time there before beginning the arduous journey home. The embassy included generals, scholars, painters, doctors, interpreters, heralds, secretaries, grooms, umbrella holders and sedan-chair carriers. Jesuit missionaries to Beijing in the 16th century (like foreigners in China today who encounter North Koreans) thought the Koreans they saw in the capital were surly, standoffish and all too self-contained – just as Europeans in the same city three centuries later spoke of 'these strangely-coated people, so proud, so thoroughly uninterested in strangers, so exclusive, so content to go their own way'.

2002	2003
Korea and Japan co-host soccer's World Cup	Six-party talks begin in Beijing

officials in Washington, he won the 2002 election and represented the rise to power of a generation that had nothing to do with the political system that emerged in 1945 (even Kim Dae-jung had been active in the 1940s). That generation was mostly middle-aged, having gone to school in the 1980s with indelible images of conflict on their campuses and American backing for Chun Doo-hwan. The result has been a growing estrangement between Seoul and Washington, really for the first time in the relationship. Still, the country's economic system remains considerably more developed and sophisticated than its political system.

In 1998 President Kim Dae-jung began a 'Sunshine Policy' aimed at reconciliation with North Korea, if not reunification. Within a year Pyongyang had responded, various economic and cultural exchanges began, and in June 2000 the two presidents met at a summit for the first time since 1945. Often seen by critics as appeasement of the North, this engagement policy was predicated on the realist principles that the North was not going to collapse and so had to be dealt with as it is, and that the North would not object to the continued presence of US troops in the South during the long process of reconciliation if the US normalised relations with the North – something that Kim Jong Il acknowledged in his historic summit meeting with Kim Dae-jung in June 2000. By now tens of thousands of South Koreans have visited the North, big southern firms have joint ventures using northern labour, and Koreans have discovered that after 50 years of division they still have a great deal in common.

> 'In 1998 President Kim Dae-jung began a 'Sunshine Policy' aimed at reconciliation with North Korea, if not reunification'

Samsung has become the new Sony in the eyes of many and Koreans have taken so quickly to the internet that it is now the most wired nation on earth. The talented younger generation has produced such a dynamic pop culture that *hallyu* (Korean Wave) is now a big phenomenon in China, Japan and Southeast Asia, and is gaining popularity in the West. Within a relatively short time and after a tumultuous 20th century, Korea has regained its place as one the great nations of the world. The single anachronism in Korea's progress in the new century is the continuing dispute over the North's nuclear programmes. The Clinton and Bush administrations had very different policies toward the North, with Clinton's people talking directly to the North and getting an eight-year freeze on its plutonium facility, and a near buy-out of its medium and long-range missiles in late 2000. The Bush administration refused bilateral talks with the North and placed it in an 'axis of evil' along with Iraq and Iran. The North responded by saying it feared a US attack along the lines of the invasion of Iraq and needed a nuclear deterrent to stop it. Deeply worried about the possibility of conflict, China sponsored six-party talks (China, Japan, Russia, the US, and both Koreas) to get Washington and Pyongyang talking and negotiating, but as of this writing the talks have yielded no significant result. The North went ahead with its threat and successfully tested a small (one kiloton) plutonium bomb in October 2006.

2004	2006
Hallyu (Korean Wave) takes East Asia by storm	North Korea tests missiles in July and a small atomic bomb in October

The Culture

THE NATIONAL PSYCHE

Korea is probably the most Confucian nation in Asia. At the heart of the Confucian doctrine are the Five Relationships, which prescribe appropriate behaviour between ruler and subject, father and son, husband and wife, old and young and between friends. People in senior positions should be authoritarian rather than democratic, which is why some teachers and company bosses act arrogantly towards those with lower status. Determining one's status is usually based on age and occupation.

Establishing a relationship of any kind implies that each person knows who is senior and junior. Based on this awareness, there is an expected behaviour that includes the appropriate usage of honorific language. That's why gestures are fraught with social landmines: use the inappropriate level of language and you may insult the other person and make yourself look uneducated. People rarely use direct questions, such as 'how old are you?', to learn about someone. Critical information of this nature is generally provided by a third party before any meeting, otherwise it's a social two-step with indirect methods of enquiry like, 'I graduated from university in 1986. When did you finish school?'

Relationships are like a circle. If you're on the inside, boundaries define obligations and expectations. If you're on the outside, well, it's a veritable state of nature. If you haven't been properly introduced, there is no obligation to be polite, let alone acknowledge the other person's existence. This worldview explains, in part, why people jump the queue, push their way through the subway door, or drive vehicles with reckless abandon.

Queue jumping and reckless driving are two manifestations of another Korean trait: tenacity. The country's recovery from the ashes of the Korean War, construction workers on the job seven days a week, or computer game addicts: they're all strands cut from the same cloth, the country's tenacious, pit-bull spirit. Once Koreans lock onto something, it's difficult to break away. Life is competitive and everything is taken seriously, be it ten-pin bowling, hiking or overseas corporate expansion.

Koreans are also fanatical about health. The millions of hikers who stream into the mountains at weekends are not only enjoying nature but are also keeping fit. Saunas and hot-spring baths are big attractions. Thousands of health foods and drinks are sold in markets and pharmacies, which stock traditional as well as Western medicines. Health drinks include vitamin-packed canned drinks and alcoholic beverages flavoured with medicinal herbs and roots such as ginseng. Nearly every food claims to be a 'well-being' product or an aphrodisiac – 'good for stamina' is the local phrase.

Another aspect of the Korean character is generosity. Fighting to pay the bill is a common phenomenon, though the *quid pro quo* is that one person pays this time and the other fights a little harder to pick up the check next time. If a Korean takes you under their wing it's difficult to pay for anything. When someone comes back from a holiday they often hand out a small souvenir to everyone. At New Year and Chuseok (Thanksgiving Day), gift-giving reaches fever pitch and stores are so filled with mountains of gift packages of grapes, pears and Spam that you can hardly squeeze inside.

LIFESTYLE

The dream of most people in an urban centre is to buy an apartment equipped with the latest gadgetry, like door locks with fingerprint recognition and high-speed internet. Although the amenities are modern, many people prefer to

THE CONFUCIAN MINDSET

The cultural divide separating Western and Korean thinking can be synthesized into two questions. Westerners ask *why* something is the case. In Korea, the great existential question is, 'how can I live in society?'

The answer comes from Confucius. Confucianism is a social philosophy, a prescription for achieving a harmonious society. Not everyone follows the rules but Confucianism does continue to shape the Korean paradigm. It's what makes Koreans different from Westerners.

- Obedience towards seniors is crucial. Never argue with parents, teachers or the boss. Be polite to older brothers and sisters. Don't start eating before your seniors. Expect a heavy penalty (including physical punishment) if you step out of line.

- Seniors get obedience, but it's not a free ride. Older sisters help out younger siblings with tuition fees and the boss always pays for lunch.

- Education defines a civilised person. A high-school graduate, despite having built a successful business, still feels shame at the lack of scholastic credentials. Students accepted into one of the country's top-three universities (Seoul National, Korea or Yonsei) are recruited by the best companies, where they quickly settle into fast-track management positions and arranged marriages with equally ambitious spouses.

- Men and women have separate roles. A woman's role is service, obedience and management of household affairs. Men don't do housework or look after children. In the past women rarely inherited anything and widows couldn't remarry. Until 2005, the courts upheld laws that barred women from being the legal head of a household.

- Status and dignity are critical. Every action reflects on the family, company and country. Don't do anything that would cause your boss to lose face, even in a minor way, and he will always pay the bill when you go out eating and drinking.

- Everything on and beyond the earth is in a hierarchy. Never forget who is senior and who is junior to you.

- Families are more important than individuals. Individuals are an insignificant part of a family that stretches backwards and forwards in time. Everyone's purpose in life is to improve the family's reputation and wealth. No one should choose a career or marry someone against their parents' wishes – a bad choice could bring ruin to a family. Everyone must marry and have a son to continue the family line. For these reasons homosexuality is considered a grossly unnatural act.

- Loyalty is important. A loyal liar is a virtuous person.

- Be modest and don't be extravagant. Only immoral women wear revealing clothes. Be frugal with praise. Life is serious rather than fun.

sleep the old fashioned way, which is on a *yo* (a mattress, similar to a futon) on the floor. Most modern homes have tables and chairs but many people sit on the floor when family comes over for a special occasion. Floors are heated from underneath by the *ondol* system.

In 1995, internet access and relatively inexpensive home computers were available but the big explosion in usage didn't occur until the late 1990s, after the government offered telecom companies a W1.5 billion package to upgrade the nation's level of connectivity. Broadband was available but demand didn't surge until the emergence of Starcraft, an online multiplayer game that captured the imagination of virtually every male from 15 to 50. But in order to play well, a fast connection was needed. Enter broadband. Today, three-quarters of all homes have broadband access. Nearly 25% of the population has a home page – called minihompy – on Cyworld, a service provider that sells gimmicky accessories like online wallpaper and music which web page owners use to spruce up their minihompy. Gaming is wildly popular; a Korean game called Lineage is the world's most popular online time waster.

Except for the important national holidays like Chuseok and Lunar New Year, Koreans rarely entertain at home. Instead, restaurants, cafés and bars are popular places to meet and entertain friends and colleagues. A proper evening of entertainment involves extensive preparation, cooking and cleanup in order to provide the banquet of side dishes and main courses normally associated with a meal. Going out to a restaurant is just a lot easier. It is precisely for this reason that the wife of the first son dreads big holidays: she's expected to prepare and serve a feast for the husband's family.

Most parents are obsessed with their children's educational progress and will spare no expense to push their kids to the top of the class. Every educational decision is geared towards the standardised university entrance exam. Parents of elementary-school children push their kids so that they attend an elite middle school, which increases the probability of getting into a top high school, which increases the odds of doing well on the university entrance exam. Going to school is never enough, however, so middle-income families send their children to after-school private institutes – called *hagwon* – to study science, math, Korean and English. Families of wealth forgo the institutes and hire private tutors. Kids from lower-income families are left to fend for themselves as best they can.

Preparing for the university entrance exam is a three-year test of endurance. Top high-school students survive on as little as four hours sleep per night while torturing their brains with multiple-choice questions on calculus and the bizarre intricacies of English grammar. It's not all doom and gloom because there's a pot of gold at the end of the rainbow: university. Schools of higher learning are little more than a four-year vacation. There is remarkably little educational value inside the classroom and virtually everyone passes.

The race to the top has created opportunities for expat teachers. Most teach English but there is a demand for professors to teach content in English, especially in the business and engineering fields. An expat English teacher can expect to receive W2 million a month as well as free accommodation, return flights, health insurance and a bonus at the end of a one-year contract. It's enough to live on but you won't be banking big money on this wage alone. The country's average household income is W3 million per month. An office worker with a degree starts at about W1.5 million a month, or W2 million in a big company, while doctors, lawyers and pilots are in the W5 million to W20 million a month bracket.

In a country like South Korea, where social pressures to conform to a rigid standard of 'normality' are intense, it's not surprising to learn that Koreans are intolerant of homosexual behaviour. Lack of tolerance is hardly unique to Korea, but what is interesting is the lengths to which Koreans will go to deny, dismiss or rationalise the existence of gay and lesbian relationships. For most of mainstream Korea, homosexuality is a) non-existent or so rare that it's hardly worth mentioning (so don't); b) a freakish crime against nature; c) the manifestation of a debilitating mental illness; or d) a social problem caused by foreigners.

There is a small gay and lesbian scene in Seoul, with a pocket of bars in Itaewon. Outside the capital, opportunities to socialise with openly gay people are spotty. Gays and lesbians coming to Korea seeking employment as English teachers are best served by keeping their sexual orientation in the closet at work.

Korean attitudes towards gays and lesbians may be changing if the experience of Hong Suk-chun is an indicator of values. His career as a TV personality seemed bright until he came out in 2000, at which point

Korea spends more on private education as a percentage of GDP than any other OECD country, but ranks 25th for public spending.

he was banished from the airwaves. As the first public figure to come out, his personal life also took a turn for the worse: he was shunned by friends and taunted by strangers. Three years later, he's back on TV with an active professional career and a public persona moulded by his efforts to change the way people think about homosexuality.

If a single truism could ever capture the essence of life in Korea, it is this: everything is in a constant state of change. As Korea zooms down the highway of modernisation, it often seems this society doesn't notice the changing landscape. The basic fabric of society – marriage, family and purity of Korean blood – is currently undergoing a shift of tectonic proportions. The traditional pattern of arranged marriages at a young age organised by parents, with the wife forced to stay home and be subservient to her husband and in-laws, is disappearing fast. A high rate of divorce – now on par with Western countries – coupled with the cost of raising a family has driven down the birth rate. With an average of 1.17 children per woman, it's the lowest rate in the world.

The number of children is on the decline, but that's only part of the statistical story. The number of girls is sharply lower than that for boys. In 2002, 109 boys were born for every 100 girls, and by the year 2010 it is estimated that there will be 128 single men at 'peak marriageable age' (27 to 30 years old) for every 100 single, eligible women (24 to 27 years old). Most young families want a maximum of two children, and one of each gender is seen as ideal – two sons are acceptable but two daughters less so. Ultrasound scans can be used to discover the sex of any foetus and if female, she will sometimes be aborted. It is illegal for doctors to inform prospective parents of the sex of their foetus, but it does happen in some cases.

Korea's demographic shift is already being felt in the countryside where many men cannot find a Korean bride. The shortage of local marriageable women has led to the birth of a new industry: imported brides. For a fee, local agencies connect Korean men – mostly from agricultural communities – with brides from poor nations such as Vietnam and the Philippines. In 2005, one in four marriages involved a Korean and a partner from another country.

Koreans are proud of what they see is a pure bloodline (even if historical evidence suggests otherwise). If current marriage trends continue and couples choose to raise a family here, the country will experience a new phenomenon: a multiracial population that will challenge the country's less-than-tolerant racial attitudes. But attitudes might change: everything else in this country does.

POPULATION

South Korea's population is 48.4 million, of whom 10.4 million live in the capital Seoul. The greater-Seoul agglomeration, including Incheon and Gyeonggi-do province, has a population of 23.5 million people, making it the second-largest urban area in the world after Greater Tokyo. The population density of 480 per sq km is one of the highest in the world, but it actually feels more crowded because half of all people live in one of the country's seven major cities.

Farming and fishing villages are in terminal decline as older people die and young people leave for a more alluring life in the cities. Villages are losing 3% of their population every year, and only 4% of the rural population is under 40 years old. Local governments are essentially powerless to stem the outflow of people who are attracted by educational facilities, health services, entertainment venues and job opportunities that aren't available in regional communities.

'If a single truism could ever capture the essence of life in Korea, it is this: everything is in a constant state of change'

ECONOMY

Out-migration from the smaller communities to urban centres is a reflection of the country's uneven pattern of economic development. Although there are pockets of industrial development scattered across the country, such as shipbuilding on Geoje Island and automobile manufacturing in Ulsan, the disparities between regions is significant. Power, finance and prestige are located in or around the capital, which is home for 90% of corporate headquarters, 70% of venture companies and 85% of state-run firms.

As part of his election campaign, President Roh Moo-hyun proposed a balanced regional-development strategy that included moving the country's administrative capital out of Seoul. When details were announced, the legal basis of the plan was challenged and the Supreme Court concluded that it was unconstitutional. Undeterred, the Roh government formulated Plan B, which called for the relocation of state-run companies to regional cities and provinces. If the programme is fully implemented, some 32,000 employees will be living in another city by 2012.

KOREA AND YOU

Almost everything you'll experience in Korea is going to be different. The food, customs and non-Romanised writing system are unlike anything in Western countries. What should you do? Embrace the differences and view your trip as a cultural expedition.

There's no sugarcoating the fact that travelling in Korea does have its annoyances. Pushy people, absent-minded pedestrians blocking escalators, scooter drivers on the sidewalk who simply don't care if you move out of the way or not and 'bali bali' (hurry, hurry) are part of the street scene. You'll also encounter a people with unsmiling faces. Koreans are often reserved initially but if you are outgoing they respond in like manner. The key to an enjoyable journey is to be open-minded and positive.

Few people speak English with any degree of communicative competency, so the onus is on you to be prepared. It only takes a few hours to memorise the Korean alphabet along with some numbers and phrases. Many restaurants in larger cities have menus with some English writing but in the rest of the country, well, that's a different matter. That's also part of the charm of exploring the countryside. To prepare yourself, study the Food & Drink chapter (p62). Korea is a relatively crime-free country, but precautions should be taken. Women travelling alone at night should, for instance, avoid taking a taxi whenever possible.

Foreigners travelling in Korea are not expected to understand or follow the complex web of rules and subtleties that define social intercourse. But you can make a favourable impression by observing a few, simple rules. When visiting temples, homes, Korean-style restaurants and guesthouses, always remove your shoes and leave them by the front door. Wearing socks or stockings is more polite than bare feet. Korean travellers leave their shoes outside the door of their motel room; it's a quaint custom but probably not appropriate for international travellers with large shoes (eg American size 12) because it's almost impossible to find a replacement pair if yours should happen to go missing.

Always remember that you are judged by your appearance. Causal clothing is fine in most situations as long as it is neat with a conservative tone. In the hot and humid summer months, men almost never wear shorts. Women with blonde hair and blue eyes who dress provocatively may be approached by Korean men enquiring if they are Russian prostitutes.

When visiting someone's home, it's customary to bring along a small gift. Fresh fruit (often more expensive than meat) or boxed sets of Spam or tuna are always appreciated. When presented with a gift, your host may at first refuse it. This doesn't mean that he or she doesn't want it – the idea is not to look greedy. You should insist that they take it, and they will accept it 'reluctantly'. For the same reason, the recipient of a gift is not supposed to open the package immediately, but rather put it aside and open it later. When receiving a gift or business card, always use two hands.

Talk to Koreans about the economy and they may use the word depression to describe both the state of national affairs and their emotional quotient. Prior to the economic crisis in 1997 that brought the country to its knees, the robust economy regularly experienced double-digit rates of annual growth. Ten years later, Koreans have had to acclimatise themselves to a comparatively modest 5% rate of growth. Although high by Western standards, it's a level that hardly fosters optimism in Korea. Things can't be all bad, however: in 2005, the number of international trips taken by Koreans passed 10 million for the first time.

SPORT
Baseball

There are eight professional teams in the Korean baseball league, all sponsored by major *jaebeol* (huge, family-run corporate conglomerates). The season generally runs from April to October and each team plays 126 games. A few Korean players have made it to the American Major Leagues, including Park Chan-ho, who had considerable success with the Los Angeles Dodgers. Another pitcher, Kim Byun-hyun, might be remembered for flipping his middle finger towards the hometown Boston Red Sox fans, but he surely will live forever in the minds of trivia buffs as the man who gave up the home run that moved Bobby Bonds past Babe Ruth on the home-run list.

Basketball

Ten teams play in the Korean basketball league and matches are played from October to March. Two foreign players (usually Americans) are allowed in each team.

Soccer

Soccer is a popular recreational sport played by men and children on the dirt fields at local schools. Outside the World Cup, which gives Koreans a reason to wear red shirts and wave the flag, interest in professional soccer is lukewarm. There are 14 teams in Korea's professional soccer league.

Ssireum

Ssireum is a traditional Korean sport. It's called Korean-style wrestling but it's actually closer to grappling. Two competitors start off kneeling, and then grab the *satba* (cloth tied around the opponent's waist and thighs). The object is to use leverage to force your opponent to the ground. This near-dead sport lacks both public and corporate support and may soon go the way of the Korean tiger. Choi Hong-man was a *ssireum* champion who left the sport to earn a living as a K-1 fighter.

Taekwondo

Taekwondo is recognised around the world as a Korean martial art. Unlike most martial arts that claim to have a history dating back thousands of years, taekwondo has been around for about 50 years. It was cobbled together at the end of WWII by fighters who wanted a sport that, on the surface at least, was unrelated to anything Japanese. Bits were taken from (ahem) karate and blended with lesser-known Korean fighting skills such as *taekkyon,* which relies primarily on leg thrusts. By the mid-1950s the name 'taekwondo' was born.

MULTICULTURALISM

Korea is a monocultural society with marginal hints of multiculturalism. About 800,000 foreigners live in Korea, half of whom are migrant workers toiling for low wages in small and medium-sized factories. Foreign residents

USEFUL WEBSITES

Witty insights into Korean society at The Marmot's Hole, www.rjkoehler.com

Learn about Korean cinema at www.koreanfilm.org

English essays about the Korean arts scene at www.clickkorea.org.

tend to congregate in pockets, such as Westerners or Nigerians in Seoul's Itaewon, Russians on Busan's Texas St or international tradespeople on Geoje Island, though none qualify as a distinct cultural community.

The Korean monoculture experience has two features: distrust of foreign cultures, which occasionally peaks into hypernationalism; and rigidity. Speak with any Korean adult about Japan and you'll be on the receiving end of an outburst detailing every wrongdoing ever committed by the Japanese during the past 500 years. You'll also hear how every cultural advancement that made its way to Japan first passed through Korea. Elementary school children will tell you they hate Japan, but they don't know why. The American military is also a common whipping horse. The deep distain which many people feel towards the US military is especially intense in these heady days of historical revisionism, as traditional allies – like the US – are seen as barriers to unification, while the North – despite it's significant cache of weapons pointing south of the 38th parallel – is viewed with greater sympathy. It should be noted that Korea's historical gripes or attitudes about the US military are almost always directed at the governmental level; protestors or angry citizens rarely target individual travellers.

Despite the country's attraction, perhaps addiction, to economic and technological change, attitudes about cultural diversity sometimes appear fossilised. A Korean university student with a good command of English was asked if he enjoyed Thai food. His answer was: 'No, I'm Korean. I like Korean food.' This simple exchange encapsulates the Korean conception of multiculturalism: it's un-Korean. It's an age-old idea, a cultural leftover from the Hermit Kingdom that may be tested in the near future as the country moves through demographics change, which include a growing multiracial population that could literally change the face of the nation. It's also a mindset that seems out of place, given the financial and human capital directed towards transforming the country into a regional centre.

In some circles, it's fashionable to claim that Korea is becoming a hub of Asia. Many kinds of hubs are bandied about: logistics hub, finance hub, hub of Northeast Asia. Noble ideas indeed but at times it sounds like hubbub. Korea lacks the social infrastructure (eg international schools, English-language access to medical and governmental services, etc) to support a sizable international population. Moreover, Korea does not possess the cultural tools to accept or work within a multicultural society. At a deep instinctual level, Koreans aren't especially fond of foreigners. They are tolerated for specific and beneficial purposes, like migrant workers doing the dirty, dangerous and difficult work (locally called 3-D work) that Koreans prefer not to do, or expats teaching English to children, but the idea that foreigners living in Korea should be treated as equals under the law is, for many people, a new idea that's difficult to accept.

> 'In some circles, it's fashionable to claim that Korea is becoming a hub of Asia'

RELIGION

There are four streams of spiritual influence in Korea: shamanism, which originated in central Asia; Buddhism, which entered Korea from China in the 4th-century AD; Confucianism, a system of ethics of Chinese origin; and Christianity, which first made inroads into Korea in the 18th century. Approximately half the nation professes to be Buddhist or Christian with the remaining 50% uncommitted.

Shamanism

Shamanism is an important part of Korean spirituality. It's not a religion but it does involve communication with spirits through intermediaries known as *mudang* (female shamans). Shamanist ceremonies are held for a variety of reasons: to cure illness, to ward off financial problems or to guide a deceased family member safely into the spirit world. A *gut* (ceremony) might be held by a village on a regular basis to ensure the safety of its citizens and a good harvest of rice or fish.

These ceremonies involve contacting spirits who are attracted by lavish offerings of food and drink. Drums beat and the *mudang* dances herself into a frenzied state that allows her to communicate with the spirits and be possessed by them. Resentments felt by the dead can plague the living and cause all sorts of misfortune, so their spirits need placating. For shamanists death does not end relationships, it simply takes another form.

On Inwangsan, a wooded hillside in northwestern Seoul, ceremonies take place in or near the historic Guksadang shrine (p116). Food offerings to the spirits include a pig's head.

Buddhism

When first introduced during the Koguryo dynasty in AD 370, Buddhism coexisted with shamanism. Many Buddhist temples have a *samseionggak* (three-spirit hall) on their grounds, which houses shamanist deities such as the Mountain God. Buddhism flourished through the unified period and contributed important works such as the Tripitaka Korea (81,340 carved woodblocks), which is at Haeinsa (p196). Buddhism was persecuted during the Joseon period, when temples were tolerated only in remote mountains. It suffered another sharp decline after WWII as Koreans pursued worldly goals. But South Korea's success in achieving developed-nation status, coupled with a growing interest in spiritual values and the environment, is encouraging a Buddhist revival. Temple visits have increased and large sums of money are flowing into temple reconstruction.

Today, about 90% of Korean Buddhists belong to the Jogye sect, which claims to have 8000 monks and 5000 nuns. Buddha's birthday is a national holiday, which includes an extravagant parade in Seoul (p102).

Confucianism

Confucianism is a system of ethics rather than a religion. Confucius (555-479 BC) lived in China during a time of chaos and feudal rivalry known as the Warring States period. He emphasised devotion to parents, loyalty to friends,

---

PROVERBS

Traditional sayings provide an uncensored insight into a nation's psyche:

▪ Koreans' strong belief in the importance of education is reflected in this proverb: 'Teaching your child one book is better than leaving him a fortune.'

▪ The hope of all Koreans of humble origins is to improve their lifestyle and be 'a dragon that rises from a ditch'.

▪ The blunt, peasant humour of the Korean character is expressed by this poor man's lament: 'I have nothing but my testicles.'

▪ Koreans distrust lawyers and governments and prefer to settle disputes in their own way: 'The law is far but the fist is near.'

▪ An unblemished character is a Korean's most treasured possession. To avoid any suspicion of being a thief, 'Do not tie your shoelaces in a melon patch or touch your hat under a pear tree'.

▪ Koreans have often needed guts and determination to overcome defeats and disasters: 'After the house is burnt, pick up the nails.'

justice, peace, education, reform and humanitarianism. He also urged respect and deference for those in authority and believed that men were superior to women and that a woman's place was in the home.

As Confucianism trickled into Korea, it evolved into Neo-Confucianism, which blended the sage's original ideas with the quasi-religious practice of ancestral worship and the idea of the eldest male as spiritual head of the family. During its 500-year history as Korea's state philosophy, it became authoritarian and ultraconservative. Today, it continues to shape the way Koreans see the world. For an account of how Confucianism underpins modern Korean values, see p44.

Christianity

Korea's first significant exposure to Christianity was via the Jesuits from the Chinese imperial court in the late 18th century. The Catholic faith spread quickly – so quickly, in fact, that it was perceived as a threat by the Confucian government and was vigorously suppressed, creating thousands of Catholic martyrs. The Christian ideal of human equality clashed with the neo-Confucius ethos of a rigidly stratified society. Christianity got a second chance in the 1880s, with the arrival of Western Protestant missionaries who founded schools and hospitals and gained many followers.

WOMEN IN KOREA

The traditional role of women as housewife and mother is changing rapidly. In the 1980s, only 15% of women in the marrying age bracket – 25 to 29 – were single. Twenty years later, more than 40% of women in that cohort are single. Women who marry are discovering that their lives look quite different from that of their mother's. Economic necessity is driving women out of the kitchen and into the workforce. Today, 60% of women with a college diploma or university degree are working, while half of all women 15 years and older hold a job, a 50% increase compared to three decades past.

Despite changes in the labour pool, the Korean workplace continues to challenge women. Sexual harassment is prevalent though it is becoming less tolerated thanks to several high profile cases, including one involving a male politician and a female reporter. Although working women put in just as many hours, they earn about one-third less than men. In the professional fields, there is still a glass ceiling based partly on the belief that women in their thirties stay home to raise a family, and therefore should not be promoted over men who are the traditional breadwinners.

'The traditional role of women as housewife and mother is changing rapidly'

MEDIA
TV

Like all countries, Korean TV is a wasteland of home-shopping channels, B-grade English-language shows and local programming that fills the void in a lonely person's life. The only English TV station in the country – excluding the TV arm of the US military, which is available in limited areas – is Arirang, broadcasting a steady stream of cheery, uplifting and thoroughly sanitised news about Korea. Korean comedies are popular and usually involve a team of wannabe celebrities who square off in contests that invariably involve a man carrying a woman sporting high-heel shoes and hot pants.

TV dramas are a refreshing change for compelling plots and superior production quality. Love triangles, revenge, odd twists of fate involving hospitalisation and memory loss, along with stirring music, are packaged into tender, innocent stories that have captivated women across the globe. Spurred on by soap operas, the growing international demand for Korean pop culture is called *hallyu*, or the Korean Wave.

The wave started in 2002 with *Winter Sonata*, the first Korean TV drama to capture the hearts, and wallets, of Japanese women, but it certainly wasn't the last. The historical drama *Dae Jang-geum* tells the story of a woman who worked as a cook in the royal court. Through perseverance she became the first female royal doctor during Joseon. Memory loss plays an important role in *Stairway to Heaven*, a serious tear-jerker about two sweethearts that become separated. The woman is involved in a car accident, loses her memory and changes her identity. The man comes back to her but his efforts to rekindle the relationship are complicated by another woman, a greedy stepmother and eye cancer.

TRADITIONAL COSTUMES

The striking traditional clothing that used to be worn all the time by Koreans is known as *hanbok* and was as much a part of the local culture as *Han·geul* and *kimchi*. Traditionally, women wore a loose-fitting short blouse with long sleeves and a voluminous long skirt, while men wore a jacket and baggy trousers. Both sexes wore socks. Cotton replaced hemp as the main clothing material during the Joseon dynasty. In winter, overcoats were worn over padded clothes and people piled on lots of undergarments to keep out the freezing cold. Men sometimes wore a wide waistcoat. The exact designs have varied over the centuries, especially female *hanbok*, but the clothes have maintained their basic pattern of simple lines without any pockets.

Hanbok style followed the Confucian principle of unadorned modesty. Natural dyes were used to create plain colours, although some parts of clothing could be embroidered, and the very rich could afford silk. In the Joseon period clothing was strictly regulated and poorer people generally had to wear white. In those days you could tell a person's occupation and status from the *hanbok* they wore. For instance, only *yangban* (aristocrats) could wear the black horsehair hats that were a badge of their rank, while a fancy *binyeo* (hairpin) in a big wig was a female status symbol. Scholars (invariably male in those days) wore a plain white gown with wide sleeves. At court, government officials wore special black hats and *heungbae* – embroidered insignia on the back and front of their gowns. Peasants and slaves wore white hemp or cotton clothes and straw sandals.

High-class women hardly ever left their home during the day, and if they did they had to wear a headscarf as a veil and were often carried about in a curtained palanquin by their slaves. Women of lower rank were not veiled and in some respects had more freedom than their wealthier sisters.

In the summer, lightweight, almost transparent ramie –a cloth made from pounded bark – provided cool and comfortable clothing for those who could afford it. Ramie clothing, with its unique texture and look, is making a comeback in the fashion world.

The problem with *hanbok* is that hardly anyone wears it. Up until the 1960s it was common but urbanisation and Westernisation have made it seem old-fashioned. The only horsehair hats you are likely to see are in dusty folk museums or on the heads of actors in historical TV dramas. *Hanbok* is usually only worn at weddings, festivals or other special occasions, and by waitresses in some traditional restaurants and residents in touristic folk villages. Men prefer Western suits or casual wear, and most women find *hanbok* uncomfortable and unflattering: it restricts their movements, has no pockets and is difficult to clean.

Today, fashion designers are reinventing the *hanbok* for the modern world. In markets and shops you can buy modern or traditional *hanbok*. The everyday *hanbok* is reasonably priced, but the formal styles, made of silk and intricately embroidered, are objects of wonder and cost a fortune.

Waistcoats are still popular but only among hikers. Elderly men sometimes wear trilby hats, which are akin to modern *hanbok*, and *ajumma* (married women) sport brightly coloured baggy trousers with clashing multicoloured patterned blouses. Men used to have long hair tied in a topknot but King Gojong had his cut off in 1895 and yet another custom gradually died out.

Hanbok: The Art of Korean Clothing by Sunny Yang (1997) gives a comprehensive history of traditional clothing with masses of pictures.

KOREAN SOAP CLEANS UP IN ASIA

Winter Sonata was the first Korean TV drama to gain an international following. It's the story of two high-school sweethearts whose innocent love was quashed by fate and a car accident. The boy discovers that the father of the girl he loves might be his long lost daddy. Overcome by the realisation that he might be in love with his half-sister, he decides to run away, only to be hit by a car. The girl thinks he is dead and moves on with her life. While he's in hospital, the boy's mother hires a shrink to erase her son's painful memories of growing up as an illegitimate child, gives him a new identity and sends him off to America. Fast forward 10 years, and the hero with a new identify is back in Korea and, coincidentally, bumps into his old high-school sweetheart. The balance of the programme is about how the relationship unfolds and how the man with a new identity recalls his past.

Bae Yong-joon plays the man with two identities. He's well known in Korea and is a certified superstar in Japan where middle-aged women fantasise about having a man like Mr Bae: soft, loving and totally into the relationship. Every shop frequented by Japanese tourists in Korea has larger-than-life images of Mr Bae.

Newspapers

The country's two English-language newspapers – *Korea Times* and *Korean Herald* – are useful resources for students studying English but receive an 'F' for news coverage. The *International Herald Tribune* is a better read. It's widely available in Seoul but hard to find in other cities (and often a day late even if you can find it).

ARTS
Architecture

The best examples of traditional architecture are in Buddhist temples, with massive wooden beams set on stone foundations, often built with notches instead of nails. Roofs are usually made from heavy clay tiles. The strikingly bold and colourful painted design under the eaves is called *dancheong*.

Modern architecture, in contrast, reflects a keen interest in budget rather than urban design. Large concrete towers that look like shoeboxes define most city landscapes. There are notable exceptions, such as Seoul's Jongno Tower, a magnificent structure with a Joseon influence. To experience how modern architecture can manipulate space in a playful manner, Seoul's Leeum Samsung Museum of Art (p104) is a must-see. For sheer power and strength, there is 63 Building on Yeouido (p114), or go even bigger with Tower G in Gangnam, which stands 73 stories.

Cinema

The Korean film industry is protected by a screen-quota system. For 40 years cinemas were required to screen Korean films for 146 days per year, but after several years of wrangling and pressure from US interests that figure was dropped in 2006 to 73 days. Korea's film culture is, however, strong and produces films that may not compare with Hollywood in terms of budget although the quality is often outstanding. Since being launched in 1996, the Pusan International Film Festival (PIFF) has grown quickly to become the most respected festival in Asia, and attracts crowds of film enthusiasts.

Visit a DVD *bang* and you can watch Korean movies with English subtitles in the comfort of your own minicinema.

Some great Korean movies include the following:

■ *The Host* (2006) has everything a great Korean monster movie needs: a beast in the Han River, family devotion and a story that blames the US military for wreaking an environmental disaster. It was a smash hit.

- *Old Boy* (2003) is a disturbing yet brilliant piece of cinema. It's the story of a man imprisoned for 15 years who seeks revenge on his captors.
- *King and the Clown* (2005) is a story of two court jesters during the Joseon dynasty with a homosexual subtext. A surprise Korean blockbuster.
- *Shiri* (1999) is about an elite squad of North Korean terrorists threatening to unleash a dastardly weapon on the South.
- *Memories of Murder* (2003) is based on a true, unsolved case. It's the story of two cops investigating the rape and murder of ten women in Gyeonggi province between 1986 and 1991. This thriller was directed by Boon Jong-ho, who also directed *The Host*.
- *JSA* (2001) is a thriller directed by Park Chan-wook about a friendship that develops between soldiers on opposite sides of the Demilitarized Zone.
- *Taegukgi* (2004) is a Korean War flick about two brothers with some terrific battle scenes.

Literature

In the 12th century, the monk Iryeon wrote *Samguk Yusa* (Myths and Legends of the Three Kingdoms), the most important work of early Korean literature. During Joseon, three-line *sijo* poems based on Chinese models continued to be written in Chinese characters even after the invention of *Han·geul* in the 15th century. In 1945 there was a sharp turn away from Chinese and Japanese influence of any kind. Western influence increased dramatically and existentialism became the guiding cultural philosophy. A growing body of modern English-language literature deals with Koreans living abroad and their struggles with identity.

Still Life with Rice by Helie Lee (1997) recounts one family's struggle during the Korean War.

The Gingko Bed (1996) blends dreams, time travel and two pieces of wood into a love story.

War Trash by Ha Jin (2004) is a gritty novel about the life of a POW during the Korean War from the perspective of an English-speaking Chinese soldier.

Native Speaker by Lee Chang-rae (1996) is a political thriller about a second-generation Korean-American man on the outside looking in. Also take a look at Lee's *A Gesture Life* (1999), the story of an older Japanese gentleman who uses grace to mask past mistakes as a soldier in Burma while overseeing Korean comfort woman.

Appointment With My Brother by Yi Mun-yol (2002) is a brilliant novella about a man from the South who meets his half-brother from the North. It's an emotional and stressful meeting for both of them, a collision of two worlds.

A BANG LIFESTYLE

In every city and town you can find plenty of *bang* (rooms) which play a large role in the modern Korean lifestyle. They always charge reasonable prices. Some of the different types of *bang* include:

Bideobang Grubby rooms with a sofa and a screen that show your video choice.

Board game bang A large room to play board games.

Da bang Teashops where the 'coffee girls' deliver more than the name suggests.

DVD bang Small rooms with a sofa and a big screen that show your choice of DVD film in English or with English subtitles. Popular with courting couples.

Jjimjilbang Sport loose fitting uniforms and partake in the Korean art of doing nothing.

Noraebang Small rooms full of happy groups of all ages singing along to their favourite songs. English songs and soft drinks are available.

PC bang Big rooms full of young, chain smoking male computer-game addicts and the occasional emailer.

A Dwarf Launches a Little Ball by Cho Se-hui (1976) is a passionate novella about a family made homeless by urban redevelopment. The story is memorable in spite of the inferior translation.

The Descendants of Cain by Hwang Sun-won (1997), one of Korea's most celebrated authors, tells the story of life in a North Korean village between the end of WWII and the beginning of the Korean War.

Music

Gugak (traditional music) is played on stringed instruments, most notably the *gayageum* (12-stringed zither) and *haegeum* (two-stringed fiddle), and on chimes, gongs, cymbals, drums, horns and flutes. Traditional music can be subdivided into three categories: *jeong·ak* is a slow court music often combined with elegant dances; *bulgyo eumak* is played and chanted in Buddhist temples; *samul·nori* is a lively style originally played by travelling entertainers. It died out during Japanese colonial rule but was reinvented in the 1970s by musicians playing four traditional percussion instruments.

Korea's traditional music is unlikely to catch on overseas, but that certainly hasn't been the case with the country's pop music, called K-pop. Riding the *hallyu*, K-pop artists have attracted significant international attention though none have attained BoA's level of commercial success. In some respects she is the Korean Madonna, a woman with considerable vocal talents and the ability to exploit new markets.

Rain's sugary love songs have a following across Asia where his third album sold one million copies. In 2006 Rain performed at New York's Madison Square Gardens to two sold-out shows. Other groups and singers that have gained notoriety include Se7en, Hyo Lee and the wildly popular boy band Shinhwa.

> 'Korea's traditional music is unlikely to catch on overseas, but that certainly hasn't been the case with the country's pop music'

Painting & Sculpture

Chinese influence is paramount in traditional Korean painting. The brush line, which varies in thickness and tone, is the most important feature. The painting is meant to surround the viewer and there is no fixed viewpoint. Zen-style Buddhist art can be seen inside and on the outside walls of hundreds of temples around the country. Murals usually depict scenes from Buddha's life.

Stone Buddhist statues and pagodas are the most common examples of ancient sculpture. Cast bronze was also common for Buddhas and some marvellous examples can be seen in the National Museum of Korea (p104). Stone and wooden shamanist guardian posts are common and Jejudo has its own unique *harubang* or 'grandfather stones' (p272). Many towns have sculpture gardens – including Seoul's Olympic Park (p113).

Korea's best-known modern sculptor, Baek Nam-june, who died in January 2006, was a Korean-American artist who used video monitors instead of stone to create inspired, sometimes bizarre, work. One of his larger creations, 'The More the Better,' is an 18m-tower with 1000 video monitors on display at the National Museum of Contemporary Art inside Seoul Grand Park (p141). His experimentation with video began in the 1960s, a time when information technology was beginning to enter the mainstream. Baek's unique artistic representations of technology's interface with society invite parallels with Marshal McCluhan, a media analyst who taught us that 'the medium is the message'.

Other modern artists include painter Kim Whanki, mixed-media artist Min Yong-soon and Kim Tschang-yeul, a painter noted for his dedication to water drops; one of the latter's paintings is at the Leeum Samsung Museum of Art in Seoul (p104). For an international taste of modern art, Gwangju hosts a two-month modern festival every two years (p254).

Pottery

Pottery on the Korean peninsula dates back 10,000 years, but the 12th century is regarded as a special moment in time when skilled artisans turned out celadon earthenware with a green tinge. Nowadays Korean celadon earns thousands of dollars at auction. Pottery fans shouldn't miss out on a visit to Icheon Ceramic Village (p148) near Seoul and two pottery villages in Jeollanam-do: the Pottery Culture Centre (p266) and the Gangjin Celadon Museum (p262).

Theatre & Dance

DANCE

Popular folk dances include *samul·nori* (drum dance), *talchum* (mask dance) and solo improvisational *salpuri* (shamanist dance). *Samul·nori* dancers perform in brightly coloured clothing, twirling a long tassel from a special cap on their heads. Good coordination is required to dance, twirl and play a drum at the same time. These dancers appear at every festival.

Talchum dance-dramas were performed by low-class travelling showmen on market days and usually satirised the *yangban* class. Masks indicated the status of the character – a *yangban*, monk, shaman, grandmother, concubine or servant – and hid the identity of the performer. Mask dance-dramas involved vigorous leaping, comedy and big gestures, together with shouting, singing and reciting. The performers usually mingled with the audience once their part was over. Today, masks are usually made of wood and every souvenir shop sells them.

There are two major modern dance festivals held in Seoul each year. The MODAFE festival (www.modafe.org) has been operating for over a quarter or a century and usually holds performances in the spring. The Seoul International Dance Festival (www.sidance.org) has been around for about a decade, with local and international performers taking the stage at numerous venues across the city including the Seoul Arts Centre. During the festival, which usually runs in October, there are workshops with noted choreographers.

> 'Good coordination is required to dance, twirl and play a drum at the same time'

THEATRE

Korea's small, modern theatrical experience is primarily based in Seoul. Commercially safe, non-verbal shows like Nanta and Tobekki appeal to an international audience (p133). There's an experimental scene in Daehangno but it's entirely in Korean, though the Hakjeon Green Theatre has subtitles on a screen (p133).

KOREAN OPERA

Changgeuk is an opera that can involve a large cast of characters. Another type of opera is *pansori*, which features a solo storyteller (usually female) singing in a strained voice to the beat of a male drummer. The performer flicks her fan to emphasise dramatic moments. For details on Seoul's traditional theatres that stage these shows, see p133.

Environment

South Korea's economic growth since 1960 has transformed the country from an agricultural to an industrial society. Sprawling apartment-block cities and huge industrial complexes have been constructed, rivers have been dammed and freeways have been bulldozed through the countryside. Authoritarian governments stamped on any opposition to development projects and the environmental impacts were ignored. Fortunately the 70% of Korea that is mountainous and forested is still largely undeveloped, and the hundreds of off-shore islands are also unspoilt. For a developed country Korea is surprisingly green, as 90% of the population is packed into high-rise city apartments.

Nowadays politics is more democratic, mayors win votes by promising green policies and citizen environmental groups are no longer ignored by the media. Unpopular construction projects can face fierce local opposition – the government has been searching for a nuclear waste site since 1986 without success, as every site suggested has been met with a storm of local protest.

THE LAND

South Korea's land area is 99,538 sq km, the same size as Portugal and almost as large as North Korea. Its overall length from north to south (including Jejudo) is 500km, while the narrowest point is 220km wide. Forested mountains cover 70% of the land, although they are not very high – Hallasan (1950m) on Jejudo is the highest peak. Many mountains are granite with dramatic cliffs and pinnacles, but there are also impressive limestone caves to visit.

Living History of the DMZ by Hahm Kwang Bok (2004) covers the unique ecological zone that separates the two Koreas.

To the south is Jejudo, a volcanic island with spectacular craters and lava tubes, and off the east coast is another volcanic island, Ulleungdo, which is remote, rural and mysterious. Korea is not in an earthquake zone, but there are dozens of mineral-laden *oncheon* (hot springs) that bubble up through the ground and have been developed into health spas. Most large rivers have been dammed, but the man-made lakes created by them are scenic. World-class ski resorts lure winter-sports enthusiasts to the snow-laden mountainous regions in the colder, northern half of the country.

The plains and shallow valleys are still dominated by irrigated rice fields that are interspersed with small orchards, plastic greenhouses growing vegetables, and barns housing cows, pigs and chickens. In the south are green-tea plantations; on frost-free Jejudo citrus fruit is grown. Despite huge government subsidies and 50% tariffs on agricultural imports, the rural population is greying and shrinking every year. In some villages everyone is over 60 years old. Very few young people want to be farmers and fewer still want to marry a farmer, so foreign wives are being imported from Southeast Asian countries.

Caves by Kyung Sik Woo (2005) is a lavishly illustrated book on Korean caves by a geological expert and cave enthusiast.

The hundreds of sparsely populated islands scattered around the western and southern coasts of the peninsula have a relaxed atmosphere, unspoiled by second-home owners, and a few have attractive sandy beaches. Here you can go way off the beaten track to islands where the inhabitants have never seen a foreigner. The west-coast mud flats are a vast larder of shellfish and crabs that not only support thousands of migrating birds, but also supply countless seafood markets and raw fish restaurants. Reclaiming the mud flats for farmland has become a highly emotive and divisive issue (p60).

ANIMALS

Korea's forested mountains used to be crowded with Siberian tigers, leopards, bears, deer, goral antelopes, wolves and foxes. Unfortunately these animals are now extinct or rare in Korea, and all that hikers are likely to see are cute little Asiatic chipmunks, squirrels and birds. Efforts are now being made to build up the number of wild animals in the country (see boxed text below). Magpies, pigeons and sparrows account for most of the birds in the towns and cities, but egrets, herons and swallows are common in the countryside, and raptors, woodpeckers and pheasants can also be seen. Although many are visiting migrants, over 500 bird species have been sighted, and Korea has a growing reputation among birders keen to see Steller's sea eagles, red-crowned cranes, black-faced spoonbills and other rarities.

> A hundred bird species can be seen in just one day on Eocheongdo, a small island off Gunsan in Jeollabuk-do.

PLANTS

Northern parts of South Korea are the coldest and the flora is alpine: beech, birch, fir, larch and pine. Further south, deciduous trees are more common. The south coast and Jejudo are the warmest and wettest areas, so the vegetation is lush. Cherry trees blossom in early spring followed by azaleas and camellias. Korea's mountainsides are a pharmacy and salad bar of health-giving edible leaves, ferns, roots, nuts and fungi. Many of these wild mountain vegetables end up in restaurant side dishes and *sanchae bibimbap* (a meal of rice, egg, meat and mountain vegetables). Wild ginseng is the most expensive and sought-after plant.

NATIONAL & PROVINCIAL PARKS

Korea has 20 national parks that cover 38,240 sq km of land (6.5% of the country). The first national park, Jirisan, was established in 1967 and is the third most-visited park with 2.6 million paying customers a year. Only Seoraksan (2.8 million) in Gang-won-do and Bukhansan (4 million), located on Seoul's doorstep, have more visitors. There are also 22 smaller provincial parks (covering 747 sq km) and 29 county parks (covering 307 sq km) that are just as worthy of a visit as the national parks. Entrance fees to the parks vary but they are all a bargain at W3000 or less. All the parks have well-marked hiking trails that can be so popular that trails have to be closed to protect them from serious erosion.

> *Field Guide to the Birds of Korea* by Lee, Koo & Park (2000) is the standard bird guide, but doesn't include all feathered visitors.

The parks can be enjoyed in every season. In spring cherry blossoms, azaleas and other flowers are a delight; in summer the hillsides and river valleys provide a cool escape from the heat and humidity of the cities;

HALF-MOON BEARS

Manchurian black bears (sometimes called half-moon bears because of the crescent moon of white fur on their chests) were thought to be extinct in South Korea. But in 2001 video-camera footage proved that a few bears were living in a remote part of Jirisan National Park, perhaps six of them. The **Jirisan Bear Project** (☎ 061 783-9120) was established with the aim to build up a self-sustaining group of 50 wild bears in Jirisan. As a start four bears from bear farms were released in late 2001. One female bear died and a second female kept pestering hikers for food and had to be removed. The two male bears, Bandol and Jangun, survived longer, but started raiding farmers' beehives. They are now involved in retraining farm and zoo bears to survive in the wild.

By 2006, 14 bears from North Korea and Russia had been released in Jirisan, and another eight were in the training programme.

The Korean bears are bigger, with a wider face and shaggier hair than the Manchurian black bears that are common in Japan. They are nocturnal and shy so hikers rarely see them, but if you do bump into a bear, stand still so as not to frighten it, and give way.

Unfortunately numerous bear products are still sold by the traditional medicine industry in Korea and throughout Asia. A bear produces around 2kg of bile a year which sells for as much as US$10,000 per kilogram.

JIRISAN NATIONAL PARK ANIMALS *Han Sang-hoon*

The last **Siberian tiger** in Jirisan was captured in 1944. Plenty of people have claimed to have seen a tiger since then, or a footprint or whatever. But there is no definite evidence or proof. Siberian tigers are critically endangered as less than 500 survive in the wild, mostly in east Russia or northeast China, but they are occasionally reported in North Korea. **Amur leopards** used to be common in Korea but the last wild one was captured in 1962: now there are less than 50 living in the wild around the world.

The **grey wolf** is probably extinct in the wild in South Korea, as there has been no confirmed sighting of one for over 10 years. However there are a few in North Korea near Paekdusan. I know that because I was lucky enough to see one when I was there on a joint project.

I estimate that 20 to 30 **red foxes** are living in the wild in the South. I've seen red foxes three times – in 1993, 1995 and 1997 – twice in Jirisan and once on Namhae island in Gyeongsangnam-do. There are perhaps less than 10 in Jirisan but they've never been photographed or videoed. If any visitor sees a fox please photograph it and send me a copy, addressed to the Bear Project at Jirisan National Park HQ.

Sika deer died out in the 1940s. Unhappily **musk deer** are also on the verge of extinction in Korea despite government protection. However the number of **water deer** is increasing, which is good news because they are a special sub-species found only in China and Korea. **Roe deer** can also be found at higher elevations in Jirisan, and many more live on Hallasan on Jejudo.

River otter numbers are decreasing due to dam and road construction disturbing their habitats. **Badger** numbers are increasing in Jirisan but illegal hunting still goes on and is reducing their numbers elsewhere – badgers are a popular food for women after they've given birth. **Racoon dogs** were doing well but recently they've been hit by a mystery virus. **Leopard cats**, **martens** and **wild boars** also live in the park but are rarely seen.

Dusk or dawn is the best time to see the park's animals. Find a little-used trail and just stand still, and they will come out if they are around.

Han Sang-hoon, Director of Jirisan Bear Project

---

during the summer monsoon, the waterfalls are particularly impressive; in autumn red-coloured leaves and clear blue skies provide a fantastic sight; and in winter snow and ice turn the parks into a white wonderland, although crampons and proper clothing are needed for any serious hikes at this time of year. Korean winters can be Arctic, especially if you're high up in the mountains.

Gaily painted wooden Buddhist temples and hermitages grace nearly every mountain, and river valleys, waterfalls and rocky outcrops abound. It's not surprising that many visitors rate the national and provincial parks as the country's top attraction.

Koreans are enthusiastic hikers, so most parks are crowded at weekends, particularly in summer and autumn. Many hikers go hiking every week and like to dress up in smart hiking gear – red waistcoats with plenty of pockets are a long-standing favourite, although ninja black is the latest hiking fashion. Proper hiking boots (not backpacker sandals!) are *de rigueur* for serious hikers, although you may see young women (usually from Seoul) struggling up a mountain trail in high heels. Korean women have the strongest ankles in the world.

Take a bottle of *soju* (Korean vodka-like drink) or *dongdongju* (fermented rice wine) and a picnic along. All the parks have tourist villages near the main entrances with restaurants, market stalls, souvenir and food shops, and budget accommodation where big groups can squeeze into a small room. Camping grounds (W3000 for a three-person tent) and mountain shelters (W3000 to W5000 for a bunk) are cheap, but provide only very basic facilities.

www.birdskorea.org has wonderful photos of Korean birds and loads of info for bird lovers.

Top national parks include:

Park	Area	Features & Activities
Bukhansan	78 sq km	Great hiking, and subway access from Seoul (p141)
Dadohae Haesang	2344 sq km	A marine park of scattered, unspoilt islands (p270) (2004 sq km marine)
Deogyusan	219 sq km	A top ski resort, a fortress and a magical valley walk (p301)
Gyeongju	138 sq km	Strewn with ancient Shilla and Buddhist relics (p197)
Hallasan	149 sq km	This extinct volcano on Jejudo is Korea's highest peak (p292)
Jirisan	440 sq km	A giant park with high peaks that is popular with serious hikers (East p247 and West p258)
Seoraksan	373 sq km	Korea's most beautiful and second-most popular park (p172)
Sobaeksan	320 sq km	Limestone caves and Gu·insa, an impressive temple complex (p343)

Top provincial parks include:

Park	Area	Features & Activities
Daedunsan	38 sq km	Granite cliffs, great views and a hot-spring bath (p300)
Gajisan	104 sq km	Scenic views and a famous temple, Tongdosa (p242)
Mudeungsan	30 sq km	Near Gwangju with an art gallery and a green-tea plantation (p253)
Namhan Sanseong	36 sq km	Take the subway from Seoul, hike round the fortress wall and eat in the restaurant village (p144)
Taebaeksan	17 sq km	Visit the Coal Museum and hike up to Dan·gun's altar (p184)

ENVIRONMENTAL ISSUES

Open any newspaper these days and you are likely to come across an environmental controversy of some kind. The NIMBY (Not In My Backyard) syndrome is starting to catch on as Korean society becomes more democratic and Westernised. Two long-running environmental issues concern where to store nuclear waste and the reclamation of mud flats at Saemangeum in Jeollabuk-do.

South Korea relies on nuclear power to generate one-third of the country's electricity, but the government has so far failed to find a permanent storage site for the radioactive waste that continues to be produced. It's all in temporary storage. Many sites have been proposed since 1986 but they have all provoked fierce opposition despite the billions of won in compensation offered to the local communities affected.

The huge US$2 billion Saemangeum project in Jeollabuk-do has involved constructing a 33km sea wall to reclaim 40,000 hectares of mud flats, mainly for agricultural use. Opponents see little economic benefit in creating more rice fields at the expense of the mud flats, which are an important fish and shellfish breeding area and provide a vital feeding ground for more than 100,000 migrant birds, including black-faced spoonbills and 12 other threatened species.

In February 2005, when the project was almost finished, at the eleventh hour a court supported the opponents and work on the project was suspended, but a year later a higher court allowed the scheme to go ahead. The sea wall was finally completed in April 2006, 15 years after it was begun. Plans are afoot to run an annual marathon along the wall and to open it up as a tourist road.

In response to the Saemangeum protests, in 2006 the government declared 60 sq km of wetlands at the Han River estuary in Gyeonggi-do a protected

Goral antelopes have been released into Woraksan National Park. Keep a lookout for them when you visit.

View www.npa.or.kr for information on all 20 national parks.

View www.greenkorea .org for a pressure group with practical ideas such as Buy Nothing Day, Car Free Day and Save Paper Day.

area. Ten smaller wetland areas (covering a total of 45 sq km) had already been protected.

Green policies have also become a hot potato in Seoul's local politics. The greening of the capital has just started after decades of delays and excuses. The new Ttukseom Seoul Forest (take subway line 2 to Ttukseom subway station, and leave by exit 8) and the expensive but splendid restoration of the Cheonggye stream (Map pp88–9) now flowing through downtown, are two examples of this new trend. One-third of Seoul's buses now run on environmentally friendly CNG (Compressed Natural Gas) rather than diesel. Seoul mayors these days are now more likely to be nicknamed 'Green' Lee rather than 'Bulldozer' Lee. Trees and gardens are part of all new property developments, and Seoul's city hall now has a grass plaza in front and some trees at the back. Hopefully the next step will be the development of fully pedestrianised streets, starting with Insadong-gil.

Most garbage is recycled and tourists can help by putting their rubbish in the appropriate bins for paper, cans and plastic. If you rent an apartment you will need separate rubbish bags for food waste, plastics, metal, paper and so on. The concierge will show you the system.

Another small way that tourists can help is by refusing unnecessary packaging. A few stores such as E-Mart and Buy The Way are already discouraging the use of plastic bags by charging for them.

Environmentalists are monitoring the impact of the Saemangeum project on migrant bird numbers – see http://english.kfem .or.kr.

Food & Drink

Korea has one of Asia's richest culinary traditions, and sampling all the quirky delights of the local food and drink is one of the joys of visiting the country. Listings in this chapter focus on Korean food, but Western fodder is nearly always available in bakeries, convenience stores and pizza and fast food outlets, which are numerous and easy to spot.

A typical Korean meal is based around boiled rice, soups and as many as a dozen side dishes, called *banchan,* which normally include Korea's national dish, *kimchi* (pickled or fermented vegetables). Diners in Korea are not expected to finish everything – in fact if you do, the side dishes will probably be refilled until you burst!

Garlic, ginger, green onion, black pepper, sesame oil, soy sauce and vinegar abound. But the big spice is chilli pepper, which usually takes the form of *gochujang* (red pepper paste). A good general rule is: red = spicy.

STAPLES & SPECIALITIES

Bibimbap

Bibimbap is a tasty and foreigner-friendly mixture of vegetables, meat and an egg on top of rice. Mix it all together with your spoon before digging in. If you don't want it too spicy, remove some of the *gochujang* before mixing. *Bibimbap* is usually served with soup but don't mix that in too! *Sanchae bibimbap* is made with mountain greens while *dolsot bibimbap* is served in a stone hotpot. Vegetarians can usually order it without meat or egg.

Bulgogi

The Korea Tourism Organisation website at www.tour2korea.com has an extensive food section, including regional recipes.

This signature Korean meal is thin slices of beef, marinated in sweetened soy sauce, that are cooked on a small barbecue grill on your table. To eat, take a lettuce or other leaf, put a slice of meat on it, add garlic, sauce or side-dish items, wrap it all up and enjoy. *Bulgogi deopbap* is slices of beef served on a hotplate with vegetables and rice.

Chicken

Samgyetang is a small chicken stuffed with glutinous rice, red dates, garlic and ginseng and boiled in broth. It's commonly eaten in summer, often accompanied by ginseng wine. *Hanbang oribaeksuk* is similar but served with medicinal herbs. *Dakgalbi* is pieces of chicken, cabbage, other vegetables and finger-sized pressed-rice cakes, which are grilled at your table in a spicy sauce. Even zingier is *jjimdak,* a hot-hot-hot mixture of chicken pieces, transparent noodles, potatoes and other vegetables. On almost every street, informal bars serve a plate of fried or barbecued chicken along with pitchers of beer.

Desserts

As in other Asian nations, desserts are not traditional in Korea, but nowadays Western-style bakeries and yogurt and ice-cream parlours have spread just about everywhere. Can't find one? Pop into a convenience store.

Sometimes at the end of a meal, you'll be served a few pieces of fruit

---

WE DARE YOU

Beondegi Silkworm larvae
Bosintang Dog-meat soup
Doganitang Cow kneecaps soup
Mettugi Fried grasshoppers
Sannakji Live baby octopus
Yukhoe Seasoned raw minced meat

GRILL YOUR OWN

If there's any food for which Korea is famous worldwide, it's barbecue. Barbecue restaurants typically have a grill set into the table, on which you cook beef ribs (*galbi*), thin slices of beef (*bulgogi*), pork (*samgyeopsal*), chicken (*dak*), seafood or vegetables. Often your server will get you started by putting the meat on the grill; after that, generally you're on your own to turn the meat and remove it when cooked. All are delicious, but *samgyeopsal* is belly pork and tends to be fatty.

The meals usually include lettuce and sesame leaf wraps. Take a leaf in one hand (or combine two leaves for different flavours) and with your other hand use your chopsticks to load it with meat, sauces and side-dish relishes to taste. Then roll it up into a little package and eat it in one go. Tip: use half a leaf for a more bite-sized package. The garlic can be eaten raw or cooked on the grill. Rice isn't usually served, so some diners order *naengmyeon* (buckwheat noodles in an icy broth) as a kind of dessert.

Barbecue meals are usually only available in servings of two or more. Sharing food goes to the heart of Korean life and culture, which is still communal. In Korea nobody likes to eat alone.

plus a tea or *sujeonggwa*, a refreshing drink made from cinnamon and ginger, served cold. Free self-serve coffee is provided in some restaurants.

Cakes are generally saved for special occasions such as weddings and milestone birthdays, but *tteok* (rice cakes), flavoured with nuts, seeds and dried fruit, are a less sweet and healthier alternative.

Gimbap & Samgak Gimbap

These cheap snacks consist mostly of *bap* (rice) rolled in *gim* (dried seaweed); often the rice is flavoured beforehand with sesame oil. Circular *gimbap* contains strips of vegetables, egg and ham in the centre, while its less famous brother, *samgak gimbap* (triangular *gimbap*), only available in convenience stores, has a savoury fish, meat or vegetable mixture on top. Nude *gimbap* has no dried seaweed cover, while some restaurants sell fancy-looking *gimbap* at even fancier prices, calling it 'Californian roll'.

> View the excellent www .koreankitchen.com for recipes to cook your own Korean meals.

Hanjeongsik

This traditional banquet comes all at once and includes fish, meat, soup, *dubu jjigae* (tofu stew), rice, noodles, steamed egg, shellfish and a flock of cold vegetable side dishes. It's a good way to sample a wide range of Korean food at one sitting. Like barbecue dishes, *hanjeongsik* almost always needs to be ordered for two or more people. In the past only the king was allowed twelve side dishes, but now anyone can order it.

Hoetjip (Fish & Seafood)

Haemul (seafood) and *seongseon* (fish) are generally served raw, but can also be broiled or grilled. Koreans love raw fish and seafood despite the high prices. When fish is served sushi-style (raw over rice) it's called *chobap*. Sashimi (without the rice) is called *saengseonhoe* and is often served with seafood side dishes and followed by a red-pepper fish-bone soup. Another preparation is *hoedeopbap*, which is like *bibimbap* except that it contains raw fish instead of egg and minced meat. Restaurants near the coast serve squid, barbecued shellfish, octopus and crab.

> *Korean Cooking Made Easy* by Kim Young-hee (2006) is a handy-sized, simple, get-you-started choice of well-illustrated and well-chosen recipes.

Jeon

These savoury pancakes usually have seafood and spring onions, but other ingredients are possible. Another kind of pancake is *bindaetteok*, which is made from freshly ground mung beans and has a meat or seafood filling, along with vegetables.

KIMCHI

The national dish is served at virtually every Korean meal, whether it's breakfast, lunch or dinner. The most common type is *baechu kimchi,* made from cabbage mixed with garlic and *gochujang* and left to pickle for months. But *kimchi* can be made from radish, cucumber and just about any other vegetable, even broccoli. Some varieties are aged for hours, others for years. Some are meant to be eaten in tiny morsels or wrapped around rice, while others, such as *bossam kimchi,* are flavour-packed little packages containing vegetables, pork or seafood. Belying its fiery reputation, *mul kimchi* is a fairly bland cold soup, similar to gazpacho. Many regions, restaurants and families have their own distinctive style of *kimchi,* and recipes are jealously guarded and handed down from generation to generation.

Traditionally, *kimchi* was made to preserve vegetables and ensure proper nutrition during the harsh winters. Even now, late-November to early December is the season for *gimjang,* or making your own *kimchi.*

Kimchi dates back to at least the 13th century, although red pepper was added only in the 17th century. Nowadays most *kimchi* is bought from stores, and some is even imported from China. It isn't just for winter anymore – it's eaten year-round to add zest and a long list of health benefits to just about every meal. Consumption of *kimchi* is reducing but still stands at 25kg per person per year.

Kimchi is the one thing that no Korean kitchen can be without. Yet *kimchi* storage can be problematic. The temperature must be kept just so – if it's too warm, the *kimchi* can over-ferment; too cold, and it will freeze. That's to say nothing of the odour it can impart to more delicate foods in the fridge. *Kimchi* is no longer buried or kept in big jars in the yard, so instead many families invest in a special *kimchi* refrigerator.

Jjigae

These stews are thicker than soups, often spicy, and served in a stone hotpot. Popular versions are made with *dubu jjigae* (tofu), *doenjang jjigae* (soyabean paste) and *kimchi.* They're served bubbling hot, so let them cool down before eating!

Juk

Juk is rice porridge, which comes mixed with almost anything: savoury versions include ginseng chicken, mushroom, abalone or seafood, while sweeter incarnations include pumpkin and red bean. The thick, black rice porridge is sesame. Look out for small, modern chain restaurants that specialise in *juk* meals, perfect if you are after a healthy, filling and fairly bland meal.

Korean Breakfasts

At fish restaurants diners choose live fish, squid, crab or shellfish from a tank, which are often served raw with side dishes and a spicy fish soup.

Traditional Korean breakfasts are centred on soup, rice and *kimchi.* If that sounds like lunch or dinner, it is, except with fewer side dishes. For something freshly baked head to a bakery, or for sandwiches, bakery items or coffee just pop into the nearest convenience store. Both are open early. Cornflakes are available in grocery and convenience stores. As in other countries, many young people make do with a quick cup of coffee and a fag.

Mandu

An inexpensive favourite, these small dumplings are filled with meat, vegetables and herbs, and are often freshly made on the premises by restaurant staff when business is slack. Fried or steamed, they make a tasty snack or light meal. *Manduguk* is *mandu* in soup with vegetables and seaweed, while *wangmandu* is a king-sized version.

Noodles

A popular noodle dish is *naengmyeon,* buckwheat noodles in an icy beef broth, garnished with finely chopped vegetables and half a boiled egg – add red pepper paste or *gyeoja* (mustard). It's especially popular in hot weather, and is often eaten after *galbi* (beef ribs) or other meat dishes as a kind of dessert.

Bibim naengmyeon pairs the noodles (still cold but not in soup) with the vegetables and other ingredients found in *bibimbap.*

Japchae are clear noodles made from sweet potatoes, stir-fried in sesame oil with strips of egg, meat, mushrooms, carrots and other vegetables. It used to be served to Joseon monarchs.

Kalguksu are thick wheat noodles in a bland clam-and-vegetable broth, while *ramyeon* is instant noodles served in fiery soup. A Koreanised Chinese dish is *jajangmyeon,* noodles in a bland dark-brown sauce that children (and nostalgic adults) adore.

Soups

Soups (*tang* or *guk*) are a Korean speciality that vary from spicy seafood and crab soups such as *haemultang* to bland broths such as *galbitang* or *seolleongtang. Gamjatang* is a spicy peasant soup with meaty bones and a potato. *Haejangguk* (bean-sprout soup) is said to cure hangovers. Some soups are served hot and some cold, even icy. Tip: if a soup is too spicy, tip in some rice.

DRINKS

Virtually every restaurant serves good old *mul* (water), either filtered or bottled, when customers arrive. If not, look for the self-serve water dispenser.

Tea is also popular. *Nokcha* (green tea) is grown in modest quantities and you can visit green-tea plantations in Jejudo (p291) and Jeollanam-do (p262), but black tea can be hard to find. Many other health teas are not made from the tea plant and include *boricha* (barley tea), *daechucha* (red-date tea), *omijacha* (five-flavour berry tea), *yujacha* (citron tea) and *insamcha* (ginseng tea). They are served hot or cold.

For a country with a tea tradition, Korea has taken to coffee in a big way. In addition to coffee shops, there are vending machines (from W300 per cup), and in some restaurants you can serve yourself coffee. Sorry decaf drinkers, you're probably out of luck but it never hurts to ask.

Bottled and canned soft drinks are everywhere, and you'll find some unique Korean choices like grape juice with whole grapes inside, and *sikhye,* rice punch with rice grains inside.

Health tonics, made with fibre, vitamins, ginseng and other medicinal herbs, are available in shops and pharmacies. They're usually sold in small (100mL) glass bottles. The top two brands are Bacchus D (박카스 D), which is only sold in pharmacies, and Vita 500 (비타 500).

A Korean Mother's Cooking Notes by Chang Sun-young (2003) proves that a mother's cooking is always the best.

SAUCY SIDE DISHES

Korean cuisine is well-known for *banchan (*side dishes), which are generally spicy and accompany nearly every meal. At least one *kimchi* (cabbage, radish or cucumber) will be included, but other common ones are green vegetables, acorn jelly, quail eggs, bean sprouts, small clams, anchovies, tofu, lettuce, seaweed, spinach, garlic or just about anything the chefs can dream up. It's always fun to try a new one.

The side-dish system is wasteful because lots of food is thrown away. The government periodically tries to reform it, but Koreans are innately conservative and resist any meddling with their culinary culture.

LOCAL SPECIALITIES

- *ureok* (raw fish) – Busan, Gyeongsangnam-do
- *dakgalbi* (spicy chicken grilled with vegetables and rice cakes) – Chuncheon, Gang-won-do
- *maneul* (garlic) – Danyang, Chungcheongbuk-do
- *oritang* (duck soup); *tteokgalbi* (grilled patties of ground beef) – Gwangju, Jeollanam-do
- *okdomgui* (grilled, semi-dried fish); *jeonbok-juk* (abalone rice porridge) – Jejudo
- *sundubu* (tofu stew) – Jeongdongjin, Gang-won-do
- *ojing-eo* (squid) served *sundae* (sausage) style – Sokcho, Gang-won-do
- *galbi* (beef ribs) – Suwon, Gyeonggi-do
- *chungmu gimbap* (rice, dried seaweed & *kimchi*) – Tong-yeong, Gyeongsangnam-do
- *gatkimchi* (leafy mustard *kimchi*) – Yeosu, Jeollanam-do

If you're looking for something stronger, *maekju* (Korean beers) are mainly lager, but recently dark beers have started appearing, and Guinness and other imported beers are increasingly available. A few microbreweries have started up, mainly in Seoul (p130). Wine is much more common than it used to be, although the choice is limited.

Soju is the local firewater (at least 20% alcohol) and is often likened to vodka in that it's clear, nearly flavourless and cheap to produce. For sale even in grocery and convenience stores, it comes in many flavours, including lemon, maple, cherry and bamboo. Innovative bartenders have been known to mix it with just about everything, including yogurt.

> Koreans consider it unhealthy to drink on an empty stomach, so bars invariably serve *anju* (snacks) such as peanuts, popcorn, dried squid or fried chicken.

A tempting range of traditional alcoholic drinks are brewed or distilled from grains, fruits, roots and anything else to hand. Koreans could make alcohol even out of rocks. Each region has its own local specialities – try *bokbunja* (made from berries), plum wine, *insamju* (made from ginseng) or whatever takes your fancy.

Makgeolli, also known as *dongdongju*, is a traditional brew made from unrefined, fermented rice wine that has a cloudy appearance and a sweetish yogurty flavour. It has a much lower alcohol content than *soju* and is traditionally served in a kettle and poured into small bowls. 'Ganbei!' ('Cheers!')

CELEBRATIONS WITH FOOD

Tteok (rice cakes) are associated with many traditional Korean festive occasions, and small family-run *tteok* shops are a common sight. Lunar New Year is celebrated with *tteokguk* (rice-cake soup); Chuseok (Thanksgiving) with *songpyeon* (crescent-shaped rice cakes with red-bean filling); and the winter solstice with *patjuk* (red-bean porridge with rice-cake balls).

WHERE TO EAT & DRINK
Restaurants

Sikdang is the general word for restaurant in Korean. Beyond major cities, few restaurants have English menus, but many have food photos or plastic food replicas.

Many Korean meals, like *bibimbap* or *samgyeopsal*, cost under W7000, while *galbi* or *bulgogi* cost from W13,000 to W20,000 but can be shared. Soups, stews and food court meals are generally around W5000. Side dishes will automatically be included in the price. If rice is not included, it's usually W1000. If you see a dish for W20,000 or up, chances are it's meant for sharing, such as a whole fish, whole duck or a large seafood stew. Most restaurants offer a very limited range of soft drinks and alcohol.

Food Courts
Department stores and shopping malls usually have a food court, often in the basement. All styles of food are available for around W5000, including Koreanised Italian pasta and pizza options and Koreanised Chinese food. Some pile up heaps of food on big platters. Coffee, fruit juice and ice cream are available too.

Street Stalls
Common street foods cost from W500 to W4000 and include *tteokbokki* (rice cakes in a spicy orange sauce), *dakkochi* (skewers of marinated, grilled chicken), *sundae* (sausages containing vegetables and noodles) and *odeng* (processed seafood).

If you're in the mood for something sweet, try *hotteok* (pitta bread with a cinnamon and honey filling), a waffle, a bag of tiny machine-made walnut cakes or an *aiseukeurim* (ice cream) cone.

In summer *soju* tents appear as if by magic in city streets, offering alcohol, snacks and meals until the sun comes up.

A night out with Korean friends often involves three stops and can be exhausting: the first stop is dinner, then it's off to a bar, before ending up in a *noraebang* (karaoke room).

Convenience Stores
Korean convenience stores are clean, well stocked and open 24 hours. With names like Mini-Stop, Family Mart, Buy the Way, LG25 and 7-Eleven, they can be found on every street corner from one end of the country to the other. They're great places to pick up snacks, soft drinks and on-the-run meals, as well as everyday items. Many have stand-up counters or a table and chairs. Staples include instant noodles (boiling water is available), *gimbap, samgak gimbap,* sandwiches, soft drinks, ice cream, biscuits and chocolate, all at reasonable prices, although fruit can be expensive. They even sell beer, wine and *soju.*

Budget Diners
Diners serve a wide variety of budget meals that cost from W2000 to W4000, including *mandu, gimbap, bibimbap, donkasseu,* fried rice and *naengmyeon* that provide a quick and simple lunch.

Fast-Food Outlets
Global fast-food restaurants like McDonald's, KFC and Subway offer the usual fare with some Koreanised additions such as *bulgogi* burger. Check out the local competitor Lotteria if you want to try a squid burger. Pizza Hut, TGIF and steakhouses all serve Western food. Koreans have taken to pizza in a big way and even the smallest towns have pizza restaurants and takeaway shops, although (like the burgers) the food may come with a Korean twist. Dunkin' Donuts and Baskin Robbins both provide dessert options.

WHY METAL BOWLS & CHOPSTICKS?
Given that Korea has one of the world's great ceramic-making traditions and is surrounded by nations which use ceramic bowls and chopsticks made of plastic or wood, many visitors find it surprising that Korea uses stainless-steel bowls, dishes and utensils.

The most common explanation dates back to the Joseon dynasty, when the kings, ever vigilant about security, would insist on using silver chopsticks and bowls because silver would tarnish in the presence of poisons. The custom caught on and was passed down to the common people, although they could only afford baser metals. Metal is also easy to clean and hard to break.

DINING DOS & DON'TS

Dos

■ Do take off your shoes in traditional restaurants where everyone sits on floor cushions. You may sit with your legs crossed or to the side. Tip: sit at a table near a wall so you can lean back against it.

■ Do pour drinks for others if you notice that their glasses are empty. It's polite to use both hands when pouring or receiving a drink.

■ Do ask for *gawi* (scissors) if you are trying to cut something and your spoon won't do it.

Don'ts

■ Don't start or finish your meal before your seniors and elders.

■ Don't touch food with your fingers, except when handling leaves for wrapping other foods.

■ Don't try to eat rice with chopsticks – use a spoon.

■ Don't pick up bowls and plates from the table to eat from them.

■ Don't leave your chopsticks or spoon sticking up from your rice bowl. This is done only in food 'presented' to deceased ancestors.

■ Don't blow your nose at the table.

■ Don't tip.

VEGETARIANS & VEGANS

Click onto www.freewebs
.com/vegetariankorea
for vegetarian views and
restaurant reviews.

Despite Korea's meat, fish and seafood reputation, there's enough variety of vegetables that vegetarians can usually find something. Plain, boiled rice is served with many meals and most side dishes are vegetables, although some are mixed with meat, fish or seafood. The same goes for *kimchi,* and watch out for stews and soups which are often made with beef or seafood stock. If all else fails, you can order *bibimbap* minus any ingredients you don't eat, or else eat rice with side dishes.

EATING WITH KIDS

Fill children up with *jajangmyeon* (noodles with a dark brown sauce), *donkkaseu* (cutlets), *juk* (rice porridge), barbecue chicken, sandwiches, bakery items, *hotteok* and ice creams. Food courts have a wide choice of food and often have play areas, and Western fast food joints are usually around as a bribe or last resort.

HABITS & CUSTOMS

Typically, you'll order a main course, such as *bulgogi,* and it will come with rice, soup, *kimchi* and other side dishes selected to create balance in terms of saltiness, spiciness, temperature and colour combinations. Don't feel guilty about leaving food as no one is expected to finish all their side dishes.

In traditional restaurants diners sit on cushions on the floor (the *ondol* heating system is beneath). Tip: take two or three cushions to be more comfortable. Remove your shoes, putting them on shoe racks if provided.

If the table is not set, there will be an oblong box containing metal chopsticks and long-handled spoons.

Meals are generally informal and eaten communally, so most dishes are placed in the centre, and diners eat a bit from one dish, a bite from another, a little rice, a sip of soup, mixing spicy and bland in whatever way they want. The main point is always to enjoy the food.

EAT YOUR WORDS
Useful Phrases

We'd like nonsmoking/smoking, please.
geumyeon seogeuro/heupyeon seogeuro juseyo
금연석으로/흡연석으로 주세요

Do you have an English menu?
yeong-eoro doen menyu isseoyo?
영어로 된 메뉴 있어요?

Do you have seating with tables and chairs?
teibeul isseoyo?
테이블 있어요?

Is this dish spicy?
i eumsik maewoyo?
이 음식 매워요?

Could you recommend something?
mwo chucheonhae jusillaeyo?
뭐 추천해 주실래요?

Excuse me! (please come here)
yeogiyo!
여기요!

Water, please.
mul juseyo
물 주세요

The bill/check, please.
gyesanseo juseyo
계산서 주세요

Bon apetit.
masitge deuseyo
맛있게 드세요

It was delicious.
masisseosseoyo
맛있었어요

I don't eat meat.
jeon gogireul anmeogeoyo
전 고기를 안 먹어요

I can't eat dairy products.
jeon yujepumeul anmeogeoyo
전 유제품을 안 먹어요

Do you have any vegetarian dishes?
gogi andeureogan eumsik isseoyo?
고기 안 들어간 음식 있어요?

Does it contain eggs?
gyerani deureogayo?
계란이 들어가요?

I'm allergic to (peanuts).
jeon (ttangkong)e allereugiga isseoyo
전 (땅콩)에 알레르기가 있어요

Han's Culinary Academy in Seoul (p118) has English-speaking staff eager to teach foreigners the secrets of Korean cooking.

Menu Decoder
FOOD
Chinese Dishes

bokkeumbap	볶음밥	fried rice
jajangmyeon	자장면	noodles in black-bean sauce
tangsuyuk	탕수육	sweet and sour pork

Fish & Seafood

chobap	초밥	raw fish on rice
garibi	가리비	scallops
gwang-eohoe	광어회	raw halibut
hoedeopbap	회덮밥	vegetables, rice and raw fish
hung-eo	홍어	ray, usually served raw
jang-eogui	장어구이	grilled eel
jeonbok-juk	전복죽	rice porridge with abalone
kijogae	키조개	razor clam
kkotge-jjim	꽃게찜	steamed blue crab
modeumhoe	모듬회	mixed raw fish platter
nakji	낙지	octopus
odeng	오뎅	processed seafood cakes in broth
ojing-eo	오징어	squid
ojing-eo sundae	오징어순대	stuffed squid

Can't find it in the Menu Decoder? View www.zkorean.com for a simple, user-friendly Korean–English dictionary.

saengseon-gui	생선구이	grilled fish
saeugui	새우구이	grilled prawns
samchigui	삼치구이	grilled mackerel
ureok	우럭	raw fish

Gimbap 김밥

chamchi gimbap	참치김밥	tuna *gimbap*
modeum gimbap	모듬김밥	assorted *gimbap*
samgak gimbap	삼각김밤	triangular *gimbap*

Kimchi 김치

baechu kimchi	배추김치	cabbage *kimchi*; the spicy classic version
kkakdugi	깍두기	cubed radish *kimchi*
mul kimchi	물김치	cold *kimchi* soup
oisobagi	오이소박이	stuffed cucumber *kimchi*

MEAT DISHES

bossam	보쌈	steamed pork with *kimchi*, cabbage and lettuce wrap
bulgogi	불고기	barbecued beef slices and lettuce wrap
dakgalbi	닭갈비	spicy chicken pieces grilled with vegetables and rice cakes
dakkochi	닭꼬치	spicy grilled chicken on skewers
dwaeji galbi	돼지갈비	barbecued pork ribs
galbi	갈비	beef ribs
jjimdak	찜닭	spicy chicken pieces with noodles
jokbal	족발	steamed pork hocks
kkwong	꿩	pheasant
metdwaejigogi	멧돼지고기	wild pig
neobiani/tteokgalbi	너비아니/떡갈비	large minced meat patty
ogolgye	오골계	black chicken
samgyeopsal	삼겹살	barbecued bacon-type pork
tongdakgui	통닭구이	roasted chicken
yukhoe	육회	seasoned raw beef

Noodles

bibim naengmyeon	비빔냉면	cold buckwheat noodles with vegetables, meat and sauce
bibimguksu	비빔국수	noodles with vegetables, meat and sauce
japchae	잡채	stir-fried noodles and vegetables
kalguksu	칼국수	thick handmade noodles in broth
kongguksu	콩국수	noodles in cold soy milk soup
makguksu	막국수	buckwheat noodles with vegetables
naengmyeon	물냉면	buckwheat noodles in cold broth
ramyeon	라면	instant noodle soup
udong	우동	thick white noodle broth

Rice Dishes

bap	밥	boiled rice
bibimbap	비빔밥	rice topped with egg, meat, vegetables and sauce
boribap	보리밥	boiled rice with steamed barley
daetongbap	대통밥	rice cooked in bamboo stem
dolsot bibimbap	돌솥비빔밥	*bibimbap* in stone hotpot
dolsotbap	돌솥밥	hotpot rice
dolssambap	돌쌈밥	hotpot rice and lettuce wraps

gonggibap	공기밥	steamed rice
gulbap	굴밥	oyster rice
honghapbap	홍합밥	mussel rice
kimchi bokkeumbap	김치볶음밥	fried kimchi rice
ojing·eo deopbap	오징어덮밥	squid rice
pyogo deopbap	표고덮밥	mushroom rice
sanchae bibimbap	산채비빔밥	bibimbap made with mountain vegetables
sinseollo	신선로	meat, fish and vegetables cooked in broth
ssambap	쌈밥	assorted ingredients with rice and wraps

Snacks

beondegi	번데기	boiled silkworm larvae
delimanjoo	데리만주	custard-filled minicakes
mettugi	메뚜기	fried grasshoppers
hotteok	호떡	pitta bread with sweet filling
jjinppang	찐빵	giant steamed bun with sweet-bean paste
norang goguma	노랑고구마	sweet potato strips
nurungji	누룽지	crunchy burnt-rice globe
odeng	오뎅	processed seafood
tteok	떡	rice cake
tteokbokki	떡볶이	pressed rice cakes and vegetables in a spicy sauce

Soups

bosintang	보신탕	dog-meat soup
chueotang	추어탕	minced loach fish soup
doganitang	도가니탕	ox-leg soup
galbitang	갈비탕	beef-rib soup
gamjatang	감자탕	meaty bones and potato soup
haejangguk	해장국	bean-sprout soup
haemultang	해물탕	spicy assorted seafood soup
hanbang oribaeksuk	한방 오리백숙	duck in medicinal soup
heugyeomsotang	흑염소탕	goat soup
kkorigomtang	꼬리곰탕	ox tail soup
mae·untang	매운탕	spicy fish soup
manduguk	만두국	soup with meat-filled dumplings
oritang	오리탕	duck soup
ppyeohaejangguk	뼈해장국	meaty bones hotpot
samgyetang	삼계탕	ginseng chicken soup
seolleongtang	설렁탕	beef and rice soup
tokkitang	토끼탕	spicy rabbit soup

Stews

budae jjigae	부대찌개	ham-and-scraps stew
doenjang jjigae	된장찌개	soybean paste stew
dubu jjigae	두부찌개	tofu stew
nakji jeon-gol	낙지전골	octopus hotpot
sundubu jjigae	순두부찌개	spicy uncurdled tofu stew
dakjjim	닭찜	chicken stew
galbi jjim	갈비찜	barbecued beef ribs stew
gopchang jeon-gol	곱창전골	tripe hotpot
kimchi jjigae	김치찌개	kimchi stew

Other

bokbunja	복분자	wild berry
bindaetteok	빈대떡	mung-bean pancake

dongchimi	동치미	pickled radish
donkkaseu	돈까스	pork cutlet with rice and salad
dotorimuk	도토리묵	acorn jelly
gujeolpan	구절판	eight snacks and wraps
hanjeongsik	한정식	Korean-style banquet
jeongsik	정식	meal with lots of side dishes
juk	죽	rice porridge
kongnamul gukbap	콩나물국밥	spicy rice bean sprout porridge
mandu	만두	filled dumplings
omeuraiseu	오므라이스	omelette with rice
pajeon	파전	green-onion pancake
sangcharim	산차림	banquet of meat, seafood and vegetables
shabu shabu	샤브샤브	DIY beef and vegetable casserole
sigol bapsang	시골밥상	countryside-style meal
siksa	식사	budget-priced banquet
sujebi	수제비	dough flakes in shellfish broth
sundae	순대	noodle and vegetable sausage
sundubu	순두부	uncurdled tofu
twigim	튀김	seafood and vegetables fried in batter
wangmandu	왕만두	large steamed dumplings

DRINKS
Nonalcoholic

cha	차	tea
daechucha	대추차	red-date tea
hongcha	홍차	black tea
juseu	주스	juice
keopi	커피	coffee
mukapein keopi	무카페인 커피	decaffeinated coffee
mul	물	water
nokcha	녹차	green tea
omijacha	오미자차	berry tea
saenggang cha	생강차	ginger tea
saengsu	생수	mineral spring water
seoltang neo-eoseo/ppaego	설탕 넣어서/빼고	with/without sugar
sikhye	식혜	rice punch
ssanghwacha	쌍화차	herb tonic tea
sujeonggwa	수정과	cinnamon/ginger punch
sungnyung	숭늉	burnt-rice tea
uyu	우유	milk
uyu neo-eoseo/ppaego	우유 넣어서/빼고	with/without milk
yujacha	유자차	citron tea

Alcoholic

dongdongju/makgeolli	동동주/막걸리	fermented rice wine
insamju	인삼주	ginseng liqueur
maekju	맥주	beer
sansachun	산사춘	rice wine
soju	소주	vodka-like drink

Korea Outdoors

Mountainous Korea is an outdoors destination that is especially attractive to hikers, with well-signed and well-maintained footpaths around the forest-covered slopes of the national and provincial parks that are served by regular bus services. Every weekend the parks fill up with Koreans of all ages who go there to enjoy nature, burn off calories and visit Buddhist temples. Fresh spring water is available at the temples and along most of the hikes, and country-style restaurants and food stalls cluster around the park entrances.

If two wheels rather than two feet is your style, cycling opportunities abound in tourist areas. Hiring a bicycle is often the best way to tour small offshore islands, and riverside cycleways in Seoul, Daejeon, Jeonju and other cities are also highly recommended. Mountain biking is yet to catch on, but you can link up with expat mountain-bike-club members in Seoul.

In July and August the nation's beaches are officially open and holiday-makers flock to the coasts to relax, eat raw fish and have fun. Korea is not known as a scuba-diving location, yet Seogwipo on Jejudo is outstanding, and all along the eastern and southern coasts are virtually virgin sites just waiting to be explored. Adrenaline junkies can go head to head with sharp-toothed sharks in Busan Aquarium.

Although mainly indoor, Korea's hot-spring spas and saunas are a health-and-beauty bargain that are popular 24 hours a day, 365 days a year. You can simmer in ginseng, green-tea and mud baths as well as bake in mugwort and jade saunas.

Korea is 70% hills and mountains and in winter the snowy slopes tempt skiers and snowboarders outdoors to Korea's fast-improving ski resorts. Ice skating outside Seoul City Hall is another great winter activity. Contact United Service Organizations (p159) in Seoul for ski package trips in winter as well as daylong water-rafting trips in summer (US$45).

> The Royal Asiatic Society of Korea (www.raskb.com) organises excellent and inexpensive weekend tours to all parts of Korea, which nonmembers are welcome to attend.

CYCLING & MOUNTAIN-BIKING

Almost every city with a waterfront and hordes of tourists has a stand where bikes can be hired. Most are geared towards leisure riders with couples and families in mind, so expect well-marked, paved, flat trails designed for pleasure rather than intense cross-country exhilaration. To hire a bike, some form of ID is usually required; a cycle helmet or lock is almost never included. If you're looking for off-road mountain-bike trails in Seoul, there are a couple of useful websites with decent maps. Try www.mtbk-adventure .com or www.angelfire.com/ga/achamtb.

People who value full mobility in their limbs rarely venture onto Seoul's streets with a bike between their legs, but the bicycle trails along the **Han River** (p114; single/tandem bicycles per hr W3000/6000) are ideal for a comfortable, car-free family outing. Watch out for speeding in-line skaters. Bikes can be hired on Yeouido, which is a good starting point for a 90-minute, 7km sprint to the World Cup Stadium or a more ambitious 38km ride to Olympic Park. The paved paths are dotted with parks, sports fields, gardens and the occasional snack bar. Further east and north of the river, bikes of similar quality and price can be hired at Ttukseom Resort.

> View www.adventurekorea .com for hiking adventures and activity tours from Seoul organised by enterprising Seok-jin.

Travellers in good shape can circumvent **Jeju Island** (p279; per day W5000-8000). The 200km pedal trek around the oval island takes about three to five days depending on the condition of the road and your legs. Hwy 12 runs around the entire island and has bicycle lanes on either side. Shore roads also have bike lanes but it's a less developed system and not always bike-friendly. The inland scenery is greener and the roads are less busy but they lack bicycle lanes. Bikes can be hired near Jeju-si bus terminal, Yongduam Rock or the seafront.

Off Jeju Island's eastern coast, **Udo** (p283; per 2hr W5000) or Cow Island offer a comparatively short but testing 17km island spin. Sights include a lighthouse perched on top of a 132m cliff, lush green fields, pretty fishing villages, and with luck, a glimpse of the famous Jeju women ocean divers. Hire your bicycle at the port near the ferry docks. May to October is a good time to ride but July and August can experience heavy rain not to mention the occasional typhoon. Other times of the year can be windy.

The Korea Plant Conservation Society (2003) will encourage you to stop and ID the flowers with photos of 200 Korean flowers.

Located in the centre of the Gogunsan Archipelago, 50km off the coast of North Jeolla province, **Seonyudo** (p305; per hr W3000) is a pretty, undeveloped island, ideal for travellers looking for a day-trip escape to a picture-postcard setting. Pedal around laid-back fishing villages, cross bridges over to neighbouring islands or follow the paved trail alongside a 2km white sandy beach and aqua ocean. Bring a picnic or enjoy a fresh seafood meal by the ocean.

Pretty and relaxing **Chuncheon** (p163; per day W5000), the antithesis of most busy Korean cities, was the setting for the popular tearjerker TV drama *Winter Sonata*. During the day, ferry your bicycle over to Jungdo for a short island

---

HIKING

Taekwondo might be the country's national sport, but hiking surely ranks as the number-one leisure activity. Over 1700 trails stream across the country with everything from easy half-day walks to strenuous mountain-ridge treks. Maybe it's the intoxicatingly fresh air, or the occasional *soju* pick-me-up, but Korea's hiking trails are frequented by some of the country's most hospitable people.

Most of the exhilarating mountain trails, like those on Jirisan and Seoraksan, are located in the country's outstanding national parks. Basic shelters are available but expect a full house during holidays, summer months and autumn weekends. If you're planning a major overnight mountain trek, shelter reservations two weeks in advance are recommended. About one-quarter of the trails may be closed at any one time to allow the mountain to regenerate itself. Visit the National Park Authority's website (www.knps.or.kr) for contact numbers, trail-closure information and online reservations.

Hallasan

Hiking up this ancient volcano is a highlight of any Jejudo trip. The best plan is to take the **Eorimok trail** for outstanding views of dwarf fir trees, hillsides of springtime azalea and the occasional midget deer. After 2¼ hours you should reach **Witseoreum shelter** (1700m), which has no accommodation but sells pot noodles. Hallasan's peak and the crater lake are up the trail but it's been closed for a lengthy period to allow for plant regeneration. On the way down, try the **Yeongsil trail** for a spectacular two-hour hike to the bus stop. The climb up is only 700m and many young children reach the top, but it is tiring and you should prepare for bad weather, which can arrive faster than a KTX train.

Nearest town: Seogwipo or Jeju-si (p292)
Entrance: adult/youth/child W1600/600/300
Information: ☎ 064 713 9950

Yeonhwado

Located off the picturesque Tong-yeong coast in Gyeongsangnam-do, this undeveloped, and largely undiscovered, island is a splendid escape for travellers looking for a leisurely three-hour hike. From the ferry terminal, walk left and follow the cement path uphill past a temple. On the mountain ridge, a dirt trail cuts left with views of a cascading rock formation that dribbles into the ocean; locals

ride amid horse-drawn carriages, while looking out for waterbirds nesting in the reeds. In the late afternoon, cruise on two wheels along the shores of Uiam Lake for a pedal-stopping sunset view. Bikes can be hired outside the lakeside **tourist information centre** (bikes per hr/day W3000/5000; ☻ 9am-7pm).

DIVING

Korea has a surprisingly active scuba-diving scene and the best place to start is on the web:

Aquatic Frontier (www.aquaticfrontier.com) Runs dive certificate courses for $300.

Deep Blue Quest (www.deepbluequest.com) An English-speaking scuba-diving club in Seoul that organises PADI certificate courses and two dives every month for all skill levels.

Scuba in Korea (www.scubainkorea.com) A top site with the low down on courses, diving clubs and dive sites in Korea, including diving with sharks in Busan Aquarium.

Suwon Scuba (www.suwon-scuba.com) The Suwon scuba club runs courses and dive trips mainly off Sokcho or in lakes.

Korea's top dive site is just off Seogwipo on Jejudo's southern coast, which has good visibility, coral as colourful as in the tropics, kelp forests inhabited by

---

call it **Yong Meori**, or Dragon's Head. At just 215m, the ridge doesn't offer a challenging hike but the ocean vistas are breathtaking. The early-morning ferry from Tong-yeong provides a spectacular sunrise view and puts you ahead of the groups that usually hit the island around lunchtime.

Nearest town: Tong-yeong (p242)
One-way ferry ticket: W7700
Information: http://tongyeong.go.kr/eng/

Mudeungsan Provincial Park

One of the country's higher peaks, **Cheonwangbong** (1187m), is in this popular park that is easy to reach from Gwangju and fills up with cheery hikers every weekend. A myriad of trails leads up to the peak, some of which can be challenging. On the way up, you pass an art gallery and the Choonsul green-tea plantation. If the steep hike to the tea bushes looks uninviting, join the masses marching over to **Tokkideung** (460m), a popular picnic spot. Odd rock formations and colourful fields of azalea, magnolia and maple trees give the mountainside a fresh look each season. There's no shortage of mountain grub; the hills are alive with the sound of ravenous eaters in shacks selling meat and vegetable meals.

Nearest town: Gwangju (p251)
Admission: free
Information: http://eng.gjcity.net/main.jsp

Responsible Hiking

- Pay any fees required by local authorities.
- Be sure you are healthy and feel comfortable walking for a sustained period.
- Obtain reliable information about route conditions.
- Be aware of local laws, regulations and etiquette about wildlife and the environment. Do not hike closed trails.
- Walk only on trails within your realm of experience.
- Be aware that weather conditions can change quickly and seasonal changes alter trails. These differences influence the way walkers dress and the equipment they carry.

schools of fish, and dolphins that swim by now and again. The subterranean ecology around Jejudo (like the land where pineapples and oranges grow alongside strawberries) is a unique mixture of the tropical and temperate.

The best diving operation in Seogwipo is **Big Blue** (p287; ☎ 064-733 1733; www .bigblue33.co.kr; 2 dives W105,000), run by Ralph Deutsch, an experienced diving enthusiast who speaks English and German.

For another unforgettable underwater experience, go scuba diving with the sharks, turtles, rays and giant groupers in **Busan Aquarium** (☎ 740 1700; www .scubainkorea.com; certified/noncertified divers W65,000/W85,000) on Hae-undae Beach. Even nondivers can do it after a two-hour training session, and there's an experienced English-speaking guide-instructor. The 30-minute dives take place on Saturday and Sunday. Don't forget an underwater camera as the lemon, sand tiger, nurse and reef sharks are big and certainly look like man-eaters. They haven't attacked anybody yet, but keep your arms by your side!

Besides Seogwipo on Jejudo; Hongdo off the south coast; Pohang, Ulleungdo and Dragon Head off Sokcho; and a wreck dive off Gangneung, all underwater sites on the east coast are worth exploring. Even the west coast has some dive operators, for instance at Daecheon beach, but visibility can be poor. Much of the country's coastal waters are unexplored, so who knows what you might discover.

Many Korean spas and saunas cost less than US$10 and even luxury ones are usually less than US$20.

HOT-SPRING SPAS

Koreans love hot food, hot baths and hot saunas – the hotter the better. Korea has many *oncheon* (hot-spring spas) where the therapeutic mineral-laden water that wells up from the depths of the earth is piped into communal baths. Equally popular are all kinds of saunas. Some saunas are fairly spartan but modern, luxury ones called *jjimjilbang* have a gym, hairdresser, café, TV, internet access and more. In Korean spas you can bathe like Cleopatra in just about anything: hot and cold mineral water, green tea, ginseng, mud, mugwort, coffee, seawater and pine needles. Prices vary with the luxuriousness of the facilities and most are open 24 hours in this nation of insomniacs and workaholics who pride themselves on not wasting much time sleeping.

Spa etiquette is simple enough. Undress completely (no swimwear or underwear!) in the locker room (Adams and Eves have separate bathing facilities) and then take a shower, as you must clean yourself thoroughly before getting into any communal bath. Soap and shampoo is supplied, as well as toothbrushes and toothpaste. A thorough cleansing is part of the bath experience. The ladies section has hairdryers, foot massagers and a line of lotions and perfumes. You can often have your hair cut or shoes shined as well.

The water in the big public baths varies from hot to extremely hot, but there may also be a cold bath, including a 'waterfall' shower. Relaxing in a hot bath is good therapy as the heat soaks into weary bodies, soothing tired muscles and minds.

Most spas also have sauna rooms, usually made of wood or stone, but all are as hot as a pizza oven. If you want to suffer more, you can be pummelled by a masseur, which costs extra. Many bathers take a nap lying down on the dormitory floor with a block of wood for a pillow. Stay all day, or all night, if you want to; nobody will hassle you to leave.

Slip into the gown supplied to visit the shared facilities outside the bathing area.

A spartan spa in the student area of Hongik is **Dongbang Sauna** (p115; admission W4000), but it has everything and is a good place to take the plunge into the Korean public-bath experience for the first time.

In Icheon, an hour south of Seoul, is the wonderful and ultramodern **Spa Plus** (p147; admission W10,000-W12,000) where you can play all day. Dip into (but don't be tempted to sip) the rice-wine bath, and try pine, fruit and herbal baths along with alternating hot and cold baths and a waterfall bath.

In the west of Daejeon city is the famous **Yousung Spa** (p309; admission W4500). Depending on the day, ladies can immerse themselves in exotic baths containing pine needles, mugwort and coffee. Coffee? Yes, coffee, which like the other baths provides aromatherapy in a bath format. Both the women's and means sections have a ginseng and green-tea bath plus hot and cold saunas.

In Geumsan, south of Daejeon, is **Geumsan Wellbeing Sauna** (p311; admission W5000). Relax in the ginseng bath and then nip smartly in and out (and in and out) of the hot and ice-cold sauna, like the Finns do, to really get your senses tingling. Then email your friends in the PC *bang* (internet room), let off some vocal energy in the *noraebang* (karaoke room; W500 a song), raise a sweat in the minigym and get thumped by an unsmiling masseur (W10,000) before finally sleeping it all off in the napping room.

A super new West Coast facility on Daecheon beach is **Mud House** (p320; admission W3000) that offers skin treatments using its special mud, as well as a sauna and an aroma spa. It's packed with merrymakers during the famous-among-expat-English-teachers, anything-goes mud festival.

Near Uljin in Gyeongsangbuk-do is **Deokgu Hot Springs Hotel** (p224; admission W6000) where the spring water is said to cure skin and digestive problems. If the water is too hot, start by dangling your feet in the water, followed by the lower half of your body. Even Koreans can find complete submersion too hot. Mixed bathing is allowed in the outdoor swimsuit section.

The country's largest spa is the domed **Hurshimchung** (p231; admission W7900), where you can spend all day and even get lost.

Yulpo Haesu Nokchatang (p262; admission W5000), on Yulpo beach on the south coast, offers you the chance to gently simmer yourself like a large *mandu* (dumpling) in green tea or hot seawater.

WINTER SPORTS

Korea offers winter-lovers so many different options for outdoor sports that the question isn't what to do, but what to do first. You will find enjoyable skiing in Seoul's many nearby resorts – the resorts in Gang·won province are modern, well maintained and beautiful. The ski season runs from December to February.

Alps Ski Resort (p174) gets the heaviest powder of the province and is set in a spectacular area right near the North Korean border. It is smaller than YongPyong, but well worth visiting for its location, views, ambience and powder. Further south, **YongPyong Ski Resort** (p179) boasts 18 sweet slopes that provide skiers with everything from bunny options to teeth-rattling, heart-racing thrills, and there are also courses for cross-country lovers as well. So this should be on the top of any ski bum's wish list. Olympic hopes or no, YongPyong Resort offers sublime skiing and snowboarding, with the usual comforts of ski-resort towns.

YongPyong Ski Resort in Gang·won-do is a leading contender to host the 2014 Winter Olympics, having missed out in 2010 by just three votes.

Getting there, or to any of the resorts, is usually only a bus ride away. All the resorts offer day packages (around W80,000) and overnight packages: prices vary with the accommodation rates, which vary from W50,000 or under for *minbak* (a room in a private home) and youth hostels, to over W250,000 for flash condos and stylish hotels). Packages can be bought in travel agents and include bus transport to and from Seoul as well as lift tickets, ski and clothing rental, and, if required, lessons and accommodation. Day, evening and night skiing is the norm. It's important to avoid the overcrowded weekends, especially at resorts near Seoul, as Koreans ski like they drive.

Travellers heading further south can still enjoy winter sports – at least for a while. In Jeollabuk-do, look for **Muju Ski Resort** (p301) in picturesque

Deogyusan National Park, which also has a beautiful and easy (three hours return) riverside hike to a temple, Baengnyeonsa. The ski resort is relatively new (it opened in 1990) and has become one of the country's top winter playgrounds – its 26 slopes have something for everyone, from bunny beginner to mogul-hardened monster. In 1997 it hosted the Universiade Winter Games and its après-ski facilities are the best. The resort has snow-making machines and Jeonju, Jeollabuk-do's capital, has an indoor skating rink.

Less than 2km from the spa hotels of Suanbo Hot Springs in Chungcheongbuk-do, **Sajo Ski Resort** (p338) is modest, but has seven slopes and three lifts, and the hot springs make for an oh-so-relaxing return after you're done conquering the slopes.

There are other winter activities besides what's on the slopes. Hiking trails in the national parks include **Bukhansan** (p141), just a short subway ride from downtown Seoul. The country's 20 national parks are as beautiful in winter as they are in summer, and snow on temple roofs provides a wonderful photo opportunity. Keep in mind though that appropriate clothes and exposure precautions are a must as temperatures can reach Siberian levels and whiteout blizzards are possible up in the mountains.

Chuncheon (p163) has lakes, bike paths and ice skating, and ice-climbers may want to try their skills in nearby **Gangchon** (p166), site of a frozen waterfall, Gugok pokpo. This 50m waterfall is spectacular any time of year, but provides ice-climbers with challenging excitement when it freezes between December and February. Ask for information about *bingbyeok deungban* (ice climbing).

Indoor **ice skating** is available all year at **Lotte World** (p113) and Koreans are ace short-track skaters. Expat workers in Seoul can join an **ice hockey** team, which is organised by **Gecko's** (p128). In winter Seoul joins in the fun as swimming pools along the Han River become ice-skating rinks, although *the* place for a magical skate is on the rink in the heart of downtown Seoul outside **City Hall** (Map pp88–9). Skates can be hired and prices are a giveaway.

After a decent snowfall, why not join the excited family groups who head for the nearest slope and sled down it on homemade sleds, which vary from fancy numbers to the basic tea tray.

Keep a lookout for **winter festivals** (p388), where barbecue snacks and *soju* are sold from igloos, ice sculptors carve wondrous (temporary) designs and everyone cuts holes in the frozen lakes to go fishing for dinner.

However cold the temperature outside, sleep on a traditional *yo* floor mattress and you'll be snug as a bug in a rug with the *ondol* (underfloor heating system) keeping even your toes as warm as toast.

'After a decent snowfall, why not join the excited family groups who head for the nearest slope and sled down it on homemade sleds'

Seoul 서울

To get the most out of this fascinating, at times frustrating, city you have to accept Seoul for what it is: the world's largest company town. The company – Korea Inc – is not a commercial enterprise in the conventional sense but a *gemeinschaft* of hypercapitalism with 10 million employees dedicated to the pursuit of capital accumulation, conspicuous consumption and social, educational and corporate ladder climbing.

Art, urban panache and public amenities are on a par with what you'd expect in an iron-ore-mining community somewhere in the hinterland – in dramatically short supply – but there are pockets of world-class quality like the Leeum Samsung Museum of Art and the War Memorial Museum. Getting workers from point A to point B is what drives municipal organisation, with little thought given to what lies between. The result is an efficient subway and inoffensive, grey urban landscape that borders on bland. There are notable exceptions, like the Jongno Tower and nearby bell pavilion, which together constitute the city's most attractive architectural juxtaposition.

Like any mining town, Seoul's precious goods are below the surface and hard to reach. If you're going to tap into this city's rich culture, which is built on 600 years of Confucius sediment, it's essential to become an explorer. Dare to stroll neighbourhoods like Samcheong-dong, where English is hardly spoken. Experiment with unusual food like crispy *bindaetteok* (빈대떡; green-bean pancake) in the Gwangjang market accompanied by a bottle of *makgeolli* (막걸리), a milky rice wine. Most importantly, challenge yourself by trying things you never imagined possible, like the public bath, the quintessential Korean experience.

HIGHLIGHTS

- Satisfy your urge for meat barbecued at your table at **Jongno Gol** (p124)
- Reflect on the possibilities of an afterlife while listening to the shaman's chants on the hills of **Inwangsan** (p116)
- Experience a euphoric sense of cleanliness at the **Hurest Spa** (p115) public bath and *jjimjilbang* (sauna)
- Behold the majesty of the Secret Garden at **Changdeokgung** (p101)
- Test your bargaining skills at the **Jang-anpyeong Antique Market** (p135)

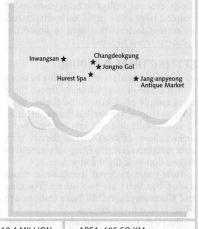

Inwangsan ★
Changdeokgung ★
★ Jongno Gol
Hurest Spa ★
★ Jang-anpyeong Antique Market

| ■ TELEPHONE CODE: 02 | ■ POPULATION: 10.4 MILLION | ■ AREA: 605 SQ KM |

SEOUL

HISTORY

With a population of almost 100,000, Seoul became the capital of Korea following the establishment of the Joseon dynasty in 1392. Confucianism was the ruling system of social order, Buddhism was banished and in the 19th century Catholics were executed. Until 1910, when Japanese colonial rule began, the rigid feudal system of kings, aristocrats, peasants, slaves and outcasts changed little. The nasty and brutish colonial masters destroyed much of the city's historical legacy. Korean culture nearly suffered a similar fate, as the country was unable or unwilling to fight against Japan's bid for regional domination. Since 1948, Seoul has been the capital of South Korea after the peninsula was formally divided into two states. Today, with a population of 10.4 million people, Seoul is one of the world's largest cities. It's also the country's centre of cultural, economic and political power, which Koreans living outside the city half-jokingly refer to as the Republic of Seoul.

NATIONAL & PROVINCIAL PARKS

On Seoul's northern boundary, **Bukhansan National Park** (p141) is known for granite cliffs, a stone fortress and lots of people at weekends. With five million annual park visitors, the easier trails leading to peaks like Insubong can be congested. Insubong is also a popular destination for rock climbers who prefer bouldering to walking.

Just 25km southeast of Seoul, **Namhan Sanseong Provincial Park** (p144) is a popular day trip from Seoul, with great hikes past ancient temples, large stone gates, tiny villages and an ancient fortress that used to guard the southern access to Seoul.

GETTING THERE & AROUND

Most international travellers arriving by plane land at Incheon International Airport; there are a couple of international flights from Japan to Gimpo Airport, but that facility now handles mostly domestic connections. From Incheon heaps of buses run into the city, with an express bus service to Gimpo if you need to make a domestic flight connection.

Most trains to Seoul terminate at Seoul station but there are two others: Yongsan and Cheongnyangni. All train stations are adjacent to subway stations.

The city's subway network is easy to use. Every station has English-language signs and the trains run frequently, though they stop around midnight. The bus system is satisfactory for people staying long enough to make sense of the routes. For short-term stays, it's tough to figure out. See p138 for transport details.

ORIENTATION

Downtown consists of Jongno, Gwanghwamun and Insadong, the city's premier tourist district. Myeongdong, Namsan and N'Seoul Tower are just to the south and easy to reach on foot if you're up for a walk. Bars, restaurants and shops of varying interest are on the other side of the mountain in Itaewon, a popular tourist district that's fast becoming the armpit of Seoul thanks to an overabundance of booze, testosterone and grime. During the day, the sidewalks are filled with shifty characters, suspicious street hawkers and an endless stream of annoying tailors who never stop asking if you want a made-to-measure suit (even though you've replied 'no' to the same person five minutes before). In the evening, there's no shortage of hookers promising to love you for a long time, drunken expat English teachers and just enough fights to warrant comparisons with a British soccer match.

Further south, the Han River cuts horizontally through the city with a mid-river island called Yeouido. South of the river, Gangnam is the city's hub of ostentation with expensive housing and Apgujeong, called the Rodeo Drive of Korea. The COEX Mall, Lotte World and Olympic Park are also south of the river and within reach of the subway.

April is not an especially good month for outdoor events in Seoul because periodic yellow dust storms reduce visibility and hamper breathing. These storms are thought to originate from China's Gobi desert. Sand, combined with air-borne particulates of industrial pollution – including heavy-metal concentrations of lead and copper largely emanating from China's booming manufacturing sector – form a potent witch's brew that on occasion requires pedestrians to wear a cloth mask over the nose and mouth to minimise health risks. Over the past few years, storms appear to have intensified, with particulate levels occasionally reaching 2000 parts per million (ppm) in a cubic metre of air, a level of pollution that is downright awful given that 300 ppm is considered hazardous.

Maps

The Korea Tourism Organisation (KTO) office (Map pp88–9) has an extensive selection of free maps.

INFORMATION
Bookshops

Bandi & Luni's (Map pp98–9; ☎ 6002 6002; 🕑 9.30am-10.30pm) The biggest selection of English-language books and mags is in the COEX Mall. There's also a branch in the Jongno Tower basement (Map pp88–9).

Kyobo Bookshop (Map pp88–9; ☎ 3973 5100) Line 5 to Gwanghwamun station, Exit 4.

Seoul Selection Bookshop (Map pp88–9; ☎ 734 9565; www.seoulselection.com; 🕑 9.30am-6.30pm Mon-Sat) Books, CDs and DVDs about Korea.

Emergency

Ambulance (☎ 119)
Fire Brigade (☎ 119)
Helpline for Foreigners (☎ 790 6783)
Police (☎ 112)

SEOUL IN...

Four Days

Walk the trails around **Inwangsan** (p116) and you might come across a shaman uttering sounds that do not seem of this world. For a spiritual journey of a different kind, go window-shopping in **Samcheongdong** (p134) and then try the *sujebi* (dough flakes in shellfish broth) at **Samcheong-dong Sujebi** (p125). Catch a taxi to Changdeokgung to join the day's last tour of the **Secret Garden** (p101). After the tour, it's a short taxi ride to Daehangno for *shabu shabu* (DIY beef and vegetable casserole) at **Opseoye** (p127) and music at **Live Jazz Club** (p132).

On day two go antiquing in the **Jang·anpyeong Market** (p135). For a different perspective on old things, head to **Leeum Samsung Museum of Art** (p104), the city's only must-see gallery. After viewing masterpieces of art, try one of two classic meals in Myeongdong: *bosintang* (dog-meat soup) at **Gye Sunok Bosintang** (p126) or *samgyetang* (ginseng chicken soup) at **Baekje Samgyetang** (p126). As long as you're in the area, take a bath at **Hurest Spa** (p115). Afterwards, enjoy the theatrical antics at **Nanta** (p133).

The third day's theme is reflection. Explore the **War Memorial Museum** (p113), which has terrific Korean War exhibitions. Then wander the streets in **Itaewon** (p104) and ask yourself why it's such a popular place. Subway over to Hapjeong and tour **Jeoldusan Martyrs' Shrine & Museum** (p104), pondering the extent of man's inhumanity. You've fed the spirit, now take care of the flesh in Sinchon, with a steak dinner cooked by a chef who worked in Paris at **Le Petit Paris** (p127). Close out the night at nearby **Noree Hanun Saramdul** (p128).

On day four explore **Seodaemun Prison** (p104) for a graphic presentation of Korean history. Then subway over to Insadong for an afternoon of browsing and drinking tea at one of the many **teashops** (p129). Dinner is barbecued pork at **Jongno Gol** (p124). In the evening tour the city's old and new sights on a **walking tour** (p117). The cable car and **N'Seoul Tower** (p103) are nearby, time and energy permitting.

Seven Days

Follow the suggested four-day plan, and...

On day five spend a few hours browsing **COEX Mall** (p113). Just be sure to be at **Bong·eunsa** (p113) in time for the two-hour temple tour if you're around on a Thursday. For good eats and drinks, head over to Gangnam and sample the home-brew at **Platinum Microbrewery** (p130).

On day six, Apgujeong is quiet in the morning so fill the time with a trip to the **National Museum of Korea** (p104). Afterwards, explore Apgujeong's Rodeo Drive and upscale department stores. Dinner is decidedly less fashionable, but the all-you-can-eat chicken wings at **Shwing** (p127) are irresistible. Be sure not to drop anything on your shirt because the next stop is **Once in a Blue Moon** (p132), the city's premiere jazz joint. When it's time for a cigar and port, walk over to the **Tribeca building** (p129).

Finally, spend the day at the track. The **Seoul Racecourse** (p143) has a lounge for international guests and is well set up for a day at the races. After, it's an easy subway ride to the **Millennium Seoul Hilton Casino** (p130).

It's unlikely that emergency service operators will be able to communicate in English, but the police department may have an interpreter available. Phone ☎ 1330 (24 hours) to contact an English-language speaker in a tourist information centre.

Internet Access

Internet rooms are on almost every street – look for the 'PC 방' sign. Most are open 24 hours and charge W1000 to W2000 per hour; after 11pm rates can be as low as W500. PC rooms are frequented by internet gamers and are often thick with smoke. Many backpacker guesthouses, hotels and cafés offer free internet access, as do these locations:

City Hall (Map pp92–3)
Gimpo domestic airport (Map pp84-5)
Incheon international airport (Map p140)
Itaewon subway station tourist information centre (Map p91)
KTO information booth (Map pp88–9)
KTO information centre (Map pp88–9)

Internet Resources

http://english.seoul.go.kr About 130,000 foreigners live in Seoul, of which 60% come from China. Learn more cool facts about Seoul on the city's website.
www.knto.or.kr Good travel information about Korea divided by region.
www.nearsubway.com An apartment locator with interactive maps.
www.rjkoehler.com The Marmot's Hole has mostly intelligent social and political commentary about Korea.

Laundry

Backpacker guesthouses usually provide free use of a washing machine with hang-dry facilities. If you stay in a *yeogwan* (budget motel), you may have to do your washing in the bathroom. Dry-cleaning shops are fairly common, but expect a hefty bill to clean your panties.

Left Luggage

Most subway stations and bus terminals have lockers. Small lockers cost W1000 a day and the ones large enough for a backpack are W2000.

Medical Services

Medical care in Seoul isn't quite on a par with western countries, but it's better than what you'll find in most Asian cities. Patients requiring hospitalisation can make their stay more bearable if friends and family visit on a regular basis, because food and room-cleaning services are minimal. Most facilities don't accept international insurance so bring cash or credit cards.

Dr Park's Dental Clinic (Map p91; ☎ 794 0551; 🕑 10am-6.30pm Mon-Fri, 10am-2pm Sat) Above Seoul Pub.
International Clinic (Map p91; ☎ 790 0857; www .internationalclinic.co.kr; 🕑 9am-6pm Mon-Fri, 9am-3pm Sat, closed noon-2pm) In the Hannam Building.
Samsung Medical Center & International Health Service (Map pp84–5; ☎ 3410 0200; 50 Ilwondong, Gangnam-gu; 🕑 8.30am-noon, 1-5pm Mon-Fri) Line 3 to Irwon station, Exit 1 and ride the shuttle bus.
Severance Hospital (Map p94; ☎ 2228 5810, emergencies 012 263 6556; www.severance.or.kr/en; 🕑 9am-12.30pm, 1.30-4.30pm Mon-Fri, 9.30-11am Sat) The International Health Care Centre is on the 3rd floor of the large building beside Yonsei University. Line 2 to Sinchon station, Exit 3.

Money

Banks are open from 9.30am to 4pm Monday to Friday and most will exchange foreign currencies. Licensed moneychangers in Itaewon keep longer hours. Near Insadong, there is a moneychanger in front of the Nakwon Arcade; look for the 'Money Exchange' sign. Compare rates and commissions before using any of these services. Expats working in Korea may be required to show a copy of their employment contract and alien registration card to open a bank account and to wire money overseas. Some banks stamp passports with the amount of remittance.

Post

Gwanghwamun post office (Map pp88–9; 🕑 9am-8pm Mon-Fri, 9am- 6pm weekends & holidays) Has extended hours. Line 5 to Gwanghwamun station, Exit 5 and walk around the corner.

Toilets

Free public toilets are available throughout the city. In a pinch, it is acceptable to enter a restaurant to use the washroom. Always carry tissue, as most restrooms do not supply this vital product. Older facilities are equipped with an oblong porcelain hole that requires users to drop their knickers and squat. Steady balance and the ability to hit the target are two skills needed to avoid a messy situation.

Tourist Information

Insadong Tourist Office (Map pp88-9; ☎ 734 0222; 🕙 10am-10pm)

Itaewon Tourist Information Centre (Map p91; ☎ 3785 2514; www.enjoy.itaewon.com; 🕙 9am-10pm)

KTO (Map pp88-9; ☎ 729 9496; www.knto.or.kr; 🕙 9am-8pm)

Seoul Station (Map pp92–3; ☎ 2392 1324; 🕙 4.30am-11pm)

Other tourist information booths include Incheon international airport, Gimpo airport, Korea City Air Terminal (KCAT), Deoksugung and the Namdaemun and Dongdaemun markets. There are also three in Itaewon and two near Lotte Young Plaza in Myeongdong.

Travel Agencies

Travel agents often advertise discounted fares in the country's English-language newspapers.

Apple Tours (Map pp86-7; ☎ 793 3478; 🕙 10am-6pm Mon-Fri, 10am-2pm Sat) The USO's overseas travel service.

Omega Top Travel (Map pp88–9; ☎ 723 6142; 🕙 9am-6pm Mon-Fri) On the 5th floor of a grungy building in Insadong. Walk down the lane between the YMCA and a convenience store.

Shoestring Travel (Map p94; ☎ 333 4151; www .shoestring.co.kr; 🕙 10am-6pm Mon-Fri, 9am-3pm Sat) Lonely Planet books are sold here.

Time Machine Travel (Map pp88–9; ☎ 778 1887; 🕙 10am-6pm Mon-Fri, 11am-5pm Sat) Room 436 of the Royal Building. Line 5 to Gwanghwamun station, Exit 7. Turn left at the street before the Sejong Center for Performing Arts and walk to the corner.

Withus Travel (Map pp88-9; ☎ 720 1123; 🕙 9am-6.30pm Mon-Fri, to 2pm Sat) On the 2nd floor in the same building as Omega Top Travel.

Xanadu Travel (Map p91; ☎ 795 7771; www.xanadu .co.kr; 🕙 9am-6pm Mon-Fri, 11am-3pm Sat) On the 5th floor of the KEB building in Itaewon.

SIGHTS
Gwanghwamun 광화문
GYEONGBOKGUNG 경복궁

At one time, this **palace** (Map pp88-9; ☎ 732 1931; adult/youth/child W3000/1500/free; 🕙 9am-6pm Wed-Mon Mar-Oct, closes 1hr earlier Nov-Feb, open to 7pm Sat & Sun May-Oct) may have been a place of pomp and ceremony. Today the uniformly brown buildings with a dirt compound in front may leave travellers with the impression that the sight is undergoing restoration work. This was the country's principal royal residence until the palace was destroyed in 1592 during the *Imjin Waeran* war with Japan. But it was not the

Japanese that razed the palace. The citizens of Seoul did that dirty deed. As the Japanese marched across the country, the king and *yangban* (aristocrats) abandoned Seoul to save their own skins. Angered by the desertion, a mob burned down the palace. It lay in waste for nearly 300 years until Regent Daewon·gun, father of King Gojong, began to rebuild it in 1865. King Gojong moved into the palace in 1868. Nearly 30 years later, the king's wife, Queen Myeongseong (Queen Min), was murdered in her bedroom by Japanese assassins. King Gojong fled the palace to sanctuary in the Russian legation.

English-language tours (🕙 9.30am, noon, 1.30pm & 3pm, not Tue) are conducted free of charge four times daily. The ceremonial changing of the guard takes place six times (not on Tuesday), though the length varies (10am for 25 minutes, 11am, noon, 1pm and 2pm for seven minutes, 3pm for 20 minutes.

Paid admission to the palace includes entry into the **National Palace Museum** (Map pp88-9; ☎ 3701 7500; 🕙 9am-6pm Tue-Fri, 9am-7pm Sat & Sun). Small and blasé, it contains clothing, furniture and artefacts from the Joseon period.

On the other side of the compound, the **National Folk Museum** (Map pp88-9; ☎ 3704 3114; www.nfm .go.kr; admission free with entry to Gyeongbokgung; 🕙 9am-6pm Mon & Wed-Fri Mar-Oct, to 5pm Nov-Feb, 9am-7pm Sat & Sun) re-creates everyday Joseon life. Farming implements, clothing and a *kimchi* display are here along with an exhibition of scholarly thought. Advanced Joseon thinkers believed the sun revolved around the Earth, heaven was round and Earth was square. Although few people subscribe to this belief system today, its impact is evident in some of the city's architecture, like the Jongno Tower, an attractive but befuddling structure until viewed through the eyes of a Joseon scholar. Take Line 3 to Gyeongbokgung station, Exit 5.

GYEONGHUIGUNG 경희궁

There are no guided tours, audio systems or admission fees at this lonely **palace** (Map pp88-9; ☎ 724 0274; admission free; 🕙 9am-6pm Tue-Sat, 10am-6pm Sun & holidays) that once served as a villa for Joseon royalty. Restored and reopened in 2002, the quiet compound blends nature with attractive architectural sightlines, created by black-tiled roofs climbing stepwise up the backside of a hill. Approach the palace at just the right angle and you'll be

(Continued on page 101)

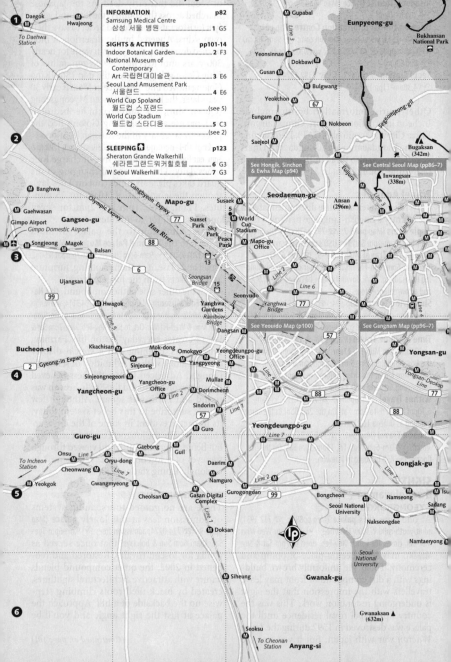

A **B** Goyang-si **C** **D**

To Wondang Station

Jichuk M

Daegok M Hwajeong M Gupabal M

To Daehwa Station

Eunpyeong-gu

Bukhansan National Park

Yeonsinnae M

Dokbawi M

Gusan M

Line 3

INFORMATION p82
Samsung Medical Centre
삼성 서울 병원..............................1 G5

SIGHTS & ACTIVITIES pp101–14
Indoor Botanical Garden...................2 F3
National Museum of
Contemporary
Art 국립현대미술관....................3 E6
Seoul Land Amusement Park
서울랜드....................................4 E6
World Cup Spoland
월드컵 스포랜드.....................(see 5)
World Cup Stadium
월드컵 스타디움......................5 C3
Zoo...(see 2)

SLEEPING p123
Sheraton Grande Walkerhill
쉐라톤그랜드워커힐호텔.............6 G3
W Seoul Walkerhill.........................7 G3

Bulgwang M

Yeokchon M 67

Eungam M Nokbeon M

Bugaksan (342m)

Saejeol M

Bugaksan (342m)

Banghwa M

Olympic Expwy Gangbyeon Expwy Mapo-gu Susaek M

See Hongik, Sinchon & Ewha Map (p94)

Seodaemun-gu

Ansan (296m)

See Central Seoul Map (pp86–7)

Inwangsan (338m)

Gaehwasan M

Gangseo-gu Sunset Park Sky Park Peace Park World Cup Stadium

Gimpo Airport
Gimpo Domestic Airport

Songjeong M Magok M Balsan M

Han River 88

Mapo-gu Office

Line 2 M M M M Line 6

Line 5

6

Ujangsan M

99

Hwagok M

Seongsan Bridge 15 Seonyudo

Yanghwa Gardens
Rainbow Bridge

Yanghwa Bridge 77

Line 3

Dangsan M

See Yeouido Map (p100) 57

See Gangnam Map (pp96–7)

Bucheon-si Kkachisan M Mok-dong Omokgyo Yeongdeungpo-gu Office Yongsan-gu

2 Gyeong-in Expwy Sinjeong M Yangpyeong M

Yongsan-Deoksu Line 77

Sinjeongnegeori M Yangcheon-gu Office Mullae M

Line 5

Yangcheon-gu Line 2 Dorimcheon M

Sindorim M 88

Line 1 57

Guro-gu Guro M

Line 7 88

To Incheon Station Onsu M Line 1 Gaebong M Guil M Dongjak-gu

Cheonwang M Oryu-dong M Daerim M

Yeongdeungpo-gu Line 7

Yeokgok M Gwangmyeong M Namguro M

Line 2

Cheolsan M Gasan Digital Complex Gurogongdan 99 Bongcheon M Namseong M Isu M

Seoul National University Sadang M

Guro-gu Nakseongdae M

Doksan M Namtaeryong M

Seoul National University

Siheung M Gwanak-gu

Gwanaksan (632m)

Seoksu M

To Cheonan Station Anyang-si

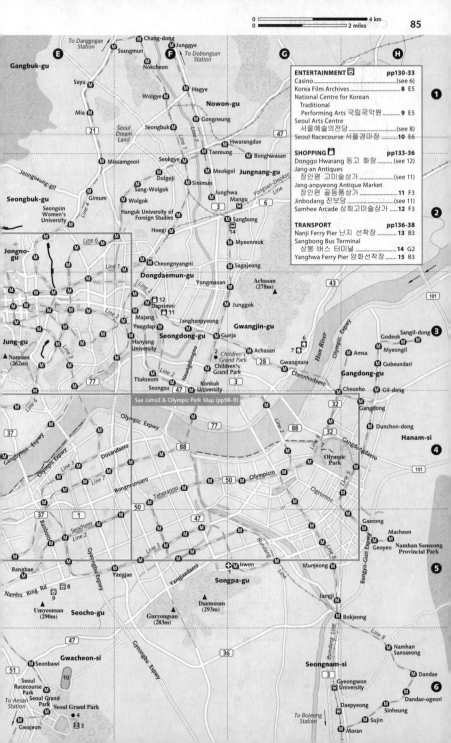

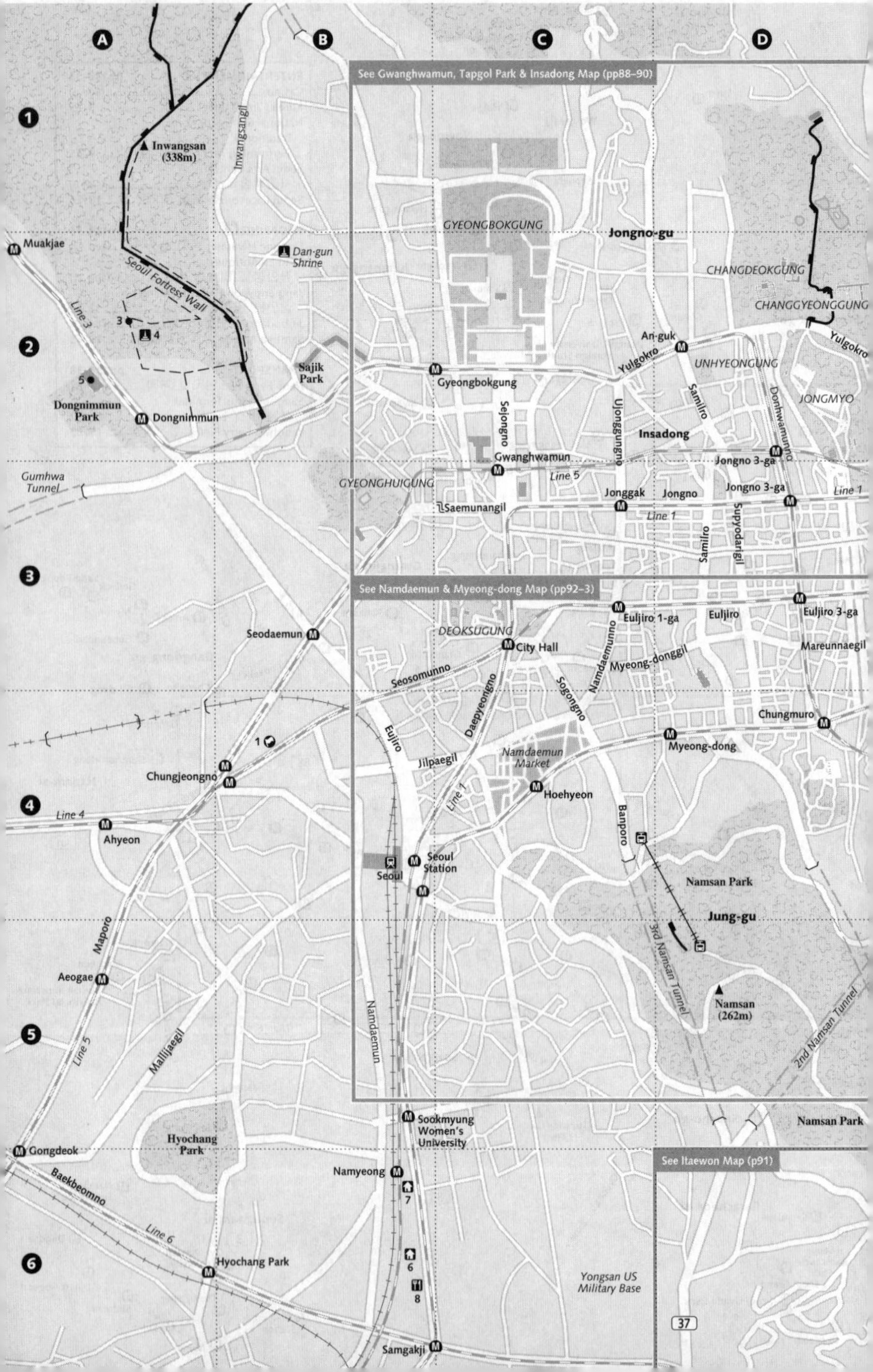

A   B   C   D

1

Inwangsan
(338m)

Inwangsangil

See Gwanghwamun, Tapgol Park & Insadong Map (pp88–90)

GYEONGBOKGUNG

Jongno-gu

CHANGDEOKGUNG

Muakjae

Dan-gun
Shrine

CHANGGYEONGGUNG

Seoul Fortress Wall

Yulgokro

Line 3

3   4

Sajik
Park

2

An-guk

Yulgokro

UNHYEONGUNG

JONGMYO

5

Gyeongbokgung

Samiro

Dongnimmun
Park

Dongnimmun

Sejongno

Ujeongungno

Insadong

Jongno 3-ga

Donhwamunro

Gumhwa
Tunnel

GYEONGHUIGUNG

Gwanghwamun

Line 5

Jonggak

Jongno

Jongno 3-ga

Samiro

Jongno 3-ga

Supyodaegil

Line 1

Saemunangil

Line 1

3

See Namdaemun & Myeong-dong Map (pp92–3)

DEOKSUGUNG

Euljiro 1-ga

Euljiro

Euljiro 3-ga

Seodaemun

City Hall

Namdaemunno

Myeong-donggil

Mareunnaegil

Seosomunno

Daepyeongno

Sogongno

Chungmuro

Euljiro

Jilpaegil

Namdaemun
Market

Myeong-dong

1

Chungjeongno

Line 1

Hoehyeon

Banporo

4

Ahyeon

Line 4

Seoul

Seoul
Station

Namsan Park

Jung-gu

Mapoto

3rd Namsan Tunnel

Aeogae

Malijaegil

Namdaemun

Namsan
(262m)

2nd Namsan Tunnel

5

Line 5

Gongdeok

Hyochang
Park

Sookmyung
Women's
University

Namsan Park

See Itaewon Map (p91)

Baekbeomno

Namyeong

7

Hyochang Park

Line 6

Yongsan US
Military Base

6   8

37

Samgakji

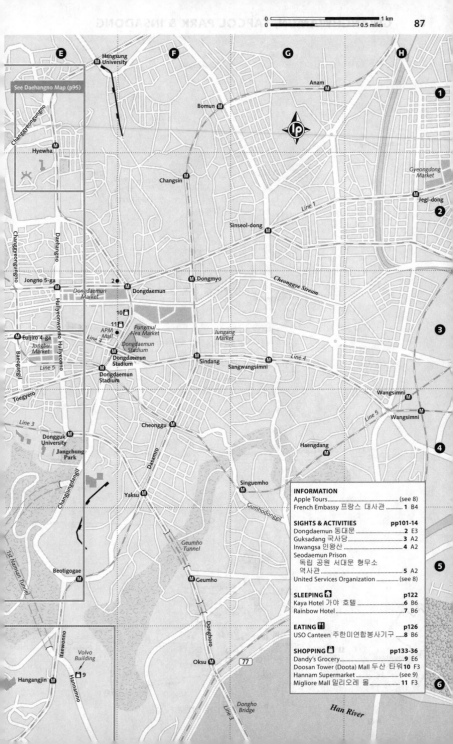

See Daehangno Map (p95)

E

Changgyeonggno

Hyewha

Changgyeonggno

Daehangno

Jongno 5-ga

Hullyeonwonno

Euljiro 4-ga
Jungbu Market

Baeogaegil

Line 5

Toegyero

Line 3

Dongguk University

Jangchung Park

Changjungdangil

Yaksu

Beotigogae

Hanoeumno

Volvo Building

Hangangjin

Hannamno

F

Hangsung University

Bomun

Changsin

Dongdaemun Market

APM Mall
Line 2

Dongdaemun Stadium

Dongdaemun Stadium

Cheonggu

Dasanno

Singuemho

Geumho Tunnel

Donghoro

Oksu

Line 3

Dongho Bridge

G

Sinseol-dong

Line 1

Dongmyo

Pungmul Flea Market

Jungang Market

Sindang

Sangwangsimni

Haengdang

Gumhodonggil

77

Han River

Cheonggye Stream

Jungang Market

Line 4

H

Anam

Gyeongdong Market

Jegi-dong

Wangsimni

Wangsimni

Line 5

1

2

3

4

5

6

2

10
11

INFORMATION
Apple Tours...................................... (see 8)
French Embassy 프랑스 대사관 **1** B4

SIGHTS & ACTIVITIES   pp101–14
Dongdaemun 동대문 **2** E3
Guksadang 국사당 **3** A2
Inwangsa 인왕산 **4** A2
Seodaemun Prison
  독립 공원 서대문 형무소
  역사관 **5** A2
United Services Organization .... (see 8)

SLEEPING 🛏   p122
Kaya Hotel 가야 호텔 **6** B6
Rainbow Hotel **7** B6

EATING 🍴   p126
USO Canteen 주한미연합봉사기구 **8** B6

SHOPPING 🛍   pp133–36
Dandy's Grocery **9** E6
Doosan Tower (Doota) Mall 두산 타워 **10** F3
Hannam Supermarket .... (see 9)
Migliore Mall 밀리오레 몰 **11** F3

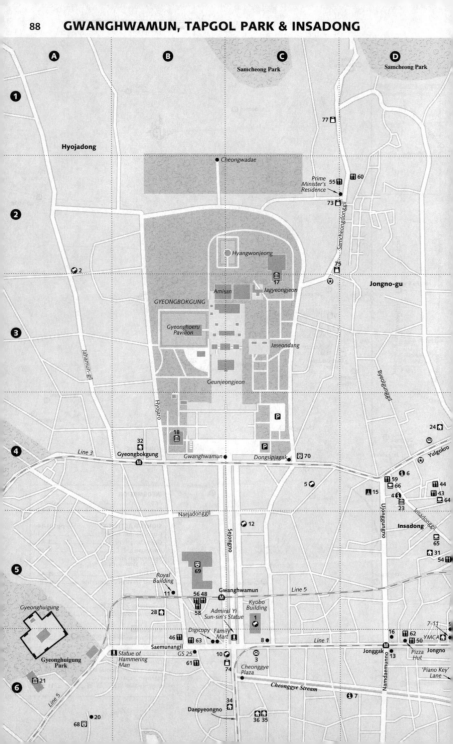

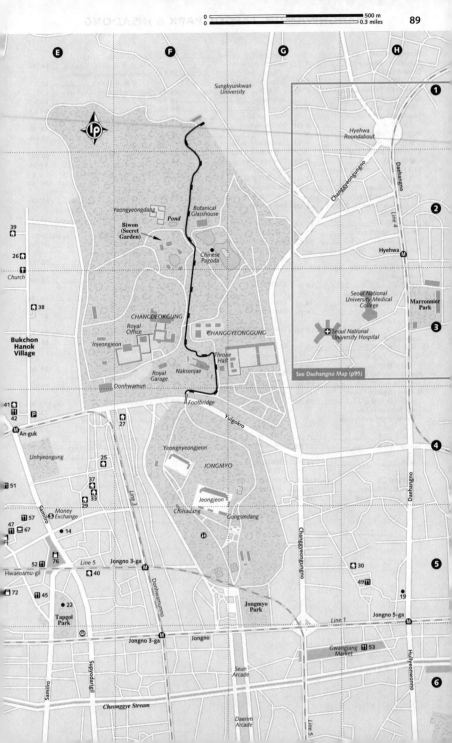

0 ———— 500 m
0 ———— 0.3 miles

E **F** **G** **H**

1

Sungkyunkwan University

Hyehwa Roundabout

2

Line 4

Hyehwa Ⓜ

Yeongyeongdang
Pond
Biwon (Secret Garden)

Botanical Glasshouse

39

26
Church

Chinese Pagoda

Seoul National University Medical College

Marronnier Park

3

38

CHANGDEOKGUNG
Royal Office

Injeongjeon

CHANGGYEONGGUNG

✚ *Seoul National University Hospital*

Bukchon Hanok Village

See Daehangno Map (p95)

Royal Garage   *Naksonjae*
Throne Hall
Donhwamun

41
42
Ⓟ

Ⓜ **An-guk**

27

Footbridge

Yulgokro

4

Unhyeongung

25

Yeongnyeongjeon

JONGMYO

Daehangno

51

37
33
29

Line 3

Money Ⓢ Exchange

57
47
67
71

● 14

Jeongjeon

Chilsadang

Gongsindang

ℹ️

30

49

5

52
Hwaenamu-gil

76
Ⓜ **Jongno 3-ga**

40

Donhwamunno

Changgyeonggungno

● 19

72
45

● 22

Jongno 5-ga Ⓜ

Tapgol Park

⊠
Ⓜ **Jongno 3-ga**   **Jongno**

Jongmyo Park

Line 1

6

Samiro

Supyogidaero

Samiro

Supyogidaero

Seun Arcade

Gwangjang Market **53**

Hullyeonwonno

Line 5

Cheonggye Stream

Daerim Arcade

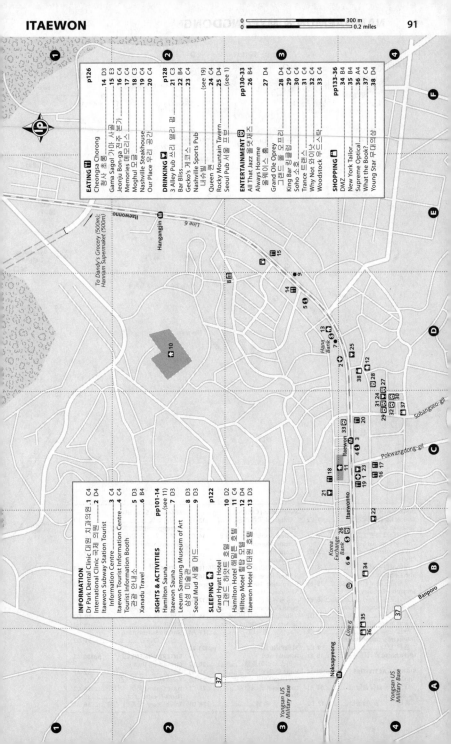

0   300 m
0   0.2 miles

INFORMATION
Dr Park Dental Clinic 대평 치과의원 1   C4
International Clinic 국제 의원 2   D4
Itaewon Subway Station Tourist
Information Centre 3   C4
Itaewon Tourist Information Centre 4   C4
Tourist Information Booth
관광 안내소 5   D3
Xanadu Travel 6   B4

SIGHTS & ACTIVITIES   pp101-14
Hamilton Sauna ....(see 11)
Itaewon Sauna 7   D3
Leeum Samsung Museum of Art
삼성 미술관 8   D3
Seoul Mud 서울 머드 9   D3

SLEEPING   p122
Grand Hyatt Hotel
그랜드 하얏트 호텔 10   D2
Hamilton Hotel 해밀튼 호텔 11   C4
Hilltop Motel 힐탑 모텔 12   D4
Itaewon Hotel 이태원 호텔 13   D3

EATING   p126
Cheongsa Chorong
청사 초롱 14   D3
Gama Sagol 가마 사골 15   E3
Jeonju Bonga 전주 본가 16   C4
Memories 메모리스 17   C4
Moghul 모굴 18   C3
Nashville Steakhouse 19   C4
Our Place 우리 공간 20   C4

DRINKING   p128
3 Alley Pub 쓰리 앨리 펍 21   C3
Bar Bliss 22   B4
Gecko's 게코스 23   C4
Nashville Sports Pub
내쉬빌 ....(see 19)
Queen 퀸 24   C4
Rocky Mountain Tavern 25   D4
Seoul Pub 서울 포브 ....(see 1)

ENTERTAINMENT   pp130-33
All That Jazz 올댓재즈 26   B4
Always Homme
올웨이스 홈 27   D4
Grand Ole Oprey 28   D4
King Bar 킹 바 29   C4
Soho 소호 30   C4
Trance 트랜스 31   C4
Why Not 와이낫 32   C4
Woodstock 우드스탁 33   C4

SHOPPING   pp133-36
DMZ 34   B4
New York Tailor 35   B4
Supreme Optical 36   A4
What the Book? 37   C4
Young Star 무미의상 38   D4

ITAEWON

DEOKSUGUNG

Deoksugunggil

Euljiro Underground Arcade

Euljiro

Euljiro 1-ga

Seoul Plaza

Seoul City Shopping Plaza

Lotte Underground Arcade

Seosomunno

Radisson Seoul Plaza Hotel

City Hall

Altar of Heaven Pavilion

Sosong Underground Arcade

Daepyeongno

Line 2

Myeong-donggil

Avatar Cinemas & Mall

Sogongno

Euljiro

Jungmuro

Namdaemun Underground Arcade

Migliore Mall

Myeongdong

Fountain & Statue

Line 4

Jilpaegil

Namdaemunno

Namdaemun Market

Myeongdong Underground Arcade

Line 1

Namdaemuno

Hoehyeon

Toegyero

Banpo

Bus No 2 Bus Stop

Line 4

Seoul Station

Sopugil

Sowolgil

Seoul Fortress Wall

3rd Namsan Tunnel

Cable Car

INFORMATION

Bank of Korea 한국은행 **1** C2
Canadian Embassy
캐나다대사관 **2** C1
Chinese Consular Section
(Visa Issuance) **3** D3
City Hall
서울시청관광안내소 **4** C1
Irish Embassy
아일랜드대사관 **5** B3
Singapore Embassy
싱가포르대사관 **6** B2
Tourist Information Booth
관광 안내 **7** D2
Tourist Information Booth
관광 안내 **8** C2
Tourist Information Booth
관광 안내 **9** C2
UK Embassy 영국대사관 **10** B1

SIGHTS & ACTIVITIES   pp101-14

Anglican Church
대한성공회대성당 **11** B1
Hurest Spa
휴레스트 웰 빙센타 **12** D2

Myeongdong Catholic
Cathedral 명동성당 **13** E2
Namdaemun
(Great South Gate) 남대문 **14** B3
National Museum of
Contemporary Art,
Deoksugung
국립현대미술관덕수궁분관 ..**15** B1
N'Seoul Tower N서울 타워 **16** E5
Panmunjom Travel Center .... (see 23)
Seokjeojeon Hall
궁중유물전시관 **17** B1
Seoul Museum of Art, Main
Building 서울시립미술관 **18** B1
Silloam Fomentation Sauna
실로암 불가마 사우나 **19** A4

SLEEPING   pp121-22

Astoria Hotel
아스토리아호텔 **20** E2
Hotel Shilla 신라호텔 **21** H3
Ibis Hotel 이비스 호텔 **22** D2
Lotte Hotel 롯데호텔 **23** C1
Metro Hotel
메트로 호텔 **24** D1

Millennium Seoul Hilton
힐튼호텔 **25** B4
Myeongdong Guesthouse
명동 게스트 하우스 **26** D2
Westin Chosun Hotel
조선호텔 **27** C1

EATING   p126

Baekje Samgyetang
백제삼계탕 **28** D2
Gye Sunok Bosintang
계순옥 보신탕 **29** D2
Myeongdong Gyoja
명동 교자 **30** D2
N'Grill .... (see 16)
Sinseon Selleongtang
신선 설농탕 **31** D2

ENTERTAINMENT   pp130-33

Chongdong Theatre
정동극장 **32** A1
Korea House 한국의집 **33** F2
Lotte Cinema 롯데 시네마 **34** C2
Nanta Theatre 난타 **35** A1
Tokebi Storm 도깨비 스톰 **36** A1

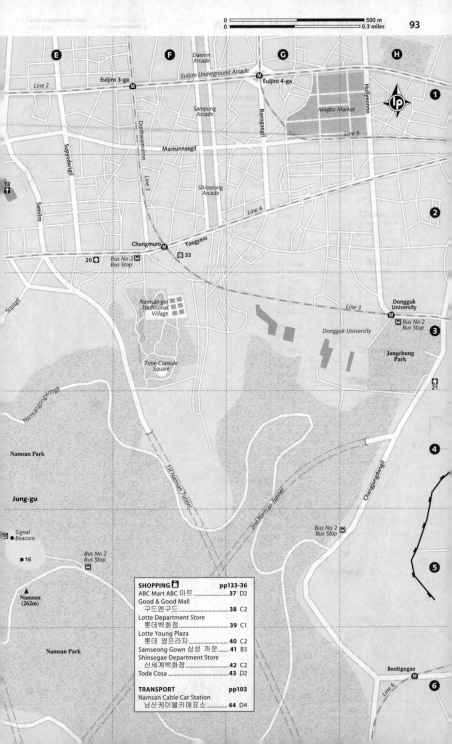

SHOPPING 🛍 pp133-36
ABC Mart ABC 마트 37 D2
Good & Good Mall
구드엔구드 38 C2
Lotte Department Store
롯데백화점 39 C1
Lotte Young Plaza
롯데 영프라자 40 C2
Samseong Gown 삼성 까운 41 B3
Shinsegae Department Store
신세계백화점 42 C2
Toda Cosa 43 D2

TRANSPORT pp103
Namsan Cable Car Station
남산케이블카매표소 44 D4

0 — 1 km
0 — 0.5 miles

INFORMATION
Severance Hospital
  세브란스 병원..**1** D4
Shoestring Travel 신발끈 여행사 **2** B5

SIGHTS & ACTIVITIES pp101-14
Bestfriend Language and Culture
  Exchange Center **3** D4
Dongbang Sauna 동방사우나 **4** B4
Jeoldusan Martyrs' Shrine & Museum
  절두산순교성지 **5** A5
Sogang University Korean
  Language Education Center
  소강 대학교......................................**6** D5

SLEEPING p122
Kims' Guesthouse
  킴스 게스트하우스 **7** A5
Queen 21...**8** D4
Seokyo Hotel 서교 호텔 **9** B4

EATING pp126-27
Agio **10** B5
Cabin Oak 캐빈 오크 **11** B4
Choonchun Jib 춘천집 **12** C4
Dokdo Tuna 독도 참치 **13** B4
Dongah Gul 동아글 **14** B5
Le Petit Paris **15** C4
Misses & Mai
  미세스 마이 ....(see 10)
Richemont **16** B4

DRINKING pp126-27
Blue Bird **17** C4
Café Atre...**18** B5
Galaxy 999 ....**19** B4
Gold II 골드바 **20** B5
Moim...(see 28)
Moon Yang 문양 **21** B5
Noree Hanun Saramdul
  놀이 하는 사람들 **22** C4
Princess **23** B5
US Bar 66..**24** B5
Watts On Tap **25** C4
Woodstock 우드스탁 **26** C4

ENTERTAINMENT pp130-33
Bebop Jazz Club
  비밥 재즈 클럽 **27** B4
Club Otwo **28** B5
Free Bird 프리버드 **29** B5
Hole **30** B5
M2 ....**31** B5
Macondo 마콘도 **32** B4
Sk@ 스카 **33** B5
Skunk Hell **34** B5
SLUG.er..**35** B5
Water Cock 워터콕 **36** B5

SHOPPING pp133-36
Ahyeon-dong Wedding Street
  아현동 웨딩거리.............................**37** D4
Hyundai Department Store
  현대 백화점 **38** C4
She's...**39** D4

TRANSPORT p137
Sinchon Bus Terminal
  신촌 시외 버스 터미널......................**40** C5

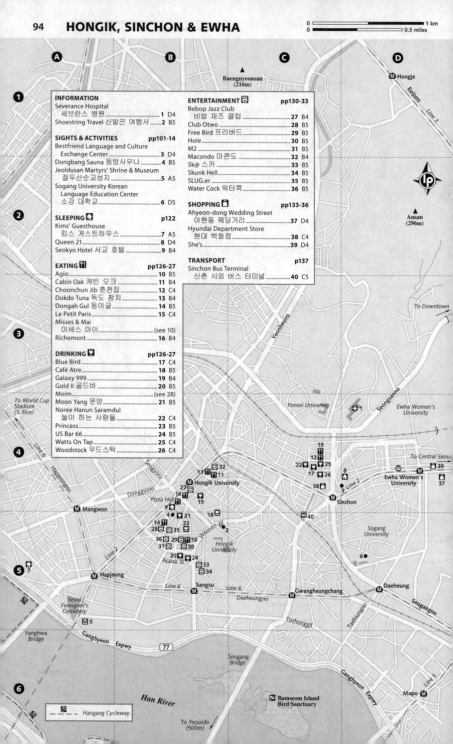

To World Cup
Stadium
(1.3km)

To Downtown

To Central Seoul

Baengnyeonsan
(216m)

Ansan
(296m)

Hongje

Yeonhuiro

Yonsei University

Ewha Women's
University

Seongsanno

Ewha Women's
University

Hongik University

Pizza Hut

Dongyoro

Seogyoro

Wausan-gil

Hongik
University

Mangwon

Hapjeong

Picasso St

Sangsu

Line 2

Line 6

Hapyeongno

Sinchon

Line 2

Sogang
University

Daeheung

Gwangheungchang

Daeheungno

Seogangno

Taehungno

Mapo

Seoul
Foreigner's
Cemetery

Yanghwa
Bridge

Gangbyeon Expwy

77

Seogang
Bridge

Tochonggil

Gangbyeon Expwy

Han River

Bamseom Island
Bird Sanctuary

To Yeouido
(500m)

Hangang Cycleway

0   200 m
0   0.1 miles

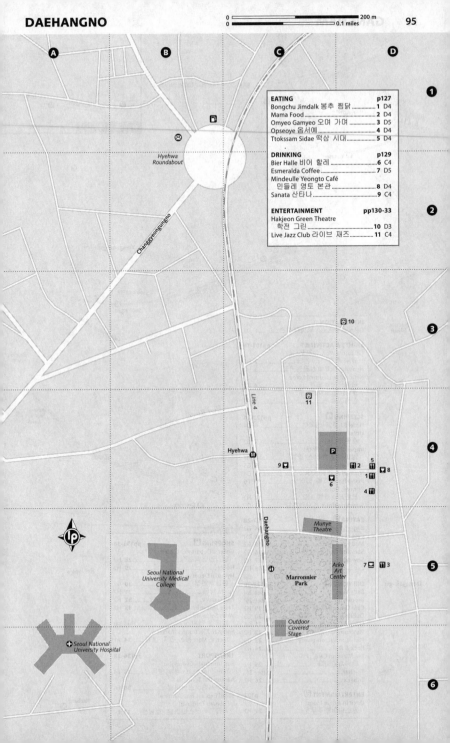

Hyehwa
Roundabout

Changgyeongungno

Line 4

Hyehwa

Daehangno

Munye
Theatre

Seoul National
University Medical
College

Arko
Art
Center

Marronnier
Park

Outdoor
Covered
Stage

Seoul National
University Hospital

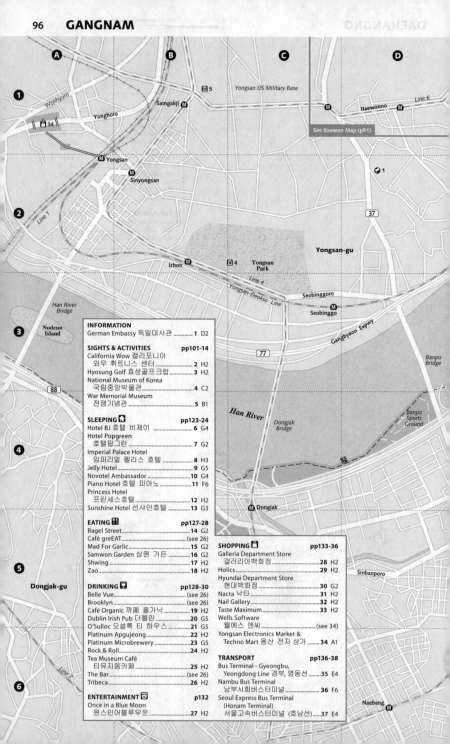

INFORMATION
German Embassy 독일대사관 **1** D2

SIGHTS & ACTIVITIES **pp101-14**
California Wow 캘리포니아
와우 휘트니스 센터 **2** H2
Hyosung Golf 효성골프크럽 **3** H2
National Museum of Korea
국립중앙박물관 **4** C2
War Memorial Museum
전쟁기념관 **5** B1

SLEEPING **pp123-24**
Hotel BJ 호텔 비제이 **6** G4
Hotel Popgreen
호텔팝그린 **7** G2
Imperial Palace Hotel
임피리얼 펠리스 호텔 **8** H3
Jelly Hotel **9** G5
Novotel Ambassador **10** G4
Piano Hotel 호텔 피아노 **11** F6
Princess Hotel
프린세스호텔 **12** H2
Sunshine Hotel 선사인호텔 **13** G3

EATING **pp127-28**
Bagel Street **14** G2
Café greEAT .... (see 26)
Mad For Garlic **15** G2
Samwon Garden 삼원 가든 **16** G2
Shwing **17** H2
Zao **18** H2

DRINKING **pp128-30**
Belle Vue .... (see 26)
Brooklyn .... (see 26)
Café Organic 까페 올가닉 **19** H2
Dublin Irish Pub 더블린 **20** G5
O'Sulloc 오설록 티 하우스 **21** G5
Platinum Apgujeong **22** H2
Platinum Microbrewery **23** G5
Rock & Roll **24** H2
Tea Museum Café
티뮤지움카페 **25** H2
The Bar .... (see 26)
Tribeca **26** H2

ENTERTAINMENT **p132**
Once in a Blue Moon
원스인어블루무운 **27** H2

SHOPPING **pp133-36**
Galleria Department Store
갤러리아백화점 **28** H2
Holics **29** H2
Hyundai Department Store
현대백화점 **30** G2
Nacta 낙타 **31** H2
Nail Gallery **32** H2
Taste Maximum **33** H2
Wells Software
웰에스 앤씨 .... (see 34)
Yongsan Electronics Market &
Techno Mart 용산 전자 상가 **34** A1

TRANSPORT **pp136-38**
Bus Terminal - Gyeongbu,
Yeongdong Line 경부, 영동선 **35** E4
Nambu Bus Terminal
남부시외버스터미널 **36** F6
Seoul Express Bus Terminal
(Honam Terminal)
서울고속버스터미널 (호남선) **37** E4

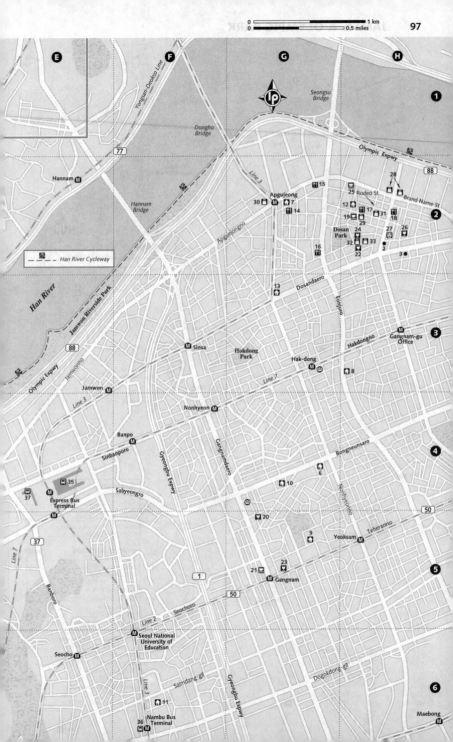

0 ——————— 1 km
0 ——————— 0.5 miles

E   **F**   **G**   **H**

1

Seongsu
Bridge

Yongsan-Deokso Line

Dongho
Bridge

Olympic Expwy

77

88

Hannam M

Hannam
Bridge

25 Rodeo St
28
Brand Name St

Line 3

Apgujeong
30 M 7
15

12 17 31 18
19 29
26
27

2

14

24
Dosan
Park
32 33
16
22

Han River Cycleway

Han River

13

Dosandaero

Jamwon Riverside Park

88

Eonju

Gangnam-gu
Office

Olympic Expwy

Jamwonno

M Sinsa

Hokdong
Park

Hak-dong

M

Hakdongno

3

Line 7

8

Janwon M

Line 3

Nonhyeon M

Gyeongbu Expwy

Gangnamdaero

Bongeunsaro

Nonhyeonno

4

Banpo M

Sinbanporo

6

Sabyeongro

10

50

37

M 35

Express Bus
Terminal

20

37

M

9

Yeoksam M

Teheranno

5

21

23

M Gangnam

Banporo

1

50

Line 2

Seochoro

M Seoul National
University of
Education

Salindang-gil

Gyeongbu Expwy

Dogokdong-gil

Seocho M

Line 3

6

11

Maebong
M

36

Nambu Bus
Terminal

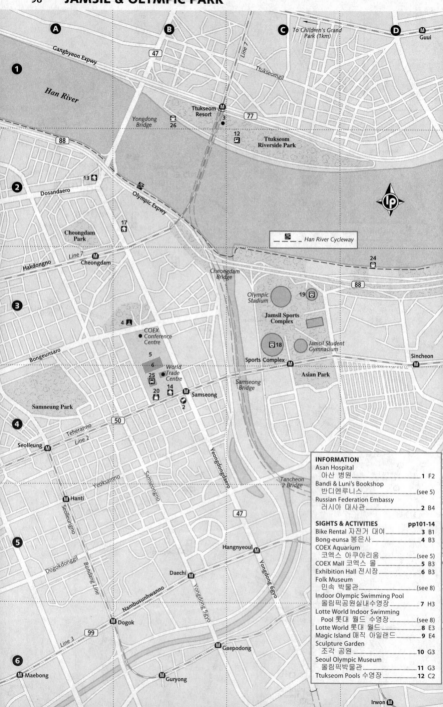

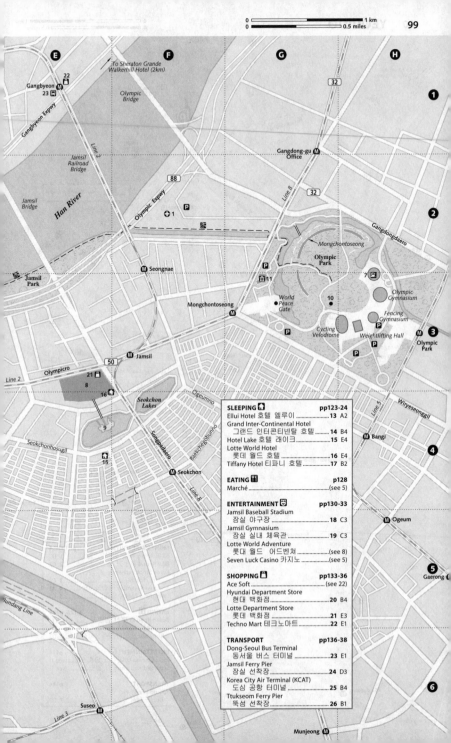

99

SLEEPING pp123-24
Ellui Hotel 호텔 엘루이 13 A2
Grand Inter-Continental Hotel
그랜드 인터콘티넨탈 호텔 14 B4
Hotel Lake 호텔 레이크 15 E4
Lotte World Hotel
롯데 월드 호텔 16 E4
Tiffany Hotel 티파니 호텔 17 B2

EATING p128
Marché .... (see 5)

ENTERTAINMENT pp130-33
Jamsil Baseball Stadium
잠실 야구장 18 C3
Jamsil Gymnasium
잠실 실내 체육관 19 C3
Lotte World Adventure
롯데 월드 어드벤처 .... (see 8)
Seven Luck Casino 카지노 .... (see 5)

SHOPPING pp133-36
Ace Soft .... (see 22)
Hyundai Department Store
현대 백화점 20 B4
Lotte Department Store
롯데 백화점 21 E3
Techno Mart 테크노마트 22 E1

TRANSPORT pp136-38
Dong-Seoul Bus Terminal
동서울 버스 터미널 23 E1
Jamsil Ferry Pier
잠실 선착장 24 D3
Korea City Air Terminal (KCAT)
도심 공항 터미널 25 B4
Ttukseom Ferry Pier
뚝섬 선착장 26 B1

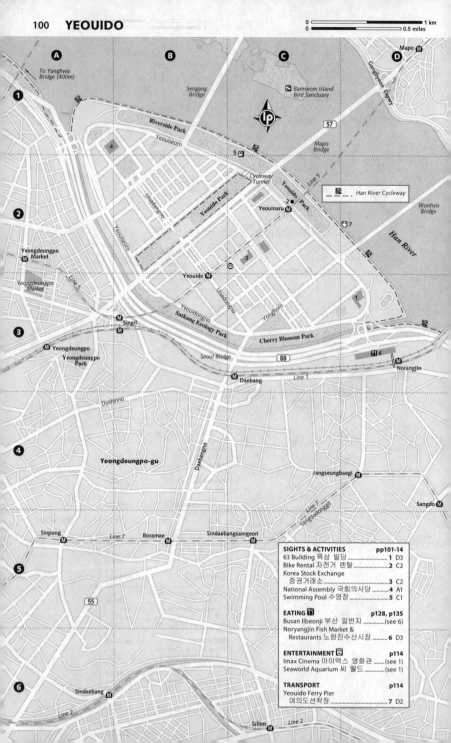

0 ————————— 1 km
0 ————————— 0.5 miles

To Yanghwa
Bridge (400m)

Seogang
Bridge

Bamseom Island
Bird Sanctuary

Mapo

Gangbyeon Expwy

57

Riverside Park

Yeouiseoro

Mapo
Bridge

Line 5

Cycleway
Tunnel

Yeouido Park

Han River Cycleway

Yeouinaru

Wonhyo
Bridge

Han River

Usadangno

Yeouido Park

Yeouiseoro

Yeongdeungpo
Market

Line 5

Yeongdeungpo
Market

Yeouido

Usadongno

Singil

Yeouidongno

Satgang Ecology Park

Yongho-ro

Cherry Blossom Park

Yeongdeungpo

Yeongdeungpo
Park

Seoul Bridge

88

Norangjin

Daebang

Line 1

Doshinno

Yeongdeungpo-gu

Daebangno

Jangseungbaegi

Sangdo

Line 7

Sangdodonggil

Sinpung

Line 7

Boramae

Sindaebangsamgeori

55

Sindaebang

Line 2

Sillim

Line 2

(Continued from page 83)

treated to a pretty view with a great depth of field: open courtyard in front, traditional building in the middle and rugged mountain in the rear. Walk to the far corner of the compound and step up on the rock to get an up-close look at the hip roof gargoyles. Take Line 5 to Gwanghwamun station, Exit 7; the palace is 10 minutes down the road.

BOSIN-GAK 보신각

Opposite the Jongno Tower, this pavilion (Map pp88–9) houses a bell forged in 1468. The bell is only rung at New Year, when crowds gather to celebrate, but during the Joseon dynasty it was struck 33 times at dawn (for the 33 heavens in Buddhism) and 28 times at sunset (for the 28 stars that determine human destiny) to signal the opening and closing of the city gates. It's best viewed at night when it's floodlit. Take Line 1 to Jonggak station, Exit 4.

SEOUL MUSEUM OF ART (GYEONGHUIGUNG ANNEXE)

Finally, an **art museum** (Map pp88-9; ☎ 723 2491; admission free; 🕑 10am-5pm Nov-Feb, 10am-6pm Mar-Oct) with a building that makes a statement. We're not sure exactly what that statement is, but the aircraft hangar interior does create a pleasant space. The museum hosts various exhibitions and an annual fine-arts competition.

TOTO

This quirky **museum** (Map pp88-9; admission W1000; 🕑 10am-9pm) gets two thumbs up from the kids and from 40-something-year-old Koreans. Filled with rare collectibles, it's a trip back in time with 20-year-old plastic model airplanes, Spiderman figurines and Korean memorabilia, like the 30-year-old school textbook that reads, 'Now our country has a highway'. Except for a few Bionic Man postcards, nothing is for sale. This 2nd-floor shop of oddities is a few doors down from the tourist information office on Insadong's main street.

Insadong 인사동

CHANGDEOKGUNG 창덕궁

Seoul has five ancient palaces, which is probably three more than most travellers need to visit. If you have time to visit just one, try to arrange your schedule to visit this **palace** (Map pp88-9; ☎ 762 9513; tours adult/youth W3000/1500; 🕑 Tue-Sun). Originally constructed between 1405 and 1412, it was Korea's centre of power from 1618 to 1896. Changdeok Palace is a World Heritage Site that can only be visited on a **guided tour** (🕑 11.30am, 1.30pm & 3.30pm, Tue-Sun). The highlight of this 2.5km, 90-minute walk is the **Secret Garden** (비원; Biwon), a magnificent forest with some of the city's freshest air and the **Royal Library** majestically overlooking a pond. Take Line 3 to An-guk station, Exit 3.

JUST FAX ME THE MAP!

There is a good reason why most hotel business cards in Korea include a map on the reverse side: street addresses are almost impossible to find. One reason why fax machines are still so popular is because Koreans often fax maps to locate a building.

In Korea, an 'address' exists in name only. There are almost no signs labelling street names. Indeed, most streets do not have names at all. Nor do houses have numbers on the outside, although every house does have an official number. Unfortunately, these 'secret numbers' mean little – numbers are assigned to houses when they are built, so house No 27 could be next to house No 324. Many larger buildings have names – knowing the name of the building will often prove more useful than knowing the address.

A *gu* (구) is an urban district in large cities like Seoul. A *dong* (동) is a neighbourhood inside a *gu*. A single *gu* contains many *dong*. An address like 104 Itaewon-dong, Yongsan-gu means building No 104 in Itaewon neighbourhood in Yongsan district. However you could wander around Itaewon for hours without finding this building, even with the help of a Korean friend. It's best to phone the place you're looking for and get directions, find a police station or tourist office – or a fax machine.

The word for a large street is *ro* (로), which is sometimes spelled as *no*. So, Jongno means Bell St. Large boulevards are divided into sections called *ga* (가). On a Seoul subway map there is a station at Euljiro 3-ga and Euljiro 4-ga – these are different sections of Eulji St. A *gil* (길) is a street smaller than a *no* or *ro* – Insadonggil is one such example.

10 GREAT ESCAPES FROM SEOUL

- Feel the heat of the Cold War at the DMZ and **Panmunjom** (p158).
- Get great views and exercise by hiking in **Bukhansan National Park** (p141) or **Namhan Sanseong Provincial Park** (p144).
- Dine on dumplings in Incheon's **Chinatown** (p152) and meander along busy **Wolmido Promenade** (p150).
- Camp in the ancient forests of **Chiaksan National Park** (p185) and hike up to its secluded temples.
- Step back into days of old in the **Korean Folk Village** (p147).
- Pick up some perfect pottery at **Icheon Ceramic Village** (p148), or try your hand at making something yourself.
- Bask in quiet solitude on **Eulwangni beach** (p153) and forget that Seoul is only two hours away.
- Get wet and wild while white-water rafting in **Inje** (p167).
- Meander **Suwon's** World Heritage **fortress grounds** (p144) and then dine on spicy but delicious *galbi* (beef ribs).
- Head to Ganghwado and hike up **Manisan** (p157) to view an ancient stone altar.

CHANGGYEONGGUNG & JONGMYO
창경궁, 종묘

This palace might fascinate historians, but travellers with less-refined sensibilities may find **Changgyeonggung** (Map pp88-9; ☎ 765 0195; adult/youth W1000/500; ☼ 9am-6pm Mon & Wed-Fri, 9am-7pm Sat & Sun Mar-Oct, 9am-5pm Nov-Feb) a bore. But the park setting is ideal for a tranquil morning walk. Cross over the footbridge to **Jongmyo**, a shrine where the spirit tablets of Joseon kings and queens are kept. If you visit both places at the same time and use the footbridge between them, you only pay one admission fee. History buffs could attend a **lecture** (☼ 11.30am & 4pm, not Tue & Sat). In October the *gwageo* (Joseon government exam) is re-enacted here.

INSADONG-GIL 인사동길

A charming district, Insadong (Map pp88–9) boasts a delightfully confusing mishmash of back alleys. Some of the shops have tried to create an old-world feel with log-beam ceilings, flagstone flooring and wooden doors. Although the commitment to restoration lacks depth, it's a likeable area that could easily occupy a day or more of exploring unusual restaurants, quirky

teashops and brusque antique dealers. Souvenir hunters will have no trouble finding something to take back home if key chains, green-tea sets and handmade paper are on the list of things to buy. It's a busy place after lunch and one of the few areas in the city where shopkeepers speak English. The main street is traffic-free Saturdays (2pm to 10pm) and Sundays (10am to 10pm), when the crowds and street vendors come out in full force.

JOGYESA 조계사

This **Buddhist temple** (Map pp88-9; ☎ 732 5292; ☼ 4am-9pm) is an urban oddity. Built in 1938 with murals of Buddha's life, it's an island of spiritual tranquillity surrounded by a sea of capitalism. Jogyesa is the headquarters of the Jogye sect, Korea's largest, which emphasises Zen meditation. It's also the heart of Seoul's annual **Lotus Lantern Festival**, several days of celebrations, exhibitions and educational programmes. The highlight is an evening parade from Dongdaemun to Jogyesa with 100,000 lanterns, usually held on the Sunday preceding Buddha's birthday. Check the website (www .llf.or.kr/eng) for details.

TAPGOL PARK 탑골 공원

This park (Map pp88–9) is a popular resting place for retired people who play cards and *baduk*, a game of strategy using stones. The main point of interest is the 12m-high **pagoda** constructed in the 1470s, with carvings that are difficult to appreciate because they're encased in a protective structure. The park's historical significance dates back to 1 March 1919, when Son Pyong-hui (1861–1922) and 32 other nationalists prepared a declaration of independence to protest Japanese rule. The declaration was read aloud here, an act that ignited nationwide protests, known as the *sam-il* (March 1st) movement. Today, March 1st is a national holiday to commemorate the uprising.

East Seoul

DONGDAEMUN

Constructed in the 14th century, Dongdaemun (Map pp86–7) served as the Great Eastern Gate of the Seoul fortress. The existing gate was built in 1869 and repaired after the Korean War. This stone gate marks the start of Dongdaemun market and, like similar structures in the city, looks stunning at night.

Namdaemun & Myeongdong
남대문 남산

N'SEOUL TOWER & NAMSAN
서울 타워, 남산

A hip moniker – N'Seoul Tower – was adopted to highlight the flashy look of this renovated **tower** (Map pp92–3; ☎ 3455 9277; adult/youth/child W7000/5000/3000; ☽ 10am-11pm) atop Namsan (South Mountain). Daytime views from the T3 observatory are great when the sky isn't filled with smog or yellow dust, and the evening views are outstanding. It's the second-best place to appreciate the scale of this megalopolis. The best view is two decks up in **N'Grill** (☎ 3455 9297; dinner for 2 W120,000; ☽ 11am-11pm), the tower's revolving restaurant. There are two different seating arrangements: window seats with the clearest view and a ring of tables a little further back.

The easiest and most scenic route to the base of the tower is by **cable car** (Map pp92–3; adult/child 1-way W5000/3000, return W6500/4000; ☽ 10am-11pm). The cable car is a 10-minute uphill walk from Myeongdong station, Exit 1, or a W2500 taxi ride from Insadong.

DEOKSUGUNG 덕수궁

This downtown **palace** (Map pp92–3; ☎ 771 9955; adult/youth/child W1000/500/free; ☽ 9am-6pm Tue & Wed, to 9pm Thu & Fri, to 7pm weekends & holidays Mar-Oct, to 5.30pm Tue & Wed, to 9pm Thu & Fri, to 5.30pm weekends & holidays Nov-Feb) is an integral part of Korea's rich history of royalty but is short on architectural pageantry. The parklike setting is, however, a welcome change from the traffic in the surrounding City Hall area.

There are no scheduled tours, but a guided walk around the compound can be arranged by calling to make a reservation at least one day in advance. From mid-February to the end of December, a modest musical **changing-of-the-guard ceremony** (☽ 10.30am, 1.30pm & 3pm, not Mon) takes place outside the main gate.

Towards the rear of the grounds, there are two neoclassical buildings. The Seokjojeon Hall (admission free with entry to Deoksugung) was completed in 1909 and holds a collection of crafts.

Far more interesting is the building next door, which houses the **National Museum of Contemporary Art, Deoksugung** (Map pp92–3; ☎ 2022 0600; adult/youth W3000/2000; ☽ 9am-5.30pm Tue & Wed, 9am-8.30pm Thu & Fri, 9am-6.30pm weekends & holidays Mar-Oct, 9am-5pm Tue, Wed, Sat, Sun, 9am-8.30pm Thu & Fri Nov-Feb). There is no permanent collection, but the curator has demonstrated an ability to put together imaginative and thought-provoking exhibitions. Line 1 or 2 to City Hall, Exit 2.

ANGLICAN CHURCH 대한 성공회 대성당

The most interesting feature of this church (Map pp92–3) is how the Renaissance-style architecture contrasts with every other building in the city. Work began in 1922, but the full design wasn't completed until 1996. The signboard beside the church describes this building's history. Line 1 or 2 to City Hall, Exit 3.

NAMDAEMUN 남대문

Constructed in 1398, rebuilt in 1447 and renovated many times, Namdaemun (Map pp92–3), the Great South Gate, is an impressive sight, especially at night, and marks the entrance to Namdaemun market.

MYEONGDONG CATHOLIC CATHEDRAL
명동 성당

This cathedral (Map pp92–3) is a surprising source of urban eye candy. The Renaissance-style construction is an architectural standout in an area dominated by neon, glass and concrete. Completed in 1898, it gained notoriety by providing protestors with sanctuary during Korea's post-war period of military rule. English-language worship occurs at 9am on Sunday.

SEOUL MUSEUM OF ART (MAIN BUILDING)

International exhibitions are the forte of this **museum** (Map pp92-3; ☎ 2124 8800; adult/youth W700/300; ⏰ 10am-10pm Mon-Fri, 10am-7pm weekends & holidays Mar-Oct, closes 1 hr earlier Nov-Feb). It's also a popular destination for school outings, judging by the number of children running around the galleries. Take Line 1 to City Hall, Exit 1; turn onto the lane close to the palace gate and follow the road along the stonewall. Opening hours are longer and admission fees are higher (up to W12,000) during special exhibitions.

West Seoul
SEODAEMUN PRISON

독립 공원 서대문형무소 역사관

Fake blood, ear-piercing screams and ingenious torture techniques are on display at this **prison** (Map pp86-7; ☎ 303 9750; adult/youth/child W1500/1000/500; ⏰ 9.30am-6pm Mar-Oct, 9.30am-5pm Nov-Feb, closed Mon). Built by the Japanese during the colonial period to house independence fighters, visitors can walk through nightmarish punishment chambers and claustrophobic cellblocks. Line 3 to Dongnimmun station, Exit 5. English-language tours are available Thursday (10am to 4pm).

WORLD CUP STADIUM & PARK

월드컵주경기장

What do you do with a $151-million football stadium in a country with a passing interest in the sport? Well, some clever person turned the **World Cup stadium** (Map pp84-5; adult/child W1000/W500; ⏰ 9am-6pm) into a retail complex. There's a Homever, a nine-screen **CGV cinema** (admission Mon-Fri/Sat & Sun W7000/W8000; ⏰ screenings 8.50am-12.30am), a gym with a six-lane, 25m **pool** (⏰ 6am-11pm), a 24-hour public bath (p115) and a food court. Visitors can enter the seating area but cannot step onto the Kentucky bluegrass pitch. Line 6 to World Cup Stadium station, Exit 1.

JEOLDUSAN MARTYRS' SHRINE & MUSEUM 절두산 순교 성지

Jeoldusan (Map p94; ☎ 3142 4434; admission by donation; ⏰ museum 9am-5pm Apr-Nov, 9am-4.30pm Dec-Mar, closed Mon) highlights a lesser-known period of barbarous behaviour in the Hermit Kingdom. It commemorates the murder of thousands of Catholics in 1866, an act put into force by Regent Daewon-gun to cleanse Joseon of the people responsible for bringing international contact. A mob mentality took force and moved Koreans to commit terrible acts against their own. The glass-enclosed show-case describes the methods used to torture Catholics before they were beheaded in public. Instruments of hate include beating sticks, whips and a chair used to bend shinbones.

Sculptures of haunting human forms dot the park surrounding the shrine, which includes a museum with a modest collection hardly worth mentioning, except for a barely perceptible piece of wood that supposedly comes from the cross used to crucify Jesus Christ. Take Line 2 or 6 to Hapjeong station, Exit 7; go left at the second corner and walk beside the covered railway line, following the brown signs – it's a 10-minute walk.

Itaewon & Yongsan-Gu 이태원
LEEUM SAMSUNG MUSEUM OF ART

If you have time to visit just one gallery, this **museum** (Map p91; ☎ 2014 6901; www.leeum.org; admission permanent collection adult/youth W10,000/6000, special collection W15,000/11,000; ⏰ 10.30am-6pm Tue, Wed, Fri-Sun, 10.30am-9pm Thu, closed Mon) should be your first choice. In Museum 1 visitors start on the 4th floor and descend a white staircase, a décor that contrasts playfully with the black galleries. The black-white interplay is particularly effective in the Buddhist gallery, where guests are greeted by a glittering bronze pagoda. Museum 2 has an entirely different look with outdoor lighting, natural construction materials and a collection of 20th-century art. Museum 3 is the Samsung Child Education & Culture Center', a head-scratching title because there's nothing here that deals with children or education. It is, instead, used for special exhibitions.

Entry into this fascinating museum requires a reservation except on Thursdays. Call between 10am and noon at least one day in advance. Take Line 6 to Hangangjin station, Exit 1; walk straight five minutes and follow the road signs. Or, in Itaewon, exit the Hamilton Hotel left and walk 12 minutes towards Hangangjin station.

NATIONAL MUSEUM OF KOREA

국립중앙박물관

This **museum** (Map pp96-7; ☎ 2077 9000; adult/child W2000/1000; ⏰ 9am-6pm Tue-Fri, 9am-7pm Sat & Sun) hosts a permanent collection of 10,000 artefacts, which includes a small but curious gallery of the history of print with a small metallic printing block. Historians cannot state with certainty when movable metallic type was invented in Korea, but believe it

(Continued on page 113)

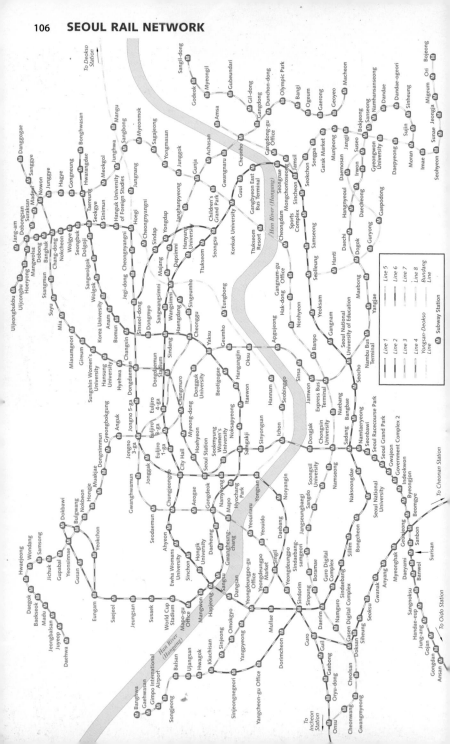

ANTHONY PLUMMER

Party-goers at a Seoul nightclub (p132)

JEFF YATES

The bright lights of Seoul (p79)

ANTHONY PLUMMER

Punters at Seoul Racecourse (p130)

Page 105: Fortress wall, Seoul (p117)
MARTIN VINCENT ROBINSON

Passengers on the N'Seoul Tower cable car (p103), Seoul

ANTHONY PLUMMER

ANTHONY PLUM

Musician at Korea House (p133), Seoul

N'Seoul Tower (p103), Seoul

ANTHONY PLUMMER

Cheonggye Stream (p117), Seoul

ANTHONY PLUMMER

Hwaseong fortress wall (p144), Suwon

MARTIN MOOS

PHILIP GAME

Carved spirit figure, Suwon (p144)

Craftsman at Korean Folk Village (p147), Gyeonggi-do

RICHARD I'ANSON

Kimchi pots, World Folk Museum (p147), Gyeonggi-do

RICHARD I'ANSON

PATRICK HORTON

Memorial at the DMZ (p158), Panmunjom

Performers, Korean Folk Village (p147), Gyeonggi-do

MANFRED GOTTSCH

Granite peaks, Mt Seoraksan, Seoraksan National Park (p172)

Traditional Buddhist monk grave-stone, Sinheungsa temple, Seoraksan National Park (p172)

Kimchi pots, Woljeongsa temple (p177), Odaesan National Park

Temple guardian, Beomeosa temple (p229), Busan

Tripitaka Koreana (Buddhist sacred texts; p196), Haeinsa

Beomeosa temple (p229), Busan

(Continued from page 104)

was developed sometime during the Goryeo dynasty, which ended in 1391. If that date is accurate, the evidence suggests Korea developed metallic movable block at least 61 years before Gutenberg, the man credited with the development of that technology in 1452.

The gallery has a replica of the first book printed with movable metallic blocks, a collection of Buddhist teachings. The original is in the French National Library. In 1866, the French launched a naval attack on Joseon and took several treasures, including this historic book. The world's oldest book printed with wooden blocks is also here. Take Line 4 to Ichon station, Exit 2.

WAR MEMORIAL MUSEUM 전쟁 기념관

Much like Iraq before the American invasion, there are no weapons of mass destruction here, but this **museum** (Map pp96-7; ☎ 709 3139; adult/youth/child W3000/2000/1000; ☉ 9.30am-6pm Mar-Oct, 9.30am-5pm Nov-Feb, closed Mon) does possess a large cache of killing technologies. Starting with rocks, arrows and bronze swords, the history of warfare ends with modern weaponry like a Soviet SCUD missile and the always-impressive B-52 bomber.

There's a substantial collection of Korean War exhibits including a video montage of gun battles, rocket launches and air bombings. English-language audio-visual stations provide descriptive images, footage and commentary on specific aspects of the war such as China's entry into the bloody fray. Glass-enclosed exhibits often lack satisfactory English-language signboards, but an audio guide is available (W2000). The big hardware – such as howitzers, aircraft and tanks – is outside. Every Friday from April to June and October to November, a military band performs at 2pm. Take Line 4 or 6 to Samgakji station, Exit 12.

South of the Han River

COEX MALL 코엑스 몰

It's a mammoth retail underworld and the best hiding place when nasty weather hits. It would be easy to spend two days browsing, eating and playing in this **mall** (Map pp98-9; www.coexmall.com; ☉ 10am-10pm), reportedly the largest underground shopping centre in Asia. Hyundai Department Store, the COEX Conference Centre, Exhibition Hall, a casino, cinema, aquarium and a *kimchi* museum are here.

BONG·EUNSA 봉은사

In some respects this **temple** (Map pp98-9; ☎ 3218 4801; ☉ 3.30am-9.30pm) is more stimulating and informative than Jogyesa. Bong·eunsa is the country's leading training centre for Buddhist monks specialising in *seon* (선; Zen) meditation. Originally founded in AD 794, it was rebuilt in 1498. The oldest building still standing, constructed in 1856, is a library with 150-year-old woodblocks carved with Buddhist scriptures and art. Twice daily (4.10am and 6.40pm) monks perform a percussion ceremony on four instruments, each designed to awaken and save beings on the ground (drum), underwater (wooden fish), in the sky (cloud drum) and under the ground (gong). English-speaking guides are available free of charge weekdays (9am to 6pm, not available noon to 1pm). Bong·eunsa also hosts a temple-stay programme and a two-hour tour (p114).

LOTTE WORLD AMUSEMENT PARK 롯데월드

A massive entertainment hub, **Lotte World** (Map pp98-9; www.lotteworld.com; ☎ 411 2000) has eight-million visitors annually. The main attraction is **Lotte World Adventure & Magic Island** (adult/youth/child W30,000/26,000/23,000, after 5pm W26,000/22,000/20,000; ☉ 9.30am-11pm), an amusement park that gets rave reviews from kids. You can swing on the Viking, twirl through rapids, plunge down a log flume and defy gravity on the Gyro Drop. If this busy park isn't enough to fill the day, there are heaps of other attractions including a folk museum, a cinema multiplex and a bowling alley. It also has an **indoor ice-skating rink** (admission plus skate rental adult/child W11,000/10,000; ☉ 10.30am-10.30pm) and a large indoor **swimming pool** (adult/child W8000/7000 Sep-Jun, W10,000/8000 Jul-Aug; ☉ 1-7pm Mon-Sat, 6am-8pm Sun). Line 2 or 8 to Jamsil station, Exit 3.

OLYMPIC PARK 올림픽 공원

It's a wonderful **park** (Map pp98-9; ☉ 5.30am-10.30pm) and one of the few places in the country where people are allowed to walk on the grass. Weekend joggers, cyclists and roller bladers are out in full force, taking advantage of the well-maintained paths that zigzag through a delightfully quirky art park. The park has several attractions, though they hardly qualify as must-see sights.

The **Seoul Olympic Museum** (☎ 410 1051; adult/youth/child W3000/2000/1500; ☉ 10am-5.30pm Tue-Sun) commemorates the 1988 games in Seoul.

SEOUL

The **Olympic swimming pool** (☎ 410 1696, 410 1353; adult/child W4500/3500; ☺ 12.15-9pm Mon-Fri) is open for public swimming, but the schedule changes. Line 8 to Mongchontoseong, Exit 1.

YEOUIDO 여의도
It's only 6 sq km in size, but this island (Map p100) in the Han River is known for parks, power and prestige. High-rise buildings dotting the island are headquarters for media, finance, insurance companies, the stock exchange and National Assembly.

The island's riverfront parks are popular places for walking and rollerblading. You can also go for a swim (opposite) or rent a bicycle (right). At the island's eastern tip, **63 Building** (☎ 789 5663; www.63.co.kr) is the city's third-tallest building (after the 73-storey Tower Palace in Gangnam and the 69-floor Mokdong Hyperion I in Yangcheon).

Purchase a package ticket (adult/youth/child W21,000/19,500/17,500) and you can feed the fish in the **Seaworld aquarium** (☎ 789 5663; ☺ 10am-10.30pm), watch a film at the **Imax cinema** (☎ 789 5663; ☺ 10am-8pm) and shoot up to the 60th-floor **Skydeck observation platform** (☺ 10am-11pm).

There are five passenger ferry terminals on the Han River: Yeouido (Map p100), Yanghwa (Map pp84-5), Ttukseom (Map pp98-9), Nanji (Map pp84-5) and Jamsil (Map pp98-9). Most **tours** (☎ 785 4411; adult/child W10,000/5000; ☺ 11.30am-10.30pm) are one hour, such as the return trip from Yeouido to the Han River Bridge. Tours operate year-round, and run every hour in July and August, and every one to two hours in other months. A 90-minute **night-cruise** (adult/child W14,600/7300; ☺ 8.40pm) departs Yeouido terminal.

North of the Han River
NATIONAL MUSEUM OF CONTEMPORARY ART
Specialising in modern Korean art, this spacious **gallery** (Map pp84-5; ☎ 2188 6018; permanent collection adult/child W1000/500, special exhibitions adult/child W3000/1500; ☺ 10am-6pm Tue-Thu, 10am-7pm Fri-Sun Mar-Oct, 10am-5pm Tue-Thu & 10am-6pm Fri-Sun Nov-Feb, closed Mon) in Seoul Grand Park is home to treasures like the late Baek Nam-june's puzzling multimedia tower. Take Line 4 to Seoul Grand Park, Exit 2. Purchase a ticket for the elephant tram and get off at the museum stop. The museum is just behind the sky lift.

TOP FIVE ART GALLERIES IN SEOUL

- Seoul Museum of Art (Main Building; p104)
- Leeum Samsung Museum of Art (p104)
- Seoul Museum of Art (Gyeonghuigung Annexe; p101)
- Toto (p101)
- National Museum of Contemporary Art (left)

ACTIVITIES
Buddhist Temple Programmes
The four-hour temple programme at **Jogyesa** (Map pp88-9; ☎ 732 5292; http://eng.jogyesa.org; W20,000; ☺ 10am-2pm last Sat each month) starts with a simple meal, during which time talk (and food waste) are not permitted. A guided tour of the temple is followed by Zen meditation. Everyone sits cross legged and a monk teaches participants to concentrate on breathing. A monk then prepares green tea, which must be served at exactly the right temperature and consumed in three sips. Reservations should be made at least 10 days in advance.

The temple-stay programme at **Bong-eunsa** (Map pp98-9; ☎ 3128 4820; by donation) sees visitors sleep at the temple – reservations are required, as is a minimum of 10 people. A less time-consuming option is the **Temple Life Program** (admission W10,000; ☺ 2-4pm Thu). This informative two-hour tour with an English-speaking guide includes a description of Buddhist history, an introduction to meditation with a Buddhist venerable and a hands-on demonstration of green-tea etiquette. Attend this worthwhile class and you'll learn why drinking green tea can be a calming experience.

Cycling
Bicycles of some vintage can be rented along the Han River on Yeouido outside Yeouinaru station, Exit 2, from a **rental hut** (Map p100; bicycles/tandems per hr W3000/6000; ☺ 9am-7pm). Similar hours and prices are found at the rental hut near the ferry-boat terminal in Ttukseom Resort (Map pp98-9). Some form of ID is required to rent a bike, which does not come with a lock or helmet.

Cycling on city streets is tantamount to suicide, but there are two trails along the Han River. The 7km ride to World Cup Stadium (Map pp84–5) takes 90 minutes. From Yeouido, cycle past the National Assembly and cross the river via the Yanghwa Bridge. Walk up the steps of the bridge. Take a look at Seonyudo in midriver – a park that used to be a water-treatment plant. Wheel your bike down the narrow path on the right of the steps on the other side of the bridge, and continue right along the cycleway along the northern side of the river. After 10 minutes turn right at the orange bridge, ride over a small bridge and then turn right again, following the green signs. Ten minutes later, you're at the large park surrounding the stadium.

For a longer ride spin out to Olympic Park (Map pp98–9). The 38km ride along a hill-free path takes four hours. Near the 18km distance marker from Yeouido, turn right (no sign), ride under a couple of bridges and follow the left side of a dry riverbed. At the road, turn left, cross over the minor road, then cross the major road using the pedestrian crossing, turn right, go over the bridge and the park is on your left.

Golf

A round of golf costs W200,000 or more with varying degrees of course quality, but it's almost impossible for travellers to book a tee time by themselves – club staff don't generally speak English and courses are busy. Your best opportunity to get into the swing is to try an indoor driving range. They're popular; just look for a large green net.

Hyosung Golf Club (Map pp96–7; ☎ 543 3046; per hr W15,000; ☉ 5am-10.30pm Mon-Fri, 5am-10pm Sat & Sun) in Apgujeong is a typical one. Most indoor driving ranges have several levels of tees. The upper deck is okay for driving but it's not an especially good location to work on your chip shot.

Public Baths & Gyms

Here's the naked truth: you can't really say you've done Korea unless you've been to a public bath. Avoiding it is akin to saying you visited Korea but didn't try the *kimchi*. International hotels have attractive facilities that nonguests can use, but the fees can be high – W20,000 or more.

Dongbang Sauna (Map p94; ☎ 332 0481; admission W4000; ☉ spa 24hr, fitness centre 5am-midnight), near Hongik University, has everything required for a relaxing time: a good selection of hot tubs, a long cold tub and a couple of saunas. The entry fee includes access to a small gym.

Black and grey stones give **Hurest Spa** (Map pp92–3; ☎ 778 8301; adult/child before 9pm W5000/3000, after 9pm W10,000/7000; ☉ 24hr) a cosy feel, but late afternoons can be busy as businesspeople prepare for a night of entertainment. The cold tub is long but it's too shallow for plunges. International travellers can use the fitness centre, public bath and *jjimjilbang* for W15,000.

Other recommendations include:

Itaewon Sauna (Map p91; ☎ 798 5855; admission W5000; ☉ 9.20am-11pm) Ideal for beginners looking for an easy place to get their feet wet.

Silloam Fomentation Sauna (Map pp92–3; ☎ 364 3944; adult/child 5am-8pm W7000/5500, adult/child after 8pm W10,000/6000; ☉ 24hr) In Seoul Station's ticketing area, walk through Exit 3 and go down the steps. At street level, walk right to the large overhead expressway ramp. Cross the street and look right.

World Cup Spoland (Map pp84–5; ☎ 302 7002; day rate W20,000; ☉ 6am-11pm) Inside the World Cup stadium. The day-rate package gets you into a well-equipped gym and public bath.

Hamilton Sauna (Map p91; ☎ 6393 1370; adult/child 5am-8pm W5000/3000, after 8pm W7000/4000; ☉ 24hr) A small but well-equipped facility with great tubs and scorching saunas.

Seoul Mud (Map p91; ☎ 749 8012; admission W80,000; ☉ 9am-midnight) You get mud, scrubbing and a massage.

California Wow (Map pp96–7; ☎ 2106 0999; day-rate W25,000; ☉ 6am-midnight Mon-Fri, 8am-midnight Sat & Sun) Everything you'd expect in Apgujeong: top-notch equipment, rich clients and a stand-offish attitude.

For further information on hot-spring baths, see p76.

Swimming

In July and August outdoor swimming pools in the parks along the Han River fill up with kids. On Yeouido parasols surround separate **swimming pools** (Map p100; adult/youth/child W4000/3000/2000; ☉ 9am-7pm Jul & Aug) for children, teenagers and adults. In the past fights erupted over prime parasol locations, a problem solved with two rules: no knives and no alcohol. Line 5 to Yeouinaru station, Exit 2.

The **Ttukseom pools** (Map pp98–9) have similar prices and hours. Line 7 to Ttukseom Resort station, Exit 2 or 3. Indoor pools are available at **Lotte World** (p113) and **Olympic Park** (p113). Most large hotels have 25m indoor or outdoor pools and some, such as the **Hamilton Hotel** pool (p122), are available to nonguests. **Caribbean Bay** (p147) is the best aquatic centre.

WALKING TOURS
Inwangsan Shamanist Hillside Walk

On this short but uphill walk, you can see Seoul's most famous shamanist shrine, visit small temples and see part of the Seoul fortress wall. The walk only takes an hour if you just want a quick look, but it's sensible to take longer and soak up the unique atmosphere.

Take Line 3 to Dongnimmun station, Exit 2, and turn left at the first alley. This area is undergoing significant redevelopment, but look for the signs pointing to Inwangsa (인왕사). Walk through the **temple gate (1)** up to the signboard with a map. The text is in Korean, but each building is numbered. Turn left and walk towards **building 2 (2)**. When the path ends, you'll find a small collection of homes and beautifully decorated temple buildings. Walk right up the cement steps and turn right as you weave through a narrow alley. The alley leads to a **bronze bell (3)** and the door to Inwangsa. Between the bell and door there is a shop that sells drinks and snacks. Beside the shop there is a set of steps leading up the hill. Walk up these steps.

Five minutes up the steps, you'll find a shamanist shrine called **Guksadang (4)**. Originally

built on Mt Namsan, it was demolished by the Japanese in 1925 and later secretly rebuilt here by Korean Shamanists. The shrine is small, but the altar inside is often filled with food offerings, as shamanists believe spirits need food and drink. Continue up the hill on the left stairs and turn left when you see a surreal collection of rocks. Erosion has transformed these **Zen rocks (5)** into semi-human forms. Exit the rock collection left and then turn left on the path leading up the hill.

Up the path, eroded rocks, dark crevices and the shaman's haunting chants give the place an *X-Files* feel of otherworldliness. Further up the hill, just past the **exercise station (6)**, there are several outdoor shrines. This is where you'll find a small **Buddha rock carving (7)**, a **Sansin statue (8)** and a trail that swings right past more rocks. The trail provides a good

---

WALK FACTS

Start Dongnimmun station
Finish Dongnimmun station
Distance 1.5km
Duration One to two hours

STRIPING DOWN THE PUBLIC BATH

The public bath is more than a place to clean up. It's a social event. Families come here for quality time, businesspeople cultivate commercial relationships and mothers gather to discuss their children's education. Bathhouses in the west may be associated with seedy behaviour, but this most definitely is not the case in Korea.

A public bath (목욕탕), sometimes called a spa or sauna, is a room with warm, hot and cold-water tubs, saunas and a massage area (for a fee). Bathhouses have separate facilities for men and women, and everybody walks around naked. Most bathhouses have a *jjimjilbang* (찜질방), a co-ed room where people watch TV, read or do nothing. There are also specialty rooms like the Cold Room (it's like the inside of your freezer) or the Oxygen Room (O^2 made from thin air!). Everybody wears a loose-fitting uniform. Most *jjimjilbang* are open 24 hours and allow guests to sleep overnight on the floor or in a bunk bed.

Enter the public bath and place your footwear in a locker near the front desk, remove the key and give it to the person at the counter, which is where you pay. The basic fee gets you into the bath. A separate charge gets you a uniform and access to the *jjimjilbang*. After paying you'll receive a locker key. Go to the locker, strip down, place your belongings inside and put the key around your wrist or ankle. Next, shower in the bathing area before jumping into the tubs.

Rotating between the hot and cold tubs is the secret to an enjoyable experience. It stimulates blood circulation, creates a tingling sensation on the skin and produces a feeling of euphoria. Many Koreans prefer to sit on the ledge and dangle their feet in the hot water for 20 minutes or more. This bathing technique slowly warms the body and stimulates a body-cleansing sweat. When you're ready to do nothing, return to your locker, put on the uniform and follow the signs to the *jjimjilbang*. Stay as long as you like. When you're done, return to the bath for another round or get changed, return the locker key and retrieve your shoes. After a few hours, the feeling of euphoria begins to dissipate. That's okay, because you can do the whole thing again tomorrow.

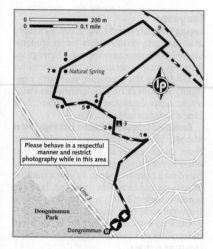

look at the recently restored **Seoul fortress wall (9)**. Follow the trail downhill and you'll end up near Guksadang. Alternatively, continue walking towards the fortress wall and you'll end up at a road that leads to steps (closed Mondays) up Inwang Mountain, or walk downhill through a residential neighbourhood to Dongnimmun station.

Respect is essential during this walk. Taking photographs or making unnecessary gestures or noise could interfere with the performance of important ceremonies.

Old & New Downtown Walk

This 90-minute walk passes through some of the downtown's most attractive and lively districts with contrasting images of Seoul, ancient and modern.

Immerse yourself in different world's of shopping, urban landscape and degrees of pedestrian congestion as you walk past and through some of the city's biggest and flashiest department stores like Lotte, the Namdaemun market (where haggling, shouting and jostling are all part of the old-world market experience) and Myeongdong, a must-visit district if you're looking for a wall-to-wall-people

WALK FACTS

Start Jonggak station
Finish N'Seoul Tower
Distance 4km
Duration 90 minutes

feel. Try the walk at night to get a different urban feel.

Take Line 1 to Jonggak station, Exit 4. At street level turn 180 degrees and you'll see **Bosin·gak (1;** p101) on one corner and the stunning **Jongno Tower (2)** on the other. Turn right around the corner and walk past a smorgasbord of street food with goodies like chicken-on-a-stick and *sundae* (순대; pig's intestines stuffed with blood, vegetables and pork).

Turn right at the first main street and you should be on a boulevard covered with giant black and white piano keys. Down the road cross the bridge, walk down the left steps, turn 180 degrees and walk straight. This is part of Seoul's **Cheonggye Stream (3)** restoration project, a US$313-million urban-renewal effort to beautify the downtown core. Ten minutes down the cement path, walk up the steps beside the small waterfall and fountain. At street level, near a **statue (4)** that looks like a giant screw, turn 180 degrees, walk straight and turn right at the first corner. Walk straight along this tree-lined street until **Seoul Plaza (5)**, a circular park with several hotels and Seoul City Hall.

Cross the street at the intersection beside the **Busan Bank (6)** and walk along the sidewalk opposite **Lotte department store (7)**. Enter Euljiro station Exit 1, pass through the sometimes-boisterous underground arcade and ride the escalator up to Exit 7. Follow the sign pointing to the Namdaemun market. At street level, walk towards **Lotte Young Plaza (8)** and cross the street at the tourist information booth. Further down the main street, you'll pass a **bronze statue (9)** with a fountain and the **Bank of Korea (10)**, an old stone building. Five minutes down the road, cross the street at the light and walk left. You should see **Namdaemun (11;** p103), the Great South Gate, and the entrance to **Namdaemun market (12;** p135) just around the corner.

Walk straight along the main lane of the market and you'll come across a **tourist information booth (13)**, which usually has a detailed map of the market. Continue walking along the lane past the information booth and **Shinsegae department store (14)**. At the first major intersection near an overpass, walk left for an up-close look at the bronze statue. Cross the street through underpass Exit 1 and come out through Exit 2. Turn left and you're in Myeongdong. At the corner with a Levis store, turn left onto a lane filled with low-cost clothes and accessories. Turn right at the corner with a

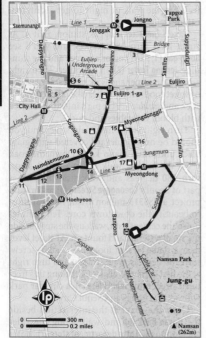

Toda Cosa (15) cosmetics shop and right again at the next street. Up the road, in a tall building called Utoo Zone, there is a coffee shop and the **Hurest Spa (16;** p115), which is where you'll find a public bath. **Migliore department store (17)**, at the end of the street, is a busy gathering place in the evening for young people.

Time and energy permitting, the **cable car (18;** p103) leading to the base of the **N'Seoul Tower (19;** p103) is a 15-minute uphill walk from here. Enter Myeongdong station and come out through Exit 1. Rotate 180 degrees, turn right at the corner and follow the main road until the cable-car station.

COURSES
Cooking

Itching to make *kimchi*? You can do that and more at **Han's Culinary Academy (**Map pp88-9; ☎ 742 3567; courses W60,000-100,000; ☺ 9am-5pm Mon-Fri), which teaches travellers how to prepare staples like *pajeon*, kimchi stew and *bulgogi*. The cost per individual varies with the number of students. Courses are taught in English. Walk upstairs to the 2nd floor office to get more information and register for a class.

Language

Sogang University (Map p94; ☎ 705 8088; www.sogang .ac.kr/~ckss) gets good reviews for its student-centred, communicative approach to language learning. New programmes commence four times during the academic year with one-month sessions during the summer and winter vacations. Costs start at W1.3 million. Take Line 6 to Sinchon station, Exit 6.

BestFriend Language & Culture Exchange Center (Map p94; ☎ 016 9499 3353; www.bestfriendcenter.com) is an unconventional language centre that offers Korean language classes (1pm to 10pm) based on a coupon system. Pay for a number of sessions and come when you can. Line 2 to Sinchon station, Exit 3, walk towards Yonsei University and turn right at the first street.

Click on www.seoul.go.kr for a long list of universities and institutes that offer Korean-language courses

SEOUL FOR CHILDREN

Children's Grand Park (Map pp84-5; ☎ 457 7054; adult/ youth/child Apr-Jun, Sep & Oct W1500/1000/free; Jul & Aug, Nov-Mar W900/500/free; ☺ 9am-10pm) is an enormous playground for 50,000 people. It's impossible to imagine a family taking in all the sights and activities available here in one day, which include a zoo, botanical garden and amusement park.

Elephants, amusement rides and contemporary art are available at the big and beautiful **Seoul Grand Park (**Map pp84-5; ☎ 500 7114; adult/youth/ child package W5500/3500/3000; ☺ 9am-7pm, Apr-Sep, 9am-6pm Oct-Mar). It includes a **zoo** (p141; ☺ shows noon, 1.30pm, 3pm & 4.30pm) with daily animal shows, Seoul Land amusement park and the National Museum of Contemporary Art (p114). There are separate entry fees for each place, though package deals are available. Walking around this expansive park takes time, so ride the elephant tram between sights (every five minutes, adult/youth/child W600/500/400). Line 4 to Seoul Grand Park, Exit 2.

Definitely get the day pass to Seoul's biggest amusement park, **Seoul Land (**Map pp84-5; ☎ 504 0011; www.seoulland.co.kr; day pass adult/youth/child W28,000/24,000/21,000; ☺ 9.30am-9pm Mon-Thu, 9.30am-10pm Fri-Sun), a miniature version of Everland. Once here, you can spend all day free falling on the Shot X Drop.

A one-hour bus ride from Seoul, **Everland** (☎ 759 1408; www.everland.com) has enchanting scenery and an exciting amusement park. A safari ride that passes remarkably sedate lions, tigers and bears is a hit with the kids. Caribbean Bay (p147) with world-class aquatic rides is next door.

Lotte World (p113; www.lotteworld.com) is a Disney-style amusement park with indoor and outdoor rides, an ice-skating rink and a swimming pool.

COEX Aquarium (☎ 6002 6200; coexaqua.co.kr; adult/youth/child W15,500/13,000/10,000; ⏰ 10am-8pm) has an amazing collection of sea creatures including piranhas, sharks, turtles and jellyfish. You could also try the Seaworld aquarium (p114) in 63 Building.

TOURS

There are three main types of tours available for English-speaking travellers. For a quick city tour, there are several circuits with stops at most of the popular spots. With a little planning, you can pack a lot of sites into a single day and, unlike the subway, develop a first-hand appreciation for Seoul's sometimes horrific traffic congestion. Travellers looking for a hassle-free escape from Seoul should check out the Royal Asiatic Society, which offers packaged excursions to different parts of the country. Trips are offered once a month, usually on weekends, so a bit of planning and schedule coordination is required.

Numerous organisations offer half-day and full-day Demilitarized Zone (DMZ) package trips, a popular excursion that can be both compelling and underwhelming. Stepping inside a building that straddles the North and South Korean border does come with a certain 'cool factor' but can be disappointing if you're expecting to see a platoon of heavily armed, goose-stepping North Korean soldiers staring down their South Korean comrades, because this type of presentation is rarely on display. On the surface, at least, Panmunjom – the truce village inside the Demilitarized Zone – has a serene, museum-like atmosphere.

Most DMZ trips leave Seoul in the morning and return in the afternoon. On the bus, the English-speaking tour guide provides historical background and a rather long list of do's and don'ts, such as the need to avoid pointing your index finger inside the DMZ (which, in the right light, could be mistaken for a handgun). At times the often repeated rules, strict controls of your movement (eg when and where you can take a picture) and frequent passport inspections (you must bring this with you on the trip) seem like an attempt

to create false drama, though the tour guide is quick to point out that controls are required to avoid an international incident.

The **Royal Asiatic Society** (Map pp88-9; ☎ 763 9483; www.raskb.com; ⏰ 10am-noon, 2-5pm Mon-Fri) organises weekend tours across Korea that cost up to W60,000. The travel schedule is prepared months in advance so check the website for details. The RSA also holds bi-weekly Tuesday lectures on Korean history and culture. Take Line 1 to Jongno 5-ga station, Exit 2 and walk straight 100m. The office (room 611) is in the tall yellow-orange building (the Korean Science Building but the sign is difficult to see) just past Dunkin Donuts.

United Services Organization (USO; Map pp86-7; ☎ 724 7003; uso.org/korea; ⏰ 9.30am-6pm Mon-Fri, 10am-2pm Sat) runs tours for American troops but civilians are welcome to join. Twice-weekly tours to Panmunjom, the DMZ and Infiltration Tunnel costing US$42 start at 7.30am and return to the city at 3.30pm. Advance bookings (sometimes a month in advance) are essential.

Panmunjom Travel Center (Map pp92-3; ☎ 771 5593; panmunjomtour.com; 2nd fl, Lotte Hotel; ⏰ 9am-6pm) has package tours to Panmunjom (W70,000), a one-day tour of Panmunjom and the third tunnel (W110,000) and a chance to speak with a North Korean defector.

Visit KTO (Map pp88–9) for additional tour options or see www.startravel.co.kr.

Seoul City Tour Bus

Designed for tourists in a hurry, these comfortable buses tour Seoul's top attractions north of the Han River. There are three routes: **Downtown** (includes Itaewon and the War Museum; W10,000; departures 9am to 7pm, every 30 minutes); the **Palaces** (the city's five ancient palaces and Insadong; W10,000; departures 9am to 4pm, every 30 minutes); and the **Night Tour** (includes N'Seoul Tower; W5000; departures 7.50pm and 8pm). Tours begin (except Monday) in front of the Dongwha Duty-Free Shop (Map pp88–9) at Gwanghwamun station (Line 5, Exit 6). A W10,000 ticket for the Downtown or Palace tour (available on the bus) allows you to jump on and off the bus all day. Visit www .seoulcitytourbus.com for details.

FESTIVALS & EVENTS

There aren't many, but Seoul does have a few festivals worth watching out for if you're in town at the right time. The big four festivals involve lanterns at night, drums, fireworks and street performances. Visit www.knto.or.kr for locations and dates that vary from year to year.

April

Insa Korean Art & Culture Festival A week-long event with parades, traditional music and even more people than usual packed onto Insadong's main street.

Yeouido Cherry Blossom Festival When the cherry blossoms bloom and the air is clear, the streets of Yeouido look great. Take Line 5 Yeouido, Exit 2 and walk towards the National Assembly.

May

Jongmyodaeje At Jongmyo shrine (Map pp88-9) on the first Sunday in May the royal spirits are welcomed and praised, fed with offerings of cooked meat and rice wine, entertained with solemn music and dance, and then respectfully farewelled.

Buddha's Birthday On the Sunday before Buddha's birthday, a huge parade is held from Dongdaemun to Jogyesa (Map pp88-9) starting at 7pm.

Hi Seoul Festival (www.hiseoulfest.org) It's 10 days of downtown street fun that the organisers believe demonstrates the cultural potential of Seoul. Events include a walking contest and tug of war.

August

Seoul Fringe Festival (www.seoulfringe.net) Mime, punk and art take over the streets, clubs and galleries around Hongik University (Map p94) during the last two weeks in August. The website is in Korean only.

September

Seokjeondaeje This ceremony is staged in the courtyard of the Confucian shrine at Sungkyunkwan University (Map pp88-9) in September.

October

Seoul World Fireworks Festival Fireworks light up the sky in front of 63 Building near Yeouido Riverside park. The two-day festival is often but not always held on two Saturdays, with the pyrotechnic show starting around 8pm.

Seoul Drum Festival (www.drumfestival.org) Three days of beating, banging and bashing in Seoul Plaza and the Seoul Arts Centre.

Sajikdaeje A re-enactment of a royal thanksgiving ceremony at the altar in Sajik Park (Map pp86-7).

SLEEPING
Gwanghwamun
BUDGET

Inn Daewon (Map pp88-9; ☎ 738 4308; dm/s/d W19,000/25,000/35,000; ✕ 🖳) Much of the charm that made this inn a budget-traveller institution is still here but in a new location. Cramped quarters, a small courtyard and rooms sharing communal facilities are now housed in a *hanok* (traditional Korean house) building. Take Line 3 to Gyeongbokgung station, Exit 4. Turn 180 degrees and walk left at the first lane.

Gwanghwa Hotel (Map pp88-9; ☎ 738 0751; r W38,000, with computer W40,000; ✕ 🖳) Central and comparatively cheap, this is a decent choice for budget travellers arriving on a late flight. The W40,000 room has a double bed, internet access and an interior that oozes 'down and out'. Take Line 5 to Gwanghwamun station, Exit 7, make a hard left and walk to the first street. It's near the Goryeo supermarket.

MIDRANGE

Hotel Lees (Map pp88-9; ☎ 762 4343; www.leeshotel.com; d/tw/tr W65,000/75,000/100,000; ✕) Here's a classic example of 'better than we expected'. Travellers who spend the day exploring and only need a clean place to crash might exclaim 'This is okay!' after entering the room for the first time. Take Line 1 to Jongno 5-ga, Exit 1, walk straight and turn right at the second street. Make a quick left and right turn, then walk 150m.

New Kukje Hotel (Map pp88-9; ☎ 732 0161; r W127,000; ✕ 🖳) The Japanese tourists who fill this busy hotel don't mind the less-than-opulent conditions. Perhaps they're impressed by the white bed linen that might have come from a hospital surplus store. Or maybe it's the central location that puts many sights within easy walking distance. Receive a W40,000 discount for taking a room without a window. Line 5 to Gwanghwamun station, Exit 5 and walk right.

New Seoul Hotel (Map pp88-9; ☎ 735 8800; d/tw/ste W140,000/160,000/290,000; ✕ 🖳) If you're accustomed to US$200 rooms where location is the best feature, this centrally located Best Western property is a good choice, behind the New Kukje Hotel.

TOP END

Koreana Hotel (Map pp88-9; ☎ 2171 7000; r W215,000; ✕ 🖳) This type-A personality hotel is designed for people on a mission who expect quality on par with their $1500 suits. The get-busy rooms are neatly decorated in neutral tones with dark woody furniture. There is also a LAN connection, though you had better bring a compact notebook because the workspace in standard rooms is minimal. Take Line 5 to Gwanghwamun station, Exit 6.

Insadong & Around

BUDGET

Holiday In (Map pp88-9; ☎ 3672 3113; www.holidayinkorea .com; dm/s/d & tw W16,000/29,000/37,000; 💈 🖵) No relation to the hotel chain with two N's in its name, this is one of the newest and nicest budget options near Insadong. The rooms are similar to what you'll find in most backpacker places, but they look cleaner. Get off at An·guk station, Exit 4. It's on a small lane south of Beewon Guesthouse.

Beewon Guesthouse (Map pp88-9; ☎ 765 0670; www .beewonguesthouse.com; dm W17,000, r W30,000-37,000, f W51,000; 💈 🖵) You thought all comfortable rooms in downtown Seoul were expensive? Well, almost every room now that Beewon is in operation. This likeable property combines motel-sized rooms with friendly staff and free use of the washing machine. If you don't mind stairs, take the *ondol* room on the 4th floor for solitude and quick access to the rooftop. It's a 10-minute walk from An·guk station, Exit 4. At street level turn 180 degrees and walk right around the corner. Turn right at the first gas station and walk straight.

Other recommendations:

Guesthouse Korea (Map pp88-9; ☎ 3675 2205; dm/s/ d & tw W15,000/27,000/37,000; 💈 🖵) A busy inn with a run-down feel. Get off at An·guk station, Exit 4.

Seoul Backpackers (Map pp88-9; ☎ 3672 1972; dm/ s/tw W17,000/27,000/37,000; 💈 🖵) Pay for six nights and get the seventh free. Get off at An·guk station, Exit 4, on a small lane south of Beewon Guesthouse.

Jongnowon Motel (Map pp88-9; ☎ 763 4249; s/d W28,000/35,000; 💈 🖵) Western travellers say good things about this place, but bring a towel. Get off at An·guk station, Exit 4. It's on a small lane south of Beewon Guesthouse.

MIDRANGE

Tomgi Hotel (Map pp88-9; ☎ 7742 6660; regular/special r W60,000/80,000; 💈 🖵) Here's that romantic getaway spot you were looking for. Special rooms in this upmarket love motel have couple-friendly features like a steam shower and two-person whirlpool. Take Line 1 or 3 to Jongno 3-ga station, Exit 4.

Hotel Sunbee (Map pp88-9; ☎ 730 3451; tw/d W77,000/88,000; 💈 🖵) Tired of hotel prices but just can't force yourself into a backpacker guesthouse? There are other options, and this is one of the best. The double bed is huge and the rooms are decorated tastefully. Many rooms come with a wide-screen TV and computer.

Bukchon Hanok Village

This quaint residential neighbourhood between Gyeongbokgung and Changdeokgung used to be home for high court officials. Today, restoration work is returning many *hanok* buildings to their past glory with traditional designs and materials.

Seoul Guesthouse (Map pp88-9Gwanghwamun; ☎ 745 0057; s/d/f W35,000/50,000/100,000; 💈 🖵) Guestrooms are in a beautiful setting with *hanok* buildings, well-maintained gardens and a 400-year-old tree. If you're awake, join the owner and his two dogs – Nurung and Ssari – for a two-hour walk starting at 8.30am. Take Line 3 to An·guk station, Exit 3 and turn left at the first main street. Follow the road signs.

Other *hanok* recommendations:

Bukchon Guesthouse (Map pp88-9; ☎ 743 8530; s/d/f W35,000/50,000/70,000; 💈 🖵) Take Line 3 to An·guk station, Exit 3 and turn left at the first main street. It's just past a church.

Tea Guesthouse (Map pp88-9; ☎ 3675 9877; s W35,000, d 50,000-70,000; 💈 🖵) On the same street as Bukchon Guesthouse but further down the road.

Woori Jip Guesthouse (Map pp88-9; ☎ 744 0536; r W50,000; 💈 🖵) Stay with Mrs Park's family and their dog. It's on a small lane off the same street as Bukchon Guesthouse.

Anguk Guesthouse (Map pp88-9; ☎ 736 8304; s/tw/d W40,000/60,000/70,000; 💈 🖵) Take Line 3 to An·guk station, Exit 1. Turn right at the street and right again.

Myeongdong & Namsan

BUDGET

Myeongdong Guesthouse (Map pp92-3; ☎ 755 5437; s W30,000, d & tw W35,000-40,000; 💈) Asian university students come here for bragging rights: 'I slummed in Seoul and spent a fortune on designer labels'. Room quality doesn't quite reach the depths of George Orwell's *Down and Out in London and Paris*, but it comes close. The bathroom's jailhouse motif almost certainly drew inspiration from *Shawshank Redemption* and is the touchstone for any legitimate claim to roughing it in Seoul. Take Line 4 to Myeongdong station, Exit 1.

MIDRANGE

Ibis Hotel (Map pp92-3; ☎ 6361 8888; r Sat W90,000, Sun-Fri W102,000 ; 💈) Every city needs a downtown hotel with rooms that look like they came out of a cookie cutter, and Seoul has one thanks to Ibis. Two-minutes from Myeongdong, rooms come with a uniform décor that isn't tedious, thanks to clever touches like the curving line of the bathroom's exterior wall. Take Line 2 to Euljiro 1-ga, Exit 6 and walk straight.

Metro Hotel (Map pp92-3; ☎ 752 1112; s/d/tw/deluxe W99,000/121,000/W145,000/157,000; ✗ 🖳) It's hard not to like the Metro Hotel: the colour-coordinated room décor is as attractive as the downtown location. Rooms lean toward small, but they're comfortable: upgrade to the deluxe twin, equipped with a double and single bed, if you need more space. Take Line 2 to Euljiro 1-ga, Exit 5. Turn right at the stone pillar. The hotel is down the street.

TOP END

Lotte Hotel (Map pp92-3; ☎ 771 1000; r from W400,000; ✗ 🖳 🖭) With 1400 rooms and 1300 staff, it's the biggest hotel in Korea. It's also one of the most stylish downtown properties. Prominent guests have included Bill Gates (he stayed in a standard room), Tiger Woods (he didn't stay in a standard room) and Brooke Shields (nobody remembers where she stayed). If it's good enough for Brooke, it should be okay for almost anyone.

Other recommendations:

Millenium Seoul Hilton (Map pp92-3; ☎ 753 7788; package W300,000; ✗ 🖳 🖭) There's a casino here. Take Line 1 to Seoul Station, Exit 8, walk straight and turn right at the street just before the green steps. The package includes a breakfast buffet.

Westin Chosun Hotel (Map pp92-3; ☎ 771 0500; deluxe/executive W370,000/420,000; ✗ 🖳 🖭) Stylish lobby. The executive option includes breakfast and access to the club lounge for an evening drink.

Hotel Shilla (Map pp92-3; ☎ 2233 3131; r W420,000; ✗ 🖳 🖭) Line 3 to Dongguk University station, Exit 5. Past the gate, walk up the stairs beside the waterfall.

Itaewon
BUDGET

Hilltop Motel (Map p91; ☎ 793 4972; r Sun-Thu W25,000, Fri & Sat W30,000; ✗) Here's that dumpy flophouse in Itaewon's hostess bar district you were looking for. A maximum-security prison most likely inspired the interior of the astonishingly bare rooms. But you do get a private bath and you're within crawling distance of Itaewon's late-night bars. Take Line 6 to Itaewon station.

MIDRANGE & TOP END

Hamilton Hotel (Map p91; ☎ 794 0171; s/d W121,000/130,000; ✗ 🖳 🖭) The whole place has an attractive look, which is a considerable improvement to what used to be a rather staid property. Families will find the twin room leans toward

spacious. Twin and ondol rooms cost the same as a double. During the summer, guests get free access to the outdoor pool. Nonguests can swim here for a fee (adult/child W10,000/7000; 10am to 6pm, mid-June to August).

Other recommendations:

Kaya Hotel (Map pp86-7; ☎ 798 5101; d & ondol W53,000, deluxe W63,000; ✗ 🖳) Close to the Rainbow Hotel. The deluxe option comes with a twin and single bed.

Rainbow Hotel (Map pp86-7; ☎ 792 9993; d/tw W55,000/63,000; ✗) Take Line 1 to Namyeong station, Exit 1. Walk right and turn right at first corner. Triple rooms are also available for W73,000.

Itaewon Hotel (Map p91; ☎ 792 3111; d & tw/ste W150,000/W200,000; ✗ 🖳) Second choice if the Hamilton is full.

Hongik, Sinchon & Ewha
BUDGET

Kims' Guesthouse (Map p94; ☎ 337 9894; dm W15,000, s W27,000, d & tw W37,000; ✗ 🖳) A great guesthouse experience isn't about facilities – it's about the quality of people you meet. Opportunities to engage a diverse group of travellers make this one of the city's best guesthouses. It's a 12-minute walk from Hapjeong station (Line 2 or 6). Take Exit 8 and walk right: when the road forks, cross the street and stay right. Just past the bend, turn right at the corner and walk straight. Turn left at the beauty shop.

MIDRANGE & TOP END

Queen 21 (Map p94; ☎ 312 2556; standard/special W40,000/50,000; ✗ 🖳) Where do students go when they want to get cuddly? They come to Queen 21, an attractive love motel in Sinchon. Rooms are filled with diversions to help pass the time during those initial moments of awkward hesitation, like internet access and a DVD system. When it's time to get horizontal, there's a queen-sized bed. Rates are W10,000 higher on Friday and Saturday. Line 2 to Sinchon, Exit 3. Turn right onto the main road, right at the first street and then a quick left turn.

Seokyo Hotel (Map p94; ☎ 330 7666; s, d & tw W157,000, deluxe W205,000; ✗ 🖳) Location is the selling point of this business-class hotel. Most rooms have been remodelled so they look clean, but the lack of upmarket furnishings gives some a downgraded appearance. The deluxe room comes with a double and single bed. Downtown Seoul is 30 minutes away and a limousine to Incheon airport stops in front of the hotel.

Other Areas North of the Han River

W Seoul Walkerhill (Map pp84-5; ☎ 465 2222; weekday package from W300,000; 🟦 🖳 ⓢ) What does the W stand for? It could be 'wow', because this fantastic property rates as one of the city's best. The rooms are chic, sassy and oh so modern. Standard rooms, called Wonderful, have a white décor with red accents on the bed cover, cushions and slippers. Other room styles – Scent, Spa, Media and Suites – simply get better. Ignore the stratospheric rack rates and enquire about weekday packages with names like Girl's Night Out.

The 'W' is beside the Sheraton Grande Walkerhill so diversions like a 24-hour casino or theatre show are minutes away. The quickest route to the hotel is a taxi (W3000) from a subway station like line 5 Gwangnaru. A shuttle bus runs between the hotel and Gwangnaru station (Exit 1) every 10 to 20 minutes.

Apgujeong

Princess Hotel (Map pp96-7; ☎ 544 0366; r/ste W80,000/120,000; 🟦 🖳) Here's the love-motel archetype complete with parking-lot curtains and well-worn interior. The property has a sturdy feel, a testament to the steady flow of in-out action that takes place at this busy hotel. There are several suite options available including a spiffy hot-pink number. Take Line 3 to Apgujeong station, Exit 2. Turn 180 degrees and walk around the corner walk. Ten minutes down the road, look for the arch with 'Rodeo' on the right. Turn right at the sign and right at the third lane.

Hotel Popgreen (Map pp96-7; ☎ 544 6623; d W126,000, tw & ondol W136,000; 🟦 🖳) Consider this your best option in Apgujeong if walking distance to upscale shopping and evening entertainment is a priority, but you just can't stomach the idea of a love motel. Rooms have a pleasant décor, most likely inspired by a Martha Stewart manual. Take Line 3 to Apgujeong station, Exit 2. At street level turn 180 degrees; the hotel is around the corner.

Other Areas South of the Han River
MIDRANGE

Tiffany Hotel (Map pp98-9; ☎ 545 0015; s W65,000, tw & ondol W78,000; 🟦 🖳) Like an on old pickup truck, this hotel doesn't look pretty but it gets the job done. Room décor demonstrates a rugged motif, thanks to the red-and-black carpet and metal doors designed to take the heavy punishment that comes with driving a busy hotel. Take Line 7 to Cheongdam station, Exit 14 and walk 200m.

Jelly Hotel (Map pp96-7; ☎ 553 4737; standard/special/VIP W70,000/100,000/120,000; 🟦 🖳) Have you ever wanted to make love on a pool table? Here's your chance. Special rooms come in a number of quirky motifs including Pocket Ball, equipped with a red-felt billiard table. For women who aren't intimately familiar with the game, here's an opportunity to work on your stroke and learn how to manipulate balls gently. Take Line 2 to Gangnam station, Exit 8. Walk straight and turn left on the lane before the Intellectual Property Office.

Sunshine Hotel (Map pp96-7; ☎ 541 1818; s/d/tw W96,000/139,000/153,000; 🟦 🖳) This sharp hotel is popular with business travellers on a budget who need to be in Gangnam. It's also ideal for travellers accustomed to the comfort and style of a US$100 hotel room. Lower-priced rooms edge towards small, but the tasteful décor, matching furnishings and modern features create a comfortable atmosphere.

Other recommendations:

Piano Hotel (Map pp96-7; ☎ 588 2044; standard/special W60,000/70,000; 🟦 🖳) Make your own fun in the whirlpool and steam shower. Line 3 to Nambu bus terminal station, Exit 6. Turn right at the second street.

Hotel BJ (Map pp96-7; ☎ 553 4100; d/tw/ste W80,000/90,000/170,000; 🟦 🖳) If you like the name, you'll love the modern rooms.

Hotel Lake (Map pp98-9; ☎ 422 1001; d & tw W95,000, ste W145,000; 🟦 🖳) Close to Lotte World and about half the price of Lotte Hotel. Take Line 2 or 8 to Jamsil station, Exit 3, walk right past the bike rack to the second light and turn right.

TOP END

Ellui (Map pp98-9; ☎ 514 3535; d & tw W196,000, luxury 260,000; 🟦 🖳) It's not quite a boutique hotel, but this smart and stylish property does demonstrate verve and creativity. Lower-priced rooms are slightly cramped but the rich décor compensates by creating a welcoming feel. The luxury room comes with a charming walkout patio surrounded by latticework and creeping vines. Take Line 7 to Cheongdam station, Exit 14, and walk 600m.

Imperial Palace Hotel (Map pp96-7; ☎ 3440 8000; superior/deluxe/ste W210,000/390,000/700,000; 🟦 🖳 ⓢ) If you're going to emblazon the words 'Imperial Palace' atop a hotel, you'd better deliver because expectations run high. This place delivers the goods. From the magnificent lobby to the well-appointed rooms, opulence runs throughout this fine establishment. Take Line 7 to Hakdong station, Exit 1, and walk straight to the first major street with a light.

Lotte World Hotel (Map pp98-9; ☎ 419 7000; r from W300,000; 🄿 🖳 🖭) You'll like it because … you believe a pricey room is appropriate compensation for the time you spend away from the family at work; because time is money and you don't want to travel to Lotte World when you could sleep in the same complex; because the W200,000 golf shirt you purchased in Apgujeong matches the lush room interior.

Novotel Ambassador (Map pp96-7; ☎ 567 1101; r W340,000; 🄿 🖳 🖭) The calculators at the front desk are a clear indication that this hotel is for dealmakers. Rack rates are negotiable with discounts of up to 50% available at different times. Most rooms come with a decent work station (LAN connection W16,000 per day), a pleasant décor and a wide bed. Access to the pool and gym are included though breakfast is extra, but that's negotiable. Take Line 2 to Gangnam station, Exit 7.

EATING
Gwanghwamun & Around
BUDGET

Witch's Table (Map pp88-9; drinks & snacks W2500-6000; ⏱ 8am-9.30pm Mon-Fri, 8am-6pm Sat) Can't start the day without a bagel and cream cheese? You can get that and more at this narrow eatery opposite the Goryeo supermarket. It is one of the few restaurants in the area to open early. Take Line 5 to Gwanghwamun station, Exit 7.

Jongno Woodong (Map pp88-9; meals W3000; ⏱ 24hr) This Korean version of a greasy spoon serves traditional favourites like *kimchi bokkeumbap* (김치 볶음밥; fried rice with *kimchi*) and *tangsu mandu* (탕수 만두; fried dumplings with sweet-and-sour sauce). Take Line 1 to Jonggak, Exit 3.

Park Ganae Maetdol Bindaeddeok (Map pp88-9; meals W4000; ⏱ 9am-10pm) Some Korean food tastes better than its name might suggest. Fried green bean is a good example; *beondegi* (번데 기; silkworm larvae) is not. Drop by this busy stall in the Gwangjang market for tasty and filling *bindaetteok* (빈대떡), a fried pancake made from ground green beans, potato, onions and bean sprouts. The stall is crowded at night with locals who wash back their pancake with *makgeolli* (막걸리), a milky rice wine. Take Line 1 to Jongno 5-ga station and follow the signs to the Gwangjang market.

Goryeo Supermarket (Map pp88-9; meals W5000) It's one of the best downtown locations to buy in-season fruit and veggies. Take Line 5 to Gwanghwamun station, Exit 7, turn right at the corner and walk to the first street.

Tosok Ma-eul (Map pp88-9; meals W5000; ⏱ 24hr) Roaming the streets of Jongno in the early hours of the morning can be stressful, especially if you're craving soup. That's why late-night prowlers come to this simple restaurant known for *gamjatang* (감자탕; ham and potato soup). Take Line 1 to Jonggak, Exit 3 – it's behind Pizza Hut.

Seolleongtang (Map pp88-9; meals W5000; ⏱ Mon-Sat) It's a scruffy restaurant on a hard-to-find lane, but getting a seat at lunch often requires a 10-minute wait. The specialty is *seolleongtang* (설렁탕; beef broth with noodles), a delicious soup ideal for people looking for a non-spicy meal. Take Line 5 to Gwanghwamun station, Exit 7, turn right at the corner and right at the second lane.

Todam (Map pp88-9; meals W5000; ⏱ noon-2pm & 6-9pm) The exterior looks like crap and it doesn't get much better past the front door, but this simple diner serves great home-style cooking. Korean food aficionados will appreciate the spicy flavour of the *chamchi kimchi jjigae* (참치 김치찌개; *kimchi* stew with tuna), while those with sensitive palates should keep a jug of water handy. Take Line 5 to Gwanghwamun station, Exit 6.

Jongno Bindaeddeok (Map pp88-9; meals W5000; ⏱ noon-2am) This is a sterling example of a dumpy-looking restaurant that serves great food. Most people come for the *bindaetteok* with beef (고기빈대떡) or seafood (해물빈대떡). The *sogogigukbap* (소고기국밥; spicy beef soup) is also delicious. Take Line 5 to Gwanghwamun station, Exit 7, walk straight and turn left at the first street.

MIDRANGE & TOP END

Samjeon Hoejeon Chobap (Map pp88-9; sushi W3000; ⏱ 11.30am-2pm & 4.30-9pm Mon-Sat) The sushi isn't served on a silver platter, but it does come to you on a silver conveyor belt. Grab a stool and pick a circulating dish. Save yourself the hassle of waiting for the next plate by ordering the W15,000 platter. Take Line 5 to Gwanghwamun station, Exit 7, walk straight and turn left at the lane beside the art centre. The restaurant is down the road.

Jongno Gol (Map pp88-9; servings W9000; ⏱ 11.30am-10pm) Barbecued meat and *soju* (local vodka) –

does it get any better? If you love pork, the answer is no. This outstanding neighbourhood restaurant specialises in *solipgama dwaeji* (솔 잎가마돼지; smoked black pig). The meat is ripened in an outdoor barbecue and brought to your tabletop grill for cooking completion. Line 1 to Jongno 5-ga station, Exit 7. Turn right at the second corner. At the end of the street, make a quick left and right turn, then turn right at the first street and walk straight.

Top Cloud (Map pp88-9; ☎ 2230 3000; meals W29,000; ☽ noon–midnight) Acrophobes beware: way up on the 33rd floor of Jongno Tower, this tasteful restaurant is ideal for special outings. Order off the menu or go with the lunch (W29,000; noon to 2pm) or dinner (W36,000; 6pm to 8.30pm) buffet. After dinner, the restaurant turns into a candle-lit bar (9pm to midnight).

Insadong
BUDGET & MIDRANGE
Minsok Jip (Map pp88-9; cake W3000; ☽ 6am–10pm) Under and around the Nakwon Arcade, there are several *tteok* (떡) shops like this one, selling rice cake. Consume a W3000 package of *yaksik* (약식), a brown-rice cake with dates and chestnuts, and you may not eat for the rest of the day.

Park-ssi Mulgo On Jebi (Map pp88-9; meals W5000; ☽ 10am–2am) It's a quaint and cluttered eatery with *sanchae bibimbap* (산체 비빔밥; fresh mountain vegetables with rice) that's as fresh and flavourful as the spinach lightly tossed in sesame oil. The meal comes with a red squeeze bottle – this is red pepper sauce, not ketchup.

Dolkemaeul Tofu House (Map pp88-9; meals W6000; ☽ 9.30am–11pm) For a low-cost meal, it's hard to beat *kimchi dubu* (김치 순두부; *kimchi* stew with tofu). Crack a raw egg into the stew and let it sit. Use the ladle to scoop rice out of the stone pot. Pour 1cm of water into the pot. Let that rest with the lid on to make a warm rice drink consumed at the end of the meal.

Dimibang (Map pp88-9; meals W6000-50,000) This restaurant proves vegetarian meals aren't all boring. Many of the set courses (W12,000 to W30,000, minimum two people) use *hamcho* (함초) root and other medicinal herbs to give the meals taste and texture. Single travellers can choose a simple meal like *doenjang jjigae* (된장 찌개; soybean stew) and *bibimbap*.

Jagun Chajib (Map pp88-9; meals W7000) Homemade *juk* (죽; porridge) is the main food served in this teashop. The brilliant orange pumpkin porridge (호박죽) has a silky smooth texture.

Chon (Map pp88-9; meals W7000-50,000; ☽ noon–midnight) Unlike most area shops, this one serves *hanjeongsik* (한정식; banquet) to single travellers. By the time the third wave of dishes hits the table, you might find yourself quietly hoping it's the last because there's a lot of food.

So Sim (Map pp88-9; meals W7000; ☽ 11.30am–10pm Mon-Sat) This quaint restaurant at the north end of Insadong serves vegetarian meals. It's a sedate place, but the full-flavour quality more than compensates for the lack of flash.

TOP END
Min's Club (Map pp88-9; lunch W15,000-45,000, dinner W30,000-75,000; ☽ lunch 11.30am-2.30pm, afternoon tea 2.30-6pm, dinner 6-11pm, last serving 9.30pm) Old-world architecture meets new-world cuisine. This attractive restaurant in a restored 1930s *hanok* building isn't the best place to experience traditional Korean cuisine, but it's popular with executives treating clients to a steak dinner.

Sanchon (Map pp88-9; lunch/dinner W19,800/35,200) This famous restaurant serves temple food, but the prices aren't very Buddhist. Sit on floor cushions in a soothing atmosphere with candles on the tables. Set meals – 16 small dishes including *japchae* (잡채; noodles with vegetables) and *pajeon* – don't change between lunch and dinner, but the price certainly does. A traditional dancer performs at 8.15pm.

Bukchon Hanok Village
Anjip (Map pp88-9; meals W6000-30,000; Mon-Sat) Eat in your own private room in this traditional restaurant noted for *hanjeongsik* (한정식), a traditional Korean banquet made for a king. Like most restaurants specialising in this fare, single travellers are not welcome. Take Line 3 to An·guk station, Exit 3, and turn left at the first street. The restaurant is down a lane opposite a parking garage.

Samcheongdong
Samcheongdong Sujebi (Map pp88-9; meals W6000; ☽ 11am-9pm) Prickly waitresses aside, the outstanding *sujebi* (수제비; dough flakes in shellfish broth) is probably the city's best. It's not spicy, but if you need a little zip, add green pepper-flavoured sauce from the tabletop container.

Son Mandu (Map pp88-9; meals W6000; ☽ 11am-9pm) High-quality *mandu* (만두; dumpling) is served in this friendly shop. The *jinmandu* (진만두; steamed dumpling) comes with six large balls stuffed with beef, pork, tofu and vegetables. After receiving your food, let it sit for a few minutes; the outside dough may be cool to the touch but the inside is hot. It's across the street from the *sujebi* restaurant.

Myeongdong

Myeongdong Gyoja (Map pp92-3; meals W6000) If you come for lunch, be prepared to stand in line because this busy restaurant has a reputation for tasty meals. *Mandu, bibimbap guksu* (비빔밥국수; spicy noodles) and *kongguksu* (콩국수; noodles in bean broth) are the specialties. Pay the woman walking around with tickets.

Sinseon Seolleongtang (Map pp92-3; meals W6000; ⏲ 24hr) Outstanding *seolleongtang* is the main dish. Like most restaurants serving this non-spicy broth, there are two side dishes of *kimchi* made from radish and cabbage. Use the scissors to cut the cabbage into bite-sized pieces.

Gye Sunok Bosintang (Map pp92-3; meals W10,000; ⏲ 10am-9pm Mon-Sat) Korean men flock here to restore their virility. In business for 50 years, this simple restaurant serves *bosintang* (보신탕; dog-meat soup), a broth thought to possess miraculous healing powers. Apparently there are believers because the place is full at lunch. Standing in front of the Catholic Church, cross the street and walk down the lane, then turn right at the first lane. The restaurant is around the bend.

Baekje Samgyetang (Map pp92-3; meals W11,000) At this impressive restaurant the outside signboard is written only in Chinese characters. The Korean classic *samgyetang* (삼계탕; chicken stuffed with rice and ginseng) is full of rich flavour and tastes even better with *insimul* (인삼술; ginseng whiskey) for W4000. Look for the signboard with the phone number 776 3267.

Itaewon

Jeonju Bon·ga (Map p91; meals W5000; ⏲ 10.30am-11pm) It's not a beautiful restaurant, which might explain why few travellers come here. Pity, because it's a hub of home-style cooking with great *dolsot bibimbap* (돌솥 비빔밥; vegetables and rice in a hot pot). By the time you've dug down to the bottom, the rice has been baked into a crispy cake, adding a new dimension of texture and taste.

Other recommendations:

USO Canteen (Map p91; meals W4000; ⏲ 7am-2pm) For ham sandwich and fries. Take Line 1 to Namyeong station, Exit 1. At street level, turn right, then right again at the corner and walk 200m.

Gama Sagol (Map p91; meals W6000; ⏲ 6am-1am) Great *seolleongtang*. Exit the Hamilton Hotel and walk left 10 minutes.

Memories (Map p91; meals W12,000; ⏲ noon-11pm, closed Aug) Authentic German schnitzel.

Our Place (Map p91; meals W12,000; ⏲ 5pm-3am) A romantic setting in Itaewon. Now that's an odd combination.

Moghul (Map p91; meals W15,000-45,000) A Pakistani restaurant with a weekend lunch (W18,000; noon-3pm) and dinner (W23,000; 6pm-10pm) buffet.

Nashville Steak House (Map p91; steaks W26,000; ⏲ 7am-11pm) Blends the best elements of a basement recreation room and a highway truck stop.

Cheongsa Chorong (Map p91; ☎ 794 1177; lunch 7000, dinner from W40,000; ⏲ 7am-10pm) A popular *hanjeongsik* restaurant with a traditional dance and music show at 7pm.

Hongik, Sinchon & Ewha
BUDGET

Richemont (Map p94; meals w4000; ⏲ 8am-11pm) When rice and *kimchi* are an impossibility, try this bakery with comfort-food staples like roast-beef sandwiches for a quick burst of energy. There's a wide selection of chocolates including caramel truffles.

Dongah Gul (Map p94; servings W5000; ⏲ noon-11pm) In the late afternoon, this is the only busy meat restaurant in the Hongik University area. Budget-conscious students are drawn to this hole-in-the-wall restaurant by the low cost, lean cuts and fun atmosphere.

Choonchun Jib (Map p94; meals W5500; ⏲ 24hr) The specialty is *dakgalbi* (닭갈비), a boneless chicken dish with chunks of cabbage, leek and carrot smothered in a spicy sauce. The staff cook the food at your table, so there's nothing to do except wait and put on the apron. Line 2 to Sinchon station, Exit 2. Turn left at the lane between Starbucks and the SK Telecom store.

MIDRANGE

Agio (Map p94; meals W9000; ⏲ noon-2am) It's not your ordinary, garden-variety pizza joint, but it does serve pizza and there is a garden. Surrounded by leafy trees, it's a romantic setting best experienced in the evening. Simple pasta dishes and pizza are the main menu items.

Misses & Mai (Map p94; meals W9000; ⏲ noon-1am Mon-Fri, noon-2am Sat & Sun) Asian fusion is the predominant menu theme in this outdoorsy restaurant next to Agio. Enjoy Pad Thai under a canopy of trees all year. A glass of wine is W8800, so consider getting a bottle, which starts at W35,000.

Cabin Oak (Map p94; meals W11,000; ☾ 9.30am-3.30am Mon-Fri, 9.30am-2am Sat & Sun) Chicken and beer – never has there been a more perfect combination since, well, ,pizza and beer. This Hongik University chicken outlet is unique because it roasts birds, stuffed with rice, over a spit.

Le Petit Paris (Map p94; ☎ 3142 0282; meals W12,000; ☾ 6-9pm, noon-2.30pm Fri & Sat) Sinchon services the food and drink needs of Yonsei University students, reputedly the country's most intelligent young minds. Given the number of crappy restaurants in the area, it seems university students aren't well-educated about food. That's what makes Le Petit Paris special. Run by a chef who worked in Paris, this small restaurant manages to find a balance between quality and budget. Steaks cooked to perfection start around W15,000.

Dokdo Tuna (Map p94; meals W17,000; ☾ 10am-2am) Not far from Hongik University (the all-night party zone for 20-somethings) this out-of-place restaurant serves comparatively expensive frozen tuna to a 35+ crowd. Pay one price and you get unlimited servings.

Daehangno
BUDGET & MIDRANGE

Omyeo Gamyeo (Map p95; meals W3500; ☾ 11am-10pm) The interior doesn't look like much, but it's been in business forever serving *gongnamul bibimbap* (공나물 비빔밥; bean sprouts with rice) and cutting-edge dishes like *picha chiju bap* (피차치즈 밥; rice with pizza cheese). One person eats for W3500 but a double order costs just W6000. Take Line 4 to Hyehwa station, Exit 2.

Ttokssam Sidae (Map p95; servings W8000; ☾ 11am-1am) This is the place to go for meat and *soju*. The meat is grilled on a slanted plate heated over a flame. Most customers throw *kimchi* on the grill to intensify the saltiness. Place a piece of pork, *kimchi* and garlic on a leaf of lettuce, wash back with *soju* and voila – you've got a gastronomical piece of heaven on Earth.

Mama Food (Map p95; meals W8000; ☾ 11am-2am) It looks like an open-air Marché restaurant (p128) without the same selection of food or steep prices. Located above a convenience store, it's a fun restaurant when you have a craving for slightly upscale Korean food under a canopy. Grilled rice with seafood or chicken is the specialty. Live music starts hourly at 8pm.

TOP END

Opseoye (Map p95; servings W10,000; ☾ 11.30am-10pm) Flowers lining the front steps and a woody interior make this one of the most attractive restaurants in the area. It's also a great option for people looking to escape spicy food. The specialty is *shabu shabu* (샤브샤브; food cooked in a hot broth) cooked at your table. Great fun with a group, it's a dining experience that should be tried at least once.

Bongchu Jimdalk (Map p95; meals W22,000; ☾ 11am-midnight) Don't let the attractive wooden tables and chairs fool you. This deceptively appealing restaurant serves only one thing: flame-thrower-hot chicken. If you can't take the heat, don't come here.

South of the Han River
APGUJEONG

Bagel Street (Map pp96-7; meals W1500; ☾ 8am-10pm) It's a long subway ride to Apgujeong, but that's the kind of sacrifice required to find a close-to-authentic bagel and cream cheese. Go the extra mile and you'll be rewarded with choices like onion, garlic or a good old plain bagel. It's behind Hotel Popgreen.

Zao (Map pp96-7; meals W3900; ☾ 8am-11pm) Some of Apgujeong's cheapest eats are here. The highlight of this thinly decorated café is the lunch (W5900; 11am to 4pm) and dinner buffet (W8900; 4pm to 11pm). Food options are limited, but it's a good opportunity to load up on fresh salad for the cost of a beer.

Shwing (Map pp96-7; meals W9500; ☾ 4-11pm Mon-Wed, 4pm-1am Thu & Fri, 3pm-1am Sat, 3-11pm Sun) This place claims to serve original Buffalo wings. Well, anyone who's been to the Anchor Bar in Buffalo, New York, will tell you these chicken parts simply don't compare in size, but they are cooked to perfection. The best deal is from 6.30pm to 9.30pm when W15,000 buys all-you-can-eat wings. Be warned, gluttony has a price: eat everything you order or pay a penalty. It's a couple of blocks behind Starbucks.

Mad for Garlic (Map pp96-7; meals W12,000; ☾ 11.20am-midnight) With dishes like 'Dracula Killer', you know what to expect. Garlic is everywhere including the air, thanks to the open-concept kitchen that unleashes an appetising aroma in this brick-and-mortar restaurant. Hard-to-find dishes like Gorgonzola pizza are the specialties, but they also serve pasta and steak. Take Line 3 to Apgujeong station, Exit 2.

Café greEAT (Map pp96-7; ☎ 3448 4556; lunch buffet W21,000, dinner/weekend buffet W23,000; ☾ 10.30am-2am, lunch buffet 11.30am-2pm, dinner buffet 5-10pm) This eatery tastefully captures the essence of the neighbourhood: it's beautiful and expensive with a dash of snobbery. The outdoor patio is ideal for a two-hour lunch amid a beautiful garden surrounded by a stonewall and greenery. The buffet has about a dozen main dishes, with an emphasis of pasta and fusion. It's on the 3rd floor of the Tribeca Building.

OTHER AREAS SOUTH OF THE HAN RIVER

Marché (Map pp98-9; meals W15,000; ☙ 11am-11pm) Inside the COEX Mall, this franchise looks like most others around the world, with food served in a marketlike atmosphere. For big eaters, the best bet is the buffet lunch (W18,900) or dinner (W24,900), which gives you access to everything except steaks, ribs and juice.

Samwon Garden (Map pp96-7; ☎ 548 3030; servings W28,000; ☙ 11.40am-10.30pm) With seating for 1000 it's the city's largest restaurant and maybe the best place to experience *sutbulgalbi* (숯불갈비; barbecued meat). It's also one of the most expensive: one serving of meat starts at W28,000 but can run up to W49,000. This immaculate facility has seven dining halls, most of which are surrounded by water wheels and lush gardens.

Busan Ilbeonji (Map p100; dinner W40,000) It doesn't look like much, but this modest shop on the 2nd floor of the Noryangjin fish market is a great restaurant. The specialty is raw fish, but it also serves an amazing lunch menu that includes *mae·untang* (매운탕; spicy fish soup); for W5000, you get a good selection of side dishes including a crispy potato cake, a baked-to-perfection fish and a pot of fish soup.

Like many good restaurants, this one requires at least two customers but Mrs Moon, the no-nonsense owner, makes an exception for foreign travellers. Take Line 1 to Noryangjin station, Exit 1, cross the bridge and walk downstairs to the restaurant section above the fish market.

DRINKING
Itaewon

Hostess Bars are concentrated on the hill opposite the Hamilton Hotel, known locally as Hooker Hill. They have suggestive names and are easy to find, but with closed-circuit cameras monitoring the streets they can easily find you.

3 Alley Pub (Map p91; drinks W3500; ☙ 4pm-1.30am Mon-Fri, noon-12.30am Sat & Sun) This English-style pub run by a Canadian and a German is popular with the 35+ crowd. Few expat teachers come here, which is fine by the owners. Great beers on tap include Krombache. Darts, pool, good pub grub and friendly people are all here.

Rocky Mountain Tavern (Map p91; drinks W5000; ☙ 6pm-2am Mon-Thu, to 3am Fri, 11.30am-5am Sat, to 2am Sun) Hockey sweaters, photos of Mounties and patrons finishing their sentences with 'eh' give this place a down-home feel for Canadian expats. If you're part of the gang, it's fun. If not, the atmosphere is as frigid as a Canadian winter.

Bar Bliss (Map p91; drinks W6000; ☙ 6pm-1am Mon-Fri, to 3am Sat & Sun) It's a wine bar with a barbecue. Bring your own steak and put it on the grill. Then enjoy a freshly cooked steak with a bottle of red wine.

Other recommendations:

Seoul Pub (Map p91; ☙ 3pm-2am Mon-Fri, noon-3am Sat & Sun) A good place to start a weekend bender.

Gecko's (Map p91; meals W8500-22,000; ☙ 11am-2am) Anyone doing the rounds in Itaewon ends up here at some point.

Nashville Sports Pub (Map p91; ☙ noon-2am, to 3am Fri & Sat) There are no team jerseys hanging on the walls, but they have pool tables and darts, which for some people qualifies as a sport.

Hongik & Sinchon

Watts on Tap (Map p94; drinks W3000; ☙ 6pm-2am Sun-Thu, to 5am Fri & Sat) Welcoming staff, cheap drinks during Happy Hour (6pm to 9pm Monday to Thursday), when a bottle of Carlsberg costs W3000, and good tunes are a recipe for fun. Take Line 2 to Sinchon station, Exit 2, walk about five minutes and turn left one block past Pizza Hut. It's down the street on the corner.

Blue Bird (Map p94; drinks W4000; ☙ 6.30pm-2am, to 3am Fri & Sat) With a collection of 1000 jazz CDs, there's only one kind of music played here. It's run by Mr Cheol, a serious jazz fan who greets international guests with humour and respect. Take Line 2 to Sinchon station, Exit 2, turn left on the lane after Pizza Hut, make a quick right then a left turn.

Noree Hanun Saramdul (Map p94; ☙ 7pm-2am, to 5am Fri-Sun) If you can appreciate George Benson's funked up cover of 'Take Five' in a Bohemian setting, you'll like it here. Exit the Blue Bird and turn right. At the corner look right and you'll see a wooden signboard with barely legible Korean characters – that's the door to this basement-level bar.

Woodstock (Map p94; drinks W4000; ⊗ 7pm-3am) This grungy bar plays rock music the way it should be: loud and on vinyl. For rock purists, nothing beats Lynard Skynard on a scratchy vinyl disc. It's across the street from Blue Bird.

Other recommendations:

US Bar 66 (Map p94; ⊗ 5pm-2am Sun-Thu, 6pm-5am Fri & Sat) A fun bar packed with American memorabilia and expats.

Moon Yang (Map p94; drinks W5000; ⊗ 11.30am-3am) A 3rd-floor bar with a birds-eye view of the area.

Moim (Map p94; drinks W8000; ⊗ 4pm-4am) A romantic hideaway on the 9th floor of the Club Otwo building.

Princess (Map p94; drinks W7000; ⊗ 10am-4am) Almost everything in this odd café has a virgin feel.

Café Atre (Map p94; drinks W5000; ⊗ 11am-10.30pm) Afternoon lattes and New York cheesecake.

Galaxy 999 (Map p94; drinks W5000; ⊗ 5pm-5am) Most curious drink? The Dr Pepper, rum and beer set ablaze.

Gold II (Map p94; drinks W2500; ⊗ 5pm-6am) Cheap drinks and busy crowds but the mandatory side dishes – like the W13,000 fruit platter – are tough to swallow. Also try Gold next door.

Daehangno

Sanata (Map p95; drinks W6500; ⊗ 3pm-2am) Unfortunately this bar lacks focus. Specialising in dark ales, there are eight beers on tap along with 12 different bottled varieties. The draft in a 1770 cc pitcher for W14,000 is pretty good value. Although the quality beer gives the place an uptown, cool feel, the overall mood is diminished by crappy tunes – from Don Henley to John Denver. Country Roads?

Bier Halle (Map p95; drinks W3000; ⊗ 3pm-midnight Mon-Fri, 2pm-midnight Sat & Sun) The plastic food in the front window should be the first hint. On the surface, it looks like a German beer hall, complete with stylized architecture, a large open-air room and sausages. But, there's one thing missing: German beer.

Esmeralda Coffee (Map p95; drinks W2800; ⊗ 11am-10pm Mon-Fri, noon-9pm Sat & Sun) It's nothing more than a coffee bar with good espresso. Sit outside near the bushes and you can pass the time people-watching.

Mindeulle Yeongto Café (Map p95; meals W10,000; ⊗ 10am-midnight) Until you sit down, this place can be a little overwhelming. It's a restaurant, café and entertainment hub packed into five floors of pink, with staff dressed in Heidi costumes constantly yelling 'hello' and 'good-bye' as they wave their hands palms up.

Apgujeong

Tribeca (Map pp96-7; ☎ 3448 4450) This large, grey building has three bars. On the 2nd floor, The Bar (open 7pm to 4am) is an expansive lounge with a Manhattan feel thanks to the high ceilings and long-reaching bar. When it's busy after 9pm, you won't mind paying W12,000 or more for a drink. At other times, it feels like you're in an empty hockey arena. Wine bars on the 5th and 6th floors appeal to cigar smokers looking for a comfortable environment to light up with a bottle of port. The 5th floor, Brooklyn (open 7pm to 2am), is a dimly lit bar with wall-to-wall wine racks. There are 1000 bottles, and customers purchase wine by the bottle. Prices start at W40,000. The upstairs

---

UNUSUAL TEASHOPS

Insadong (Map pp88–9) has many teashops serving traditional hot and cold drinks made from fruit, leaves, herbs and roots. Many teashop owners make a big effort to create a memorable décor. A cup of tea costs W6000, but it's a quality product. Birdsong, running water and ethereal music add to the atmosphere.

Yetchatjip (Old Teashop; Map pp88–9) This has a bric-a-brac décor and little birds that fly around the teashop. Getting a seat in the afternoon can be difficult, as it's popular with Japanese travellers.

Meosi kkeokjeong inga? (What are you worried about?; Map pp88–9) Overflows with plants, flowers and remarkably fresh air. Lights in wicker baskets give the place a soft, relaxed feel, hence the name.

Insadong (Map pp88–9) A simple teahouse in a relaxing setting. The inside seating area has a cosy feel, thanks to the cordwood and pots of tea brewing on the stove. Go straight to the back and you'll discover a small outdoor courtyard surrounded by private rooms with floor seating.

Dawon (Map pp88–9) Opposite Kyongin Gallery. Sit in a splendid courtyard under the trees or on floor cushions inside a 19th-century building. The omijacha is a delicious, cold, pink tea made from schisandra berries – it's said to have five flavours.

Belle Vue (open 7pm to 2am) has an uneven, almost kitschy décor. Both bars have a selection of cigars in humidors, including Cohibas and Montecristos starting at W20,000.

Platinum Apgujeong (Map pp96-7; drinks W5000; 4pm-4am Mon-Sat, 4pm-2am Sun) It's the second outlet of this notable microbrewery, which, unlike some less-successful micros in Korea, has clear and tasty beer. This basement-level bar has a battleship-grey interior that creates the impression you're inside a brew tank. Quaff back a couple pints of the Morphine brew with 8.1% alcohol and you might imagine you're in most any place. It's 100m from the Rock & Roll bar.

Other recommendations:

Café Organic (Map pp96-7; drinks W5000; 11am-11pm) The latte might be the finest in the area.

Tea Museum (Map pp96-7; 10.30am-8.30pm Mon-Sat) A teashop, exhibition room and emporium in one.

Rock & Roll (Map pp96-7; drinks W8000; 3pm-5am) Apgujeong's original western bar started in 1990 but still looks good.

Gangnam

Dublin Irish Pub (Map pp96-7; 4pm-2am Mon-Fri, 4pm-3am Sat & Sun) Not many Irish people come here, but that's not the point. With a dark woody design and high ceilings, the atmosphere's fine for sampling five imported beers on tap and a good selection of bottled brew, including Leffe. Good taste has a price: pints start at W12,000 plus 10% VAT.

Platinum Microbrewery (Map pp96-7; 2052 0022; drinks W7700; 11.30am-1am Mon-Sat, 11.30am-midnight Sun) Seven yummy brews on tap but the main draw is the all-you-can-eat-and-drink buffet (W30,000; 6pm to 10pm, except Sunday). Take Line 2 to Gangnam station, Exit 8. Telephone reservations are required at least two days in advance for the buffet.

O'Sulloc (Map pp96-7; drinks W3000; 9am-11pm) Green is the dominant design motif and ingredient in this fusion shop that pushes the limits of green-tea experimentation including Carmel Can Panna, a noble idea but a disastrous concoction.

ENTERTAINMENT
Casinos & Betting

Sheraton Walkerhill Hotel (Map pp84-5; 450 4826; 24hr) Seoul's original casino in the offers the usual games including Black Jack and Roulette. There is no dress code, though shorts and slippers are not permitted. Korean nationals cannot enter casinos. Take Line 5 to Gwangnaru station and catch a taxi (W3000). On the way back to the city, board a shuttle bus to the subway.

The city's two other 24-hour casinos operated by **Seven Luck** (www.7luck.com) are in the **Millennium Seoul Hilton** (Map pp92-3; 2021 6000). Line 1 to Seoul station, Exit 8; and **COEX Mall** (Map pp98-9; 3466 6000), Line 2 to Samseong station, Exit 5 or 6.

Seoul Racecourse (Map pp84-5; 509 1221; www.kra.co.kr; admission W800; races 11.30am-5pm Sat & Sun Sep-Jun, 1-9pm late Jul - late Aug) If cards aren't your calling, try the ponies at this well-organised facility with a surprising number of English-speaking staff. International guests use the lounge on the 4th floor of the Lucky Ville Grandstand, where interpreters help visitors place a wager. Bets range from W100 to W100,000. Take Line 4 to Seoul Racecourse station, Exit 2.

Cinemas

You will find multiplex cinemas in most malls and busy commercial districts. Tickets cost about W7000 and films are usually screened from 10am to 11pm, though some theatres like **Lotte Cinema** (Map pp92–3) in Myeongdong screen films after midnight. English-language films are usually shown in their original language with Korean subtitles. Most cinemas sell tickets with assigned seating.

Korea Film Archives (Map pp84-5; 521 3147; www.koreafilm.or.kr) Located in the basement of the Seoul Arts Centre, this body occasionally screens classic Korean films with English subtitles.

Seoul Selection Bookshop (Map pp88-9; 734 9564; 9.30am-6.30pm Mon-Sat) This bookshop shows Korean films with English subtitles (W3000; 11am Saturday).

DVD Rooms

The ubiquitous DVD *bang* (room) serves multiple social functions: it is a good place to escape nasty weather and one of the few chances travellers have to watch a Korean movie with English subtitles. DVD *bangs* are also the Korean equivalent of a drive-in theatre: instead of making out in a car, young people come here. The cost is generally W7000 per person. Busy commercial districts around universities have heaps of DVD *bangs*.

Gay & Lesbian Venues

Itaewon has the only openly gay and lesbian bar scene that attracts foreigners and English-speaking Koreans. The small venues are clustered on an alley near Hooker Hill. Not much happens until 9.30pm or later, even on Friday and Saturday.

Trance (Map p91; ☺ 10pm-4am) Drag-queen shows take the stage every Saturday night at 2.30am or whenever there's a big crowd.

Other recommendations:

Queen (Map p91; ☺ 8pm-3am, to 6am Fri, closed Mon) Happy hour 8pm to 11pm.

Always Homme (Map p91; ☺ 8pm-4am, to 6am Fri & Sat) Open every night.

Why Not (Map p91; ☺ 8pm-6am) A moody blue interior with disco lights.

Soho (Map p91; ☺ 8pm-4am Tue-Thu, 6pm-4am Fri-Sun, closed Mon) Drinking three Long Island Ice Teas here is like having a temporary frontal lobotomy.

Live Music
ITAEWON

All That Jazz (Map p91; admission W5000; ☺ 6pm-1am Mon-Fri, 6pm-2am Sat & Sun) This is one of the classier joints in Itaewon, with an interior reminiscent of the Rat Pack days. Live jazz sets take place from 8.30pm to 11pm on weeknights, and from 7pm to 1.30am on weekends.

LIVING IN SEOUL

You've landed your first teaching job in Seoul. Now what? To make your sojourn an enjoyable one, you'll need to tackle three pieces of business as soon as you arrive.

The first is housing. Employers provide foreign workers with an apartment or a monthly stipend. Private-language schools that retain good teachers generally provide housing with a short commute to work. Other schools and most universities offer a monthly allowance of about W400,000, a paltry sum insufficient to rent a studio apartment near a subway station. For this size and location expect to pay at least W600,000 per month plus W50,000 in maintenance fees. Some apartments require a refundable deposit (전세) between W3 million and W100 million, which your employer may or may not provide.

Apartment hunting usually begins online. Websites like nearsubway.com list vacancies by district. The *Korea Herald* online newspaper (www.koreaherald.co.kr) has a small listing of affordable accommodation with many places located in distant areas like Bundang, a suburb just outside Seoul. Work in this quiet, wealthy residential community and you'll enjoy a comfortable, perhaps dull, lifestyle. If you don't work here, it's best to avoid Bundang because long subway commutes into Seoul can be draining. If you have a Korean-speaking friend, walk around any neighbourhood you like and visit a real-estate office (부동산). For proximity to a party zone, Hongik University or Sinchon are good areas (Map p94). If quality of life is important, expats report good things about living south of the Han River in Jamsil (Map pp98-9). It's expensive, but comparatively fresh air and quick access to nearby sights like Olympic Park (Map pp98-9) make life comfortable. Housing with oil heat may look inexpensive, but the winter heating bills can be shocking, so choose gas whenever possible.

Your quality of life will increase exponentially once you're able to make sense of restaurant menus and street signs. Learning the Korean alphabet is easy and the three hours you invest by memorizing word sounds will never cease to yield dividends. Most large bookstores, such as Bandi & Luni's (p81), have Korean-language books. Learning to speak Korean at a rudimentary level is equally advantageous. Some universities offer a language instruction program, though quality varies. For a relaxed atmosphere with a flexible schedule try BestFriend Language & Culture Exchange Center (p118).

Finally, be adventurous. Seoul is a big city with many diversions, but it can also be a lonely place, especially for new arrivals. Avoid the unproductive trap that some expats fall into: go to work, hit the bar, bitch about Korea and hide at home. Start a new hobby or join a travel group like the Royal Asiatic Society (p119). Its weekend programmes are popular with singles interested in travel and meeting new people. Working out is also a great way to meet people. Taekwondo studios and fitness centres can be found in almost every neighbourhood. Small gyms with basic equipment cost as little as W30,000 per month. Seoul is a tough city, but it rewards those who dare to explore.

Woodstock (Map p91; admission free; ⏰ 6pm-4am) Classic rock music lives in this bar. Live music with a Stevie Ray Vaughn and Hendrix bent is on most Fridays, funk on Saturdays. Sets start around 9pm.

HONGIK UNIVERSITY

Hongik's claim to fame is dance clubs and a small indie-music scene. Live shows start around 7pm and finish at 10pm. Entry is usually W5000 to W10,000 and includes a drink, but can jump to W20,000 for special events.

Skunk Hell (Map p94; www.skunklabel.com/eman.html; admission up to W20,000; ⏰ 8-11pm) Seoul's home for punk with an attitude. Foreigners are welcome, but there are rules: don't trash-talk Korea and don't try to hook up with the local women.

Bebop Jazz Club (Map p94; admission free; ⏰ 5.30pm-2am Mon-Fri, 5.30pm-1am Sat & Sun) Live sets 9.30pm, 11pm and midnight.

Free Bird (Map p94; admission W7000, Sat & Sun W10,000; ⏰ 6.30-11pm Tue-Sun) Check the schedule outside the door.

SLUG.er (Map p94; admission free Mon-Thu, W10,000 Fri-Sun; ⏰ 6-11pm) Indie groups perform 8pm-10.30pm.

Water Cock (Map p94; admission W5000; ⏰ 8pm-midnight Tue-Sun) Live sets 9pm to 11.30pm.

DAEHANGNO

Live Jazz Club (Map p95; admission Mon-Fri W5000, Sat & Sun W8000; ⏰ 7pm-1.30am Mon-Fri, 6.30pm-3am Sat & Sun) In a student ghetto overrun with cute cafés that encourage men to get in touch with their feminine side, there is one den of masculinity, and this is it. Completely done up in black, it's the coolest place in Daehangno and gets busy when the first of three bands takes the stage at 8pm.

APGUJEONG

Once in a Blue Moon (Map pp96-7; ☎ 549 5490; admission free; ⏰ 5pm-2am, 5pm-1am Sun) You're not likely to catch the next Keith Jarrett here, but there is some kicking jazz. Bottled beer starts at W12,000. One-hour sets on stage at 7pm, 8.30pm, 10pm and 11.30pm.

Nightclubs

ITAEWON

Grand Ole Oprey (Map p91; ⏰ 6pm-midnight Sun-Thu, 6pm-3am Fri & Sat) It's everything you'd expect from a country-and-western bar: Dwight Yoakam tunes, Jack Daniels posters and a confederate flag. Gets busy on Friday and Saturday nights when the good ol' boys from the US army garrison drop by to square dance.

King Bar (Map p91; ⏰ 6pm-5am Mon-Fri, 6pm-6am Sat & Sun) A GI institution, this bar has a rough-and-tumble feel. If you've been in a bar where two guys scrap because one guy didn't like the way the other looked at the bar girl, you know what this place is like.

HONGIK UNIVERSITY

Samba, techno, hip-hop and whatever else comes along is played in this clubbing area. Entry usually costs W5000 to W10,000 but increases on Friday and Saturday if the club hires a special guest DJ. **Hongik Club Day** (www .clubculture.or.kr) happens on the last Friday of the month: W15,000 gets you free entrance to 15 clubs and a map.

Hole (Map p94; admission W5000 Mon-Fri, W10,000 weeknights; ⏰ 8pm-5am) Break out your best oversized football jersey and twist that baseball cap sideways, because American hip-hop is full on at this smoky basement club. Oh, and don't forget the badass attitude.

M2 (Map p94; admission W10,000-15,000; ⏰ 8pm-5am Mon-Fri, 6pm-6am Sat & Sun) Everybody dances facing the DJ.

Macondo (Map p94; admission free Mon-Thu, W5000 Fri & Sat; ⏰ 7-11.30pm Mon-Thu, 7pm-5am Fri & Sat) Free meringue and salsa lessons (7.30pm to 8.30pm, Monday to Thursday, and Saturday).

Club Otwo (Map p94; admission W10,000; ⏰ 9pm-2am Mon-Fri, to 4am Sat & Sun) Features a DJ booth modelled after the bridge of the *USS Enterprise*.

Sk@ (Map p94; admission Sun-Thu W5000, Fri & Sat W10,000; ⏰ 6pm-5am, to 6am Sat & Sun) The volume may cause ears to bleed.

Sport

Seoul has two pro basketball teams, the SK Knights and the Samsung Thunders. Home court for both is the Jamsil Gymnasium (Map pp98–9); take Line 2 to Sports Complex station, Exit 8. Seoul's professional football club, FC Seoul, plays in the World Cup Stadium (Map pp84–5).

Baseball is supposedly Korea's number-one sport but that's hard to figure because weeknight attendance can be thin. The LG Twins and Doosan Bears play at Jamsil Baseball Stadium (Map pp98–9); take Line 2 to Sports Complex station, Exit 5 or 6. Advanced ticket purchases are almost never required. Walk up to the ticket booth on game day (adult/youth W8000/6000 weekdays, add W2000 weekends) and you might be asked what team you prefer: boisterous home-team fans sit on the first base line, more sedate visitors near third base. Food options outside the stadium include *pajeon* and dried squid, and inside the stadium a cup of frothy draft beer costs W3000.

Most weekday and Saturday games begin at 6.30pm. Sunday and holiday games start at 2pm in April, May, June and September, and at 5pm in July and August.

Theatre Restaurants

Korea House (Map pp92-3; ☎ 2266 9101; www.koreahouse .or.kr; ☺ lunch noon-2pm, dinner 5.30-7pm & 7.20-8.50pm Mon-Sat, 6.30-8pm Sun) Dining like royalty isn't cheap. Choose the dinner-show package, which includes a one-hour dance, *pansori* (traditional opera) song and music spectacle in a *hanok* building, and pay between W59,000 and W100,000 per person. Skip the meal and attend the show for W29,000. Performances begin at 7pm and 8.50pm except Sunday (one show at 8pm). Lunch is available in the *hanok* building, but there's no performance. Take Line 2 or 3 to Chungmuro station, Exit 3.

Sheraton Grande Walkerhill Hotel (Map pp84-5; ☎ 455 5000; walkerhill.co.kr) This glitzy 1½-hour show hits the stage in the Gayagum Theatre at 6pm and 8.40pm (except Wednesday, every night in December), with traditional Korean music and dance and a Western-style cabaret. Dinner and show costs W90,000 to W130,000; the wine-and-show option costs W65,000.

Theatres

Nanta Theatre (Map pp92-3; ☎ 739 8288; nanta.co.kr; ticket W20,000-60,000) This long-running percussion show set in a kitchen blends drumming, audience participation and slapstick comedy. Shows start at 4pm and 8pm (Monday to Saturday) with an extra performance at 1pm on Saturday and two shows Sunday and holidays (3pm and 8pm). Take Line 1 to City Hall, Exit 1, turn onto the lane close to Deoksugung's gate and follow the road along the stonewall.

Chongdong Theatre (Map pp92-3; ☎ 751 1500; www .chongdong.com; ticket W30,000-40,000) Traditional Korean music, *pansori* singing, *samul·nori* (Koran percussion) and fan-dancing take the stage six days a week (not Monday). The 70-minute performance starts at 8pm (April to November) and 4pm (December to March). English subtitles on a screen explain the songs. It's on the road to Nanta Theatre.

Tokebi Storm (Map pp92-3; ☎ 739 8288; www.tokebi storm.com; ticket W40,000-50,000; ☺ 8pm Tue-Sun, 4pm & 8pm Sat, 3pm Sun & holidays, closed Mon) What do producers do when they see a nonverbal, percussion show become a hit? They make another one. Looking like Nanta, which looks like Stomp, this show uses spirits from another world. It's in a newspaper building past Nanta Theatre.

Other recommendations:

Seoul Arts Centre (Map pp84-5; ☎ 580 1300; www .sac.or.kr) You can see *Carmen* and *The Nutcracker* here. Take Line 3 to Nambu bus terminal station, Exit 5, walk straight to the second light and turn left. The centre is five minutes down the road.

National Centre for Korean Traditional Performing Arts (Map pp84-5; ☎ 580 3300; www.ncktpa.go.kr/eng /index_eng.jsp; tickets W8000-10,000) Holds weekly performances Tuesday (7.30pm March to December except mid-July to mid-August), Thursday (7.30pm March to July, September to December) and Saturday (5pm weekly). It's down the road from the Seoul Arts Centre.

Sejong Centre for the Performing Arts (Map pp88-9; ☎ 399 1700; www.sejongpac.or.kr) The sopranos regularly appear at this attractive downtown complex along with baritones, mezzo-sopranos and, if you're 'lucky', Michael Bolton.

Hakjeon Green Theatre (Map p95; ☎ 742 8454; www.hakchon.co.kr; W28,000; ☺ 7.30pm Tue-Fri, 4pm Sun, 4pm & 7.30pm Sat) Mostly Korean musicals with English subtitles on a screen (Wednesday, Friday, Sunday).

SHOPPING

Are you struggling with this year's fashion decisions? Answers to all your stylish questions can be found in Seoul's classy and unabashedly over-the-top department stores. One Galleria department store (Map pp96-7) in Apgujeong wasn't sufficient to meet the demand for W200,000 golf shirts so they built another across the street. Running low on Coco Chanel? Skip over to Lotte department store (Map pp92-3) in Myeongdong where a bottle of scent costs W154,000.

It's never too early to get the kids hooked on the Lotte brand, so walk across the street to **Lotte Young Plaza** (Map pp92-3; ☺ 11.30am-9pm). Comparatively downmarket Hyundai department stores are in Apgujeong (Map pp96-7), the **COEX Mall** (Map pp88-9; ☺ 10am-10pm) and Sinchon (Map p94). In Namdaemun, there's a Shinsegae department store (Map pp92-3).

Duty-free shops are scattered around Seoul with the usual perfumes, cameras, watches, cigarettes and souvenirs. Centrally located **Donghwa** (Map pp88-9; ☺ 9.30am-8.30pm) has a wide choice of luxury items. It's in the tall building near the corner. Line 5 to Gwanghwamun, Exit 6.

If you're after electronics, head to **Techno Mart** (Map pp98-9; 10am-8pm), which has eight floors filled with digital cameras, TVs, computers and software. Most major brand names are represented here. The Microsoft dealer, **Ace Soft** (☎ 3424 7911), on the 7th floor sells OEM XP in English (home W120,000, professional W160,000). Take Line 2 to Gangbyeon station, Exit 2.

Ahyeondong Wedding Street

It's probably a coincidence that this street (Map p94) of fairy-tale dreams, with 200 wedding outfitters, is located next to Ehwa Women's University. Stroll down the street and you've got yourself a free fashion show. One of the more unique shops is **She's** (Map p94; ☎ 393 9925; 10am-8pm, closed 2nd & 4th Tue), where Rococo dresses cost up to W1 million. Line 2 to Ewha Women's University station, Exit 4.

Apgujeong

This posh area (Map pp96-7) has deluxe department stores, boutiques and high-class hairdressers as well as a dazzling array of nail boutiques and plastic surgeons all promising to beautify, tonify and electrify.

Nail Gallery (Map pp96-7; ☎ 549 0101; 10.30am-10.30pm) When was the last time you took a good look at your cuticles? If you frequent Apgujeong with any regularity, the answer is probably last week. Manicures cost W20,000, pedicures W45,000. Men are welcome, but they have bigger digits, so add W5000.

Nacta (Map pp96-7; ☎ 512 9947; 11am-10.30pm) Getting a tattoo is *verboten* in Korea, so the next best thing is piercing. You can get just about any body part stuck, including the navel (W40,000).

Holics (Map pp96-7; ☎ 3444 0599; frames W250,000; 11am-10pm Mon-Fri, to 9pm Sat & Sun) Walk around Apgujeong for an afternoon and it will become obvious that the most fashionable ladies are sporting gaudy frames like Jackie Onassis used to wear. If you simply must have the latest in eyewear, Holics is the choice.

Taste Maximum (Map pp96-7; ☎ 3444 7021; noon-10pm) With designs by up-and-coming Korean designer Kim Gyu-sik, this is the vogue boutique for Korean-Americans looking to spruce up their nightclub wardrobe. Jeans start at W100,000 while a custom-fitted vest starts at W300,000.

Insadong

Small art galleries display paintings, while art-and-craft shops sell pottery, antiques and calligraphy brushes. Cassettes of chanting and clothing can be bought in shops around Jogyesa.

Antique Watch (Map pp88-9; ☎ 735 2700; 10.30am-7pm Mon-Sat) Hey buddy, wanna buy a watch? Then step inside this curio of eclectic timepieces. Some time machines date back to 19th-century France including the 2m-high swing clock that costs W35 million. Cuckoos, grandfathers and mantelpieces are available as well as a sizeable collection of pocket and wristwatches dating from around the early 20th century.

Beautiful Tea Museum (Map pp88-9; ☎ 735 6678; 10am-10.30pm) This exquisite building houses a delightful collection of tea paraphernalia. It's also a place to learn about the surprisingly complex world of green tea. Premium tea – which can run as high W18,000 per pot – is as full bodied as good wine. Sets of premium tea cost W30,000 to W80,000.

Samcheongdong

The shops here are so interesting men often find themselves unexpectedly engrossed in a feminine form of behaviour: window shopping. One-of-a-kind clothing, funky jewellery and antiques are all part of the mix, with prices that sometimes make Apgujeong look affordable.

Vintage (Map pp88-9; ☎ 722 2509; noon-9pm) Clothing, furniture and jewellery imported from Europe are found here. Some items, such as the W700,000 dress, appear overpriced, while the stunning cameo looks like a bargain at W150,000.

Comble (Map pp88-9G; ☎ 720 1146; 10.30am-8.30pm) Here's a fun hat store. These beautiful pieces designed by Choi Hye-jung cover the spectrum of headgear, from flappers to straw brims. Most cost between W100,000 and W300,000. Customers are welcome to try on a hat and admire themselves in the mirror.

Lamove (Map pp88-9; ☎ 736 4067; noon-7pm) One-of-a-kind accessories are available in this artsy shop with an avocado décor. Jewellery, bags and broaches are priced between W45,000 and W500,000.

Itaewon

Dandy's Grocery (Map p91; ☎ 796 2390; 9am-8pm) Craving macaroni and cheese? Then this shop

TOP MARKETS

Dongdaemun Market

This massive collection of traditional markets, street stalls and department stores (Map pp86–7) has a dizzying array of choices that would take most serious shoppers a week to plough through. The eastern side of the market generally caters to the wholesale trade and opens late (10.30pm), while stores in the western section, such as Migliore and Doota, open early and close late (10.30am to 5am). A market map is available in the tourist information office near the old baseball stadium (9am to 10pm). Take Line 1 to Dongdaemun station, Exit 7.

Jang·anpyeong Antique Market

If it's old and Korean, you'll probably find it in this delightful antique market (Map pp84–5) spread out over several buildings. Just outside the subway exit, Samhee buildings 5 and 6 contain ceramics, paintings, stone statues and more all piled up in small, cluttered shops. Interesting pieces include a stunning 1m swinging bell in a wooden frame at **Donggo Hwarang** (☎ 927 7650; stall 131, Samhee Bldg 6; 10am-9pm, Mon-Fri). The asking price is W5 million.

Down the street, the Jang·anpyeong building has a wider selection of large pieces including a 3m stone pagoda at **Jinbodang** (☎ 2249 0002; stall 112; 10am-7pm, closed 1st & 3rd Sun), costing W4 million. Upstairs, there's a collection of Chinese medicine cabinets with 40 or so drawers, each with a different Chinese inscription. At **Jang·an Antiques** (☎ 2244 1922; 10am-7pm, closed 1st & 3rd Sun) reproductions cost W250,000, while the asking price for a 150-year-old piece is W7.5 million.

Take Line 5 to Dapsimni station, Exit 2. At street level, look left and you'll see a sign pointing to Samhee 5 and 6. Walk straight for 10 minutes to the Jang·anpyeong building; it's just past the German-car dealership. Many shops are closed weekends and most shut down for summer vacation, which usually runs from the end of July to mid-August.

Namdaemun Market

It doesn't have the same range of goods as Dongdaemun, but this fun market (Map pp92–3) is easier to navigate, which makes for a more interesting day of exploring. There's a good mix of traditional shops as well as day-and-night retail and wholesale markets, fashion malls and **Shinsegae department store** (10.30am-8pm). Souvenir hunters looking for a gift for someone who likes to cook should visit the **Samseong Gown** (Map pp92–3; ☎ 752 0081; 6am-6pm Mon-Sat), where a Japanese sushi-chef jacket costs W24,000. A market map is available from the tourist information booth (8.30am to 6pm).

Noryangjin Fish Market

Every kind of marine life is swimming around in tanks, buckets and bowls at this large fish market (Map p100). It's like a free aquarium show, except you can eat the animals. Giant octopuses, stingray and mussels along with a selection of unknown sea creatures are on view and on sale. A kilogram of prawns costs W20,000, while a king crab goes for W17,000 per kilogram. Take Line 1 to Noryangjin station, Exit 1, cross the bridge and walk down the stairs to the fish market.

Yongsan Electronics Market & Techno Mart

It would take several days to fully explore the merchandise available at this **market** (Map pp96-7; 9.30am-7.30pm, closed 1st & 3rd Sun), thought to be the largest in Asia. There are hundreds of shops spread around 22 markets, though the biggest collection is concentrated in a few buildings such as Terminal Electronics Market, Sonin, Najin and iPark Mall. The latest computers, mobile phones, cameras, DVD players and wide-screen digital TVs are here. Be sure to enquire about warranties and inspect your purchases carefully because not everything is on the up-and-up.

English-language computer software is available at **Wells Software** (☎ 701 8188; 10am-7pm Mon-Fri), which stocks OEM XP Home (W120,000) and Professional (W180,000). It's located on the 4th floor of the Terminal Electronics Market building. Take Line 1 to Yongsan station, Exit 3.

SEOUL

of imported goods in front of Hannam Supermarket is a must-visit. Cereals, Quaker Oats, Crisco shortening and impossible-to-find salt-and-vinegar chips are here. Expats outside Seoul can phone in an order (minimum W50,000), which will be shipped by Mr Kim. Before shipment, you pay through a bank transfer. You also pay transport costs COD.

Hannam Supermarket (Map p91; ☎ 702 3313; ☺ 8.30am-8pm) The selection of Western food is not exceptional, but they have hard-to-find items like lasagna pasta. It's a 20-minute walk from Itaewon, or take Line 6 to Hangangjin station, Exit 2, turn right at the corner and mount the overhead crosswalk steps, then walk right – it's in the basement of the Volvo building.

Young Star (Map p91; ☎ 795 1939; ☺ 9am-10pm) Men struggle to find meaningful souvenirs. Ornamental key tags look good but usually end up in the trash. That's why intelligent male shoppers come to Young Star to buy their partner a handmade belly-dancing outfit. There are heaps of options including a stimulating aqua-blue number. It's the gift that keeps on giving. English is not spoken here, so you'll need measurements in hand. It's located at the top of the staircase opposite the International Clinic.

New York Tailor (Map p91; ☎ 749 8222; ☺ 10am-8pm) You may wonder why there are so many photographs of generals and admirals – this is where US military heavy hitters come for a civilian suit. A 100% wool, made-to-measure jacket and two pants start at W390,000.

What the Book? (Map p91; ☎ 797 2342; www .whatthebook.com; ☺ 10am-8pm Mon-Sat, noon-8pm Sun) A good selection of new and second-hand English-language titles is available here. This shop also operates a reliable online service with access to thousands of titles.

Supreme Optical (Map p91; ☎ 795 6423; ☺ 9.30am-8pm, closed 2nd & 4th Tue) You've heard that Korea has great prices on glasses – check it out for yourself because seeing is believing. The selection isn't large, but the staff speak English. Frames start at W30,000 and you can get an eye examination onsite.

DMZ (Map p91; ☎ 794 7930; ☺ 9.30am-9pm, closed 2nd & 4th Wed) Need a WWII German tank helmet? How about a Korean War compass watch? You'll find both and a lot more in this musty military surplus store. MP helmets, military insignia and an LA police badge are also here. From the Hamilton Hotel, cross the street and walk right, turn left at the street just before McDonalds.

Myeongdong

If it's got a label, you'll probably find it in Myeongdong (Map pp92–3). The streets fill up every evening with shoppers, hawkers and people shouting out the latest sale into a megaphone. It can be an overwhelming experience that borders on sensory overload, as street vendors take over a couple of roads offering unusual snacks – like peanut-butter-flavoured squid – and an inexhaustible selection of plastic accessories.

GETTING THERE & AWAY
Air

For details of airline companies and flights in and out of Seoul, see p395.

INCHEON INTERNATIONAL AIRPORT

Spacious **Incheon International Airport** (Map p140; ☎ 032 741 0114; www.airport.or.kr), 52km west of Seoul, handles most of the country's international flights with limited domestic connections to Jejudo, Busan and Daegu.

International arrivals are on the 1st floor, where you'll find **tourist information centres** (☺ 7am-10pm), ATMs and **foreign currency exchange booths** (☺ 5am-9pm); a currency-exchange booth near the baggage-claim area inside the arrivals terminal is open until the last flight arrives. Mobile phones can be rented at **KT** (☺ 24hr) and **LG Telecom** (☺ 24hr) – hire rates are W3000 per day plus a local calling charge of W600 per minute. If you lose the phone there's a W600,000 replacement fee. Outside the airport doors, buses depart for destinations in Seoul and elsewhere. In the basement, **Inha University Hospital** (☎ 743 3119; ☺ 24hr) charges W20,000 for a consultation. A **dentist** (☺ 9am-5pm Mon-Fri) is also available.

The 3rd-floor departures area has places to eat and drink. Banks in the retail section beyond immigration control allow you to exchange *won* before leaving the country. To obtain a tax refund on goods purchased at shops participating in the tax-refund scheme, show the goods and receipts to a customs officer at the check-in counter. Once past immigration control, take the stamped receipt to a **Global Refund counter** (☺ 7am-9pm) to get your money.

Incheon Airport Transit Hotel (☎ 743 3000; www .airgardenhotel.com; 6hr r/deluxe/ste W45,000/55,000/80,000; ✖ ▣) rents nonsmoking rooms to transit passengers on a short-term basis. Add 21% for tax and service and W12,000 for double occupancy.

GIMPO INTERNATIONAL AIRPORT

Direct flights link **Gimpo International Airport** (김포국제공항) (Map pp84-5; http://gimpo.airport .co.kr), 18km west of the city centre, with 11 cities via Korean Air and Asiana. The 1st floor is for arrivals, the 2nd floor is for checking in and the 3rd floor is for departures. The **tourist information centre** (✆ 9am-9pm) offers free internet access. Airport services include banks, car-hire counters and restaurants. The **First Aid Centre** (✆ 6am-10pm) has a doctor available or on call.

KOREA CITY AIR TERMINAL

Check your luggage and go through customs and immigration procedures at the **Korea City Air Terminal** (KCAT; www.kcat.co.kr; ✆ approx 5.30am-6.30pm). Located in the **COEX Mall's** (Map pp98-9; ☎ 551 0077) World Trade Centre, this service is available only for Korean Air and Asiana passengers. Passengers with goods to declare at customs that are stored inside checked bags may use this terminal: anyone with goods to declare in a carry-on bag must check-in at the airport. Nonstop buses run every 10 minutes to Incheon (W13,000) or Gimpo (W6000) airports. Allow 90 minutes to get from KCAT to Incheon and 60 minutes to Gimpo airport.

Bus

There are three kinds of buses. Inter-city buses are usually older vehicles and may make frequent stops. The major differences between express and deluxe buses are price and comfort: deluxe buses have fewer but wider seats, ample legroom and more expensive tickets. Some deluxe buses depart after midnight, which comes with a 10% surcharge.

The Seoul express bus terminal (Map pp96-7)connects with major cities and has two buildings: the Gyeongbu-Gumi-Yeongdong terminal and Honamseon terminal. The former connects with cities like Busan (W20,000), Daegu (W14,000) and Daejeon (W7600); the latter – connected to the Central City complex – has routes to the Jeolla provinces and southern coastal area. Destinations include Mokpo (W16,000) and Jeonju (W10,000). Take Line 3 to Express Bus Terminal station and follow the signs for the Gyeongbu or Honamseon line.

Seoul's other bus terminals include the following:

Dong-Seoul Bus Terminal (Map pp98-9) Has connections to some major cities and communities in the eastern part of the country. Take Line 2 to Gangbyeon Station, Exit 4.

Nambu Bus Terminal (Map pp96-7) Services towns south of Seoul. Take Line 3 to Nambu Bus Terminal station, Exit 5.

Sangbong Bus Terminal (Map pp84-5) Has limited service to cities north and east of Seoul. Take Line 7 to Sangbong station, Exit 2. It's opposite an E-Mart store.

Sinchon Bus Terminal (Map p94) Has services to Gwanghwado, an island northwest of Seoul. Take Line 2 to Sinchon station, Exit 7.

Train

There are three major train stations in Seoul, all close to a Line 1 subway station. Most trains leave Seoul station (Map pp92-3), which has high-speed Korea Train Express (KTX), *Saemaul* (express) and *Mugunghwa* (semi-express) services to many parts of the country. KTX destinations and one-way fares from Seoul station include Busan (W44,800) and Daejeon (W19,500). Current KTX trains take about two hours and 40 minutes between Seoul and Busan. If the last leg of track construction is completed on schedule in 2008, that ride will take less than two hours.

Yongsan station (Map pp96-7) handles KTX and train connections with South Chungcheong and the Jeolla provinces; KTX fares include Gwangju (W33,300) and Mokpo (W38,000). There is no KTX service from Cheongnyangni station (Map pp84-5), but there are *Saemaul* and *Mugunghwa* connections. *Saemaul* services include Wonju (W9000) and Andong (W21,000). For current fares and detailed schedules visit the Korea National Railroad website (www.korail.go.kr).

Yeongdeungpo Station (영등포역) near Yeouido is a major *Saemaul/Mugunghwa* station for those south of the river (like the other three, it's also a short walk from a Line 1 subway station). Yeongdeungpo was, until recently, a KTX station as well, but the government is pushing people to use the Gwangmyeong Station built exclusively for KTX service. Gwangmyeong is technically outside Seoul city limits, but it is accessible to those in the southwestern part of the capital (but not on Line 1).

GETTING AROUND
To/From the Airport

Two types of buses run from Incheon international airport to Seoul: standard city limousine buses (W8000) operate from 5am to 11pm, KAL deluxe limousine buses (W13,000) take passengers to major hotels. Buses usually run every 15 minutes and take up to 100 minutes.

Regular taxis to Seoul cost around W40,000, while a deluxe could cost W80,000 depending on traffic. Expect an expressway toll of W6700 to be added to the fare, and if you travel after midnight a 20% premium.

Buses run between Incheon and Gimpo airports (W4500, 30 minutes, every 10 minutes) along a special road. If your accommodation in Seoul is near a subway station, you could take a bus to Gimpo airport. Walk 10 minutes and you've got access to Line 5 and a 50-minute ride to downtown. A regular taxi ride from Gimpo to the city centre costs W20,000, while a deluxe taxi could set you back W30,000.

At the time of writing, a rail link promising to simplify travel to and from Incheon airport was under construction. Stage 1, scheduled for completion during the first half of 2007, will establish a 41km train connection between Incheon and Gimpo airports, while Stage 2 will connect Gimpo airport and Seoul station, with trains travelling up to 150km/h. The projected completion date for Stage 2 is 2009.

CITY LIMOUSINE BUS ROUTES

Limousine buses from Incheon International Airport are listed below, with bus numbers, route names and major stops.

600 (Jamsil) Seoul express bus terminal, Samseong station, Lotte World

601 (Dongdaemun) Hapjeongdong, Sinchon, City Hall, Jongno, Dongdaemun

602 (Cheongnyangni) Hapjeong station, Seokyo Hotel, Sinchon station, Gwanghwamun, YMCA

602-1 (Sungshin Women's University) World Cup Stadium, An-guk-dong, Daehangno

603 (Guro) Mokdong Ogeori, Guro station

604 (Geumcheon-gu Office) Nambu cargo terminal, Novotel Hotel

605 (City Hall) Mapo, Seoul station, City Hall, Gwanghwamun

606 (Jamsil) Seoul express bus terminal, Samseong station, Lotte World, Olympic Park

607 (Songjeong station)

608 (Yeongdeungpo station) Dangsan station

609 (Daechi station) Seoul express bus terminal, Gangnam station, Yangjae station

KAL LIMOUSINE BUS ROUTES

KAL1 (City Hall) KAL Building, Lotte Hotel, Koreana Hotel.

KAL2 (Namsan) Seoul Station, Hilton Hotel, Shilla Hotel, Holiday Inn

KAL3 (Gangnam) Renaissance Hotel, Grand Inter-Continental Hotel, COEX Inter-Continental Hotel

KAL4 (Jamsil) Sheraton Grande Walkerhill Hotel, Dong-Seoul bus terminal, Lotte World

Direct (KCAT) Korea City Air Terminal

Direct (Seoul express bus terminal)

Direct (Seoul station)

Itaewon 63 Building, Itaewon Hotel

Dobong & Nowon Gireum station, Hagye station, Sofia

Public Transport

BUS

The bus system is good but it's complex and ill suited for travellers who don't understand Korean. Buses have different colours indicating different travel areas: yellow buses circulate downtown; red buses travel in the metropolitan area; green buses connect subway stations with downtown; blue buses travel to the suburbs. Fares start at W800 and increase depending on the distance travelled. Bus fare can be paid using the rechargeable transport card called the T-Money card, which can be bought for W2500 at any subway station booth; add credits in multiples of W1000. You can also use it at stores that display the T-Money sign.

SUBWAY

Seoul's **subway system** (www.seoulsubway.co.kr, www.smrt.co.kr) is reliable and cheap. Trains run every few minutes from 5.30am to around midnight and many subway stations have lifts or stair lifts for wheelchairs. Lockers are available, though most are too small to take a full-sized backpack. Every station is well-signed in English and the system is very user friendly. The basic one-way subway fare is W900 and covers most of Seoul. Hour-long trips cost around W1500. The T-Money card provides a small discount on fares and saves the hassle of buying a ticket for each trip.

Taxi

Regular taxis are a good deal for short trips. The basic fare for 2km is W1600 and rises W100 for every 168m or 41 seconds after that. A 20% surcharge is levied between midnight and 4am. Deluxe taxis are black with a yellow stripe and cost W4000 for the first 3km and W200 for every 205m or 50 seconds, but they don't have a late-night surcharge. Few taxi drivers speak English, but most taxis have a free interpretation service whereby an interpreter talks to the taxi driver and to you by phone. All taxis are metered and tipping is not required.

Gyeonggi-do 경기도

The province of Gyeonggi-do hugs Seoul like a reverse letter 'C,' providing excellent day trips or longer expeditions to some of Korea's gems. Often overlooked due to its proximity to the *Bladerunner*-esque cityscape that is Seoul, Gyeonggi-do is a varied province: rivers and rice fields, shrines and scenery, timeless temples and ever-present smiles. Slip into the quiet fishing life on a West Sea island, walk on a deserted beach or a wave-smoothed mud flat, or go inland and take in fantastic vistas from hiking destinations such as Bukhansan National Park or Namhan Sanseong Provincial Park.

For a chilling reminder of cold-war animosities and the almost anachronistic threat of war, hop on a DMZ-bound tour bus and catch glimpses of North Korea, barbed wire and the paradox of Panmunjom. Shoppers looking to take home a piece of Korean art should hit the Korean Folk Village or Icheon Ceramic Village. When you've seen enough museums, travellers with children can enjoy Seoul Grand Park and Everland, or hit the slopes in winter for great skiing.

Suwon and Incheon are the area's biggest cities; the latter has its own local government and telephone code and is the port for ferries to nearby islands, Jejudo, and even China. Ganghwado, a nearby island, is still relatively unspoilt, and has dolmen (ancient tombs), a mountain-top altar, fortifications and an interesting history, making it a perfect place to recharge your batteries if Seoul's nightlife starts to wear thin.

HIGHLIGHTS

- Hike up to granite peaks and an ancient fortress in **Bukhansan National Park** (p141)
- Get dirty on the amazing mud flats of the **West Sea Islands** (p153)
- Feel the chill of the Cold War at **Panmunjom** (p158) in the DMZ
- Go back in time at the rustic, laid-back **Korean Folk Village** (p147)
- Stroll around **Suwon** (p144) and admire its neon charms
- Head to **Icheon** (p147) for pottery and relaxing hot spas

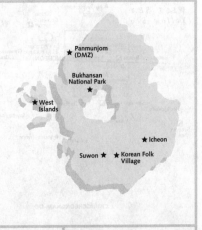

- ★ Panmunjom (DMZ)
- ★ Bukhansan National Park
- ★ West Islands
- ★ Icheon
- ★ Suwon
- ★ Korean Folk Village

| ▪ TELEPHONE CODE: 031 | ▪ POPULATION: 10.3 MILLION | ▪ AREA: 10.189 SQ KM |

History

Gyeonggi-do's history is rife with pilgrimages, plundering, plots and plans, infiltrations, defeats and surrenders. Its nearby islands and many coves have been used repeatedly to gain access to Seoul or defend against attacks from China, Japan, France and the United States. Its current border with North Korea makes it a front line for this war (technically, a formal peace treaty ending the Korean War was never signed), and even today tunnel-detection teams operate in hopes of fending off North Korean incursions.

National & Provincial Parks

Gyeonggi-do is so close to Seoul that most of its parks are easy day trips, though hikers may want to budget more time to stop and smell the flowers along the way. The closest is Bukhansan, a beautiful park with a serene peak that overlooks Seoul. Its proximity to this giant metropolis means that the serenity is often shared with hundreds of other folks also looking to get away from it all; minimise the crowds by starting early or visiting during the week.

Namhan Sanseong Provincial Park is nearby, an easy day trip from Seoul that offers hiking, wildflower and bird viewing, and interesting meandering along ancient fortress walls.

Also nearby is Suraksan (p143), not a national park proper, but still a beautiful area well worth visiting if time allows.

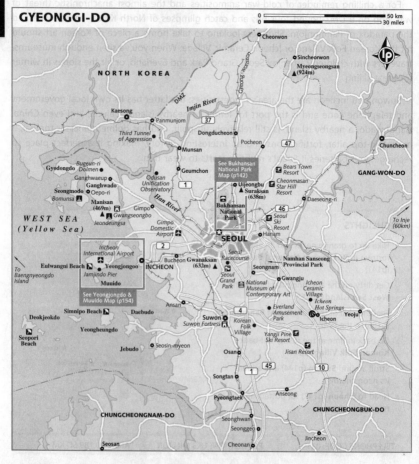

GYEONGGI-DO

0 — 50 km
0 — 30 miles

Getting There & Around

All of Gyeonggi-do is within day-trip distance of Seoul, making it a great place to escape to, even if you don't have a lot of time. Buses and trains, and in some places even subway lines, make for speedy, inexpensive travel. Taxis are economical, even for longer jaunts, but are especially useful for quick trips once you've reached your destination.

SEOUL GRAND PARK 서울대공원

The **zoo** (☎ 02-500 7114; http://grandpark.seoul.go.kr; adult/youth/child W3000/2000/1000; ♥ 9am-7pm Apr-Sep, 9am-6pm Oct-Mar) in the park is set among the forested hillsides south of Seoul. A river runs through the park and families picnic along its shady banks. You can hike along a number of marked trails which are 2km to 6km long. Admission is cheaper from November to March (adult/youth/child W1500/1200/700).

The zoo is home to a long list of exotic creatures including the popular African ones, and has a long history of breeding successes, including tigers and panda bears. Cage quality varies: some are lush and green (especially the aviary), others are muddy and a bit depressing. The zoo features cranes, swans, pelicans and other large birds, and an indoor botanic garden houses a forest of cacti, numerous orchids and carnivorous pitcher plants. Ants and swimming beetles are on display in a 'miniature creature' exhibit, plus there's 'Squirrel Plaza' and other displays.

A fun dolphin-and-seal show costs W1500 and shows three to four times per day. If you still haven't gotten your fill of animal shows, you can watch a girl dressed in pink chase flamingos around to the cheers of kids and crowds. It's cute, and the birds probably need a little exercise, but they don't do much more than run around.

The large and striking **National Museum of Contemporary Art** (☎ 02-2188 6000; www.moca.go.kr; adult/youth/child W1000/500/free; ♥ 9am-6pm Tue-Sun, 9am-5pm Nov-Feb) is spread over three floors and also has sculptures in the garden. You are unlikely to miss one exhibit: a huge pagoda-shaped video installation that is 18m high and uses 1000 flickering screens to make a comment on our increasingly electronic universe. It's the work of Paik Nam-june, a video artist with an international reputation, and is entitled *The More the Better*. Free films are shown on Saturday during August, concerts are held in July and music and dance performances are put on in

October. To get there, walk up to the entrance of Seoul Grand Park and bear left.

Getting There & Away

Take subway Line 4 to Seoul Grand Park station (W900), which is 45 minutes from City Hall. Leave by Exit 2 and then either walk (10 minutes) or take an elephant-inspired **tram** (adult/child W600/500) to the entrance of the park. Another option is to take the **cable car** (adult/child W4000/2000). A free shuttle bus runs every 20 minutes from the subway station (outside Exit 4) to the National Museum of Contemporary Art, or it's a 20-minute walk. A combo ticket includes the tram, chairlift and zoo admission at a slight discount off the individual fares.

BUKHANSAN NATIONAL PARK
북한산 국립공원

This **national park** (☎ 02-909 0497; www.npa.or.kr; adult/youth/child W1600/600/300; ♥ sunrise-sunset), made up of a granite peak and surrounding area, is visible from the city itself (and is so close that it's possible to visit by subway). It offers sublime vistas of mist-shrouded mountains, maple leaves, rushing streams and remote temples. The park is sometimes crowded, especially on weekends. Rock climbers particularly enjoy Insubong (810m), which is a free-climber's dream, with some of the best multipitch climbing in Asia and routes of all grades.

Camping is possible in summer or you can stay in basic mountain huts, but they are not usually open in winter. During peak periods (10 July to 20 August and 1 October to 14 November), on public holidays and weekends, some huts and camping grounds have an online reservation system (www.npa.or.kr).

The following two hikes are recommended – both are all-day hikes so you need to be reasonably fit to complete the full course. If your energy begins to flag, consider taking a swig of the Korean hiker's friend: pine-needle *soju* (local vodka-like brew). One mouthful should be enough to help you make it to the top. Well, that's what Koreans claim anyway.

Baegundae Hike 백운대

This moderate-to-strenuous hike takes six hours, including short breaks.

Leave Gupabal station by Exit 1, walk straight for 100m to the bus stop and take bus 704 (W900, 10 minutes, every 15 minutes) to the Bukhansan bus stop. Get off with the other

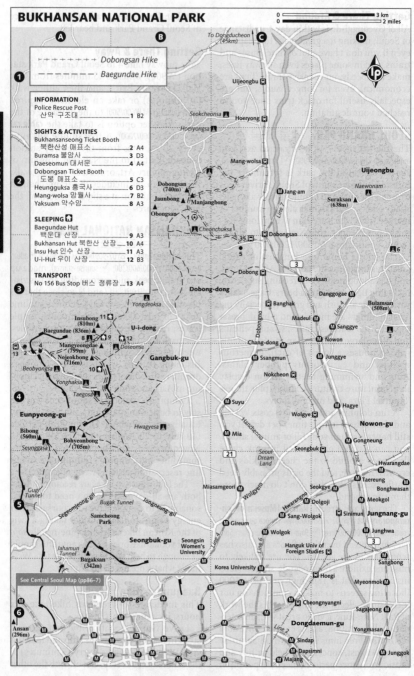

BUKHANSAN NATIONAL PARK

0 —————— 3 km
0 —————— 2 miles

├─┼─┼─┼─┼─┼─┤ *Dobongsan Hike*

─ ─ ─ ─ ─ ─ ─ *Baegundae Hike*

INFORMATION
Police Rescue Post
산악 구조대 **1** B2

SIGHTS & ACTIVITIES
Bukhansanseong Ticket Booth
북한산성 매표소 **2** A4
Buramsa 불암사 **3** D3
Daeseomun 대서문 **4** A4
Dobongsan Ticket Booth
도봉 매표소 **5** C3
Heungguksa 흥국사 **6** D3
Mang-wolsa 망월사 **7** B2
Yaksuam 약수암 **8** A3

SLEEPING
Baegundae Hut
백운대 산장 **9** A3
Bukhansan Hut 북한산 산장 **10** A4
Insu Hut 인수 산장 **11** A3
U-i-Hut 우이 산장 **12** B3

TRANSPORT
No 156 Bus Stop 버스 정류장 **13** A4

hikers, walk straight and then turn right. The ticket office is 500m from the bus stop.

The park's highest peak, Baegundae (836m), is 4km or two hours away. A five-minute walk brings you to the fortress wall and Daeseomun gate. Fifteen minutes after leaving the gate, the road crosses a bridge. Fork left following the sign to Baegundae and keep a look out for little striped ground squirrels. Spring water is available at Yaksuam, a hermitage that you reach 45 minutes after leaving the road. Past Yaksuam there are stairs up to another fortress gate, and then you use metal cables to haul yourself up Baegundae peak. Surrounded by granite cliffs and with a 360-degree view, it's a top-of-the-world feeling.

Dobongsan Hike 도봉산

Dobongsan is a mountain with three rocky peaks. This cool, shady 10km hike takes about five hours, but add time for a picnic lunch. Moderate fitness is required.

Take subway Line 1 north to Dobongsan station (W900). It takes 45 minutes from City Hall if your train goes all the way (not all do). Exit the station and follow the other hikers across the road, through the market and food stalls and past a bus terminal to the ticket booth.

Keep on the main path, following the sign to Jaunbong, one of Dobongsan's peaks, which is 2.7km away. Five minutes past the spring, turn right, following the sign to Manjangbong (another Dobongsan peak). Keep a look out for woodpeckers and squirrels.

About an hour from the subway station, you arrive at Dobong Hut. Bear right following the sign to Mang·wolsa. Then follow signs to Jaunbong, go past the police rescue post and up the final steep and rocky stretch to the top which is between two rocky peaks. Here the adventure begins as you scramble down a ravine helped by metal cables, then up and along a rocky ridge and through narrow crevices.

Follow the signs, descend via Mang·wolsa or turn right at the sign marked 'Wondobong Ticket Box' for a less-used short cut down the hillside past a small spring. Half an hour from the right turn you join the main track down to the car park. Follow the road, bearing left as you enter the town, to Mang·wolsa subway station (Line 1).

SURAKSAN 수락산

To the east of Bukhansan National Park is Suraksan (638m), another attractive climbing

---

TOP FIVE CAMPING ESCAPES OUT OF SEOUL

- Bukhansan National Park (p141) – great hikes, awesome views and right in Seoul's backyard.

- Seoraksan National Park (p172) – one of the most gorgeous parks in all Korea, pretty at any time of year.

- Chiaksan National Park (p185) – lush greenery, rushing rivers and ancient temples abound.

- Gyeongpo Beach (p176) – hang out on the beach and party with a mellow, young-ish crowd.

- West Sea Islands (p153) – highlands, mud flats, beaches and ancient tombs.

---

and hiking area. It's not a national or provincial park, but expect crowds at the weekends or other peak times. One relatively easy hike is to take subway Line 4 to Danggogae station and hike up past Heungguksa to Suraksan peak, and then descend to Jang-am subway station. A shorter hike from Danggogae station is up to the top of Bulamsan (508m) and then on to Buramsa and down to Sanggye station. Either way you'll be glad you got out of the city, if only for the afternoon.

SEOUL RACECOURSE 서울 경마장

The **racecourse** (Map pp84-5; ☎ 509 2054; www.kra .co.kr; admission W800; ⊙ 9.30am-6pm Sat & Sun) has a comfy lounge area in the grandstand on the left for foreigners – take a lift to the 4th floor, turn right and it's near Block A. Short races over 1km or 2km take place every half hour between 11am and 5.30pm at the weekend, and there are night races in July and August as well. The racecourse is closed four weekends of the year – check the racing calendar on the website for details. There are plenty of canteens and fast-food outlets. The small **Equine Museum** (☎ 509-1287; admission free; ⊙ 9.30am-6pm) is worth a peek, with a modest but interesting collection of horse-related artefacts and displays.

Getting There & Away

To get there, take subway Line 4 to Seoul Racecourse station (W800) and leave by Exit 2. A covered walkway leads almost all the way to the entrance.

NAMHAN SANSEONG PROVINCIAL PARK 남한산성 도립공원

Completed in 1626, **Namhan Sanseong** (☎ 743-6610; www.namhansansung.or.kr), a temple/fortress complex and wall 20km southeast of downtown Seoul, is famous for its beautiful pine forests, wildflowers and oaks. It once guarded the city's southern entrance, while Bukhan Sanseong guarded the northern approaches. Buddhist monks – soldiers rather than pacifists in those days – lived here and kept watch. Numerous hiking options wind through the forests, some of them paralleling the old fortress wall, providing fantastic recreation in a site that's very accessible from Seoul.

SUWON 수원

pop 1.04 million / 120 sq km

Suwon, 48km south of Seoul, is the provincial capital of Gyeonggi-do and a city of sensual neon, exotic flavours, all-night discos and ancient history. The faithfully restored fortress of Hwaseong draws tourists from around the globe. It was built between 1794 and 1796 during the reign of King Jeongjo and has been designated a World Heritage site. Suwon is also close to the Korean Folk Village (p147) and makes an easy day trip from Seoul.

Information

The **main tourist information centre** (☎ 228 4672; www.suwon.ne.kr; ☯ 9am-6pm Mar-Oct, 9am-5pm Nov-Feb) is outside the railway station, and another **tourist information booth** (☯ 9am-6pm) is near Paldalmun at the start of the fortress walk. Numerous PC *bang* (PC방; internet room) offer internet access for about W1000 per hour.

Sights

HWASEONG 화성

Suwon's impressive **fortress wall** (admission free; ☯ 24hr), made of earth and faced with large stone blocks, stretches for 5.7km: 95% of it has been restored. Hiking round the wall with its command posts, observation towers, entrance gates and fire-beacon platform makes for a fascinating two-hour historical walk. Start at **Paldalmun**, also known as Nammun (South Gate), and follow the sign. Walk along the wall up to the top of **Paldalsan** (143m), a good viewpoint, where you might hear and see cuckoos.

HWASEONG HAENGGUNG 화성행궁

Before setting off around the fortress wall, you can visit the **palace** (http://ehs.suwon.ne.kr; admission W1000; ☯ 9am-5pm, Tue-Sun) that was originally built by King Jeongjo. Courtyard follows courtyard as you wander around the large walled complex where King Jeongjo's mother held her grand 61st-birthday party (the 61st is considered particularly auspicious and marked a major date in an ancient Korean's life). The palace was destroyed during the Japanese occupation, after which a hospital and school were built on the site. You can try your hand at traditional Korean archery here (W1000 for five arrows).

Festivals & Events

Every October a grand **royal procession** is re-enacted as part of Suwon's annual festival. It's a grand affair, with colourful costumes and lots of onlookers taking photographs. Visit http://shcf.or.kr for more info.

KING SEJONG THE GREAT: FATHER OF HAN·GEUL

Honoured as one of only two Korean rulers to have the moniker 'the Great,' Gyeonggi-do's own King Sejong might have had less impact on Korean history were it not for the wisdom of his two elder brothers. Both felt that it was their younger brother who was right for the throne, yet for him to ascend they would first have to be banished. By pretending to be boors, the two elders were deemed unfit to rule and the mandate finally fell on the third brother.

A good thing, too, as Sejong was indeed a remarkable man. Grasping that literacy was a key to a powerful nation, he created the *Han·geul* writing system, a simple alphabet that (it was said) 'anyone could learn within two months'. In addition to following the already accepted Confucian rules of yin and yang, the characters' shape actually instructed readers where they should place their tongues – making it even easier for uneducated peasants to grasp.

King Sejong was hated by the scholarly elite, who felt literacy was a birthright reserved solely for nobility. Many scoffed at the idea of learning *Han·geul*; some refused. Yet his effectiveness dealing with the scores of Japanese pirate ships and his understanding of technology won him a revered place in Korean hearts and history – and a spot on the face of the W10,000 note.

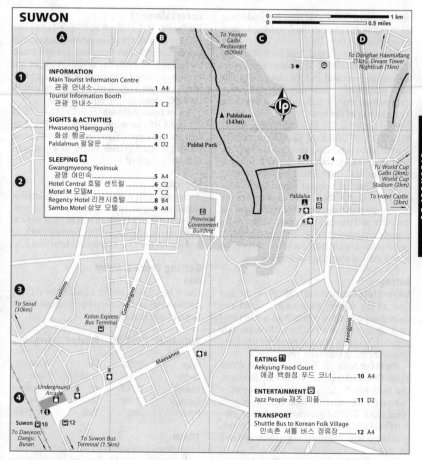

On weekends from March to November, a re-enactment of the **changing of the guard** occurs at 3pm (Saturday) or 2pm (Sunday), with a procession, drums and fanfare.

Sleeping

There are very few midrange and top-end hotels. The best deals are love hotels, which offer squeaky-clean rooms, amenities and often internet for about W35,000 (sometimes less).

Gwangmyeong Yeoinsuk (☎ 254 3701; r with/without bathroom W15,000/10,000; 🗷) Right in front of Suwon Station, this typical budget *yeoinsuk* (family-run hotel) has no beds, only *yo* (padded quilts) on the floor. The sign, down a dark alley off Maesanno, is easy to miss.

Motel M (☎ 254 4673; r W30,000; 🗷) Rooms in this definite love motel (can't miss the racy DVDs or the gratis condoms!) are sparsely furnished, but the owner is kind (though no English is spoken). Look for it near the fortress wall, where a long, green carpet of astroturf leads up to the doorway from the street.

Sambo Motel (☎ 242 5776; r W30,000, Sat W35,000; 🗷) Almost impossible to find without calling ahead, the Sambo is in a nest of similar motels; the rooms have cable TV, video, attractive wood linoleum floors, and beds rather than *yo*.

Regency Hotel (☎ 246 4141; www.htregency.co.kr; r incl breakfast W88,000; 🗷 🖳) Glitzy, big and noisy at times if the function rooms are being rented, this top-end choice offers small rooms, comfy beds, carpeted floors, gold trim and a fake rose on the table. It's close to the Gyodong Sageori intersection.

Hotel Central (☎ 246 0011; fax 246 0018; d/tw/ste W88,000/99,000/180,000; 🏧 🖳) Some rooms overlook the fortress wall, but it's a bit pricey. The hotel has a funky restaurant/bar with retro-style purple couches that's oddly incongruous with the rest of the hotel.

Hotel Castle (호텔 캐슬; ☎ 211 6666; d/tw/ste W225,000/275,000/350,000; 🏧 🖳) The expansive marble lobby sets high expectations. Helpful, English-speaking staff, rooms with internet access and AC inverters, a business centre, men's sauna and popular nightclub all help make the Castle stand out. Downsides are minor: the plush rooms are a bit cramped for the price and the dark, carpeted hallways are vaguely reminiscent of *The Shining*. The white grand piano is a tasteful touch, and there's live easy-listening music in the evenings.

Eating

Aekyung Food Court (meals up to W6000) On the 2nd floor of the railway station, this smart and clean food court has a bunch of outlets that cook up more than 60 different Korean-style dishes. It's a great place to meander until you find something that suits you.

World Cup Galbi (월드컵 갈비; meals W5000-25,000) Overlooking the World Cup Stadium, the best lunch deals are *galbi jeongsik*, a banquet with excellent side dishes or *galbi* (beef ribs). Try the *galbitang* and *naengmyeon* (buckwheat noodles in an icy beef broth, garnished with chopped vegetables and half an egg).

Yeonpo Galbi Restaurant (연포; ☎ 255-1337; meals W6000-25,000) Scrumptious smells will guide you here; halfway round the fortress-walk at Hwahongmun, walk down the steps to this popular restaurant, which serves *galbi* and the famous Suwon version of *galbitang*: big portions of beef ribs in a broth served with spicy side dishes.

Donghae Haemultang (동해해물탕; ☎ 206-5333; 🕒 11.30am-11.30pm; platters small/large W40,000/60,000) Huge seafood paella-style platters so spicy that your eyeballs scald just looking at it, but mouth-wateringly good if you can stand the capsaicin. The smallest platter will feed a decent army. If you're still hungry afterwards, ask for rice – they fry it to crispy with the platter leftovers. It's in the same building as the Dream Tower Nightclub (see right).

Entertainment

Jazz People (째즈피플; ☎ 243 8802; 🕒 11.30am-2am, 11.30-4am Sat) With a bird's-eye view of Suwon, this comfortable 8th floor hang-out has live music for half an hour every day at 9pm. A mix of soft Korean or foreign love songs make it a popular blind-date spot, and affordable beers and coffees (W4000) probably help out as well.

Dream Tower Nightclub (드림타워나이트클럽; ☎ 205-7163; women/men W35,000/39,000; 🕒 8pm-4am) In the upper floor of a neon-washed building, this hip club caters to a younger, college-age crowd.

Shopping

At the end of the fortress-walk is a large market with fruit, veggies and a variety of other comestible and clothing items, as well as some department stores offering stylish Korean clothing and goods. Prices are comparable to Seoul.

Getting There & Away

BUS

Catch bus 5, 5-1 or 7-1 outside the railway station to go to the Suwon bus terminal. Buses depart from there for:

Destination	Price (W)	Duration	Frequency
Busan	25,200	5hr	10 daily
Daegu	12,200	3½hr	7 daily
Gwangju	11,800	4hr	every 30min
Gyeongju	18,000	5hr	9 daily
Incheon	3600	1½hr	every 15min

TRAIN

From Seoul take subway Line 1 to Suwon but make sure the train has 'Suwon' (수원) on the front. It costs W1200 and takes an hour.

From Suwon, trains depart frequently to cities all over Korea:

Destination	Price (W) S class	Price (W) M class
Busan	30,500	20,800
Daegu	21,400	14,500
Daejeon	9500	6400
Jeonju	17,700	12,100
Mokpo	28,200	34,700

Getting Around

Outside the train station on the left, buses 11, 13, 36, 38 and 39 go to Paldalmun (W700) for the 'round-the-fortress' walk. A taxi is W3000.

KOREAN FOLK VILLAGE
한국 민속촌

This beautiful **folk village** (☎ 288 0000; www.korean folk.co.kr; adult/youth/child W11,000/8000/7000; 🕙 9am-6pm Mar-Oct, 9am-5pm Nov-Feb) has a large collection of thatched and tiled traditional houses that take at least half a day to look around. Set around a quiet river are a temple, a Confucian school and shrine, a market, a magistrate's house with examples of punishments, storehouses, a bullock pulling a cart, and all sorts of household furnishings and tools. In this historical and rural village atmosphere, artisans wearing *hanbok* (traditional Korean clothing) create pots, make paper and weave bamboo, while other workers tend to vegetable plots, pigs and chickens. Even the confections (some of them anyway) are handmade: look for the 'magician' making dragon's beard candy – it's made from honey hand-pulled to widths of a human hair.

Traditional musicians, dancers, acrobats and tightrope walkers perform, and you can watch a wedding ceremony. These events happen twice daily and usually start around 11am and 3pm.

Next door is an **amusement park** (adult/youth/child W16,000/14,000/13,000) aimed at children (price includes admission to the folk village), an **art gallery** (admission W3000) and a **world folk museum** (adult/youth/child W3000/2500/2000). A combo ticket to all three gives you a discount off the separate admission fees.

Getting There & Away
To get there take subway Line 1 to Suwon station (W1400, one hour). Leave the station, turn left and walk a short distance to the Tourist Information Centre. Here you can purchase tickets for the Korean Folk Village and catch the free shuttle bus (30 minutes, every hour). The last free shuttle bus leaves the folk village at 4pm. After that time, walk to the far end of the car park and catch city bus 37 (W900, 30 minutes, every 20 minutes) back to Suwon station.

EVERLAND 에버랜드

An expensive amusement park, **Everland** (☎ 759 1408; www.everland.com), an hour southeast of Seoul, is divided into four separate parts.

The **Ho-Am Art Museum** (호암미술관; ☎ 320 1801; www.hoammuseum.org; adult/child W3000/2000; 🕙 10am-6pm Tue-Sun) houses one of Korea's major art collections with 91 Korean national treasures, foreign 20th-century art and a sculpture garden. A free shuttle bus runs on the hour from outside Festival World Entrance B, which is near the buses to Seoul.

Caribbean Bay (adult/child W45,000/35,000 Jun & Sep, W55,000/45,000 Jul & Aug; 🕙 9.30am-6pm, closes later Jul & Aug) has an **outdoor section** (🕙 1 Jun-15 Sep) with a wave pool, sandy beach, tube rides, body slides, spa pools, a surf pool, lazy pool, an adventure pool and a scuba diving pool. The **indoor section** (adult/child W25,000/18,000) is all that is open from September to May.

Festival World (adult/child day pass W28,000/20,000; 🕙 9.30am-6pm, closes later Jul & Aug) follows the Disneyland formula with fantasy buildings, thrill rides, impressive gardens and so on.

Getting There & Away
To get to Everland take subway Line 2 to Gangnam station, leave by Exit 6 and walk to the Everland bus stop (Map pp96–7); take bus 5002 (W1400, one hour, every 15 minutes). Other buses go to Everland from outside Suwon's train station – take bus 66 or 6000 (W1400, one hour, every 30 minutes). See the Everland website for up-to-date transport details.

ICHEON 이천
pop 187,000
Just 60km southeast of Seoul is the mountain-surrounded city of Icheon (not to be confused with Incheon on the west coast), famous for its numerous potters, ceramic vendors, Ceramic Village and a relaxing spa. There's no nightlife, but the city has a quiet charm. Shoppers and ceramic lovers may want to stay here overnight to have time to look around or dabble in making something at a hands-on workshop.

There are excellent maps at the **visitors centre** (☎ 644 2020; 🕙 9am-5pm) near the Seolbongho reservoir. Along with pottery, Icheon is famous for its rice, which some claim is so good that 'it needs no side dishes'. Tourists may find that to be stretching the truth, but the good news is that it's always served with side dishes – and the rice is certainly good, often proudly served in Seoul's finer restaurants.

Miranda Hot Spring Spa 미란다 온천
The splendid **Spa Plus** (스파 플러스; ☎ 633 2001; www.mirandahotel.com; adult/child W10,000/7000, Sat & Sun W12,000/10,000; 🕙 6am-9pm) is a large complex that has ultramodern facilities. Treat yourself to hot, warm and cold baths, a waterfall bath, and rice wine, herbal, pinewood and fruit baths. The spa is next to the Miranda Hotel, which is just a five-minute walk from Icheon bus terminal.

GYEONGGI-DO

Yeong·woram Hermitage 영월암

Founded by the Jogye sect in the interests of promoting self-cultivation, this 1000-year-old hermitage is perched high above the town, a steep 20-minute walk uphill from the visitors centre. Ancient ginkgo trees shade the brightly painted buildings (burned, unfortunately – the hermitage was carefully restored in 1991). Moss, a giant bell and a carved cliff-face Buddha overlooking the sleepy city all make this a fun place to visit.

Icheon Ceramic Village 이천 도예촌

Don't come here expecting picturesque riverside huts or wispy-bearded characters labouring over kick wheels: the Icheon Ceramic Village (Icheon Doyechon) is a busy town with a main street full of traffic, and the many potteries are spread out over a wide urban area. It's not as scenic as some places, but the huge selection of wares make it a fascinating destination for ceramics lovers or shopping aficionados.

Catch a taxi (W5000) or local bus 114 (W1300) from outside the bus terminal and get off after 15 minutes near **Songpa Pottery** (송파 도예; ☎ 633-6587; www.songpadoye.com; ⏰ 9.30am-4.30pm), the large traditional building with blue-green tiles. Inside is unusual crystalline pottery with fern–like designs as well as traditional inlaid celadon and *buncheong*-style pottery. Don't break anything – it could cost you W1 million. Some household items are W10,000 but a tea set is W60,000.

Walk along the main road and over the bridge to the town and you'll come to a sign in *Han·geul* indicating a right turn to Haegang Museum (a 20-minute walk from Songpa Pottery). **Haegang Ceramics Museum** (해강 도자 미술관; ☎ 634 2266; adult/youth/child W2000/1000/500; ⏰ 9.30am-5pm Tue-Sun) has some interesting old kilns outside that are still used.

If you fancy making your own cup, bowl, or million-won vase, visit **Namyang** (남양; ☎ 632 7142; adult/child W15,000/10,000; ⏰ 10am-5pm) where you can don a smock and sit down at a slippery mass of spinning clay, or handbuild something. If you like what you create, Namyang's friendly owners can ship it to you (even overseas) for an additional postage and handling fee (W40,000 or so, depending on weight and destination).

Festivals

From late April through early June, the yearly **World Ceramics Festival** (www.wocef.com/biennale/eng) is held, a massive event with potters, vendors and viewers world wide.

Sleeping

You probably want to do Icheon as a day trip from Seoul, but if not, there are numerous options to choose from.

Jeong·eon Park Motel (정언 파크 모텔; ☎ 635 1661; r W30,000; 🏷) Rooms are small, musty and have deep-red track lights if you need 'ambience'; however, it's the nearest accommodation to the bus terminal, only a one-minute walk away, and the owners are welcoming (though no English is spoken).

Hiwon Hotel (하이원호텔; ☎ 637 3100; r W40,000; 🏷 🖥) Rooms are clean, dark and utterly characterless, but it's a nice option for folks who don't want a love hotel and it's not far from the bus station. Japanese tour groups often stay here, which can sometimes mean a bit of noise.

Now It's The Moon Time (☎ 633 7373; r W45,000; 🏷 🖥) Gets points for the crazy name, but it's also (admittedly, a love hotel) spotlessly clean, brand new and very tastefully done, with heated toilet seats, a DVD collection (not only racy titles, but normal ones too). Many rooms have Jacuzzi-style baths.

Miranda Hotel (미란다호텔; ☎ 633 2001; www .mirandahotel.com; r W236,000; 🏷 🖥) Located next to Spa Plus (p147), where guests receive a 20% discount, and overlooking a small lake with a pavilion on an island, this is the snazziest hotel in Icheon. It has a small business centre and a bowling alley (per game W2800, shoe hire W1000; open from 10am to 10pm). The lobby has fine examples of locally made ceramics.

Other motels can easily be found around Icheon bus station and in Icheon Ceramic Village.

Eating

Near the bus station there are lots of small eateries and restaurants, with the usual Korean fare: *ssambap* (assorted ingredients with rice and wraps), *sundae* (noodle and vegetable sausage), noodles and beef. If you want something more authentic, try one of these:

Yetnal Ssalbapjip (옛날 쌀밥집; ☎ 633 3010; meals W9000-15,000; ⏰ 9.30am-10pm) Near the Songpa Pottery showroom, you sit on cushions on the floor and eat a banquet of over 20 dishes. Cold plum tea rounds off an excellent feast. The more expensive options include additional steak, crab and fish dishes.

Gomijeong (고미경; ☎ 634 4811; meals W10,000-30,000; ⏰ 11.30am-9.30pm) On a hillside outside town, Gomijeong claims its rice is 'so good no side dishes are needed'. They may not be needed, but the side dishes are fantastic – a wonderful assortment of preset courses that vary by price. The paper screens, floor seating and delicate lotus-patterned walls all make this a treat worth taking a taxi for. If they have it, the sweet-pumpkin soup is as good as it gets.

Getting There & Away

Buses run from Seoul's Gangnam bus terminal (Map pp96–7) and Dong-Seoul bus terminal (Map pp98–9) to Icheon (W3600, one hour, every 30 minutes).

INCHEON 인천

☎ 032 / pop 2.5 million / 958 sq km

Incheon, a bustling, industrial port 36km west of Seoul, is big enough to warrant its own subway line. The international airport sits on an offshore island, so be sure (if you're heading to the airport) that you don't go to Incheon proper. Instead, take a direct bus from Seoul. (A subway service is scheduled to open in late 2007.) The city has a nice waterfront area with amusement rides, sushi shops, stores and ferries, as well as a very accessible Chinatown right opposite the Line 1 Incheon terminus. Come here for a great day trip out of Seoul, sample some different foods, stroll along with the dating couples or tour groups in Wolmido waterfront, or use Incheon as a skipping stone to the more remote islands.

Incheon became briefly famous in 1950 when the American General Douglas MacArthur led UN forces in a daring landing there behind enemy lines. Military experts doubted that such a tactic could succeed, but it did and within a month the North Koreans were all but defeated. The tide turned again in November of the same year when large numbers of Chinese troops stormed across the border.

Today the Chinese are still crossing the sea to South Korea, though now they have tourist or business visas. Incheon is a cosmopolitan city with docks full of container ships and giant cranes. It has its own metropolitan government, is not part of Gyeonggi-do and has its own telephone code. Ganghwado and other West Sea islands are also part of the Incheon municipality.

SKI RESORTS

Gyeonggi-do has a handful of ski resorts within easy reach of Seoul (an hour or less by bus) and they all provide shuttle buses (around W12,000 return) to and from the capital during the ski season from December to February. Prices vary and travel agents sell package deals that include transport, accommodation, ski-equipment hire and lift passes. Some Koreans ski and snowboard like they drive, so expect a few bumps.

Bears Town Resort (☎ 02-594 8188, 031-540 3156; www.bearstown.com) Located 50 minutes northeast of Seoul, this resort has 11 slopes, two sledding hills and nine lifts, including the Life Line Little Bear, Big Bear, Polar Bear and (you guessed it) Panda Bear. Accommodation includes a youth hostel and a condominium; facilities include a supermarket, heated pool, sauna, bowling alley and tennis courts. English-speaking instructors, snowboarding and night skiing are available. USO, the American troops' activities organisation (see p159), runs ski tours to this resort and anyone is welcome to join. The resort also has its own golf course to attract visitors outside the winter period.

Cheonmasan Star Hill Resort (☎ 02-2233 5311, 346-594 1211; www.starhillresort.com) Just 40 minutes northeast of Seoul, this place has five slopes and seven lifts. The hotel has a heated pool and a 'plastic slope' so skiing is available year-round. English-speaking instructors are available.

Jisan Resort (☎ 02-3442 0322, 031-638 8460; www.jisanresort.co.kr) This resort has nine slopes, snowboarding slopes and four lifts. English-speaking instructors are available. Because it's close to Seoul it gets a lot of office workers and couples. There's even a dedicated 'couples slope' as well as summer grass-skiing. It's located 60 minutes southeast of Seoul.

Seoul Ski Resort (☎ 02-3487 0761, 031-592 1220; www.seoulresort.co.kr) One of the oldest and closest resorts to Seoul (just 40 minutes east of the city), Seoul Ski Resort has three slopes, three lifts, a sledding hill and hotel accommodation (66 rooms).

Yangji Pine Ski Resort (☎ 02-540 6800, 031-338 2001; www.pineresort.com) Fifty minutes southeast of Seoul, this resort has seven slopes, one sledding hill, six lifts and great views from the top. Accommodation is in a hotel or condominium and the latter has a heated pool and bowling alley.

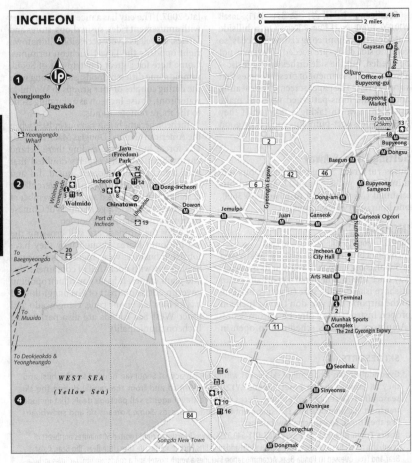

Information

The principal **tourist information centre** (☎ 435 7257; ☼ 9am-6pm) is outside Incheon subway station and the staff are very helpful, with lots of excellent maps, tourist info and suggestions not only for the city, but for the surrounding islands as well. Smaller information centres are in the bus terminal and on **Wolmido promenade** (☎ 765 4169; ☼ 10am-noon & 1-6pm).

Sights

Songdo Resort (☎ 832 0011; admission W3000) has a fairground with thrill rides, paddle boats, a water slide and swimming in a large salt-water lake that is popular in summer. A Big Three ticket is W10,000, a Big Five ticket costs W15,000.

Also in Songdo is the **Incheon Landing Memorial Monument Hall** (☎ 832 0915; admission free; ☼ 9am-6.30pm Mar-Oct, 9am-5pm Nov-Feb, closed Mon). Old newsreel films of the Korean War reveal the ugly reality of modern warfare. Sixteen countries sent troops or medical units to help South Korea, and 70,000 UN and South Korean troops took part in the surprise landing in Incheon in 1950, supported by 260 warships.

Next door is **Incheon Municipal Museum** (☎ 832 2570; adult/child W400/free; ☼ 9am-6pm Mar-Oct, 9am-5pm Nov-Feb, closed Mon), which has an excellent collection of celadon pottery that spans 19 centuries.

Wolmido enjoys sea breezes and is one of the nicer places in Incheon, though nice depends on your definition. The bus/taxi ride passes some amazing container ships, port loading docks, cranes and machinery… interesting, yes, but not quite 'scenic' beauty. The waterfront promenade is a popular place with dating couples. In summer young people gather here in the evening to listen to music, drink alcohol and let off fireworks. On off days or when it rains there is very little to do.

An amusement park has the usual rides for around W3000 each. Frequent ferries leave from here to Yeongjongdo, the airport island with a popular spa, beach and seafood restaurants.

Walking Tour

The walk is only 2km and takes an hour, but more if you linger and explore.

Take the subway to **Dong-Incheon station (1)**. Follow the exit signs for the **Sinpo underground shopping arcade (2)**, and spend some time window shopping. Turn right at the Gyeongdong-sa 4 Geori intersection and onto **Sinpo Fashion Street (3)**. Turn left after the Keum Kang shoe store and head for **SC First Bank (4)**. Turn right again and look on the left for three historical **Japanese bank buildings (5,6,7)**, which date back to the 1890s when Korea was opened up to foreign companies.

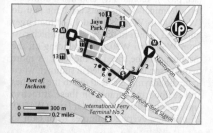

Chinatown (8) deserves a good meander. It has a new gate, new lamp posts and interesting murals. Stores sell souvenirs, clothes, shoes and other goods, but restaurants can be pricey.

You can munch scrumptious dumplings at the **Wonbo Dumpling Shop (9)**, where three big dumplings filled with meat, mushrooms, noodles or tofu cost just W3000.

Up the steps is Jayu Park (Freedom Park) with commanding views over the city, and several statues: the **US Treaty Memorial** and the **Korean Centennial (10)**, and the statue of **General MacArthur (11)**, who changed the course of Korean history with his daring landing at Incheon in 1950.

From the park, walk back down to Chinatown and **Incheon subway station (12)**. If you want a drink, a meal or to play with a one-armed bandit, head to the **Paradise Hotel (13)** with its views over the busy port.

Tours

You can pick up two tours outside Incheon subway station. The **City Tour** (adult/youth/child W1000/500/300) takes four hours and runs eight times daily.

The **Airport Island Tour** (adult/youth/child W4000/3000/1300) takes about three hours. Contact the Incheon subway station tourist information centre (see Information opposite) for tour departure times, which vary depending on the season.

Sleeping

Old-fashioned *yeogwan* (motels with small en suites) are scattered all over Incheon, but they cluster around Bupyeong subway station (take Exit 6 and walk towards the golf driving range) and in Wolmido and Songdo.

NEAR INCHEON SUBWAY STATION

Hong Kong Motel (☎ 777 9001; r W30,000; ❄) One of the best budget options, this place has love-hotel touches but is clean, with crisp sheets, linoleum floors and even small sofas in the rooms. It faces the Paradise Hotel on the opposite side of the street.

Paradise Hotel (☎ 762 5181; www.paradiseincheon .co.kr; d/tw W192,000/276,000; ❄ ⬛) Built on a hill overlooking the port, this long-established hotel has a small casino. Steak meals cost W36,000 in the Western-style restaurant. Korean or Western-style rooms are available and there's a sauna as well (W15,000). Turn right as you exit the subway station and follow the road, looking to the right for the hotel on the hill.

NEAR BUPYEONG SUBWAY STATION

Venus Motel (베니스모텔; ☎ 524 0945; r W25,000, Fri & Sat W45,000; ❄) Some rooms are a bit stale, but this is one of the nicest cheap options in Incheon and the staff are friendly. Triple rooms are available for W30,000 (W45,000 on Friday and Saturday). It's located on a small side street to the left of the station, just next to the larger, fancier (and less friendly) Plaza Motel.

A number of other motel and *yeoinsuk* (family-run hotel) options are on the same street, and there are other options nearby.

WOLMIDO

A number of motels are dotted around Wolmido, although many of them have seen better days. Among the better options are the **Utopia Motel** (☎ 764 6353; r W30,000, Sat W35,000; ❄), which is a far cry from utopian, and the **Sophia Motel** (☎ 773 1783; r W25,000; ❄).

SONGDO

Songdo Hilltop Hotel (송도힐탑호텔; ☎ 834 3500; r W40,000, VIP room W60,000; ❄ ⬛) Dark, almost gothic décor. VIP rooms are slightly fancier and all include PCs, but some standard rooms have computers as well at no extra charge.

Ramada Songdo (라마다송도텔; ☎ 830 2200; www.ramada-songdo.co.kr/eng/default.asp; r W252,000; ❄ ⬛) The luxury-accomodation choice with posh furnishings, beach and ocean views, three restaurants, a sauna and gym, a business centre and an internet line in every room. *Ondol*-style rooms (with underfloor heating systems) are slightly cheaper than Western-style ones.

Eating & Drinking

WOLMIDO

Prices are high here, but dishes are meant for sharing and you can order *gonggibap* (steamed rice) to cut down on the number of seafood dishes. Sushi, sashimi and beef are popular.

If you want something easier on the wallet, try the spotlessly clean **Jjanggu Jonghap Bunsik** (짱구종합분식; ☎ 765-6501; meals W2000-6000; ⏲ 9.30am-10pm), right across the street from the noisy carnival, for nice *gimbap* (Korean sushi) and *mandu* (filled dumplings). It's open 365 days of the year.

SONGDO

Restaurants in this touristy neighbourhood tend to be more Western than Korean, but by Ramada Songdo is **Multeombeong** (meals W20,000), which offers fish and crab meals.

CHINATOWN

From the Line 1 Incheon subway stop, head across the street and up the hill for a variety of Chinese restaurants.

Buanbu (부앤부; ☎ 765-7787; www.bunbu.co.tw; meals W4000-6000, set menus from W15,000; ⏲ 11am-10pm) On the left at the top of the first intersection, Buanbu ('Bu and Bu') offers great spicy noodles, clam soups and a variety of other scrumptious dishes.

Café Castle (☎ 773 2116; www.cafécastle.co.kr; coffee, sweets W2000-7000; ⏲ 11.30am-midnight) Enjoy fantastic views of the port from this small, leafy, intimate café. It's at the top of Chinatown, right near the steps to the park. Be sure to tell them beforehand if you don't like your coffee sweet.

Getting There & Away

BOAT

Yeonan Pier and International Ferry Terminal 2 are the departure points for regular international ferries to a number of Chinese cities (see p399). Yeonan Pier also has a domestic ferry terminal where boats leave for Jeju-do (W46,000 to W90,000) and 14 of the larger inhabited islands in the West Sea, which cost from W5500 to W30,000 depending on the distance and the speed of the ferry. A more frequent service is provided in summer, when many holidaymakers head out to the beaches and seafood restaurants on these attractive and relaxing islands. A regular ferry (W1500, 25 minutes, every 20 minutes from 6am to

9.30pm) runs from Wolmido promenade to Yeongjongdo.

BUS

From Seoul, it's faster, cheaper and easier to take the subway to Incheon. But from other cities it is not necessary to go to Seoul first, as there are direct buses to Incheon. From Incheon you can get a bus to these destinations:

Destination	Price (W)	Duration	Frequency
Cheonan	6000	1½hr	every 30min
Cheongju	8300	2hr	every 30min
Chuncheon	9900	3hr	hourly
Gongju	9500	2½hr	every 1½hr
Incheon Int'l Airport	5000	1hr	every 30min
Jeonju	10,300	3hr	hourly
Suwon	3400	1hr	every 20min

The bus terminal has a department store, chemist shop, post office, cinema and a tourist information centre.

TRAIN

Take subway Line 1 from Seoul (W1400), which takes around 70 minutes, though it branches at Guro and not all trains go all the way to the Incheon terminus. Incheon city has its own subway system, which doesn't cover the tourist areas but does go to the bus terminal.

Getting Around
BUS & TAXI

Buses (W900) and taxis leave from outside Dong-Incheon and Incheon subway stations.

To get to Songdo, hop on bus 6, 9 or 16, or take a taxi (W5000).

To Wolmido, it's a 20-minute walk from Incheon subway station or a W2200 taxi ride. To get to Yeonan Pier, take bus 12, 24 or 28, or hail a taxi (W5000).

For the International Ferry Terminal 2, take bus 23 or a taxi (W1900). If you go to the wrong ferry terminal, a taxi between the two costs W5000.

Bus 306 goes to Yeongjongdo (W3600, every 20 minutes), the airport island, where Yeongjongdo market and Eulwangni Beach are worth a visit (see right).

SUBWAY

Incheon has one subway line, running in a north–south direction. It intersects with the

KNR line at Bupyeong station, where there is Lotte Mart, an underground shopping arcade, a budget food court, cinemas and a cluster of older-style *yeogwan*. If you arrive at Incheon bus terminal, you can walk down to the subway station. The basic subway fare is W800 and Seoul subway cards can be used on the Incheon line.

ISLAND HOPPING IN THE WEST SEA

Sandy beaches, sea views, rural scenery, vineyards, fresh air and fresh seafood – the West Sea islands are a different world to Seoul. Dozens of islands are technically part of the Incheon municipality, even though it can take hours to reach them by boat. The islands are mostly rocky, though coves hide a few excellent sandy beaches. Some islands have rare smooth-stone beaches. The stones are called *mongdol* and it takes centuries of tidal action to produce them. It is illegal to collect these stones, so don't try to take any home with you.

For the Koreans, a major reason to visit the islands is to indulge in a *saengseon hoe* (raw fish) culinary safari. Island restaurant menus typically include *saengseon chobap* (vinegared rice with raw fish), *saengseon·gui* (grilled fish) and *mae·untang* (spicy fish soup). If seafood appeals to you, be sure to ask the price first – the species of fish as well as the season and the cooking (or noncooking) method greatly influence the price, which can vary from so-so reasonable to 'Oh-my-god-it-costs-*that*-much?' outrageous.

Before embarking for the islands, stock up with sufficient cash – money-changing facilities and ATMs are next to nonexistent in this far-flung corner of Korea.

Minbak (private homes with rooms for rent) and *yeogwan* cost W20,000 to W30,000, but prices double in July and August when the island beaches become crowded. However, at other times (even warm weekends in June and September) you'll probably have the beach to yourself.

Yeongjongdo & Muuido
영종도, 무의도

Although Yeongjongdo is home to Korea's busiest international airport, the western beaches are not disturbed by the air traffic. The seafood market at Yeongjongdo Wharf and a flashy seawater hot spa are other popular attractions. In the north of the island, Airport

Town Square has been developed with half a dozen new midrange hotels, a guesthouse and apartments for airport workers.

Yeongjongdo Wharf Market sells fish, shellfish, crabs and other varied seafood, which nearby restaurants will cook and serve for you (see opposite).

Behind the market, take bus 202 (W1200, 20 minutes, hourly) and ask the driver to drop you near Jamjindo if you want to visit Muuido. From the bus stop, walk over the causeway from Yeongjongdo to the islet of **Jamjindo** (잠진도) and enjoy the views. A 15-minute walk brings you to the small ferry to Muuido (W1000, at least hourly).

On **Muuido Wharf**, try a delicious, fresh shellfish barbecue – a big bowl costs W25,000 (feeds three or four people) and octopus *pajeon* (green-onion pancake) is W4000. Then it's a 10-minute walk to the fishing village, where you can turn right and walk over the hill past cherry trees and grapevines for 15 minutes to **Keunmuri Resort** (큰무리 리 조트; admission Jun & Sep/Jul & Aug W1000/2000, huts W30,000/42,000) where there are camp sites, pine trees, a sandy beach and a swimming pool. At

low tide you can walk across to the unspoilt and uninhabited islet of **Silmido** (실미도).

Return the same way you came, and on Yeongjongdo you can catch a bus or hitch a lift to the popular western beaches. **Eulwangni Beach** (을왕리 해수욕장) is 10 minutes from the Jamjindo drop-off point by bus and has new motels, *minbak, noraebang* (karaoke rooms) and many restaurants. This beach is the most popular because the sea doesn't recede at low tide leaving behind huge mud flats, as it does along most of the west coast.

For a quieter beach, walk north to **Wangsan Beach** (왕산 해수욕장). The western beaches, set among rice fields and vineyards, are attractive (nearby Incheon International Airport doesn't affect them) and the mud flats harbour clams, sea worms, birds and mudskippers. Take bus 301 or 316 (W1300, 15 minutes, every 30 minutes) and get off at the last stop.

Haesupia Spa (해수피아 스파; ☎ 886 5800; adult/child W6000/4000; ⏰ 6am-8pm) is a luxury seawater hot spa with nice views and restaurants, located on the road between Yeongjongdo Wharf and Jamjindo. Shuttle buses run there from Yeongjongdo Wharf.

YEONGJONGDO & MUUIDO

SIGHTS & ACTIVITIES	
Haesupia Spa	1 C2
Wolmido	2 D2

SLEEPING	
Carib Beach Hotel	3 A2
Chowon Motel	4 A2
Guesthouse Korea	5 B2
Hotel Airpark	6 B1
Hotel Sky	7 B2
Hub Herb Hotel	8 B1
Incheon Airport Hotel	9 B1
Keunmuri Resort	10 A3

EATING	
Jeonju Sikdang	(see 3)
Keunjip	11 B1
Yeongjonghoesenta	12 D1

TRANSPORT	
Bus Stop	13 B2
Bus Stop	14 B2
Ferry Ticket Office	15 D2

SLEEPING
Eulwangni Beach

A wide range of accommodation is available by Eulwangni Beach – everything from small bare rooms to luxury suites with a balcony. From the airport, use bus 301 or 316 and get off at the last stop. There's beachside camping near the pine groves.

Chowon Motel (초원 모텔; ☎ 746 3369; r W30,000; Sat & Sun W40,000; ✸) Small but modern rooms right on the beach; prices double in summer.

Carib Beach Hotel (카리브 모텔; ☎ 751 5455; r W50,000-80,000; ✸) Shaped like a ship, but this love motel isn't as ship-shape as it could be. That said, views are fantastic from the 'porthole' windows and it's just steps away from the water. There's a karaoke bar in the basement. Prices are up to 50% higher on Saturdays and during summer.

Airport Town Square

Airport Town Square is a relatively new town that has been built on Yeongjongdo a few kilometres from the airport, not to be confused with the even-closer-to-the-tarmac Airport Business District; the latter is essentially a few large business hotels and accompanying stores. Most accommodation in both places is quite new, and either town could be good for an overnight stay after you come or before you leave. Bus 223 (W900, 10 minutes, every 30 minutes) and 203 (W1300, 10 minutes, every 30 minutes) run between Airport Town Square and Incheon International Airport. There is also a free shuttle bus service (10 daily) from the airport (3rd floor exit, Gate 5). Some hotels provide a free pick-up or drop-off service to and from the airport, but others charge up to W20,000. Bus 111-1 runs between Town Square and Incheon city.

Guesthouse Korea (게스트하우스코리아; ☎ 747 1872; www.guesthousekorea.co.kr; s/d or tw W38,000/48,000; ✸ 🖵) This unusual guesthouse has large, light, modern, motel-style rooms on various floors in a new building in the Airport Business District. Spacious rooms have kitchenettes, cable TV and free internet. Deluxe rooms are nicer, bigger and (amazingly!) cost the same; some even have a washing machine. Free pick-up from the airport is also provided.

Hotel Airpark (호텔 에어파크; ☎ 752 2266; www.hotelairpark.com; r W80,000; ✸ 🖵) Another newish hotel with a restaurant, bar and a coffee shop. Rooms have real-wood floors

and a feng-shui feel. Baths are attractive, with frosted glass walls.

Hub Herb Hotel (허브허브 모텔; ☎ 752 1991; r W80,000; ✸ 🖵) Ask for a discount, as the price varies on availability. Lamé bedspreads seem more Versailles than Korea. Rooms are cramped but clean.

Hotel Sky (호텔 스카이; ☎ 752 1101; www .hotelsky.co.kr; r W90,000; ✸ 🖵) Faded but friendly, with black marble in the lobby and one building that's entirely reserved for nonsmokers. Facilities include a business centre, restaurant and coffee shop.

Incheon Airport Hotel (인천에어포트 호텔; ☎ 752 2066; www.incheonairporthotel.co.kr; s/d & ondol W115,000/135,000; ✸ 🖵) All rooms have a TV, DVD players and (yes, ugly) fridge-sized vending machines, while special rooms have snazzy triangular whirlpool baths, desktop PCs and fax machines. A golf driving range is on the roof. Advance reservations can drop the price by W20,000 or so.

EATING

You can buy fish, shellfish, prawns or blue crabs at Yeongjongdo Wharf Market and take them to a restaurant such as **Yeongjonghoesenta** (영종 회센타; ☎ 032-746 0155), where you can have it cooked and served with quail eggs and shellfish soup for W5000. Popular raw fish such as the black-skinned *ureok* or *gwang·eo* (flounder) cost around W10,000 each, while prawns or blue crab are around W20,000 per kg. It's a much better deal than you get in Wolmido.

Keunjip (큰집; ☎ 752 1442; meals W5000-10,000; ⏲ 6am-10pm) In Airport Town Square, this place cooks up a tasty *ppyeohaejangguk*, a hotpot of big meaty bones served with rice.

Jeonju Sikdang (전주식당; ☎ 746 2115; soup W5000; ⏲ 7am-11pm) Handmade, udon-style noodles in a delicious, nonspicy broth make the seafood soup a winner. Look for this greasy-spoon in the first floor of the Carib Beach Motel.

GETTING THERE & AWAY

To visit Yeongjongdo and Muuido, take subway Line 1 to Incheon station and then a taxi (W1500) to Wolmido. On the promenade is the ticket office for the car ferry to Yeongjongdo. The adult/child fare is W2000/1500 for the 20-minute trip and ferries run every half hour from 7am to 9pm daily. Cars cost an additional W6500. An alternative way

GYEONGGI-DO

to or from Muuido is by a high-speed ferry (W8900, 20 minutes, 10.30am) or regular ferry (W5650, one hour, 8am and 5pm), which travel between Incheon's Yeonan Pier and the port on the south of Muuido island.

If you don't need to go to the port (and onward to Muuido or other islands), just take an express bus to the airport (W8000) from Seoul and then use local buses, shuttles, or taxis from there.

Jagyakdo 작약도

In summer the landscape of this tiny island is decked out with jagyak (peonies), thus the island's name. The island is also heavily forested with pines. Jagyakdo is just 3km north of Wolmido, but you don't get the boat from there. If you'd like to spend the night, there is one yeogwan and 15 bungalows for rent on the island.

Ferries (W7000, 30 minutes, hourly from 10am to 5pm) depart from Incheon's Yeonan Pier.

Yeongheungdo 영흥도

Simnipo Beach, at the northwest corner of the island, is 30km from Incheon. The beach has a 4km-long pebbly stretch and a 1km sandy stretch.

The ferry (W25,000, four hours, four a week, but more often in summer) leaves from Incheon's Yeonan Pier. With the new bridge to the island, you can also reach the island by bus (four a day).

Deokjeokdo 덕적도

This is one of the most scenic islands that can be reached from Incheon, and the high-speed ferries make a one-day excursion from Seoul possible. But why be in a rush to leave? Sit back and relax. The island is 77km from Incheon, and along its southern shore is Seopori Beach, which is 2km long and lined with a thick grove of 200-year-old pine trees. The beach is spectacular and easily the most popular on the island. The island also has many unusual rock formations and it's worth climbing the highest peak, Bijobong (292m) for the grand view.

There are plenty of yeogwan and minbak as well as a camping ground at Seopori Beach.

No matter which ferry you take, you will be dropped off at Jilli Pier on Deokjeokdo. From there, it's a 20-minute bus ride to Seopori Beach. The high-speed ferry (W17,500,

50 minutes, 9.30am and 3pm) is the best option, although there is a cheaper regular ferry (W12,000, 2½ hours, 1.30pm and 7.30pm).

Baengnyeongdo 백령도

Far to the northwest of Incheon and within a stone's throw of North Korea is Baengnyeongdo, a scenic island that is attracting an increasing number of tourists. The island is South Korea's westernmost point and is notable for its remoteness and dramatic coastal rock formations – taking a tour around the island by boat to view these unusual rock shapes is a 'must do'. With North Korea a stone's throw away, the military presence is visible.

Sagot Beach is 3km long and consists of sand packed so hard that people can (and do) drive cars on it. In contrast, some of the other beaches in the area are pebble. The Koreans like to walk barefoot on the pebbles or even lie down on them, because they believe that the resulting acupressure is good for their health.

The island is served by a high-speed ferry (W43,700, four hours, twice daily) and a regular ferry (W29,500, eight hours, once daily). Both ferries leave from Incheon's Yeonan Pier.

GANGHWADO 강화도
☎ 032 / pop 57,700 / 319 sq km
Famous for its 'stamina producing' ginseng, Ganghwado is still a rural island that seems oddly distant from the bustle and craziness of Seoul, despite the fact that it is less than a two-hour bus ride away. Egrets stalk through verdant rice fields, gulls chase french fries from the ferries and the pace of life is slow – boring even, but boring in the best of ways.

Attractions include numerous small fortifications; one of Korea's largest dolmen (a prehistoric burial chamber) which is a World Heritage monument; Manisan with an ancient stone altar on its summit; and a 10km coastal bicycle track.

A short ferry trip away on Seongmodo is one of the country's most important temples, Bomunsa, with a cliff-carved Buddha and beautiful old pines. Numerous sashimi and seafood restaurants make dining a pleasure, though you may find seafood is the only item and it can be pricey.

Ganghwa-eup 강화읍
The main town, Ganghwa-eup, is not particularly scenic, but is just 2km beyond the

northern bridge and makes a good base for visiting the island's attractions. The **tourist information centre** (☎ 930 3515; www.ganghwa.incheon .kr; ⏰ 9am-6pm Mar-Oct, 9am-5pm Nov-Feb) in the bus terminal has helpful English-speaking staff.

A palace surrounded by an 18km **fortress wall** was built in 1231 and 2km of walls and three major gates have been renovated. The fortress was destroyed in 1866 by French troops, who invaded Korea in response to the execution of nine French Catholic missionaries. The French army burnt many priceless books and took 300 back to France where they still remain, though recently the French government has been less opposed to returning this part of Korean heritage.

The **market** near the bus terminal sells locally grown ginseng and *hwamunseok* (화문석), which are large reed mats with floral designs that are beautiful but very expensive. Woven baskets are cheaper, easier to transport and have similar designs.

Springtime brings the Dolmen Cultural Festival (celebrating this unique ancient burial ground with festivities that include a dolmen construction re-enactment) and the Ganghwado Azalea Festival, both held in October.

Gourmands will want to try the grilled eel and the (in season) Large Eyed Herring sashimi, both of which are island specialities.

There are *yeogwan* scattered around the town centre.

The accommodation nearest the bus terminal, **Hyatt Motel** (하얏트 모텔; ☎ 933 0710; r W35,000, Sat & Sun W50,000; ☒ ▯), has large, comfortable rooms, dark hallways and a friendly owner. Internet rooms cost W5000 more. Turn left outside the bus terminal and it's a five-minute walk along the main road.

Namsan Youth Hostel (남산 유스호스텔; ☎ 934 7777; dm/f W12,000/40,000) offers cheap beds for solo travellers but is a 20-minute, 2km walk southwest of the bus terminal, so you might want to take a taxi.

Ganghwa Bus Station restaurants (☎ 934-1239; meals W2000-6000; ⏰ 10am-9pm), in the bus terminal on the second floor, offer various Korean meals. There's a coffee shop as well (open 8.30am to 8pm).

GETTING THERE & AWAY

Buses to Ganghwa-eup (W4400, 1½ hours, every 10 minutes from 5.10am to 9.45pm) leave from Sinchon bus terminal in Seoul.

Around Ganghwa-eup

The small but modern **Ganghwa History Hall** (강화역사관; ☎ 933 2178; adult/youth & child W1300/700; ⏰ 8.30m-7pm Mar-Oct, 9am-5.30pm Nov-Feb) reveals the island's interesting history and is located near a fortification (Gapgot Dondae) close to the northern bridge. If you want to visit ask the bus driver to drop you off there rather than in Ganghwa-eup bus terminal, or else you'll need to take a taxi.

Even if history isn't your thing, there's a fun cycle path here that goes to Gwangseongbo, 10km away along the coast. It's a scenic, mainly flat jaunt, though the summer sun can be scorching. Rent bikes from the **bicycle rental shop** (☎ 933 3692; mountain bike/tandem per hr W2000/4000, per day W8000/12,000) but return them by 6pm. Eel restaurants, rice fields, flowers and seagulls will greet you along the way.

Buses (W900, five minutes, every 1½ hours from 6.20am to 7.45pm) go from the museum to Ganghwa-eup bus terminal, which is 2km away. Otherwise hitching a lift into town should not be a problem.

Manisan 마니산

This **park** (☎ 937 1624; adult/youth/child W1500/800/500; ⏰ 6am-6pm) is in the island's southwest, 14km from Ganghwa-eup. On the 468m-summit is **Chamseongdan** (참성단), a large stone altar said to have been originally built and used by Dan-gun, the mythical first Korean, who was born in 2333 BC. Every 3 October on National Foundation Day (a public holiday), a colourful shamanist ceremony is held here. The 3km walk to the top from the bus stop includes over 900 steps, takes an hour and on a fine day the views are splendid.

Buses from Ganghwa-eup run to Manisan (W1300, 30 minutes, every 50 minutes from 6.50am to 7.30pm).

Jeondeungsa 전등사

This **temple** (☎ 937 0125; adult/youth/child W1800/ 1300/1000; ⏰ 6am-sunset) built inside a fortress is famous for the 80,000-plus wooden blocks of Buddhist scriptures, the Tripitaka Koreana, that were carved here between 1235 and 1251 and later moved to Haeinsa Temple (see p195).

Bugeun-ni Dolmen 부근리 고인돌

The biggest **dolmen** (admission free; ⏰ 24hr) on Ganghwado is an impressive sight and has a top stone weighing more than 50 tonnes. Replicas of other ancient relics such as Stonehenge and the Easter Island statues can be seen there too. The site can be visited by bus (W900, 15 minutes, hourly from 6.20am to 8pm) or taxi (W2500, 10 minutes).

Oepo-ri 외포리

If you have been yearning for a close look at seagulls, come to Oepo-ri, a fishing village on the west coast about 13km from Ganghwa-eup. 'Flocks' is too small a word to describe the number of happy 'rats with wings' that follow the ferries between Oepo-ri to Seongmodo.

Even if you stay on land, there's a quiet beauty here. The views of the harbour, mud flats and (yes) seagulls seem to be cut from a Korean silk painting. Fishing trawlers, either sun dappled or mist cloaked, chug in and out of the port, through a backdrop of lavender-coloured islands; it's not hard to imagine that life here has been little changed for decades.

The seafood market (turn right after you get to the water) has good prices and there are decent restaurants and *yeogwan*. It's also the terminal for the ferry to Seongmodo (석모도), where the main attraction is the temple Bomunsa.

Ganghwa Youth Hostel (강화 유스호스텔; ☎ 933 8891; www.gh-yh.co.kr; dm/f W12,000/70,000), an institutional-style youth hostel, doesn't have the ambience of some and is a bit off the beaten path, but offers a cheap night's sleep for the budget traveller.

At the **Blue Moon Motel** (블루문 모텔; ☎ 933 4056; r W30,000, Sat W40,000; ⊠) rooms are smallish and a bit stuffy, but clean, with the usual love-hotel amenities and a choice of *ondol* or Western options. Tinted windows offer privacy whether it's needed or not, and the location makes it a good choice for those planning to head to Bomunsa the following day.

Buses from Ganghwa-eup (W1100, 30 minutes, every 30 minutes from 6.40am to 6.40pm) take a scenic cross-island route. Ferries depart from the two tiny terminals for Seongmodo (right), as well as other islands.

Bomunsa 보문사

Situated high (steep walk, many stairs, catch your breath at the top) in the pine-forested hills of Seongmodo island, this **temple** (☎ 933 8271; adult/youth/child W1500/1200/800; ⊗ 8am-7pm) has some superbly ornate painting on the eaves of its various buildings. The grotto and 10m rock carving are standout features. Korean women come here in hopes of conceiving sons, and

the Korean grandmothers you see are not praying for sons for themselves but for their daughters. Resorts and restaurants are dotted around the island's coastline, but you can also make this a day trip from Seoul if you don't mind getting up early and returning late.

Ferries (☎ 932 6007) depart Oepo-ri for Seongmodo (adult/child W1600/800, 10 minutes, every 30 minutes) between 7am and 8.30pm. The ferry also transports cars (W14,000 return). On Seongmodo a bus (W1000, hourly on weekdays, every 30 minutes on weekends) takes you to near the temple but it's a steep climb up. *Steep.*

PANMUNJOM & THE DMZ TOUR
판문점

Panmunjom, only 55km north of Seoul, is the only place in the Demilitarized Zone (DMZ) where visitors are permitted. This is the village established on the ceasefire line at the end of the Korean War in 1953. In the blue UN buildings in Panmunjom, peace discussions still take place, though there's something surreal, almost comic, about the pomp and precautions. Perhaps even more surreal is the giant, ultramodern train station at the border, empty save for tourists, yet ready to serve a united Korea the minute the boundary lines are lifted.

There's nowhere else in South Korea where you can get so close to North Korea and North Korean soldiers without being arrested or shot, and the tension is palpable. And yet, at the same time, there's a theatrical aspect here too, with posturing on both sides. Though your tour will likely be a quiet one, the soldier 'tour guides' will happily remind you that gun battles erupt in this frontier village – and that North Korean spies still slip across the border from time to time. (Such incidents usually end with the spies getting caught, being shot, or swallowing poison and committing suicide. And you thought that only happened in B-grade Hollywood movies, right?) Sabre rattling or no, the threat of North Korea remains a big issue in the region and conflicts flare up from time to time. Shots were fired in 2001 and 2003, and in 2006 North Korea successfully tested missiles and seemed bent on attaining nuclear capabilities despite international pressure for disarmament.

The DMZ, a strip of land 4km wide and 248km long, divides the two Koreas and is one of the most heavily fortified borders in the world. Even a hungry opossum would have a tough time slipping through the high fences topped with barbed wire, watchtowers, anti-tank obstacles and minefields that line both sides of the DMZ.

Both US and South Korean troops live in Camp Bonifas, which is 'In Front of Them All' and would face the brunt of any surprise attack from the North. At one point around 1800 soldiers were stationed here. Now it is about 600, most of which are South Korean men serving their required two years of military service.

There are only two villages in the DMZ, and they're both near Panmunjom – and within hailing distance of each other if you have a big enough loudspeaker. On the south side is Dae-seong, a subsidised village with a church and high tax-free incomes. Each family there lives in a modern house with high-speed internet connection, and each farms seven hectares. All 230 residents must be at home by the 11pm curfew, and soldiers stand guard while the villagers work in the rice fields or tend their ginseng plants.

Gijeong, the North Korean village in the DMZ, is even more unusual because all the buildings are empty and always have been. According to the US soldiers, it's a ghost town whose only function is to broadcast propaganda to anyone around for six to 12 hours a day, using ultra-powerful loudspeakers as big as a house that any rock band would love to own. The village also has a 160m-high Eiffel Tower–like structure, flying a flag that weighs nearly 300kg. The North Korean flag

is larger than the one on the South Korean side. Giant *Han-geul* letters on the northern hillsides spell out slogans such as 'Follow the way of the Leader', while on the South Korean side the message 'Freedom, Abundance and Happiness' is lit up at night.

The tour includes a visit inside one of the UN buildings, where official meetings are still sometimes held, and which look like temporary classrooms with simple tables and chairs. Both sides constantly monitor the rooms so everything you say can be overheard. On the ceasefire line soldiers from the North and South stand only centimetres apart. The South Korean soldiers stand guard in a modified 'taekwondo' stance, and North Korean soldiers sometimes peer – expressionless – into the windows (making for great photo ops). Dangerous or not, posturing or not, it's a surreal experience that will make a clear impression.

See the excellent film *JSA* for a dramatic story set in the DMZ about what happens when ordinary soldiers from both sides meet by accident.

Getting There & Away

Access to Panmunjom is permitted for tour groups only – this is not a do-it-yourself trip. You must have your passport or you won't be allowed to board the tour bus, and unlike the immigration checks at most world airports, here they actually look at your photograph closely and compare it with your face. Vital too is that you follow the dress and behaviour codes (which, among other things, forbids wearing jeans!), and before you enter the DMZ all visitors must sign a document absolving the UN and the South Korean government of responsibility in case of any injuries due to 'enemy action' while on the tour.

The **United Service Organizations** (USO; ☎ 724 7003; www.uso.org/korea), the US army's social and entertainment organisation at the Yongsan base, runs **tours** (Tue-Sun, US$40/W40,000, cash only) that include the Third Tunnel, which was dug by the North Koreans, but not lunch. They start at 8am and finish at 3pm. To reach the USO take subway Line 1 to Namyeong station. It's about 10 minutes' walk from Exit 2 – go straight, looking to the left for the USO entrance gate.

Most foreigners will find the USO tour is fine, but if you'd rather not take it, there are other options. Half-day tours with Korean

---

DMZ NATIONAL PARK?

The DMZ separates North and South Korea. It is surrounded by tanks and electrified fences, and is virtually sealed off to all people. Ironically, this has made it something of an environmental haven. No other place in the world with a temperate-zone climate has been so well preserved. This has been a great boon to wildlife: for example, the DMZ is home to large flocks of Manchurian cranes. Environmentalists hope that the day the two Koreas cease hostilities, the DMZ will be kept as a nature reserve. With undetonated landmines still in place, the zone won't be seeing tour groups anytime soon.

THE UNDERGROUND WAR

A brass plaque in Panmunjom gives the following account of the North Koreans' tunnelling activities.

'On 15 November 1974, members of a Republic of Korea Army (ROKA) patrol inside the southern sector of the DMZ spotted vapour rising from the ground. When they began to dig into the ground to investigate, they were fired upon by North Korean snipers. ROKA units secured the site and subsequently uncovered a tunnel dug by the North Koreans that extended 1.2km into the Republic of Korea. On 20 November, two members of the UN Command (UNC) investigation team were killed inside the tunnel when dynamite planted by the North Koreans exploded. The briefing hall at Camp Kitty Hawk is named after one of the officers killed, Lieutenant Commander Robert N Ballinger.

In March 1975, a second North Korean tunnel was discovered by a UNC tunnel detection team. In September of 1975, a North Korean engineer escaped and provided valuable intelligence concerning the communist tunnelling activities. Acting on the information, a tunnel-detection team successfully intercepted a third tunnel in October 1978, less than 2km from Panmunjom.

Today the North Koreans continue to dig tunnels beneath the DMZ. The UN and ROKA have fielded tunnel-detection teams, which drill around the clock in hope of intercepting new tunnels.'

Since the plaque was put up, a fourth tunnel extending 1km into South Korean territory was discovered (in 1990).

---

companies cost around W40,000 and full-day tours cost around W60,000. Not all the tours are the same, and use caution before putting money down. Ensure they include Panmunjom. Some trips include a visit to the Third Tunnel and some don't. Visiting the tunnel is worthwhile and you should make sure it's included in the tour before handing over the cash. Also be sure to check the refund/rescheduling options if a tour is cancelled.

ODUSAN UNIFICATION OBSERVATORY
오두산 통일 공원

The **Unification Observatory** (Tong-il Jeonmangdae; ☎ 945 3171; www.jmd.co.kr; adult/youth W2500/1300; ☿ 9am-6pm Apr-Sep, 9am-5.30pm Oct, Nov & Mar, 9am-5pm Dec-Feb) at Odusan is as close as most Korean civilians can get to the DMZ. Panmunjom, north of Seoul, is actually inside the DMZ and can be visited by foreigners, but Korean civilians are not normally allowed there (so make sure you don't plan on bringing a Korean friend when you take the USO tour). This large, futuristic building has a viewing area, museum, gift shop and auditorium. Festivals and events are sometimes held here; check the website for details.

Since the Unification Observatory does offer South Koreans a rare peek at the forbidden North, tourists by the bus load turn up here daily throughout the summer months, and it's also popular with tours from Japan and Taiwan. It isn't quite the same as going to Panmunjom – there's little of the tension since the Unification Observatory isn't actually in the DMZ but is instead a few kilometres away. If you want to see anything at all (such as the UN post, the North Korean post – only just – and the North's propaganda signs), you have to use the pay telescopes for viewing. It's calm and non-threatening, but still interesting.

Getting There & Away

To get to the observatory from Seoul's Seobu bus terminal in Bulgwang-dong, take a bus (50 minutes, every 40 minutes) to Geumchon (buses to Munsan stop in Geumchon). Or from Seoul train station, take a train to Geumchon (one hour, hourly). From Geumchon bus station, take a local bus (30 minutes, every 40 minutes) to the Unification Observatory (these buses are marked Songdong-ri).

Gang·won-do
강원도

Gang·won-do, northeast of Seoul and bordering the ocean and North Korea, holds many of Korea's natural gems. Roads wind through wildflower-dappled valleys, rivers chase and meander their way to the sea, and verdant green mountains cloaked in mist rise up suddenly. Come here to trade the crazy neonscape of Seoul for rural majesty, or visit the quiet but still fun cities of Chuncheon or Gangneung.

Gang·won-do has several of South Korea's most beautiful national parks, including Seoraksan, whose evocative, jagged peaks seem like giant, nature-made sculptures and whose trails offer hours – even days – of hiking. More sedate pleasures can be found in the beaches of Gangneung and Naksan, where Seoulites arrive in droves in the summertime to sunbake on smooth, white-sand beaches and splash in the sea. Bungee jumping, skiing, cycling, and white-water rafting are other outdoor options. Most of the more beautiful parts of the province are found in obscure valleys with dramatic gorges, raging rivers and dense forests, and the sandy coves and rocky headlands south of Samcheok provide serene sea views.

Approaching the northern border you'll see tank blockades, barbed wire and lots of military: North Korean spies still slip through from time to time, and it's a bit odd to see lines of spotlights that illuminate the beaches – they're not for tourists, they're to spot intruders.

GANG·WON-DO

HIGHLIGHTS

- Hike the breathtaking peaks of **Seoraksan National Park** (p172)
- Tour the North Korean villas and view lots of barbed wire at **Hwajinpo** (p171)
- Marvel at the giant penis totems at Sinnam's **Haesindong Gong·won** (p183)
- Lounge in the white-sand splendour of **Gyeongpo Beach** (p176)
- Sample delicious, scaldingly spicy chicken at **Chuncheon** (p163)
- Explore the Coal Museum and Dan·gun's mountain-top altar in **Taebaeksan Provincial Park** (p184)
- View the artistic Buddhist treasures at **Woljeongsa** (p177) and **Sang·wonsa** (p177) in Odaesan National Park

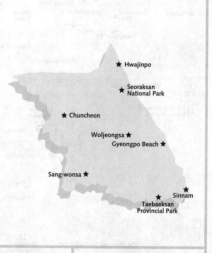

★ Hwajinpo

★ Seoraksan National Park

★ Chuncheon

Woljeongsa ★

Gyeongpo Beach ★

Sang·wonsa ★

★ Sinnam

Taebaeksan Provincial Park ★

■ TELEPHONE CODE: 033   ■ POPULATION: 1.5 MILLION   ■ AREA: 16,874 SQ KM

History

Historically the province has been isolated due to its rugged terrain, and during the Korean War it was the site of many fierce battles for strategic mountain tops. After the war, the area's rich natural resources, including coal and timber, were industrialised, bringing road and rail links. With the closure of many coal mines during the 1990s, the province was forced to create alternative employment opportunities. Tourism was the solution.

In summer 2006 a 100-year rainy season brought torrential downpours, and with it flooding, landslides and death. The disaster killed over 60 people, washed away roads and trails (including many in the Seoraksan National Park and other hiking areas) and destroyed homes and businesses. By the time this book is published much will be back to normal thanks to aid and industrious rebuilding, but the memory of the loss is fresh and painful.

National Parks

Seoraksan National Park and Chiaksan National Park are the two biggest and most famous parks of the province. Both are spectacular. Seoraksan offers grand vistas, forest-darkened hiking trails, rushing rivers, beautiful autumn and winter trips, and stunning scenery all year round. Chiaksan, smaller and less visited, has a more subtle beauty that is just as charming, and its temples and peaks are some of the highest in the country. While both parks are well-equipped to handle large

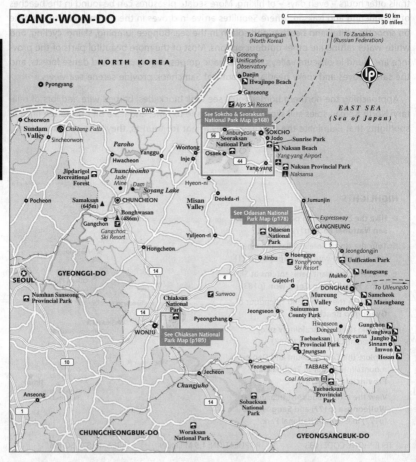

numbers of visitors, at peak times (usually July and August) the swarms of visitors take a bite out of the beauty. Escape them by hiking in the early morning, just after the trails open, or choosing to come at other times of the year.

Getting There & Around
Public transport is so good in South Korea that getting there and around is deceptively easy, and inexpensive too. The roads are probably the quietest in the country, except in July and August when crowds flock to the east-coast beaches. Buses and trains run frequently from Seoul to all major cities. From there, local buses or taxis go the rest of the way.

CHUNCHEON 춘천
pop 260,000
The 'City of Lakes', proud birthplace of the scrumptious yet mouth-scalding *dakgalbi* (chicken, rice cakes and veggies cooked with spicy chilli paste), still retains the charm and quiet of a small town, despite its size. Four pretty artificial lakes surround the city (the provincial capital), making for beauty, nice bike rides and (in season) mosquitoes. Whether you are up in the surrounding mountains, on the shoreline, or in the lakes themselves, you'll find that it's a gorgeous spot; however, outside the obvious outdoor activities and the *dakgalbi* restaurants, there's not a lot to do and the water, pretty at a distance, is quite dirty up close. In spring a section of rice fields outside town becomes a haven for visiting cranes. Fans of Asian TV dramas will recognise this as the setting for the wildly popular *Winter Sonata*, posters of which still fly all over town.

Orientation
Nam (South) Chuncheon train station is the main station, but it is located 2km (about a 30-minute walk) from the town centre and the bus terminal. You'll need to walk or take a taxi to reach the lake shore, bike rentals or the town centre. Much of the city proper is clustered near the shoreline. Jungdo is a small island just offshore.

Information
A large and helpful **tourist information centre** (☎ 250 3896; www.iccn.or.kr; ☉ 9am-6pm) is near the bus terminal and has free internet access and brochures on the whole of Gang·won-do. A smaller **office** (☎ 252 3600; ☉ 9am-6pm) is near the lake, Uiamho.

Activities
BICYCLE TOURS
Jungdo Cycle Ride
Hire a bicycle from the **bicycle rental stall** (per hr/day W3000/5000; ☉ 9am-7pm) near the lakeside tourist information centre. You will need to leave some form of ID. Cycle to Talbang Makguksu (p165) for lunch and then pedal to the ferry pier for Jungdo (중도). Alternatively catch bus 74 (W900, 10 minutes, many daily).

This pretty little lake island has horse-and-carriage rides (per person W5000 for 10 minutes), water skiing (W30,000 for 10 minutes), rowing boats (W5000 per hour), an outdoor swimming pool (open in July and August), sports fields and picnic areas. Herons, ducks and other water birds occupy the reeds, more so at the island's western end. You can look for ancient tombs as well. At the bicycle rental stall, Heukyeomsotangjip Restaurant sells *bulgogi* (barbecued beef and vegetables) and *seolleongtang* (beef and rice soup) but most visitors picnic under the trees.

The **Jungdo Ferry** (adult/child W4300/2400 return, every 30min; ☉ 9am-6pm) takes 10 minutes and bicycles are charged W1000 (return fare).

Lakeside Cycle Ride
A cycle path runs along Uiam Lake to the Korean War Memorial and beyond. It's a magical ride if you do it as the sun sets behind the mountains. The War Memorial is a reminder of the Chuncheon battle when the North Koreans lost 6600 men and 18 tanks.

BOATING
Row boats (W6000 per hour) and swan paddle boats (W10,000 per hour) can be hired from near the Ethiopia Café. Don't fall in – the water is nasty.

ICE SKATING
The **ice skating rink** (☎ 263 7302; adult/youth W3000/2500; ☉ 1pm-6pm Tue-Sun) can be reached by bus 75 or you could cycle there.

Sleeping
Grand Motel (☎ 243 5021; Okcheondong 39-6; r W30,000; ✗ 🖳) Dark rooms are brightened by art on the walls, and some have balconies. The lino floors are a bit characterless, but the owners are kind and they provide a free pick-up service from the bus terminal and train station.

Youngbinjang Hotel (☎ 253 1530; www.hotel-youngbin.co.kr; Gunhwadong 1727; r W30,000; ✗ 🖳) Nicely

GANG·WON·DO

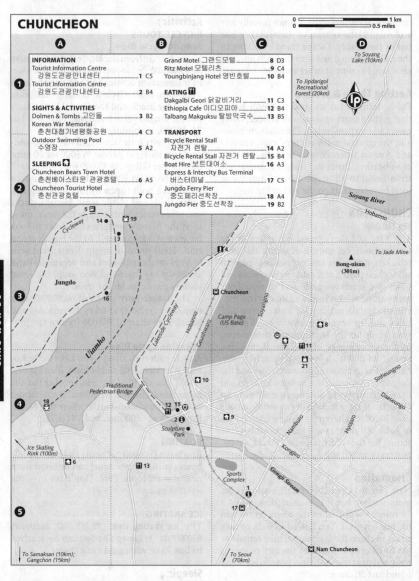

CHUNCHEON

0	1 km
0	0.5 miles

INFORMATION
Tourist Information Centre
강원도관광안내센터 **1** C5
Tourist Information Centre
강원도관광안내센터 **2** B4

SIGHTS & ACTIVITIES
Dolmen & Tombs 고인돌 **3** B2
Korean War Memorial
춘천대첩기념평화공원 **4** C3
Outdoor Swimming Pool
수영장 **5** A2

SLEEPING
Chuncheon Bears Town Hotel
춘천베어스타운 관광호텔 **6** A5
Chuncheon Tourist Hotel
춘천관광호텔 **7** C3

Grand Motel 그랜드모텔 **8** D3
Ritz Motel 모텔리츠 **9** C4
Youngbinjang Hotel 영빈호텔 **10** B4

EATING
Dakgalbi Geori 닭갈비거리 **11** C3
Ethiopia Cafe 이디오피아 **12** B4
Talbang Makguksu 탈방막국수 **13** B5

TRANSPORT
Bicycle Rental Stall
자전거 렌탈 **14** A2
Bicycle Rental Stall 자전거 렌탈 ...**15** B4
Boat Hire 보트대여소 **16** A3
Express & Intercity Bus Terminal
버스터미널 **17** C5
Jungdo Ferry Pier
중도페리선착장 **18** A4
Jungdo Pier 중도선착장 **19** B2

located in the centre of town, the Youngbin-jang is unassuming and clean and the owners are friendly. Three 'special' rooms have desktop computers; all rooms have hair dryers and carpeted floors. Rooms are smallish but not at all musty. There's a restaurant below.

Ritz Motel (☎ 241 0797; r W30,000, Sat W40,000; ✕ ☑) This motel has small, ultramodern

rooms that are a bit heavy on the air freshener, and 'deluxe' rooms that have giant televisions and mammoth baths. A bar downstairs is open from 6pm to 1am. In case you've forgotten that this is a 'loooooooove' motel, there's an underwear vending machine in the lobby and a huge racy DVD collection. Yes, you read that right: underwear.

Chuncheon Tourist Hotel (☎ 255 2222; fax 243 9457; r W70,000; ✕ 🖵) An English sign would make this 'tourist' place much easier to find – look out for the church spire and you will be very close. It's got nice character, with wooden floors, pretty embroidered sheets and paper screens on the windows. A restaurant, a coffee shop and even a slot-machine room are all on the premises. If you didn't bring your own laptop, just ask: they'll be able lend you one.

Chuncheon Bears Town Hotel (☎ 256 2525; fax 256 2530; r & ondol W77,440, Sat W96,800; ✕ ✕ 🖵) A peek at the parking lot says this place has seen better days, but this clean, modern hotel offers great lake views. Internet comes in two flavours: rooms with a computer or wireless. The koi pond, no-smoking lobby and several restaurants are additional pluses. Downsides? It's a bit far from the centre of town…but well worth it for those wonderful views.

Eating

Dakgalbi Geori is a famous food street where more than 20 restaurants serve up delicious *dakgalbi* (grilled spicy chicken pieces). Other restaurants (some of them excellent) are a short taxi ride away. You need at least two people and it's a good idea to order the boneless chicken and extra rice or noodles to mop up the leftover sauce.

Umji Bunsik (☎ 244 2969; meals W1000-3000; 🕙 9.30am-9.30pm Mon-Sat) *Gimbap* (Korean sushi), *ramyeon* (instant noodles), fried rice – dirt-cheap eats that can be taken on the go, but it's worth 'ducking' (pun intended) into their curious backroom: anyone over 4ft tall will have to crouch. If time permits, ask for a sticky note and pen so you can help out with the wallpaper.

Talbang Makguksu (☎ 254 2518; meals W3500) This small, greenery-covered traditional restaurant with masks on the wall is famous for *makguksu* (cold buckwheat noodles with a garnish). You can eat them dry or add broth to them from the kettle. Don't mix in all the *gochujang* if you want to keep the chilli content down.

Drinking

Ethiopia Café (🕙 10am-11pm, closed for rain) This is an old established café with river views and Ethiopian artefacts. Coffees and beers are W2000 to W3000.

Getting There & Away

Buses and trains take about the same time from Seoul if there aren't any traffic jams. Buses will also get you right into Chuncheon, whereas the train stations are further away. On weekends, seats on both can be sold out.

BUS

Departures from the **express bus terminal** (☎ 256 1571) include the following:

Destination	Price (W)	Duration	Frequency
Daegu	16,600	3½hr	5 daily
Gwangju	17,500	4½hr	4 daily

From the intercity bus terminal:

Destination	Price (W)	Duration	Frequency
Cheongju	14,300	3½hr	hourly
Cheorwon	10,300	2½hr	every 20min
Dong-Seoul	6700	1¾hr	every 20min
Gangneung	10,200	3½hr	every 20min
Sangbongdong	6700	1¾hr	every 30 min
Sokcho	13,800	3½hr	hourly
Wonju	5000	1½hr	every 15min

TRAIN

Trains to Chuncheon depart from Seoul's Cheongnyangni Station (W5200, 1¾ hours, hourly between 6.15am and 10.20pm), which can be reached by subway Line 1. Chuncheon's two train stations are both inconveniently located, so you'll need to deal with the city buses, take a taxi or walk about 1.5km. Returning to Seoul, the last train leaves at 9.45pm.

AROUND CHUNCHEON
Sundam Valley 순담 계곡

This valley, 8km from Cheorwon (up near the DMZ) is the base for various adventure sports companies, including **Hantangang Rafting** (☎ 452 8006; fax 452 6011), that organise kayaking, canoeing or rafting on the Hantang River. The season runs from mid-April to October. There are a few rapids, but they're not scary except after the monsoon season.

A 1½-hour rafting trip (9km) along a scenic ravine costs W30,000, while a longer 18km, eight-hour trip costs W60,000. Kayaking and canoeing cost about the same and mountain bikes can be hired (from W5000 to W15,000).

GREEN GOLD: THE CHUNCHEON JADE MINE 옥 채석장

If you've ever wanted to sleep on pure jade, you've come to the right place. The **Jade Mine** (☎ 242 0447; admission W7000; ⏲ 9am-6pm) is difficult to get to, so check with the tourist information centre before you go. The jade is a very pale green, almost white. The water that trickles through the jade rock is said to be good for your health and bottles of it are for sale. Apparently onions grow well when watered with it, and some people believe that jade 'radiation' is good for their health, so the mine has mattresses on the floor where you can take a health-giving rest. A shop sells jade items: prayer beads for W10,000, rings for W45,000 and necklaces for W250,000. And yes, beds too: a bargain at only W400,000...mattresses of solid jade.

A taxi from Chuncheon to the jade mine and back, with a 30-minute waiting time at the mine, costs W20,000. Bus 65 (W950, 40 minutes) runs to the mine but only three times daily. A bus to nearby Dongmyeon runs hourly; from there the mine is only a 1km walk.

To get there, catch a bus to Cheorwon or Sincheorwon (www.cheorwon.gangwon.kr) from Dong-Seoul bus terminal (W6500, two hours, every 30 minutes). You can then ring **Hankook Leisure Gaebal** (☎ 452 7578) to pick you up – but staff only speak Korean, so it is far easier to log on to www.adventurekorea.com and go on one of the tours from Seoul. Call ahead as the summer 2006 floods may still be affecting the rafting routes, with changed or altered outdoor conditions.

GANGCHON 강촌

Gangchon is a popular resort village that in many ways – with its DVD rooms, bars, *dakgalbi* restaurants, scooters and bikes – is like the university areas of Seoul. It's a much prettier place to stay than nearby Chuncheon city, but if you're solo (or nursing a broken heart) be warned: you may find the ubiquitous cooing couples on tandem bicycles (often wearing matching outfits) a bit hard to stomach.

Hire a **bicycle** (per hr/day W2000/5000) and ride along the cycleway towards **Gugok Pokpo** (구곡 폭포; ☎ 261 0088; adult/youth/child W1600/1000/600; ⏲ 8am-sunset), which is 6km from the train station. Park your bike at the entrance. Market ladies sell black rice, dried apricots, sweet potatoes, *omijacha* (five flavours tea), pumpkin jelly sweets and *dongdongju* (rice wine) homebrew (mmm, homebrew!). Walk for 15 minutes to the delightful waterfall, which cascades down a 50m cliff. The signs on the ropes say 'Danger: Do not Cross', but you might not be able to read them since so many people are ducking under to get closer for picture taking.

In winter it's a popular spot for *bingbyeok* (ice climbing). From near the waterfall you can also hike up **Bonghwasan** (봉화산; 486m; closed in April due to chance of fire), which takes around 30 minutes. Buses 10, 50 and 50-1 (W950, 10 minutes, hourly) make trips from Gangchon to the waterfall entrance.

The **Gangchon Ski Resort** (☎ 02-449 6660, 033-260 2000) has 10 slopes and six lifts, and there is a shuttle bus from Gangchon train station in the ski season. It's 6km back towards Seoul – follow the river.

Sleeping & Eating

Reservations are a good idea, as peak times can see most places fill.

White Bell Minbak (화이트벨 민박; ☎ 262 0083; www.whitebell.co.kr; r W40,000, Fri & Sat W60,000; ⊠) Conveniently located in the centre of town, this has charming rooms with pot plants and a balcony. 'Frilly' doesn't even begin to describe the décor. Larger rooms (W70,000) include kitchenettes.

Riverwalk Pension (리버웍; ☎ 011-9042-6185; www.riverwalk.co.kr; 1 r/2 r weekdays W60,000/80,000, weekends W80,000/100,000) On the other end of the scale, this beautiful, intimate cabin is a stone's throw from the river, far enough out of town so that things are quiet and peaceful (except when the train rumbles by). Rooms are inside the cabin and are cute and well-furnished, with small desks and balconies – some baths even have bidets. Cornfields, flowers, a deck, loveseats and free bikes make this feel like a retreat. It even offers free pickup at the train station.

Gangchon Tojong Dakgalbi (강촌토종닭갈비; ☎ 261 5949; meals W4000-10,000; ⏲ 10am-10.30pm) Simple, spicy and good. Floor seating only means you have to stand up to enjoy the river-valley view outside, but that's this humble establishment's only fault. It stays open later if diners are still eating.

Getting There & Away

Gangchon is a short bus ride away from Chuncheon (W950, every 40 minutes between 6am to 10pm). The bus stop is outside Gangchon train station. Trains from there go to Seoul's Cheongnyangni station (W4200, 1½ hours, one to two per hour between 6am and 10pm). Subway access is expected to come through by the time this book is printed, so expect even more teens and 20-somethings than are here already.

SOYANG LAKE 소양호

The most interesting way to travel from Chuncheon west across Gang·won-do is to start via a short ferry ride across Soyang Lake, a large artificial lake with gentle green hills and slightly opaque water held back by one of Korea's largest dams. Catch bus 11 (W900, 30 minutes, hourly) from Chuncheon's inter-city bus terminal to Soyhang Dam, and walk 1km past the market stalls (some of which sell *mettugi* – fried grasshopper – for W2000 a cup) to the ferry pier.

There are **hydrofoils** (per trip W30,000), which can be rented at Yanggu Pier to the northeast. The hydrofoils are small, and can only transport two to three people at a time.

Rent a **boat** (adult/child return W4000/2000) from the pier and head to the scenic temple, **Cheongpyeongsa** (adult/child W2000/1000). There's an easy 30-minute hike when you arrive.

At Yanggu Pier, a bus (W940, 15 minutes) runs to Yanggu, from where you catch a bus for a ride through the mountains to Wontong (W2700, 30 minutes) and then another bus (W750, 10 minutes) to Inje bus terminal.

INJE 인제

pop 30,000

Inje (www.inje.gangwon.kr) is a small town and an adventure sports centre – white-water rafting, kayaking and bungee jumping are becoming increasingly popular with young Koreans. It was hit hard by the 2006 flooding, however; many homes and businesses were damaged or destroyed. You can use the internet free (not all day, please) at the terminals in the **tourist information centre** (☎ 460 2170; ☼ 9am-6pm). Find it by going left out of the bus terminal and downhill to the T-intersection. The centre will be on your right.

X-Game (☎ 461 5216; www.injejump.co.kr; admission W30,000; ☼ 9am-sunset, closed Nov-Mar & very wet days) operates a 60m bungee jump from a tower above the river on the edge of the town. It even has an elevator so you don't have to climb up any stairs.

White-water rafting is organised by more than 20 rafting companies, including **Naerincheon Rafting** (☎ 461 5859; ☼ May-Oct) who provide a pick-up service from Inje. Others, including **Naerincheon Adventure Leisure** (☎ 463-0031; rafting@moheom.co.kr), provide an all-day package out of Seoul that includes pick up, lunch and return (W45,000 per person).

Next to Inje bus terminal are several small eateries, but vegetarians will want to cross the street and look straight ahead on the right for **Han·gukgwan** (한국관; ☎ 461 2139; 3 people W30,000; ☼ 10.30am-9.30pm), where you can order *sanchae jeongshik* (temple food), small side dishes of marinated roots, herbs and seasonal veggies, plus miso soup and salt-encrusted fish. The brown, creaky building has character too: it was once a brothel and 'performance house' due to its proximity to the 38th Parallel. If you can't find it, look for the silver lettering and a sign that says 'Since 1990' in English.

Getting There & Away

Buses from Inje to Sokcho (W6500, every 40 minutes) go via Osaek in Seoraksan National Park's southern part and Yang·yang. Buses also run to Chuncheon (W7000, every 1½ to two hours) and Dong-Seoul (W12,600, hourly between 7am and 7pm, three hours,).

SOKCHO 속초

pop 84,000

Sokcho is the biggest city near Seoraksan National Park and enjoys more tourism than most port cities. Fishing is still a major industry and Dongmyeong Port is worth a wander round with its sea views, fishing boats, seafood restaurants and lighthouse. Barbed wire lines every inch of shoreline. At night remember that lights in the water are to attract squid; lights on the beaches are to detect spies.

From here ferries leave for Russia and for tours of Paekdusan (p372) on the Chinese border with North Korea.

There is a small **tourist information centre** (☎ 639 2689; ☼ 9am-6pm, closed Jan) outside the express bus terminal.

Sleeping

Room rates go up 50% in July and August. Motels surround the express bus terminal and are within easy walking distance of the beach.

GANG·WON·DO

SOKCHO & SEORAKSAN NATIONAL PARK

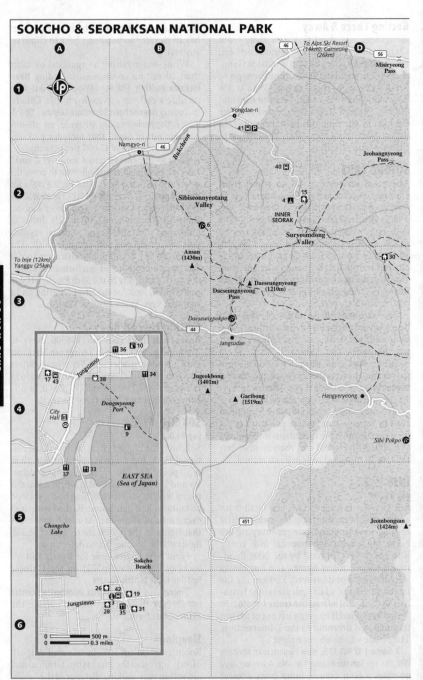

To Alps Ski Resort
(14km); Ganseong
(26km)

Misiryeong
Pass

Yongdae-ri

Namgyo-ri

Bukcheon

Jeohangnyeong
Pass

Sibiseonnyeotang
Valley

INNER
SEORAK

Suryeomdong
Valley

Ansan
(1430m)

To Inje (12km);
Yanggu (25km)

Daeseungnyeong
(1210m)

Daeseungnyeong
Pass

Daeseungpokpo

Jangsudae

Jungsimno

Jugeokbong
(1401m)

Garibong
(1519m)

Hangyeryeong

Sibi Pokpo

City Hall

*Dongmyeong
Port*

*EAST SEA
(Sea of Japan)*

Jeombongsan
(1424m)

*Chongcho
Lake*

Sokcho
Beach

Jungsimno

0   500 m
0   0.3 miles

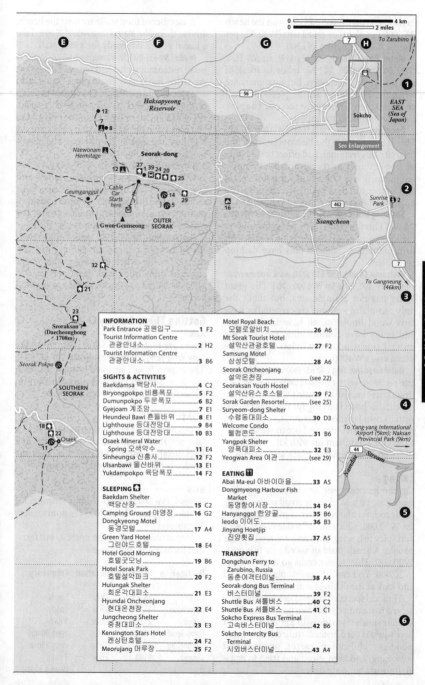

INFORMATION

Park Entrance 공원입구 **1** F2
Tourist Information Centre
관광안내소 **2** H2
Tourist Information Centre
관광안내소 **3** B6

SIGHTS & ACTIVITIES

Baekdamsa 백담사 **4** C2
Biryongpokpo 비룡폭포 **5** F2
Dumunpokpo 두문폭포 **6** B2
Gyejoam 계조암 **7** E1
Heundeul Bawi 흔들바위 **8** E1
Lighthouse 등대전망대 **9** B4
Lighthouse 등대전망대 **10** B3
Osaek Mineral Water
  Spring 오색약수 **11** E4
Sinheungsa 신흥사 **12** E1
Ulsanbawi 울산바위 **13** E1
Yukdampokpo 육담폭포 **14** F2

SLEEPING

Baekdam Shelter
  백담산장 **15** C2
Camping Ground 야영장 **16** G2
Dongkyeong Motel
  동경모텔 **17** A4
Green Yard Hotel
  그린야드호텔 **18** E4
Hotel Good Morning
  호텔굿모닝 **19** B6
Hotel Sorak Park
  호텔설악파크 **20** F2
Huiungak Shelter
  희운각대피소 **21** E3
Hyundai Oncheonjang
  현대온천장 **22** E4
Jungcheong Shelter
  중청대피소 **23** E3
Kensington Stars Hotel
  켄싱턴호텔 **24** F2
Meorujang 머루장 **25** F2

Motel Royal Beach
  모텔로얄비치 **26** A6
Mt Sorak Tourist Hotel
  설악산관광호텔 **27** F2
Samsung Motel
  삼성모텔 **28** A6
Seorak Oncheonjang
  설악온천장 .... (see 22)
Seoraksan Youth Hostel
  설악산유스호스텔 **29** F2
Sorak Garden Resortel .... (see 25)
Suryeom-dong Shelter
  수렴동대피소 **30** D3
Welcome Condo
  웰컴콘도 **31** B6
Yangpok Shelter
  양폭대피소 **32** E3
Yeogwan Area 여관 .... (see 29)

EATING

Abai Ma-eul 아바이마을 **33** A5
Dongmyeong Harbour Fish
  Market
  동명항어시장 **34** B4
Hanyanggol 한양골 **35** B6
Ieodo 이어도 **36** B3
Jinyang Hoetjip
  진양횟집 **37** A5

TRANSPORT

Dongchun Ferry to
  Zarubino, Russia
  동춘여객터미널 **38** A4
Seorak-dong Bus Terminal
  버스터미널 **39** F2
Shuttle Bus 셔틀버스 **40** C2
Shuttle Bus 셔틀버스 **41** C1
Sokcho Express Bus Terminal
  고속버스터미널 **42** B6
Sokcho Intercity Bus
  Terminal
  시외버스터미널 **43** A4

GANG·WON·DO

In July and August you can camp on the beach (W6000 per night) or rent a tent (W12,000 per night). A shower costs W1300.

Motel Royal Beach (☎ 633 5599; fax 635 5588; r W30,000, Sat W40,000; ✷) No lobby to speak of and no English is spoken, but foreigners are welcome. The rooms are simple, with small beds, and there's no internet access. The pink elevator brightens the mood.

Dongkyeong Motel (☎ 631 6444; r W30,000; ✷ ▢) This large motel is the best option near the intercity bus terminal, and offers three hours of free internet at its terminals. It's noisy but inexpensive, with a funky spiral staircase that's more fun than taking the elevator. The uppermost floors have distant water views.

Samsung Motel (☎ 636 0069; r W30,000, Sat W40,000; ✷ ▢) This fairyland castle has gemstones in the lobby and good, comfortable rooms with firm mattresses. Some rooms have desktop computers.

Welcome Condo (☎ 631 8711; www.welcomecondo .co.kr; r W50,000, Fri & Sat W70,000; ✷) The giant lobby has not a single sofa, but that's the only complaint – rooms are carpeted or have faux-wood linoleum, all have kitchenettes, and many have commanding views of the water. Large windows let in lots of light. The sauna costs W4000.

Hotel Good Morning (☎ 637 9900; www.goodmorning hotel.net; Hae-oreumgil; r W60,000, Sat W70,000; ✷ ▢) Brand new and just a stone's throw from the beach, this hotel is trying for the snazz factor with its own Japanese restaurant, karaoke, and rooms with balconies and ocean views. They haven't loaded them up with kitsch, either – the décor is minimalist, black and tasteful.

Eating
On the harbour side of Dongmyeong Harbour Raw Fish Market are small stalls serving *modeumhoe* (a large platter of mixed raw fish) for W80,000, which includes side dishes, sauce and spicy fish soup, and can be shared by four people. A small plate of sliced raw fish costs W20,000, while spider crabs go for W9000 to W20,000. You can sit outside on the sea wall and look at the fishing boats while you eat.

The local speciality is squid *sundae* (sausage), served in quantities that two people can share. Usually *sundae* is made with a pork casing, but here squid is used instead, stuffed with minced noodles, tofu, onion, carrot, seaweed and seasoning, and then sliced and fried in egg – an unusual but tasty dish.

A number of food stalls are near the beach, among them **Abai Ma·eul** (meals W5000-10,000). Take a taxi if you're not ready for a long walk.

Ieodo (☎ 635 4673; Jungsimno; meals W5000-10,000) A small restaurant with squid *sundae*, *Saengseongui* (fried fish), *ojing·eo deopbap* (squid rice) and spicy squid *bibimbap*. The stuffed penguin on the shelf appears to want a piece of the squid. It's a bit difficult to find: go to the port and as you walk (with the water on your right) past the KTF building, look for the pale-green building – Ieodo is across the street.

Jinyang Hoetjip (☎ 635 9999; meals W10,000-120,000; ⏱ 9am-10.30pm) Upscale, fancy and famous, with lots of greenery and delectable scents from the kitchen. It offers sashimi platters, squid *sundae* and *mulhoe* (water raw fish). Meals include numerous side dishes.

Hanyanggol (☎ 635 7588; meals W5000; ⏱ 9am-10pm) Cheap eats near the express bus terminal. Try the delicious *wang·mandu* (large steamed buns filled with meat and vegetables) or *kalguksu* (thick noodles in seafood broth).

Getting There & Away

AIR
There are flights from Seoul (Gimpo) to the new **Yang·yang International Airport** (☎ 670 7114). The airport is well serviced by buses that run north to Sokcho and Goseong Unification Observatory and south to Gangneung.

BOAT
Dongchun runs a ferry to Zarubino in Russia (see p399) with onward travel to China and Paekdusan, a mountain that straddles the border between China and North Korea.

BUS
Buses leave Sokcho express bus terminal for Seoul Gangnam (W13,900, 4½ hours, every 30 minutes).

Departures from Sokcho intercity bus terminal include the following:

Destination	Price (W)	Duration	Frequency
Busan	33,200	7½hr	hourly
Chuncheon	11,600	3½hr	hourly
Daegu	23,000	3½hr	9 daily
Dong-Seoul	13,900	4hr	every 30min
Gangneung	5900	1½hr	every 20min
Yanggu	9100	2¼hr	3 daily (9am-4.30pm)

Buses also leave the intercity bus terminal for Jinburyeong (W4600, six daily from 6.10am to 2.20pm) and stop at Baekdamsa and Yondae-ri on the way. From Jinburyeong shuttle buses go to the Alps Ski Resort.

Local buses leave from outside the intercity bus terminal in the north of Sokcho, but southward-bound bus 7 (W900, 25 minutes, every 15 minutes) to Seorak-dong and bus 9 (W900, 15 minutes, every 15 minutes) to Naksan can both be picked up along their routes, which include the express bus terminal.

NORTH OF SOKCHO
Hwajinpo 화진포
This sandy beach is popular in July and August but almost deserted at other times. Nearby is a lake and three **summer villas** (admission adult/child W2000/1500 for all three; ☺ 9am-6pm) that belonged to former politicians (see below). Everything is within walking distance. 'English body language' is spoken by the staff at the **tourist information centre** (☎ 680 3677; ☺ 9am-6pm Apr-Oct, 9am-5pm Nov-Mar).

Shaped like a giant whale, **Hwajinpo Aquarium** (해양 박물관; ☎ 682 7300; adult/child W1000/800; ☺ 9am-5pm) has displays of shellfish, fossils, coral and rare fish. On the 3rd floor is a **teashop** (teas W2000), which offers 10 strongly flavoured medicinal teas that are brewed on the premises, and views of the beach and lake.

January Pension (제뉴어리; ☎ 682 2630; www .januarypension.com; r W60,000) A brand new, spic-and-span pension that's a stone's throw from the water. It has an English-speaking owner, a café and computer. Giant plate-glass windows in the dining room make it a great place to watch the sun rise. A simple breakfast of toast, jam and coffee is included. From mid-July to mid-August rooms are W90,000.

Hwajinpo Condo Restaurant (화진포 콘도 식당; ☎ 682 0500; meals W4000-10,000; ☺ 8am-9pm) The only restaurant in the area, this has *bibimbap* or a good fish meal for two people with seaweed soup and side dishes.

GETTING THERE & AWAY
Take local buses 1 or 1-1 (W4120, one hour, every 15 minutes) from the bus stand outside Sokcho intercity bus terminal. Get off at the access road to Hwajinpo (15km south of Goseong Unification Observatory) near the Daejin High School and turn left. From there it's a 10-minute walk (800m) down to the Hwajinpo Aquarium (left).

Goseong Unification Observatory
고성 통일 전망대
The **Unification Hall** is to your left as you enter the **complex** (☎ 682 0088; adult/child W2000/1000; ☺ 9am-4.30pm Mar-Jun & Sep-Oct, 9am-5.30pm Jul & Aug, 9am-3.30pm Nov-Feb), which is surrounded by souvenir shops and restaurants. Binoculars are available to take a closer look at the forbidden North and you should be able to see the Geumgang mountain range.

POLITICIANS VILLAS

The site of **Kim Il Sung's Villa** (김일성 별장) is a pleasant 20-minute walk from the Hwajinpo Aquarium. Nothing remains of the North Korean leader's original summer residence except for some steps that feature in a fascinating 1948 photograph of his six-year-old son, Kim Jong Il, with his younger sister and the young son of a Russian general. A small exhibition hall has some old photos, which show the original building to have been a large European-style villa built of stone. The reason it is here in South Korea is that before the Korean War, this area was ruled by North Korea. At the 1953 Armistice, South Korea gained land here on the east side but lost Kaesong and the Ongjin Peninsula.

Yi Gibung's Villa (이기붕 별장) was built in 1920 and used by English missionaries who made a crazy-golf course in the garden. Between 1945 and 1953 the house was used by North Korean Communist Party members, then it became the summer retreat of Vice President Lee and his Austrian wife. When President Syngman Rhee fled to Hawaii in 1960, Vice President Lee's son shot his parents dead and then turned the gun on himself.

A 10-minute walk away is **Syngman Rhee's Villa** (이승만 별장), furnished with many of his personal belongings. Educated at Princeton and Harvard, Rhee was South Korea's president from 1948 until 1960. A tough autocrat, he was finally forced out by student and trade union protests in 1960, and he went to live in Hawaii where he died in 1965.

See Getting There & Away (above) for details on getting to the villas.

Catch bus No 1 or 1-1 (W3400, 1½ hours, every 15 minutes) from Sokcho to Daejin, a pleasant 50km ride up the coast with barbed-wire fences, fortifications and tank traps to remind you of the threat from the North's armed forces. From Daejin Education Centre catch the shuttle bus (W2000, 20 minutes) to the observatory. If you're driving, remember to stop first at the Daejin Education Centre to get your entry ticket; otherwise polite but firm MPs will turn you around at the barricade. A pass costs adult/child W5000/2000.

SOUTH OF SOKCHO
Naksan Provincial Park
낙산 도립공원

This small coastal **park** (☎ 670 2518; admission free; ⊙ 24hr), 12km south of Sokcho, is famous for the temple **Naksansa** (☎ 672 2448; adult/youth/child W2500/1500/1000; ⊙ 5am-7pm). A 15m white statue of Gwaneum, the Goddess of Mercy, completed in 1977, looks out over the East Sea from atop a small, pine-covered rocky outcrop. Overnight temple stays are normally possible, but the temple is closed to overnight visits for rebuilding following a 2005 fire. The pavilion, Ulsangdae, is a good spot to watch the sunrise.

Down below the temple is **Naksan Beach**, popular in summer, with motels, *minbak* (private homes with rooms for rent) and restaurants. Beach **camping** (per site W2000-4000) is possible in July and August.

Euisangdae Condotel (의상대콘도텔; ☎ 672-3201; www.euisangdae.tc.to; r W40,000) has not a speck of character, but not a speck of dirt either. It's clean, friendly, reasonably priced and is right on the beach too. Rooms have kitchenettes and most have balconies. There's sometimes noise on the beach at night, so light sleepers should ask for an upper-floor room.

Hotel Naksan Beach (☎ 672 4000; www.naksanbeach .co.kr; r from W117,000; ✷ ▯ P) offers upmarket accommodation with either Western or *ondol*-style rooms, plus restaurants, a nightclub and a seawater sauna (nonguests/guests W6000/4000; ⊙ 5:30am to 8pm).

GETTING THERE & AWAY
Catch bus 9 (W900, 15 minutes, every 15 minutes) from outside either of Sokcho's bus terminals. It runs between Sokcho and Yang·yang.

There are direct buses from Naksan to Dong-Seoul bus terminal (W13,700, 4½ hours).

SEORAKSAN NATIONAL PARK
설악산 국립공원

This **park** (☎ 636 7700; http://npa.or.kr/sorak/eng /npa/intro.htm; adult/youth/child W3400/1300/700), open two hours before sunrise and closed two hours before sunset, is one of the most beautiful on the entire Korean peninsula – North and South. It boasts oddly shaped rock formations, dense forests, abundant wildlife, hot springs and ancient Shilla-era temples. Unesco has designated the area a Biosphere Protection Site and Seoraksan itself (Snowy Crags Mountain) will leave you in awe. Sinhe-ungsa Temple is also a must see, and if you tire of the park itself head down to the nearby coast for some of Korea's best sandy beaches.

The peak season is July and August, though the mid-October leaf-changing show attracts coachloads of visitors. Prices for accommodation more than double at these times. Accommodation can become completely full, so make reservations early.

Sadly, this park was creamed by 100-year downpours in the summer of 2006, washing out numerous hiking trails. Check conditions with the **tourist information centre** (☎ 635 2003) before you visit.

Orientation
The park is divided into three sections.

Outer Seorak is the most accessible and popular area and is nearest to Sokcho and the sea. Seorak-dong has hotels, motels, restaurants, bars, *noraebang* (karaoke rooms) and a 24-hour supermarket. The left-luggage facility by the ticket office costs W1000 for most items and W2000 for a big backpack.

Inner Seorak, at the western end of the park, is the least commercialised area. It has three entrance points: from Hwy 46 at Yongdae-ri to Baekdamsa; at Namgyo-ri, where a hiking trail goes through Sibiseonnyeotang Valley; and from the south (Hwy 44), where a trail goes north from Jangsudae.

Southern Seorak is the name given to the Osaek (Five Colours) area, which is famous for its cold mineral spring for drinking, and hot mineral springs for bathing and soothing those aching muscles after a long day's hike.

Information
A helpful **tourist information centre** (☎ 635 2003; ⊙ 9am-6pm Mar-Oct, 9am-5pm Nov-Feb) is located rather inconveniently at Sunrise Park, where the Seorak-dong access road joins the main coast

road. A left-luggage facility costs W1000 to W3000 per bag, depending on its size.

Outer Seorak

GWON·GEUNSEONG 권금성
A 1.1km **cable car** (☎ 636 7362; return W8000) runs every 20 minutes and the views (and queues!) on a nice day are amazing. It drops you a 10-minute walk away from the fortress remains and summit.

HEUNDEUL BAWI (TOTTERING ROCK) & ULSAN BAWI 흔들바위, 울산바위
Heundeul Bawi, a massive 16-tonne boulder, can be rocked to and fro by a small group of people, and half the Korean population has played at being Superman here! Other boulders have Chinese characters carved on them. Nearby is **Gyejoam**, with a prayer hall inside a cave.

From Heundeul Bawi carry on and scale the imposing granite cliff known as **Ulsan Bawi**. To reach the 873m summit, you have to climb up an 808-step staircase. It takes 45 minutes and is hard going but the reward is a spectacular view from the top.

TWO WATERFALLS HIKE 쌍폭포
A 45-minute hike from Seorak-dong brings you to a couple of impressive waterfalls, **Yukdamp Pokpo** and **Biryong Pokpo**. This relatively easy 2km hike starts at the stone bridge beyond the cable-car station.

DAECHEONGBONG 대청봉
This is the highest peak in the park at 1708m, but is currently closed for a five-year rotational restoration/preservation; it will reopen in 2011.

Southern Seorak

It's easier to hike up Daecheonbong from **Osaek Hot Springs** in the south. The hike is steep and difficult but is reckoned to take four hours up and three hours down, after which you can soak your aching body in the **hot spring pools** (adult W8000). Alternatively you could continue and descend to **Seorak-dong** (six hours down).

Inner Seorak

BAEKDAMSA 백담사
In the relatively uncrowded northwestern section of the park lies **Baekdamsa** (☎ 462 2554; adult/youth/child W3200/1200/600; ☼ sunrise-sunset).

Shuttle buses (adult/child W2000/1000, every 20 minutes, 7am to 5.30pm) run from the car park 4km up the valley. It's another 3km hike to the temple (50 minutes). The hike beyond the temple along Suryeom-dong Valley (another two hours) is highly recommended.

SIBISEONNYEOTANG VALLEY 십이선녀탕 계곡
This legendary Seoraksan valley is strewn with waterfalls, cascades, pools and large boulders.

The 2½-hour hike to **Dumun Pokpo** is a real treat, and after another two hours uphill you can turn right for a 30-minute hike up **Anson** (1430m) or turn left for **Daeseungnyeong** (1210m), which takes the same length of time.

Sleeping

Yeogwan (motels with small en suite rooms) tend to charge W30,000, but W50,000 on busy weekends and even more in peak season (July and August).

Camping sites are available in Seorak-dong, Jangsudae and Osaek for around W5000, but don't expect any fancy facilities.

There are mountain shelters – **Jungcheong** (☎ 672 1708), **Huiungak**, **Yangpok**, **Suryeom-dong** (☎ 462 2576) and **Baekdam** – which are basic and cost W5000.

SEORAK-DONG 설악동
The first big section of *yeogwan*, shops and restaurants is on the left as you head west.

Seoraksan Youth Hostel (☎ 636 7115; www.sorakyhostel.com; dm/f W30,000/50,000; ✄ 🖳) This large, multileveled institution is the cheapest option for solo travellers.

Further on is another bunch of facilities on the right.

Sorak Garden Resortel (☎ 636 7474; www.sorakgardenresortel.com; d & ondol W30,000; ✄ 🖳) Rooms are clean and sparsely furnished, with décor that has a child's bedroom feel. Some have a kitchen.

Meorujang (☎ 636 8790; www.meorujang.co.kr; r W30,000) Simple rooms painted in bright colours. Each has a small table and chairs, a fridge and the like.

Kensington Stars Hotel (☎ 635 4001; www.kensington.co.kr; d & ondol/tw W169,000/199,000; ✄ 🖳) With English-style décor and more than a touch of class, this hotel has the best view and is very near the park entrance. Some rooms are shrines to Korean film stars. From September to June, the price drops to W129,000 including breakfast.

Hotel Sorak Park (☎ 636 7711; www.hotelsorakpark .com; tw & ondol W193,600; ✵ ▨) There's a white décor thing going on here, which will either make you feel peaceful or make you think you've died; this fancy hotel features balconies and mountain views and is within walking distance of the park entrance. Facilities include a casino, karaoke lounge and restaurants. The saunas are undergoing repairs. Discounts of 20% to 50% are possible in off-season.

Mt Sorak Tourist Hotel (☎ 636 7101; www.sorak hotel.co.kr; r W121,000; ✵) This simple, natural wood-furnished hotel is the only one inside the national park. Substantial discounts are offered during off-peak periods.

SOUTHERN SEORAK
Accommodation clusters around the Osaek hot-spring pools.

Hyundai Oncheonjang (☎ 672 4088; r W30,000, Sat & Sun W35,000-40,000; ✵) No *oncheon* (hot spring) but hot-spring water in the bathrooms. All rooms have kitchenettes.

Seorak Oncheonjang (☎ 672 4111; r W30,000, Fri & Sat W40,000; ▨) The *oncheon* is free for guests, as is internet use. Rooms cost up to W70,000 during peak periods.

Green Yard Hotel (☎ 672 8500; r W60,000, Fri & Sat W85,000; ✵ ▨) Green Yard is due to reopen in June 2007 after suffering massive flood damage in summer 2006. And not a moment too soon, as this is the top accommodation here – with an *oncheon* (W5000), nightclub, billiards and restaurants. Rooms have balconies and cost up to W180,000 in July, August and October.

INNER SEORAK
Access to Baekdamsa is by way of Yongdae-ri, where you can find *minbak* and restaurants.

Eating
Seoraksan is not noted for its food, but popular meals are *sanchae bibimbap* (rice topped with egg, meat, vegetables and sauce; W5000) and *sanchae jeongsik* (W8000), which features mountain vegetables. Trailside stalls sell snacks such as roast potatoes (W2000) and potato starch cakes with red-bean filling (W1000).

Getting There & Away
The access road to Outer Seorak branches off the main coast road halfway between Sokcho and Naksan. Buses 7 and 7-1 run every 10 minutes between Sokcho and Seorak-dong (W950).

Buses from Sokcho intercity bus terminal run every 30 minutes to Osaek Hot Springs (W3000) and Jangsudae (W4400).

Baekdamsa and Namgyo-ri can be accessed by buses that go from Sokcho intercity bus terminal to Jinburyeong (eight daily from 6.10am to 3.50pm).

ALPS SKI RESORT
알프스 스키 리조트
This **resort** (☎ 681 5030; fax 681 2788; www.alpsresort .co.kr; ✵ 9am-4.30pm, 6pm-10pm Dec-Mar; pass with/without skis W76,000/48,000) was opened in 1984 and is nowhere near as large as the nearby Yong-Pyong Ski Resort (see p179), but it receives the heaviest snowfalls of any resort in Korea and has some of the most spectacular scenery, due to its proximity to Seoraksan National Park. There are eight slopes and five lifts, and English- and Japanese-speaking instructors are available.

The resort can be reached by buses that go from Sokcho intercity bus terminal to Jinburyeong (eight daily from 6.10am to 3.50pm) or from Yang-yang International Airport. A free shuttle also runs from Seoraksan's Haemaji Park, and there are direct buses to and from Seoul (one-way/return W14,000/26,000).

GANGNEUNG 강릉
pop 220,000
Gangneung is the largest city on the northeast coast of Korea and hosts an annual Dano Festival (p176), held for the past 400 years. It is the gateway to Jeongdongjin beach, Odaesan National Park and Korea's top ski resort, YongPyong. It's also pretty in itself, with a lagoon, beach, 'tofu town' and more.

The main **tourist information centre** (☎ 640 4414; www.gntour.go.kr; ✵ 8am-10pm) is near the bus terminal and there is a smaller booth in front of the train station. They have both English- and Japanese-speaking staff.

Sights
OJUKHEON 오죽헌
This expansive **complex** (☎ 648 4271; adult/youth/child W1000/500/300; ✵ 9am-6pm Mar-Oct, 9am-5pm

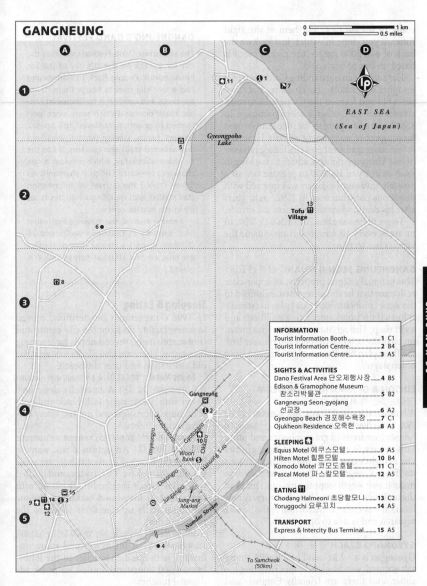

GANGNEUNG

0 — 1 km
0 — 0.5 miles

EAST SEA
(Sea of Japan)

Gyeongpoho Lake

Tofu Village 13

Gangneung

Woori Bank

Jung-ang Market

Namdae Stream

To Samcheok (50km)

INFORMATION
Tourist Information Booth 1 C1
Tourist Information Centre 2 B4
Tourist Information Centre 3 A5

SIGHTS & ACTIVITIES
Dano Festival Area 단오제행사장 4 B5
Edison & Gramophone Museum
    참소리박물관 5 B2
Gangneung Seon-gyojang
    선교장 6 A2
Gyeongpo Beach 경포해수욕장 7 C1
Ojukheon Residence 오죽헌 8 A3

SLEEPING
Equus Motel 에쿠스모텔 9 A5
Hilten Motel 힐튼모텔 10 B4
Komodo Motel 코모도호텔 11 C1
Pascal Motel 파스칼모텔 12 A5

EATING
Chodang Halmeoni 초당할모니 13 C2
Yoruggochi 요루꼬치 14 A5

TRANSPORT
Express & Intercity Bus Terminal 15 A5

GANG·WON·DO

Nov-Feb, closed Tue), 4km from downtown, has numerous buildings, expansive gardens and lotus pools, and is famous for its black-stemmed bamboo groves. It's a relaxing, fun, beautiful place to wander around and it's worth stepping off the beaten path to see the forests and lesser-visited gardens too. Iris, blooming in June, is stunning.

Sin Saimdang (1504–51) was born here as was her son Yi Yulgok (1536–84), whose pen name was Yiyi. Sim Saimdang is regarded as a model daughter, wife and mother, and was an accomplished poet and artist who liked to paint detailed studies of plants and insects. Many of her paintings are on display beside the real-life plants (obviously, you've got to come in season to catch them at the right time). If you come in winter, just look on the back of a W5000 note – the melon motif is based on one of her works.

Her son was an outstanding Confucian philosopher and scholar. He could read at three years old and learned the Chinese Confucian classics from his mother at a very young age. In 1564 he won first prize in the state examination for prospective government officials. He served in various government posts including minister of war. Unfortunately his advice to the king to raise an army of 100,000 to prepare against a possible invasion by Japan was ignored with disastrous consequences in 1592, eight years after his death, when the Japanese did invade.

To get there, take bus 202 or 300 (W950, 10 minutes, every 10 minutes) from outside the express bus terminal.

GANGNEUNG SEON·GYOJANG 강릉선교장
This national cultural property, an upper-class residence that has been restored, belonged to the same family for 300 years (10 generations). It has a lotus pond, interesting buildings and a gift shop. Though the restoration has meant much of the original timbers and tiles are lost, the floor plan has remained unchanged since olden days.

EDISON & GRAMOPHONE MUSEUM
에디손&촌음기박물관장
A bit surreal in rural Korea, this **museum** (☎ 652 2500; www.edison.or.kr; admission W4500; ☺ 9am-6pm) houses hundreds of gramophones and other Edison paraphernalia, plus odd incongruities like a knight's coat of armour. Though the tour itself is in Korean only, there's enough here to make it well worth stopping by – and many of the antiques are very self-explanatory. A new location was under construction at the time of research and is due to open in 2007.

GYEONGPO BEACH 경포 해수욕장
Gyeongpo is a white-sand beach with pretty salt-stunted, wind-twisted pines rimming the shore, and there are friendly English- and Japanese-speaking staff in the **tourist information booth** (☎ 640-4537; ☺ 9am-5pm). The water is warmer than one would expect, but doesn't have the azure hues of the tropics – it's still beautiful, but a flat steel grey. In peak season (July 10 to August 20) camping is possible for W20,000. Tents can be rented for W10,000 a night, and showers cost W2000.

GANGNEUNG'S DANO FESTIVAL

The shamanist Dano Festival overtakes the city for a week on the 5th day of the 5th lunar month. People flock to Gangneung and a tent city rises to house them. There are circus and carnival acts, shamanist rituals, mask dramas (which were once performed by government slaves), folk operas, farmers' bands, *ssireum* (Korean wrestling) and assorted stalls and hawkers. It has the air of a medieval fair, which provides a rare chance to see Korea's original shamanist religion. During the festival, an information stall staffed with multilingual guides is set up in the market centre.

Another festival, the Yulgokje Festival, is held annually at Ojukheon on 25 and 26 October, when traditional rites of respect are enacted and classical Korean music is played.

Sleeping & Eating
In 1996 Gangneung's bus terminal moved to a new facility far from the city centre and (not surprisingly) several hotels have sprung up nearby. There are also places to stay at the old bus station and near the beach.

Equus Motel (☎ 643 0114; r without/with computer W30,000/40,000; ☒ ☐) A tastefully done love motel with a luxurious feel, black-and-gold trim, huge televisions and not too many coloured strobe lights.

Komodo Motel (☎ 644 1855; r without/with computer W30,000/35,000; ☐) An option if you want to be near the beach. The rooms here are well-appointed and have TVs, fridges and bottled water. The décor is refreshingly bland, with not a hint of love-hotel tackiness. Follow the spiral stairs up one floor to get to the reception desk.

Hilten Motel (힐튼 모텔; ☎ 647 3357; r W30,000, Sat W40,000; ☒) A bit newer and more upmarket, with a red chandelier in the lobby. Faux-wood floors and bottled water are additional touches.

Pascal Motel (파스칼 모텔; ☎ 646 9933; r W40,000, Sat W55,000; ☒ ☐) A bit bland, but the hallways have pretty Korean paper decorative screens. Small tables make the rooms feel a weensy bit more homey.

Yoruggochi (☎ 643 8613; meals W3000-9000; ☺ 6pm-2am) A great place to put back a few beers, this tiny *odeng* (processed seafood) shop has beer, *soju* (local vodka), skewers of chicken and other simple dishes. It's right near the bus terminal.

Chodang Halmeoni (☎ 652 2058; www.chodang dubu.com; meals from W8000; ☯ 6.30am-9pm) Simple setting and great soft tofu in one of the most renowned shops of this village. Tipplers will want to try the buckwheat *dongdongju*, which hisses slightly from the natural carbonation.

Tofu lovers and vegetarians will want to head to 'Tofu Village,' a cluster of numerous restaurants all specializing in *sundubu* (soft tofu), which is often served warm in a bowl. Wash it down with *dongdongju* for the true experience.

Getting There & Away

BUS

Gangneung's express and intercity **bus terminals** (☎ 643 6093) share the same building, a shiny new facility near the expressway entrance.

Express bus departures from Gangneung include the following:

Destination	Price (W)	Duration	Frequency
Dong-Seoul	11,700	3hr	every 30min
Seoul Gangnam	11,700	3hr	every 20min

Intercity departures include the following:

Destination	Price (W)	Duration	Frequency
Chuncheon	10,200	3½hr	every 20min
Daejeon	13,000	3½hr	hourly
Donghae	2600	½hr	every 10min
Hoenggye*	2100	½hr	every 20min
Jinbu**	3200	¾hr	every 10min
Samcheok	3800	1hr	every 10min
Sokcho	5700	1½hr	every 20min
Wonju	6300	1½hr	every 30min

* get off here for the shuttle bus to YongPyong Ski Resort
** get off here for the hourly bus to Odaesan National Park

TRAIN

Seven daily *Mugunghwa* trains connect Gangneung (W20,100, 6½ hours) with Seoul's Cheongnyangni station via Wonju.

Getting Around

Buses 202 and 303 (every 15 minutes) connect the bus terminal with the train station. Schedules in English are available at the tourist information centres.

ODAESAN NATIONAL PARK
오대산 국립공원

Like Seoraksan, Odaesan (Five Peaks Mountain) is a high-altitude massif. The **park** (☎ 332 6417; adult/youth/child W2800/1300/700; ☯ 9am-7pm) has great hiking possibilities, superb views and two prominent Buddhist temples: **Woljeongsa** and **Sang·wonsa**. Near the southern entrance, the **Korea Botanical Garden** (☎ 332 7069; www.kbotanic .co.kr; adult/youth/child W5000/3000/2000; ☯ 9am-6pm) is 1.7km down a lane and has over 1000 native plants, orchids and a café.

Birobong (1563m) is the highest peak in the park. From Sang·wonsa you can hike it (it's steep and not for the faint-hearted) and continue along a ridge to **Sang·wangbong** (1493m), then back down to the road and along to the temple (five hours). If you have the stamina, continue along the ridge to **Durobong** (1422m) and **Dongdaesan** (1433m) before heading down to Hwy 446.

As with Seoraksan, the best times to visit are late spring and early to mid-autumn when the hillside colours are prettiest, but it's pretty any time of year.

Woljeongsa 월정사

The temple was founded in AD 645 by the Zen Master Jajang during the reign of Queen Seondeok of the Shilla dynasty to enshrine relics of the historical Buddha. Over the next 1350 years the temple was often destroyed by fire and rebuilt. During the Korean War it was completely flattened. Yet today you would never suspect these disasters had ever occurred. The **paintings** inside the main hall are masterpieces of religious art. Not even in Tibet will you find anything so colourful, imaginative and intricate. One of them could be compared to Hieronymus Bosch.

The temple has a **teashop** (per mug W3000-W4000) and a **museum** (adult/child W1000/500; ☯ 9am-5pm Wed-Mon) of Joseon-era Buddhist art.

Sang·wonsa 상원사

A further 10km beyond Woljeongsa is Sang·wonsa where the hiking trails begin. The intricately decorated bronze bell, one of the oldest and largest in Korea, was cast in AD 663, one year after construction of the temple commenced. Check out the graceful features and hairstyle of the famous statue of a Buddhist saint, Munsu the Bodhisattva of Wisdom. Not much has survived in Korea that reveals the artistic talent of its people

GANG·WON·DO

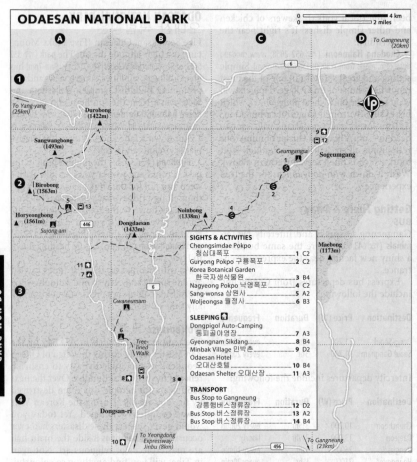

ODAESAN NATIONAL PARK

from over a millennium ago, so it is a prized possession, a symbol of an advanced Buddhist culture.

Sleeping & Eating

A small village of *minbak* and restaurants is on the left side of the access road, a 40-minute walk south of Woljeongsa. If you want more comfort there are two *yeogwan* near the ticket office. Halfway between the temples is Dongpigol Auto-camping and Odaesan Shelter, which both cost W5000.

A large camping ground and numerous *minbak* are also available at the entrance to Sogeumgang.

Odaesan Hotel (☎ 330 5000; www.hotelodaesan .co.kr; r from W180,000;) This is the only deluxe option in the park. Rooms have plush sofas and soft lighting and many have balconies with scenic views. The hotel offers a generous 50% discount during off-peak months (from September to November and February to June).

Gyeongnam Sikdang (☎ 332 6587; meals W6000-13,000) This establishment serves tasty *sanchae bibimbap* (rice, egg, meat and mountain vegetables in hot sauce); delicious *sanchae baekban* (rice with mountain vegetable side dishes); and huge *gamjabuchim* (감자부침; potato pancake). Order a bottle of delicious *memilkkotsul* (메밀꽃술; W3000), which is *makgeolli* (fermented rice wine) flavoured with buckwheat flowers. There's also free coffee.

Getting There & Away

Take an intercity bus from Gangneung (W3100, 45 minutes, every 10 minutes) to **Jinbu intercity bus station** (☎ 335 6307). From Jinbu, local buses (12 per day) run from outside the bus terminal to Woljeongsa (W1420) and Sang·wonsa (W2320) in Odaesan National Park.

Take local buses 303 or 7-7 (W900, one hour, 12 daily) from outside Gangneung bus terminal to Sogeumgang.

YONGPYONG SKI RESORT
용평 스키 리조트

With world-class facilities and lots of trees, **YongPyong** (☎ 033-335 5757; www.yongpyong.co.kr) is one of Asia's best ski resorts. It only missed out on hosting the 2010 Winter Olympics to Vancouver by 56 votes to 53. The season runs from December to March and there are 31 slopes for skiers and snowboarders, plus mogul bumps, cross-country trails and two half-pipes.

A lifts-and-gondola day pass costs W56,000/42,000 (adult/child), while a day's ski equipment rental is W25,000/19,000 (adult/child). Snowboards cost W33,000 for half-day hire, while cross-country skiing (including skis and entry fee) costs W20,000 and sledding W15,000. Day-long ski classes (in English) for beginners are W45,000/33,000 (adult/child), but you need a group of 10. Package deals including transport and accommodation are offered with discounts outside the peak season.

Sleeping

There are a number of sleeping options, most pretty pricey. Check the internet for deals in advance.

YongPyong Hostel (☎ 335 5757; fax 335 0160; r for up to 5 people W70,000) Peeking out of the pines like a Swiss chalet, this is a good option for friends on a budget who don't mind sharing a room. It's closed from March to October, except for group bookings.

Dragon Valley Hotel (☎ 335 5757; r W242,000; ❄ ☎) Nicely situated, with 50% discounts from March to October.

Condominiums (☎ 335 5757; fax 335 0160; basic condos from W252,000 ❄) Discounted 50% from March to October.

Getting There & Away

Buses leave from Gangneung intercity **bus terminal** (☎ 335 6307) to Hoenggye (W2000,

½ hour, every 20 minutes). From Hoenggye a free shuttle bus leaves for YongPyong (10 minutes, 12 daily from 5.30am to 11.30pm), more frequently during the ski season.

Direct buses run to the resort from Seoul, Incheon, Busan, Daejeon and other cities.

JEONGDONGJIN 정동진

Twenty kilometres south of Gangneung is a holiday resort with novel tourist attractions, including a North Korean submarine. The town is famed for having a train station on the beach with a swifts nest in its eaves. The sand-timer hourglasses in the souvenir stalls relate to a popular Korean TV soap opera *Hourglass*, which used the station in some scenes. On a hilltop you can see a giant cruise ship and a sailing ship – a surreal sight.

Unification Park 통일 공원

In this **park** (☎ 640 4469; adult/child W2000/1000; ◷ 9am-5.30pm Mar-Oct, 9am-4.30pm Nov-Feb) you can venture inside a small North Korean spy submarine and a large American warship. There is also a tourist information centre.

The **North Korean submarine** weighs 325 tonnes, is 35m long and had a top speed of 13km an hour. The conditions must have been unbearably cramped for the 11 crew, 15 soldiers and agents inside.

On 17 September 1996 the submarine got stuck on some nearby underwater rocks. The commander burnt important documents (the fire-blackened compartment is still visible), shot the crew members, then landed with the soldiers and agents and attempted to return to the North. None succeeded, but it took 49 days to capture or kill them, and in the process 17 South Korean civilians and soldiers were killed and 22 injured.

The **warship** has a less dramatic story, having been built in America in 1945 and donated to the South Korean government in 1972.

To get there, take bus 11-1 (W900, 15 minutes, every 30 minutes) from Jeongdongjin train station or Gangneung. Taxis charge W8000 for the 5km drive south along the coast from Jeongdongjin.

Sleeping & Eating

Numerous motels (with names like Paradise and Sun Lovehouse) offer comfortable, modern rooms from W25,000 (but double that in July and August). Try to find a room with a balcony overlooking the sea and the sunrise.

GANG-WON-DO

Jijunghae Motel (지중해 모텔; ☎ 642 1518; r W25,000; ❷) Clean rooms with a balcony and an almost palatial en suite toilet and shower.

Halmeoni Chodang (할머니 초당; meals W4000-15,000) Try the *sundubu* (순두부), a bowl of unset tofu that you mix with seasoning and eat with rice and vegetable side dishes.

Beachside tent restaurants serve up crab, raw fish and squid *sundae*. Some offer a bowl of exotic-looking shellfish, which are barbecued at your table for W30,000 and make a delicious hors d'oeuvre for three people.

Getting There & Away

BUS
Buses 109 (W1100, six daily) and 112 (W700, every 30 minutes) leave from outside Gangneung bus terminal for Jeongdongjin. Other buses leave from near the Gangneung train station.

TRAIN
Trains leave Gangneung station for Jeongdongjin 12 times daily and cost W2100. The same service operates to and from Donghae and costs W5200.

Getting Around
The attractions are spread out so seeing them involves either leg-work, working out the bus routes and times or taking a taxi.

DONGHAE 동해
pop 93,000
Donghae is far from quaint and verges on unattractive, but this east-coast port has popular beaches, ferry service to Ulleungdo island (p212), buses to nearby Mureung Valley and a small cave in the downtown area.

A useful **tourist information centre** (☎ 530 2868; ❧ 9am-6pm) is outside the Cheon·gok Donggul entrance.

Sights & Activities

CHEON·GOK DONGGUL 천곡 동굴
The most interesting thing about this **cave** (☎ 532 7303; adult/youth/child W4000/1100/700; ❧ 9am-6pm Mar-Oct, 9am-5pm Nov-Feb) is that it was only discovered in 1991…and that it is in the centre of town! While it's not that big (700m long), it is well lit and the many different kinds of calcified formations make it a worthwhile visit. Keep an eye out for cave insects with incredibly long feelers. There are bats but you probably won't see any.

MUREUNG VALLEY 무릉 계곡
This valley southwest of Donghae is considered by locals to be one of the prettiest in the country.

BEACHES
Mangsang Beach (망상 해수욕장) is a large, popular stretch of sand north of Donghae, with shallow water and many amusements and accommodation in July and August.

Chuam Beach (추암 해수욕장), to the south, is an attractive sandy cove with rocky headlands.

Festivals
They take their cuttlefish seriously in Donghae: a three-day **Cuttlefish Festival** at Mangsang Beach every July includes a cuttlefish-slicing contest, a catching-cuttlefish-by-hand competition and a cuttlefish quiz.

Sleeping
There are some good options next to Donghae intercity bus terminal.

New World Motel (☎ 532 1212; r without/with computer W30,000/35,000; ❷ ▣) Across from the bus station. Head for the (tacky, yes, but very visible) red-and-yellow palm trees. It's a budget place, but some rooms have trippy blue linoleum. Other rooms are far more subdued, with a few faux-Victorian touches that seem a bit out of place.

Picasso Motel (☎ 531 5109; r W40,000; ❷ ▣) Swanky and spotless, with gold-embroidered sheets and softly lit rooms. Channel flipping will remind you (yowza!) that it's a love motel, but the front desk is friendly, welcoming and English speaking.

New Donghae Tourist Hotel (☎ 533 9215; www .hotelnd.com; s & d/tw W60,000/80,000; ❷ ▣) There's a 30% discount in the off-peak season; however, with no in-room computers this may not be an option for anyone needing the internet. On the plus side, it has a small goldfish aquarium in the lobby…and a (men only) sauna.

Donghae Hilton Hotel (☎ 533 7722; www.dhhilton .com; r W80,000; ❷ ▣) Not to be confused with the 'other' Hiltons, the Donghae Hilton offers Mozart, not muzak, computers in every room, and large rooms with firm beds and balconies (looking out, um, over the parking lots). Off peak is discounted up to 50%, a great deal.

There are a bunch of shabby places near the express bus terminal; do-it-yourselfers can likely start there.

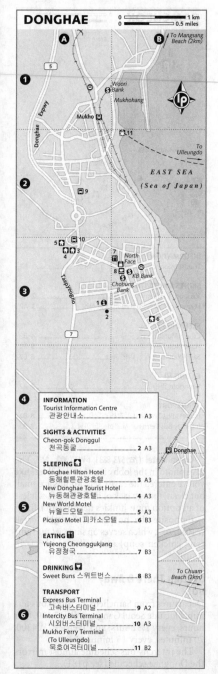

DONGHAE

0 ———————— 1 km
0 ———————— 0.5 miles

To Mangsang
Beach (2km)

Woori
Bank

Mukhohang

Mukho

Donghae Expwy

To
Ulleungdo

**EAST SEA
(Sea of Japan)**

North
Face

KB Bank

Chohung
Bank

Taepyeongdo

To Donghae

To Chuam
Beach (2km)

Eating & Drinking

This is a good place to wander, as there are lots of small cafés and restaurants scattered around. Chances are you'll find a gem on your own, but if not, head for one of the following:

Yujeong Cheonggukjang (☎ 533 7222; meals W5500-9000; ⊗ 9.30am-9.30pm) Fantastic spicy miso soup served with 21 different side dishes (most of them spicy too!). Fish (obvious) and a pork dish (ask) are the only meats, so this is a good choice for vegetarians. The friendly owners can bring only veggie options if you ask.

Sweet Buns (☎ 535 6568; www.sweetbuns.co.kr; coffee & breads W1700-3000; ⊗ 10am-11pm) A clean, well-lit place with remarkably tacky figurines, Sweet Buns has the usual coffees and espresso drinks along with some more unusual ones, like sweet potato or pumpkin lattes. Unfortunately, the cheesecakes are nothing special.

Getting There & Away

BOAT

The Ulleungdo **ferry** (☎ 531 5891; one way W45,000) sails at 10am daily from March to October, departing from the island at 5.30pm, but times vary. The crossing takes three hours. Non-Korean citizens must have their passport. If possible, ask a Korean speaker to ring for details.

BUS

From Donghae's **express bus terminal** (☎ 531 3400; www.kobus.co.kr), buses leave for Seoul's Gangnam bus terminal (every 40 minutes) and Dong-Seoul (nine daily). The standard bus fare is W13,500 and the journey takes around three hours and 20 minutes. Local buses leave from outside the intercity bus terminal next to the SK gas station.

Intercity terminal (☎ 533 2020) bus destinations include the following:

Destination	Price (W)	Duration	Frequency
Busan	24,600	5hr	18 daily
Daegu	24,500	6½hr	24 daily
Gangneung	2600	40min	every 10min
Samcheok	1200	20min	every 10min
Sokcho	8600	2½hr	9 daily
Taebaek	6100	2hr	12 daily
Yang·yang Airport	7000	2¼hr	7 daily
Wonju	8900	3hr	3 daily

TRAIN
Seven trains a day run to Seoul's Cheong-nyangni station (W16,200). Trains head to Busan, Danyang, Jecheon, Taebaek and Gang-neung as well.

SAMCHEOK 삼척
pop 68,000
Samcheok is a gateway to some gorgeous coast-lines, fascinating caves and sculptures. It's the gateway to Hwanseon Donggul (opposite), a huge cave complex under mountains, and is promoting itself as the City of Caves with plenty of cave exhibitions. The area has twice hosted a Penis Sculpture Festival, including a giant phallus-carving contest. Though the festival was shut down by Christian protesters, you can view many of the curious (often comic) contest entries at the shrine and museum at Sinnam (opposite). For more about the phallus 'phascination', see opposite.

The **tourist information centre** (☎ 575 1330; www .samcheok.go.kr; ⊙ 9am-6pm) has English-speaking staff. It's outside the intercity bus terminal.

Mystery of Caves Exhibition
동굴 신비관
This **exhibition** (☎ 574 6828; adult/youth/child W3000/2000/1500; ⊙ 9am-6pm Mar-Oct, 9am-5pm Nov-Feb) is housed in a funky building that resembles a wedding cake dripping with brown icing, and is packed with modern displays and films on caves and cave creatures. An IMAX film is shown at 10.30am, 2pm and 3pm. A building with a bat-shaped roof of solar panels houses an exhibition of cave mock-ups.

Jukseoru 죽서루
This **pavilion** (⊙ 9am-6pm Mar-Oct, 9am-5pm Nov-Feb) is just an old building in a small park perched on a cliff overlooking the river.

Sleeping & Eating
The usual motels can be found around Sam-cheok's bus terminals.

Samil Yeoinsuk (☎ 573 2038; r W15,000) It's the cheapest and is clean and fan-cooled, with a choice of Western or *ondol*-style rooms. Faux-wood vinyl flooring brightens things…a little. The lobby sports a cute 'bird and flower' style Korean painting.

Hanil Motel (☎ 574 8277; r W30,000; ✷ 💻) Some rooms have computers, making this clean, simply furnished place the town's best option, although others are slightly cheaper.

Crown Motel (☎ 573 8831; r W30,000; ✷) The cave photo in the lobby is so big you'll feel like you've entered the cave itself. Rooms are small but clean, though lack of internet makes it less of an option for e-junkies needing an i-fix.

Opposite the hospital is **Yeongbin** (meals W5000-12,000), which serves up *samgyetang* (gin-seng chicken soup) and *galbitang* (beef-rib soup).

Getting There & Away
BUS
Departures from Samcheok's express bus ter-minal include Seoul Gangnam (W13,100, four hours, every 1½ hours) and Taebaek (W4300, 70 minutes, every 15 minutes).

The intercity bus schedule almost mirrors the Donghae schedule (see p181).

TRAIN

The train schedule is the same as the Donghae schedule (opposite), although trains from Seoul arrive in Samcheok about 15 minutes earlier.

AROUND SAMCHEOK
Hwanseon Donggul 환선 동굴

This immense limestone **cave** (☎ 570 3255; adult/youth/child W4000/2800/2000; ⊗ 8am-5pm Apr-Oct, 8.30am-4pm Nov-Mar) is one of the largest in Asia. Inside are cathedral-sized caverns, waterfalls, cascades and pools. Nearly 2km of steel stairways inside the cave allow visitors to get a good look at the many and varied features. Some formations have fanciful names, and there are good English-language information boards.

It gets quite cool inside (10°C to 14°C), so take a jacket. The cave is located in a majestic valley and it's a steep 35-minute uphill climb from the ticket office.

Near the ticket office are a couple of *gulpijip* (bark shingle houses), typical of the style once common in the mountains.

Bus 50 (W2000, 50 minutes, nine daily between 6.30am and 5.10pm) leaves Samcheok intercity bus terminal for the cave. The last bus back leaves at 6.40pm.

South of Samcheok

The coast becomes rocky with high cliffs and sandy coves, making a picturesque getaway.

MAENGBANG BEACH 맹방 해수욕장

About 12km down the coast from Samcheok is Maengbang Beach, one of the more popular spots to swim. The water is very shallow, making it a big hit with families with young children.

A small freshwater creek, also okay for swimming, runs nearby.

YONGHWA BEACH 용화 해수욕장

This beach, 25km south of Samcheok, has pine trees and is an attractive sandy cove between two rocky headlands.

JANGHO BEACH 장호 해수욕장

Next to Yonghwa is this sandy beach with a fishing village and harbour at the end of it.

SINNAM 신남 해수욕장

This small fishing village is home to an impressive **Fishing Village Folk Museum** (어촌 민속 전시관; ☎ 570 3568; adult/youth/child W3000/2000/1500; ⊗ 9am-6pm Mar-Oct, 9am-5pm Nov-Feb, closed Mon). There's a lot to see here, though English signage is currently limited. Displays include shamanist rituals to ensure a good catch, taboos observed by local fishermen (such as not eating eggs before going on board), holographic projections and a fun fishing-boat simulation. Many of the exhibits are made with real creatures of the sea.

Outside the museum is **Haesindang Gong·won** (Penis Park; 해신당 공원), which is full of giant wooden penis carvings (see below). Sinnam is 20km south of Samcheok and the bus ride takes 50 minutes.

IMWON BEACH 임원 해수욕장

Only 200m long, this beach has a dramatic setting in a cliff-lined cove. Nearby is a sea cave and a freshwater creek.

HOSAN BEACH 호산 해수욕장

The southernmost beach in Gang·won-do, Hosan is 1km in length and has good white sand. There is a pine-tree grove next to the beach where camping is popular.

Getting There & Away

Buses 20, 30, 70, 90 and 90-1 go to Maengbang Beach. Bus 20 continues to Jangho Beach, bus

---

SHOW ME A PENIS

While phallic symbols are nothing new, the origins of this town's penis fetish are not the usual fertility or stamina preoccupations one would expect. Sinnam legend has it that a young virgin drowned within sight of her boyfriend on a small rocky island offshore. The boy had hoped to save her but was unable to because of the rough seas. Shortly after her death, fishermen noticed that the catch was dwindling and soon the town was sure that this 'unfulfilled' girl had cursed the fishing grounds. All hope seemed lost, but when a fisherman heeding the call of nature did so facing the ocean, the next day's catch increased. Soon the village erected, um, erections in hopes that the penises would placate the frustrated ghost. The fishing yields returned to normal, and Sinnam's custom of showing Mr Willy to the water remains to this day.

30 goes to Gungchon Beach, bus 70 goes to Yongeunsa, bus 90 (nine daily) turns round at Imwon Beach, and bus 90-1 (five daily) continues to the end of the line at Hosan Beach. The standard buses charge W900 and deluxe buses charge W1300.

TAEBAEK 태백
pop 55,000

The train station, bus terminal, information centre and *yeogwan* are all conveniently within sight of each other in the town centre, and the **tourist information centre** (☎ 550 2828; ☑ 9am-5pm) has kind English-speaking staff.

The Taebaeksan Snow Festival takes place at the end of January with giant ice sculptures, sledding and igloo restaurants.

Getting There & Away

Numerous buses connect Taebaek to various destinations:

Destination	Price (W)	Duration	Frequency
Dong-Seoul	15,900	5½hr	every 30min
Samcheok	4300	1¼hr	every 15min
Taebaeksan	1000	25min	every 45min

Trains depart for Seoul train station (W12,900, 11 daily) and Gangneung (11 daily).

TAEBAEKSAN PROVINCIAL PARK 태백산 도립공원

Taebaeksan (☎ 550 2740; adult/youth/child W2000/1500/700; ☑ sunrise-sunset), meaning Big White Mountain, is the sixth-highest mountain in South Korea. The mountain actually consists of twin peaks, **Janggunbong** (1568m) and its neighbour, **Munsubong** (1546m). The mountain is one of the three most sacred for shamanists, and on the summit is **Cheonjedan** (천제단), an altar connected with Dan-gun, Korea's mythical founder, where ceremonies are still occasionally performed (3 October to 5 October, and 1 January). A rare outdoor **Statue of Dan-gun** (단군산) is in front of the Dan-gun shrine near the entrance to the park. The shrine is a simple, bare wooden hall with Dan-gun's portrait and some food offerings in brass bowls.

The Taebaek region was once South Korea's main coal-mining area, and the **Coal Museum** (태백 석탄 박물관; ☎ 550 2743; adult/youth/child W2000/1500/700; ☑ 9am-5.30pm Tue-Sun Mar-Oct, 9am-4.30pm Nov-Feb) by the park entrance is well worth a visit. You can't miss the building, which has a mine-head contraption at one end. Don't miss the simulated roof collapse – accidents and deaths were common, and more than 200 miners were killed between 1970 and 1996. At some mines in the remote mountains, tigers were another hazard and miners killed by tigers were given a special gravestone.

In front of the park entrance is a 'tourist village' of identical two-storey houses. There are plenty of restaurants as well.

Buses from Taebaek bus terminal (W1000, 25 minutes, every 45 minutes) provide a good service to the park.

JEONGSEON 정선
pop 41,000

This remote, mountain-locked town can be visited on a one-carriage, gaily decorated train. Catch a train from Taebaek to Jeungsan (증산; W4400, 35 minutes, 11 daily) and change to the Jeongseon line, which goes to Jeongseon (35 minutes) and on to the end of the line at Gujeolli (one hour). It's one of the prettiest routes in Korea, with classic Gang·won-do scenes of densely wooded mountains and rivers bordered by terraced rice fields, vegetable gardens and orchards. Very occasionally there'll be an ox pulling a plough, a scene from a previous era.

Jeongseon train station is 2km from the town centre and the nearest *yeogwan*, so you may need to take a taxi (W1500) as there are not many buses. It's another 2km from the town centre to the express bus terminal. Daewangjang (대왕장) is a typical old-fashioned *yeogwan* but a reasonable deal at W30,000.

Getting There & Away
BUS

Buses leave Jeongseon for a number of destinations:

Destination	Price (W)	Duration	Frequency
Dong-Seoul	14,600	4hr	7 daily
Gangneung	7000	1¾hr	13 daily
Jecheon	5900	2hr	6 daily
Taebaek	4700	1¼hr	7 daily

WONJU 원주
pop 283,000

Wonju is a relaxed, youthful city with a large Korean army base. Yonsei University has a campus here; its green lawns overlook a man-

MARKET WATCHING

The food section of Jeongseon's five-day market is what catches the eye: middle-aged women are frying up vegetable pancakes, putting red beans into small doughnuts, and stirring big cauldrons of bubbling brown soup. *Maemilmuk* are thick strips of noodle that are put into the brown soup and garnished with dried seaweed. Under a multicoloured golf umbrella, a woman is making green rice cakes that look like strips of plasticine. The inevitable *kimchi* (pickled vegetables) sellers guard tables groaning under the weight of 20kg jars of fiery, glowing *kimchi* – some of them containing small, whole pickled crabs. Nearby, strips of pungent but tasty dried squid are being heated up and passed through a small mangle. Next up are containers of soy-bean paste – the basis of millions of soups that are enjoyed every day throughout Korea. An *ajumma* (older woman) with a towel wrapped round her head is selling homebrew. The next stall has a monstrous octopus laid out on a bed of ice, and further on, table-sized slabs of white tofu are for sale – something bland at last – together with grey intestines that are steaming in a big metal pot. Finally there is the 'popping man' with his ancient machine. He puts a handful of grain into a metal cup, there's a puff of steam, and hey presto– a rice cracker pops out. Now that's real magic. No wonder a gang of small kids is watching him intently.

made pond and make for a relaxing place to stroll among students who generally jump at the chance to practice their English with a 'real live' foreigner. 'A', 'B' and (yes, you guessed it!) 'C' streets have a host of restaurants, hotels, motels and bars. The street market (open from 6am to 9pm) has an amazing variety of fruits and veggies. Local buses cost W950 and many of the stops are GPS-enabled, allowing you to know exactly when the next one will arrive.

Getting There & Away

There are two terminals, **Wonju terminal** (☎ 746 5223; www.wonjuterminal.co.kr) and **Wonju express bus terminal** (☎ 747 4181). The latter serves Seoul.

BUS

Destination	Price (W)	Duration	Frequency
Cheongju	8000	1½hr	hourly
Gangneung	6300	1½hr	every 30min
Seoul Gangnam	5700	1½hr	every 15min

TRAIN

Trains (W4800, nine daily) run between Wonju and Seoul's Cheongnyangni station.

CHIAKSAN NATIONAL PARK
치악산 국립공원

Chiaksan means 'Magpie Crags Mountain' and this **park** (☎ 732 5231; adult/youth/child W3600/1300/700; ☻ sunrise-sunset) is 20km northeast of Wonju, making it a very do-able weekend trip from Seoul. The dense forests, mist-cloaked mountains, rushing rock-strewn rivers and wildlife make it well worth checking out. The most

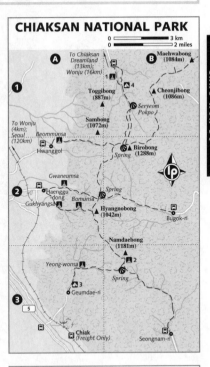

CHIAKSAN NATIONAL PARK

SIGHTS & ACTIVITIES	
Guryongsa 구룡사	1 B1
Sang·wonsa 상원사	2 B3

SLEEPING 🛏	
Geumdae-ri Camping Ground 금대리야영장	3 A3
Guryong-sa Camping Ground 구룡사야영장	4 B1

popular hike starts from **Guryongsa** (Nine Dragon Temple, partially burned and recently restored) and goes up to **Birobong** (three hours) and then either back down again to Guryongsa or down to **Hwanggol**. The hike down takes about two hours, whichever route you take. The hikes are quite tough and there are no mountain shelters in the park.

In the southern part of the park is **Sang·wonsa**. Perched on top of a 50m cliff, it commands a mind-liberating view across the valley. Talk with an official about the current trail conditions before you make hiking plans.

Sleeping & Eating

The main *minbak* and restaurant area is outside the Guryongsa entrance. For those who prefer the great outdoors, camping is possible at **Geumdae-ri** and **Guryong-sa** (☎ 731-1289; small/ large tent W3000/W6000).

Getting There & Away

From Wonju, you can take buses 41 or 41-1 (W950, 40 minutes, every 25 minutes) to Guryongsa. Buses 82 or 82-1 run to Hwanggol, while buses 21 to 25 run to Geumdae-ri and Seongnam-ri.

Gyeongsangbuk-do
경상북도

Gyeongsangbuk-do's natural beauty is seconded only by its profusion of spectacular temples, Confucian schools, ancient pagodas, rock-carved Buddhas, teashops and tombs. Gyeongju, once the capital of the Shilla dynasty (57 BC–AD 935), is often called 'the museum without walls' for its historical treasures, many of which are outdoors. The oddly symmetrical 'hills' in the centre of town are serene, peaceful pyramids – stately reminders of the dead they still honour. Thankfully, this beautiful city was spared the ravages of bombings in the Korean War; even today it retains a 19th-century feel.

Come here and find treasures in all directions. Andong, in the north, offers mouthwatering mackerel, a fascinating folk village, strong *soju* (locally brewed vodka) and many temples as well, including the oldest wooden building in South Korea. To the south, check out Daegu's medicinal herb market or peek at the anachronistic 'pink light district' that still operates despite new laws banning prostitution.

While technically in Gyeongsangbuk-do's southern sister (Gyeongsangnam-do), Haeinsa is a must-see temple-library most easily accessed via Daegu: check out the 1000-year-old wooden tablets, preserved in a building so ahead of its time that modern science hasn't improved it.

In the 'Sea of Korea', as Koreans call it, is the rugged, mist-kissed island of Ulleungdo, where fishing villages dry squid in quantities that boggle the mind. Even further east lies Dokdo (aka Takeshima), a fishing ground still disputed today.

GYEONGSANGBUK-DO

HIGHLIGHTS

- See and smell the fascinating **medicinal herb market** (p192) in Daegu
- Marvel at the 80,000-plus wooden tablets of the Buddhist sutras at the temple **Haeinsa** (p195)
- Slip back into the Shilla era in **Gyeongju** (p197)
- Experience the Confucian academies **Oksan Seowon** (p208) and **Dosan Seowon** (p220)
- Watch squid dry on the rugged, gorgeous island of **Ulleungdo** (p212), 135km offshore
- See centuries-old papermaking and masks at the villages of **Hahoe** (p220) and **Andong** (p220)

| ■ TELEPHONE CODE: 054 | ■ POPULATION: 5.1 MILLION | ■ AREA: 20,023 SQ KM |

History

This beautiful province holds many of South Korea's oldest treasures. Whether you plan on meandering through Gyeongju's 'open-air museum' or want to create your own elixir of eternal life in Daegu's Herbal Medicine Market, you will find that the area's historical events are more tangible here, less a part of the distant past and more a part of the present. At the centre of South Korea, this area was once the capital of the Shilla empire (57BC–935AD), and as such was a central part of Korean government and trade. During this almost 1000-year-long empire, the Shilla rulers created alliances with China to defeat Japanese threats, as well as to repel other Korean invaders. During this time Confucian laws were widely adopted and informed all aspects of Korean life including who, where, and when a person could marry. In many ways these traditions are still held by modern Koreans, who often follow Confucian rules (as well as their parents' wishes) in deciding how to marry.

National Parks

Gyeongsangbuk-do's national parks are not as famous as those of its neighbour, Gang·won-do, but they provide wonderful hiking and photograph opportunities and are surprisingly close (thanks to KTX high-speed trains) to Seoul. Weekend trips to Gyeongju National Park, Palgongsan Provincial Park or Juwangsan National Park will bring you face

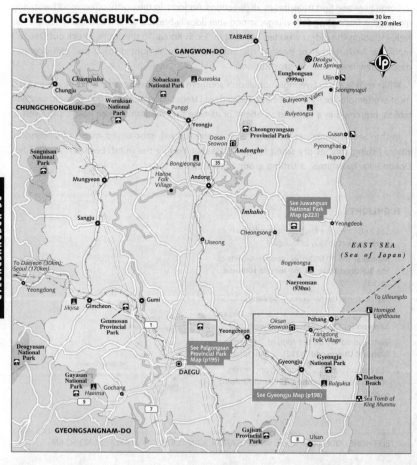

to face with stunning scenery and temples, and will be less peopled (even in the peak seasons) than some of the parks closer to Seoul.

The remote island of Ulleungdo, although not a park proper, might just as well be one: its jagged cliffs plunge down into steel-blue waters, populated only by seabirds. The small villages subsist on squid and other marine crops, and you will not be disappointed to be so far away from Seoul.

Getting There & Around

The area is serviced by Daegu's International Airport, by KTX and express trains, and by buses (the latter are cheap, quick and usually direct, often arriving faster than a train or flight). Some of the more remote areas are best accessed by car or (in the case of Ulleungdo) by ferry.

DAEGU 대구

☎ 053 / pop 2.45 million

Daegu's fascinating traditional-medicine market is its biggest tourist draw. Come here to see strange roots the size of human thighs, jars of honey-coloured liquids, baskets of flowers, dried leaves and medicinal herbs. Even if it's pouring rain the avenues smell fragrantly of these ancient cures, which many Koreans still swear by today (though Viagra is gaining a foothold in the 'stamina-producing' arena).

A simple, two-line subway system makes getting around easy, and the country's third-largest city has great restaurants, good nightlife and neon that puts parts of Seoul to shame.

Daegu makes a great hub for day trips: be sure to check out Haeinsa (p195) and Jikjisa (p196), both of which offer temple stays for those wishing to get a closer look. Note that Daegu, while surrounded by Gyeongsangbuk-do, is its own administrative district and has its own telephone area code.

Orientation

At 885 sq km Daegu covers a larger area than Seoul. Its subway was the site of a horrific fire (caused when a passenger set himself and others ablaze in 2003), but things are back to normal now – a second line opened up in 2005. Most of the city's attractions are within easy walking distance of the subway or train. The airport is a 30-minute drive from the city, to the northeast.

Information

Daegu has a **tourist office** (☎ 053 1330, 939 0080; 9am-5pm) at all major transit points and destinations including the airport, outside Dongdaegu station, inside Seomun Market, at Duryu Park (all Map pp190–1) and in the central shopping district and by the Herbal Medicine Market (Map p193). All have comprehensive local maps in English, reams of pamphlets, and at some (including the one at Dongdaegu station), free internet terminals.

Kyobo Books (Map p193; ☎ 425 3501; 2nd floor, Kyobo Bldg; 9.30am-5pm) is a good place for English-language books. It's near Jungangno subway station.

Sights & Activities
MARKETS & SHOPPING STREETS

Daegu is a shopper's dream. In addition to good prices on all kinds of 'normal' and brand-name goods (clothes, shoes, bags etc) at the various department stores, Daegu has numerous speciality markets that make for a fascinating stroll even if you're not going to part with any won.

Start at the **Seomun Market** (Map pp190-1; 9am-6pm Mar-Oct, 9am-5pm Nov-Feb), a hulking, multistorey complex with over 4000 shops in six sections. Bustling yet orderly, it's been one of Korea's big-three markets since 1669, even if the current buildings have little of that historic character. The market is closed on the second and fourth Sunday of each month.

Yasigolmok (야시골목; Map p193) is the heart of Daegu's shopping district, with clothing and fashion outlets, bustling day and night.

While anti-prostitution laws were recently tightened and the sex trade is supposed to be gone, **Jagalmadang** (Map pp190–1) is one of Korea's 'big-three' red-light districts; the other two are in Busan and Seoul. Apparently the streets of Jagalmadang were once paved with small stones so that any girls trying to escape (or customers trying to get some action for free) would be heard. Although the lights are mostly pink, not red, it's a curious scene and can be interesting for foreigners, even women. Don't expect gratis nudity though – the women read or slurp noodles.

DAEGU NATIONAL MUSEUM
국립 대구 박물관

This national **museum** (Map pp190-1; ☎ 768 6051; http://daegu.museum.go.kr/; adult/child W1000/500;

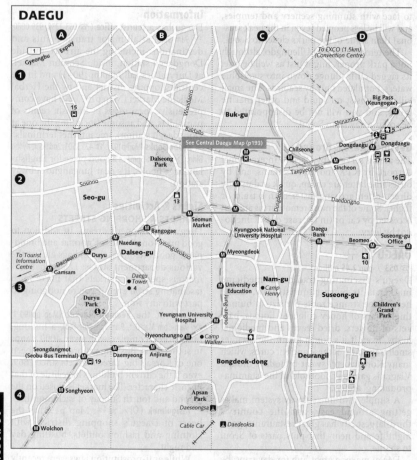

DAEGU

🕙 9am-6pm Mar-Oct, 9am-5pm Nov-Feb, closed Mon)
is home to a fine collection of pottery, Buddhist icons and various dioramas showing the local history. The English-language
signage is reasonably good. The museum is
well served by bus lines: from central Daegu
take bus 242 or 427 to Daegu National Museum, or from Dongdaegu station take bus
814 or 514.

WOOBANG TOWER LAND 우방 타워랜드
Visitors with kids will want to head to this
amusement park (Map pp190-1; ☎ 620 0100; www
.woobangland.co.kr/english; adult/youth/child
W8500/6300/5300), in the huge Duryu Park west
of the city centre. Opening hours vary – check
the website before visiting.

BULLO-DONG TUMULI PARK
불로동 고분 공원
North of town, not far from Daegu airport,
Bullo-Dong Tumuli Park (☎ 940 1224; admission free;
🕙 9am-6pm) covers some 330,000 sq metres.
The grassy hillocks rising like bumps across
the valley are *tumuli* (burial mounds, similar
to those in Gyeongju). Dating from the 2nd
to the 6th century AD, the *tumuli* are for
both nobles and commoners – the higher the
location on the hill: the higher the status of
the person.

Tours
The city **tourist information centre** (☎ 627 8900; www
.daegutour.or.jp; 🕙 9am-6pm, 9am-7pm Jul & Aug) offers a
series of seven tours that are free for foreigners

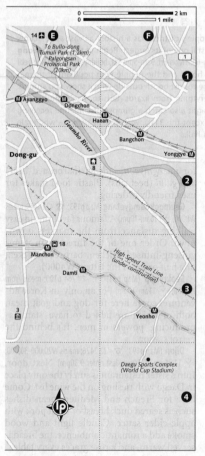

GYEONGSANGBUK-DO

(not including admission, meals etc). Tour programmes change weekly.

Sleeping
BUDGET

Rojan Motel (Map pp190-1; ☎ 766 0336; r W18,000) By far the best deal in Gyeongsangbuk-do, this spotless motel offers clean, crisp sheets and free coffee and candy – even energy drinks in the fridge. No English is spoken, but foreigners are welcome. Payment by credit card ups the price to W20,000.

Amoreu Motel (Map pp190-1; ☎ 955 8155; r W30,000; ✶ ▣) Décor is dark here but it's not love-motel tacky: the rooms are clean and all have TVs, combs and free coffee. Turn right out of Dongdaegu station and cross over the pedes-

trian bridge, then go right (down the steps to the street). It's straight ahead on the left, with a pink sign.

MIDRANGE

Hotel Ariana (Map pp190-1; ☎ 765 7776; www.ariana .co.kr; d/tw from W88,000/98,000; ✶ ▣) A great deal on new crisp, characterless rooms, near the Deurangil restaurant district. Some English is spoken by the staff. Ice cream–lovers will drool when they see the Haagen-Dazs freezer in the lobby.

Garden Hotel (Map pp190-1; ☎ 471 9911; www .gardenhotel.co.kr; d W95,800; ✶) Near the US military camps and used to catering to English-speaking guests. Cosy, up-to-date rooms have minibars and hair dryers.

DAEGU'S HERBAL MEDICINE MARKET 한약 시장

This market (Map p193), west of the central shopping district, has a history as vast as its scope. It dates from 1658, making it Korea's oldest and still one of its largest. Begin at the **Yangnyeong Exhibition Hall** (☎ 257 4729; admission free; ☉ 9am-6pm Mon-Fri, 9am-5pm Sat, holidays & Mon-Fri Nov-Feb) for an introduction to *insam* (ginseng), reindeer horns and the people who popularised them – there's usually someone who speaks English at the tourist booth outside who'll show you around. Then head out to the street to stock up on everything from lizards' tails to magic mushrooms (the latter with a prescription, of course); you might also catch a glimpse of someone receiving acupuncture. On the days ending with 1 or 6 (except the 31st), *yangnyeong sijang* (a wholesale market) takes place downstairs in the exhibition hall.

TOP END

Hotel Inter-Burgo (Map pp190-1; ☎ 952 0088; www .hotel.inter-burgo.com; r W193,600-257,000; ▨) Snazzy, with Spanish touches that give it more character than some top-end clones. The hotel boasts a parklike setting, contemporary lines, river views, pool, sauna and even a putting green.

Taegu Grand Hotel (Map pp190-1; ☎ 742 0001; www .taegugrand.co.kr; d/tw from W260,000/270,000; ▨ ▣) A kilometre or two south of Dongdaegu station, newly renovated, with live music Monday to Saturday. Amenities include a business centre, health club and saunas (both male and female). Suites have computers.

Eating

Around the Yasigolmok district (Map p193) are literally hundreds of cafés, bars and nightclubs.

Gimbapjang (Map p193; ☎ 425 0343; dishes W2000-4000; ☉ 10am-2am) Nearly across the street from Kaejung, with *naengmyeon* (buckwheat noodles in an icy broth) and *mandu* (dumplings) on the menu at rock-bottom prices. Folk music is incongruously festive in this well-lit greasy spoon.

Into (Map p193; ☎ 421 3965; dishes W4000-12000; ☉ noon-9pm) The Into is a European café that serves fine pastas and tasty salads. There are just four tables, but it has a nice variety of French and Italian items on the changing menu.

Kaejung (Map p193; ☎ 424 7051; dishes W5000-8000; ☉ 10am-10pm) A popular and respected place specialising in chewy and very tasty *naengmyeon*, and soft tofu. An English menu is available. Jazz tunes croon, and a faux chia-pet hamster add flair.

Gangsan Myeonok (Map p193; ☎ 426 6878; dishes W5000-9000; ☉ 10am-10pm) One of Daegu's oldest establishments, this eatery is well regarded

for *naengmyeon, bulgogi* (barbecued beef) and *galbi* (beef ribs). Plastic food makes for user-friendly ordering.

Geumgok Samgyetang (Map p193; ☎ 424 4449; meals W8000; ☉ 10am-10pm) A famous favourite, in easy walking distance from the markets downtown. Order one of the three menu items: ginseng-infused chicken, barbecue chicken, or a half order of the latter (W4000).

Seokryujip (Map pp190-1; ☎ 764 6100; meals from W8000; ☉ 11am-10pm) For an only-in-Korea adventure, come here for dog and goat meat, both of which are fabled to have 'stamina-producing' powers in men. It's behind the petrol station.

Dijon (Map p193; ☎ 422 2426; mains W20,000-30,000; ☉ 11.30am-10.30pm, last order 9.30pm) Next door, Into's sister restaurant is surely the only place in Daegu with riesling on the wine list. Come here for French and Mediterranean dishes such as seared duck breast or roast pork with apple-cider sauce. Candle light and wood smoke add a romantic ambience, the bread is served warm, and a rose graces every table.

Drinking

Being Korea's third-largest city, Daegu has a gay district with many bars near the express bus terminal (Map pp190-1).

The central shopping district is teeming with *hof* (local pubs), karaoke bars and cafés.

Bus (Map pp190-1; ☎ 427 3312; side dishes W10,000, beers W3500-5000; ☉ 5pm-noon, yes, noon) Unmistakable, this bus-turned-pub is on a side street right near G2. It's a popular hang out.

Ariana Bräu (☎ 762 0900; ☉ 5pm-2am; dishes W9000-35,000) This place has food and then turns into a pub after 8pm, with live music six nights a week.

Tombo (☎ 745 5425; drinks W3000-10,000) Foreign visitors might start at this tiny shot bar for a

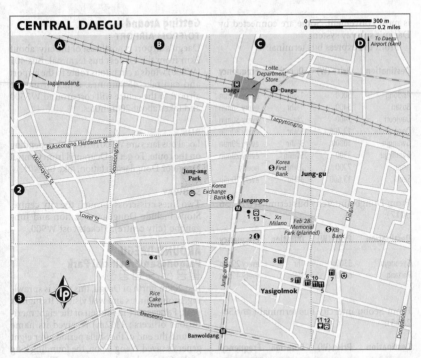

CENTRAL DAEGU

mix of 20- to 40-somethings, both local and foreign.

Entertainment

There is a huge Xn Milano complex that houses the Hanil Gukjang cinema (Map p193), where there are often English-language movies.

G2 (Map p193; ☎ 246 1623; www.clubg2.co.kr; admission incl 1 drink W5000-10,000; ⏰ 7pm-5am) Come here to bump around in trance-inducing, black-lit darkness. The funk and hip-hop is ear-splitting – just the way most of the crowd wants it. Come after 11pm or you'll have the place to yourself. Soldiers are asked to leave by 12.30am.

Getting There & Away

AIR

Asiana and Korean Air connect Daegu with Seoul and Jeju. International destinations include Shanghai and Bangkok.

BUS

There are five bus terminals (Map pp190–1): an **express bus terminal** (☎ 743 3701), by Dong-daegu train station), plus Dongbu, Seobu,

Nambu and Bukbu (east, west, south and north) intercity terminals. This list is not meant to be comprehensive, and note that buses to some destinations leave from multiple terminals, so it's best to inquire which is most convenient. Some are connected by Daegu's subway system.

From the express bus terminal:

Destination	Price (W)	Duration	Frequency
Andong	5000	1½hr	every 20min
Busan	5400	1¾hr	every 30min
Daejeon	7400	2hr	every 30min
Dong Seoul	13,700	3¾hr	every 30min
Gwangju	10800	3¾hr	every 30min
Gyeongju	3300	50min	every 20min
Jinju	7200	2¼hr	hourly
Seoul	13,600	3¾hr	every 10min

From Dongbu intercity bus terminal (☎ 756 0017):

Destination	Price (W)	Duration	Frequency
Gyeongju	3300	1hr	every 25min
Pohang	6000	1½hr	every 45min

From Seobu intercity bus terminal (☎ 656-2825):

Destination	Price (W)	Duration	Frequency
Busan	8400	2hr	8 daily
Haeinsa	4000	1½hr	every 20min

From Bukbu intercity bus terminal (☎ 357 1851):

Destination	Price (W)	Duration	Frequency
Andong (nonstop /express)	6800	1½/2¼hr	every 20/ 30min
Chuncheon	16,600	5½hr	5 daily

TRAIN

Dongdaegu station (Map pp190–1), on the eastern side of the city, is the main station for long-distance trains. It's also next door to the express bus station.

You'll find that there are good connections to Busan and Seoul. *Mugunghwa* (limited express) trains run every 30 minutes to Seoul (W15,800 to W19,800, 3½ to four hours) and Busan (W6200 to W7300, 1½ hours). KTX service has frequent trains to Daejeon and occasional ones all the way to Dongdaegu. Check www.korail.go.kr for exact schedules and fares.

Getting Around
TO/FROM AIRPORT

Daegu's airport is northeast of the city, about 2km from the express bus terminal. Bus 401 (W900) winds a circuitous route to the airport and can take 45 minutes. A taxi from the airport to the centre will cost around W3500 and takes about 20 minutes.

BUS

Local bus fares are W900 or W1300, depending on the route. To get to Deurangil from Central Daegu or Dongdaegu station, take bus 401.

SUBWAY

Two lines crisscross through the city centre. Stops include Dongdaegu station and Jungangno (city centre). Tickets cost W900.

AROUND DAEGU
Palgongsan Provincial Park
팔공산 도립공원

Just 20km north of Daegu, this park is sprawling, mountainous and well visited. Its highest peak, **Palgongsan** ('mountain of the eight meritorious officers'; 1192m) received its name around the end of the Shilla period after eight generals saved Wang-Geon, the founding king of the Goryeo kingdom.

The park's most popular destination is **Donghwasa** (☎ 982 0101; admission W2500; ⏱ 9am-6pm), the province's leading temple, with a history stretching back to 493.

Gatbawi (☎ 983 8586; www.seonbonsa.com; admission free) is a medicinal Buddha and national treasure, some 850m above sea level and said to date back to 638. This Buddha is famed for the flat stone 'hat' hovering over its head, 15cm thick. Incense wafts and the mountain mist makes it quite a spiritual experience. It takes about 45 minutes to walk up the (numerous!) stone steps to Gatbawi from the tourist village.

The **Palgongsan Skyline Cable Car** (☎ 982 8801; return W5500; ⏱ 9.45am-sunset) is the quickest way to ascend Palgongsan. The 1.2km-long ride drops you at the observatory (820m), which affords a panoramic view of Daegu. There's a tourist village at the base of the cable car that has many restaurants – Sanjungsikdang (meals W5500 to W18,000) is known for mushroom cuisine including tasty mushroom *pajeon* (pancakes).

Bus 401 (W900) runs between Dongdaegu station and the tourist village below Gatbawi.

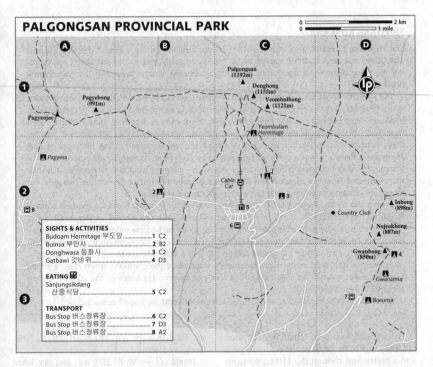

PALGONGSAN PROVINCIAL PARK

SIGHTS & ACTIVITIES
Budoam Hermitage 부도암 1 C2
Buinsa 부인사 2 B2
Donghwasa 동화사 3 C2
Gatbawi 갓바위 4 D3

EATING 🍴
Sanjungsikdang
산중식당 5 C2

TRANSPORT
Bus Stop 버스정류장 6 C2
Bus Stop 버스정류장 7 D3
Bus Stop 버스정류장 8 A2

Bus 급행 (Geuphaeng; W1300) connects Donghwasa and the bus stop near Dongdaegu station, running at least once every 12 minutes and taking 50 minutes to complete the journey.

Haeinsa 해인사

This Unesco World Heritage **temple** (☎ 055-931 1001; admission W3500; ⏱ 8am-11am, noon-5pm Wed-Mon) should be on every visitor's not-to-be-missed list.

Haeinsa holds 81,340 woodblock scriptures, making it one of the largest Buddhist libraries of its kind. Known as the **Tripitaka Koreana** (see p196), the blocks are housed in four enormous buildings at the temple's upper reaches, complete with simple but effective ventilation to prevent deterioration. Also housed here are an additional 2835 blocks from the Goryeo period containing more Buddhist scriptures, literary works and an illustration of Avatamsaka Sutra. Although the buildings are normally locked, the blocks are easily visible through slatted windows.

As well as being one of Korea's most significant temples, Haeinsa is also one of the most beautiful. Part of its beauty lies in the natural setting of mixed deciduous and coniferous forest. It's a romantic's paradise in wet weather, when wisps of cloud drift through the forest. At prayer times (3.30am, 10am and 6.30pm), the place can feel otherworldly (try listening with your eyes closed), and on our visit we were able to create our own print from an actual woodblock in the **exhibition hall**.

The main hall, **Daegwangjeon**, was burnt down during the Japanese invasion of 1592 and again (accidentally) in 1817, though miraculously the Tripitaka escaped destruction. It escaped a third time when a South Korean pilot working for the Allied forces refused to allow them to bomb it.

A **Haeinsa museum** (☎ 055-934 3150; admission W2000; ⏱ 10am-6pm Mar-Oct, 10am-5pm Nov-Feb, closed Tue), built in 2002, showcases some of the temple's treasures and has a reverie on Haeinsa in contemporary art upstairs. It is a short walk from the main road, and the temple is a further 15-minute walk. At the time of research the museum was closed for remodelling.

TRIPITAKA KOREANA

The **Tripitaka Koreana**, also known as the Goryeo Buddhist canon, is one of the world's most significant complete Buddhist sacred texts. Tripitaka literally means 'three baskets', representing the three divisions of Buddhism: the Sutra (scriptures), Vinaya (laws) and the Abhidharma (treatises).

The Tripitaka Koreana has been preserved on more than 80,000 beautifully carved woodblocks, which took 16 years to complete. From carefully selecting appropriate birch wood, then soaking it in brine and boiling it in salt before drying it, to locating and constructing a sophisticated repository, the techniques involved were so complex and the artwork so intricate that they remain an inspiration today. The woodblocks are housed and preserved in the 15th-century hall, **Janggyong Pango**, a masterpiece of ingenuity in its own right; its techniques include charcoal beneath the clay floor and different-sized windows to minimise variations in humidity. Despite the ravages of Japanese invasion and fires that destroyed the rest of the temple complex, the repository remained standing with the woodblocks preserved intact.

During the 1970s, President Pak Chung-hee ordered the construction of a modern storage facility for the woodblocks. The facility was equipped with advanced ventilation, temperature and humidity control. However, after some test woodblocks began to grow mildew the whole scheme was scrapped. Today the four storage halls and woodblocks are inscribed on the Unesco World Heritage List to ensure their continued preservation. In a bold attempt to ensure accessibility to more people, Haeinsa's monks have completely transcribed the complete works onto a single CD-ROM and translated the classical Chinese text into modern-day Korean – the 20-plus-volume set costs a mere W3,000,000.

Excellent additional info is at www.cha.go.kr/english/world_heritage/haeinsa.jsp.

Hikers will want to challenge **Gayasan** (1430m), the main peak in the national park and a pretty one, though the 1100m up from Haeinsa are known to be tough. With luck you might spot an otter on a riverbank.

SLEEPING & EATING

Haeinsa is a popular day trip from Daegu, but there are options to spend the night. Probably the most interesting is Haeinsa itself, which participates in the Temple Stay Korea (p384). Don't expect luxury – men and women sleep in separate *ondol* (underfloor heating) dorms, but it's a worthwhile option to experience the 3.30am service.

Gobau (고바우; ☎ 931 7311; r W30,000; meals W9000) A beautiful place to stay, with kind owners and interesting Korean poetry on the walls. Rooms are simple and floor heated, with yellow linoleum and a fat tube of toothpaste by the sink. Try the restaurant (7am to midnight) where *sanchae jongsik* (rice with many assorted side dishes) is the main dish. Try for a table in the back room, where windows look out over a stream and trees.

Haeinsa Hotel (해인관광호텔; ☎ 055-933 2000; www.haeinsahotel.co.kr; d/tw W78,650/84,700; 🔀 🖵) Comfort at the top of the hill, with fountains and a polished lobby, coffee shop and restaurant. English is spoken. The hotel offers a 20% weekday discount.

Jeonju (전주; ☎ 931 2323; www.jjbab.com; dishes W5000-10,000; ⏱ 7am-9pm) On the 2nd floor of the bus terminal, this clean, cheap shop serves good *bibimbap* (vegetables, meat and rice), pancakes and veggies, with the peaceful sound of the river in the background.

GETTING THERE & AWAY

While actually in Gyeongsamnam-do, Haeinsa is most easily accessed by bus (W4000, 1½ hours, every 30 minutes) from Daegu's Seobu terminal. The subway connects Seobu terminal to Dongdaegu station, making it (if you are unbelievably crazy and enjoy getting up at the crack of dawn) a possible day trip from Seoul. Most people will want to plan an overnight in Daegu.

Jikjisa 직지사

One of Korea's largest and most famous temples, **Jikjisa** (Map p188; ☎ 436 6175; admission adult/youth/child W2500/1500/1000; ⏱ 7am-6.30pm Mar-Oct, 7am-5.30pm Nov-Feb) is one of the most picturesque – with quiet forests, a river and ancient stone monuments covered with lush, green moss. The delicate paintings on the temples have a refinement and grace that is very appealing, as are the giant timbers that support the structures, and the faded, cracked wood.

Situated in the foothills of Hwang-aksan, amid ancient pines and hardwoods (many trees are labelled), it was first constructed during the reign of the 19th Shilla king, Nulji (AD 417–58). Priest Jajang, who had spent many years studying in China and brought back to Korea the first complete set of the Tripitaka Buddhist scriptures, rebuilt it in AD 645. Further reconstruction was done in the 10th century but the temple was completely destroyed during the Japanese invasion of 1592 and reconstructed in 1602.

SIGHTS

Of the 40 original buildings, about 20 still exist, the oldest dating from the 1602 reconstruction. Highlights include the **Daeungjong**, with stunning Buddhist triad paintings on silk (1774) that are national treasures, and the rotating collection in the temple's **Buddhist art museum** (☎ 436 6009; admission W1000; ⏰ 10am-5pm Mar-Oct, 10am-4.30pm Nov & Dec, closed Mon). The museum is closed in January and February.

Jikjisa's most famous monk was called Samyeong (aka Son-gun or Yujeong), a militant monk who spent many years in Geumgangsan (the Diamond Mountains in North Korea). He organised troops to fight against the Japanese in 1592 and later became the chief Korean delegate to the Japanese court when a peace treaty was negotiated in 1604. Following the completion of the treaty, Samyeong returned to Korea with over 3000 released prisoners of war.

SLEEPING & EATING

Many visitors day trip to Jikjisa, and the temple participates in **Temple Stay Korea** (☎ Jikjisa 436 2773; www.templestaykorea.net; per night W30,000); programmes are arranged on a one-on-one basis. Otherwise, there's a well-established tourist village by the bus stop with a range of *minbak* (private homes with rooms for rent), *yeogwan* (budget motels) and restaurants.

GETTING THERE & AWAY

Jikjisa is reached via Gimcheon (pop 152,000), about 20 minutes by bus. Local buses 11, 111, and 112 (W1300) depart every 10 minutes from Gimcheon's **intercity bus terminal** (☎ 432 7600), just to the right of the train station parking lot. The temple complex is a pleasant 15-minute walk from the bus stop.

Gimcheon can be reached by train on the line connecting Daegu (50 minutes) and Seoul. If you're using KTX from Seoul, transfer at Daejeon and take a local line to Gimcheon.

By bus:

Destination	Price (W)	Duration	Distance
Andong	10,200	2hr	125km
Daegu	4600	1¼hr	88km
Daejeon	5400	1¼hr	88km
Gochang*	5700	1¼hr	65km

*for Haeinsa & Gayasan National Park

GYEONGJU 경주
pop 266,000

Known as 'the museum without walls', Gyeongju holds more tombs, temples, rock carvings, pagodas, Buddhist statuary and the ruins of palaces, pleasure gardens and castles than any other place in South Korea. *Tumuli* (grass-covered burial mounds) are only the most conspicuous and accessible of the sights.

In 57 BC, around when Julius Caesar was subduing Gaul, Gyeongju became the capital of the Shilla dynasty, and it remained so for nearly 1000 years. In the 7th century AD, under King Munmu, Shilla conquered the neighbouring kingdoms of Goguryeo and Baekje, and Gyeongju became capital of the whole peninsula. The city's population eventually peaked at around one million, but as empires do, Shilla eventually fell victim to division from within and invasion from without.

The city began a cultural revival in the early 20th century – with much preservation and restoration work thanks to the dictator Park Chung-hee in the 1970s – which continues today.

One can not truly know Gyeongju's charms without visiting its outlying districts. Gyeongju covers a vast 1323 sq km, and you should allow several days to take it all in.

Orientation & Information

Central Gyeongju is compact, encompassing the bus and train terminals (under 20 minutes' walk apart) and, between them, sights, lodgings and dining.

About 5km east of the centre is Bomunho, a lakeside resort with a golf course, luxury hotels and posh restaurants. A 16km drive southeast brings you to Bulguksa, one of Korea's most

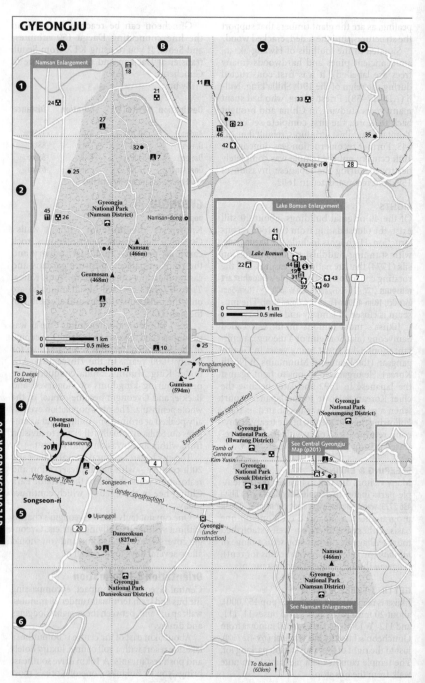

GYEONGJU

GYEONGSANGBUK-DO

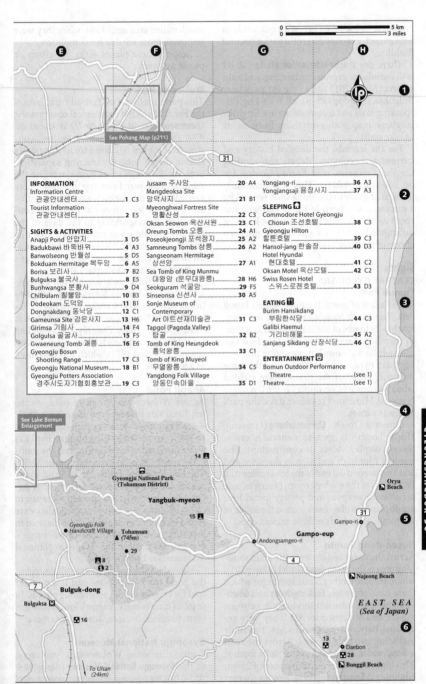

famous temples. From here it's a quick ride to Seokguram, a mountain grotto with a historic Buddha.

There are **tourist-information kiosks** (☎ 772 3842) outside the express bus terminal and train station (Map p201) and in the car park near Bulguksa (Map pp198–9), all with English-speaking staff and a comprehensive English-language map with everything from sights to bike trails.

For the legends, the detailed history and current archaeological debate surrounding the Shilla remains, read *Korea's Golden Age* by Edward B Adams. This is a beautifully illustrated guide to the Shilla sites, written by a man who was born in Korea and who has spent most of his life there. The book can be difficult to buy in Gyeongju, so pick up a copy at one of the large bookshops in Seoul.

Sights

CENTRAL GYEONGJU
Tumuli Park

In the heart of town, the huge walled **Tumuli Park** (Map p201; ☎ 746 6020; admission W1500; ⏰ 9am-9pm) has 23 tombs of Shilla monarchs and family members. From the outside, they look like grassy hillocks – much more subtle than the Egyptian pyramids, but they served the same purpose; many of the *tumuli* have yielded fabulous treasures, on display at the Gyeongju National Museum. On colder days, the park closes at sunset.

One of the tombs, **Cheonmachong** (Heavenly Horse Tomb), is open to visitors. A cross-section display shows its construction. The tomb is 13m high and 47m in diameter and was built around the end of the 5th century AD. Facsimiles of the golden crown, bracelets, jade ornaments, weapons and pottery found here are displayed in glass cases around the inside of the tomb; other finds include ancient eggs.

Noseo-dong Tombs

Across the street and closer to the main shopping area is the **Noseo-dong district** (Map p201), where there are other Shilla tombs for which there is no entry fee. **Seobongchong** and **Geum-gwanchong** are adjacent tombs built between the 4th and 5th centuries AD. They were excavated between 1921 and 1946, the finds including two gold crowns. Across the road is **Bonghwadae**, the largest extant Shilla tomb at 22m high and with a circumference of 250m; adjoining is **Geumnyeongchong**. Houses covered

much of this area until 1984, when they were removed; more are due for demolition.

Respect these places – do not climb or picnic on them.

Wolseong Park

This park, southeast of Tumuli Park, houses the Far East's oldest astrological observatory, **Cheomseongdae** (Map p201; ☎ 772 5134; admission W300; ⏰ 8am-6pm Apr-Oct, 9am-6pm Nov-Mar), constructed between 632 and 646. Its apparently simple design conceals amazing sophistication: the 12 stones of its base symbolise the months of the year. From top to bottom there are 30 layers – one for each day of the month – and a total of 366 stones was used in its construction, corresponding to the days of the year (OK, so time was calculated a little differently back then!). Numerous other technical details relate, for example, to the tower's position in relation to certain stars.

A few minutes' walk south from Cheomseongdae is the site of **Banwolseong** (Castle of the Crescent Moon; Map pp198–9; admission free), once a fabled fortress. Now it's attractive parkland, with some walls and ruins. The only intact building is Seokbinggo or 'Stone Ice House' (early 18th century, restored 1973), which was once used as a food store.

Anapji Pond

Across Wolseongno, the main road, on the left-hand side is **Anapji Pond** (Map pp198–9; ☎ 772 4041; admission W1000; ⏰ 8am-sunset Sep-May, 7.30am-7pm Jun-Aug), constructed by King Munmu in 674 as a pleasure garden to commemorate the unification of the Korean peninsula under Shilla. The buildings here burned in 935 and many relics ended up in the pond itself, to be rediscovered only when it was drained for repair in 1975. Thousands of well-preserved relics were found including wooden objects, a die used in drinking games, scissors and a royal barge – you can see them in the Gyeongju National Museum (see below).

Nowadays the buildings are still gone, but the pond has been refilled and is a popular spot for couples to take prewedding photos. In season (June to early August), lotus blossoms seem to fill the horizon. Bring the camera.

Gyeongju National Museum

Continuing along Wolseongno, you come to the **Gyeongju National Museum** (Map pp198–9; ☎ 740 7518; http://gyeongju.museum.go.kr; admission adult/

CENTRAL GYEONGJU

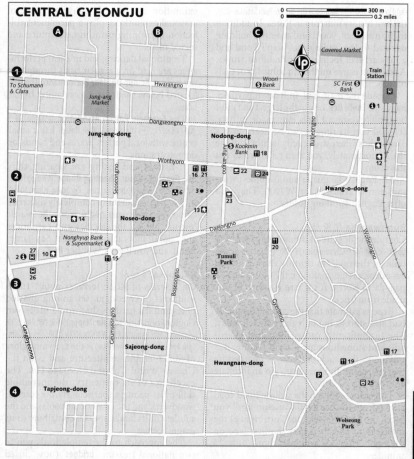

GYEONGSANGBUK-DO

child W1000/500; 9am-6pm Tue-Sun, 6-9pm Sat May-Oct), the best history museum in Korea. In addition to the main hall, you'll find an entire building devoted to the findings at Anapji Pond and a new art hall focusing on Buddhist works. Admission is free on the 4th Saturday of each month.

Outside the main hall, in its own pavilion, hangs the **Emille Bell**, one of the largest and most beautifully resonant bells ever made in Asia. It's said that its ringing can be heard over a 3km radius when struck only lightly with the fist. Unfortunately, you aren't allowed to test this claim.

An English-language audio guide to the museum is available for W3000. They also offer English-speaking guides.

Bunhwangsa 분황사

Completing this circuit is this large **pagoda** (Map pp198-9; 742 9922; admission W1000; sunrise-sunset), built in the mid-7th century during Queen Seondeok's reign, making it the oldest datable pagoda in Korea. It's a rare example of one made from brick.

Experts estimate that the pagoda originally had nine storeys, but only three are left today. The magnificently carved Buddhist guardians and stone lions are a main feature; it is unique in that each entrance is guarded by two guardians. Bunhwangsa is in an intimate courtyard.

To get there follow the willow-lined road across from the National Museum until you reach the first intersection. Turn right at the intersection and then take the first lane on the right. The walk will take about 20 to 25 minutes.

EASTERN GYEONGJU
Bomunho Resort 보문 단지

Bomun is a newer district (Map pp198-9) around an artificial lake some 5km east of central Gyeongju. Tradition seekers will find the tandem bikes, paddleboats, conference centres and such less appealing, but it is home to Gyeongju's top-end lodgings as well as some midrange options. The lake and extensive parklands are great for strolling or bike riding, though the area doesn't have the character of the town centre.

The **Sonje Museum of Contemporary Art** (Map pp198-9; 745 7075; www.artsonje.com; admission W3000; 10am-6pm, closed Mon), just in front of the Hilton Hotel, holds three cavernous

exhibition spaces with a diverse range of seasonal exhibitions, plus a permanent collection containing paintings, sculpture and mixed media.

Traditional dancing and musical performances are held on a regular basis throughout the year at **Bomun Outdoor Performance Theatre**, located below the information centre by the lake.

The **Gyeongju Potters Association** (Map pp198-9; 748 8071; 10am-6pm, often closed) has a small centre with local potters' wares and hands-on demonstrations.

If history and hiking are wearing thin, the **Gyeongju Bosun Shooting Range** (Map pp198-9; 741 7007; www.kjshooting.com; 10am-10pm; 10 bullets W20,000) is something completely different. Choose a (yes, real) pistol from the plastic 'menu', put on the goggles and earphones and take 10 shots at a paper target. Say 'James Bond' and you'll get a Walther PPK.

Bulguksa 불국사

On a series of stone terraces about 16km southeast of Gyeongju, set among gnarled pines and iris gardens that would make Van Gogh swoon, this **temple** (Map pp198-9; 746 9913; admission adult/youth/child W4000/3000/2000; 6.30am-6pm Apr-Oct, 7am-5pm Nov-Mar) is the crowning glory of Shilla temple architecture and is on the Unesco World Cultural Heritage List. The excellence of its carpentry, the incredible skill of its painters (particularly the interior woodwork and the eaves of the roofs) and the subtlety of its landscapes all contribute to its magnificence.

The approach to the temple leads you to two national treasure '**bridges**' (now closed for preservation), actually stairways to the main hall. One of these bridges has 33 steps, representing the 33 stages to enlightenment. Two more national treasures are the pagodas that stand in the courtyard of the first set of buildings and that somehow survived Japanese vandalism. The first, **Dabotap**, is of plain design and typical Shilla artistry, while the other, **Seokgatap**, is much more ornate and typical of the neighbouring Baekje kingdom. The pagodas are so revered that replicas appear on the grounds of the Gyeongju National Museum.

You can reach Bulguksa from central Gyeongju via buses 10 or 11 (W1300). There's a **tourist information booth** (746 4747) in the car park, near the bus stop.

Seokguram Grotto 석굴암

In the mountains above Bulguksa is the famous grotto of **Seokguram** (Map pp198-9; ☎ 746 9933; admission adult/child/youth W4000/2000/3000; ⏱ 6.30am-6pm Apr-Oct, 7am-5.30pm Nov-Mar), also on the Unesco World Cultural Heritage List. Chipmunks dance in the thick woods leading up to the rotunda, where sits an image of the Sakyamuni Buddha surrounded by over three dozen guardians and lesser deities, all considered masterpieces. This Buddha's position looking out over the East Sea (visible in clear weather) has long made him regarded as a protector of his country. He also bears striking resemblance to similar figures found in China and India, especially those at Badami, north of Mysore.

Seokguram was quite a feat of engineering when it was constructed in the mid-8th century. Huge blocks of granite were quarried far to the north at a time when the only access to the Seokguram site (740m above sea level) was a narrow mountain path. Seokguram can be a magical place, especially when it is raining and the mists cloak the mountaintops.

Buses run hourly between the car parks for Bulguksa and Seokguram (W1300, 15 minutes). From the Seokguram car park, it is a 400m walk along a shaded gravel track and up the stairs to the grotto. Alternatively, there is a hiking trail between Seokguram ticket office and Bulguksa (about 3.2km).

Girimsa 기림사

Once you've descended through the pass in the eastern district of Gyeongju National Park, you will reach the turnoff to **Girimsa** (Map pp198-9; ☎ 744 2922; admission W2500; ⏱ 8am-6pm), one of the largest complexes in the vicinity of the Shilla capital. Its size (14 buildings in all) compares with that of Bulguksa, yet it receives a fraction of the visitors because of its location. While you'll see all the usual temple elements (gates, heavenly kings, musical instruments, Buddhas in various forms), the relative peace and quiet may help you feel somehow closer to them here than elsewhere.

From Gyeongju intercity bus terminal, take a bus towards Gampo-ri or Yangbuk-myeon (bus 100 or 150) and ask the driver to drop you off at Andongsamgeo-ri, where the turnoff to the temple goes off to the left. From there you will either have to walk, hitch or take a taxi the 4.5km to the temple (along a paved road).

Golgulsa 골굴사

This **temple** (Golgulam; Map pp198-9; ☎ 744 1689; www.sunmudo.com; admission free) with a kick features a cliffside Buddha carved out of solid rock in the 6th century, part of an interesting cave hermitage. Visitors come here to study *sunmudo*, a Korean martial art which has taekwondo characteristics and involves principles of the Buddhist eight-fold path and four noble truths. Demonstrations (1½ hours) occur at 8.30am and 7pm daily at Sunmudo University on the temple grounds. The cost is W15,000 to join morning or evening training sessions and two-day, one-night training sessions are available (US$50 including meals). Reservations are needed for all training; English translation may be arranged.

To reach Golgulsa, take the bus to the same stop as for Girimsa. From the bus stop it's a 15-minute walk, or someone may be able to pick you up if you ring the temple.

Gameunsa Site 감은사지

About 1km before the coast, along the main road to Gyeongju, stand the remains of this large **Shilla-era temple** (Map pp198-9; admission free; ⏱ 24hr). A diagram by the entrance shows the one-time layout, but for now all that remain are two three-storey pagodas – among the largest in Korea – and foundation stones. The pagodas are prototypes of those constructed following the unification of Shilla. A huge bell, some four times larger than the Emille Bell in the Gyeongju National Museum, once hung in Gameunsa but was stolen during the 1592 invasion by the Japanese, who tried to take it back to their homeland. They didn't get far and the bell was lost in the sea nearby. A team from Gyeongju National Museum searched for the bell several years ago but was unsuccessful. There are reportedly plans to try again.

Sea Tomb of King Munmu
대왕암(문무대왕릉)

A group of small, rocky islets 200m off the coast is the setting for the famous **tomb** (Map pp198-9) of the Shilla king Munmu (r 661–81), who unified the peninsula in 668. It is billed as the world's only underwater tomb.

Munmu had made it known that on his death he wished to be cremated and his ashes buried at sea close to Gameunsa. The idea was that his spirit would become a dragon and protect the eastern shores of the Shilla kingdom from Japanese pirates. His wishes were carried out by his son, Sinmun, who became the next Shilla king.

The rock visible in the pool at the centre of the islets is presumed to cover Munmu's ashes, though no investigations have been carried out and some experts dismiss it as a flight of fantasy. Don't plan on researching it yourself, however; the islets are off-limits, and even if visits were permitted, strong tides can make them dangerous to reach.

The tomb sits off **Bonggil Beach**. Both it and **Daebon Beach** (a cove to the north) are popular with Koreans, especially during the summer holiday period, but there's nothing special about this stretch of coastline. There are plenty of *minbak* (private homes with rooms for rent) and seafood restaurants located in the area.

From Gyeongju take bus 150 toward Yangnam (W2700, one hour, every 15 minutes) and get off at Bonggil.

SOUTHERN GYEONGJU (NAMSAN)

This mountain, south of the city centre, is one of the region's most rewarding areas to explore, a place where you can easily combine the athletic with the spiritual. It's beautiful, and strewn with relics, active temples, monasteries and sites for impromptu religious observance. Among the relics found (so far) are 122 temple sites, 64 stone pagodas, 57 stone Buddhas, and many royal tombs, rock-cut figures, pavilions and the remains of fortresses, temples and palaces.

You can choose from hundreds of paths, many of which run alongside streams that tumble down the mountain. The paths and tracks are well trodden, though at times you will need to head off the main trails to scout for relics that are not immediately visible, since only a few of them are signposted. See opposite for some day-hike suggestions.

You can also check with tourist offices at Gyeongju or Bomun for additional maps and information about trail conditions.

Buses 11, 500, 501, 503, 505, 506, 507 and 591 all pass by Namsan.

Oreung Tombs 오릉

South from the city over the first bridge, these **tombs** (Map pp198-9; ☎ 772 6903; admission W300; ☺ 8am-6pm) are five of the region's most ancient. The 2000-year-old tomb of the kingdom's founder, King Hyeokgeose, can be found here.

Poseokjeongji 포석정지

Quite a walk down the road is this **former banquet garden** (Map pp198-9; ☎ 745 8484; admission W500; ☺ 9am-6pm Mar-Nov, 9am-5pm Dec-Feb) in a glade of shade trees. The site is known for one symbol of Shilla elegance: a thin, shallow, abalone-shaped granite waterway, several metres in diameter, through which a stream once flowed. It's now dry.

Samneung 삼릉

This **pine grove** (Map pp198-9; admission free; ☺ 24hr) has the *tumuli* of three Shilla kings, mostly thought to be one of the earliest (Adalla, r 154–84) and two of the last (r 912–27). Another tomb, located away from the others, is said to contain King Gyeongae, who was killed when robbers raided Poseokjeongji during an elaborate banquet, setting the stage for the dynasty's collapse.

Samneung is also a good place to start your hike up Namsan; see opposite.

WESTERN GYEONGJU
Tomb of King Muyeol

The main tomb of the Muyeol group is that of **King Muyeol** (Map pp198-9; ☎ 772 4531; admission W500; ☺ 9am-6pm summer, 9am-5pm winter). In the mid-7th century he paved the way for the unification of Korea by conquering the rival Baekje kingdom; the peninsula was fully unified by his son, King Munmu. An interesting monument to his exploits (and national treasure) sits near the entrance to the tomb compound: a tortoise carrying a capstone finely carved with intertwined dragons, symbolising his power.

Tours

Public tour buses (☎ 743 6001; 7hr tours excl lunch & admissions W10,000) access all the sights and depart from the intercity bus terminal (Map p201) at 8.30am and 10am.

Sleeping

Lodgings are everywhere, so do-it-yourselfers can find something whether you arrive by train or bus. Most restaurants are between the two terminals. Higher-end lodgings and restaurants are at Bomunho, with some less expensive options just east from the lake.

Other motels are sprinkled around the western area of Central Gyeongju and offer a similar price and similar quality to those listed.

BUDGET

Arirang-jang Yeoinsuk (Map p201; ☎ 772 2460; r W15,000) Shabby but inexpensive, it has tiny, odd-shaped *ondol* rooms and is also close to the train station, right behind the bakery.

Hanjin Hostel (Hanjin-jang Yeogwan; Map p201; ☎ 771 4097; http://hanjinkorea.wo.to; dm/s/d W15,000/20,000/30,000; 🖳) You'll either love it here or it will freak you out. The rooms are dingy, but the walls are covered with beautiful paintings by the owner's daughter. The kitchen, courtyard and roof deck are great places to commune with other travellers. The yoga-practising owner speaks English and Japanese and hands out free maps.

Nakwonjang Yeoinsuk (Map p201; ☎ 742 4977; r W20,000) Clean, simple, fan-cooled *ondol*-style rooms steps away from the train station. Some (W12,000) have no bathroom, just a hose with which to splash yourself.

Sarangchae (Map p201; ☎ 773 4868; www.kjstay .com/eng.htm; s/d & tw incl breakfast from W25,000/30,000; 🖳) This place has lots of character and a hostel-type atmosphere. It's in a traditional Korean house offering rooms with *ondol* or beds. It's well decorated, has a courtyard, kitchen, internet, laundry machines and friendly owners. It is centrally located, right across from the *tumuli* park. Bookings ahead are essential.

NAMSAN DAY HIKING ROUTES

Central Namsan

There are numerous trails through Namsan; the most convenient starting at Samneung (Map pp198–9). Whichever route you take, be sure to include detours – necessary to hunt for relics off track. There's virtually no English signage, but with some *Han-geul* (Korean phonetic alphabet) skill you should do fine. If the weather's clear, you can be assured of fine views and reasonable trails.

Three-hour course Head up from Samneung, breaking to take in several relief carvings and statues along the way, to the hermitage **Sangseonam** (상선암), where you'll find lovely views across the valley and maybe a monk chanting. Continue up past the rock formation **Badukbawi** (바둑바위) and along the ridge to **Sangsabawi** (상사바위), then walk back the way you came.

Five-hour course Instead of doubling back from Sangsabawi, continue on to the summit of **Geumosan** (금오산, 468m) to **Yongjangsaji** (용장사지, Yongjang temple site), where you can view the seated Buddha image carved in stone and the three-storey stone pagoda. Descend to **Yongjang-ri** (용장리, Yongjang village), from where you can catch a bus back to central Gyeongju.

Eight-hour course Follow the route as far as Yongjangsaji, but instead of heading down towards Yongjang-ri head across the ridge to **Chilbulam** (칠불암, hermitage of seven Buddhas), Namsan's largest relic with images carved in natural rocks and stone pillars. From here it's mostly downhill towards the road and about another 1km to **Namsan-dong** (남산리, Namsan village) on the eastern side of the park, from where it's an easy bus ride back to town.

Northeastern Namsan

Take local bus 11 from Gyeongju and get off as soon as the bus crosses the river, about 2.5km past the National Museum. Off the main road is a fork – take the left branch and you can wind your way to **Borisa** (보리사), a beautifully reconstructed nunnery set amid old-growth trees and ancient images. It is possible to head over the hill behind Borisa to **Tapgol** (탑골, Pagoda Valley), but it's a rough climb. It's easier to backtrack down to the fork and take the other branch. Follow the river for several hundred metres until you come to a small village. Turn left here and head up the road through Tapgol and you'll reach the secluded hermitage **Okryongam** (옥룡암). In the upper corner are ponderous boulders covered with Korea's greatest collection of **relief carvings**.

Returning to the bridge and looking towards the main road, you will see two **stone pillars** standing in a thicket of trees amid rice paddies. These pillars are all that remain standing of **Mangdeoksa**, a huge Shilla-era temple complex. From there it's an easy trip back towards the National Museum, about 20 minutes. Depending on your route, this itinerary might take you a half-day.

Taeyang-jang Yeogwan (Map p201; ☎ 773 6889; r Sun-Fri/Sat W25,000/30,000; 🍴) Right near the Hanjin, this spotlessly clean motel has a small rock garden in the lobby and a very friendly owner. Thick velour curtains give the otherwise plain rooms a Victorian feel.

MIDRANGE

Two nice choices are in Bomunho. There are other options near the bus terminals.

Hansol-jang (Map pp198-9; ☎ 748 3800; fax 748 3799; r from W40,000; 🍴) Rooms here, both *ondol* and bed, each have a tiny balcony. Free video rentals are also available.

Bellus Hotel (Map p201; ☎ 741 3335; www.bellushotel .com; d/tw W40,000; 🍴 🖥) This has modern décor in both *ondol* and Western rooms (*ondol* rooms have nicer decoration), all with bathtubs. There's internet access in the lobby and even a microbrewery downstairs (open from 5pm to 2am).

Swiss Rosen Hotel (Map pp198-9; ☎ 748 4848; www .swissrosen.co.kr; r from W48,000; 🍴) Across from Hansol-jang, the Swiss Rosen is a nice deal even if the rooms are not enormous. Add W20,000 and get breakfast, coffee, beer and even barbecue. From September to May rates are 20% less.

Gyeongju Park Tourist Hotel (Map p201; ☎ 777 7744; www.gjpark.com; d/tw W78,000/92,000; 🍴 🖥) One of the few places in Korea to offer no-smoking options, this friendly place was renovated in 2006. Some rooms on the 2nd floor are above a nightclub, but these have in-room internet terminals to compensate. There's a 30% discount in the off-peak season.

TOP END

Gyeongju's top lodgings sit along the lake at Bomunho.

Commodore Hotel Gyeongju Chosun (Map pp198-9; ☎ 745 7701; www.chosunhotel.com; r from W205,700; 🍴 🖥) This hotel was renovated in 2002 and is already getting Korean celebs as guests. There's nice woodwork in the rooms, Gyeongju green and terracotta-coloured motifs downstairs, and one of the city's favourite spas.

Hotel Hyundai (Map pp198-9; ☎ 748 2233; www .hyundaihotel.com; r from W242,000; 🍴 🖥 🍴) Marble everywhere, gardens by the lake, balconies and internet connections in each room, plus fitness club. Disabled travellers will appreciate the care given to accessibility.

Gyeongju Hilton (Map pp198-9; ☎ 745 7788, toll free 00798-651 1818; www.hilton.com; r from W254,100;

🍴 🍴) A real Miró hangs in the lobby of this Gyeongju chain. It has a sauna, squash courts, gym and a World Cup floor where the German and Danish teams stayed. The Hilton owns the nearby museum, so a night's stay includes free admission should you care to see more art than is in the lobby.

Eating

Gyeongju's greatest concentration and diversity of choices is in the city centre. Southeast of Tumuli Park is a street full of *ssambap* restaurants (*ssambap* is lots of tasty side dishes, which you wrap up in lettuce and other leaves).

Galibi Haemul (Map pp198-9; meals W3000-10,000) Across from the car park at Samneung, serving seafood *pajeon* and *haemul galgaksu*, wondrous homemade noodles with seafood – the noodles are greenish because they contain seaweed.

Burim Hansikdang (Map pp198-9; ☎ 748 8098; Bomunho; meals W6000-12,000; 🕐 7am-midnight) Where mushrooms are the speciality, often with either beef or octopus, boiled tableside in a scrumptious broth.

Pyeongyang (Map p201; ☎ 772 2448; meals W6000-18,000; 🕐 9.30am-10pm) Don't be put off by the sign out front reading 'tourist restaurant'; plenty of locals love it too for *bulgogi, naengmyeon* and other Korean faves.

Kisoya (Map p201; ☎ 746 6020; meals W6500-23,000) Next door to Terrace (see below) with a similar setting and decent menu of Japanese standards with Korean touches. Veggie options are available. As with Terrace, the *tumulus* adds excitement to the meal.

Kuro Ssambap (Map p201; ☎ 749 0600; www.web town.org/kuro; per person W8000; 🕐 10am-9pm) Eclectic collection of birds, rocks, figurines, pottery and other folk arts make this a unique place to dine. Orders include 28 refillable side dishes.

Terrace (Map p201; ☎ 773 8084; meals W8300-27,000; 🕐 10.30am-midnight) Clean and contemporary, offering Korean and Western food. Outdoor seating next to a *tumulus*, which is dramatically lit at night (more pleasant than it sounds).

For dessert, try Gyeongju *bang* (baked barley pancakes with red-bean paste sandwiched inside). **Danseokmyeongga** (Map p201; ☎ 741 7520; 🕐 8am-11pm) claims to have originated the trend. The owner speaks Korean and Japanese, but almost no English.

Drinking

There are numerous clubs, bars, pubs, and live houses in the streets near Rio and Dongguk University. At some the custom is to purchase *anju* (snacks, often W10,000 to W20,000) and chat in Korean with the female waitstaff. You may find yourself ignored if you go in with a few friends expecting to sit somewhere and chat by yourselves over beers. Bars change names frequently, but chances are the university students walking around speak enough English to recommend a place or two.

Mahayeon (Map p201; ☎ 745 0072) Tucked on a side street (across from the peach-coloured church) on the 2nd floor, Mahayeon offers traditional teas and *dongdongju* (rice wine) served in traditional style, with floor seating, dark wood tables and delicate paper screens. If you drank tea in Insadong, come here to experience the real thing.

Buzz (Map p201; ☎ 742 7642; www.buzzcoffee.co.kr; coffee W3000; ⏲ 10am-10pm) If you can't wait until 11am to get your coffee fix at Schumann & Clara, try Buzz, a sparsely decorated store with espresso drinks, coffee and shaved ice.

Schumann & Clara (☎ 749 9449; coffee W3500-10,000; ⏲ 11am-8pm) Jamaican Blue Mountain–lovers can get their fix at this classy café, along with classical music and understated contemporary décor. It's northwest of the centre, on the student-populated street east of the bridge that heads to Dongguk University, diagonally across from the 7-Eleven and right next to Baskin-Robbins. Coffees here are prepared by hand, the way they should be; the only downside is that coffee addicts will be shaking from DTs by the time the place opens at 11am.

Rio (☎ 745 2325; admission free, beers W4000-7000, cocktails W7000-10,000; ⏲ 7pm-4am) An intimate, mellow, yellowlit retro place with fun photos of jazz greats…and Sting. Owned by a guy who teaches at the university, this place is likely to feature local student talent, which sometimes isn't that talented but is still fun. The menu features classics like domestic and imported 'Bear' and cocktails such as the 'Orenge Blossom'. Be sure to ask for something strong if you want to taste any alcohol.

Entertainment

There are outdoor traditional dance and music performances every Saturday during April, May, September and October (3pm to 5pm) on the stage (Map p201) in Wolseong Park. More regular traditional performances

are held at Bomunho (Map p201) between April and November. In April and November, these performances are held at 2.30pm and during summer in the evenings at 8.30pm. Check with **KTO** (☎ 1330) for more details (p393).

For more contemporary fare, there's a cluster of cinemas (Map p201) in central Gyeongju.

Getting There & Away

AIR

There is no airport at Gyeongju itself, but the airports at Busan (Gimhae) and Ulsan are readily accessible. Ulsan's airport is closer, but Gimhae has more flights. For information on airport transport, see below.

BUS

Gyeongju's **express bus terminal** (Map p201; ☎ 741 4000) and **intercity bus terminal** (p201; ☎ 743 5599) are adjacent to one other. Buses from the express bus terminal:

Destination	Price (W)	Duration
Busan	4000	1hr
Daegu	3300	1hr
Daejeon	10,600	3hr
Seoul	16,300	4½hr

Buses from the intercity bus terminal:

Destination	Price (W)	Duration
Busan	3500	1hr
Daegu	3300	1hr
Gangneung	23,100	6hr
Uljin	13,100	4hr
Ulsan	3800	1hr

TRAIN

Gyeongju–Seoul *Mugunghwa* services run twice daily (W17,900 to W22,700) from the **train station** (Map p201 ☎ 743 4114). Several *Saemaul* (luxury express) from Seoul (W33,700 to W38,800) make the trip as well. There are more services on weekends and holidays. Trains also connect Busan and Gyeongju, but buses are more frequent. Coin lockers (W1000) are available in the train-station lobby.

Getting Around

TO/FROM THE AIRPORT

Several direct buses link Gyeongju with both the Ulsan airport (W4500, four daily) and

Busan's Gimhae airport (W9000, 12 daily). Buses leave from Gyeongju's main terminal.

BICYCLE

Hiring a bicycle for a day or two is a great way of reaching the sites in the close vicinity of Gyeongju. There are some bike trails around Namsan (but it's rather hilly) and Bomunho. Most of the roads are quite safe.

There are bicycle-rental shops everywhere, and the rates are standard: a mountain bike costs about W5000 hourly or W10,000 to W12,000 daily.

BUS

Many local buses (regular/deluxe W900/1300) terminate just outside the intercity bus terminal, alongside the river. For shorter routes (eg to Bulguksa), buses can be picked up along Sosongno and Daejeongno.

Buses 10 (which runs clockwise) and 11 (counterclockwise) run a circuit of most of the major sights including Bulguksa, Namsan and Bomunho, as well as the bus terminals and Gyeongju train station (every 15 minutes). Bus 150 departs from the train station to the eastern sights, via the Bomunho Expo arena (every 30 minutes). Bus 100 makes a similar initial route and then veers north after Eoilri.

TAXI

If your time is limited and you want to cover a lot of ground in a short time, taxis are often available for day hire outside the train and bus stations. Rates are negotiable but hover around W70,000/100,000 for five/seven hours. Do not expect the driver to speak much English.

AROUND GYEONGJU

Many tourists do this area as a day trip out of Gyeongju – and wish they'd budgeted time to stay overnight. It's hard to improve on the outstanding examples of traditional Korean architecture in sublime settings.

Yangdong Folk Village
양동 민속 마을

This beautiful and peaceful hillside Joseon-dynasty village (Map pp198–9) is full of superb mansions and traditional wooden houses. It's been designated as a preservation area.

The village was established in the 15th and 16th centuries and consists of around 150 houses typical of the *yangban* class – a largely

hereditary class based on scholarship and official position. Yangdong was the birthplace of Son-so (1433–84), a scholar-official who was one of the key figures in quashing the revolt against King Sejo in 1467. His grandson, the great Confucian scholar Yi Eon-jeok (pseudonym Hoejae; 1491–1553), was born in the same house. Much of the area around Oksan Seowon (below) is devoted to him.

Highlights among the larger buildings include the Yi Hui-tae (1733; with its many outbuildings), Simsujeong (1560; the village's largest structure) and Hyangdam (1543; known for tight-knit spaces) houses. Most of the houses here are still lived in, so you need to observe the usual courtesies when looking around; some of the larger mansions stand empty and are open to the public. There are descriptive plaques with English explanations outside some of the more important structures. If buildings are locked, you may be able to ask for a key nearby. The people who live here tend to be very friendly. There are no entry fees to any of the buildings. You should plan on spending several hours here.

Uhyangdasil (dishes W4000-13,000), just behind the church, is a friendly café in a traditional building, serving tea, wine, snacks and small meals. There are also some simple restaurants and shops for snacks and drinks.

From Gyeongju, buses 200, 201, 202, 203 and 206 (all 200 buses go toward Angang-ri) will get you to within 1.5km of Yangdong. From the bus stop, follow the train line and then go under it. There's only one road into the village, about a 30min walk.

It's easy to catch buses back to Gyeongju or continue on to Angang-ri and from there to Oksan Seowon.

Oksan Seowon & Around
옥산 서원

A *seowon* is a Confucian academy, and Oksan Seowon (Map pp198–9) was one of the most important. It was established in 1572 in honour of Yi Eon-jeok (1491–1553) by another famous Confucian scholar, Toegye (see p220). Oksan Seowon was enlarged in 1772 and was one of the few *seowon* to escape destruction in the 1860s. However, an early-20th-century fire destroyed some of the buildings here; today only 14 structures remain.

During the summer holiday period, the banks of the stream are popular camping spots, and swimming is possible in the rock pools below the waterfall. It's also a great place for a picnic.

SIGHTS
Dongnakdang 독락당

A 10-minute walk beyond Oksan Seowon, along the road up the valley, will bring you to **Dongnakdang** (Map pp198-9; admission free; ☺ by appointment), a beautiful collection of well-preserved buildings, constructed in 1515 and expanded in 1532 as the residence of Yi Eon-jeok after he left government service. The walled compound is partly occupied by descendants of Master Yi himself.

Due to past vandalism, the family requests visitors to book appointments in advance (ask at tourist offices). They will open up the inner rooms and answer any questions (in Korean). Even if you don't speak Korean, a visit feels like a private tour of a special place.

Dodeokam 도덕암

About 1.75km beyond Dongnakdang, up in the forested mountains near the end of the valley, is this tiny, intimate **hermitage** (Map pp198-9; ☎ 762 9314; admission free). It's a rustic place perched on a rock outcrop from which two springs emerge. The views, both above and below, are magnificent.

Dodeokam is a steep walk up from the road, meaning that it's about as far as you can get from the madding crowd. Barely any Koreans even know about it. To get here, take the main road through the valley past Dongnakdang and Jeonghyesa. Follow the stream for another 600m and you'll see a rusty sign on the left. Turn left and follow the zigzag path up the mountain. It's about 900m from here to the temple.

SLEEPING & EATING

Home stays and basic info on this area can be arranged by phoning ☎ 017-533 2196, where a lady sets up accommodations for families or groups.

Oksan Motel (Map pp198-9; ☎ 762 9500; d W30,000; ☒) Near the sights, the late-1990s Oksan has *ondol* or bedrooms with shower and an attractive setting.

Sanjang Sikdang (Map pp198-9; ☎ 762 3716; chicken/duck stew for 2-4 people W25,000/35,000) specialises in free-range duck and chicken. *Tojongdak baeksuk* and *orihanbang baeksuk* are chicken and duck stews served with rice porridge. Note: stews will take up to 40 to 50 minutes

to prepare, so you can take it easy (there's outdoor seating if the weather's nice) or have a Korean speaker phone before you arrive. It's not far from Dongnakdang.

GETTING THERE & AWAY

Bus 203 (W900 to W1300, every 30 to 40 minutes) to Angangri connects Gyeongju train station and Oksan Seowon.

Tomb of King Heungdeok 흥덕무덤

The farthest of the royal tombs (Map pp198-9) from central Gyeongju, this was also one of the last ones constructed during the Shilla dynasty. It's one of the most complete and has a pretty setting among the trees.

The tomb is 4km north of Angangri, about halfway between Oksan Seowon and Yang-dong Folk Village.

Songseon-ri 송선리

Close to the summit of the thickly forested mountain Obongsan (640m), **Bokduam hermitage** (Map pp198-9) features a huge rock face out of which 19 niches have been carved. The three central niches hold a figure of the historical Buddha flanked by two *bodhisattva* (Munsu and Bohyeon); the remainder house the 16 *arhat* monks who have attained Nirvana. The carving is recent and although there's an unoccupied house up here, the actual hermitage was burned down in 1988 after an electrical fault started a blaze. There is also a recently erected statue of Gwanseeum, the Goddess of Mercy, just beyond the rock face. Just below the hermitage is a stunning viewpoint from the top of a couple of massive boulders. It's a great place for a picnic lunch.

The trail is well maintained and easy to follow, but bring water as there are no springs along the way. The walk up will take around an hour. From the bus stop in Songseon-ri, follow the creek up along the narrow road about 500m to a small temple (Seongamsa). The trail starts just to the left of this temple and is well marked with *Han·geul*.

A further 3.8km up the road from the bus stop for Bokduam and Jusaam, remote **Sinseonsa** temple near the top of Danseoksan (827m) was used as a base by General Kim Yu-shin in the 7th century. It has seen a bit of renovation work since then. About 50m to the right as you face the temple are some ancient rock carvings in a small grotto – it's believed to be one of the oldest cave temples in Korea. It's about a

1½- to two-hour circuit walk from the bus stop. There's a little village along the way, about 2.5km from the bus stop.

En route to Sinseonsa, Danseok Sanjang sells drinks and light meals.

Bus 350 (W1300, every 40 minutes) from Gyeongju passes Songseon-ri for Bokduam and Jusaam. If you're continuing on to Sinseonsa, tell the driver that's where you'd like to get off.

POHANG 포항

pop 488,000

Pohang is a good springboard to Ulleungdo or the even more remote Dokdo, but isn't particularly scenic in itself. The largest city on Korea's east coast and an important industrial centre, Pohang is dominated by Posco (Pohang Iron & Steel Company), the world's second-largest steel maker. The city centre is quite lively, however, and Bukbu Beach on the north side of town is popular with both visitors and locals. The two central intersections, Ogeori and Yukgeori, ('five-road' and 'six-road' junctions) brim with cafés, clothing stores, hofs, restaurants and game parlours. Another lodging, dining and entertainment strip faces lively Bukbu Beach.

Orientation & Information

Bukbu beach, adjacent to the ferry terminal, is 1.7km long, making it one of the longest sandy beaches on Korea's east coast. **Information booths** (☎ 245 6761; ☺ 9am-6pm Mon-Sat) are by the bus and ferry terminals, which are about 3km apart. Buses 105 and 200 go to Bukbu Beach from the intercity bus terminal.

Sights

BOGYEONGSA 보경사

This **temple** (☎ 262 1117; admission W2000; ☺ 7am-7pm), 30km north of Pohang, is a gateway to a beautiful valley boasting 12 splendid waterfalls, gorges spanned by bridges, hermitages, stupas and the temple itself. There are a number of good hikes including ascending **Naeyeonsan** (930m). The summit itself is called Hyangnobong and the return trip from Bogyeongsa is about 20km (around six hours).

The temple is 15 minutes' walk from where the buses from Pohang terminate, and there's a tourist village with a collection of souvenir shops, restaurants, minbak and yeogwan.

The trail to the gorge and waterfalls branches off from the tourist village and is well maintained. It's about 1.5km to the first waterfall, 5m-high **Ssangsaeng pokpo**. The sixth waterfall, **Gwaneum pokpo**, is an impressive 72m and has two columns of water with a cave behind it. The seventh waterfall is called **Yeonsan pokpo** and is a respectable 30m high.

As you head farther up the trails, the going gets difficult and the ascent of Hyangnobong should only be attempted if the day is young.

Buses run between Pohang's intercity bus terminal and the temple (W2350, 25 minutes, hourly).

HOMIGOT 호미곶

This district, on a natural cape that protects Pohang's harbour, is a popular spot at sunrise, especially 1 January. The **lighthouse museum** (☎ 284 4657; admission W700; ☺ 10am-5.30pm Tue-Sun) has a large collection of memorabilia relating to lighthouses in Korea and overseas.

Catch bus 200 or 200-1 from the bus terminal. Hop off at Guryongpo, the final stop (W1300, every 12 minutes), then catch a bus going to Daebo (W900, 20 minutes, every 40 minutes).

Sleeping

There are about two dozen yeogwan around the intercity bus terminal with rooms from W25,000. Note that rates in all categories may go up in peak times. The nightlife district in the town centre has similar options. For better scenery and more choice, head up to Bukbu Beach.

Ibeu-jang Motel (☎ 283 2253; d from W25,000) Fancy mirrors seem tragically out of place in these otherwise stark, linoleum-floored rooms. The red lamp is the only hint that this is a love motel.

Manstar Motel (☎ /fax 244 0225; www.manstarmotel .com; Bukbu Beach; r W30,000) Down a street off the main drag, the Manstar has nice rooms, seashell-design baths and the kind owner speaks English.

S Motel (☎ 247 0073; d from W30,000; ☒ ☐) The yellow linoleum is off-putting and the rooms are smallish (but not stuffy) and have PCs and TVs . It's in a great location, making it a good deal for the price. Fridges include the usual gratis energy drinks.

Miseagull Hotel (☎ 242 8400; fax 248 1818; Bukbu Beach; d/tw from W50,000/70,000) Looking out over Bukbu Beach, so some rooms have sea views, but unless you're just going to the beach it's a bit far from the centre.

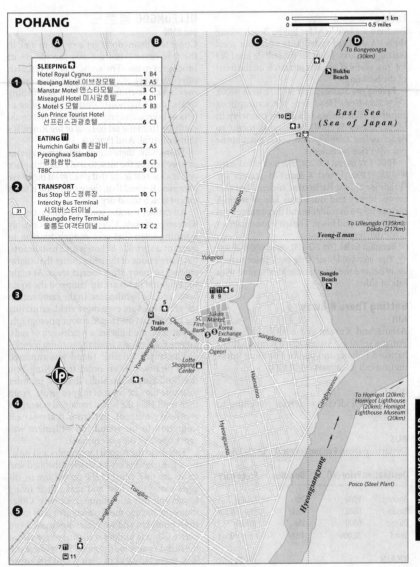

POHANG

0 ———— 1 km
0 ———— 0.5 miles

SLEEPING 🏠
Hotel Royal Cygnus 1 B4
Ibeujang Motel 이브장모텔 2 A5
Manstar Motel 맨스타모텔 3 C1
Miseagull Hotel 미시갈호텔 4 D1
S Motel S 모텔 5 B3
Sun Prince Tourist Hotel
선프린스관광호텔 6 C3

EATING 🍴
Humchin Galbi 훔친갈비 7 A5
Pyeonghwa Ssambap
평화쌈밥 8 C3
TBBC 9 C3

TRANSPORT
Bus Stop 버스정류장 10 C1
Intercity Bus Terminal
시외버스터미널 11 A5
Ulleungdo Ferry Terminal
울릉도여객터미널 12 C2

Bukbu Beach

East Sea
(Sea of Japan)

To Bongyeongsa
(30km)

To Ulleungdo (135km);
Dokdo (217km)

Yeong-il man

Songdo Beach

Yukgeori

Hangguro

Jukdo Market

SC First Bank

Korea Exchange Bank

Cheonggyecheongno

Train Station

Songdoro

Ogeori

Lotte Shopping Center

Haenamno

To Homigot (20km);
Homigot Lighthouse
(20km); Homigot
Lighthouse Museum
(20km)

Yongheungno

Hyeongsanno

Gangbyeonno

Posco (Steel Plant)

Hyeongsangyang

Tongilro

Jungheungno

Sun Prince Hotel (☎ 242 2800; fax 242 6006; d from W60,000; ❄) Newly remodelled, with a shiny marble lobby and both *ondol* and Western rooms available, the Sun Prince is a nice option for those not wanting a love motel. Red-tile floors, sculpted bathtubs and flowered quilts are just a few of the nice touches. The downsides: there's no internet (just LAN outlets) and a (possibly noisy) nightclub downstairs.

Hotel Royal Cygnus (☎ 275 2000; fax 283 4075; d from W120,000) A snazzy place that is popular with conference groups. The hotel is within walking distance of the train station, and has a business centre and natural hot-spring baths.

Eating

For fresh seafood head for Bukbu Beach, where there's a string of restaurants with your meal waiting in tanks. Look for the telltale *hoe* (회) for 'raw seafood', usually in a circle on the front of the building.

Pyeonghwa Ssambap (☎ 247 3779; meals W6000; ☽ 10.30am-10pm) Head here for scrumptious *ssambap* (side dishes which you can wrap in lettuce leaves; W6000). No English menu, so order *dolsot ssambap* and you'll get a stone pot with rice included.

TBBC (☎ takeout 080 208 9292; chicken/duck meals W10,000/12,000; ☽ lunch & dinner) It stands for 'Traditional Best Barbecue Chicken,' but also serves turkey and duck plus lots of beer. A picture menu is available and there are several locations around town. The telephone number is for delivery only.

Humchin Galbi (☎ 272 5592; meals W5000-20,000; ☽ 11am-midnight) Diner-style pork place tucked away behind the bus station. Meals come with lots of sides.

Getting There & Away

AIR

Asiana and Korean Air both have Seoul–Pohang services. Asiana also operates a flight between Pohang and Jejudo. For more information call the **airport** (☎ 284 0111).

BOAT

See p217 for details of ferries travelling to Ulleungdo.

BUS

Departing from **Pohang terminal** (☎ 272 3194):

Destination	Price (W)	Duration	Frequency
Andong	9900	2hr	7 daily
Busan	6600	1½hr	every 10min
Daegu	6000	2hr	30 daily
Seoul	20,000	4½hr	every 40min

TRAIN

There are a few trains from **Pohang station** (☎ 275 2394) including to Seoul (*Saemaul*; W35,800, five hours, two daily at 7.25am and 5.25pm).

Getting Around

Local buses cost W900/1300 (regular/deluxe). Bus 200 runs between the airport and the intercity bus terminal.

ULLEUNGDO 울릉도

pop 8300

Come to Ulleungdo to get away from it all in the true sense – not the way the spa-resort brochures mean. The scenery is spectacular, offering vistas of spun-cotton clouds lazing over volcanic cliffsides, seabirds and fishing boats, quiet harbours dotted with piles of nets or buoys, and jagged coastline that could easily be from the set of *Lord of the Rings*. It's that beautiful. And that's it.

Thankfully, there are no amusement parks or huge resorts; the most touristy that this place gets is a lone cable car that gives great birds-eye glimpses. Beyond that, there's not much to do except watch squid dry.

An extinct volcano some 135km east of the Korean peninsula, Ulleungdo today is mainly a fishing town that sees enough tourism to warrant a sprinkle of hotels and restaurants, but there's none of the neon clutter that characterises so many other tourist areas. At night the brightest lights are the lamps on the squid boats and the lighthouses. In the rainy season the green hues are even more vivid, saturating the hills like an overtoned colour photograph. In autumn, the hills are a patchwork of reds, greens and yellows from the turning leaves.

This small volcanic island was captured from pirates after an order from King Yeji, the 22nd king of the Shilla dynasty, in order to secure the east coast of the peninsula. From then until 1884 the island remained essentially a military outpost, but from that year on migration to the island for settlement was sanctioned by the government.

Thanks to the rugged topography and isolation, the island is only sparsely inhabited and farms are tiny. Most of the people live in villages along the coast and make their living harvesting fish and summer tourists. Other industries include the production of taffy made from pumpkin and woodcarvings made from native Chinese juniper – all offered for sale at the island's many tourist shops. Everywhere you look there are racks of drying squid, seaweed and octopus.

Orientation & Information

Most visitors arrive from the mainland to the port of Dodong-ri, on the island's southeastern side. A new port in nearby Sadong-ri has been underway for years, but typhoons keep hammering the island and the current opening date will be sometime in 2007. Pre-

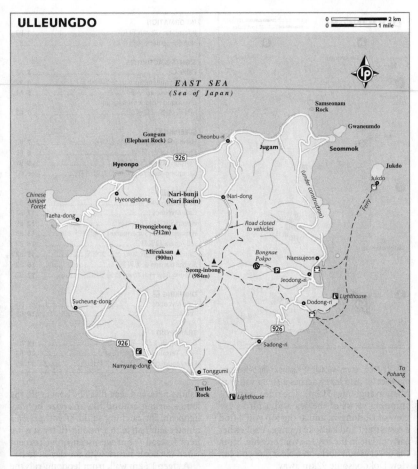

ULLEUNGDO

0 _____ 2 km
0 _____ 1 mile

EAST SEA
(Sea of Japan)

Samseonam Rock

Gwaneumdo

Gong-am (Elephant Rock)   Cheonbu-ri

Jugam   Seommok

Hyeonpo   926

Jukdo

Jukdo

(under construction)

Chinese Juniper Forest

Hyeongjebong   Nari-bunji (Nari Basin)   Nari-dong

Taeha-dong

Hyeongjebong ▲ (712m)   Road closed to vehicles

Mireuksan ▲ (900m)

Bongnae Pokpo   Naessujeon

Seong-inbong ▲ (984m)   Jeodong-ri

Sucheung-dong   Lighthouse

Dodong-ri

926

Sadong-ri

926

Namyang-dong

Tonggumi   To Pohang

Turtle Rock   Lighthouse

sumably, once open it will radically alter the island's tourist flow. On the coast north of Dodong-ri is the busy village of Jeodong-ri, which retains a traditional fishing-village feel. The other main point of interest to tourists is Nari-bunji, a basin in the north of the island.

There's no English spoken at the **information booth** (Map p214; ☎ 790 6454; ☼ 9am-6pm, 9am-11pm mid-Jul–mid-Aug) by the Dodong-ri ferry terminal; however, there are bilingual maps as well as bus schedules in Korean. The friendly owner of the Cafe Myconos (p216) just up the road speaks English and is a great source of local information. Detailed maps of the island can be bought from tourist shops. You can change money at Nonghyeop Bank in Dodong-ri.

Sights
DODONG-RI 도동리
Dodong-ri is the island's administrative centre and largest town. Like a pirate outpost, its narrow harbour is almost hidden away in a narrow valley between two forested mountains, making it visible only when approached directly. It's also the island's main tourist hub, meaning the greatest selection of lodging and dining, but the number of tourists can be a little overwhelming. By the ferry terminal, a staircase leads around the base of the cliffs to a **lighthouse** (allow one hour to walk).

Mineral Spring Park 약수 공원
The highlight of this park, a 350m climb above Dodong-ri, is the **cable car** (Map p214;

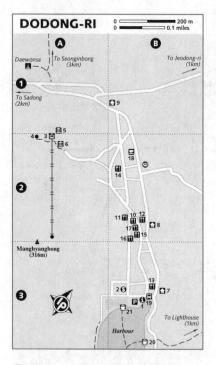

☎ 791 7160; return W6500; ☼ approx ½hr before sun-rise-when last visitor leaves) across a steep valley to Manghyangbong (316m). The ride up affords stunning views of the sea and a bird's-eye view of Dodong-ri, and at the top you'll find a restaurant and karaoke lounge. Visit either early or late in the day to avoid crowds. From the observation deck, on a clear day you can view Dokdo, some 92km away.

The park's namesake *yaksu gwangjang* (mineral-water spring) is near the top. The water has a distinctive flavour (think diet citrus soda-meets-quartz) and some claim drinking it has all sorts of medicinal benefits, though there are always risks with drinking untreated water. Nearby, you'll also find a rack cliff (artificial rock-climbing wall).

Also in the park are two **museums** (Map p214; ☎ 790 6421; admission free; ☼ 9am-6pm), the elaborate Dokdo Museum and Ulleungdo's simple historical museum; the exhibits are in Korean.

JEODONG-RI 저동리
Jeodong-ri (Map p213) retains a fishing-village character, with picturesque seawalls,

fishing nets, and seagulls. The boats with the lamps strung around like oversize holiday lights are for catching squid. If you prefer a quieter alternative to Dodong-ri, try staying here instead – but we mean quiet (except when the boats return with the day's catch).

A steep 1.5km walk from Jeodong-ri is the car park to **Bongnae pokpo** (Map p213; ☎ 790 6422; admission W1200; ☼ 6am-7pm Apr-Oct, 8am-5pm Nov-Mar). Source of the island's drinking water, it's quite spectacular during the summer. From the car park, a path (20 minutes) takes you to the lookout. Hourly buses serve the car park from Dodong-ri via Jeodong-ri (W1500, mid-spring to mid-autumn).

Namyang-dong 남양
The road from Dodong-ri follows a stunning, path along spectacular coastal cliffs (Map p213), passing **rock formations** and ocean cliffs covered with Chinese juniper. The journey can be made by public bus or taxi.

Sunset Point Pavilion (Ilmoljeon Mangdae) is a steep 15-minute walk above the town, commanding great views of the ocean and, yes, of the sunset. Follow the western creek out of town and cross the bridge after the school. A small trail continues up to the pavilion.

Nari-bunji 나리 분지
Nari Basin (Map p213) is on the northern slope of **Seong-inbong** (984m), the island's highest peak and the summit of a dormant volcano. Nari is the only place on the island that's reasonably flat, so there are several farms here and a couple of reconstructed traditional thatched-roof houses. It's a popular place to start or conclude a hiking expedition (right).

Minbak, camping and restaurants are available. At the restaurants by the campground, you might try *hanjeongsik* (Korean banquet; W6000) or *sanchae deodeokjeon* (mountain vegetable pancake; W7000) and wash it down with some local *dondongju* (rice wine; W6000).

Activities
BOAT TRIPS
A **round-island tour** (W15,000) is a great way to admire Ulleungdo's dramatic landscape. Tours depart from Dodong-ri ferry terminal (Map p214) and last around two hours. They run up to four per day, depending on demand, with more tours possible during summer. In nonpeak seasons they may be cancelled.

Other sightseeing boats serve the island of Jukdo (Map p213), a nature preserve 4km from Ulleungdo. Boats (W10,000, up to four daily) offer excellent views of Ulleungdo as well as Jukdo's own cliffs. Visitors are welcome to take

---

WAITING FOR DOKDO
In 1905, during the Japanese occupation, Japan annexed Dokdo – fishing grounds marked by two small, rocky islands – and renamed it Takeshima. Korea protested, but as a colony did not have much say. Following WWII, US general Douglas MacArthur designated the island part of Korea, and US forces erected a monument there to Korean fishermen accidentally killed nearby by American ordnance. However, Japan destroyed the monument in 1952, prompting Korea to send a defence unit and Japan to put the island under surveillance. It remains disputed territory because of its fishing rights, and fuels Korean ire at the Japanese..

---

a picnic to eat on the island. It takes about 1½ hours including walk or picnic time.

On Saturday in summer, boats offer trips around Dokdo, with a reservation and sufficient demand (W37,500; three or 5½ hours return). The three-hour boats are speedier, but you can't go outside; the 5½- hour boats are slower and have open decks for sightseeing. If time permits, the latter are more enjoyable.

During the annual squid festival (three days in mid-August), you may be able to board boats and even ride a vessel out to sea. The rest of the year it's interesting to watch them in the evening when they head out to sea with their lanterns glaring.

CAR TRIPS
Another popular way to see the island is by taxi. Fees are negotiable, but you can expect to spend about W80,000 per day. Try asking at the Cafe Myconos (p216) first – the owner's husband owns a taxi, but if he is unavailable, she may be able to recommend another. It takes about one hour from Nari-bunji to Dodong-ri.

HIKING
Various pathways lead to the summit of **Seong-inbong**, but the two main routes run from Dodong-ri (about five hours return) or Nari-bunji (four to five hours return).

From Dodong-ri, take the main road towards the temple Daewonsa. Just before you reach the temple, there is a fork in the trail and a sign (in Korean) pointing the way to Seong-inbong (a steep 4.1km).

From Nari-dong, enter the forest, adhering to the right-hand path, and you'll arrive at signboarded fields of chrysanthemum and thyme. Farther on you'll pass some traditional homes. Finally, at the entrance to the virgin forest area and picnic ground, the steep ascent of Seong-inbong takes you (one hour) through a forest of Korean beech, Korean hemlock and Korean lime.

Just below the peak, as you descend to Dodong-ri, is a trail off to the right, down to Namyang-dong (1½ hours).

Sleeping
Ulleungdo has loads of choices (starting at around W25,000), although luxury travellers will be disappointed – even shocked. Love motels will be the fanciest; nothing here (yet) is five-star. Room rates rise steeply in peak

season (from W50,000 to W60,000 in July, August and holidays), so book ahead.

Camping is available on the beach at Namyang-dong, Naessujeon and Sadong-ri. Toilets and showers are available at the latter two during summer. Camping (free) and *minbak* are also available at Nari-dong.

DODONG-RI

Hanil-jang Yeogwan (Map p214; ☎ 791 5515; d W30,000) Nicer than some surrounding options; *ondol* rooms are fairly large and come with a fat tube of toothpaste, but the price doubles in high season (July and August). It's very close to the port, right across from the supermarket.

Sanchang-jang Yeogwan (Map p214; ☎ 791 0552; d W30,000) Orchids brighten up an otherwise grim stairway, but this aging *yeogwan* has good, clean *ondol* rooms (with faded photos of the island's attractions) and is conveniently in the centre of town. If no-one is at the reception desk, inquire in the restaurant (open 7am to 7pm) below.

Pension Skyhill (Map p214; ☎ 791 1040; d/ondol W60,000/50,000; 🕸) This newish place (opened 2003) near the top of town has a shared kitchen, rooftop barbecue facilities, VCRs and videos to borrow.

Khan Motel (Map p214; ☎ 791 8500; www.motelkhan .com; d W70,000; 🕸) Tourists are welcome at this clean love motel, with both *ondol* and Western-style rooms. Shiny tile floors, large televisions, embroidered sheets and a nightclub (open 5pm to 1am) are all pluses. Prices are up to W30,000 cheaper from September to June.

JEODONG-RI

Many lodgings in town offer free pick-up from Dodong ferry terminal with advance notice.

Kaiser Motel (☎ 791 8900; basic/deluxe W30,000/ 40,000) Basic rooms are stuffy but clean. It's a good non-*yeogwan* option for those wanting Western style.

Nakwon-jang Yeogwan (☎ 791 0580; r from W30,000; 🕸) Basic, no-nonsense rooms, some without windows, with a choice of *ondol* or Western style. It's very central and close to the bus stop.

Jeil Minbak (☎ 791 5170; ondol W50,000; 🕸) All *ondol* rooms, one with a kitchenette (same price). Yellow linoleum is off-putting, but the rooms air out well and the owner is extremely kind. Don't confuse with the Jeil Motel nearby. Some rooms have port views. Rooms are W30,000 from September to June.

Jeil Motel (☎ 791 2637; r from W30,000, VIP W50,000; 🖵) Lions greet you at the top of the stairs. Smallish rooms have faux-wood floors and not much of a view, but they are spotless. VIP rooms are enormous, with couches, computers, internet, sculptures and snazz. Don't confuse with the much simpler Jeil Minbak.

Eating & Drinking

Outdoor seafood stalls are so ubiquitous in Ulleungdo that you have to be careful not to trip over a squid; October is peak season.

There are also a few scattered *mandu/naengmyeon/gimbap* shops where you can eat for as little as W2000, and some casual outdoor restaurants by the harbour allow you to watch the boats unload squid for the women to clean and sell. Nari-dong has restaurants too.

DODONG-RI

Cafe Myconos (Map p214; ☎ 791 0532; http://blog.naver .com/ingridpark; coffee W2000-3000, sandwiches W3000; ⊙ 10am-10pm) Tiny, cute, turquoise-and-white café with an English-speaking owner and certainly the best coffee on the island. It's a great place to unwind as you wait for the ferry or to find out local information after you arrive.

Sutbul Garden (Map p214; meals W5000-13,000) is known for organic beef from 'medicinal cows' raised on medicinal herbs.

99 Sikdang (Map p214; ☎ 791 2287; dishes W5000-20,000) Potted plants outside the doorway mark the door of this friendly place that's received press throughout Korea for its *ojing-eo bulgogi* (squid grilled at table with vegetables and hot pepper sauce; W8000). *Taggaebibap* (shellfish with rice; W13,000) is also a favourite, and adventurous eaters can try *buk-eo* (blowfish; from W20,000).

Ulleung Raw Fish Town (Map p214; meals W6000-10,000) Serves mainly seafood stews, or raw fish for sharing (raw-fish prices vary).

Haeun Sikdang (해운식당; (Map p214; ☎ 791 0002; ⊙ 6.30-9pm; entrees W6000-15,000) Across the street from the 99, offering similar fare that's just as delicious. There's clean table seating and the usual Ulleungdo sea-related fare: shellfish with rice, grilled squid, squid *bulgogi* (W10,000) and so on.

Sanchang-hoe Sikdang (Map p214) Downstairs from Sanchang-jang Yeogwan, specialising in *honghapbap* (mussel rice) and *mulhoe* (sliced raw fish), both W10,000.

Tema (Map p214; ☎ 791 3122) Across from the Ulleung Hotel, this is a pleasant café to relax or enjoy a drink; it's on the 2nd level above Soul clothing shop. It means 'my glass is empty' (implication: please refill it). Otherwise, there's loads of karaoke during the summer months.

Koreaned-out? Jeil Jegwa is a comfy bakery with a table for you to enjoy your treats. Self-caterers will find numerous tiny groceries and the larger Hannam Chain Supermarket just up from the ferry terminal.

JEODONG-RI
Gyeongju Sigyuk Sikdang (☎ 791 3034; 9am-10pm; dishes W6000-15,000) Serves tasty *yaksut bulgogi* (medicinal herb-marinated beef; W15,000), but you have to order a minimum of three serves. The mixed-vegetable dishes and *san-chae bibimbap* (*bibimbap* made with mountain vegetables) are just as tasty.

Byeoljang Sigyuk Sikdang (☎ 791 0028; 9am-9pm; dishes W6000-15,000) Diagonally across the street, this has a similar menu and has recently redone the interior, with attractive bamboo and paper screens. Seating is on the floor.

Getting There & Away
You should carry your passport – you'll need the number in order to board the ferry and you may need it to register your arrival on Ulleungdo.

FERRY
You can get to Ulleungdo by **ferry** (☎ 242 5111; www.daea.com) from Pohang (standard/1st class W51,100/56,200, three hours, one to three daily) or Donghae (W54,500, three hours, one daily at 10am), but ferries are subject to cancellation in poor weather. The departure timetable varies month to month. Other ferries from Hupo and Sokcho may only run during July and August.

It is best to reserve all your tickets to and from the island, especially during summer. Otherwise you can buy your ticket at the boat terminal first thing in the morning, but you may go on a waiting list. Advance bookings and news about cancelled ferries can be obtained in Seoul (☎ 02-514 6766), Ulleungdo (☎ 791 0801) and Pohang (☎ 242 5111). Ring **KTO** (☎ 1330) for more details. Some travel agents make reservations and sell tickets.

Getting Around
BUS
Buses run between Dodong-ri and Jeodong-ri every 30 minutes (W900, 10 minutes). Eleven

daily buses go from Dodong-ri via Namyang-dong (25 minutes) to Cheonbu (50 minutes), where you can transfer to Nari-bunji (10 minutes, eight daily). For an up-to-date timetable, ask at the tourist information booth.

TAXI
Taxis, usually 4WD, regularly ply between Dodong-ri and Jeodong-ri – wave them down if a seat is empty (per person W2400). All day trips can be arranged as well for about W80,000 to W100,000. Try asking at the Cafe Myconos (p213) first.

ANDONG 안동
pop 169,000
The whole area surrounding Andong, roughly in the middle of Gyeongsangbuk-do, is peaceful, rural and notable for having preserved much of its traditional character.

Famous for its mackerel, its strong *soju* and its wooden masks, Andong makes a good base for exploring the numerous sights outside the city.

Orientation & Information
Some sights are a considerable distance away and getting to them requires a series of bus rides, often with inconvenient schedules. Ask at the tourist information booth for help planning your trip.

Hiring a taxi (W120,000) for the day is an air-conditioned luxury that's well worth it if you're enduring summers heat.

The **tourist office** (☎ 852 6800; www.andong.go.kr; 9am-6pm) is to the left as you exit the train station. It is brand-spanking new, with English, Chinese and Japanese information and snazzy computerised displays.

Sights & Activities
ANDONG FOLK VILLAGE & FOLKLORE MUSEUM 안동 민속 마을, 박물관
On a hillside 40 minutes' walk from the centre of town, **Andong Folk Village** serves as a repository for homes moved to prevent them from being submerged by the construction of Andong Dam in 1976. Relocated and partially reconstructed traditional-style buildings range from simple, thatched peasant farmhouses to the more elaborate mansions of government officials and the like, with their multiple courtyards. The village looks so authentic that the TV network KBS has used it as sets for historical dramas.

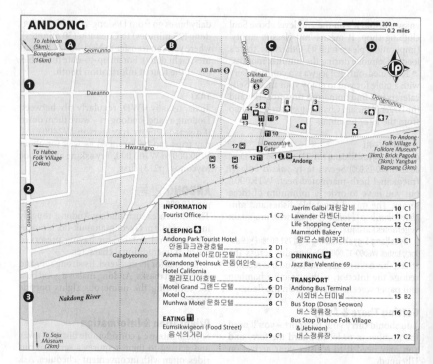

ANDONG

0 ———————— 300 m
0 ———————— 0.2 miles

INFORMATION	
Tourist Office....................................	1 C2

SLEEPING 🏠	
Andong Park Tourist Hotel	
안동파크관광호텔.............................	2 D1
Aroma Motel 아로마모텔................	3 C1
Gwandong Yeoinsuk 관동여인숙....	4 C1
Hotel California	
캘리포니아호텔................................	5 C1
Motel Grand 그랜드모텔................	6 D1
Motel Q..	7 D1
Munhwa Motel 문화모텔................	8 C1

EATING 🍴	
Eumsikwigeori (Food Street)	
음식의거리.......................................	9 C1

Jaerim Galbi 재림갈비.....................	10 C1
Lavender 라벤더...............................	11 C1
Life Shopping Center.......................	12 C2
Mammoth Bakery	
맘모스베이커리.............................	13 C1

DRINKING 🍸	
Jazz Bar Valentine 69......................	14 C1

TRANSPORT	
Andong Bus Terminal	
시외버스터미널..............................	15 B2
Bus Stop (Dosan Seowon)	
버스정류장.......................................	16 C2
Bus Stop (Hahoe Folk Village	
& Jebiwon)	
버스정류장.......................................	17 C2

Just next door to the folk village is **Andong Folklore Museum** (Andong Minsok Bangmulgwan; ☎ 821 0649; admission W1000; ⏰ 9am-6pm Mar-Oct, 9am-5pm Nov-Feb). It offers clear and fascinating displays of Korea's folk traditions from birth through to death.

The village is about 3km east of Andong, close to the dam wall on the opposite side of the river from the road alongside the train track. To get there catch bus 3 (every 35 minutes) and hop off at *minsokchon* (folk village). A taxi will cost around W2500.

If you're walking (about 40 minutes) or have your own transport, stop off at the seven-storey Shilla-period **brick pagoda**, the largest and oldest brick pagoda in Korea. It looks oddly like someone went wild with oversize Lego and is well worth a quick peek.

SOJU MUSEUM 소주 박물관

Mmmm, alcohol…mmm. This **museum** (☎ 858 4541; www.andongsoju.net; ⏰ 9am-5pm closed Sun; admission free) has decent English explanations and displays of interesting seasonal traditional meals, plus other oddities such as 'The Birthday Table of Queen Elizabeth Herself' when

she visited Andong in 1999, and a 'bamboo wife' (no, not something sexual), a kind of pillow meant to allow for more airflow during oppressively humid summer nights. The heady *soju* of Andong may or may not be to your taste, but its significance has been preserved with its designation as a provincial intangible cultural property. With 45% alcohol content you will need to keep the lid on tight to avoid evaporation.

On the grounds of the Andong Soju Brewery, the museum houses a couple of displays that detail the distilling process, the drinking ceremony and a history of *soju* labels. A (thimble-sized) taste of the liquor is given at the end of your visit.

The museum is in the south of Andong, across the Nakdonggang, and best reached by taxi (W3000) or by buses 34 or 36 (W900).

JEBIWON 제비원

No, it's not a Star Wars character, though this huge rock-carved **Amitaba Buddha** (Icheon-dong Seokbulsang; admission free; ⏰ 24hr) does bear a faint resemblance to Jabba the Hutt. The body and robes of this Buddha are carved on a boulder

GYEONGSANGBUK-DO

over 12m high, on top of which are the head and hair – carved out of two separate pieces of rock. Interestingly, the head was actually added at a later date.

Catch bus 54 (every 30 minutes) and ask the driver to drop you off at Jebiwon. Local buses to Yeongju can also drop you at Jebiwon.

BONGJEONGSA 봉정사

This Shilla-period **temple** (☎ 853 4181; admission W1500; ⏰ 7am-7pm Jun-Aug, 8am-sunset Sep-May), 16km northwest of Andong, has a rushing stream, small waterfall, lush moss and (in season) shrill cicadas. The ornately decorated **Geungnakjeon** (Paradise Hall) is seen as the oldest wooden structure in Korea. Repair work on the Daeungjeon (main sanctuary) has revealed a Goryeo-era mural.

From bus 51 (W900, seven daily), it's a 500m walk to the temple.

Festivals & Events

Andong Mask Dance Festival (held at the of end of September to early October) is a great time to visit Andong. It brings together a colourful array of national and international mask dance troupes. It is usually held in tandem with Andong's folk festival, showcasing many traditional performances of music and dance. Check with **KTO** (☎ 1330) for details.

Sleeping

There are plenty of inexpensive *yeoinsuk* (family-run hotels with small rooms and shared bathroom) around the bus terminal, though they're not pretty.

Gwandong Yeoinsuk (☎ 859 2487; d W10,000) Your best deal on a tight budget, set around a courtyard on a quiet side street east of the train station. A wood shop is on the corner. It also serves simples soups from 8am to 9pm.

Motel Q (☎ 857 6878; r W25,000; 🅿 🖳) White walls, pink cushions and leafy trim seems a bit campy, but it's a good deal for the price. All rooms have desktop PCs and real bathtubs.

Motel Grand (☎ 859 0014; r Sun-Thu W25,000, Fri & Sat W30,000; 🅿) Opposite Motel Q, it has red 'mood' lighting, dark faux-wood floors and bamboo patterns.

Munhwa Motel (☎ 857 7001; d W30,000; 🅿 🖳) Features a fancy lobby devoid of all furniture, and dark hallways, some lit with black lights. Rooms are very clean, with 'MoonHwa' embroidered on the sheets, and there are large TVs and 'mood' lights. Some rooms have

closets the size of wine cellars. A coffee shop (open 8.30am to 7pm) is on the 1st floor.

Aroma Motel (☎ 856 6644; d from W35,000; 🅿 🖳) Unfortunate name, but the large rooms have TVs, coffee, wood-grain linoleum, and the lobby has large photos of area attractions. *Ondol* rooms are nicer, but rooms with beds are available.

Hotel California (☎ 854 0622; d from W40,000; 🅿 🖳) Neat, sweet and central, though cheaper places are just as nice. It's a love motel with tasteful, contemporary style that won't jar sensibilities.

Andong Park Tourist Hotel (☎ 859 1500; www .andonghotel.com; d/tw W60,000/65,000) Andong's establishment choice, though unless you need a business centre or the sparkling, marbled lobby, there's not much reason to pay twice as much for essentially the same thing as the love hotels offer. Rooms are so-so clean, comfortable, and charmless, the way a business hotel should be.

Eating & Drinking

You could eat each meal in Andong on Eumsikwigeori, the restaurant row in the town centre, marked by the decorative gate off the main street.

Mammoth Bakery (☎ 857 6000; coffee W3000, breads W1000-4000; ⏰ 7am-11pm) Clean, well lit and friendly, with good lattes and fresh breads, this bakery has been around for more than 30 years.

Jaerim Galbi (☎ 857 6352; meals W4000-17,000) Four items on the menu; the spicy chicken makes a hot day seem cool.

Lavender (☎ 855 8550; set meals W5000-16,000; ⏰ 11am-11pm Tue-Sun) White and airy, this is a very civilised pasta and salad place – pastas come with garlic bread, salad and coffee. The wines are reasonably priced, and you're welcome to bring your own bottle for a W15,000 fee.

Yangban Bapsang (☎ 855 9900; www.yangban .net; meals W6000-15,000; ⏰ 10.30am-9pm) Mackerel served golden, skin crispy, flesh tender – melts on the tongue the way mackerel was meant to. There's floor seating and the wax fish hanging from the rafters look real. From the bus station, turn right and walk about 4km until you come to a bridge and a dam; it's on your left.

The streets around Eumsikwigeori are packed with bakeries, fast food, convenience stores and *hofs*. Try **Jazz Bar Valentine 69**

(☎ 843 0069; ◷ 7pm-4am) for friendly service and plush chairs, though the 'jazz' is more easy listening. For self-caterers, Life Shopping Center is conveniently located between the bus terminal and the train station.

Getting There & Away

BUS

The **bus terminal** (☎ 857 8296) serves both express and regular buses.

Destination	Price (W)	Duration	Frequency
Busan	13,500	3¾hr	7 daily
Cheongsong*	4700	1hr	4 daily
Daegu	7300	2¼hr	frequently
Daejeon	16,600	2hr	4 daily
Pohang	9900	2hr	7 daily
Seoul	15,100	5¼hr	frequently

*for Juwangsan National Park

TRAIN

Destination	Price (W)	Duration	Frequency
Dongdaegu (transfer for Busan)	6900	2hr	3 daily
Gyeongju	7400	2hr	4 daily
Daegu	7100	2hr	1 daily
Seoul	14,300	5½hr	6 daily
Seoul	21,200	4hr	2 daily

Getting Around

The tourist office hands out a helpful local bus timetable with English explanations. The town is small enough to get around on foot, and the local buses serve all the sights.

HAHOE FOLK VILLAGE 하회 민속 마을

This **village** (Hahoe Minsok Maeul; ☎ 854 3669; admission W2000; ◷ 9am-6pm Mar-Oct, 9am-sunset Nov-Feb) is 24km west of Andong and centuries back in time. A river carves a 'C' around the village enclosing mud-daubed houses, tiled walls overrun with squash vines, magpies and vistas that seem right out of the history books. While other Korean folk villages can be tourist productions, this one has residents maintaining old ways, and the government helps with preservation and restoration. There is a tourist information booth at the entrance to the village, and a lotus pond that (in season) is filled with beautiful blooms. Remember to respect people's privacy if you step beyond the entrance gates.

Two kilometres back in the direction of Andong, **Hahoe Mask Museum** (☎ 853 2288; www.maskmuseum.com; admission W1500; ◷ 9.30am-6pm) houses a remarkable collection of traditional Korean masks, plus masks from across Asia and countries as diverse as Nigeria, Italy and Mexico. The English signage here is excellent.

If you're lucky, you can catch one of two daily buses to Hahoe that follow a very bumpy dirt road to stop at **Byeongsan Seowon** (☎ 853 2172; admission free; ◷ 9am-6pm Apr-Oct, 9am-5pm Nov-Mar), a riverside former Confucian academy dating from 1572 and renamed in honour of Ryu Seong-ryong. This spot, boasting some original buildings (with impressively bowed support posts), is way off the tourist map except during summer – then the river bank is busy with young people picnicking and enjoying the relaxing atmosphere.

There are a couple of places to buy snacks by the river, and Hahoe has a number of *minbak* (W20,000 to W25,000, usually quite spartan).

Bus 46 (regular/deluxe W900/1300, 50 minutes, eight daily) runs out to Hahoe from Andong. Two buses daily stop by Byeongsan Seowon and stay about 20 minutes to allow you to look around.

ANDONG HANJI 안동한지

Minutes away from the folk village, this fascinating **paper museum** (☎ 858 7007; www.andonghanji.com; shop ◷ 9am-6pm daily, factory to 6pm Mon-Sat) offers the chance to see modern paper made in the traditional way. Mulberry bark is stripped, soaked, bleached and mashed to make pulp, which is then screened out into giant blocks – the sheets of paper are removed one by one and dried by hand on a large metal 'iron'. Samples of the paper, plus fascinating exhibits of its uses, are in the museum. There are even evening gowns made from it, worn yearly in a fashion show in Seoul.

Take bus 46 (regular/deluxe W900/1300, 50 minutes, eight daily), which leaves from Andong.

DOSAN SEOWON 도산 서원

If the sloping setting and attractive buildings of **Dosan Seowon** (☎ 856 1073; adult/youth/child W1500/700/600; ◷ 9am-6pm Mar-Oct, 9am-5pm Nov-Feb) give you a feeling of *déjà vu*, open your wallet – you'll find an image of this revered Confucian academy on the back of the W1000 note.

ANDONG'S MASKED BALL

In late September/early October, masks and their admirers come from all over the world to join in a host of mask-related festivities. In Hahoe village, masked dancers perform traditional dances in the pine forests to the delight of crowds. Andong City has numerous mask-related shows, and a mask-making contest pits artisan against artisan in a delightful 'mask off' to see who can make the best mask. Firework displays are another popular attraction.

Every weekend at 3pm from May to October (as well as Sunday at 3pm in March, April and November), **Byeolsingut Talnori** performances take place in a small stadium near Hahoe's car park. These shows are a must-see; plus, they're free, although donations are demanded by hard-working *halmeoni* (grandmas). If you can't make it to a performance, you can view many masks at the Hahoe Mask Museum.

According to legend, the Hahoe mask tradition came about when the residents of Hahoe got frustrated with their hoity-toity noble clan. One clever craftsman carved a likeness of one of the most obsequious, much to the delight of his peers. Byeolsingut Talnori is a traditional dance style created by the common folk for the common folk to satirise the establishment. Characters wear masks representing social classes including corrupt monks and the rich, some with bulging eyes and crooked mouths. The conflicts among them are portrayed in amusing combinations of popular entertainment and shamanism. Accompanying the dance are the sounds of *nong-ak*, a traditional farmers' musical percussion quartet. For more information, visit www.maskdance.com or call Andong's tourist info booth (p217).

Some 28km to the north of Andong, Dosan Seowon was founded in 1574 in honour of Yi Hwang (aka Toegye 1501–70, see p208), Korea's foremost Confucian scholar – he's on the *front* of the W1000 banknote. For centuries during the mid-Joseon dynasty, this was the most prestigious school for those who aspired to high office, and qualifying examinations for the civil service took place here. It's a beautiful spot, with mountains on one side and farm fields below. On the grounds, small lotus ponds harbour hundreds of frogs, which glisten on their lily leaves like jewels.

Toegye was also a prolific writer, publishing dozens of volumes summarising and explaining the Chinese classics. Some of his most famous expressions: 'When you are alone, behave decently' and 'In practising virtue one should perform it with perseverance, suppressing one's desires'. The buildings are beautifully preserved (and are often used by Korean film makers) and an exhibition hall gives clues about Toegye's life and work.

Continuing along the main road, you'll find the **Ocheon-ri Traditional Houses** (Ocheon-ri Yujeokji; admission free; 9am-6pm), rescued from destruction before the building of the Andong dam. These buildings (12th to 18th centuries) housed the local Kim clan, which included scholars and government officials. The hillside setting is relaxing, relatively unvisited and excellent for picnicking.

Bus 67 (W900, 40 minutes) runs along the main road, dropping you off about 2km from the *seowon;* four buses daily continue the last 2km.

CHEONGNYANGSAN PROVINCIAL PARK
청량산 도립공원

Beyond Dosan Seowon, this **park** (679 6321; admission W800; 8.30am-6pm) boasts some spectacular views and tracks wandering along cliff precipices. In addition to the mountain Cheongnyangsan, the summit of which is **Changinbong** (870m), there are 11 scenic peaks, eight caves and a waterfall, **Gwanchan pokpo**. A spider web of tracks radiates out from Cheongnyangsa, most are well signposted and marked. The largest temple in the park is **Cheongnyangsa** and there are a number of small hermitages. Built in AD 663, the temple is quite scenic, sitting in a steep valley below the cliffs. **Ansimdang**, at the base of the temple, is a pleasant teahouse. By the time you read this, a folk museum should have opened near the bus stop.

It takes about five hours to complete a round trip of the peaks, returning to the bus stops, or about 90 minutes to the temple and back again.

Sanseong Sikdang (672 1133; r W20,000) is a restaurant and *minbak*. Try washing down your meal with some of the local *dongdongju* (W5000). There is also a small store near the restaurant.

It's a 1.5km walk from the bus stop to the restaurant and first trail. Bus 67 (W1300; one hour, six daily) continues past Dosan Seowon to the park; note that not all buses stop here.

BUSEOKSA 부석사

This **temple of the floating stone** (☎ 633 3258; admission W1200; ◷ 6am-8pm Apr-Sep, 6am-6pm Oct-Mar) is small, serene and way-out-of-the-way, about 60km north of Andong, but well worth trekking to, as it has sublime views over a misty valley and a peacefulness that even the non-spiritual will feel. It was established in 676 by the monk Uisang after he had returned from China, bringing with him the teachings of Hwaeom Buddhism. Though burnt to the ground in the early 14th century by invaders, it was reconstructed in 1358 and escaped destruction during the late-16th-century Japanese invasions.

This stroke of good fortune has resulted in the preservation of the beautiful main hall, **Muryangsujeon**, making it one of the oldest wooden structures in Korea. It also has what are considered to be Korea's oldest Buddhist wall paintings, as well as a unique, gilded-clay, sitting Buddha. The small exhibition room houses some of Korea's oldest paintings of Indra, Brahmadeva and four Deva kings.

Below the entrance there is a small tourist village with restaurants and *minbak*.

Transport to Buseoksa is from Yeongju or Punggi, (city bus/deluxe W950/3600, one hour, hourly). From the bus stop it's a steep but pretty climb up a graded hill, through cornfields and peach groves.

JUWANGSAN NATIONAL PARK 주왕산 국립공원

Far to the east of Andong and reaching almost to the coast, this 106 sq km **park** (admission W2600; ◷ sunrise-1hr before sunset) is dominated by impressive limestone pinnacles that seem to appear from nowhere. Beautiful gorges, waterfalls and cliff-face walks also feature strongly, and with any luck you'll glimpse an otter or protected Eurasian flying squirrel, among the 900-plus species of varied wildlife here.

Orientation & Information

The main gateway to the park is the town of Cheongsong, about 15km away. There is a **national park information centre** (☎ 873 0014; 2nd fl bus terminal) with English-language park maps (W1000). Be sure to check here for local trail conditions.

Sights & Activities

Most visitors to the park are content to see the waterfalls and caves, but for a more rigorous experience try hiking up from Daejeonsa temple to **Juwangsan** (720m; once known as Seokbyeongsan or 'Stone Screen Mountain'; 1¼ hours), along the ridge to **Kaldeung-gogae** (732m, 15 minutes) and then down to **Hurimaegi** (50 minutes), before following the valley back to Daejeonsa (1¾ hours).

On the way back down take the side trip to **Juwang Cave**; the track first passes **Juwang-am Hermitage**, from where a steel walkway takes you through a narrow gorge to the modest cave.

Also within the park is **Naewonmaeul**, a tiny village where craftspeople do woodworking.

Sleeping & Eating

There is a *minbak* village *(minbakchon)* opposite the Juwangsan bus terminal and a **camping ground** (☎ 873 0014; sites W3000) on the other side of the stream.

Bangalo Minbak/Restaurant (☎ 874 5200; r W40,000) This place has a log-cabin exterior with central courtyard, and rooms have *ondol* or beds; some have a space for you to bring your own camping stove. It's just outside the parking lot on the way back to town. From May to September the rates are around W10,000 cheaper.

Juwangsan Spa Tourist Hotel (☎ 872 6801; Cheongsong; d W80,000; ✖) This is the region's most upmarket hotel and lives up to its name with hot-spring baths. Doubles are W55,000 from May to September.

Dubu (tofu) lovers will appreciate the several restaurants making their own tofu in the busy tourist village between the bus terminal and the park entrance.

Getting There & Away

Virtually all buses to Juwangsan stop in Cheongsong (W1300, 20 minutes, every 30 minutes).

Destination	Price (W)	Duration
Andong	7300	1hr
Busan	17,800	3¾hr
Dongdaegu	14,200	3hr
Dongseoul	22,700	5hr

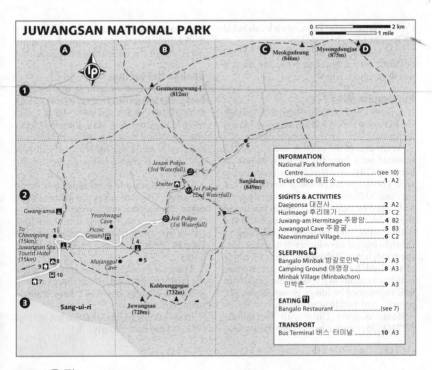

JUWANGSAN NATIONAL PARK

INFORMATION
National Park Information
Centre...(see 10)
Ticket Office 매표소..**1** A2

SIGHTS & ACTIVITIES
Daejeonsa 대전사 **2** A2
Hurimaegi 후리매기 **3** C2
Juwang-am Hermitage 주왕암.......................**4** B2
Juwanggul Cave 주왕굴................................**5** B3
Naewonmaeul Village.....................................**6** C2

SLEEPING
Bangalo Minbak 방갈로민박..........................**7** A3
Camping Ground 야영장................................**8** A3
Minbak Village (Minbakchon)
민박촌 **9** A3

EATING
Bangalo Restaurant.....................................(see 7)

TRANSPORT
Bus Terminal 버스 터미널 **10** A3

ULJIN 울진
pop 51,000

There's not much to see in this sea-coast town – its claim to fame is as the home of four of Korea's nuclear power plants. However, some regional attractions are worth a look.

The bus terminal is in the south of town with the main shopping area at least 1km away, across a bridge. If you need to cash up, the Nonghyeup Bank in the shopping district handles foreign exchange.

A stay near the bus terminal is convenient for quick getaways, but the atmosphere is typical bus-terminal grim.

The shopping district, a quick taxi ride away (W1600), is a nicer setting at similar prices. Rates all over town can climb steeply in summer. **Daerim-jang** (☎ 783 2131; d W25,000;), just north of the bus terminal, is a decent, basic *yeogwan*. **Yongkkum-jang** (☎ 783 8844; d W30,000;), at the northern end of town, is slightly better kept (rooms have bathtubs) and near restaurants, shopping and bakeries.

You can catch intercity express buses from Uljin to the following:

Destination	Price (W)	Duration
Busan	16,4000	4hr
Daegu	15,700	4hr
Seoul	23,600	5hr
Gangneung	9100	2½hr
Gyeongju	11,700	2½hr
Pohang	9500	2hr

AROUND ULJIN
Seongnyugul 석류굴

To spot the Buddha, the Virgin Mary, a Roman palace and a wild boar all in one place, head for this 470m-long **cave** (☎ 782 4006; admission W2200; 8am-6pm Apr-Oct, 8am-5pm Nov-Mar). Impressive stalactites, stalagmites and rock formations are said to resemble images of these icons and dozens more, alongside a number of large caverns and pools. It was Korea's first cave to be developed for tourism. Although there are walkways and bridges inside, larger visitors (height and/or girth) may find some passages a tight squeeze – hard hats are provided.

Spooky legend has it that human bones have turned up here over the years, said to date from the 1592 Japanese invasion, when locals holed up inside only to be sealed in.

The easiest way to get there is by taxi (W5500) from Uljin. Otherwise five buses a day depart from Uljin.

Bulyeongsa 불영사

It's a pretty forest- and river-lined road through the Bulyeong Valley, but you may wonder, is it worth the 15km drive? Emphatically yes.

At the end of the canyon, and another 15 minutes' walk from the car park, **Bulyeongsa** (admission W2000; ☯ 6.30am-6.30pm) is an idyllic spot. The temple is a centre for ascetic practice for some 50 Buddhist nuns, set around a pond and ringed by mountains. It is said that one of the boulders topping one mountainside is a natural representation of the Buddha and, in the right light, the boulder casts its image onto the pond; hence 'Bulyeongsa' means 'Temple of the Buddha's Shadow'. The atmosphere is as harmonious as the name suggests, with well-maintained buildings, groomed grounds, pagodas and Buddhist paintings.

Buses connect Uljin with the temple (W2100, 35 minutes, hourly) but the best way to get around is independently: either riding a bike (note that there is a rather long uphill part through the valley) or driving a car.

Deokgu Hot Springs 덕구 온천

The chief attraction here is the water at **Deokgu Hot Springs Hotel** (☎ 782 0677; fax 785 5169; r from W121,000, spa admission W6000; ✕ ♨), said to cure digestive and skin ailments. Separate men's and women's baths are large and attractive, while the hotel's new, outdoor Spa World is mixed bathing (requiring a swimsuit).

Deokgu has some good walks further up the valley. One walk takes you 4km to **Yongso pokpo**, the original hot springs (no bathing facilities). A much more strenuous hike (about five hours) takes in the mountain **Eungbongsan** (999m) returning via **Minssimyo** (five hours).

There are a couple of other *yeogwan* below the Hot Springs Hotel, which charge around W30,000 a night but don't have mineral springs on tap.

Buses connect Uljin and the hot springs (W2350, one hour, hourly).

Gyeongsangnam-do
경상남도

South Gyeongsang province is a study in contrasts. Travellers looking for big-city action are unlikely to go away disappointed as Busan is full of interesting restaurants, thousands of places to drink and enough cultural assets to fill a few days of exploring. It's the country's second-largest city and one of the world's busiest container ports, but Busan is not a high-energy Asian megacity. It is evolving into an interesting place thanks to a number of ongoing and proposed megaprojects. Chief among these is Lotte World 2, a 107-storey tower currently under construction in slightly dilapidated Nampodong.

The goal of turning Busan into Korea's movie capital took a great leap forward when the city government announced plans to build MGM Studio City, an amusement park with studio sets and a film academy in conjunction with US media giant Metro-Goldwyn-Mayer. With the closure of the US military installation at Camp Hialeah, the city is left with a difficult question: what to do with a large, valuable tract of land that's 10 minutes on foot from Seomyeon?

While developers are busy rearranging the urban landscape, change comes slowly in the towns and fishing villages dotting the expansive countryside. Adventurous travellers willing to hop on a bus and explore will be rewarded with pristine islands, scenic mountains and lush rice paddies. While wandering the streets of a quiet village, don't be surprised if a local resident asks if you need help and then insists that you join his or her co-workers for dinner. Find yourself lost on the back roads? Stick your thumb out and you might be surprised to learn that hitchhiking works here. Few people speak English, but all you really need to succeed is a warm smile, patience and the ability to read body language.

HIGHLIGHTS

- Shock your taste buds with Busan seafood specialities like raw fish at **Gwang-an beach** (p237)
- Go island-hopping off the coast of **Tong-yeong** (p242)
- Rejuvenate your body at **Hursimchung** (p231), one of the world's largest hot spas
- Explore **Jirisan** (p247), one of the best places to hike in Korea
- Take a stroll on the soft, white sand at **Sangju Beach** (p246)

★ Jirisan

Gwang-an Beach ★

Hurshimchung ★

Tong-yeong ★

Sangju ★

| ■ TELEPHONE CODE: 055 | ■ POPULATION: 7.9 MILLION | ■ AREA: 10,500 SQ KM |

History

South Gyeongsang province has a long history of warfare, though it's difficult to beat the *Imjin Waeran* for destruction, treachery and the birth of an icon. In 1592 the Japanese were eager to secure a land route to China. The Joseon government refused assistance, so the Japanese attacked. Led by Toyotomi Hideyoshi, the Japanese landed 160,000 troops at several places including Busan, Sangju Beach and Jinju, where the Koreans made a valiant yet unsuccessful stand against a superior enemy.

The war's star was Admiral Yi Sun-sin, a brilliant tactician credited with the development of the turtle ship, an ironclad vessel instrumental in harassing Japanese supply lines. Despite his significant wartime contributions, Yi was arrested in 1597 for disobeying orders thanks to a clever ruse concocted by the Japanese, who were eager to see the good admiral removed from the war. With Yi behind bars, the Japanese launched a massive assault that destroyed all but 13 of Korea's 133 vessels. Shaken by the loss, the King released Yi and put him in charge of the tattered navy. In a classic case of size doesn't matter, the admiral destroyed or damaged 133 Japanese vessels. One year later, Yi defeated a Japanese armada near Namhae Island that cost the invaders 450 ships. It also cost Admiral Yi his life. In September of 1598, Hideyoshi died and the Japanese leadership lost its appetite for the war.

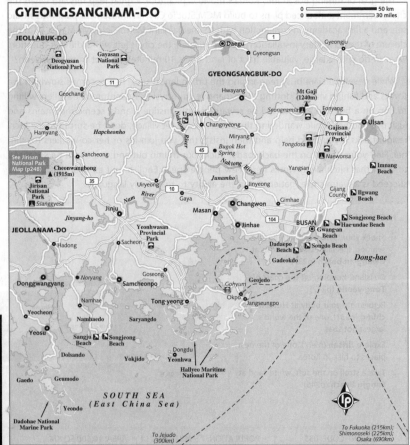

National & Provincial Parks

There are five national parks scattered across the province. On the western flank, **Jirisan National Park** is noted for serious climbs. **Hallyeo National Maritime Park** is a spectacular ocean playground encompassing coastal islands from Namhae to Geoje. Along the border separating South and North Gyeongsang provinces, **Gayasan National Park** is famous for Haeinsa, one of the country's most important temples (although it's located in South Gyeongsang province, access is easiest from Daegu p195). Tucked into the northwest corner of the province, **Deogyusan National Park** is where you'll find downhill skiers and snowboarders hitting the slopes at **Muju Resort** (p301).

There are two provincial parks: **Yeonhwasan** (40 minutes southeast of Jinju) and **Gajisan** (40 minutes north of Busan). Travellers looking for stimulating day trips from Busan should consider visiting **Gajisan Provincial Park** for terrific temples like **Seongnamsa** and a challenging hike up **Mount Gaji** (1240m).

Getting There & Around

Most train travellers stop at Busan station, a big glassy facility close to the city centre. Some inbound trains also stop at Gupo, a handy west-end terminal ideal for travellers who don't need to go downtown. Train travel in the rest of the province is possible, though schedules are not always convenient. For regional trips, the bus is a superior option with departures from Seobu and Dongbu bus terminals. By air, travellers land at Gimhae International Airport, about 30 minutes west of central Busan.

BUSAN 부산

☎ 051 / pop 3.66 million / 763 sq km

There's a noticeably absent cosmopolitan feel in this port city known for raw fish and a harsh dialect that people in Seoul sometimes find incomprehensible. Underneath the drab urban landscape created by an unimaginative use of concrete, quirky people jump the queue, shout while conversing and giggle at the sight of international travellers. Rough around the edges indeed, but like any rogue there's a charming side that begins to emerge once formal barriers have been dropped over dinner and drinks. Cultural mores prevent most people from initiating contact with foreigners. But if you take the first step, the level of kindness and generosity extended your way can be surprising.

Orientation

Busan is a sprawling coastal city tucked into the southeastern corner of the peninsula. The city's manufacturing centre and new container port are at the western end in Gangseo-gu (Map p230). Gimhae International Airport is further west, 27km from Busan's city centre. Agricultural and fishing communities continue to survive in Gijang County in the city's east end, though development pressures may bring significant changes over the next decade.

The heart of the city is concentrated in a band of north–south development running through the centre of Busan. Busy container ports dominate the southern coastline in and around Nampodong, an ageing commercial district with a mishmash of back alleys. Two passenger ferry terminals, the immigration office and a community of draggletailed buildings that serve as a living museum of 40 years past are one subway stop north at Jungangdong. Further north, Line 1 and 2 of the subway intersect in Seomyeon (Map p233), the city centre packed with bars, restaurants and street vendors. Continue north on Line 1 (Map p232) to find Hurshimchung spa, Beomeosa temple and a trail leading to Geumjeong Mountain. Gwang·an and Hae·undae (Map p235) beaches are easy to reach on the eastern section of Line 2.

Information

EMERGENCY

Fire & rescue ☎ 119
Police ☎ 112

INTERNET RESOURCES

City government (http://english.busan.go.kr) For basic socio-economic and travel data.
Pusanweb (www.pusanweb.com) A site to find teaching employment and chronic kvetchers.
South Gyeongsang (http://english.gsnd.net/default.jsp) Learn about South Gyeongsang's sites and geography.

MEDICAL SERVICES

Dong-ui Medical Centre (Map p228; ☎ 850 8523) Marie Kim is an RN who can help travellers. Take Line 1 to Yangjeong station; outside Exit 4, take local bus 8 or 8-1.
Dr Hyun (Map p228; ☎ 897 2283) For dental problems. His 2nd-floor office is near Line 2 Gaya station, Exit 2.
Dr Seo (Map p228; ☎ 755 0920) For general medical maladies. Dr Seo speaks English well. His clinic is at a major intersection beside a pharmacy in Milak-dong, 10 minutes on foot from Line 2 Gwang·an station, Exit 1. Turn right at the second corner and walk 600m.

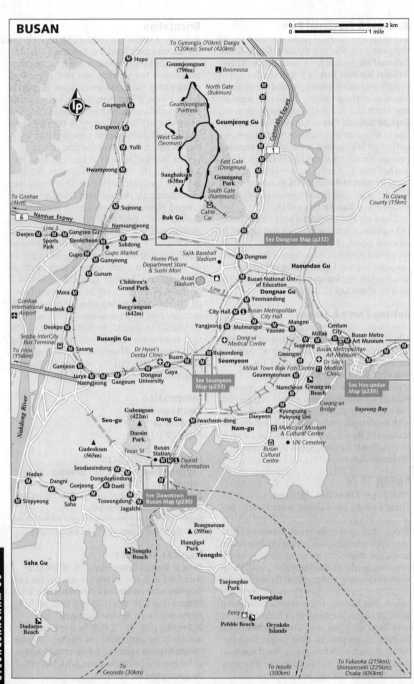

BUSAN

0 — 2 km
0 — 1 mile

To Gyeongju (70km); Daegu
(120km); Seoul (420km)

Hopo

Geumjeongsan
(790m)

Beomeosa

North Gate
(Bukmun)

Geumgok

Geumjeongsan
Fortress

Geumjeong Gu

Dongwon

West Gate
(Seomun)

Yulli

Hwamyeong

East Gate
(Dongmun)

Sanghaksan
(638m)

Geumgang
Park

Buk Gu

South Gate
(Nammun)

To Gimhae
(4km)

Namhae Expwy

Sujeong

Cable
Car

See Dongnae Map (p232)

To Gijang
County (15km)

Namsangjeong

Daejeo

Line 3

Gangseo Gu

Sports
Park

Deokcheon

Sukdong

Sajik Baseball
Stadium

Dongnae

Haeundae Gu

Gupo

Gumyeong

Gupo Market

Home Plus
Department Store
& Sushi Mori

Busan National Uni
of Education

Gunam

Children's
Grand Park

Asiad
Stadium

Line 3

Dongnae Gu

Mora

Baegyangsan
(642m)

City Hall

Busan Metropolitan
City Hall

Yeonsandong

Gimhae
International
Airport

Modeok

Yangjeong

Mulmangol

Mangmi

Centum
City

Busan Metro
Art Museum

Deokpo

Yeonmi

Dong-ui
Medical Centre

Millak

Suyeong

Seobu InterCity
Bus Terminal

Busanjin Gu

Busan Metropolitan
Art Museum

To Jinju
(156km)

Sasang

Dr Hyun's
Dental Clinic

Buam

Bujeondong

Seomyeon

Gwangan

Dr Seo's
Medical
Clinic

Gamjeon

Gaya

Millak Town Raw Fish Centre

Geumnyeonsan

See Hae-undae
Map (p235)

Jurye

Naengjeong

Gaegeum

Dongeui
University

See Seomyeon
Map (p233)

Namcheon

Gwang-an
Beach

Suyeong Bay

Gubongsan
(422m)

Seo-gu

Dong Gu

Daeyeon

Kyungsung –
Pukyong Uni

Gwang-an
Bridge

Daesin
Park

Jwacheon-dong

Nam-gu

Gudeoksan
(565m)

Texas St

Busan
Station

Municipal Museum
& Cultural Centre

Hadan

Seodaesindong

Tourist
Information

UN Cemetery

Dangni

Goejeong

Dongdaesindong

Daeti

Busan
Cultural
Centre

Sinpyeong

Saha

Toseongdong

See Downtown
Busan Map (p230)

Jagalchi

Bongnaesan
(395m)

Saha Gu

Songdo
Beach

Hamjigol
Park

Yeongdo

Taejongdae
Park

Taejongdae

Ferry

Dadaepo
Beach

Pebble Beach

Oryukdo
Islands

To
Geojedo (30km)

To Jejudo
(300km)

To Fukuoka (215km);
Shimonoseki (225km);
Osaka (690km)

MONEY

Most banks exchange currency, though the level of service varies; your chances of finding reasonably efficient service are greatest at the Korea Exchange Bank (KEB). There's a black market for US dollars in Jungangdong and Nampodong; look for women sitting on chairs clutching black purses and whispering, 'changee'.

Gimhae International Airport currency exchange
domestic terminal (Map p228; 9:30am-4:30pm); international terminal (8:30am-9pm).

POST

Is Korea a wired country? Hell yes, even the post office has free internet access.

Central post office (Map p230; 8am-6pm Mon-Fri, 8am-1pm Sat & Sun) Line 1 to Jungangdong station, Exit 9.

TOURIST INFORMATION

Busan station office (Map p228; 441 6565; 8:30am-8pm) There's a modest selection of maps and knowledgeable staff.

Gimhae International Airport desk (Map p228) domestic terminal (973 4607; 9am-9pm); international terminal (973 4537; 7am-9pm) Try these when you need help finding a bus into the city.

Hae-undae office (Map p235; 749 4335; 9am-6pm) A great selection of material; beside the Busan Aquarium on Hae-undae beach.

TRAVEL AGENCIES

It's easy to find a travel agency. Finding one with English-speaking staff, well that's a different matter.

Kangsan Travel (Map p235; 747 0031; www .kangsantravel.com; 9am-6pm Mon-Fri, to 2.30pm Sat) provides English-language services geared towards expats. Take Line 2 to Hae-undae station, Exit 7; the agency is on the 2nd floor above a Family Mart.

Dangers & Annoyances

It's best to avoid Texas St – a small commercial district opposite Busan station that's home for shifty people, Russians, hostess bars and the occasional street hold up – at night. Never drink tap water; don't even cook with it. Typhoon season – roughly mid-July to the end of August – brings heavy rain, ferry cancellations and on occasion severe property damage. Yellow dust storms in the spring don't compare with the thick sheets of gunk that blanket Seoul, but there are days when it's best not to go outside.

Sights & Activities

BEOMEOSA 범어사

Magnificent **Beomeosa temple** (Map p232; adult/youth/child W1000/700/500; 7am-7pm) is Busan's best sight. Founded in AD 678, all of the original structures have been rebuilt at some point during Korea's history of invasions and conquests. Despite its city location, Beomeosa temple is a world away from the urban jungle, with beautiful architecture neatly set against an extraordinary mountain setting. It's a busy place, as the path leading to the temple serves as the northern starting point for trails across Geumjeong Mountain. Before heading back to the city, visit the restaurants near the bus stop to enjoy *pajeon* (파전; green onion pancake) for W6000. Take Line 1 to Beomeosa station, Exit 5. At street level spin 180 degrees, turn left at the corner and walk 200m to the terminus. Catch bus 90 (W900, 15 minutes, every 15 minutes from 8am to 8pm) or take a W2500 taxi to the temple entrance.

GEUMJEONG FORTRESS 금정산성

Travellers climbing **Geumjeongsan** (Geumjeong Mountain) expecting to see a fort will be disappointed because there isn't one. **Geumjeong fortress** (Map p232) is a long stone wall with four gates serving as expensive trail markers. Not all is lost because this is where you'll find some of the city's best hiking. Outdoor enthusiasts seeking an intimate experience with nature should avoid the mountain on holidays and weekend mornings – peak times for maddening crowds of fashionable hikers.

The journey to Geumjeong Mountain is as good as the destination. Most hikers start at the north end of the trail that begins with a mildly steep climb along the left side of Beomeosa temple. This trail eventually leads to the **North Gate** (북문). The 8.8km hike from Beomeosa to the **South Gate** (남문) is a comfortable hike with a couple of steep stretches. Trails are well marked in Korean with a handful of English signs, though there is a need for signage at the **East Gate** (동문). Travellers coming from Beomeosa temple should pass under the gate and walk down hill to a paved road. Turn right at the road and walk to a large signboard. Turn left here to pick up the trail to the South Gate.

The least arduous route is by **cable car** (Map p232; one way/return adult W3000/5000, child W2000/2500; 9am-6.30pm) inside **Geumgang Park** (Map p232;

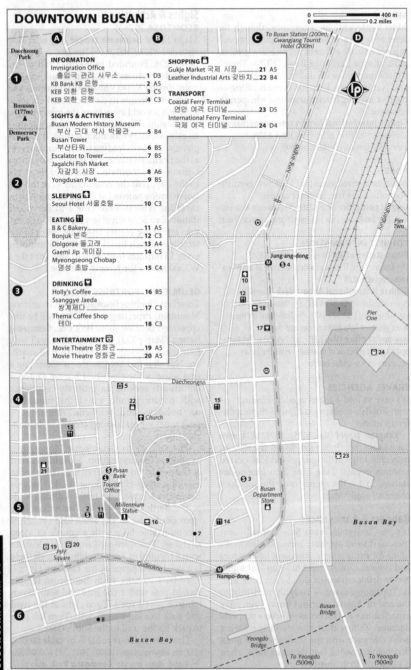

DOWNTOWN BUSAN

0 — 400 m
0 — 0.2 miles

INFORMATION
Immigration Office
출입국 관리 사무소 **1** D3
KB Bank KB 은행 **2** A5
KEB 외환 은행 **3** C5
KEB 외환 은행 **4** C3

SIGHTS & ACTIVITIES
Busan Modern History Museum
부산 근대 역사 박물관 **5** B4
Busan Tower
부산타워 **6** B5
Escalator to Tower **7** B5
Jagalchi Fish Market
자갈치 시장 **8** A6
Yongdusan Park **9** B5

SLEEPING
Seoul Hotel 서울호텔 **10** C3

EATING
B & C Bakery **11** A5
Bonjuk 본죽 **12** C3
Dolgorae 돌고래 **13** A4
Gaemi Jip 개미집 **14** C5
Myeongseong Chobap
명성 초밥 **15** C4

DRINKING
Holly's Coffee **16** B5
Ssanggye Jaeda
쌍계제다 **17** C3
Thema Coffee Shop
테마 **18** C3

ENTERTAINMENT
Movie Theatre 영화관 **19** A5
Movie Theatre 영화관 **20** A5

SHOPPING
Gukje Market 국제 시장 **21** A5
Leather Industrial Arts 갖바치 ... **22** B4

TRANSPORT
Coastal Ferry Terminal
연안 여객 터미널 **23** D5
International Ferry Terminal
국제 여객 터미널 **24** D4

To Busan Station (200m);
Gwangjang Tourist
Hotel (200m)

Daecheong
Park

Bosusan
(177m)

Democracy
Park

Jung-ang-dong

Pier
Two

Pier
One

Daecheongno

Church

Pusan
Bank
Tourist
Office

Millennium
Statue

Busan
Department
Store

Busan Bay

PIFF
Square

Gudeokno

Nampo-dong

Busan
Bridge

Busan Bay

Yeongdo
Bridge

To Yeongdo
(500m)

To Yeongdo
(500m)

GYEONGSANGNAM-DO

adult/child W600/300; ☺ 9am-6pm Mar-Oct, 9am-5pm Nov-Feb) at the southern base of the mountain. Climbing 540m, the ride provides a splendid view of the city's valley development. From the cable car, it's a comfortable 10-minute walk to the South Gate.

The cable car is a 15-minute walk from Oncheonjang station on Line 1. Take Exit 1 and walk left towards the overhead pedestrian crosswalk. Cross the street, walk down the left staircase and turn right at the first corner. Down the street, there's a sign pointing to Geumgang Park. Once through the park's gate, take the middle paved road to the cable car, called Rope Way in English.

SEOKBULSA 석불사

Hard to find, difficult to reach and a wonder to behold, **Seokbulsa temple** (Map p232; admission free; ☺ 7am-7pm) is a hermitage carved into rock. Two massive boulders stretching 40m in height jut out from the mountainside to form a U-shaped enclave with three rock facings that is now a place of worship. Inside the enclave, enormous Buddhist images have been meticulously etched into stone. Visually powerful in scale and impact, it's the kind of work that moves first-time visitors to exclaim 'Wow' as they step back and arch their necks to get the full picture. Quietly walk past the women bowing on the 'shoes-off' platform and step into the small caves for a close-up look at the Buddha glowing in soft candlelight.

Getting to Seokbulsa is a worthwhile challenge for anyone with a desire to explore out-of-the-way places. The most interesting – and strenuous – route is to add this stop to your Geumjeongsan Mountain hike. From the **South Gate** (남문), the path indicated by the Mandeokchon (만덕촌) sign leads to a collection of restaurants and foot-volleyball courts in **Namman Village** (남만 마을). At one point, the path stops at a court; walk right and pick up the trail on the other side.

About 500m down the trail, look for a sign that reads 석불사 입구 (Seokbulsa entrance). Turn right and walk down the steep hill to the road sign pointing the way to a 600m uphill hump to the temple. On the way back, there's no need to return to Namman Village. Take the trail to the top of the mountain and ride the cable car down. Bottom line: add 4km and 1½ hours to the Geumjeongsan Mountain hike to experience one of the most unique temples in Busan.

PUBLIC BATHS

You can't really experience Korea unless you've been to a public bath.

With 4300 sq metres of floor space, **Hurshimchung** (Map p232; adult/youth/child W7900/4000/5000; ☺ 5.30am-10pm, last entry 9pm) is the best place to take the plunge. Reportedly the largest *jjimjilbang* (bathhouse) in Asia, the soaking tubs, saunas and domed roof make this spectacle a great place to relax, wash and exfoliate. Guests can stay as long as they like and take a break in the 3rd-floor snack bar; put on the *jjimjilbang* uniform (Monday to Saturday W1000/Sunday free)in the change room and use the locker key to pay. The bill is settled as you leave the spa. Located opposite the Nongshim Hotel, it's a 15-minute walk from Oncheonjang station or the cable car.

Vesta Spa & Jjimjilbang (Map p235; adult/youth spa W5000/5000; spa & jjimjilbang W7900/5000; ☺ 24hr) can not compare with Hurshimchung in terms of size. It does however have a cosy atmosphere with an attractive interior design that relies heavily on wood and flagstone. What's the coolest feature of this must-try facility? The outdoor balcony where guests can stand in the buff overlooking the sea. Located on Dalmaji Hill, a W3000 taxi from Hae·undae beach is the only practical way to get here.

BEACHES

Hae·undae (Map p235) is the country's most famous beach. During the peak travel season in August, umbrellas mushroom across the 2km beach while frolickers fill the water with truck-size inner tubes rented from booths behind the beach. It's a fun family outing with 500,000 friends, though the marketing bumph portraying Hae·undae as a world-class resort is bunk. Take Line 2 to Hae·undae station, Exit 3, and walk to the beach.

Among the city's seven other beaches, **Gwang·an** (Map p228) is the best option for access and quality (the other beaches are Dadaepo, Songdo, Songjeong, Ilgwang, Imnang and Pebble Beach). Although the ugly wall of commercial development behind the beach diminishes the daytime experience, Gwang·an really shines at night. The multicoloured light show illuminating the bridge is grand. The shortest route to Gwang·an is Line 2 to Geumnyeonsan station, Exit 3. Rotate 180 degrees at street level and turn right at the corner; the beach is five minutes down the road.

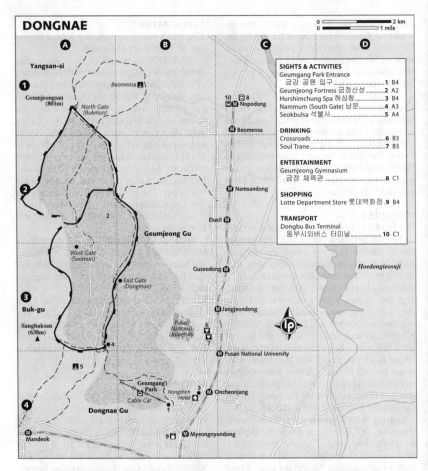

DONGNAE

0 ————— 2 km
0 ————— 1 mile

SIGHTS & ACTIVITIES
Geumgang Park Entrance
금강 공원 입구 **1** B4
Geumjeong Fortress 금정산성 **2** A2
Hurshimchung Spa 허심청 **3** B4
Nammum (South Gate) 남문 **4** A3
Seokbulsa 석불사 **5** A4

DRINKING
Crossroads **6** B3
Soul Trane **7** B3

ENTERTAINMENT
Geumjeong Gymnasium
금정 체육관 **8** C1

SHOPPING
Lotte Department Store 롯데백화점 .**9** B4

TRANSPORT
Dongbu Bus Terminal
동부시외버스 터미널 **10** C1

Yangsan-si

Geumjeongsan
(801m)

Beomeosa

North Gate
(Bukmun)

10 8
Nopodong

Beomeosa

Namsandong

Dusil

Geumjeong Gu

West Gate
(Seomun)

Guseodong

Hoedongieosuji

East Gate
(Dongmun)

Buk-gu

Sanghaksan
(638m)

Pusan
National
University

Jangjeondong

6

7

Pusan National University

4

5

Geumgang
Park

Nongshin
Hotel

3

Oncheonjang

Cable Car

1

Dongnae Gu

Mandeok

9

Myeongnyundong

YONGDUSAN PARK 용두산 공원

In the centre of this humble park stands
the 118m **Busan Tower** (Map p230; adult/youth/child
W3500/3000/2500; ⏱ 8.30am-10pm Apr-Oct, 9am-10pm
Nov-Mar). If the haze is not too thick, daytime
views of container-ship traffic in the harbour
provide a sense of the port's scale of opera-
tions. Other things to do: buy corn from a
kiosk or watch pigeons swoop for food.

JAGALCHI FISH MARKET 자갈치 시장

Anyone with a love of seafood and a tolerance
for powerful odours could easily spend a
couple of hours exploring the country's
largest **fish market** (Map p230). Waterfront
warehouses, tiny shops and elderly women
perched on street corners sell an incredible

variety of seafood. Sea-weathered sailors offering a 20-minute boat tour of the harbour
might approach you on the pier.

MUSEUMS & EXHIBITIONS

Busan frowns upon bourgeois pursuits like art
and urban design, so it isn't surprising that the
arts scene is, well, lacking.

The **Busan Metropolitan Art Museum** (Map p228;
☎ 744 2602; adult/youth/child W700/300/free, Sat free;
⏱ 10am-6pm) is hardly a must-see but it does
come in handy during the typhoon season
when you need a place to escape the rain. Take
Line 2 to Metro Art Museum station, Exit 5
and walk 150m.

In Hae-undae, the **Busan Aquarium** (Map p235;
☎ 740 1700; adult/youth/child W15,000/12,500/10,000;

GYEONGSANGNAM-DO

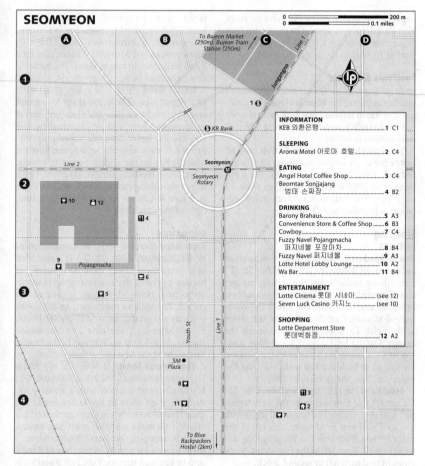

SEOMYEON

INFORMATION	
KEB 외환은행	**1** C1

SLEEPING	
Aroma Motel 아로마 호텔	**2** C4

EATING	
Angel Hotel Coffee Shop	**3** C4
Beomtae Sonjjajang 범태 손짜장	**4** B2

DRINKING	
Barony Brahaus	**5** A3
Convenience Store & Coffee Shop	**6** B3
Cowboy	**7** C4
Fuzzy Navel Pojangmacha 퍼지네불 포장마차	**8** B4
Fuzzy Navel 퍼지네불	**9** A3
Lotte Hotel Lobby Lounge	**10** A2
Wa Bar	**11** B4

ENTERTAINMENT	
Lotte Cinema 롯데 시네마	(see 12)
Seven Luck Casino 카지노	(see 10)

SHOPPING	
Lotte Department Store 롯데백화점	**12** A2

10am-7pm Mon-Fri; 9am-9pm Sat, Sun & holidays, to 11pm Jul-Aug) is a large fish tank with 50,000 creatures. The aquarium also hosts a shark diving class open to nondivers. Visit www.scuba inkorea.com for details.

The **Busan Modern History Museum** (Map p230; ☎ 253 3845; admission free; 9am-6pm; closed Mon) is a modest effort but it does display hard-to-find information about Busan's development. It's located north of Yongdusan Park, 300m west of the Jungangdong central post office.

In Uamdong, the **Busan Municipal Museum** (Map p228; adult/youth/child W500/300/free; 9am-6pm, closed Mon) has a small collection of Korean War photos and film footage.

Across the street, the **UN Cemetery** (Map p228; www.unmck.or.kr; ☎ 625 1608; admission free; 9am-

5pm) appeals to history enthusiasts, though the photo exhibition is an embarrassingly modest tribute. English-speaking tour guides are inside the kiosk. Line 2 to Daeyeon station, Exit 5. At street level turn 180 degrees and you'll see a sign pointing to the UN Cemetery.

Tours

Mipo Wharf (Map p235), the small wharf at the eastern end of Hae-undae beach, is home base for two ocean tours.

The 50-minute circuit (round trip adult/child 13,000/7000; tours 7.30pm, 8.20pm, 9.10pm and 10pm) runs around Gwang-an Bridge.

An 80-minute tour-shuttle service to the Coastal Ferry Terminal in Jungangdong (Map p230; one way adult/child 14,900/7450) departs Hae·undae every 90 minutes from 9am (last departure 4pm). On the return trip, departures from the Coastal Ferry Terminal start at 10.30 (last departure 5.30pm).

Festivals & Events

In August special events are held on the city's beaches as part of the **Busan Sea Festival**, including the **Busan International Rock Festival** (www .rockfestival.co.kr/birof_english; Dadaepo beach). Limited information is online.

The **Pusan International Film Festival** (www.piff .org) is the city's largest and most significant festival. First launched in 1996, the 10th version in 2005 screened 307 films from 73 countries. The festival is held sometime between September and October.

Sleeping

BUDGET

Blue Backpackers Hostel (☎ 634 3962; www.busanback packers.com; dm W15,000, tw W25,000-35,000 ✪ ▯) Everything today's discriminating budget traveller needs is here: free washing machine, breakfast and internet. Take Line 1 to Beomnaegol station, Exit 3, and cross the street at the light. Turn left and walk towards the bridge. On the bridge, look for a door leading to a staircase. Walk down to the parking lot and go to building 106 with '1-2' over the entrance. Take the elevator to 1802.

Seoul Hotel (Map p230; ☎ 469 7001; d W25,000; ✪) Unremarkable rooms close to the ferry terminal. You get a simple bed in a small room with a crap TV. If you need more, this is not the place for you. Take Line 1 to Jungangdong station, Exit 17. Turn left at the first street. Walk straight and turn left at second block.

Arpina Youth Hostel (☎ 731 9800; www.busanyouth hostel.co.kr; dm W28,600; ste from W150,000; ✪ ▯ ▣) Hostel and golf anyone? You get both and more at Arpina, a nonsmoking, mixed-use

facility with dorm bunks, a five-lane pool, health club and driving range. For W100,000, you can rent a dorm room. Take Line 2 to Metropolitan Art Museum station; take Exit 3 and walk straight two minutes. The hostel is down the road beside the green net.

Haotel Motel (모텔 하오텔; ☎ 863 0413; d W30,000; ✪) Spend W30,000 at any love motel and you might be disappointed, but spend your money here and be charmed by the country-inn feel of this understated property. From hallways adorned with green vine on white lattice to the wicker basket of towels, this place embodies cosiness. Take Line 1 or 3 to Yeonsan-dong station, Exit 1, walk straight and turn left at the second block then turn right at the first block.

MIDRANGE

Sugar Motel (Map p235; ☎ 747 8620; standard/special/ VIP W40,000/50,000/60,000; ✪ ▯) If your idea of a romantic getaway includes a supply of battery-operated devices, this motel is worth inspecting. Hae·undae beach is around the corner, but with so much stuff in the room you may not get that far. Add W10,000/20,000 Friday/Saturday. Take Line 2 to Hae·undae station, Exit 3 and walk towards the beach; turn right at the first major intersection.

Four Season Motel (포시즌 모텔; ☎ 866 1712; standard/deluxe/ste W40,000/50,000/80,000; ✪) It's finally here: a motel with a water park. Aqua fans go weak at the knees inside the Blue Hawaii room when they see the tub big enough to make a splash with any group. Friends stopping by later? No problem – there's room for a party in the shower. Line 1 or 3 to Yeonsan station. Take Exit 5 and walk right at street level. The hotel is on the 12th floor of the CMC building.

Gwangjang Tourist Hotel (광장 광광 호텔; ☎ 464 3141; d/tw/ondol W43,000, ste W60,000; ✪ ▯)

BUSAN IN FILM

Chin·gu begins in the 1970s with four boys running behind a truck spewing a thick cloud of insect repellent, a powerful image underscoring this gangster film's theme of blindly chasing after something without considering the reasons or consequences. By the 1990s the boys are men and their lives have taken radically different directions, with two friends ending up as leaders in rival gangs, leading to a compelling courtroom scene. Artfully directed and skilfully acted, the semiautobiographical story based on director Kwak Kyungtaek's life is set in Busan, with local sites such as Jagalchi fish market and a gang fight inside a movie theatre – which today sits as an underutilised skin-flick venue. *Chin·gu*, which is Korean for friend, is the highest grossing movie in the country, and attracted eight million viewers. The DVD version has English subtitles.

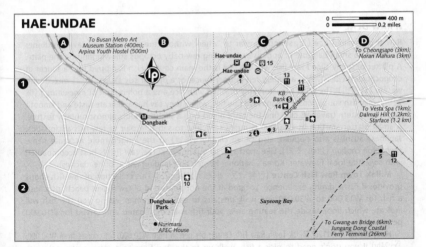

HAE·UNDAE

To Busan Metro Art Museum Station (400m); Arpina Youth Hostel (500m)

Hae-undae

To Cheongsapo (3km); Noran Mahura (3km)

Hae-undae

KB Bank

Dongbaek

To Vesta Spa (1km); Dalmaji Hill (1.2km); Starface (1.2 km)

Dongbaek

Dongbaek Park

Nurimaru APEC House

Suyeong Bay

To Gwang-an Bridge (6km); Jungang Dong Coastal Ferry Terminal (26km)

Perhaps the city's best tourist-class hotel, it's ideal for travellers who require only a proper place to lie down after a busy day of sightseeing but can't stomach the idea of slumming in a comparably priced love motel. Line 1 to Busan station, Exit 8, and walk across the plaza.

TOP END

Westin Chosun Beach Hotel (Map p235; ☎ 749 7201; r W193,000; 🛇 🖵 🕱) It's Busan's oldest international hotel, but gets better with age. A hint of retro shaken, not stirred, with modern touches, creates a James Bond – à la Sean Connery – dashing cool. Inside and out, this is the best hotel on Hae·undae beach.

Other recommendations include:

Novotel Ambassador Busan (Map p235; ☎ 743 1234; d W190,000; 🛇 🖵 🕱) Staff could benefit from a customer-relations training seminar.

Grand Hotel (Map p235; ☎ 740 0114; d W200,000; 🛇 🖵 🕱) Better-than-average facilities (like a 50m pool) across the street from Hae·undae beach.

Paradise Hotel (Map p235; ☎ 749 2111; tw W240,000; 🛇 🖵 🕱) Busan's first casino is here.

Eating

The food in Busan is salty, spicy and raw, just like the people of this fair metropolis. Seafood in various shapes and forms – like eel, octopus, and swellfish – is popular and plentiful.

BUDGET

Dolgorae (Map p230; meals from W2500) The interior looks like a penitentiary but the stern women who run this shop serve some of the city's best

doenjang jjigae (된장찌개; spicy soy-bean stew). The soup bowls are small but with prices this low, order another set. Located at the end of a narrow lane one block west of the KB bank near B&C Bakery.

B&C Bakery (Map p230; meals from W3000; 🕙 8.30am-10.30pm) One of the best places to stock up on carbohydrates before exploring Nampodong's

A RAW DEAL

Raw fish is called *hoe* (회; sounds similar to 'when' without the 'n'). A typical raw-fish dinner starts with a small banquet of appetisers including raw baby octopus still wiggling on the plate. A platter of thinly sliced raw fish without rice is the main course. Fish is dipped into a saucer of *chogochujang* (초고추장), a watery red-pepper sauce, or a dish of soy sauce (간장) mixed with wasabi (와사비). The meal is customarily finished with rice and a boiling pot of *mae·untang* (매운탕; spicy fish soup). Most Koreans love raw fish, which they say has a delicate taste and smooth texture. Western travellers may find the taste bland with a slightly tough, almost rubbery texture. A small platter starting at W40,000 is rarely sufficient to satisfy a pair of raw-fish aficionados. Japanese sushi is also popular, also called *chobap* (초밥) or the longer, more accurate name *saengseon chobap* (생선 초밥). Like most special outings in Korea, raw fish is best accompanied with *soju* (the local firewater, Korea's national hootch and leading cause of headaches).

Millak Town Raw Fish Centre (민락타운 외 센터; Map p228) This collection of raw-fish shops provides a rustic dining experience. Located at the northeast end of Gwang·an beach, purchase a fish for W15,000 to W30,000 and walk upstairs to eat; the woman selling you the fish will indicate which floor. Inside the seating area, your fish will be prepared and served for W10,000 per person.

Haryu (☎ 753 1126; Millak Town Raw Fish Centre; per person from W20,000, set courses from W40,000; ⊗ 24hr) If you don't need to pick a fish, walk up to the 2nd floor to a restaurant run by the English-speaking owner, Mr Jeon. Take Line 2 to Gwang·an station, Exit 5. At the top of the stairs, turn 180 degrees and then right at the first street. Walk 600m and turn left at the beach. The raw-fish centre is the large, brown building 300m down the road.

Grandmother Lee's Raw Fish House (Map p235; per serving W20,000; ⊗ 10am-sunrise) Stop by for raw fish and you might end up partying until sunrise. It's a small restaurant with ground-floor fish tanks and space for groups upstairs. The affable Mr Lee speaks English well and takes the time to explain the features of each fish. Walk to the eastern end of Hae·undae beach, turn left at the first street past the Mipo ferry terminal and then a quick right turn. It's the first restaurant on your right.

Myeongseong Chobap (Map p230; sushi sets from W12,000, raw fish W30,000-60,000) A popular Japanese-style restaurant serving *saengseon chobap* and *saengseonhoe koseu* (생선회 코스, Korean raw-fish set menu). Located in Jungangdong, it's 100m north of the Tower Hotel with 'sushi' written on the signboard.

The **Jagalchi Fish Market** (p232) in Nampodong is the city's sprawling wholesale and retail centre for all things fishy. There are heaps of waterfront restaurant options to enjoy raw fish, all surrounded by boats off-loading their catch, enormous seafood warehouses and salty characters. Although it's a popular destination for Japanese tourists who seem to enjoy the 'roughing it on the pier' dining experience, the primitive interior design of many shops does not hold the same level of attraction for local citizens who prefer a less rustic environ, like that found in the restaurants in and around Gwang·an and Hae·undae beaches.

back alleys. Pastries, cakes and coffee are on the 1st floor; light meals are served upstairs.

Beomtae Sonjjajang (Map p233; meals from W3500) Here's a sterling example of a successful restaurant owner who won't update, modernise or even clean up the shop interior. According to superstition, the good fortune a successful shop enjoys could be lost if the interior were changed. Consequently, some shoddy-looking restaurants, like this one, serve great food. The *jjambbong* (짬뽕; spicy seafood soup) and *tangsuyuk* (탕수육; sweet-and-sour fried pork) are all excellent.

Ops Bakery (Map p235; meals from W3500; ⊗ 7am-11pm) You thought everything in Hae·undae was overpriced? Well, almost everything, now that Ops serves bacon and eggs for breakfast. Located on the street opposite the Novotel.

Podo Cheong (Map p233; ☎ 806 9797; per serving W5000; ⊗ midday-midnight) It's not the best *sutbul galbi* (숯불갈비; charcoal-fired barbecue) restaurant but it is very good. The main draw of this busy restaurant is the backyard barbecue feel in the outdoor patio. Lean *moksal* (목살) pork chop) tastes great, though most Koreans choose *samgyeopsal* (삼겹살; bacon). Unless you're hoping to accelerate the likelihood of a heart attack, avoid this cut, which is essentially a slab of fat with a hint of pork.

Bonjuk (Map p230; meals from W6000; ⓨ 8am-10pm, closed Sun) When you need a break from Korea's flamethrower-hot food, try porridge. *Juk* (죽) comes in several flavours including vegetable and silky smooth pumpkin. It's outstanding stick-to-your-ribs food suitable for breakfast, lunch or dinner.

Seafood

Sushi Mori (수시 모리; sushi plates from W1500) The environs are not especially attractive but this restaurant in the Home Plus department store (p231) food court has sushi on a conveyor belt. If you'd prefer to eat on the run, go to the back of the store's grocery section and buy a box of sushi for the unbelievably low price of W390 per piece. It's not outstanding quality but it is good.

Pungmi Chueotang (풍미추어탕; meals W6000; ⓨ 11am-9pm Sun-Fri, 11am-10pm Sat) This scruffy-looking restaurant draws people from great distances for the *chueotang* (추어탕; loach soup). Made from ground loach and leafy cabbage, the dark-green soup has a mild taste. If it's too mild, dip into the plastic tubs of seasoning, which includes *sancho* (산초), a brown spice that adds a rich, earthy flavour when used sparingly. With a self-serve counter of unlimited side dishes like baked fish and seaweed, it's an outstanding meal and one of the city's best deals.

Getting here is not easy, though. Take a taxi from Seomyeon or Sports Complex station, Exit 11, and go to the main gate of Children's Park. Walk along the road to the right of the park entrance then follow the cement lane another 200m.

Halmae Jaecheopguk (할매 재첩국; per serving W6000; ⓨ 24hr) Hungover in Gwang·an beach? Do what many Koreans do and stumble over to this restaurant respected for hangover remedies disguised as food. *Jaecheopguk* (재첩국; marsh clam soup) is a clear shellfish broth. Located on Gwang·an's one-way street opposite the Giant Step jazz bar; look for the 24-hour restaurant with a blinding yellow interior.

MIDRANGE & TOP END

Angel Hotel Coffee Shop (Map p233; meals from W8000; ⓨ 8am-11pm) When the idea of rice and *kimchi* for breakfast has you considering the benefits of fasting, try this economical and tasty

option: bacon and eggs with change back from a W10,000 note.

Gaboja Eonyang Bulgogi (가보자 연양불고기; ☎ 751 9232; per 150g serving W20,000; ⓨ 10am-6am) Located on Gwang·an's Eonyang Bulgogi one-way street, this *sutbul galbi* restaurant serves sumptuous though stratospherically expensive Eonyang beef. There is a belief in Korea that domestic beef – called *Hanu* – is superior in quality to imported meat and therefore warrants high prices. Maybe, but at W130,000 per kilogram it better rock your world.

Seafood

Gaemi Jip (Map p230; meals from W7000; ⓨ 9am-11pm) The speciality is *nakji bokkeum* (낙지볶음; octopus stew), a fiery dish that can cause customers to sweat profusely, so keep a good supply of beverages close at hand. Located on a small lane in Nampodong near the steps to Yongdu-san Park, it's worth the effort to find this place if you want to try something different.

Geumsu Bokguk (Map p235; meals from W8000; ⓨ 24hr) Remember the Simpson's episode when Homer ate blowfish and was told he had 24 hours to live? This restaurant serves that fish. A worthwhile restaurant for anyone who wants to experience a seafood delicacy and earn bragging rights: 'I ate poisonous fish and survived'. Stay on the 1st floor for relatively inexpensive dishes. Head upstairs and join the Japanese tourists who have a strong yen for the pricey sets. Located on a lane across the street from the Paradise Hotel.

Drinking

There are thousands of places to drink, ranging from sophisticated hotel bars to *pojangmacha*, Korean late-night drinking establishmens fashioned out of tarpaulin and plastic chairs.

PUSAN NATIONAL UNIVERSITY

It's the original party zone for expats, with heaps of places to drink and eat, all geared towards fickle university students.

Soul Trane (Map p232; drinks W4000) It's a dance club that falls in and out of fashion with English-language teachers and Korean women hoping to brush up on their conversation skills. It's near the front gate of the university.

Crossroads (Map p232; drinks W4000) Across the street from Soul Trane, Crossroads often plays the foil for people looking for a less intense place to quaff. On occasion, a rowdy place in its own right.

GYEONGSANGNAM-DO

KYUNGSUNG-PUKYONG UNIVERSITIES

The commercial district in front of Kyungsung and Pukyong universities is an electric party district with eating and drinking options catering to 40,000 hungry, thirsty and frugal students. Most expats hang out in one or two places.

Ol' 55 (drinks W4000; ☾ 7pm-2am Tue-Thu, 7pm-5am Fri & Sat, closed Sun) A testosterone-charged tavern with everything a beer-chugging man needs: ale to match budget and taste, a prohibition on hip-hop music, and women who play billiards in high-heel shoes and cut-offs. Take Line 2 to Kyungsung-Pukyong station, Exit 3, turn 180 degrees, walk to the corner and turn left. Turn left at the second street and right at next block.

Vinyl Underground (drinks W4000; ☾ 7pm-5am) Bring your A-game to this hip-hopping dance club that's wall-to-wall flesh late Fridays and Saturdays. Mingle with local women sporting the latest music video–inspired club wear and the baddest home boyz to come out of Saskatchewan. It's up the street from Ol'55.

HAE·UNDAE BEACH

Drinks in Hae·undae can put a serious dent in your wallet. The beachfront hotel bars are popular with the corporate crowd who can set up a tab, though travellers with a refined sense of budget head elsewhere. If you're looking for a low-cost option, grab some beverages from a nearby convenience store and plop down on the beach.

U2 (Map p235; drinks W3000; ☾ 7pm-3am, 7pm-5am Fri & Sat) Finding a bar that plays George Thorogood isn't easy. Luckily, Busan has one and this is it: a fine rock-and-roll bar with bourbon, scotch and beer. It's opposite the Marriott Hotel.

Starface (Map p235; drinks W4000; ☾ 7pm-4am) Everything a fun neighbourhood pub needs is here: decent bar selection, regular specials and the occasional brawl. Friday night is all-you-can-drink for W15,000 (some limitations). Located on Dalmaji Hill, a W3000 taxi from Hae·undae is the only practical way to get here. Not many drivers are familiar with Starface but they all know 김성종 추리문학관, the next-door bookstore.

Noran Mahura (Map p235; drinks W4000; ☾ 2pm-sunrise) It's a tent restaurant on Cheongsapo (청사포), an out-of-the-way harbour where people come for a drink to watch the sunset and unexpectedly stay for the sunrise. The harbour road is packed with tent restaurants so if this one happens to be busy, walk along the pier to find another. Snacks include *garibi* (가리비), grilled clams with a salsalike sauce that tastes great. It tastes even better with *soju* at sunrise. Catch a W3000 taxi from Hae·undae beach.

GWANG·AN BEACH

Gwang·an's interesting bars are located on the busy beachfront road and the small lane one block behind the drag.

Fuzzy Navel (drinks W4000; ☾ 7pm-6am) Most of the stimulating places are beside or behind this funky bar, where the recipe is simple: take one shack and decorate liberally with California beach-bum graffiti. Add Plexiglas windows and presto, one of the city's most interesting concoctions.

SEOMYEON

Cowboy (Map p233; drinks W4000; ☾ 4pm-2am) Anyone doing the rounds in Seomyeon at some point pulls into Cowboy. Dark and smoky with thumping Korean pop music interspersed with classic-rock tunes, the open-floor concept and wooden bar make it possible to mingle and on occasion hook up.

Lotte Hotel Lobby Lounge (Map p233; drinks W4000) Here's the upscale lizard lounge you've been looking for. Palm trees, comfy chairs and live muzak created by the duo with a piano and iMac. Throw in a decent Irish coffee and you've got the perfect place to impress a date.

Barony Brahaus (Map p233; drinks W5000) Formerly known as Dojima, it's Busan's first microbrewery and a popular after-work watering hole for the upwardly mobile crowd. With a 550cc mug starting at W5000 it's easy to run up a substantial tab quickly. That's why prudent drinkers drop W16,000 on the all-you-can-eat-and-drink option; gorge and binge daily from 6pm to 10pm. Located on a small lane one block behind Lotte Department Store.

Other recommendations:

Fuzzy Navel (Map p233; drinks W5000; ☾ 6.30pm-6am) The newest Fuzzy Navel and a real party for the 20-something crowd on Seomyeon's Youth Street. It's on the 4th floor.

Fuzzy Navel Pojangmacha (Map p233; drinks W5000; ☾ 8pm-5am) There's a long line of orange pojangmacha tents behind Lotte Hotel. This is the black one.

Wa Bar (Map p233; drinks W5000; ☾ 5pm-6am) A big open-concept ice bar. On Seomyeon's Youth St half a block from Fuzzy Navel.

NAMPODONG

Most of the drinking establishments in Nampodong cater to Japanese and Korean business travellers. But there are a number of shops where you can experiment with unusual teas or sip espresso.

Holly's Coffee (Map p230; drinks W2000; ☻ 8am-11pm) Where else in the world can you drink great espresso and free high-speed internet access? Well, lots of places in Nampodong actually, and this is one of them.

Thema Coffee Shop (Map p230; drinks W2500; ☻ 8am-8pm) Fine espresso with a bacon-and-eggs breakfast from 8am to 11am. From Jungangdong station, Exit 13, turn left at the first street.

Ssanggye Jaeda (Map p230; drinks W3000; ☻ 10am-9pm) A teahouse with medicinal drinks like the dark and slightly bitter *ssanghwa* (쌍화차). Take Line 1 to Jungangdong station, Exit 11, then walk two blocks past the post office.

Entertainment

LIVE MUSIC

Giant Step Jazz Bar (drinks W5000; ☻ 5pm-3am, closed Sun) You've got friends coming to town and you need a place to impress. The usual haunts are out because you've earned a reputation for table dancing after multiple shots of *soju*. Enter the Giant Step, a jazz bar with all the trappings you'd expect in an upscale joint, like burgundy wood, black-and-white photos and a good supply of recordings, plus live 30-minute sets on stage Wednesday to Saturday (9pm, 10pm and 11pm). It's near Gwang·an beach on the street behind the Fuzzy Navel (opposite).

Monk (drinks W4000; ☻ 6pm-2am) Before and after jazz sets (9pm to 11pm, Wednesday to Saturday), Monk can be an empty sound stage with a few offbeat characters. When live music hits the stage, the place is full of offbeat characters. Poetry Plus runs one Saturday every six weeks (9pm to 11pm). It's across the street from Ol' 55 (opposite).

SPORTS

Professional sports provide a day of fun with ticket prices in the W5000 to W10,000 range. Perennial bottom feeders, the Lotte Giants , play baseball at Sajik Stadium (Map p228). From October to March, the KTF Magicwings play pro basketball at Geumjeong gymnasium (Map p232; Line 1 Nopodong station, walk 1.2km from Exit 1). The Busan Icons of the Korean soccer league play in Asiad Stadium

(Map p228), located behind the Asiad Home Plus department store and a 10-minute walk from Sajik baseball stadium.

CINEMA

Several theatres show first-run English-language movies including the multiscreen cinemas in Nampodong next to PIFF Sq (Map p230), the **Lotte Cinema** (Map p233; 10th fl, Lotte department store, Seomyeon), and the 10-screen facility at **Megabox** (Map p235; Hae·undae), 100m from Line 2 Hae·undae station, Exit 1; the ticket booth is on the 1st floor and screens are on the 6th floor.

GAMBLING

Paradise Casino (Map p235; ☎ 742 2110; Hae·undae; ☻ 24hr) Anyone who understands the science of gambling can test his or her skill.

Seven Luck Casino (Map p233; ☎ 665 6000; Lotte Hotel, Seomyeon; ☻ 24hr) Downtown travellers with an itch could try here.

Shopping

Busan's traditional markets offer a unique and occasionally shocking experience.

Bujeon Market (Map p233) The city's largest downtown traditional, open-air emporium and best place to buy low-cost, in-season fruit and vegetables. It's accessible from Bujeon-dong station (Exit 5).

Gukje Market (Map p230) West of Nampodong; has hundreds of small booths with a staggering selection of items, from leather goods to Korean drums.

Gupo Market (Map p228) A large selection of clothing, pungent Korean food and butcher shops specialising in fowl and dog meat. Whatever one's take on the ancient practice of using man's best friend for human nourishment, images of an eviscerated canine carcass are bound to produce lasting memories. Take Line 3 to Deokcheon station, Exit 3, turn right at the first street and then left at the first street.

Leather Industrial Arts (Map p230) Handcrafted leather goods are made at this small shop with an impressive selection of bags, belts and wallets. It's around the corner from the Busan Modern History Museum.

Experience the country's department-store culture of saturating the floor with sales assistants and free food samples. All stores have ready-to-eat food and some Western goods.

Hyundai department store Slightly downmarket compared to Lotte, which usually means lower prices. Take Line 1 to Beomil-dong station, Exit 7.

Home Plus department store (Map p228) Beside Asiad stadium, with a multiscreen movie theatre, 10-pin bowling lanes, health club (you only need to bring running shoes) and a decent supermarket. Take Line 3 to Sports Complex station, Exit 11. At street level follow the sidewalk and turn left at the first lane.

Lotte department store (Map p233; Seomyeon) The biggest; there's also a smaller version outside Myeong-nyun-dong station, Exit 1, on Line 1 (Map p232).

Getting There & Around

AIR

Korean Air Lines (KAL) runs one airport limousine service from Gimhae International Airport to the major hotels in Hae·undae (adult/child W6000/3500, one hour, every 30 minutes). A taxi from the airport to Seomyeon takes 30 minutes and costs W20,000, depending on traffic. A 10-minute taxi to Deokcheon station costs W7000. The most economical link between the airport and city is a W1500 bus: the 307 to Deokcheon station, 201 to Seomyeon station (Lotte department store) or the 300 to Hadan. There are also buses from the airport to regional cities including Gyeongju (W9000), Masan (W5700) and Ulsan (W7400).

International flights are mostly to Japan (Tokyo, Osaka, Nagoya and Fukuoka), with infrequent departures to Beijing, Shanghai, Hong Kong, Bangkok, Manila and Vladivostok.

On domestic routes, the Busan–Seoul run on Korean Air or Asiana (one hour, every 30 minutes from 7am to 9pm) usually requires reservations for weekend and holiday travel. Most flights from Busan to Seoul land at Gimpo Airport, which has few international connections. If you're flying out of the country, you'll need to catch the express bus from Gimpo to Incheon International (see p137). Flights also connect Busan and Jejudo (one hour, every 30 to 90 minutes from 7am to 8pm).

FERRY

There are two ferry terminals located near the immigration office (Map p230). From Jungangdong station, take Exit 12 and walk towards the containers visible down the road and cross the major street. To find the International Ferry Terminal continue straight and turn right past the immigration office; the terminal is about 150m down the path. To find the Coastal Ferry Terminal (domestic departures), do not walk towards the immigration office. Instead, turn right and walk 200m along the waterfront to the large building on the left.

First-floor booths in the International Ferry Terminal sell tickets for overnight ferries to three Japanese cities: Fukuoka (round trip W152,000, departs 10.30pm, arrives 6am); Shimonoseki (round trip W161,000 to W608,000, departs 8pm, arrives 8am); and Osaka (round trip W237,000, departs 4pm, arrives 10am).

For a quick trip to Fukuoka on the Kobe or Beetle hydrofoils, go to the 2nd floor. There are five daily departures (round trip W171,000, three hours, departs 8.45am, 10am, 2pm, 3pm and 3.45pm) and an additional departure Friday morning (9.30am). Add a W2600 departure tax for all international trips.

The Coastal Ferry Terminal handles domestic departures to Goeje Island: Gohyun (one way W19,700, 75 minutes, departs 10.30am, 12.30pm, 2.30pm, 4.30pm and 5.45pm); Okpo (one way W19,200, 55 minutes, departs 6.30am, 9am, 11am, 1pm and 3pm); and Jangseungpo (one way W19,200, 45 minutes, departs 8am, 10am, midday, 2pm, 4pm, 5pm and 6pm). There is one departure daily (except Sundays) for Jeju Island (one way W36,000, departs 7pm, arrives 6am).

BUS

Dongbu bus terminal (Map p232) is located at Nopodong station on Line 1. Intercity buses travelling to Dongbu allow passengers to get off at Dusil station, a great time-saver if you don't need to go to the terminal. Departures from Dongbu include the following:

Destination	Price (W)	Duration	Frequency
Daegu	9800	2hr	every 30-120min
Gyeongju	5300	1¼hr	every 10min
Seoul	30,000	5½ hr	every 10-30min

Seobu intercity bus terminal (Map p228) is located outside Sasang station on Line 2 with street level access through a department store. Westbound departures include:

Destination	Price (W)	Duration	Frequency
Hadong	9500	2½hr	every 30-60min
Jinju	6000	1½ hr	every 10 min
Namhae	9800	2½hr	every 30min
Ssanggyaesa	11,400	3½hr	every 2hr

SUBWAY

Busan's three-line subway uses a two-zone fare system: W900 for one zone and W1000

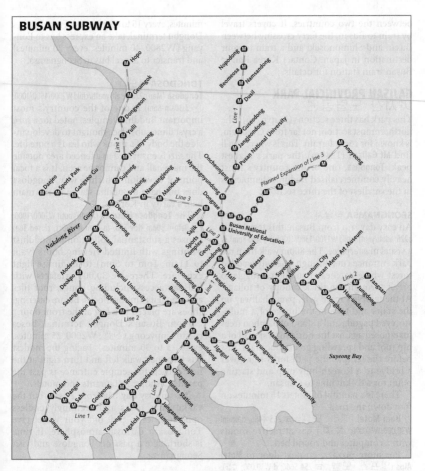

BUSAN SUBWAY

for longer trips. Purchasing a Hanaro card (W2000 plus travel credits, available at ticket booths) is handy: you get a small discount on fares and avoid the hassle of buying a ticket for each trip. See p241 for a subway map.

TRAIN

Most trains depart from and arrive at Busan's downtown station (Map p228). There are also departures from Gupo (Map p228), a station with easy subway access to Line 3 that saves the hassle of going downtown. Between Busan and Seoul, KTX is the quickest service with most trips taking three hours or less (adult/child W44,800/22,400; every 30 to 60 minutes). First-class tickets are more expensive, though the wide seats have ample legroom.

The *Saemaul* used to be known as the express service. Today, the 4½-hour ride to Seoul seems like an eternity (adult/child W36,800/18,400, departures every 60 to 90 minutes). Travellers desperate to save a buck – or wanting to read an entire book on the train – could try the painfully slow *Mugunghwa* service, which wheezes to Seoul in 5½ hours (adult/child W24,800/12,400, departures every one to three hours).

Bujeon station has limited *Saemaul* and *Mugunghwa* regional connections to places like Mokpo (adult/child W23,100/11,650, three times daily). The **Korea Rail** (www.korail .go.kr) website has detailed schedules.

If you're heading to Japan, a Korea–Japan Through Ticket provides discounted travel between the two countries. It covers travel by train to Busan, the ferry crossing between Busan and Shimonoseki and a train to your destination in Japan. Contact Korea Rail at Busan train station for details.

GAJISAN PROVINCIAL PARK
가지산 도립공원

This park has three sections (Map p226). The northernmost section, not far from Gyeongju, is known for rocky terrain. This is where you'll find **Mt Gajisan** (1240m), the park's highest peak. **Tongdosa**, one of the country's most heavily commercialised Buddhist temples, is in the smallest of the three sections.

SEONGNAMSA 석남사

An easy day trip from Busan, this **temple** (Map p226; adult/youth/child W1700/1300/1000; ⊙ 3am-8pm) is a visual masterpiece. The 800m walk from the park entrance cuts through a heavily wooded forest where patches of sunlight struggle to break through the thick canopy of foliage. At the temple's main gate, pause halfway up the stairs and take in the image of a multi-storeyed pagoda and a stand of bamboo trees juxtaposed against the horizontal spread of a hip roof and sprawling green mountain. Just before the temple, the path forks right over a bridge to a Korean-only map and starting point for a 6.4km hike to Gajisan.

There is a handful of motels 15 minutes on foot down the road.

Hera Motel (헤라 모텔; ☎ 263 4466; d/ondol W30,000/W50,000; ✖ ▣) has attractive rooms with a computer and round bed.

For more pizzazz, go next door to **Motel Alps** (알프스 모텔; ☎ 254 5666; d W30,000; ✖). No computers, but it does have beautiful rooms decorated in rich earthy colours and a whirlpool or steam sauna.

Buy snacks from the shop near the park entrance or try one of the few restaurants in the area like **Jangbaeksan Saeng Galguksu** (장백산 생 칼국수; meals W4500; ⊙ 10am-9pm) where hand-made noodles take 15 minutes to prepare.

The most scenic route to Seongnamsa leaves Miryang bus terminal (W4500, 60 minutes, every 30 to 60 minutes). During the second half of the trip, the bus climbs a steep, winding road carved into the mountainside with stunning views of peaks and valleys smothered in a green forest. Sit on the right side of the bus to get the best view. Originating from points east, local buses depart Eonyang (언양; W900, 25 minutes, every 15 to 45 minutes). From Busan's Dongbu terminal, take an express bus to Eonyang (W2800, 40 minutes, every 20 minutes) and transfer to a local bus to Seongnamsa.

TONGDOSA 통도사

Tongdosa (Map p226; adult/youth/child W2000/1500/1000; ⊙ 3.30am-8pm) is one of the country's most important Buddhist temples, noted for a *sari*, a crystalline substance thought to develop inside the body of a monk who leads a pure life. The *sari* is enshrined in a fenced area outside the main hall and cannot be seen. It is a focal point of devotion, which is why Tongdosa does not have a Buddha statue in the main hall, a rarity in Korea.

The **Tongdosa Museum** (adult/youth W2000/1000; ⊙ 9am-4.30pm Nov-Feb, to 6pm Mar-Oct, closed Tue) houses a substantial collection of Buddhist paintings with limited viewing hours (9am to 11am, 1pm to 5pm) to minimise light exposure. There are 30,000 artefacts with full-day access including gongs, roof tiles and wooden printing blocks. Before entering, shoes are placed in a bag at the front door.

From Busan's Dongbu terminal, buses run to Sinpyeong (신평; W2000, 25 minutes, every 15 to 30 minutes). Facing the modest bus terminal, walk left and turn right at the first corner; the temple entrance is past the parade of shops, restaurants and motels.

It is an easy day trip from Busan, but the yakkity bus tours and seemingly endless opportunities to pull out your wallet give Tongdosa a carnival atmosphere. If time is short, take a pass on Tongdosa and visit Seongnamsa.

TONG-YEONG 통영
pop 134,000 / 235 sq km

On the southern tip of Goseong Peninsula, Tong-yeong (Map p226) is a coastal city wedged between Namhae and Geoje islands. Most of the picturesque sights are in and around Gangguan (강구안), a pretty harbour just made for sunset strolls. Visiting Tong-yeong's truly spectacular sights – the 190 or so islands dotting the coastline – usually requires an overnight stay and early-morning ferry departure to some of the most pristine territory in the province.

The tourist information booth outside the bus terminal has maps available but it might not be staffed by anyone who can speak English.

Sights & Activities
GANGGUAN 강구안
It's not the only harbour in the city, but Gang-guan is the prettiest. It's also a busy pier anchored by a promenade that serves multiple civic functions including dock, basketball court and picnic ground for package-tour travellers who aren't squeamish about a mid-morning *soju* pick-me-up. Towards the north end of the promenade, there's a **turtle ship replica** (admission free; ☻ 10am-5pm) and the **Jung-ang Live Fish Market**, an open-air building with grannies selling seafood out of plastic tubs.

Not long ago, the narrow zigzagging streets west of the promenade were ideal for an hour of window-shopping. Today it's a commercial block straight out of a developer's cookie cutter. Fortunately the far more interesting **Seoho Bay** (서호만) road is just around the corner. Set aside an hour in the early evening to get the full neon show as you walk past the **Passenger Ferry Terminal** (여객선 터미널; Yeogaekseon Terminal), a string of fishing-gear shops and raw-fish restaurants. Locally promoted as an important sight, the **Undersea Tunnel** (해저 터널) is a dull (imagine a long cement corridor) but necessary step if you're going to take in the panoramic view from the other side of the bay.

YEONHWA ISLAND 연화도
Anyone with the vaguest interest in independent exploration should take a ferry to one of the nearby islands. There are heaps of options departing the Passenger Ferry Terminal, which together could easily involve a fortnight of island hopping. If time is limited, the day trip to Yeonhwa Island is such a pleasurable experience it's hard to imagine how even the crustiest of souls wouldn't be stirred by the beauty of this unspoiled island. The trip begins with a 45-minute ride through islands silhouetted by the early-morning sun.

Once on land, there are a couple of trail options. Travellers looking for a stimulating yet mildly challenging walk will probably be satisfied by turning left and following the cement road past garden plots of lettuce, a school and a brown cow. Turn right at the fork and walk up the hill past **Yeonhwasa** (연화사), a small Buddhist temple. At the top of the hill near a pagoda, turn left and follow the narrow trail for outstanding views of the ocean and **Yongmeori** (용머리; Dragon's

Head), a string of rocks cascading into the sea which islanders say resembles a dragon's head. The trail eventually leads back to a road that terminates at a fishing outpost called **Dongdu** (동두). On the road to Dongdu, there are several dirt trails that might appeal to hikers eager to get above the treeline. Travellers unable to rappel boulders stay on the road, which is where you might meet Pastor Lee, a friendly island resident who walks this course twice a day.

In Dongdu, the path behind the second *minbak* (a home that rents rooms to travellers) crosses the back end of a mountain and passes a herd of black goats not far from a rocky oceanfront. On the return trip, get back to the pagoda and follow the dirt path to the mountaintop (215m) for a photogenic view of Yongmeori and, if you use your imagination, a dragon's head.

At a leisurely pace this walk will take about three hours excluding breaks. Back at the terminal, there's a convenience store plus half a dozen raw-fish restaurants and *minbak*. Raw fish and *soju* – staples of any seaside trip for Koreans – cost W30,000 per person. For an inexpensive meal, try the *mae-untang* at the tent restaurant called **Four Rocks Raw Fish House** (Naebawi hoetjip; 네바위 횟집; soup W5000). It's typically served as a side dish rather than a separate menu item, but the accommodating restaurant makes an exception for hungry international travellers.

Eating & Drinking

Gangguan's promenade is the place for *chungmu gimbap* (충무 김밥), a spicy squid-and-radish dish made famous in Tong·yeong, while the Seoho Bay road is known for raw fish. The city's evening entertainment district is in Mujeon-dong, a 10-minute walk behind the bus terminal.

Ddongbo Halmae Gimbap (똥보 할매 김밥; per serving W3500; ⏰ 7am-2am) Hungry travellers with limited Korean skills come here because there's no need to speak or read: this place only serves *chungmu gimbap*. The waitress will ask how many servings you want and if necessary she'll use her fingers to count. One serving of this spicy dish, which will test the red-pepper tolerance of the hardiest Korean food-lover, should be enough for a single person.

Paldo Sikdang (팔도 식당; meals W4500; ⏰ 6.30am-9pm) Blue-collar workers come here for hearty meals including *kimchi jjigae* (김치찌개; *kimchi* stew), served with a stack of dried seaweed that tastes great folded over a dollop of rice and dipped into seasoned soy sauce. Exit the bus terminal, turn right and then right at the first corner. The restaurant is down the street on the right.

Hoerak Hoetjip (희락 횟집; meals W10,000) It looks like all the other raw-fish restaurants opposite the Passenger Ferry Terminal, but the food is outstanding. *Mae·untang* comes with an impressive array of colourful side dishes including glazed squash and baby shrimp.

Prowstar Espresso Coffee (drinks W2500) Travelling without good coffee isn't just painful – it's pointless. That's why java lovers flock to this haven of joe, a remarkably uncommon sight in the province where coffee usually means a W300 cup of vending-machine swill. It's near the Gangguan harbour beside an entrance to the Jung·ang Live Fish Market.

Paseo del Rio (drinks W4000; ⏰ 6pm-4am) If a small Korean town could ever have a bar like the TV show *Cheers*, this is it. Stop by a second time and everybody remembers your name. Unlike *Cheers*, customers have to pay. Hell, the bar owner even charges his mother for a drink.

Sleeping

The streets immediately behind and beside the bus terminal are good places to start looking for a room. Near Gangguan, there is a handful of motels on or near the lane next to the KB bank, which is where Tong·yeong's seedy side comes to life at night.

Saejongjang (세종장; ☎ 645 5711; d W20,000; ❄) It's not going to win any awards for interior design – unless they start handing out prizes for nouveau grunge – but the price and location are right for travellers catching an early departure from the nearby Passenger Ferry Terminal. From the southern end of the Gangguan promenade, exit Paseo del Rio and walk left. The motel is down a small lane near the Lotteria restaurant.

Sweet Motel (스휘트 모텔; ☎ 642 6381; d W30,000; ❄) This place has simple, clean rooms unlikely to disappoint or amaze. Older than the more expensive properties in the area, it's a decent option for budget travellers who want to be close to the bus terminal and Mujeon Dong's nightlife. It's on the street immediately behind the bus terminal.

Motel Palace (펠레스 모텔; ☎ 645 8533; d W40,000; ondol W35,000-50,000; ❄) This is one of the newer properties near Gangguan's waterfront with rooms that don't yet have the dents, scratches and cigarette burns customarily found in love motels. Despite the curious selection of ornate furnishings that give rooms a dollhouse feel, there's tremendous value for a group that doesn't mind an *ondol* room. It's near Gangguan harbour on a small lane beside the KB bank.

Getting There & Around

The bus terminal is 2km north of Gangguan. Express buses connect Tong·yeong with Jinju (W7600, 1½ hours, every 10 to 20 minutes) and Busan (W9100, 2½ hours, every 30 minutes) with frequent local buses to Gohyeon (W900, 30 minutes, every six minutes). Immediately outside the terminal, all city buses (W900) pass through Gangguan. Ferries depart Tong·yeong's Passenger Ferry Terminal daily for Yeonhwa Island (W7700, 6.50am, 11am and 3.30pm) with three daily return trips (W7700, 8.30am, 1.20pm and 5.20pm).

JINJU 진주

pop 342,000 / 713 sq km

Jinju is known as 'the education city.' Students driven to succeed leave Jinju and the best way to escape is to study hard and enter a university in Seoul. Migration of the youth pool gives Jinju a laid-back feel, a refreshing change for anyone looking for a day trip to escape Busan's comparatively frantic pace.

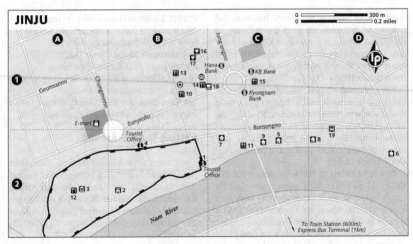

JINJU

0 ———— 300 m
0 ———— 0.2 miles

Orientation

Jinju's interesting sights are located north of the Nam River. East of the Jinju Fortress, Jung-angno separates two worlds: a traditional market to the east and modern trappings like coffee shops, bars and cinemas to the west. Jinju is the largest city in the area and a convenient transport hub from which to explore the province's western region.

Sights & Activities

Jinju Fortress (adult/youth/child W1000/500/300; 🕙 9am-6pm Sun-Fri, 9am-7pm Sat) is the city's most interesting and historically important site. Local street signs call it a castle, but it's actually a well-preserved fortress partially destroyed during the Japanese invasion of 1592. It was here that one of the major battles of the campaign was fought, in which 70,000 Koreans lost their lives. Inside the fortress walls, traditional gates, shrines and temples dot the grassy knolls of this heavily wooded park. Enter the fortress from the North Gate, not

far from a large E-Mart department store, or the East Gate. Information booths (9am to 6pm) with a good supply of English-language maps are at both gates. The East Gate booth is closed weekends; the North Gate booth is open seven days.

Inside the fortress, the **Jinju National Museum** (☎ 742 5951; adult/youth/child W1000/500/free; 🕙 9am-5pm Tue-Fri, 9am-7pm Sat, Sun & holidays, closed Mon) specialises in artefacts from the *Imjin Waeran* War (임진왜란), a seven-year bloody tussle between Joseon and Japan's Toyotomi Hideyoshi Shogunate that began with the latter invading the former in 1592.

Festivals & Events

In October several important festivals take place, including the **Nam River Lantern Festival** and **Jinju Bull Fighting Contest**.

Sleeping

With the exception of October, finding a room to match your budget won't be a problem. The river road behind the north-end bus terminal is lined with motels ranging from dungy to delightful. There is a good selection of low-cost *yeoinsuk* (family-run motels with small rooms and shared bathrooms) two blocks from the fortress's East Gate.

Ewha Yeoinsuk (☎ 747 7417; ondol W10,000; ❂) You probably won't find a cheaper place than this anywhere. Rooms come with dangling light fixtures, flimsy doors and common baths. If full, there are at least six more *yeoinsook* of comparable quality and price within a one-block radius.

New Tema Motel (☎ 741 1467; d/internet r W30,000/ 35,000; ❂ ▣) Standard rooms are slightly larger than nearby competitors but they also look a little more beat up. The most intriguing feature is the sex machine available in some 'special' rooms (W50,000). It's an odd piece of engineering, though the card providing detailed instructions on safe use is helpful. Experimentation costs W5000 for 30 minutes, W10,000 for the power hour.

Other recommendations:

Byeoksan Hwang Tobang Motel (☎ 741 7738; d W30,000; ❂) It ain't pretty but it's got a private bath.

Dong Bang Tourist Hotel (☎ 743 0131; d & tw W106,000, ste from W165,000; ❂) An oasis of quality behind the bus terminal with satisfying though underwhelming rooms.

Versace Motel (☎ 741 4888; d W40,000; ❂) One of the newest and most attractive properties behind the bus terminal. Bigger rooms are W50,000; add W10,000 Saturday and Sunday.

Eating & Drinking

For something different, try one of the eel restaurants along the waterfront near the fortress. They're all about the same quality and price (W13,000 per person).

Won-gung Galbi (per serving W6000; ☻ 11am-5am) This is the place if you're looking for *sutbul galbi* (숯불갈비), charcoal-barbecued meat. Each table comes with a pull-down vent to exhaust smoke. Around the corner from the police station, it's one block north on the east side of the street.

Zio Ricco (meals W8000; ☻ 10am-midnight) With low chairs and cool music, it's a popular eatery with the locals and expats. Pasta and pizza are the specialities with Chilean wine starting at W32,000 per bottle.

Other recommendations:

Bobos (W5000; ☻ 7pm-7am) A dimly lit bar with a convivial atmosphere.

Charles & Johnson (drinks W5000; ☻ 6pm-6am) Ask any university student on the street and they'll know where to find this popular bar and dance club.

Gwannamgaek Sikdang (meals W2500; ☻ 9am-5pm) A simple place to relax inside the Jinju museum.

Holly's Coffee (drinks W2500; ☻ 9am-11pm) Great espresso and inspired potato cake.

Yoo Gane (meals from W5000; ☻ 11am-11pm) The *dakgalbi* (닭갈비; spicy chicken) is more hot than not.

Getting There & Around
AIR

The closest airport is in Sacheon, 20km from Jinju. Three daily flights connect with Gimpo Airport in Seoul via Korean Air and Asiana. Korean Air also has two flights per week to Jeju Island. Local buses connect Jinju's northend bus terminal to Sacheon airport (W900, 30 minutes).

BUS

There's an express bus terminal south of the river. Most travellers use the terminal north of the river. Departures from the north terminal include the following:

Destination	Price (W)	Duration	Frequency
Busan	6700	1½hr	every 10-20min
Hadong	4100	1hr	every 30min
Namhae	4500	1½hr	every 20min
Ssanggyaesa	6100	1½hr	every 1-1½hr
Tong-yeong	5700	1½hr	every 15min

TRAIN

The train station is south of the Nam River. *Mugunghwa* connections include Daegu (adult/child W9600/4800, 3¼ hours, six daily); Daejeon (adult/child W18,400/9200, seven hours, twice daily); and Seoul (adult/ child W27,700/13,900, seven hours, twice daily). One daily *Saemaul* departs for the capital (adult/child W41,100/20,600, six hours, 9.50am) and Daejeon (adult/child W27,300/13,700, 5½ hours, 6.25pm).

NAMHAE ISLAND 남해도
pop 67,000 / 357 sq km

It's the country's third-largest island and a terrific place to explore a slower pace of life, so clearly evident in the countryside where some farmers continue to use oxen to plough rice paddies. Some of Korea's nicest **beaches** are located on the southern coast, including **Sangju** (상주 해수욕장) and **Songjeong**

(송정 해수육장). Sangju is an especially attractive beach thanks to its soft white sand and a stand of trees that create an illusion of isolation. Public transport to Sangju from Namhae City is available (W1800, 40 minutes, every 30 minutes to two hours) but the return trip can involve long roadside waits. It's not popular, but hitching a ride back to Namhae City is possible.

Budget sleep options and the town's best drinking street are a short walk from the bus terminal. Inside the terminal go up one floor, walk out the main door and turn right. Follow the path past the garden plots to a stone wall. Turn right and follow the road to the intersection with a Baskin Robbins. One block before that intersection, turn right and walk down the road to find **Jangsujang Yeogwan** (장수장 여관; ☎ 864 2172; d & ondol W25,000; ❄), a respectably clean and quiet inn.

The small lane immediately behind Baskin Robbins is famous for economical boozing. Many shops are called *silbi* (실비), a one-woman operation with expensive *soju* and a parade of free side dishes – including mussels and *pajeon* – that easily qualify as a meal. **Mullae Bang·a Silbi** (물레방아 실비; ❄ 4pm-2am) is a good one but there are also many others.

There are six daily buses to Hadong (W3400, one hour, 6am, 7.10am, 10am, 1.05pm, 3.35pm and 6.05pm) as well as frequent service to Jinju (W4500, 1½ hours, every 30 to 60 minutes) and Busan (W10,100, 2½ hours, every 30 to 60 minutes).

JIRISAN NATIONAL PARK – EAST
지리산 국립공원
Jirisan National Park (Map p248; adult/youth/child W3400/1300/700; ❄ 2hr before sunrise-2hr after sunset) offers some of Korea's best hiking opportunities with 12 peaks over 1000m forming a 40km ridge. Many peaks are over 1500m high, including **Cheonwangbong** (1915m), the country's second-highest mountain. If you plan to hike here, the Jirisan National Park map (W1000, available at the park entrance) lists topographical information as well as trails, camp sites, springs, shelters and other points of interest. There are three principal park entrances, each with a temple. Two of the three temples, Ssanggyesa and Daewonsa, are in South Gyeongsang province. From the west, Hwa·eomsa is accessible via Gurye in Jeollanam province (see p258).

The **Jirisan Bear Project** (p58).was established with the aim to build up a self-sustaining group of 50 wild bears in Jirisan, so keep a look-out on your travels

SSANGGYESA 쌍계사
The visual imagery of this **temple** is a feast for the eyes, and like any exquisite dinner should be consumed with deliberation in order to enjoy every morsel. Stone walls supporting multiple levels of buildings notched into the mountainside, combined with mature trees and a trickling creek, create a pleasant sensory experience. Three gates mark the path to the main hall; take time to read the signs to appreciate the symbolism of your visit. One of the most attractive temples in the province, it's a long day trip from Busan. For a more relaxing pace, consider an overnight stopover in Jinju and an early-morning departure to the mountain.

HIKING
It's impossible to describe the myriad of trails within this great park. The traditional course runs east to west (Daewonsa to Hwa·eomsa), which experienced Korean hikers say requires three days. Some LP readers have suggested an alternate three-night route that puts hikers in position for a sunrise view atop Cheonwangbong. The route starts with a night at the Nogodan shelter. The next two nights are spent at the Baemsagol and Jangteomok shelters. On the final day, follow the trail to Jungsan-ni and then catch a bus to Jinju or Busan.

Travellers with less-ambitious plans, but who want to experience Mt Jirisan's beauty, hike the popular trail to **Buril Pokpo** (불일폭포; Buril Falls). Starting from Ssanggyesa, the mildly challenging trail (2.4km each way, three hours return) winds through a forest along a rippling creek. About two-thirds along the way, just when you've noticed the sound of the creek has disappeared, the trail bursts onto an open field. Down the path, hikers can buy beverages and snacks at a hermit's home. At the foot of the falls, there's a large rocky pool where hikers meditate to regain their chi.

Sleeping
CAMPING
There are nine camping sites (from W3000): Hwangjeon, Daewonsa, Jungsan-ni, Baemsagol 1 and 2, Dalgung, Daeseong, Buril Pokpo and Baengmu-dong. Facilities are basic.

JIRISAN NATIONAL PARK

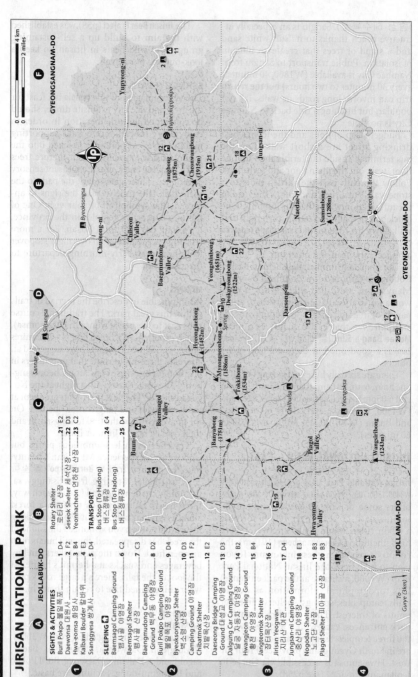

SIGHTS & ACTIVITIES

Buril Pokpo 불일폭포	1 D4
Daewonsa 대원사	2 F2
Hwa-eomsa 화엄사	3 B4
Kalbawi Boulder 칼바위	4 E3
Ssanggyesa 쌍계사	5 D4

SLEEPING

Baemsagol Camping Ground 뱀사골 야영장	6 C2
Baemsagol Shelter 뱀사골 산장	7 C3
Baengmudong Camping Ground 뱀무동 야영장	8 D2
Buril Pokpo Camping Ground 불일폭포 야영장	9 D4
Byeoksoryeong Shelter 벽소령 야영장	10 D3
Camping Ground 야영장	11 F2
Chibatmok Shelter 치밭목 산장	12 E2
Daeseong Bridge Camping Ground 대성교 야영장	13 D3
Dalgung Car Camping Ground 달궁 자동차 야영장	14 B2
Hwangjeon Camping Ground 황전 야영장	15 B4
Jangteomok Shelter 장터목산장	16 E2
Jirisan Yeogwan 지리산 여관	17 D4
Jungsan-ni Camping Ground 중산리 야영장	18 E3
Nogodan Shelter 노고단 산장	19 B3
Piagol Shelter 피아골 산장	20 B3

Rotary Shelter 로타리 산장	21 E2
Seseok Shelter 세석산장	22 D3
Yeonhacheon 연하천 산장	23 C2

TRANSPORT

Bus Stop (To Hadong) 버스정류장	24 C4
Bus Stop (To Hadong) 버스정류장	25 D4

SHELTERS
There are 10 shelters (W5000 to W7000). From west to east, they are: Nogodan 1 and 2, Piagol, Baemsagol, Yeonhacheon, Byeoksoryeong, Saeseok, Jangteomok, Chibatmok and the Rotary shelter. Jangteomok has enough space for 150 bodies, and sells film, torches, noodles and drinks. Seseok is the largest shelter, with space for 220 people. For overnight hikes bring bedding, food and tea/coffee, as most shelters have limited supplies. Online bookings are recommended and are essential for weekends and holidays. See the Korea National Park Service's website (www.npa .or.kr) for details.

MINBAK & YEOGWAN
The path to Ssanggyesa is lined with restaurants, souvenir shops, a water wheel and a grandmother selling *saengchikjeup* (생칙즙; per glass W1000), a muddy juice thought to provide hikers with a blast of energy. A few metres before the wheel, **Jirisan Yeogwan** (지리산 여관; ☎ 883 1668; ondol W30,000) has basic *ondol* rooms overlooking a creek. A group of travellers will find better value in a *minbak*; turn right past the water wheel to find a dozen or more places with rooms for W30,000.

Getting There & Away
Buses to Ssanggyesa often pass through Hadong, a small village and useful transfer point in the region. If you can't get a direct bus to Ssanggyesa, travel to Hadong and catch one of the frequent buses to the temple (W2000, 30 to 60 minutes, 13 times daily). On route to Ssanggyesa from Hadong, buses pass a large bridge and shortly thereafter make a quick stop in Hwagae; don't get off there. Further down the road (usually the next stop), the bus stops beside a concrete bridge. Do get out here, cross the bridge and follow the winding road to the park entrance. Return-trip tickets are purchased inside the restaurant beside the concrete bridge. The signboard lists times for several destinations, though most travellers are best served by heading to Hadong, where frequent buses connect with Busan (W9700, 2½ hours, every 30 to 60 minutes) and Jinju (W4100, 1½ hours, every 30 minutes).

Jeollanam-do
전라남도

South Jeolla is one of Korea's least developed and greenest provinces, where 25% of households are farmers against a national average of 7%. The province is pioneering pesticide-free and organic farming, while fish farming has breathed new life into coastal fishing villages and the many small, offshore islands, more and more of which are being linked by bridges to the mainland. A feature of rural life these days is farmers marrying Vietnamese and other Asian brides, so that Jeollanam-do has more international marriages than Seoul.

Irrigated rice fields, marine and land-based national parks, dramatic coastal views, fresh seafood and political dissent sum up the province. But – just as a one-time radical can become part of the establishment – Jeollanam-do is slowly but surely becoming more like the rest of Korea: it is now crisscrossed by expressways and its expanding cities are filling up with anonymous apartment blocks. Despite this, the province retains a rebel edge and is proud of its ceramic and artistic traditions, its Naju pears and green tea, its exiled poets and its pro-democracy martyrs.

The region's two heroes are Admiral Yi Sun-sin, who defeated the Japanese navy in the 1590s, and Kim Dae-jung, a 20th-century democracy warrior who became president in 1997 and finally ended the stranglehold on political power and patronage held by politicians from the eastern provinces. He received almost 100% support from the Jeolla provinces.

HIGHLIGHTS

- Savouring the scenic location and the flavours of a **green-tea plantation** (p262) at Boseong

- Enjoying breathtaking coastal views from **Hyang-iram** (p262) at Dolsando

- Voyaging to the scattered, unspoilt islands of **Heuksando** (p270) and fabled **Hongdo** (p270)

- Admiring art and crafts in Gwangju's **Art Street** (p256) and nearby Damyang's **Bamboo Crafts Museum** (p257)

- Creating your own ceramic masterpiece at the **pottery workshop** (p262) in Gangjin

★Damyang

★Gwangju

Boseong
★

Heuksando
★ & Hongdo

★ Gangjin   Dolsando ★

| ■ TELEPHONE CODE: 061 | ■ POPULATION: 3.5 MILLION | ■ AREA: 12,400 SQ KM |

History

Jeollanam-do, far from the centre of power in Seoul during the long Joseon era, was a place of exile, and was used as a dumping ground for political and religious dissidents. The tradition of political dissent has continued and the province was a hotbed of opposition to the military governments that favoured the eastern provinces and ruled South Korea in the 1960s and 1970s. Students and trade unionists led countless pro-democracy protests and demonstrations, until army tanks crushed an uprising in Gwangju city in May 1980. The soldiers' brutality stained the reputation of the military rulers, although it was not until 1992 that a civilian, Kim Young-sam, was finally elected president.

National & Provincial Parks

Cruise around thousands of islands in **Dadohae Haesang National Park** (p270) and take a cable car ride in **Duryunsan Provincial Park** (p263). You could bump into a bear in **Jirisan National Park** (p258), which spreads over three provinces, while two Zen Buddhist temples attract pilgrims to **Jogyesan Provincial Park** (p258). At weekends hikers stand in queues at **Mudeungsan Provincial Park** (p253) just outside Gwangju, while remote **Wolchulsan National Park** (p266) can be traversed in under five hours.

Getting There & Around

Most travellers arrive by train or bus and then use buses and ferries to travel around, although trains do run to the southern ports of Mokpo and Yeosu and east to Busan.

GWANGJU 광주

☎ 062 / pop 1.4 million

Gwangju may look like any other city with its shop-filled central area, an attractive riverside, busy restaurants, pubs and bars – all encircled by apartment blocks – but within this everyday exterior resides the heart of an artist and the soul of a revolutionary. Civic Gwangju emphasises the arts and the city has an important place in the history of Korea's democracy and human-rights movement.

Information

Central post office (Chungjangno) Free internet.
Fine Bank (Jukbongno) Foreign exchange.

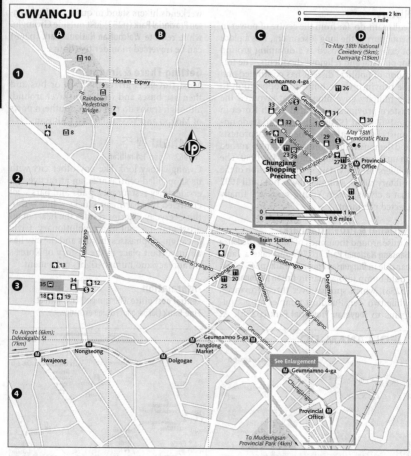

GWANGJU

Global ATM (bus terminal) Near the ticket booths.
Gwangju Bank Foreign exchange.
Standard Chartered Bank (Geumnamno) Global ATM and foreign exchange.
Tourist information centre bus terminal (☎ 360 8733); Gwangju airport (☎ 942 6160); Geumnamno (☎ 062 1330; ☺ 9am-9pm); train station (☎ 522-5147) The main centre (Geumnamno) has free internet.

Sights & Activities
GWANGJU NATIONAL MUSEUM & VICINITY 광주국립박물관

The highlight of this **museum** (☎ 570 7014; adult/child W1000/500; ☺ 9am-6pm Tue-Sun), to the north of the city, is its fine collection of perfectly preserved Chinese ceramics that were discovered in 1975 inside a 14th-century shipwreck. The display ranges from elegant, classical vases to homey mortars and pestles. Other galleries show Joseon and Buddhist art, two Korean art genres neglected by Western art critics.

Take a 15-minute walk through a tunnel under the expressway to **Gwangju Folk Museum** (☎ 521 9041; adult/youth/child W500/300/200; ☺ 9.30am-5pm, closed day after national holidays). It uses dioramas, models, sound effects, videos and more to show off Jeollanam-do's traditional culture. Historical photographs at the end reveal how quickly Koreans have morphed from feudal farmers to 21st-century whiz kids.

Around the Folk Museum is a pleasant park that contains the Biennale Exhibition Hall. Walk back down through the park to the Gwangju Art Museum and the bus stop.

The **Gwangju Art Museum** (☎ 222 3574; adult/youth/child W460/300/250; ☽ 9am-5pm Tue-Sun), part of an ugly art plaza with concert and performance halls, displays highlights from the avant-garde Gwangju Biennale (p254). Thought-provoking exhibits could include a portrait of the back of someone's head, a cow made of leather or a landscape inside a suitcase.

Take bus 23 (W900, 10 minutes, every 15 minutes) from outside the bus terminal and get off at the Gwangju Art Museum stop (Munhwa Yesul Hoegwan), a 15-minute walk from Gwangju National Museum. Bus 50 (W900, 20 minutes, every 30 minutes) runs from the train station to the Folk Museum; bus 55 runs from Geumnamno to the National Museum.

MAY 18TH NATIONAL CEMETERY
국립 5.18 민주묘지

This sombre **memorial park** (☎ 266 5187; admission free; ☽ 8am-7pm Mar-Oct, to 5pm Nov-Feb), which opened in 1997, contains a simple burial site for 325 civilian casualties of the 1980 Gwangju Uprising. A small but emotionally charged museum shows photographs, and a hard-hitting video film gives a dramatic account of the traumatic events of over 25 years ago (p254) that still scar the country's political landscape. 'History which does not speak the truth and does not remember the past is bound to be repeated' is the message.

On the right, a memorial hall displays photographs of the ordinary folk – from students to grandmothers – who paid the ultimate price during the military government's so-called 'crackdown on communists'.

A five-minute walk through the memorial garden leads to the reinstated original cemetery, where the victims were first hurriedly buried without proper ceremony. Later the bodies were dug up and reinterred in the new cemetery.

Bus 518 (W900, 20 minutes, every 30 minutes) drops you off at the cemetery entrance and can be picked up at the Gwangju Hospital stop, near the large Home Plus store, or along Geumnamno. Bus 311 (W900, 15 minutes, every 15 minutes) runs from the bus terminal to Gwangju hospital.

ASIAN CULTURE COMPLEX
아시아문화중심도시홍보관

This complex, in the old Provincial Hall overlooking the May 18th Democratic Plaza, features art displays and cultural performances from around Asia. Local bands let rip in the small park outside on warm weekends.

MUDEUNGSAN PROVINCIAL PARK
무등산도립공원

Overlooking Gwangju, **Mudeungsan Provincial Park** (☎ 265 0761; admission free) is a gorgeous green mountain range with a spider's web of well-signed trails leading to the peak, **Cheonwangbong** (1187m). About 1km (a 30-minute walk) from the bus stop (fork right to Saeinbong) is **Uijae Misulgwan** (☎ 222 3040; admission W1000; ☺ 9.30am-5.30pm Tue-Sun), a chic art gallery that displays landscape, flower and bird paintings by Heo Baek-ryeon (1891–1977), whose pen name was Uijae. His modern-style house is in an idyllic spot, a five-minute walk away on the other side of the path.

Walk up from the gallery to the famous **Choonsul tea plantation** that Uijae established. It's a steep 15-minute walk up, but turn left and then right to join the well-trodden main track up to **Tokkideung** (460m), a popular picnic spot with views of dramatic scree slopes, which takes half an hour. Otherwise walk downhill and the track comes out at the fork, a five-minute walk before the museum (20 minutes).

Alternatively, a 10-minute walk on from the art gallery takes you to **Jeungsimsa**, a temple with a Shilla-era iron Buddha backed by red-and-gold artwork, housed in an insignificant-looking shrine behind the main hall. The tiny shrine perched on a rock next to it is dedicated to the Shamanist Mountain God. From the temple you can continue on to Saeinbong (1.3km) or further afield.

The park is alive with Gwangjuites at weekends, and restaurant shacks that cling to the hillsides or overlook cascading streams sell pork, chicken and mountain-vegetable meals.

Buses 15, 27, 52, 555, 771 and 1001 go to the Jeungsimsa entrance to Mudeungsan Park, east of Gwangju. Bus 555 (W900, 30 minutes, every 15 minutes) can be picked up outside Exit 3 of Nongseong subway station (a 10-minute walk south of the bus terminal) or along Geumnamno.

BASEBALL 야구

Catch the local Kia Tigers baseball team in action at **Mudeung Stadium** (adult/youth/child W5000/3000/1000) near the bus terminals, and spot the differences with the American game. Many buses, including buses 1 and 23, can drop you there. Matches start at 2pm or 6.30pm.

Festivals & Events

The **Gwangju Biennale** (www.gb.or.kr) is a major two-month contemporary art festival that takes place every two years (next held in autumn 2008). With international curators, each biennale has a different theme and is based in the Biennale Exhibition Hall, near the Gwangju Folk Museum. The city always fills with colourful and mind-expanding performances, displays, lectures, exhibitions and music, most of it experimental and some of it at the joyfully wacky end of the modern art spectrum.

Sleeping

BUDGET

The usual mixture of *yeogwan* (motels with small en suites) stuck in a 1980s time warp,

---

MAY 18TH MASSACRE

What the 1989 Tiananmen Square Massacre is to China, the 1980 Gwangju Massacre is to South Korea, a mass demonstration and protest against an authoritarian regime with deadly consequences that became an icon for its time.

Following large-scale student protests against military rule, on 18 May 1980 the army was ordered to move into Gwangju on the pretext of quelling a communist uprising. The soldiers had no bullets, but they used bayonets to murder dozens of unarmed protesters and passers-by. Outraged residents broke into armouries and police stations and used the seized weapons and ammunition to drive the troops out of their city.

For over a week pro-democracy citizen groups were in control, but the brutal military response came nine days later on 27 May, when soldiers armed with loaded M16 rifles, supported by helicopters and tanks, retook the city. Most of the protest leaders were labelled 'communists' and summarily shot. At least 154 civilians were killed during the uprising, and an additional 4089 were wounded or arrested. Many of those arrested were tortured. For eyewitness accounts of the still-controversial street fighting, read *Memories of May 1980* by Chung Sang-yong (2003) or view www.518.org.

In memory of the pro-democracy martyrs, the Gwangju Prize for Human Rights has been awarded since 2000, and recipients have included Aung San Suu Kyi, the pro-democracy leader struggling to overthrow the military rulers in Myanmar.

and smart new motels surround the bus terminals.

Eunhasu (☎ 367 0511; r W20,000; ✗ ⬛) Among a plethora of *yeogwan* with dated furniture and fittings in the alleys north of the bus terminals, this good-value one is clean, with large-sized bathrooms and round beds.

Asia Motel (☎ 367 5001; r W25,000; ✗ ⬛) Light-coloured decor and a computer in the room are the plus points in this *yeogwan* north of the bus terminals, which could do with some TLC.

Classic Motel (☎ 363 1751; r W30,000; ✗ ⬛) Just 100m north of the bus terminal is this brand new motel inside a fancy-looking black-and-silver tower. Despite the exterior, the rooms are more alpine than love motel in design. Rooms are a tad cramped but are stylish and welcoming, and you could hunt around for hours to find a better room at this price. Add W5000 for a computer or W10,000 for a superior DVD room.

Noblesse Motel (☎ 351 6161; r W30,000; ✗ ⬛) Don't be put off by the quirky naked-lady door handles and love-hotel exterior – regular overnight rooms are just that. Its location south of the bus terminals surrounded by restaurants and bars is a plus. Rooms with a computer are W5000 extra.

Lawrence Motel (☎ 366 1900; r W30,000; ✗ ⬛) A well-lit lobby in this no-fuss, cream-coloured motel in a busy area south of the bus terminals creates a favourable impression, maintained by rooms that go for a plain and simple Zen-style look.

Koreana Tourist Hotel (☎ 526 8600; ksc7812@hanmail.net; r W30,000; ⬛) A stuffed tiger guards the lobby and chandeliers light the large coffee shop of this well-priced and well-maintained hotel set amid a bevy of love motels near Gwangju train station. Rooms are spacious with ornate furniture and have a computer.

MIDRANGE

Hotel Palace (☎ 222 2525; www.hotelpalace.co.kr; r W50,000; ✗ ⬛) In the heart of the city, amid the shopping frenzy of Chungjangno, are these quiet, quality rooms which have been recently renovated and are all stocked with smart computers. Pop into the pop-art coffee shop if you like lurid velour.

Gwangju Prince Hotel (☎ 524 0025; r W60,000; ✗ ⬛) You might meet some Korean baseball stars staying at this modest but reasonably priced hotel near the museums. The lift is scruffy but this is a real hotel with a lobby,

---

KIMCHI FESTIVAL

Jeollanam-do has always been Korea's premier rice-growing region, and is known for the country's freshest and best food. So Gwangju is the perfect location for showing off the country's top *kimchi* (pickled vegetables). Every October, Gwangju hosts a five-day *kimchi* extravaganza with a fairground, market stalls, pottery making, folk music and a *hanbok* (traditional clothing) fashion show. The festival is the best opportunity to make, taste, purchase or just enjoy the visual sensation of Korea's most famous dish in all its hundreds of varieties. Shuttle buses run to the often-changing venue.

---

sauna, restaurants, coffee shop and bar, and yet the price is not much more than a smart motel. Rooms have computers.

Hotel Hiddink Continental (☎ 227 8500; www.hotel-continental.co.kr; r from W84,000; ✗ ⬛) The discounted price makes this hotel – named after Korea's revered 2002 World Cup soccer coach – a reasonable option, but the suites are not worth the extra. The sky-lounge bar (beer W5000) is its best feature with armchairs, great city views, an outdoor terrace and a mixed bag of live music nightly at 8pm.

Eating

BUDGET & MIDRANGE

Hyundai department store (⏰ 10am-8pm) Near Gwangju train station, it has a bright and clean food court (meals W3500 to W5000) in the basement.

Shinsegae department store (⏰ 10am-8pm) Next to the bus terminals, this classy store has 10 small, reasonably priced restaurants (W4000 to W10,000) and a café on the 8th floor, and the food plaza in the basement sells takeaway barbecue chicken, big *mandu* (dumplings) and *hotteok* (sweet pita-bread snack).

Yero (meals W5000) Down an alley off Art Street is this very informal *ssambap* (wraps and side dishes) restaurant made up of three rooms in the owner's house. It's all very rustic and untidy but people come for the food and Yero is as near to Korean home cooking as you can get.

Minsokchon (meals W4500-13,000; 11.30am-midnight) A popular barnlike but attractive and cheery restaurant that echoes to *so galbi* (소갈비; beef) and *dwaeji galbi* (돼지갈비; pork) sizzling on table barbecues. The *galbitang* (갈비탕) is excellent with chunky, lean meat and 'wellbeing' additions. If this restaurant has a long queue outside, try the branch in Gwangsan-gil.

Moojinjoo (meals W6000-13,000; 11.40am-midnight) With an architecturally adventurous design, this classy restaurant is often packed out on all floors, although its speciality, *bossam* (보쌈; steamed fatty pork with *kimchi*, cabbage and lettuce wraps), may not appeal to everyone. The lunchtime-only *bossam jeongsik* (W6000) is a cheaper deal.

TOP END

Yeongmi (meals W20,000-32,000) One of the many duck restaurants in Duck Street alongside Hyundai department store, it has starred on TV. The speciality is *oritang* (오리탕), which is meant for sharing and bubbles and thickens away at your table together with a pile of vegetables. Ignore the tatty décor; it's the taste of the food that counts.

Songjukheon (meals from W40,000; noon-2pm, 6-10pm) An atmospheric *hanok* where *hanbok*-clad staff serve a full-on *yangban hanjeongsik* (banquet) in your own antique-decorated room, with *gayageum* (12-stringed zither) music in the background. The restaurant is expensive but special.

Drinking

Soul Train (Hwanggeumgil; 6pm-5am) This dark basement pub, patronised by both Koreans and foreigners, has a square bar, a pool table and a nightclub feel.

Mike & Dave's Speakeasy (7pm-3am Thu-Sun) A popular live band rocks this informal and friendly bar, hidden down an alley, on Fridays at 10pm. The bar was set up by two enterprising Canadians and the beers include ABC stout.

Shopping

Chungjangno, Gwangju's buzzing, semi-pedestrianised shopping district, is bursting with clothing and accessory stores, bars, nightclubs, buzzing restaurants and all the usual fast-food chains. A tsunami of young people sweeps along the streets every night, both above ground and in the Chunggeum underground shopping arcade.

If-U (11.30am-10pm) Here are six floors of fashion shopping for the very young at heart, and a food court (meals W3000 to W10,000;

) downstairs with screens and vehicular décor.

25 (10am-11pm) This music shop sells Western and Korean rock CDs downstairs, while classical and jazz selections can be found upstairs.

Migliore (11.30am-11pm) It has stacks of fashion outlets, five cinemas on the 11th floor, a 24-hour *jjimjilbang* (luxury sauna; admission W5000) and an event stage outside. The *jjimjilbang* has great facilities including aroma, cucumber and green-tea pools while a full-body massage, oil and scrub beauty treatment will set you back W12,000.

Art Street (Yesurui Geori) This is Gwangju's answer to Seoul's Insadong with art galleries, a woodcarver's studio, a leather workshop, teashops, and stores selling *hanbok* (traditional Korean clothing), *hanji* (handmade paper), art books, ethnic jewellery, calligraphy brushes, tea sets and dolls.

Shinsegae department store (10am-8pm) Brand-name outlets rub shoulders in this department store in a gleaming, luxury ambience. There's a Starbucks (drinks W3000 to W5000), the favourite haunt of local *doenjangnyeo* (a derogatory term for young women who only care about style and fashion), and next to it is an art gallery (admission free) showcasing changing exhibitions.

Getting There & Away

AIR

A dozen Gwangju–Seoul and nine Gwangju–Jeju flights run daily, and international flights operate to Shanghai and Macau.

BUS

Gwangju's huge, brand-new bus terminal houses both express and intercity buses, a tourist information centre and fast-food outlets, with a department store and other shops nearby.

Express bus destinations include:

Destination	Price (W)	Duration	Frequency
Busan	13,800	4hr	every 20min
Daegu	10,800	3hr	every 40min
Daejeon	8900	2½hr	every 30min
Jeonju	5300	1¼hr	every 30min
Seoul	14,100	4hr	every 10min

Intercity buses departing Gwangju include the following services:

Destination	Price (W)	Duration	Frequency
Boseong	5400	1½hr	every 30min
Gangjin	7200	1½hr	every 30min
Haenam	8200	2hr	every 30min
Jindo	12,400	3hr	hourly
Mokpo	6300	1¼hr	every 30min
Songgwangsa	5600	1½hr	8 daily
Suncheon	5800	2hr	every 30min
Wando	11,900	2½hr	hourly
Yeongam	5000	1½hr	every 20min
Yeosu	8600	2¼hr	every 30min

TRAIN

KTX trains (W33,300, 2¾ hours, 11 daily) run between Gwangju and Yongsan station in Seoul.

Saemaul (W29,700, 3¼ hours, two daily) and *Mugunghwa* (W20,000, four hours, four daily) trains also run along the route. A *Tonggeun* (commuter) train (W2000, one hour) runs once a day at 6.55am from Gwangju train station to Mokpo or three times a day from Songjeong-ni train station (W1600), west of Gwangju past the airport.

Getting Around
TO/FROM THE AIRPORT

Bus 1000 (W1000, 30 minutes, every 15 minutes) runs from the airport to the bus terminals and Geumnamno. A taxi costs around W7500. Soon the new subway will provide an alternative.

BUS

Gwangju has over 80 city bus routes, and most run past the bus terminal that has bus stops on all sides. Bus 17 (W900, 20 minutes, every 15 minutes) runs between the bus terminal and Gwangju train station.

SUBWAY

The subway (W800, every 10 minutes) is being extended west to the airport. Buy a disc ticket and at the subway barrier hold the disc ticket over the yellow pad. When you reach your destination put the disc ticket into the slot at the exit barrier.

AROUND GWANGJU
Unjusa 운주사

This intriguing **temple** (☎ 374 0660; adult/youth/child W2000/1500/600; ⏰ 7am-7pm Mar-Oct, 8am-5pm Nov-Feb) occupies a river valley and its hillsides in Hwasun-gun, 40km south of Gwangju.

Legend has it that the site originally housed 1000 Buddhas and 1000 pagodas, built because according to traditional geomancy, the southwest of the country lacked hills and needed the pagodas to 'balance' the peninsula. The remaining 23 pagodas and some 100 Buddhas are still the greatest numbers of any Korean temple. According to another legend they were all built in one night by stonemasons sent down from heaven, but another theory is that Unjusa was the site of a school for stonemasons.

Whatever their origins, many works are unique and some are national treasures. Back-to-back twin Buddhas face their own pagodas, while another pair of Buddhas lying on their backs are said to have been the last works sculpted one evening; the masons returned back to heaven before the Buddhas could be stood upright.

To reach Unjusa, catch bus 218 or 318 from Gwangju bus terminal (W2700, 1½ hours, hourly) and the temple is a 10-minute walk from the bus stop. Check with the driver as only some of the buses (eight 218s and eight 318s) go all the way to Unjusa. The last bus back to Gwangju currently leaves around 6.20pm.

Damyang Bamboo Crafts Museum
담양대나무박물관

This **museum** (☎ 381 4111; adult/youth/child W1000/700/500; ⏰ 9am-5.30pm) in Damyang, north of Gwangju, has an amazing range of bamboo products, both ancient and modern. Furniture, exquisitely woven baskets – even a bamboo teapot and bamboo jewellery – are more interesting than you'd expect. Next door is a free display of exquisite bamboo wonders from around the world. Bamboo has 101 uses and the shops in front of the museum prove it. A few of the 46 kinds of bamboo grow behind the museum.

A two-minute walk down the road is the busy but superb **Bakmulgwan Apjip** (박물관앞집; meals W10,000-20,000; ⏰ 24hr) The *daetongbap* (대통밥) is excellent – rice and nuts cooked inside a bamboo stem, bamboo-shoot *doenjang*, and a dozen dazzling side dishes are served up with free bamboo-leaf tea. The side rooms have glorious views over the rice fields. Ask for a bag to carry home your bamboo rice container as a souvenir. *Tteokgalbi* (떡갈비), two big sizzling meat patties, is another option.

JEOLLANAM-DO

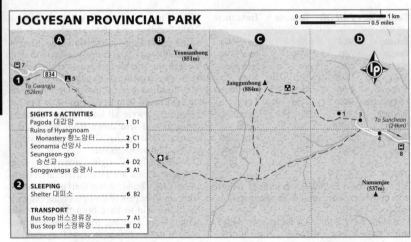

JOGYESAN PROVINCIAL PARK

0 _____ 1 km
0 _____ 0.5 miles

Yeonsanbong
(851m)

To Gwangju
(52km)

Janggunbong
(884m)

To Suncheon
(24km)

Namamjae
(537m)

SIGHTS & ACTIVITIES
Pagoda 대갑암 1 D1
Ruins of Hyangnoam
　Monastery 향노암터 2 C1
Seonamsa 선암사 3 D1
Seungseon-gyo
　승선교 4 D2
Songgwangsa 송광사 5 A1

SLEEPING
Shelter 대피소 6 B2

TRANSPORT
Bus Stop 버스정류장 7 A1
Bus Stop 버스정류장 8 D2

Try and visit Damyang on the 2nd, 7th, 12th, 17th, 22nd and 27th of each month as the bamboo market is held on these days. A bamboo crafts festival is held in May.

Local bus 311 (W1200, 40 minutes, every 15 minutes) runs from gate 23 of the bus terminal northwards to Damyang, dropping off at the museum, but you have to walk for five minutes to the main road to catch the return bus. Bus 303 runs from Gwangju train station to Damyang. If you end up in the Damyang bus terminal it's a 15-minute walk to the museum.

JOGYESAN PROVINCIAL PARK
조계산도립공원

This **park** (☎ 755 0107; adult/youth/child W2500/1500/free; ⊗ 8am-7pm Mar-Oct, 8am-5pm Nov-Feb) centres around two noteworthy temples, their beauty complemented by the attractive surrounding forest.

To the west, 80km from Gwangju, **Songgwangsa** is considered one of the three jewels of Korean Buddhism (along with Tongdosa and Haeinsa, in Gyeongsangnam-do). It starred in the *Little Monk* movie and is a regional head temple of the Jogye sect, by far the largest in Korean Buddhism. It is also one of the oldest Zen temples in Korea, originally founded in AD 867 although most of the buildings date from the 17th century. Songgwangsa is known for having produced many prominent Zen masters over the years, and today the temple is home to a community of monks.

On the eastern side of the mountain is **Seonamsa**, a quieter hermitage dating back to AD 529, where the monks study and try to preserve the old ways. Below Seonamsa is **Seunseon-gyo**, one of Korea's most exquisite ancient granite bridges, with a dragon's head hanging from the top of the arch.

A spectacular hike over the peak of **Janggunbong** (884m) connects the two temples. The walk takes six hours if you go over the peak, or four hours if you go around it. Either route is fantastic.

Accommodation and restaurants are available by the car park at Songgwangsa. Lodgings here range from W20,000 to W25,000. There's also a tourist village near Seonamsa.

From Gwangju buses (W5600, 1½ hours, every 1½ hours) run to Songgwangsa, but only one bus a day (W6000, ¼ hours) runs from Gwangju to Seonamsa, leaving at 7.45am.

JIRISAN NATIONAL PARK – WEST
지리산국립공원

The highlight of this part of the park is **Hwa-eomsa** (☎ 783 9105; adult/youth/child W3800/1800/1300; ⊗ 6am-7pm), 86km northeast of Gwangju, which was founded by priest Yon-gi in AD 544 after his return from China. Dedicated to the Birojana Buddha, the temple has suffered five major devastations including the Japanese invasion of 1592, but luckily much remained despite the various cataclysms. It was last rebuilt in 1636.

On the main plaza is **Gakgwangjeon**, a huge two-storey hall. There are some massive pillars and striking scroll paintings inside, but there are paintings that are national treasures nearly 12m long and 7.75m wide, featuring Buddhas, disciples and assorted holies. These are displayed outdoors only on special occasions. Korea's oldest and largest stone lantern fronts Gakgwangjeon, which was once surrounded by stone tablets of the Tripitaka Sutra (made during the Shilla era). These were ruined during the Japanese invasion. Many pieces are now preserved in the temple's **museum**.

Up many further flights of stairs is Hwa·eomsa's most famous structure, a unique three-storey pagoda supported by four stone lions. The female figure beneath the pagoda is said to be Yon·gi's mother; her dutiful son offers her tea from another lantern facing her.

The temple is about 15 minutes' walk from the ticket office. It is possible to continue from the temple and along Hwa·eomsa valley. After about 2½ to three hours the trail begins to ascend to a shelter, **Nogodan Sanjang** (a strenuous four-hour hike). From the shelter the trail continues to rise until you are finally on the long spine of the Jirisan ridge. For hiking details and a map see p247.

The large tourist village is located at the park entrance, with most restaurants having mountain-vegetable *sanchae jeongsik* (산채정식) and *dolsot bibimbap* (돌솥비빔밥) on the menu. Accommodation includes the recently renovated and smart **Jirisan Prince** (☎ 782 0740; r W40,000; 🔀), behind the car park with a log-cabin effect on the front, but prices can rise W10,000 on Friday and Saturday.

Buses (W6400, 1½ hours, every 90 minutes) run from Gwangju bus terminal to Jirisan National Park and Hwa·eomsa.

NAGAN FOLK VILLAGE 낙안읍성민속마을

Among Korea's many folk villages, **Nagan** (☎ 749 3893; adult/child W2000/1500; 🕑 9am-6pm) is unique for its setting, surrounded by 1410m of Joseon-period fortress walls, built to protect the inhabitants from marauding Japanese pirates. It's Korea's best-preserved fortress town, crammed with narrow, dry-stone alleyways leading to vegetable allotments, and adobe and stone homes thatched with reeds. Some are private homes while others house working artisans or are *minbak* (private homes with rooms for rent), restaurants or souvenir shops. Some points of interest are

labelled in English and there's the inevitable folk museum.

The **Namdo Food Festival** (which receives 200,000-plus attendees) is usually held here early in October. It features about 300 Korean dishes, plus eating contests and traditional cultural events.

Catch a bus (W850, 15 minutes, every 30 minutes) from Beolgyo (platform 11) or bus 63 or 68 from Suncheon (W850, 40 minutes, hourly).

YEOSU 여수
pop 327,000

The port city of Yeosu is about halfway along Korea's steep, island-pocked and deeply indented southern coast. By the time you reach Yeosu you will have seen comparable city centres, but its shoreline, peppered with cliffs, islands and peninsulas, is spectacular.

Orientation

Yeosu is shaped like a molar. The two roots (hilly, dramatic island coastlines) straddle a bay, crowned by the city centre. The island of Odongdo, linked by a pedestrian causeway, sits east of town, and the much larger Dolsando, now joined by a bridge to the mainland, is to the southeast. Yeosu bus terminal is 4km north of Jung·ang Rotary and the harbour, reachable by bus or taxi.

Information

Gyodong post office (Chungmuro) Free internet access.
Korea Exchange Bank (near Jung-gang Rotary) Exchanges foreign currency.
Tourist information centre (☎ 664 8978; www.yeosu .go.kr) At the entrance to Odongdo pedestrian causeway.
Yeosu post office (Gosoro)

Sights
ODONGDO 오동도

This small, craggy **island** (☎ 690 7301; adult/youth/ child W1600/600/500; 🕑 9am-5.30pm), a favourite destination for locals, is joined to the mainland by a 750m causeway that can be traversed by a **road train** (adult/youth/child W500/400/300). The island is one large botanical garden with bamboo groves and camellia trees, which are full of birdsong and can be walked round in 20 minutes. Take the lift up the **lighthouse observatory** (admission free; 🕑 9.30am-5.30pm) for the best harbour views.

Shops, restaurants, a dancing fountain, a turtle-ship replica and boat trips around the

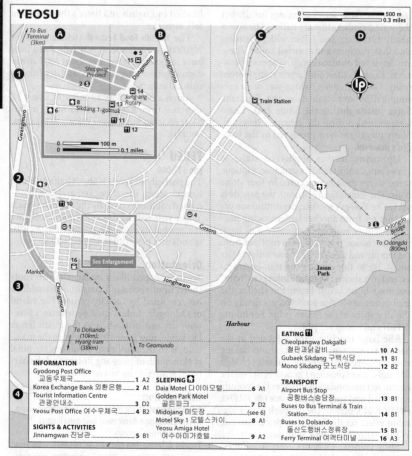

YEOSU

harbour or around Dolsando are also available.

Ten city buses (W850) run to the pedestrian causeway: buses 2, 8, 10, 17, 18, 85-1, 101, 103, 107 and 555. Otherwise it's a 30-minute walk from Jung-ang Rotary to the causeway.

JINNAMGWAN 진남관
In the centre of town stands this national treasure, Korea's largest single-storey wooden structure (75m long and 14m high). The beautiful **pavilion** (admission free), first constructed in 1716 with 68 pillars supporting its massive roof, was originally used for receiving officials and holding ceremonies. Later it became a military headquarters.

On the right, a small but modern **museum** (admission free; 10am-5pm) focuses on Admiral Yi Sun-sin (1545–98) and has maps explaining his naval tactics and victories over Japan in the 1590s.

Sleeping
Most accommodation is in a street of motels, with *yeogwan* and *yeoinsuk* (family-run budget hotels) in an ideal location near the harbour front.

Midojang (663 2226; Sikdang 1-golmuk; r W20,000;) Cramped but light rooms and bathrooms are kept very clean at the area's best budget option.

Motel Sky (662 7780; Sikdang 1-golmuk; r W30,000;) A friendly welcome awaits you at this well-maintained smart and modern motel. The 6th floor has the best views, and some rooms have round beds or computers (W5000 extra).

Golden Park Motel (☎ 665 1400; Chungminno; r W30,000-40,000; ✖) The harbour view from room 805 is so fabulous that it earns a mention for this otherwise ordinary motel at the Yeosu end of Odongdo's pedestrian causeway.

Daia Motel (☎ 663 3347; Sikdang 1-golmuk; r W35,000-50,000; ✖ 🖳) This new motel with a kindly owner has some stylish features with big TVs and new computers, although bathrooms are small. The more expensive rooms are very spacious with comfortable armchairs, and room 606 has the best sea view.

Yeosu Amiga Hotel (☎ 663 2011; standard/deluxe W77,000/133,000; ✖ 🖳) White décor and large windows make for pleasant rooms with hillside views, and deluxe rooms are spacious. Guests can surf the internet, dine and enjoy a cup of coffee without leaving the hotel.

Eating

The harbour front is loaded with restaurants serving fresh fish and seafood, although none of them are cheap.

Cheolpangwa Dakgalbi (meals W3000-6000) Cook up your own chicken and vegetables in a big metal pan and then ask for rice to mix with the remnants at this top budget option. Side dishes include salad, mussels and lettuce wrap. The friendly young staff can help out with the barbecuing.

Gubaek Sikdang (meals W10,000; ✖ 7am-8pm) The *ajumma* (older women) staff is friendly and used to dealing with foreigners. *Saengseon·gui* (생선구이; grilled fish) with rice and refillable side dishes is the best deal.

Mono Sikdang (meals W10,000-30,000; ✖ 8am-9pm) On the 2nd floor above the police station is this small fish restaurant, where a couple of tables have harbour views. Try *galchigui* (갈치구이) or the spicy and more expensive *saengseon chorim* (생선초림).

Getting There & Away

AIR

Yeosu airport, 17km north of the city, has flights to Seoul and Jejudo.

BOAT

The ferry pier for island ferries is at the western end of the harbour.

BUS

The express and intercity bus terminals are together, 4km north of the port area. Buses include:

Destination	Price (W)	Duration	Frequency
Busan	11,200	4hr	hourly
Gwangju	8600	2¼hr	every 30min
Mokpo	13,900	3½hr	hourly
Seoul	19,200	5hr	hourly

TRAIN

Trains from Yongsan in Seoul to Yeosu are provided by *Saemaul* (W35,900, 5½ hours, three daily) and *Mugunghwa* (W24,200, six hours, 12 daily) services.

Getting Around

BUS

The express and intercity bus terminals are 4km north of the port. Cross the pedestrian overpass to Pizza Hut and from the bus stop,

---

KOREA'S ADMIRABLE ADMIRAL

Yi Sun-sin was Korea's greatest admiral. Based in Yeosu, he inflicted a series of defeats on the Japanese navy in the 1590s before being killed in battle in 1598. He introduced a new type of warship, the *geobukseon* or turtle ship, which was protected with iron sheets and spikes against the Japanese 'grapple and board' naval tactics. Although only a handful were deployed, *geobukseon* replicas can be found on Odongdo as well as in museums throughout the country.

The standard Korean warship was the flat-bottomed, double-decked *panokseon*, first built in the 1550s and also powered by two sails and hard-working oarsmen. It was stronger and more manoeuvrable than the Japanese warships and had more cannons on board. With these advantages, clever tactics and an intimate knowledge of the complex patterns of tides and currents around the numerous islands and narrow channels off the southern coast, Admiral Yi was able to defeat the Japanese navy time and time again. His forces sank hundreds of Japanese ships and thwarted Japan's ambition to seize Korea and use it as a base for the conquest of China.

almost any bus (W890, 15 minutes) can take you to Jung·ang Rotary. Check the destination with the driver. From the train station the same situation applies. From the airport, buses (W2500, 40 minutes, every 30 minutes) run to Jung·ang Rotary.

DOLSANDO 돌산도

This large scenic island, where you might even see a bullock pulling a plough, is now connected to Yeosu by a bridge. Perched halfway up on a cliff on its southern tip is a popular temple and small monastery called **Hyang·iram** (☎ 644 3650; adult/youth/child W2000/1500/1000; ⊙ 8am-6pm), which has superb coastal views over clear blue seas when the mist disperses.

It's a steep 10-minute walk from the bus stop through the tourist village up to the temple, passing through narrow clefts in the rock. Outside one shrine are 75 stone turtles, each with a W10 coin on its back.

Walk to the right and down the access road for 50m for the signposted walk up **Geumosan** (323m). Climbing up the 350 steps takes about 30 minutes, and your reward is a fantastic vista of distant islands and a 360-degree view from the rocky summit. Carry on and the loop track brings you back down to Hyang·iram (25 minutes).

Every restaurant in the tourist village sells locally made *gatkimchi* (갓김치), which has a mustard taste; even if you don't usually like *kimchi* you might like the mildish ones here.

By the ticket office is **Geumohoegwan** (meals W4000-12,000), which offers *saengseon·gui* (생선구이; spicy crab soup) or seafood *kalguksu* (칼국수; noodles). If the weather's fine, sit outside in one of the thatched shelters with a sea view.

Buses 101 and 111 (both W890, one hour, six daily) run from outside Jinnamgwan to Hyang·iram. Check the times as the timetable has gaps.

GEOMUNDO 거문도

Ferries (adult/child one way W28,200/6250, two hours, twice daily) from Yeosu ferry terminal visit this far-flung and rarely visited group of three islands, 112km south of Yeosu. The islands were grabbed by British warships in April 1885 for a naval base that was called Port Hamilton. It was occupied until February 1887, but all that remains is a British cemetery with some gravestones. The islands also have an attractive beach.

BOSEONG 보성

This town is the gateway to **Boseong Daehan Dawon** (☎ 853 2595; adult/child W1600/1000; ⊙ 9am-6pm). Imagine standing on a hillside, its slopes covered with rows and rows of green tea bushes – that is what you find here in a very attractive setting. Photo opportunities abound as you walk around the tea plantation.

Dine in the **restaurant** (meals W4000-6000), overlooking the tea bushes, on *jajangmyeon* made with green-tea noodles, *bibimbap* with green tea-rice, or other green-tea themed favourites. Downstairs you can buy green-tea shakes or green-tea yogurt. Nearby is a green-tea ice-cream stall, or for just W1000 you can enjoy a cup of green tea. A shop sells green tea in leaf, teabag or powder form as well as green-tea soap.

Local buses to the tea plantation continue to Yulpo beach, where **Yulpo Haesu Nokchatang** (☎ 853 4566; adult/child W5000/3000; ⊙ 6am-8pm, last entry 7pm) offers you the chance to bathe in green-tea water or seawater.

Buses pass through Boseong every 30 minutes along the Mokpo–Suncheon route. From Boseong bus terminal take a local bus (W850, 10 minutes, every 30 minutes) to the green-tea plantation.

GANGJIN 강진

One of two important ceramic centres in Jeollanam-do, Gangjin has been associated with celadon for over 1000 years. Across the district are the remains of nearly 200 kilns. Gangjin is specifically known for etched celadon, in which shallow patterns are cut out of the piece while it's still wet and filled in with special glazes through an inlay process. The celadon is fired at 800°C before glazing and at 1300°C after glazing. Another distinctive feature of Gangjin celadon is no ice-crackles. Most celadonware has crackles because the soil and glazes are a tiny bit mismatched – this wasn't the case in Gangjin.

The **Gangjin Celadon Museum** (강진청자박물관; ☎ 430 3524; adult/youth/child W1000/500/400; ⊙ 9am-6pm) is 18km south of Gangjin and 300m from the road. There is little English explanation but the exquisite examples of Goryeo-dynasty celadon speak with their own voices. On the left is a **pottery workshop**, where visitors start with a lump of black clay, spinning or moulding their own cup or artwork and then etching it. It is later fired and posted to you for W10,000 plus postage.

GREEN TEA

The 'wellbeing wave', the name given to the trend towards healthy food and drinks, has boosted sales of *nokcha*, green tea, which was introduced in the 7th century. Like ginseng it is used as a flavouring for a wide variety of products from ice cream, chocolates, cakes and milk shakes to noodles, pasta and *hotteok* (sweet pita bread). Some spas even offer green-tea baths.

Korean Buddhist monks have always regarded green tea as an ideal relaxant and an aid to meditation, especially when prepared, served and drunk in the correct ceremonial way known as *dado*. They usually settle any disputes over a cup of green tea.

Korean green tea is only grown in the southern provinces and has a subtle flavour, but experts can tell when and where the tea was picked. Green tea, like wine, is a blend of flavours, a mix of aroma and taste, with its own special vocabulary and rituals.

On the right is an excavated kiln site, discovered in 1968, that dates back to the 12th century.

The museum and shops outside sell reproduction Goryeo celadon. The **Gangjin Ceramic Festival** is held here during midsummer.

To get there, take a local bus from Gangjin bus terminal (platform 13) for Maryang and get off at the museum (W1600, 25 minutes, every 30 minutes), which is called Cheongja Doyoji in Korean.

Buses to Gangjin include:

Destination	Price (W)	Duration	Frequency
Boseong	3300	45min	every 30min
Gwangju	7200	1½hr	every 20min
Mokpo	4000	1hr	hourly
Yeosu	10,900	2hr	every 30min

DURYUNSAN PROVINCIAL PARK
두륜산도립공원
Sights & Activities
One highlight of this park, southeast of Haenam, is **Daedunsa** (Daeheungsa; ☎ 534 5502; adult/youth/child W2500/1500/1000; ⏱ sunrise-sunset), a major Zen temple complex. The temple is thought to date back to the mid-10th century, but it remained relatively unknown until it became associated with Seosan, a warrior monk who led a group against Japanese invaders in 1592–98. Since then it's been very popular with Koreans, yet it maintains an atmosphere of rusticity. A museum houses a Goryeo-dynasty bell, other Buddhist treasures and a tea-ceremony display (Seosan was also a tea master). The temple is a 40-minute walk from the bus stop.

The park's highest peak, **Duryunbong** (700m), provides a dramatic backdrop. To climb it, turn left after the temple museum. It takes 1½ hours to reach the top, and you

are rewarded with a very picturesque view of Korea's southern coastline and, on clear days, out to Jejudo. Head back via the other trail and turn right at the first junction (20 minutes); it's another hour back down to Daedunsa, via Jinburam.

For an easier ascent, walk back down the access road from the bus stop and turn right up the road for 800m to the **cable car** (☎ 534-8992; one way/return W4000/6800; ⏱ 7am-7pm). It takes you 1.6km up **Gogyebong** (638m) but does not operate on windy days. On the way is **Duryusan Oncheonland** (☎ 534 0900; admission W6000; ⏱ 5am-11pm), a smart new sauna and spa.

Sleeping & Eating
Haenam Youth Hostel (☎ 533-0170; dm/r W7000/25,000; ⏱ ▯) A three-minute walk beyond the cable car is the best budget option, with clean modern rooms. All have *yo* (padded quilt mattresses on the floor), and nondorm rooms have en suite facilities.

Yuseonggwan (유성관; ☎ 534 2959; d W30,000) This idyllic traditional inn, built around a courtyard and filled with art, is inside the park about two-thirds of the way between the car park and Daedunsa. It offers breakfast (W7000) and dinner (W10,000).

Jeonju Restaurant (meals from W10,000; ⏱ 9am-10pm) It's famous for mushrooms – choose *pyogojeon·gol* (mushroom casserole) or *pyogosanjeok* (minced beef, seafood, mushrooms and vegetables). Look for the English sign halfway along the line of restaurants leading to the ticket office.

Getting There & Around
Access to the park is by bus (W850, 15 minutes, every 30 minutes) from Haenam bus terminal. A minibus runs from the parking lot to Daedunsa (W500).

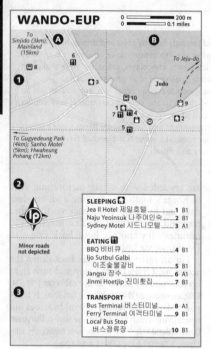

WANDO-EUP

0 --- 200 m
0 --- 0.1 miles

To Sinjido (3km); Mainland (15km)

To Jeju-do

Judo

To Gugyedeung Park (4km); Sanho Motel (5km); Hwaheung Pohang (12km)

Minor roads not depicted

SLEEPING
Jea Il Hotel 제일호텔 **1** B1
Naju Yeoinsuk 나주여인숙 **2** B1
Sydney Motel 시드니모텔 **3** A1

EATING
BBQ 비비큐 **4** B1
Ijo Sutbul Galbi
이조숯불갈비 **5** B1
Jangsu 장수 **6** A1
Jinmi Hoetjip 진미횟집 **7** B1

TRANSPORT
Bus Terminal 버스터미널 **8** A1
Ferry Terminal 여객터미널 **9** B1
Local Bus Stop
버스정류장 **10** B1

Bus connections from Haenam include:

Destination	Price (W)	Duration	Frequency
Busan	20,600	6hr	hourly
Gwangju	8200	1¾hr	every 30min
Jindo	4200	1hr	hourly
Mokpo	4500	1hr	every 30min
Wando	4500	1hr	hourly

WANDO 완도

pop 70,000

Another island now connected by a bridge to the mainland, Wando is scenic with everchanging views of scattered offshore islands. Ferries to Jejudo leave from the main town ,Wando-eup, which has stacks of flashy new motels. There are other ferries running to nearby islands.

Sights & Activities

The best and most convenient swimming beach is **Myeongsasim-ni** on neighbouring Sinjido, an island now joined to Wando by an impressive bridge that is lit up at night. Take a bus (W2000, 15 minutes, hourly) from the bus terminal in Wando-eup to this sandy beach that is lined with pine trees.

On Wando's south coast is **Gugyedeung Park** (☎ 554 1769; adult/youth/child W1600/600/300; 9am-5pm), a tiny park that offers views of distant cliffs and offshore islands, a pebbly beach and a 1km nature trail that runs through a thin slither of coastal woodland to the Sanho Motel (below). Swimming is dangerous.

The Seobu (western side) bus (W850, five minutes, hourly) runs from Wando-eup bus terminal, not from the local bus stop. Get off at Sajeong and walk 600m down to the park entrance.

Sleeping

Smart new motels topped by neon signs run all the way along the western side of Wando-eup harbour. Rates rise in July and August if the town is busy. Jeongdo-ri (at the entrance to Gugyedeung Park) and Bogildo have many *minbak* options.

Naju Yeoinsuk (☎ 554 3884; r W15,000) Rock-bottom prices are charged at this basic budget pad that couldn't be closer to the ferry terminal. Some rooms, though bare, are less cell-like than its brother *yeoinsuk*, and most have beds and en suite bathrooms, although with a bowl rather than hand basins.

Jea Il Hotel (☎ 554 3251; fax 554 3250; r W20,000;) A brilliant location for this *yeogwan*, with its faded furniture and fittings overlooking the fishing boats. Ask for a room such as No 101, which has an enclosed balcony and views.

Sanho Motel (☎ 552 4004; d from W30,000;) In a remote location at the far end of Gugyedeung beach is this hilltop motel with wonderful views, a coffee shop and artworks on the wall. It's a special place with a guesthouse atmosphere in a get-away-from-it-all spot that's popular with arty types.

Sydney Motel (☎ 554 1075; r W35,000;) Tired of small rooms and bathrooms? Then stay at this modern motel located halfway between the bus and ferry terminals. Great sea views, too. Opened in 2003, it's still one of the spiffiest in town. There's nice wood panelling and all rooms have shower stalls (hooray!); *ondol* rooms are larger.

Eating

Wando's speciality is raw seafood, but *saengseon-gui* (생선구이; grilled fish) and *jang-eogui* (장어구이; grilled eel) are cooked-food options.

BBQ (meals W4000-9000; 11.30am-11pm) Come to this casual and laid-back cubbyhole of an eatery for pizzas, burgers and chicken that arrives fried, barbecued or smoked. An English menu is available.

Ijo Sutbul Galbi (meals W5000-12,000) Dine in your private room in this 2nd-floor restaurant with traditional Korean food, including a *hanjeong-sik* (한정식) banquet that includes oysters or other seafood.

Jangsu (meals W6000) Escape from spicy soups and raw fish at Jangsu, which offers a good-deal rice hotpot meal that includes grilled fish, omelette, salad and ginseng water.

Jinmi Hoetjip (meals W8000-30,000) At the start of the busy fish market alley is this typical harbourside restaurant that serves up the ubiquitous raw fish, including *hoedeopbap* (회덮밥).

Getting There & Away
BOAT
From **Wando Ferry Terminal** (555 0655), Onbada 1 ferry (W18,250 to W28,000) sails to Jejudo daily at 8am and takes five hours. **Hanil Car Ferry 1** (554 8000) departs at 2.20pm (Monday to Saturday) and Hanil Car Ferry 2 departs at 3.30pm (Sunday to Friday). Both cost W19,800 and take around 3 to 3½ hours. Other ferries run to a dozen nearby islands.

BUS
Buses depart from Wando for the following destinations:

Destination	Price (W)	Duration	Frequency
Busan	25,100	6hr	6 daily
Gwangju	11,900	2¾hr	every 30min
Haenam	4500	1hr	hourly
Mokpo	8700	2hr	every 1½hr
Yeong-am	7000	1½hr	every 30min

Getting Around
From Wando-eup bus terminal, one local bus heads west (Seobu bus) while another heads east (Dongbu bus). Both go to the bridge to the mainland before heading back to Wando-eup. The ferry terminal is a 25-minute walk from the bus terminal or a short taxi ride.

BOGILDO 보길도
This island southwest of Wando is popular in summer thanks to the sandy beaches at **Jung-ni** and **Tong-ni**, 2.3km from Cheongbyeo port. Walk or take a bus or taxi to reach them.

Getting There & Away
Car ferries (555 1010) ply between Bogildo and Wando (adult/child W7000/3500, 70

THE BARD OF BOGILDO

A new day warms itself, the bigger fish swim near the surface.
Pull the anchor, pull the anchor!
In twos and threes the seagulls rise, then glide low and rise again.
Jigukcheong, jigukcheong, oshwa!
The fishing rods are ready, where did we put the wine bottle?

Yun Seondo (1587–1617) wrote his 40-verse masterpiece of *sijo* poetry, *The Fisherman's Calendar* (http://thewordshop.tripod.com), while living in seclusion on Bogildo, a quiet and relaxing island off Jeollanam-do's southern coast. While there he planted a natural-style Korean garden, **Seyeo-njeong** (세연정; adult/youth/child W1000/700/500; 9am-5pm), featuring big boulders, lily ponds and tree plantings surrounding a viewing pavilion.

Walk on for another 10 minutes and on the right is **Munhakcheheon** (문학체현), a small park that has Yun's poems (in *Han-geul*) hanging from the trees. Cross the stream to climb up the rocky hillside (15 minutes).

The garden is a pleasant 20-minute walk from the ferry terminal (follow the English signs) or else take a bus or taxi.

Too much wine: I must have dozed; my boat drifts into rough water.
Make fast the lines, make fast the lines!
Now peach blossoms float around us; maybe paradise is near.
Jigukcheong, jigukcheong, oshwa!
Good! At least we're far away from the dusty world of men.

minutes, 10 daily). To reach the ferry, take the free hourly shuttle bus from Wando-eup bus terminal to the port at Hwaheung Pohang, 12km to the west.

JINDO 진도
pop 43,000

Korea's third-largest **island** (http://tour.jindo.go.kr /english), south of Mokpo and connected to the mainland by a bridge, boasts some of the world's largest tides. During low tide for a few days each year (usually in March or April), a 2.8km-long, 40m-wide causeway appears, which connects to a small island, Modo, off Jindo's southeastern coast. Some 300,000 people make the crossing each year – in long rubber boots (available for rent, naturally).

The experience is known as the *Ganjuyuk Gyedo* (Mysterious Sea Rd) and has long been celebrated among Koreans in legend. With the spread of Christianity in Korea, the similarity to the Israelites' crossing of the Red Sea has only brought more enthusiasts. The **Yeongdeung festival** that coincides with the crossing includes local folk music and dances, a Jindo dog show and fireworks.

Jindo is also famous for its unique breed of dog, the Jindogae (see p259), which is designated as a precious natural monument and is the only natural monument that can be described as faithful, brave and adorable.

The **Jindo Dog Research Centre** (진돗개시험 연구소; ☎ 540 3396; admission free; ⏰ 9am-6pm) is dedicated to their study and training. If you want to see a training session, telephone first (note that no English spoken). Otherwise, the dogs can be viewed in their pens. To reach the centre from the bus terminal, walk back along the main road into Jindo-eup for 1km and at the blue sign (in English) turn right. It is about a 20-minute walk from the bus terminal.

Getting There & Around

Buses connect Jindo-eup (Jindo's main town) with many places:

Destination	Price (W)	Duration	Frequency
Busan	24,800	6hr	2 daily
Gwangju	11,300	2¾hr	every 30min
Mokpo	4700	1¼hr	hourly
Seoul	18,900/28,100	6hr	4 daily

A free shuttle takes visitors to the Mysterious Sea Rd (Bbonghalme Dongsan) during the festival.

YEONG·AM 영암

The Yeong·am district was a centre of Korea's famed ceramic industry in the 7th to 9th centuries, and the **Pottery Culture Centre** (☎ 470 2566; admission free; ⏰ 9am-5pm) has modern and traditional wood-fired kilns, some dark-glazed pots on display, and potters in a workshop delicately smoothing their pots.

Some buses from Mokpo (W3170, 20 minutes, hourly) stop outside the pottery centre, but otherwise you must take a bus from Yeong·am to Gurim (W850, 10 minutes, hourly) and walk 1.2km (20 minutes) to the pottery centre and the folksy tiled houses around it.

WOLCHULSAN NATIONAL PARK 월출산국립공원

East of Yeong·am, 42-sq-km **Wolchulsan** (☎ 473 5210; adult/youth/child W1600/600/300; ⏰ 5am-7pm Mar-Oct, 8am-6pm Nov-Feb), Korea's smallest national park, invites a day of hiking. There are crags, spires and unusual shaped rocks around every corner as well as an 8m Buddha rock carving, steel stairways and at one point a 52m steel bridge spanning two ridges. Beautiful and rugged rock formations include **Cheonwangbong** (809m), the park's highest peak.

GRANDMA BBONG, A KOREAN MOSES

Grandma Bbong is a folk hero on Jindo, credited with originating the 'Moses Miracle' of the parting of the waves. According to legend, over 500 years ago a family of tigers was causing so many problems on Jindo that all the islanders moved to nearby Modo, but somehow Grandma Bbong was left behind. She was broken-hearted and prayed to the Sea God to be reunited with her family. In answer to her fervent prayers, the Sea God parted the sea, enabling her to cross over to Modo and meet her family again. Her statue and shrine can be seen on Jindo and even a karaoke has been named after her. At certain times every year, the sea still parts, revealing a muddy causeway between Jindo and Modo.

JINDO DOGS

Jindo is home to a special breed of Korean hunting dog, Jindogae, which is as brave, intelligent, loyal and cute as any canine on the planet. They can be a challenge to train and control, but they possess an uncanny sense of direction – one Jindo dog was taken to Daejeon but somehow made its way back to the island, a journey of hundreds of kilometres. Expect to fork out around W370,000 for a young one. Being hunting dogs, they are an active, outdoor breed that is not suited to an urban environment. Any other breed of dog found on Jindo is immediately deported to the mainland in order to maintain the breed's purity. View www.kang.org/jindo.html or www.jindojunkie.com for adorable photos and more information.

The popular route is the 8km, six-hour hike from Dogapsa in the west to Cheonhwangsa in the east or vice versa as the bus service to both ends is frequent. *Minbak* and restaurants can be found at both ends. Tracks are well signposted, but steep and strenuous in places due to the rocky terrain.

Getting There & Away

The gateway to the park is Yeong·am, from where buses run the 11km to Dogapsa (W1000, 20 minutes, every 20 minutes) in the west and the 4km to Cheonhwangsa (W850, 10 minutes, every 15 minutes).

MOKPO 목포

pop 246,000

The sprawling port city of Mokpo is the end of the line for train and expressway traffic, and a starting point for sea voyages to Jejudo and the western islands of Dadohae Haesang National Park. Korea's National Maritime Museum is appropriately located here, and the craggy peaks of Yudal Park rear up in the city centre and offer splendid sea, city and sunset views.

Information

KB Bank (Jung·angno) Foreign exchange and a global ATM.
Post office (Jung·angno) Free internet access; behind it is an historical Japanese colonial building.
Tourist information centre (☎ 270 8599) At the train station.

Sights

GATBAWI PARK MUSEUMS 갓바위공원

This complex of museums and art galleries, situated between rocky hillsides and a wide river, is 4km northeast of downtown Mokpo.

Jeonsigwan (전시관) is a grand four-floor atrium building that displays the work of local artists who work in all genres – from traditional ink to colourful modern splodges, from photographs to the Asian art of bonsai trees.

The twin highlights of the small **National Maritime Museum** (국립해양유물전시관; ☎ 270 2000; adult/child W600/300; ☺ 9am-6pm Tue-Sun) are two shipwrecks, one dating from the 11th century and the other from the early 14th century. Thousands of priceless items of Korean and Chinese celadon, coins and other trade items were salvaged from them. Fascinating film footage shows the treasures being salvaged, and part of the actual boats have been preserved. Next door is Badatga restaurant (p269).

The **Local History Museum** (문여역사관; admission free; ☺ 9am-6pm Tue-Sun) has a natural rock collection – a popular Joseon-era hobby was collecting and displaying unusual-shaped rocks. Also on display are vigorous and colourful oil paintings by the 20th-century artist Oh Soong-woo, and more traditional works by four generations of artists from one family.

Namnong Memorial Hall (남농기념관; adult/child W1000/500; ☺ 9am-6pm Tue-Sun) has more artworks by the same talented family, some of which are excellent, but it's a pity there aren't more of the modern ones.

The brand-new **Mokpo Natural History Museum** (목포자연사박물관; ☎ 276 6331; adult/youth/child W3000/2000/1000; ☺ 9am-6pm Tue-Sun) is aimed at children, with large dinosaur skeletons, live lizards and fish, and colourful but dead butterflies. There are snacks available at the cafeteria.

The riverside **Gatbawi rocks** have been heavily eroded into shapes that are supposed to look like two monks wearing hats, but from land you only get a side or top view. Carry on from the Gatbawi rocks to hike up the rock-strewn hills behind the museums.

Catch bus 15 (W850, 15 minutes, every 30 minutes) from outside the train station (across the overbridge). A taxi costs W4000 from the train station.

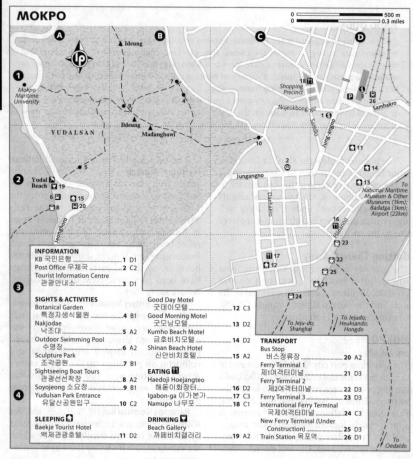

MOKPO

YUDALSAN PARK 유달산

This attractive **park** (☎ 242 2344; adult/youth/child W700/500/300; ⏰ 8am-6pm) offers splendid views across the island-scattered sea as you clamber around balancing rocks and rocky cliffs. From the train station, walk down Jungangno to the park entrance (20 minutes) and then past pavilions and an old cannon on the left.

You can turn right for 700m to the glass **botanical garden** (adult/youth/child W700/500/300) to see orchids and rare Korean plants, and nearby is the **sculpture park** (adult/youth/child W1000/600/400). But stay on the main path for **Madangbawi** (great views and two rock carvings), followed by **Ildeung** (228m), another peak where swallows zip by and cuckoos can be heard. It's a 30-minute walk from the park entrance.

Turn left (no sign) just before **Soyojeong** (소요정), a white pavilion, to head down to Yudal beach. Turn left at the sign to Arirang Gogae (아리랑고개) and then follow the sign to **Nakjodae** (낙조대), a pavilion that you reach 30 minutes after leaving Ildeung. From Nakjodae pavilion it's a 10-minute walk down the steps to the beach.

The beach is just a tiny patch of sand, rocks and seaweed, so the main attractions are the island views, the boats coming and going, and the **outdoor swimming pool** (adult/child W4000/2800; ⏰ 10am-7.30pm Jul & Aug). Restaurants offer salmon, raw fish and chicken meals, and the Beach Gallery (opposite) is here. Sightseeing trips (adult/child W10,000/5000) cruise around the nearby islands but don't land.

Bus 1 and most of the other buses that pass by can take you back to Mokpo train station.

Sleeping

Kumho Beach Motel (☎ 242 5700; r W30,000; 🗙) The best accommodation between the train station and the ferry terminal is this white high-rise motel run by a friendly and helpful owner. The modern and clean rooms have a dash of style thrown in.

Good Morning Motel (☎ 245 3357; r W30,000; 🗙) A good, modern motel with a convenient central location, and the young owner provides guests with plenty of free soft drinks.

Good Day Motel (☎ 243 6633; r W30,000; 🗙 💻) Probably the best of the half-dozen newish motels near the ferry terminals, with wide corridors leading to smart rooms that have water views.

Baekje Tourist Hotel (☎ 242 4411; fax 242 9550; d from 40,000; 🗙) A five-minute walk from the train station and the ferries, the light and natural wood decor is appealing, especially in end rooms like No 501. It costs more than the motels, but has a bar.

Shinan Beach Hotel (☎ 243 3399; www.shinanbeach hotel.com; mountain/ocean view r from W99,500/119,500; 🗙) Traditionally regarded as Mokpo's top hotel, it towers over Yudal Beach and is classy in an old-fashioned way. Rooms (mainly *ondol* or twin) are welcoming with large windows, but the sky lounge is a disappointment. Ask for a 50% discount in the off-peak season.

Eating

Namupo (meals W6000-14,000; 🕙 10am-midnight) Not in a seafood mood? Try the *galbi* (갈비) grills at this thrillingly clean local favourite in the city centre. The meat of the *namupo galbi* (나무포갈비) is beautifully seasoned. A hotpot rice meal with good side dishes is another option.

Badatga (meals W6000-20,000) This glass box with comfy armchairs next to the National Maritime Museum is perfect for lunch or just to rest your feet and have a coffee while enjoying the river views. The wide-ranging menu covers Western, Korean and fusion food.

Igabon·ga (meals W15,000) Highly recommended is *tteokgalbi* (떡갈비), an outsize meat patty with seafood, bamboo-shoot and salad side dishes that is served on leaves and decorated with flowers.

Haedoti Hoejangteo (meals W30,000) A typically scruffy and expensive raw fish and hot seafood soup restaurant along the seafront. Meals are for sharing and you can order *hung-eo* (홍어; raw ray), the local speciality.

Drinking

Beach Gallery (Yudal Beach; 🕙 10am-4am) A café with nightly live music in summer, outside or inside.

Getting There & Away

AIR

Flights operate on the Gimpo–Mokpo route and sometimes on the Jejudo–Mokpo route, but the airport is 22km from the city.

BOAT

Mokpo's boat terminals handle ferries to Jejudo and the smaller islands west and southwest of Mokpo. See the corresponding destination sections for details. From Ferry Terminal 1, the Continental fast ferry runs to Jeju-si at 8am daily, takes 3½ hours and costs W45,200. From the International Ferry Terminal, slower car ferries run to Jeju-si leaving at 9am (Tuesday to Sunday) and 3pm (Monday to Saturday), and take 4¼ hours. Fares start at W21,800, with children under 12 half-price.

Four Season Cruise (☎ 243 6633; fare W125,000) runs between Mokpo and Shanghai, departing on Monday at 5pm and Friday at 2pm.

BUS

Mokpo's bus terminal is some distance from the centre of town. Turn left outside the bus terminal, then left at the end of the road and walk down to the main road where bus 1 (W850, 10 minutes, every 20 minutes) stops on the left. It runs to the train station, the ferry terminals and then on to Yudal beach.

Departures include:

Destination	Price (W)	Duration	Frequency
Busan	22,400	5hr	hourly
Gwangju	6300	1¼hr	every 30 min
Haenam	4500	1hr	every 30 min
Jindo	4700	2hr	hourly
Seoul	24,400	4½hr	every 20min
Wando	8700	2hr	7 daily
Yeong-am	3170	30min	every 30min
Yeosu	13,900	3½hr	hourly

TRAIN

KTX provides a fast service to Yongsan station, Seoul (W38,000, 3¼ hours, 11 daily), as well as *Saemaul* (W34,200, 4½ hours, two daily) and *Mugunghwa* (W23,100, 5½ hours, five daily) services. Infrequent but cheap trains run to Gwangju, Boseong and Yeosu.

Getting Around

It's a 15-minute walk from the train station to the ferry terminals or to the entrance to Yudal Park.

Airport buses (W2500, 30 minutes) depart from near the train station and are timed to meet flights. They also stop by the bus terminal.

Local bus 1 (W850, 10 minutes, every 20 minutes) runs from the bus terminal to the train station and on to Yudal beach. Local bus 15 (W850, 15 minutes, every 30 minutes) runs to the Gatbawi Park museums.

OEDALDO 외달도

Tiny 1km by 1km Oedaldo, an island of fig trees and swallows, is worth a visit, but only in July and August when the huge outdoor swimming pool is open. Car ferries (W7000 return, one hour, five daily) run there from Ferry Terminal 2 in Mokpo.

DADOHAE HAESANG NATIONAL PARK 다도해해상국립공원

Consisting of over 1700 islands and islets and divided into eight sections, Dadohae Haesang (Marine Archipelago) National Park occupies much of the coast and coastal waters of Jeollanam-do. Some of the isles support small communities with income from fishing and tourism; others are little more than tree-covered rocks.

Mokpo is the gateway to the western sector, including Hongdo and Heuksando, the most visited and scenic of the islands. They are great places to beat the heat of July and August, so booking of ferries and accommodation is advised in those months.

Hongdo 홍도

The most popular and beautiful of the islands west of Mokpo is **Hongdo** (Red Island; visitor fee W2300). Some 6km long and 2.5km wide, it rises precipitously from the sea and is bounded by sheer cliffs, bizarre rock formations and wooded hillsides cut by steep ravines. The island is ringed by islets and sunsets can be spectacular, but the only way you can see most of it is by boat, because with the exception of the villages, Hongdo is a protected nature reserve; entry is prohibited.

Ferries to Hongdo land at Ilgu village, which like the smaller, northerly village of Igu has a tiny cove that provides shelter to the fishing boats. A boat connects the two villages.

Boat tours (W15,000, two hours, twice daily) around the island are the way to appreciate the island and its rocky islets and arches.

Ilgu has *minbak* and *yeogwan* at the usual prices. **Royal-jang** (☎ 246 3837; ondol r W50,000) is clean and rooms are just three minutes from the beach, but beware of the karaoke downstairs. **Yuseongjang** (☎ 246 3723; ondol W30,000, r 50,000-80,000; 🛇) is next to the KT office and meals can be arranged. From September to June rates for both are W30,000.

Heuksando 흑산도

Heuksando, on the way to Hongdo, is the larger, more populated and more accessible of the two islands. Views from its peaks show why Dadohae Haesang means 'marine archipelago'. Fishing villages are linked by trails, but walking around the island would take around nine hours. Fortunately, local buses circle most of the island – a recommended trip is up the peak **Bonghwadae**, on the north coast hill, Sangnasan.

The largest village, **Yeri**, formerly a whaling centre, is where ferries dock. With sufficient demand, tourist boats will take you around the island (W13,000, two hours). The island's other major village is **Jinni**.

Gecheonjang (☎ 275 9154; Yeri; r W30,000; 🛇), a stone-fronted *yeogwan* by the post office, has bright yet rustic rooms with views of the harbour. Rates from September to June are W25,000. **Daedo Minbak** (☎ 275 9340; Yeri; d W25,000; 🛇), with just a few rooms, is pleasant and unpretentious.

Seafood restaurants are plentiful but prices can be steep. The speciality is *hung·eo* (홍어; ray, usually served raw).

GETTING THERE & AWAY

The same ferries serve Heuksando, 90km west of Mokpo, and Hongdo, another 20km further on. Leaving from Mokpo's **Ferry Terminal 1** (☎ 243 2111), ferries run to Heuksando (adult/child one way W26,700/5750, 1½ hours, three daily) and continue on to Hongdo (adult/child one way W32,600/5750, 2¼ hours).

Jejudo 제주도

JEJUDO

Hawaii, the Mediterranean, Disneyland, paradise…Jejudo has been compared to all four, and each is at least partly true. The volcanic island features swaying palm trees, cactus plants, orange orchards, circus shows, casinos, a dozen sandy beaches, 14 golf courses, scuba diving and much more. Jejudo is Korea's holiday and honeymoon island, where even bank tellers sport colourful, open-necked aloha shirts.

Most spectacular though are the volcanic landscapes. South Korea's highest mountain, Hallasan (1950m), is a special national park with varied ecological zones, cute little roe deer and wonderful azalea blooms in May. Out east is an awesome volcanic crater, Ilchulbong, while Udo island has dramatic, black-lava cliffs and a glaringly white coral-sand beach. Along the southeast coast are incredibly eroded and pockmarked cliffs at Yongmeori and a sheer-sided rock, Sanbangsan, which is a spiritual mountain with a grotto temple and water with healing powers. Then there's the world's longest lava tube at Manjanggul, folk villages, museums, sculpture parks and Asian-style gardens – masses to see and do. The sea temperature is the warmest in Korea and the coral near Seogwipo is as colourful as in the tropics.

Festivals and events include marathons, triathlons and iron-man contests, and outdoor concerts and movies are held on the fun-filled beaches in summer. Stay in world-class resorts, smart new motels or classy *minbak*. Dine on barbecued pheasant and grilled *okdom*, a local fish that used to be reserved for Joseon monarchs.

HIGHLIGHTS

- Be inspired by volcanic **Hallasan** (p292), South Korea's highest mountain, with its spectacular views and four distinct ecological zones

- Be awed by the world's longest **lava-tube cave** (p281) at Manjanggul

- Be entranced by forested volcanic craters atop **Seongsan Ilchulbong** (p282) and **Sangumburi** (p281), and dramatic eroded cliffs along the **Yongmeori coast** (p290)

- Be amazed by the **colourful coral** (p287) around Munseom Island, off Seogwipo

- Be thrilled by gravity-defying **acrobats** (p291, p291 and p291) on and off motorbikes and horses

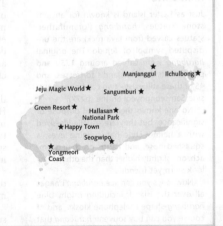

Manjanggul ★ Ilchulbong ★
Jeju Magic World ★ Sangumburi ★
Green Resort ★ Hallasan ★ National Park
★ Happy Town
Seogwipo
★ Yongmeori Coast

■ TELEPHONE CODE: 064   ■ POPULATION: 560,000   ■ AREA: 1847 SQ KM

JEJUDO

History

Despite being just 85km from the mainland, Jejudo was little visited for centuries. As a result it acquired its own history, traditions, dress, architecture and dialect.

According to legend, Jejudo was founded by three brothers (p277) who came out of holes in the ground and established the independent Tamna kingdom. Early in the 12th century the Goryeo dynasty took over, but in 1273 Mongol invaders conquered the island, contributing a tradition of horsemanship, a special horse *jorangmal* (p291) and quirks in the local dialect.

Over the years the island developed a unique architectural style: stone houses with a thatched roof that was tied down by rope against the strong winds. Different generations lived together in a walled compound, but unlike the rest of Korea, each generation had separate cooking facilities. Visit Seong-eup Folk Village (p284) to explore some traditional housing compounds that include outdoor toilets next to pigsties.

Local clothing was made from hemp and dyed with persimmon, and this orange-tinted clothing is a popular souvenir.

In 1653 a Dutch trading ship was wrecked on the island (p290). The 36 survivors were looked after by a kindly Jejudo governor, but when a few tried to escape they were severely beaten. After 10 months they were taken to Seoul and were forced to stay in Korea for 13 years until some of them escaped in a boat to Japan. One of the escapees, Hendrick Hamel, published his experiences (see www.hennysavenije.pe.kr), the first detailed account of the 'Hermit Kingdom' by a European.

During the later Joseon period, the island became home to over 200 exiles: intellectuals, Catholic converts and political undesirables who spent their time teaching the islanders and composing wistful poems.

Through it all, the locals carried on earning their living by fishing and farming. The island is famous for tangerines, which are grown on the southern coastal lowlands and are on sale throughout the year. Inland, pastures support horses and cattle.

Like the rest of the country, the past few decades have seen the island change radically – most of the coastline is now built up and many farm pastures have been turned into golf courses. The catalyst has been a flood of tourists from the mainland and abroad, which peaks from mid-July to mid-August. The numbers of *haenyeo* (see p284), hardy and hard-working female divers who still free-dive for seafood and seaweed, are in steep decline. Their daughters have opted for an easier life on dry land.

Recently the island has been given self-governing status and this may open the door to further economic development.

HARUBANG

Just as Easter Island is known for ancient stone statues, *harubang* ('grandfather' statues carved from lava rock) are the undisputed symbol of Jejudo. The original *harubang* were carved around 1750 and placed outside the island's fortresses, and 45 of these still exist – two can be seen outside Samseonghyeol Shrine (p277).

No one knows their original purpose or significance, but they are usually life-sized with a helmet-style hat, bulging eyes, a squashed nose, and hands on their stomach, one slightly higher than the other. They look stern yet friendly.

Nowadays you can see *harubang* images all over the island, including bright blue *harubang*-shaped telephone kiosks, and of course you can buy souvenir *harubang* that will fit inside your pocket.

Climate

The island's climate is less extreme than that of the Korean peninsula, and the mild winters mean palm trees, cacti, orange orchards and even pineapple plants thrive. Despite this, don't expect tropical temperatures, but rather a moderate but fickle, four-seasons-in-a-day climate, typical of islands.

Jejudo is also the rainiest place in Korea thanks to the country's highest mountain, Hallasan (1950m). But while most of the nation gets up to 60% of its rainfall during the summer rainy season, Jejudo's is more spread out. Downpours are least likely during autumn.

The island is noted for its strong winds, but they are usually brief. Conditions are often misty or hazy, except in autumn.

Hallasan is the dividing line between the subtropical oceanic southern side and the temperate north. Conditions on the peak can change rapidly, as it's a cloud trap.

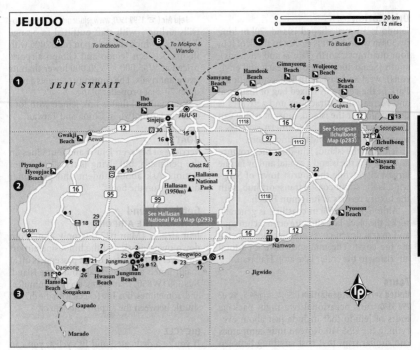

JEJUDO

	0 ——————— 20 km
	0 ——————— 12 miles

JEJU

Despite the heavy rainfall, surface water is a rarity due to the island's porous volcanic rock. The riverbeds are usually dry and the waterfalls are spring-fed. Underground water, by contrast, is abundant – Jejudo is basically one giant sponge.

Swimmers: being 33° north of the equator, you'll want a wetsuit unless you're swimming in July and August – or in a swimming pool.

View http://jeju.kma.go.kr for a detailed daily weather forecast in English.

National & Provincial Parks

Jejudo has only one national park but volcanic Hallasan (p292) is one of the best with roe deer, varied vegetation and wonderful views on the way up and down South Korea's highest peak.

Orientation

Jejudo is an oval-shaped island, 70km long by 30km wide, but it is easiest to think of it in four quadrants: north (Jeju-si and environs), south (Seogwipo, Jungmun Beach and environs), west and east, with Hallasan National Park in the centre. A mixed bag of historical and recreational attractions and activities is dotted all over the island, most of which can be reached by bus. The southern side has a more easy-going, holiday atmosphere.

Jejudo is the island, Jeju-do is the province and Jeju-si is the island's capital and by far the largest city, while the tourist town of Seogwipo is the south coast's transport hub, with the luxury resorts at Jungmun Beach.

Although the 250km coastline is generally rocky, the black-lava cliffs are often picturesque and over a dozen coves and beaches punctuate the coast. The midlands have a pastoral air, rising to the crater lake atop Hallasan.

Tours

United Services Organization (USO; Map pp84-5; ☎ 02 792 3380) runs occasional two-night package tours of Jejudo that include just about everything for US$340. Korean tour companies run similar trips that cost anything between W199,000 and W880,000.

Getting There & Away

AIR

Korean Air (Map p276; ☎ 1558 2001; www.koreanair.co.kr) and **Asiana Airlines** (☎ 1588 8000; www.flyasiana.com) operate flights from Jejudo airport to numerous Korean cities.

Jeju Air (☎ 1599 1500; www.jejuair.net) is a new no-frills airline – with staff outfitted in orange T-shirts – which started up in June 2006 with flights between Jejudo and Gimpo airports priced at W55,000 – W20,000 lower than its two giant rivals. The company operates a new, quiet 70-seat propeller plane.

International flights link Jejudo with four cities in Japan, two in China and Taiwan.

BOAT

Ferries sail between Jeju-si and four cities on the peninsula, but flying is usually a better option. Ask about student and pensioner discounts on the boats.

Getting Around

TO/FROM THE AIRPORT

Jeju airport (Map p273) is only 4km from downtown Jeju-si, and the limousine airport bus (every 20 minutes) drops passengers off at major hotels and resorts all round the island. Bus 300 (W850, 15 minutes, every 20 minutes) and, sometimes, bus 100 (check with the driver) shuttle between the airport and Jeju city.

BICYCLE

If you're a dedicated and fit cyclist, you can hire a bicycle (p279) and pedal yourself around the island (250km) in four or five days. Some coastal and city roads have cycleways alongside. Don't forget rain gear.

BUS

Buses radiate from the terminals in Jeju-si (Map p276) and Seogwipo (Map p286), cover-

---

FERRIES FROM JEJU-SI

All ferries use the Jeju Ferry Terminal (Map p276) except New Sea World and Car Ferry 2, which use the International Ferry Terminal, 2km further east. City bus 92 (W850, every 20 minutes) runs from both ferry terminals, but a taxi is more convenient.

Destination	Ship's name	Telephone	Price (W)	Duration	Frequency
Busan	Cozy Island	751 1901	32,000-150,000	11hr	Mon, Wed, Fri
	Seoul Bong Ho	751 1901	36,000-150,000	11hr	Tue, Thu, Sat
Incheon	Ohamana	721 2173	53,500-190,000	13hr	Tue, Thu, Sat
Mokpo	New Sea World	758 4234	21,800-86,350	4¼hr	daily Tue-Sun
	Car Ferry Rainbow	758 4234	21,800-50,100	4¼hr	daily Tue-Sun
	Continental	726 9542	45,200	3hr 30min	1 daily
Wando	Onbada	721 2171	18,250-28,000	5hr	1 daily
	Hanil Car Ferry 1	751 5050	19,800	3½hr	daily Tue-Sun
	Hanil Car Ferry 2	751 5050	19,800	3hr	daily Mon-Sat

JEJUDO CUISINE

The island is well known for certain foods that are difficult or impossible to find elsewhere in Korea. *Okdomgui* (p281) is ubiquitous and tasty, a local fish that is semi-dried before being grilled and has a gourmet taste that appealed to Joseon monarchs. *Heukdwaeji* (pork from the local black-skinned pig) is also common – look for a picture of a black pig on restaurant signs. *Jeonbok juk* (abalone rice porridge) is another island favourite, but abalone is so expensive these days that the amount of abalone in the porridge is declining. A few restaurants serve up *kkwong* (Jejudo pheasant) including Kkwong Memil Guksu (p280) and Gombawi (p283). If you love raw fish, you won't want to leave Jejudo as every kind of *hoe* (raw fish) and seafood is available from restaurants and direct from *haenyeo*, the island's traditional female divers.

For gifts, tangerines (especially the knobbly *hallabong*) are number one, but there is also prickly-pear jam, black *omija* tea, honey and the less appealing local chocolates. Hallasan *soju* is smoother than some.

---

ing most of the island with services running round the coast road every 20 minutes. Some cross-island buses also run every 20 minutes. Carry an ample supply of W1000 notes as changing a higher note can cause difficulties. One problem is that buses don't always go all the way to the beach or tourist site, so that some legwork is necessary. Also you must always check with the driver where the bus is going as not all the buses to some destinations follow the same route. Ask for a copy of the current bus timetable from a tourist information centre.

CAR

Since the sights and activities are scattered all over the island, it almost makes sense to rent a car. Many road signs are in English and the hire cost is reasonable. The problem is that, despite speed traps and road humps, driving techniques on the island are only slightly less mad than on the mainland. Still if you're brave enough to give it a go, there are four car-hire companies with desks at Jeju-si airport. Don't pay the official rates as they are invariably discounted 60% or more, except during the real summer peak from mid-July to mid-August. Expect to pay around W46,000 a day for a modest car plus around W12,000 a day for insurance, although the exact amount depends on the excess (the amount a hirer must pay in case of an accident).

To rent a car in Korea, government regulations insist hirers must have an international drivers licence and be 21 years old. Car-rental agencies include the following:
Avis (☎ 1544 1600; www.avis.co.kr)
Jeju Rent (☎ 747 3301; jrent@jejurentcar.co.kr)
Kumho/Hertz (☎ 751 8000; www.kumhorent.com)

SCOOTER

Definitely the coolest and most fun way to see Jejudo is on a scooter, which can be hired in Jeju-si (p279).

TAXI

Taxis charge W2000 for the first 2km or so, while a 15km journey costs around W10,000. You can hire a taxi driver for around W100,000 a day (plus meals and lodging), but the price goes up to W150,000 for an English-speaking driver. Agree on the route and negotiate a price beforehand.

JEJU-SI 제주시
pop 294,000

Jeju-si (Jeju City), the island's capital, sits at the middle of the north coast. The city centre, a mere 4km east of Jeju airport, is hardly glam but does have a few historic structures, a large market, the Chilseongno shopping precinct and lively student bars and restaurants opposite the old city hall. The seafront has no beach but still manages a seaside atmosphere in summer with a funfair and swimming pool. A new suburb, Sinjeju, has midrange hotels but little else.

Information

Central post office (Gwandeongno; ☯ 9am-6pm Mon-Fri, 1-6pm Sat) Has a global ATM, armchairs, toilets and free internet access.
City Hall post office (Jung-angno)
KB Bank (Jung-angno) Money exchange.
KTO tourist information office (☎ 742 0032; 1st fl airport terminal) Free internet.
Ramada Plaza Jeju (Tapdongno) Global ATM.
Shinhan Bank (1st fl, airport terminal) Global ATM.
Tourist information centres Jeju-si ferry terminal (☎ 758 7181; ☯ 6.30am-8pm); Jeju airport (☎ 742

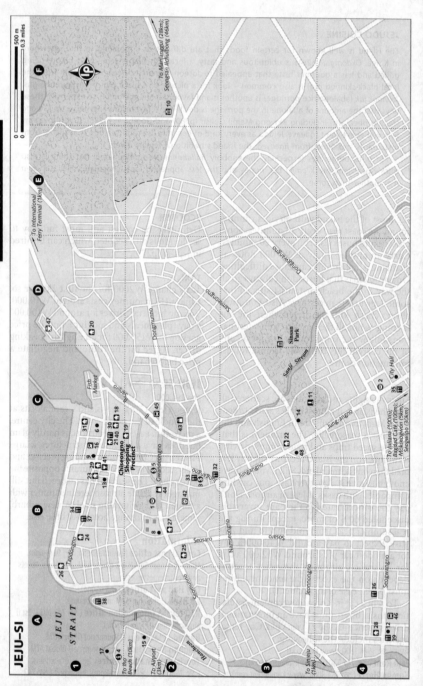

JEJUDO

JEJU-SI

JEJU
STRAIT

Chiseongno
Shopping
Precinct

Fish
Market

Sinsan
Park

Samji Stream

City Hall

To Manjanggul (28km);
Seongsan Ilchulbong (46km)

To International/
Ferry Terminal (1km)

To Billiara (100m);
Bagdad Café (100m);
Moksegwon (5km);
Seogwipo (30km)

To Iho
Beach (10km)

To Airport
(3km)

To Sinjeju
(1km)

Dongmunno

Samseongno

Dongseogwangno

Jungangno

Jungangno

Sosaro

Namseongno

Seosaro

Jeonnongno

Seogwangno

Seomunno

Tapdongno

Gwandeongno

0   500 m
0   0.3 miles

8866; ⏱ 6.30am-8pm); Yongduam Rock car park (☎ 750 7768; ⏱ 9am-8pm) Free internet access at the airport and Yongduam Rock car-park centres.

Woori Bank (Gwandeongno) Money exchange.

Sights & Activities

JEJU-SI SEAFRONT 제주시해안
Hotels, motels, restaurants and fast-food outlets are strung along the seafront, but there is no beach. It can be lively in the evenings at the eastern end where you can hire skates and Rollerblade along the promenade or shoot some hoops on the outdoor basketball courts. The small amusement park **Fantasia** (rides W1000-3000) produces more screams than a rock concert, the outdoor swimming pool complex called **Water Park** (adult/child W8000/6000; ⏱ 10am-6pm Jul & Aug) makes a good beach substitute, and the outdoor concert hall hosts summer shows.

SAMSEONGHYEOL SHRINE 삼성혈
The main feature of this very unusual **shrine** (☎ 722 3315; Samseongno; adult/youth/child W2500/1700/1000; ⏱ 8am-7pm Mar-Oct, to 6pm Nov-Feb) is a hole in the ground, or rather three holes in the ground. Legends say that three brothers, Go, Bu and Yang, came out of the three holes and

founded the Tamna kingdom with help from three princesses who arrived by boat together with cattle and horses. The brothers divided the island kingdom into three sections by each shooting an arrow and taking the third where his arrow landed.

The shrine was originally built in 1526 and the spirit tablets of the island's first ancestors are honoured with food and music in a ceremony held three times a year: on 10 April, October and December. At the entrance are two of the 45 remaining original *harubang*, which are over 250 years old.

Ask to see the English version of a 15-minute film about the legend that's shown in the exhibition hall on the right.

FOLKLORE & NATURAL HISTORY MUSEUM 민속자연사박물관
This wide-ranging **ecomuseum** (☎ 722 2465; Samseongno; adult/youth/child W1100/500/free; ⏱ 8.30am-6.30pm) in Sinsan Park has well-labelled exhibits on Jejudo's varied volcanic features including volcanic bombs, lava tubes and trace fossils. Fortunately the volcanoes have all been dormant for the last 1000 years, although earthquakes were felt in the 16th century. Other highlights to look out for are excellent

JEJUDO

ADVENTURE JEJUDO

Jejudo is Activity Island, particularly in August when water sports take off from the more popular beaches. Jungmun beach on the south coast is the main focus of events with **kayaking, jet-skiing, water skiing, jet-boating** and **parasailing** on offer, and even some **surfing** for those surfie newbies. In nearby Seogwipo you can float upwards on a **balloon ride**, but the star activity is **scuba diving** (www.bigblue33.co.kr), which is highly recommended, although you can also view fish and coral without getting wet from the cramped comfort of a **submarine**. Jejudo is famous for wind, so **windsurfing** is popular, and Pacific Land near Jungmun beach offers **sailing trips**, though they are on the pricey side. For **golf, horse rides** or **quad bike** and **go-kart** action head into the island's green interior. If you'd rather watch horses than ride them, join the crowds at the race track near Jeju-si for the weekend **racing**. Jejudo's unique volcanic landscapes can be explored on foot, above ground up craters and below ground along lava caves. Hire a **bicycle, scooter** or **car** for go-where-you-please freedom. You don't need any special equipment to enjoy the fun, just a sense of adventure. Some activities are seasonal and companies tend to come and go, so if you see your favourite activity going on, just vault the language barrier and join in.

---

wildlife films, the bizarre oar fish and panoramas of the island's six ecological zones.

MOKSEOGWON 목석원
About 6km south of Jeju-si, **Mokseogwon** (☎ 702 0203; adult/youth/child W2000/1500/1000; ☽ 8am-6.30pm Feb-Nov, 8am-5.30pm Dec-Jan) is both a garden and art park with oddly shaped rocks and gnarled roots. It's a labour of love, put together over many years by a local resident, and if your switch is flipped 'on', you could find it a wondrous place.

Installations are creations of wood and stone (Mokseogwon translates as 'Wood-stone garden'). Some are fanciful, some meaningful, some beautiful, some weird, and all comprise objects found around the island. Look for the apocryphal story of a couple and their life together told via trees and rocks. Many of the works are made from the roots of the *jorok* (yew) tree, which symbolises longevity and is found only on Jejudo.

To reach Mokseogwon, take the city bus 500 (W850, 30 minutes, every 15 minutes) bound for Jeju National University – pick it up along Jungangno.

MOK OFFICE & GWANDEOKJEONG 관덕정, 목관아
The island's administrative centre under the Joseon dynasty, the **Mok Office** (☎ 702 3081; Seomunno; adult/youth/child W1500/800/400; ☽ 7am-7pm), has been reconstructed. The cluster of historical buildings has an austere style that designed to promote virtue. Next door is 15th-century **Gwandeokjeong** (admission free; , an impressive and recently renovated

pavilion that was used for receiving official guests and hosting banquets.

NATIONAL JEJU MUSEUM 국립제주박물관
This **museum** (☎ 720 8000; adult/youth/child W1000/500/free; ☽ 9am-6pm Tue-Sun) is housed in a large, inconveniently located building. It's a clone of the many other local museums dotted around the country but antiques addicts can get their fix here. Many city buses stop outside, including bus 26 (W850, every 15 minutes).

YONGDUAM ROCK 용두암
On the seashore to the west of city, **Yongduam Rock** (Dragon's Head Rock) attracts coach loads of Korean tourists, but foreign visitors usually wonder why these oddly-shaped black basalt lava rocks attract such large crowds. Still, looking at people looking at rocks appeals to some…

IHO BEACH 이호해수욕장
The nearest **beach** to Jeju-si along the west coast is blessed with an unusual mixture of yellow and grey sand, which means that you can build two-tone sandcastles. The beach is a decent size with shallow water that makes for safe swimming, and changing-room facilities are open in July and August. Further out to sea you can pit your free-diving skills against *haenyeo* divers searching around the rocks for seafood and edible seaweed. A small fishing port is on one side, and terns dive for fish too.

Buses (W850, 20 minutes, every 20 minutes) leave Jeju-si bus terminal for Iho Beach – get off at Heonsa Village stop and it's a 150m walk to the beach.

CYCLE, SCOOTER & SKATE HIRE

Pedal west along the coast road (lunching in one of the many restaurants) or even all the way round the island on bicycles rented from **Smart Bicycle** (☎ 755 1134; Seogwangno; per day W6000; ⏰ 8am-7pm) or **Tabalo Bicycle** (☎ 751 2000; per day W8000; ⏰ 8am-8pm), which has new bikes.

Tom and Suji at **Travel Story** (☎ 713 4778; Yongunno; ⏰ 6am-7pm Mar-Oct, 8am-6pm Nov-Feb) speak English and hire out bicycles (per day W5000) and cute Taiwanese scooters (per day W25,000 to W30,000) which can take two people. The scooters range from 50cc to 125cc and insurance is another W5000. A scooter is a cool and convenient way to tour Jejudo. Telephone and they will pick you up from the airport or ferry port.

On the western end of the seafront, **Jeju Inline Skate Proshop** (Tapdongno; skates & bicycles per hr W2000; ⏰ 11am-10pm) hires out skates either from the shop or from a truck parked round the corner on the esplanade.

Sleeping

Seafront motels and hotels are a 10-minute walk from the ferry terminal.

BUDGET

Chincheol Minbak (☎ 755 5132; s/d W15,000/17,000) Mrs Kim runs the city's best under-W20,000 budget option. *Chincheol* means 'friendly' and guests can mingle in the communal kitchen and outside in the patch of garden where a table and chairs are shaded by an awning. It's untidy but close to the ferry terminals and some rooms have beds, a TV and a toilet/shower cubicle.

Sin·gangnamjang (☎ 753 8770; r W25,000; 🖭) Located opposite the bus terminal, the rooms are small but not too gloomy and should satisfy those on a tight budget who plan to use the buses to tour the island.

Ruby Motel (☎ 755 5565; r W30,000; 🖭) The owner is friendly and may offer cups of coffee and help with the laundry. The rooms are a reasonable size with artworks on the walls, but the atmosphere in this *yeogwan* near the bus terminals needs brightening up and a lick of paint would work wonders.

Geullobeol Motel (☎ 756 5943; r W30,000-40,000; 🖭) Down by the seafront, and run by friendly *ajumma* (middle-aged women), the cheaper rooms are smallish but blissfully modern, smart and clean, which makes them the city's best W30,000 deal.

MIDRANGE

The smart new motels are worth the extra money.

Tapdong Hotel (☎ 723 3600; Haejingno; r W40,000; 🖭 🖳) One of the best high-rise motels near the seafront with spacious, stylish rooms and bathrooms. Rooms are fully equipped with a computer as well as unusual extras like shower partitions and an electric kettle. A pot plant makes it seem almost like home.

Bobos Motel (☎ 727 7200; Haejingno; r W40,000; 🖭 🖳) A classy, posh motel, opposite Tapdong Hotel, where the staff is welcoming and most rooms have ornate furniture as well as modern fittings. Ask for room 507 if you prefer something less like a love motel.

cf Motel (☎ 726 3230; r W40,000; 🖭 🖳) A modern, smart motel with appealing rooms – a computer is W5000 extra. Choose between regular or more lavishly furnished rooms with a round bed.

White Beach Hotel (☎ 753 8460; r W60,000; 🖭) The seafront location is the reason for staying here as long as you don't mind a small bathroom. It feels like a genuine hotel rather than a motel, and everything is new and smart. Rooms with a sea view are W10,000 extra. The ground-floor restaurant serves Jejudo specialities (W12,000 to W15,000), while the rooftop bar (p281) is a hidden gem.

Jeju Palace Hotel (☎ 753 8811; www.cjpalace.co.kr; Tapdongno; r W70,000; 🖭 🖳) On the seafront, the rooms are fine if you turn a blind eye to the small bathrooms with dated fittings. Other retro features like chandeliers have some charm and the restaurant has a sea view when the mist lifts. You can email from the lobby and male guests can steam in the sauna, but there's no bar for that après-sauna pick-me-up.

Robero Hotel (☎ 757 7111; www.roberohotel.com; Gwandeongno; r from W100,000; 🖭 🖳) The downtown location overlooking Gwandeokjeong pavilion suits shoppers, but the business centre is just a computer and fax machine in the lobby and room TVs are old. This is compensated by plenty of modern art, which adds a boutique style to the hotel. Exchange rates are 10% lower than the banks.

Pacific Hotel (☎ 758 2500; r from W105,000; 🖭 🖳) Despite the name, this downtown haunt of tour groups has an Egyptian theme, from its pyramid shape to hieroglyphics in the lift. It's smart enough but needs new TVs, showers and balcony furniture to receive an unequivocal recommendation.

Oriental Hotel (☎ 752 8222; www.oriental.co.kr; Tapdongno; r standard/sea view W123,420/145,000;) This seafront hotel verges on top end so the lobby is impressive, overlooks a grotto and echoes to atmospheric live music in the evening. As is usual the public rooms and the casino are grander and more impressive than the guestrooms. Still, room windows are large, the décor is light, and sheets are whiter than snow, so small imperfections can be forgiven.

TOP END

Jeju KAL Hotel (☎ 724 2001, www.kalhotel.co.kr; Jung-angno; r weekday/weekend W160,000/210,000;) This plush Korean Airlines high-rise in the heart of downtown has the best city views and all the top-end bells and whistles including a casino, a lap pool, aerobics and yoga classes, and a 19th-floor sky bar (beer W8000) with a live band.

Ramada Plaza Jeju (☎ 729 8100; www.ramadajeju.co.kr; Tapdongno; r W200,000;) This brand-new hotel, with a casino and conference centre, makes the most of its absolute seafront location with an overall nautical design that gives guests the illusion that they're at sea on a luxury liner. The atrium lobby has 'wow' factor, and the usual corridors have been replaced with open balconies. Rooms have floor-to-ceiling windows, staff go the extra mile, and the only negative is the small toilet cubicles. Prices rise at weekends and rooms with sea views cost more, but breakfast is included.

Eating

E-Mart Food Court (Tapdongno; meals W2500-6000; 10am-9pm) The food court on the 5th floor has sea views and a smorgasbord of cheap eats but is on the tatty side. Hidden away at the far end of the basement supermarket is a great takeaway section – sushi, kebabs, spare ribs, chicken and raw-fish platters (hung·eo, raw ray) are W12,000.

El Paso (meals W5000-10,000; off Jung-angno; noon-1am) This new (you guessed it) Mexican restaurant, decorated with quality Mexican artworks, has a chef who learnt his trade in Mexico City. All your faves are here along with soft music, Mexican beers and of course tequila.

Kkwong Memil Guksu (Seogwangno) A tiny five-table eatery near the bus terminal, it has one staff member and two items on the menu: the kkwong-gui (꿩구이; W15,000) is simple and highly recommended – half a pheasant is grilled at your table. Order rice to go with it as the side dishes are nothing to write home about. The other option is kkwong memil guksu (꿩메밀국수; W4000) – pheasant pieces share a soup with homemade noodles wide enough to drive along.

Bagdad Café (meals W9000-11,000; 11am-2am;) With a Nepalese chef, this new Indian restaurant-café-bar, named after the film not the city, has music, stylish English-speaking staff and an outside terrace. It has more character and atmosphere than all the city's other restaurants put together. The curries, naan bread and mango lassi taste authentic, and weekends can be busy with a mixed crowd of Koreans and homesick Brits. Beers are W5000.

Jeil Hyangto Eumsik (Tapdongno; meals from W10,000; 11am-11pm) Jeil Hyangto Eumsik even has an English menu, which includes raw-fish platters (W30,000 to W60,000), with local okdom fish priced at W100,000 raw or W20,000 grilled. Grilled abalone is W30,000 while abalone rice porridge is W10,000.

Opposite E-Mart on the seafront are fish and seafood restaurants with prices and replicas of the food on show outside.

Other recommendations include:

Bonjuk (Jung-angno; meals W5000-8000) Enjoy one of the 16 flavours of rice porridge in this neat and clean chain restaurant on the high street.

Daebokseong (meals W7000-12,000) Sit at the counter, at a table or in your own private room and enjoy Japanese-style sushi, sea-bream soup or abalone rice porridge.

I Want Pizza (Samnyeong 1-ro; pizzas W7900-10,000; 11am-11pm) Sit inside among the mountains of pizza boxes for a reasonably priced 13-inch pizza at this takeaway near the bus terminal.

Taphyang Samgyetang (meals W7000-15,000) A popular place near the seafront for samgyetang (삼계탕; ginseng chicken) or duck dishes served as a soup or dry with vegetables.

Jeongdaun (meals W7000-25,000; 24hr) With views over the sea, this 2nd-floor restaurant serves up fresh fish and hoedeopbap (회덮밥; vegetables, rice and raw fish).

Drinking

Cheongsong Eoreum Makgeolli (Jung-angno; meals W4000-8000; 5pm-5am;) Don't leave without popping into this traditional 'makgeolli and mackerel' pub restaurant near the seafront that offers a wide choice of wholesome grub plus beers and kettles of makgeolli (fermented rice wine; W3000). Join the locals (children welcome) for traditional food and good cheer in a friendly atmosphere. Ask for the English menu.

White Beach Hotel Bar (beers/cocktails W3000/6000; 2pm-2am) Enjoy a wonderful sea view from a modernist glass box atop this seafront hotel. On a fine day the outside terrace, decorated with flower boxes, is the perfect spot for a date or a sundowner.

Entertainment

Juliana (Haksasaero; admission W35,000; 7pm-late) This nightspot in the student entertainment zone opposite City Hall operates on the Korean system and the high admission price buys three beers and *anju* (snacks). The music is mixed but mainly hip-hop. Extra beers are W4000.

Academy Cinema (admission W7000) Like all Korean cinemas, Academy screens foreign films in their original language, subtitled in *Han·geul*.

Shopping

The city's three prime shopping zones are Dongmun market, which spreads bustling and cheerful retail therapy over a large area in the city's heartland, nearby Jungang underground shopping centre, and the Chiseongno shopping precinct with its youthful fashion stores and brand-name boutiques stocked with clothes, accessories and cosmetics.

E-Mart (Tapdongno) Has a souvenir section near the lift exit on the 4th floor, which stocks gift boxes of oranges and *harubang*-shaped jars of *omija* (berry) tea and cactus honey tea. Soaps are another option, but sample the chocolate before you buy. Another souvenir is *dojang*, Korean name seals, which take 10 minutes to make and cost W6000. For eating options at E-Mart see opposite.

Getting Around

There are streams of city buses, most of which can be picked up outside the bus terminal or along Jung·angno, and taxis are cheap and convenient.

EASTERN JEJUDO

Samyang Beach 삼양해수욕장

The first beach along the coast road east of Jeju-si is Samyang, which has the darkest sand on the island and is jet black when wet. In the summer, join the locals and bury yourself in the iron-rich sand for a therapeutic sand bath, said to relieve dermatitis, arthritis and athlete's foot.

Take the Seongsan Ilchulbong bus (W1000, 25 minutes, every 20 minutes) or else several local buses, such as bus 26, go there too.

Gimnyeong Beach & Sailing Club
김녕해수욕장, 김녕세이링클럽

The white sand of Gimnyeong beach contrasts with the black-lava rocks at this small beach where the **Emerald Pension Castle** (에메랄드펜션개슬; ☎ 782 1110; r W50,000-80,000), five steps from the beach, has super sea views. Emerald room is lovely and worth every won.

West of the beach is a small harbour and the **Gimnyeong Sailing Club** (☎ 011-639 5379), where English-speaking Mr Kim can sort you out some sailing in a dinghy or cruiser. Check the prices and telephone before turning up. Just take the boat out, or lessons can be arranged. The harbour is a perfect spot for novices to learn and Jeju is famous for its wind – you can see wind turbines spinning round nearby.

Take the Seongsan Ilchulbong bus from Jeju-si bus terminal to Gimnyeong (W1000, 50 minutes, every 20 minutes) or else a number of local buses go there.

Sangumburi 산굼부리

Halfway between Jeju-si and Seong·eup Folk Village, this impressive green **volcanic crater** (☎ 783 9900; adult/youth & child W3000/1000; 9am-6pm) is 350m in diameter and 100m deep, a perfect spot for a bungy jump. It's just one of the 360 'parasitic cones' (secondary volcanoes) found on Jejudo, but has the easiest access, a five minute walk. Another five-minute walk goes a short way around the crater rim. That's all that's allowed so it's a short stop. The crater is lush and forested with over 420 varieties of plants. In the distance, across the plains, are more of Jejudo's volcanic humps. Some buses (W1800, 30 minutes, hourly) that run between Jeju-si bus terminal and Seong·eup and Pyoseon stop at the entrance to the crater – look out for ivy-covered walls.

Manjanggul 만장굴

East of Jeju-si and about 2.5km off the coast road is the world's longest system of **lava-tube caves** (☎ 783 4818; adult/youth & child W2000/1000; 9am-6pm Mar-Oct, 9am-5pm Nov-Feb). The caves are 13.4km long, with a height varying from 2m to 30m and a width of 2m to 23m. If you've never been inside a lava tube before, don't miss this chance. Venturing inside the immense black tunnel with its swirling walls and pitted floor, it looks like the lair of a giant serpent and it's hard to imagine the titanic geological forces that created it aeons ago, moulding rock as if it was Play-Doh.

Take a jacket, as the cave ceiling drips and the temperature inside is a chilly 10°C. The lighting is dim so a torch is a good idea. You can walk for 1km along the black tube to a 7m lava pillar, the cave's outstanding feature. The walk takes 30 minutes as the floor is pitted and full of puddles.

Lunch at **Daesikdang** (대식당; meals W5000-12,000; ☷ 8am-6.30pm) where the local fish speciality, *okdom* (옥돔), comes with rice and good side dishes. For a light lunch, two people can share one *okdom*. It's on the 2nd floor of the tourist complex with an outside balcony.

A 20-minute walk back down the access road is **Gimnyeongsagul** (김녕사굴, Snake Cave), which is officially closed, but just follow the sign to walk through the first double-decker lava-tube cave and on to the even larger second lava cave, which you can venture down if you have a torch.

On the other side of the road, on the right by the shop, is another lava-tube cave with an unusual lava-platform feature.

GETTING THERE & AWAY

Take the Seongsan Ilchulbong bus (W1900, one hour, every 20 minutes) from Jeju-si bus terminal, which leaves from platform 4. It drops you on the main road, 2.5km from Manjanggul, but the 35-minute walk down the access road is lined with oleander trees and goes past fields bordered by dry-stone walls, woodland inhabited by pheasants, lava-tube caves and an excellent maze (see below). A bus (W850, five minutes, 11 daily) runs along the road but the service is usually irregular.

Gimnyeong Maze 김녕미로공원

A 10-minute walk from Manjanggul is this popular **hedge maze** (☎ 782 9266; adult/youth/child W3300/1650/550; ☷ 8.30am-7pm Mar-Oct, 8.30am-6pm Nov-Feb), which is as much fun for adults as for children. It's fiendishly clever and a real challenge. Owner Fred Dunstin is often around if you enjoy a good yarn.

Woljeong Beach 월정해수욕장

This small, white, sandy beach is so little known that it's not on most maps. Stay here for an off-the-beaten-track experience where you can even spot dotterels on the beach. **Miworld Pension** (미월드펜션; ☎ 7847447; r W60,000-120,000) has smart rooms with kitchens and balconies, though bathrooms are cramped. Take

the Seongsan Ilchulbong bus from Jeju-si bus terminal, get off at the Manjanggul stop, and walk down the road to the beach (500m).

Seongsan Ilchulbong 성산 일출봉

Seongsan-ri (Fortress Mountain Village) is at the extreme eastern tip of Jejudo, at the foot of the spectacular, extinct volcano **Ilchulbong** (Sunrise Peak; ☎ 784 0959; adult/youth & child W2000/1000; ☷ before sunrise-sunset). The summit (182m) is shaped like a punchbowl, though there's no crater lake here because the volcanic rock is so porous. The crater is a forested Lost World ringed by jagged rocks and the sides of the mountain plunge vertically into the surf. It is one of Jejudo's most impressive sights.

Climbing to the summit only takes 20 minutes and doing it in time to catch the sunrise is a life-affirming journey for many Koreans – expect plenty of company on the trail. To do the sunrise expedition, you'll have to spend the night in Seongsan-ri. The path is clear, but if you're concerned you can carry a torch. Not an early riser? It's also a popular daytime hike.

Over to the left, small **speedboats** (per trip W10,000) can whisk you out to sea for another perspective on Ilchulbong.

On Seongsanpo seafront you can see **haenyeo**, Jejudo's famous female divers (p284). A group of *haenyeo*, middle-aged or older, goes out on a boat every morning to dive for seafood and seaweed. Please don't take photographs without their permission.

Mr Park at **Sea Life Scuba** (제주성산포 해양스쿠버리조트; ☎ 782 1150; Seongsanpo; ☷ 7am-6pm) speaks some English and can take you diving inside underwater caves and around coral reefs. A day trip with two dives costs US$200, including a guide and all equipment.

SLEEPING

Accommodation usually includes fully equipped kitchenettes and varies from W15,000 for a *yo* mattress in a tiny cell with shared facilities to stylish and spacious rooms with superb views for up to W40,000.

Yonggung Minbak (용궁민박; ☎ 782 2379; r W25,000; ☒) This redbrick *minbak* offers the best deal with great in-your-face Ilchulbong views and a varied collection of sizable and comfortable rooms. It's on the left on the way from the bus stop to the Ilchulbong ticket office access road.

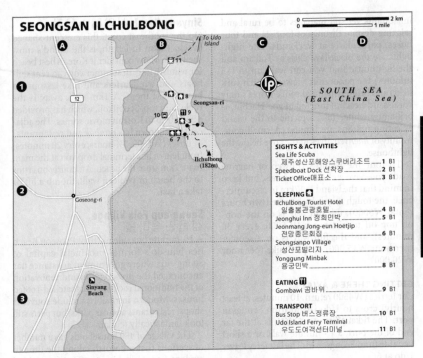

SEONGSAN ILCHULBONG

SOUTH SEA
(East China Sea)

SIGHTS & ACTIVITIES
Sea Life Scuba
제주성산포해양스쿠버리조트 **1** B1
Speedboat Dock 선착장 **2** B1
Ticket Office매표소 **3** B1

SLEEPING
Ilchulbong Tourist Hotel
일출봉관광호텔 **4** B1
Jeonghui Inn 정희민박 **5** B1
Jeonmang Jong-eun Hoetjip
전망종은회집 **6** B1
Seongsanpo Village
성산포빌리지 **7** B1
Yonggung Minbak
용궁민박 **8** B1

EATING
Gombawi 곰바위 **9** B1

TRANSPORT
Bus Stop 버스정류장 **10** B1
Udo Island Ferry Terminal
우도도여객센터미널 **11** B1

JEJUDO

Jeonghui Inn (정희민박; ☎ 782 2169; r W30,000; ✗) Large rooms here – opposite Gombawi restaurant and near Ilchulbong ticket office – have no views, but there is room enough for a soccer team to sleep on the floor on *yo* mattresses.

Jeonmang Jong-eun Hoetjip (전망종은횟집; ☎ 784 1568; r W30,000-40,000; ✗) Above a fish restaurant on Seongsanpo seafront, room 202 is the best, enhanced by a wonderful sea view. Look for the castle-shaped building with pebbles.

Ilchulbong Tourist Hotel (일출봉관광호텔; ☎ 782 8801; r W39,000; ✗) The red-and-white hotel at the entrance to Seongsan-ri is nothing special and lacks atmosphere, but the rooms (although not the bathrooms) have been recently renovated and have Ilchulbong views. It's a good standby if the better places are full.

Seongsanpo Village (성산포빌리지; ☎ 782 2373; r W40,000; ✗ 💻) Sit out on a balcony with a wonderful view of the sea and anything going on along the harbour. The rooms are almost as good as the view and have computers. Look for a large red-and-green building, 100m along the Seongsanpo seafront.

EATING

Most restaurants specialise in raw fish and hot-pepper soups but grilled fish, *galchi gui*, *okdom gui* (grilled, semi-dried fish) and *jeon-bok-juk* (abalone rice porridge) are also available. The latter is a local speciality, though you don't get much abalone for your W10,000.

Gombawi (곰바위; meals W5000-25,000; ✗ 7am-4pm) The best view and the best food are here, on the 2nd floor above LG 45 convenience store on the access road to Ilchulbong. Try the local speciality, pheasant and buckwheat noodle hotpot (W10,000) or the tofu casserole (W5000). It has an English menu but is not open for dinner.

GETTING THERE & AWAY

Buses (W3800, 1½ hours, every 20 minutes) run to Seongsan-ri from Jeju-si bus terminal. Make sure that the bus goes right into Seongsan-ri as a few stick to the main road and drop you 2.5km from Seongsan-ri.

Udo Island 우도

Northeast of Seongsan-ri, 3.5km off the coast, is Udo Island (Cow Island), which has 1750 inhabitants yet still manages to be rural and relaxing despite throngs of tourists and tour buses, particularly at weekends. The highlights are the black-lava cliffs at Tolkani and the lighthouse that you can walk up to (15 minutes) for panoramic views of patchwork fields and brightly painted roofs. Korea's only coral-sand beach, Hongjodan-goe Haebin, is brilliantly white. Take a picnic to the island as eating options are limited. A small community of *haenyeo* dives in the cove below the lighthouse.

To tour the island's cobweb of narrow roads you have a choice of wheels, but keep in mind that the island is 17km in circumference: the tough way is by bicycle (two hours rental W5000), the soft way is on the hop-on hop-off tourist buses (W5000, every 30 minutes), and the fun way is on a scooter (per hour W15,000) or quad bike (per hour W20,000).

GETTING THERE & AWAY

Car ferries (W4500 return, 10 minutes, at least hourly) cross to Udo island from Seongsan port. The **ticket office** (☎ 782 5671) is at the far end of the port, a 15-minute walk or a short taxi ride from Seongsan-ri. The last ferry leaves Udo at 6pm.

Sinyang Beach 신양해수욕장

On the southeast coast, this crescent-shaped beach, 1.5km in length, is the island's most sheltered. Many consider it Korea's best beach for windsurfing; in summer you can rent sailboats and windsurfers and take lessons on how to use them. A 1km walk away is the rocky outcrop, Seopjikoji, which has provided a backdrop to Korean movie scenes. The adjacent small town has *minbak* and restaurants.

Buses (W3800, 1¾ hours, every 20 minutes) from Jeju-si bus terminal drop you at the main road, 2km from the beach. An hourly bus runs to the beach or you can walk, thumb a lift or take a taxi.

Seong-eup Folk Village
성읍민속마을

A 10-minute bus ride north of Pyoseon Beach lies Jeju-do's former provincial capital of Seong-eup, where government assistance has encouraged the preservation and renovation of the traditional rock-walled, thatched-roofed houses. Modern intrusions include souvenir shops, restaurants and car parks, but parts still look fantastically feudal.

The village of 480 households has a number of sections that are worth taking the time to explore. Some inhabitants offer a free guided

---

HAENYEO

At 9am on Seongsan-ri harbour, 30 or so wrinkled grandmas are pulling on wetsuits, diving masks, weight belts and gloves, prior to a boat ride out to sea where they will use their low-tech gear – polystyrene floats, flippers, nets, knives and spears – to gather seaweed, shellfish, sea cucumbers, spiky black sea urchins, octopus and anything else edible that they can catch. Great physical stamina is a prerequisite. They use no oxygen tanks, but are able to hold their breath underwater for up to two minutes and reach a depth of 20m.

The women divers look so old and bent that it's amazing that they continue to dive for hours on end every day and in all weathers. They work as a cooperative and share their catch. They shout at each other because most wear earplugs and are probably a bit deaf as well.

Watching them getting organised on the harbour front, you can only marvel at their toughness and communal spirit. They are a special breed – instead of staying home with their feet up in front of the telly, they are out at sea every day braving the elements.

Haenyeo have been free-diving for generations not only in the waters around Jejudo but further afield off the coasts of Japan and China. Sadly they will be the last generation of divers because their daughters have not followed in their mothers' slipstream – instead they have much easier jobs in shops, offices or the tourism industry.

At their peak in the 1950s, there were almost 30,000 *haenyeo* on Jejudo but now fewer than 3000 are left and some are in their mid-60s.

My Mother the Mermaid is a memorable Korean movie about a feisty, overbearing mother and her daughter, which is intercut with flashbacks to when the mother was a shy young *haenyeo* on Jejudo and courting the local postman. The daughter and the mother-as-a-young-girl are played by the same talented actress.

tour of their compound, but afterwards they want you to buy local products such as black *omija* tea (W25,000 per kilogram) or paper-thin dried fish called *myeongtae,* both of which are delicious.

Just take off down the narrow lanes and discover the place for yourself. Remember the houses are still occupied, but if the gate poles are down (see below) you are welcome to enter.

Buses (W2300, 45 minutes, every 20 minutes) leave from Jeju-si bus terminal and from Pyoseon or Jeju Folk Village (W850, 10 minutes, every 20 minutes).

ACTIVITIES

Along the road north of Seong·eup Folk Village and before the turning to Sangumburi Crater are ATV tracks, go-kart racing courses and horse riding (a steep W80,000 an hour). A bus runs along the road every 20 minutes.

Jeju Folk Village 제주민속촌

Just outside Pyoseon and close to the town's extensive beach, **Jeju Folk Village** (☎ 787 4501; www.jejufolk.com; adult/youth/child W6000/4000/2000; ⏱ 8.30am-6pm) is more re-creation than preservation, but in its way is more educational than Seong·eup Folk Village. Various sections cover Jejudo's culture from shamans to *yangban* (aristocrats), and the differences between mountain, hill-country and fishing villages. Some of the buildings are *hanok* (traditional Korean houses) brought intact from other parts of the island and are 200 to 300 years old; the modern construction has been done in authentically traditional style.

The folk village has its own flora and fauna, country-style restaurants and traditional song and dance performances. The English-

---

GATE POLE MESSAGES

Jejudo has traditionally described itself as having lots of rocks and wind, but no beggars or thieves. In Jejudo's folk villages, instead of locked gates in front of homes you'll often see two stone pillars with a column of three holes carved through each. Three wooden poles straight across means 'We're not home, please keep out'. However if one end of the poles is in their holes but the other ends are on the ground, it means 'We're home, please enter'.

---

language audio guide (W2000) is worth the investment.

Direct buses (W3600, one hour, every 20 minutes) run to the entrance gate from Jeju-si bus terminal. Otherwise the folk village is a 1km walk from the bus stop in Pyoseon-ri.

Pyoseon Beach 표선해수욕장

At low tide a huge expanse of white sandy beach appears that stretches as far as the eye can see, and in the middle a lagoon forms. If you like plenty of space, this is the beach to visit. Behind is a small town with all facilities.

Buses run here from Jeju-si via the 97 road cross-island route (W3400, one hour, every 20 minutes) or via the east coast road (W5100, two hours, every 20 minutes).

Namwon 남원

Just 100m along the coast road west of Shinyoung Cinema Museum, turn right at the hamburger sign, then left at another sign to reach the two-storey wood cabin that is **Red Pond Herb Farm** (붉은못허브팜; hamburgers W15,000; ⏱ 10am-9pm; 🖳). The English-speaking staff sells unique hamburgers the size of Frisbees – enough for four people or you can take away what you cannot eat. In a giant herbal bun packed with salad and even apple is a thin patty made from Jeju black-pig pork or else soy bean for a vegetarian option. Free herb tea is included.

SOUTHERN JEJUDO
Seogwipo 서귀포
pop 84,300

Amid the tangerine groves on the lower slopes of Hallasan sits touristy Seogwipo, Jejudo's second-largest town. It's much smaller and more laid-back than Jeju-si, and scuba diving and ballooning are available. The town centre (up a steep slope from the harbour) is chock-full of motels and hotels. A short distance away are two spring-fed waterfalls – this is one of the few places on the island where water is not immediately absorbed into the porous volcanic rock.

INFORMATION
KB Star Bank (Jung-angno) Foreign exchange only.
Post office (Jung-angno) Free internet access.
SC First Bank (Standard Chartered; Jung-angno) Foreign exchange and global ATM.
Tourist information centre (☎ 064-1330; ⏱ 9am-10pm) Free internet access.

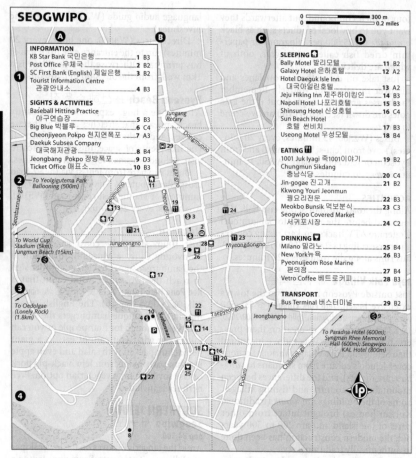

SEOGWIPO

0 ——— 300 m
0 ——— 0.2 miles

INFORMATION
KB Star Bank 국민은행 **1** B3
Post Office 우체국 **2** B2
SC First Bank (English) 제일은행 **3** B2
Tourist Information Centre
관광안내소 **4** B3

SIGHTS & ACTIVITIES
Baseball Hitting Practice
야구연습장 **5** B3
Big Blue 빅블루 **6** C4
Cheonjiyeon Pokpo 천지연폭포 **7** A3
Daekuk Subsea Company
대국해저관광 **8** B4
Jeongbang Pokpo 정방폭포 **9** D3
Ticket Office 매표소 **10** B3

SLEEPING
Bally Motel 발리모텔 **11** B2
Galaxy Hotel 은하호텔 **12** A2
Hotel Daeguk Isle Inn
대국아일호텔 **13** A2
Jeju Hiking Inn 제주하이킹인 **14** B3
Napoli Hotel 나포리호텔 **15** B3
Shinsung Hotel 신성호텔 **16** C4
Sun Beach Hotel
호텔 썬비치 **17** B3
Useong Motel 우성모텔 **18** B4

EATING
1001 Juk Iyagi 죽1001이야기 **19** B2
Chungmun Sikdang
충남식당 **20** C4
Jin-gogae 진고개 **21** B2
Kkwong Youri Jeonmun
꿩요리전문 **22** B3
Meokbo Bunsik 먹보분식 **23** C3
Seogwipo Covered Market
서귀포시장 **24** C2

DRINKING
Milano 밀라노 **25** B4
New York뉴욕 **26** B3
Pyeonuijeom Rose Marine
편의점 **27** B4
Vetro Coffee 베트로커피 **28** B3

TRANSPORT
Bus Terminal 버스터미널 **29** B2

SIGHTS & ACTIVITIES
Waterfalls
The 22m-high **Cheonjiyeon Pokpo** (천지연폭포;
☎ 733 1528; adult/youth/child W2000/1000/600; 7am-
10pm), west of Seogwipo, is a 15-minute walk
via a path through a beautifully forested, steep
gorge. After heavy rain the waterfall can be
impressive, but at other times it's more noisy
than wide.

Jeongbang Pokpo (정방폭포; ☎ 733 1530;
adult/youth/child W2000/1000/600; 7.30am-6.30pm
Mar-Oct, 7.30am-5.30pm Nov-Feb) is 23m high and
up to 8m wide, depending on the levels of
recent rainfall. It's said to be the only waterfall in Asia that falls directly into the sea.
Jeongbang Pokpo is a 15-minute walk east of
the town centre.

Submarine & Sightseeing Boat Tours
잠수함, 유람
Daekuk Subsea Company (☎ 732 6060; submarine
tours adult/youth/child W51,000/40,600/30,200, sightseeing
boat tours adult/child W16,500/11,000) operates well-
established and popular 30-minute submarine tours down to a depth of 30m around
Munseom island, which has coral and fish
dressed up in carnival colours. Tours run at
least hourly and reservations are advised.

The same company also runs sightseeing
boat tours around the port and nearby islands,
which last an hour.

Oedolgae (Lonely Rock) 외돌개
About 2km west of Seogwipo, the 20m-tall
volcanic basalt pillar called **Oedolgae** (Lonely

Rock) juts out of the ocean. Like other unusual-shaped rocks there's a legend associated with it – a Korean general is said to have scared away Mongolian invaders by dressing the rock up to look like a giant soldier. Oedolgae is a pleasant walk through pine forests to a beautiful cliffside lookout.

Bus 200 or 300 (both W850, five minutes, eight daily) run to Oedolgae or else it's an easy and pleasant 30-minute walk from town.

Syngman Rhee Memorial Hall
이승만기념관
This small private **museum** (☎ 763 2100; adult/youth/child W2000/1500/1000; ☷ 10am-7pm May-Oct, 10am-6pm Nov-Apr) has lots of English descriptions and is dedicated to South Korea's first president, Syngman Rhee (1875–1965). Jailed by King Gojong for his political activities, later he became an independence leader and the Japanese colonial government put a price of W300,000 on his head. He was South Korea's president during the Korean War and up to 1960, when he fled with his Austrian wife to Hawaii after widespread public demonstrations against his rule.

Scuba Diving 스쿠버다이빙
Diving off Seogwipo is surprisingly good with walls of very colourful soft coral, 18m-high kelp forests (March to May), schools of fish and the occasional inquisitive dolphin. Diving here always surprises first-timers because it's a mixture of the tropical and temperate – rather like diving in Norway and the Red Sea at the same time! Visibility is best from September to November but is around 10m at other times, and water temperature varies from 15°C to 27°C.

A recommended dive operator is **Big Blue** (☎ 733 1733; www.bigblue33.co.kr; ☷ 9am-7pm), run by English-speaking Ralph Deutsch, a genuine diving enthusiast. A day's diving (two dives) costs W105,000 with all equipment and a guide. Diving is from a boat and the maximum group size is eight persons. A five-day NAUI certificate course costs W480,000.

Ballooning 열기구테마파크
Rise gently into the air with **Yeolgigutema Park Ballooning** (☎ 732 0300; Dong-iljudoro; adult/youth/child W25,000/18,000/10,000; ☷ 9am-6.30pm). Although the balloon stays tethered to the ground, it doesn't operate when Jejudo's notorious wind is blowing.

The balloon site is not on a bus route, so take a taxi (W2000) or walk (15 minutes from Jung·ang Rotary).

Baseball 야구
At **Baseball Hitting Practice** (Jung·angno; per 10 pitches W500) pick up a baseball bat, put a coin in the box and the robot pitches 18 balls in quick succession.

World Cup Stadium 월드컵주경기장
The graceful **soccer stadium**, 6km west of Seogwipo, is the centrepiece of a cluster of buildings that includes a cinema multiplex, an E-Mart discount store, a water park, an Eros museum and Seogwipo's new bus terminal.

SLEEPING
The town has hundreds of motels and hotels, so visitors are spoilt for choice.

Budget
Jeju Hiking Inn (☎ 763 2380; www.hikinginn.com; r W20,000; ☐) Kevin speaks English and runs Seogwipo's best W20,000 budget option. Smart computers are free for guests, cyclists can keep their bikes in the lobby bicycle rack, and you can buy fresh fish or seafood in the covered market and cook it in the communal kitchen.

Bally Motel (☎ 732 8881; Cheonji 3-ro; r W30,000; ☒) The most modern and best motel is in the northern part of town and has a metallic, modernist facade and spacious, high-quality rooms, with a style that is more busness hotel than love motel. Check that your room window has mosquito netting and a hairdryer. Drawback: the receptionist is often absent and you may have to telephone.

Other recommendations:
Galaxy Hotel (☎ 733 6678; r W25,000; ☒) This motel is well kept, has friendly staff and the upper rooms are light and airy.
Useong Motel (☎ 732 5700; r W30,000; ☒) Simple but well-kept rooms are more cheerful and welcoming than others at this price, and the ones on the 4th floor (no lift), such as room 405, have sea views.
Napoli Hotel (☎ 733 4701; fax 733 4802; r W30,000; ☒) There's nothing Italian here, but the standard motel rooms are pleasant enough and some have sea views.

Midrange
Shinsung Hotel (☎ 732 1415; fax 732 1417; r W50,000; ☒ ☐) A classy new midcity motel with a hard-to-miss metal-and-chequerboard exterior. Rooms have a computer and Jacuzzi, but

don't try to use both at the same time. A room with a sea view costs W10,000 extra, even if it's too misty to see the sea.

Hotel Daeuk Isle Inn (☎ 763 0002; www.isleinn hotel.co.kr; r W73,000; ✗ ▢) Sorry to spoil the illusion, but the bright balcony flowers are not real, although they do add to the hotel's continental European feel and style. Although the rooms are nothing special, it is a real hotel with no hint of a love motel, and the lobby has email access.

Sun Beach Hotel (☎ 732 5678; Taepyeongno; r incl breakfast W80,000; ✗) A reasonable option if you're into retro and hanker for these mid-range tourist hotels that resemble a grand dame somewhat past her prime but still retaining an air of faded gentility.

Top End

Paradise Hotel (☎ 763 2100; www.paradisehoteljeju .co.kr; r from W210,000; ✗ ▢ ▣) Three cheers for a rare-as-hens'-teeth genuine boutique hotel with a dramatic adobe design, full of organic curves and African art. The five eclectic room styles all share the striking combo of barn doors and gold taps. Dream of lion safaris in the African rooms that have four-poster beds with mosquito netting. During the 2002 World Cup, Ronaldo slept in room 209, David Beckham in room 302 and Michael Owen in room 303. The extensive garden has superb coastal cliff views as well as a popular restaurant and bar.

Seogwipo KAL Hotel (☎ 733 2001; www.kalhotel.co.kr; r from W245,750; ✗ ▢ ▣) An overall design of muted colours and pastels pervades this calm and soothing luxury hotel that has a trout farm in the garden. Add W50,000 for ocean views and another 20% at weekends.

EATING

Fish restaurants cluster round the harbour, but food is not Seogwipo's strong point. Seogwipo Covered Market (Jungjeongno) has wonderful fruit and live seafood direct from local orchardists and fishermen.

Kkwong Yori Jeonmun (meals W3500-15,000; ☽ 11am-8.30pm) A modest eight-table Chinese restaurant with an English menu and four styles of 'gourmet' *jajangmyeon* (자장면; noodles including minced pork and seafood versions). *Kkwong* (꿩), the only pheasant dish on the menu, is a pile of battered pheasant, bones and all, meant for sharing, that costs W30,000.

1001 Juk Iyagi (Jung-angno; meals W5000-10,000; ☽ 9am-9.30pm) Big bowls of rice porridge with a choice of 20 almost-diced-to-death ingredients are offered in this squeaky clean chain restaurant. Mini side dishes plus tea or coffee are free.

Other recommendations:

Meokbo Bunsik (meals W1000-4000; ☽ 24hr) Just down the road opposite the covered market is this cheap diner with homemade *mandu* (만두; dumplings) steaming in big pots outside.

Chungmun Sikdang (meals W4000-10,000) A simple, clean restaurant with a good-deal *jeongsik* (정식; meal with lots of side dishes) or *sundubu* (순두부; soft tofu) for W4000.

Jingogae (meals W6000-17,000; ☽ 9am-10pm) If you want meat, head to this traditional restaurant for *galbi* (갈비; beef ribs) or Jejudo pork.

DRINKING

Vetro Coffee (Jungjeongno; drinks W2000-5000; ☽ 10am-11pm) Buy a cake from the bakery opposite and eat it with one of Vetro's special home-roasted coffees. Iced latte is popular.

Pyeonuijeom (Rose Marine; ☽ 10.30am-4am) This tumbledown shack is as quirky and informal a bar as you'll find anywhere on planet Korea – sit outside by the water or even in a wigwam. You want tuna stew? The staff will open a can and cook it up for you (meals W5000 to W8000).

Milano (밀라노; beers/cocktails W3000/5000; ☽ 7pm-4am) Sit inside on the red seats or outside near the barbecue (meals W6000 to W15,000) under the trees with harbour views.

New York (Myeongdongno; local beer/cocktails W3000/6000; ☽ 7pm-6am) This dark, classy bar has a long list of imported beers and attracts expats and their friends at the weekends. Meals are W10,000 to W13,000.

GETTING THERE & AROUND

From Jeju-si, buses (W7500, two hours 40 minutes, every 20 minutes) run along the east or west coast to Seogwipo, while buses on cross-island routes take half the time and cost half as much. The Seogwipo bus terminal is being moved 6km west to the World Cup Stadium, but frequent buses (W850, 10 minutes) will link the town with the new bus terminal.

Seogwipo is small enough to walk around its wooden pavements, but taxis are plentiful and cheap. Local buses can be picked up at Jungang Rotary.

HONEYMOON ISLAND

Jungmun, with its three luxury resorts, is a favourite haunt for Korean honeymooners, especially around May or June, although these days honeymooning abroad is becoming popular. Couples holding hands under the palm trees and wearing matching outfits are likely to be honeymooners, as are tandem-bike riders and couples putting food into each other's mouths. Locals say if you see a couple and neither of them is talking on a mobile phone, then they must be on honeymoon. Horse riding, regarded as an exotic and romantic activity, is popular with honeymooners, as is the Teddy Bear Museum. Thanks to digital and video cameras, almost every second of the honeymoon can now be recorded for posterity and usually is.

The island also attracts business and professional conferences, so your hotel might be swarming with Asian dentists or telecom execs from five continents. In spring, waves of high-school students spread over the island on school trips, excited to be in what is almost a foreign country.

Jungmun & Vicinity 중문

A 25-minute bus ride west of Seogwipo is the tourist town, luxury resorts and surprisingly unspoilt beach at Jungmun, surrounded by tourist attractions and activities.

SIGHTS & ACTIVITIES

Just before the Jungmun Beach access road off Hwy 12 is the legendary waterfall **Cheonjeyeon Pokpo** (천제연폭포; ☎ 738 1529; adult/youth/child W2500/1370/850; ☼ sunrise-sunset), a three-tier cascade tucked deep inside a forested gully. Above soars a footbridge with sculptures of the seven nymphs who served the Emperor of Heaven and who, it is said, used to slide down moonbeams to bathe here every night.

At the start of the access road to the resorts and beach is a huge, glass botanical garden, **Yeomiji** (여미지; ☎ 738 3828; www.yeomiji.or.kr; adult/youth/child W6000/4500/3000; ☼ 8.30am-5.30pm Mar-Sep, 8.30am-5pm Oct-Feb). Indoor sections mimic rainforests, deserts and other landscapes, while outdoor plantings and designs include Italian, Japanese, palm and herb gardens.

Overlooking Jungmun Beach is **Pacific Land** (퍼시픽랜드; ☎ 738 2888; adult/youth/child W12,000/10,000/8000; ☼ shows 11.30am, 1.30pm, 3pm & 4.30pm), an ageing complex that puts on animal shows featuring dolphins, sea lions and monkeys doing all sorts of tricks. The entertaining shows run four times a day. Camel rides in the car park add a surrealist touch.

The same company also runs **sailing cruises** (adult/child per hr W60,000/50,000) on a catamaran.

Business visitors may well find themselves at **Jeju International Convention Centre** (제주국제컨벤션센터), 600m east of Pacific Land, as Jejudo builds up its convention business. The building, completed in 2003, is a striking glass cylinder design with ocean views.

Just south of the Convention Centre is **Jusangjeolli Rocks** (주상절리), a dramatic 2km stretch of coastline, known for hexagonal rock columns that look as if they were stamped out with a cookie cutter. The formations are the result of the rapid cooling and contraction of lava (just what you'd expect to happen when molten lava pours into the sea).

Although the Buddhist temple **Yakcheonsa** (약천사; ☎ 738 5000; admission free; ☼ sunrise-sunset) was only constructed between 1987 and 1997, it is one of Jejudo's most impressive buildings. The four-storey main hall is filled with vibrant murals of scenes from Buddha's life and illustrations of his teachings. Climb the stairs to the 3rd floor, and you'll also see cases containing some 18,000 tiny Buddhist figurines. Flash photography is not permitted (time exposures are OK). Overnight temple stays are possible.

The temple is less than 1km east of the Convention Centre, and can be reached by local bus 100, 110, 120 or 130 (W850, 15 minutes) from Seogwipo.

Water Activities

Parasailing (☎ 739 3939), **jet-skiing** and **water-skiing** (☎ 738 5111; W20,000-40,000) operators are based between Pacific Land and the International Convention Centre, while **jetboats** (☎ 739 3939; W25,000) operate from an inlet east of the Convention Centre. **Sit-on kayaks** (per 2hr W15,000) can be hired on Jungmun Beach.

Jungmun Beach (중문해수욕장), a 500m stretch of golden sand with its jungly backdrop, only becomes crowded in summer when it's patrolled by lifeguards. Walk along the beach, up the steps to the Hyatt Regency Hotel, continue along the boardwalk and down the steps to reach an even more scenic beach: aquamarine water and golden sand backed by sheer black cliffs eroded into cylindrical shapes. It has a surprisingly Lost World feel, as if dinosaurs are about to appear along with a David Attenborough voiceover.

You may see surfers at Jungmun Beach but the waves are generally unexciting.

SLEEPING & EATING

Minbak, pension and restaurants are strung out along Hwy 12 near the 1km-long access road to Jungmun Beach, while luxury hotel resorts are down towards the beach.

Yeohang Donghwa Guesthouse (여행동화; ☎ 713 47779; dm/r W10,000/30,000; ✗ 🖵) This blue-and-white guesthouse is above a fish restaurant, set back from the main road and overlooking Yeomiji botanical glasshouse. The dorms are big (25 beds in the men's dorm, 15 in the women's) but the accommodation is brand new with a youthful vibe. Upstairs, wood-panelled rooms are very attractive and some have kitchenettes.

Gold Beach Minbak (골드비치민박; ☎ 738 7511; r W50,000; ✗) Smart wood-panelled rooms with balconies and kitchenettes can be found here. Room 305 is one of the best. Look for a peach-and-green building above a restaurant, 200m east of the Jungmun Beach access road.

Hyatt Regency Jeju (☎ 733 1234; www.hyattcheju .com; r from W170,000; ✗ 🖵 🖲) This white, bee-hive-shaped edifice around a soaring atrium sports a beautiful spa/fitness facility, It's the closest resort to the beach and offers the best sea views. Stylish rooms have a computer, and Sunday brunch (11.30am to 2pm) is accompanied by live jazz.

Shilla Jeju (☎ 738 4466; www.shilla.net; r weekday/ weekend with breakfast from W200,000/300,000; ✗ 🖵 🖲) If Lotte (below) is brash Las Vegas, Shilla drips designer cool with muted colours, modernist artworks and an understated Zen décor beneath a Spanish-style, red-tile roof.

Lotte Hotel Jeju (☎ 738 7301; r from W300,000; ✗ 🖵 🖲) This palatial resort brings Las Vegas to Jejudo with an over-the-top fantasy garden containing windmills, a boating lake and a swimming pool. A nightly Las Vegas outdoor show involves music, lights, fountains, volcanoes and dragons. It's the most glitzy hotel and has a foreigner-only casino.

GETTING THERE & AWAY

Buses (W1100, 20 minutes, every 20 minutes) leave Seogwipo bus terminal for Jungmun,

dropping you at the Jungmun Beach access road, 1km from the beach. Local buses such as bus 100 also run to Jungmun.

Sanbanggulsa & Yongmeori Coast 산방굴사, 용머리해안

A steep, 10-minute walk up the south-facing side of the dramatic and craggy **Sanbangsan** (395m) is a simple stone Buddha in a cave known as **Sanbanggulsa** (☎ 794 2940; adult/youth/ child W2500/1500/free; ✆ 8.30am-7pm). This atmospheric cave has been a sacred site since Goryeo times, and the water flowing from the ceiling is said to be magically curative.

Lower down, by the ticket office, are other shrines and statues of more recent origin.

Across the road, a footpath leads downhill to the spectacular **Yongmeori coast**, an oceanside promenade of soaring cliffs, heavily pockmarked by erosion into catacombs, narrow clefts and natural archways. It's a *National Geographic* opportunity for photographers. Note that the walk along the Yongmeori cliffs closes during very high seas.

At the promenade exit is a replica of the **Sperwer**, a Dutch merchant ship that was wrecked here long ago in August 1653. A sailor on board, Hendrick Hamel (1630–92), survived the shipwreck but was forced to stay in Korea for 13 years before managing to escape in a boat to Japan: he wrote the first book on Korea by a Westerner (p272). You can look over the boat and learn about Hamel's adventures.

The entry ticket to Sanbanggulsa includes entry to the Yongmeori coast and Hamel's ship. Hwasun Beach is only 1km away but is marred by the power station at one end.

Buses (W2300, 45 minutes, every 40 minutes) leave from Seogwipo bus terminal for Sanbangsan. Make sure the bus is going all the way there as not all the west coast buses do.

Jeju Art Park 제주조각공원

Get off at the stop before Sanbangsan for this **art park** (☎ 794 9680; adult/youth/child W4500/3500/2500; ✆ 8.30am-8pm Apr-Oct, 8.30am-5.30pm Nov-Mar) that features over 180 modern sculptures in a garden setting. All genres are represented so you should find some that say something.

Marado & Gapado 마라도, 가파도

These two islets, both flat as pizzas with black rocky crusts, lie off Jejudo's southwest tip. Marado is Land's End, the most southerly point of Korea, and is so windswept that there are virtually no trees. Around 20 families live there and they have to collect their own water. It has an isolated, wild mood despite the tourists and only takes 30 minutes to walk around. Gapado, the nearer and larger of the two, is more ordinary and attracts fewer visitors.

Buses (W2700, one hour, every 20 minutes) leave Seogwipo bus terminal for Moseulpo, the port from which ferries service the islands. Get off the bus at the Hamo-ri stop, walk back up the road, turn right at the crossroads, then take the second right at the next intersection, and the ferry ticket office is at the far end of the port, next to the police box. It's a 15-minute walk from Hamo-ri bus stop.

From Moseulpo, **ferries** (☎ 792 1441; adult/child return W10,000/6000; 30 minutes) run to Marado daily at 10am, 11.30am and 2pm, with a 3.30pm sailing on weekends. Ferries (adult/child return W8000/4000, 15 minutes) also run daily to Gapado at 8.30am and 2pm.

O'Sulloc Tea Museum
오설록차박물관

On the rolling, 52-hectare plantation of Sulloc, one of Korea's largest growers of *nokcha* (green tea), the teacup-shaped **museum** (☎ 794 5312; admission free; ⏲ 10am-5pm) has swell views of tea fields and a rather on-the-nose video about tea. There is a great collection of ancient tea implements, some of which date back to the 3rd century. Visitors are welcome to stroll the fields, and in the shop you can enjoy green tea, a slice of green-tea cake and green-tea ice cream. Unfortunately no buses pass by.

WESTERN JEJUDO
Bunjae Artpia 분재예술원

Bunjae (bonsai) trees may seem esoteric, but this **bonsai park** (☎ 772 3701; adult/youth/child W7000/5000/4000; ⏲ 8am-6.30pm, 8am-10pm late Jul–mid-Aug) has some excellent examples. It's the life's work of Mr Sung Bum-young, who opened the park in 1992 and has never looked back. The park has hosted dignitaries from all over the world.

Mr Sung has filled the park with hundreds of dwarf trees – the oldest is some 500 years old. Signs translated into English espouse his personal philosophy. A quick walk through can take 20 minutes, but why not put yourself in a Zen mood and contemplate nature in miniature along with the rocks and water? Some visitors make the most of the experi-

---

> ### MARADO'S ORIGINAL INHABITANTS?
>
> The first settlers on remote Marado arrived in 1883, apparently to escape from gambling debts. This was considered a desperate move as the island was believed to be haunted by ghosts. However the skilful flute-playing of one Mr Kim is said to have driven the island's original inhabitants away.

---

ence, spending up to 1½ hours here. No buses pass by.

Jeju Racetrack 제주경마장

Enjoy a weekend afternoon at the races at the popular **Jeju Racetrack** (☎ 741 9412; admission W800; ⏲ 12.30-5.35pm Sat & Sun Sep-Jun, 4.20-9.10pm Sat & Sun Jul & Aug), 15km from Jeju-si. The facilities are first class and foreigners have their own lounge with executive chairs on the 3rd floor of the brand-new Happy Ville grandstand. What is unique is that all the horses are local *jorangmal*, Jeju horses descended from the ones brought over by invading Mongols centuries ago.

Cross-island (road 95) buses (W1300, 30 minutes, every 20 minutes) between Seogwipo and Jeju-si stop outside the racetrack. A taxi from Jeju-si costs W10,000.

Acrobat Shows

There are three shows along the cross-island 95 road, all of which are worth seeing.

Green Resort (제주그린리조트; ☎ 792 6102; admission W12,000; ⏲ shows 10.30am, 2.30pm, 4.30pm & 5.40pm) hosts hour-long shows that combine Chinese acrobatics (tumbling, bicycle tricks, plate spinning) and Mongolian acrobatics on horseback (handstands on a horse at full gallop). Some of the tricks are amazing in this traditional-style show but the music and announcers are overloud.

Smarter and more high-tech is the circus at **Happy Town** (해피타운; ☎ 794 4444; adult/child W15,000/8000; ⏲ shows 10.30am, 2pm, 3.30pm & 5pm) that stars contortionists, motorbike stunt riders and unbelievable acrobats who perform in midair and on the ground.

Stunning aerial acrobatics plus motorbike tricks are the show highlights at **Jeju Magic World** (제주매직월드; ☎ 746 9005; www.jejumw .co.kr; adult/youth/child W15,000/10,000/7000; ⏲ shows 10am, 2pm, 4pm, 6pm Mar-Sep, 10am, 2pm, 3.30pm & 5.20pm Oct-Feb).

MYSTERIOUS & GHOST ROADS
신비의도로, 도깨비도로

For a 'Twilight Zone' moment, drive on to one of these stretches of road, turn off the engine, shift to neutral, and your car will appear to roll uphill. If you pour water or roll a ball on the pavement, there's a similar effect. It's really an optical illusion due to the angle of the road relative to sight lines, but it certainly looks convincing. If you decide to test it, watch out for other vehicles trying the same thing!

The first stretch to be discovered (allegedly by a taxi driver taking a break) is **Sinbiui Doro** (Mysterious Rd), in the hills about 7km south of the airport. **Dokkaebi Doro** (Ghost Rd) is to the east.

The cross-island (road 95) bus passes by all three venues every 20 minutes from Seogwipo and Jeju-si.

Hallim Park 한림공원

No time to explore Jejudo? Just visit **Hallim Park** (☎ 796 0001; adult/youth/child W6000/4500/3500; ⏰ 8.30am-5.30pm), which has everything – a botanical and bonsai garden, a mini folk village and a 500m walk through a lava-tube cave – all in one place. The park is filled with such beautiful plantings, most notably in a botanical garden full of local plants, that it's hard to believe that the area was originally barren rocks. The cave, **Hyeopchaegul**, only discovered in 1981, is one of the few lava tubes in the world with stalagmites and stalactites, usually only found in limestone caves. They're here thanks to the large quantities of pulverised seashells in the soil above the cave, which were blown in from the shore over thousands of years.

HALLASAN NATIONAL PARK
한라산국립공원

Hiking up **Hallasan** (☎ 713 9950; adult/youth/child W1600/600/300) is a highlight of any trip to Jejudo. The best plan is to hike up the **Eorimok trail**, which starts after a 15-minute walk from the bus stop. It's 4.7km, starting with a steep climb up through a deciduous forest (gorgeous coloured leaves in autumn). Halfway up, the dense trees give way to an open, subalpine moorland of bamboo, grass, dwarf fir trees and hillsides of azaleas that flower in April and May. Small, light brown roe deer now number over 1000, and you have a good chance of spotting one here. After 2¼ hours you should reach **Witseoreum shelter** (1700m), which has no accommodation but sells instant noodles (W1500) to hungry hikers. Ahead are the craggy cliffs of Hallasan's peak, but the path there is closed on a long-term basis to allow for plant regeneration (see below).

After lunch, head down the 3.7km **Yeongsil trail**, which is wetter but has grand scenery – panoramas of green *oreum* (craters) and pinnacle rocks atop sheer cliffs as you hike through a dwarf-fir forest, before reaching the mixed deciduous and evergreen forest lower down. It's a 1½-hour hike down to the road and then a 30-minute walk along a roadside footpath to the bus stop. The climb is only 700m in altitude (it starts at 1000m) but it's tiring – this is Korea's highest mountain – and you need to be prepared for bad weather that can arrive in the blink of an eye. However small children can make it, so you can too.

The other two routes are longer and more difficult – the Gwaneumsa trail is 8.7km and takes five hours (no bus service to the start) and the Seongpanak trail is 9.6km and takes 4½ hours. These routes go to the peak (1950m) with views of the famous crater lake.

RESTORING HALLASAN

The very popularity of the trek up Hallasan was threatening to destroy the area's unique and fragile ecosystem. Hikers were literally trampling plants to death and threatening the wildlife that the plants supported. Drastic action was required to save Korea's highest mountain from an eco-disaster. Even the roe deer were under threat.

Wooden boardwalks were constructed to reduce the impact of hikers' feet and to encourage them to stay on the track. The trail around the crater lake and the trail from the lake to Witseoreum shelter was closed for at least a decade to allow the worst affected and most fragile sections to recover. This meant that hikers up the popular and easier western trails could no longer view the crater lake. However, the mountain ecology is slowly recovering, and at the last count the number of roe deer had increased to 1249.

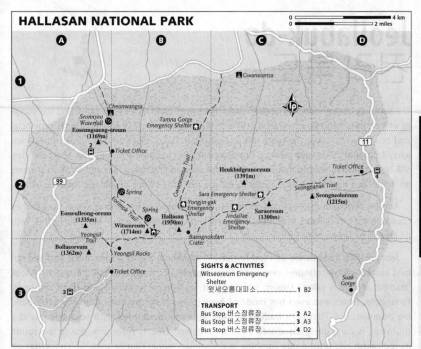

HALLASAN NATIONAL PARK

SIGHTS & ACTIVITIES
Witseoreum Emergency
Shelter
윗세오름대피소 **1** B2

TRANSPORT
Bus Stop 버스정류장 **2** A2
Bus Stop 버스정류장 **3** A3
Bus Stop 버스정류장 **4** D2

All the shelters are for emergency use only and cannot be booked for overnight stays.

Buses to Eorimok run from Jeju-si bus terminal (W2100, 35 minutes, nine daily) and from Jungmun (W3000, 50 minutes, nine daily). They also stop at Yeongsil, a W3500, 45-minute ride from Jeju-si and a W1600, 30-minute ride from Jungmun. Buses leave Jeju-si bus terminal (W1700, 35 minutes, every 15 minutes) for Seongpanak and Seogwipo.

Jeollabuk-do
전라북도

The southwestern province of Jeollabuk-do has always been Korea's rice bowl, and the image of white egrets standing in terraced rice fields is a provincial icon. Unspoilt national, provincial and county parks cover the more mountainous parts and offer some of Korea's finest get-away-from-it-all hikes and scenery. Buddhist temples, frequently rebuilt over the centuries, still house shaven-headed monks who find the surrounding rocks, hills and trickling streams an aid to Zen meditation as they try to escape from the chains of material desires.

Another form of escape is to off-shore islands, sun drenched in summer, when the beaches could almost be Thailand. In winter thrill-seekers head to the slopes of Muju Ski Resort, with its European alpine atmosphere.

Jeonju city is famous for its food (especially *bibimbap*, a dish of rice, meat and vegetables served up by countless restaurants nationwide), its traditional culture and its *hanok* (traditional house) village suburb with its craft workshops, museums and rustic teashops. Fans, dolls, boxes and even ties made of *hanji* (paper made by hand from mulberry bark) are popular buys. *Pansori,* a traditional musical drama performed by a solo singer and a drummer, is particularly associated with the province. Like its sister province to the south, its radicalism and artistic side combine in the annual Jeonju Film Festival, which focuses on indie films from around the world.

Jeollabuk-do has recently faced conflict over two major environmental issues: the storage of nuclear waste and the Saemangeum reclamation project on the west coast (p60).

HIGHLIGHTS

- Explore Jeonju's fascinating **hanok village** (p297)
- Be amazed by the unique rock-pinnacle temple garden in **Maisan Provincial Park** (p300) in the shadow of 'Horse Ears' mountain
- Zip round **Seonyudo** (p305) on a nippy quad bike before relaxing on the beach
- Amble through pretty **Seonunsan Provincial Park** (p303) to a giant Buddha carving on a cliff
- Ski, skateboard or sled down the slopes at **Muju Ski Resort** (p301)
- Take a cable car up to the skyline in **Daedunsan Provincial Park** (p300) or **Naejangsan National Park** (p302)

| TELEPHONE CODE: 063 | POPULATION: 2 MILLION | AREA: 8050 SQ KM |

History

The Donghak rebellion, led by Chon Pong-jun, took place mainly in Jeollabuk-do in 1893 when a raggle-taggle force of peasants and slaves, armed with various homemade weapons, seized Jeonju fortress and defeated King Gojong's army, before being destroyed by Japanese forces. Their demands included the freeing of slaves, better treatment of the *chonmin* or low-born, the redistribution of land, the abolition of taxes on fish and salt, and the punishment of corrupt government officials.

National & Provincial Parks

An atmospheric temple, coastal views and a waterfall are features of **Byeonsanbando National Park** (p304). A cable car takes you near the peak in **Daedunsan Provincial Park** (p300) and afterwards you can relax in a hot-spring spa. Skiers and hikers both enjoy the super scenery in **Deogyusan National Park** (p301). **Maisan Provincial Park** (p300) is famous for its 'horse ears' mountains and mystical stone towers, while the big drawcard at **Moaksan Provincial Park** (p299) is its superb temple. **Naejangsan National Park** (p302) has a great ridge hike and a cable car up to it for softies. Pretty **Seonunsan Provincial Park** (p303) has a giant Buddha carving on a cliff.

Getting There & Around

If you arrive by train or bus, you can then base yourself in Jeonju, the *hanok* city, where buses radiate to every nook and corner of the province.

JEONJU 전주

pop 622,000

Jeonju (www.jeonju.go.kr), the provincial capital, is famous for being the birthplace of both the Joseon dynasty and *bibimbap* (rice, meat, egg and vegetables with a hot sauce). Centrally located, the city is the perfect base from which to explore Jeollabuk-do as it's the hub for all the bus services. The historical area of the city has many outstanding *hanok* buildings, old and new.

Information

KB Bank (Girinno) Global ATM and foreign currency exchange.

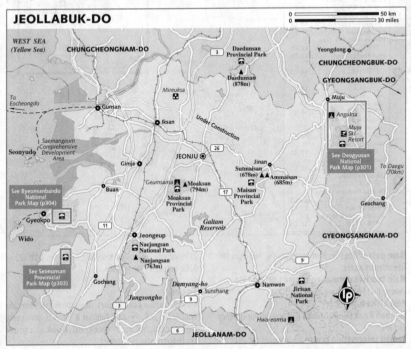

JEONJU

0 —— 600 m
0 —— 0.4 miles

SLEEPING
Apeulleoseu Motel 아플러스모텔 ...**23** D3
Good Morning Motel 굿모닝모텔 ...**24** C4
Jeonju Core Riviera Hotel
　전주코아리베라호텔 ...**25** D4
Jeonju Tourist Hotel
　전주관광호텔 ...**26** B4
Jeonju Traditional Life Experience Park
　전주한옥생활체험관 ...**27** C4
Kkumui Gungjeon Motel
　꿈의궁전모텔 ...**28** D3
Mint Motel 민트모텔 ...**29** A2
Munhwa Sauna Motel 문화여관 ...**30** D4
Seunggwangje 승광제 ...**31** C4

EATING
Banya Dolsotbap
　반야돌솥밥 ...**32** C5
Gimbap Ma-eul 김밥마을 ...**33** C5
Hankookkwan 한국관 ...**34** A1
Nadeulbeol 나들벌 ...**35** B4
Sambaekjip 삼백집 ...**36** B4
Traditional Culture Centre
　전통문화센터 ...**37** D5

DRINKING
Daho Teahouse 다호찻집 ...**38** D5

SHOPPING
Core Department Store
　코아백화점 ...**39** B3
Dongbu Market 동부시장 ...**40** C5
Hanbok Shops 한복거리 ...**41** B5
Ntepia 엔테피아 ...**42** C4

TRANSPORT
Express Bus Terminal
　고속버스터미널 ...**43** C4
Intercity Bus Terminal
　시외버스터미널 ...**44** D4
Local Bus Stop 버스정류장 ...(see 1)

INFORMATION
KB Bank 국민은행 ...**1** A2
Main Post Office 우체국 ...**2** C4
Main Tourist Information
　Centre 관광안내소 ...**3** D5
Post Office 우체국 ...**4** B5
Shinhan Bank 신한은행 ...**5** C4
Tourist Information Centre
　관광안내소 ...**6** C5
Tourist Information Centre
　관광안내소 ...**7** C4

SIGHTS & ACTIVITIES
Craft Treasures Centre
　공예품전시관 ...**8** D5
Folding Fan Museum
　전통부채박물관 ...**9** C5
Gang-am Calligraphy
　Museum 강암서예관 ...**10** C5
Gyeonggijeon 경기전 ...**11** C5
Hanbyeokdang Pavilion
　한벽당 ...**12** D5
Imokdae Pavilion 이목대 ...**13** D5
Jeondong Catholic Church
　전동성당 ...**14** C5
Jeonju Hyanggyo
　전주향교 ...**15** D5
Jeonju Korean Paper
　Institute
　전주전통한지원 ...**16** D5
Jeonju Traditional Life
　Experience Park
　전주한옥생활체험관 ..(see 27)
Kkotsugi Gongbang
　꽃숙이공방 ...**17** C5
Nambu Market
　남부시장 ...**18** C5
Omokdae Pavilion
　오목대 ...**19** D5
Oriental Medicine Centre
　전주한방문화센터 ...**20** C5
Pungnammun 풍남문 ...**21** C5
Traditional Wine Museum
　전통술박물관 ...**22** C4

0 —— 200 m
0 —— 0.1 miles

Main post office (9am-8pm Mon-Fri, 9am-6pm Sat)
Free internet access.
Main tourist information centre (282 1338;
Gyeonggiro) Free internet access.
Post office (China Street)
Shinhan Bank (Girinno) Global ATM and foreign-currency
exchange.
Tourist information centre bus terminal (281

2739; outside Express bus terminal); Gyeonggiro (232
6293; outside Gyeonggijeon)

Tours
Good-value **coach tours** (tours/tours incl Seonyudo
W9000/W19,000; 8am-7pm Sat & Sun Mar-Nov) visit
different sights every weekend. Book at a tourist information centre.

Sights & Activities

JEONJU HANOK VILLAGE 전주한옥마을

This historical urban village can take all day to look around – ask at a tourist information centre for the excellent 'Invitation to Our Tradition' brochure.

The **Oriental Medicine Centre** (☎ 232 2500; www .hanbangcenter.com; admission free; ☯ 10am-6pm) offers medical tests and diagnosis from an Asian-medicine perspective for a fee of W1000 to W4000, and recommends herbal, acupuncture, moxibustion and massage therapies, but language can be a problem.

Housed in a beautiful old *hanok*, the **Traditional Wine Museum** (☎ 287 6305; admission free; ☯ 9am-6pm Tue-Sun) has a *gosori* (traditional still). You can learn how to make your own *soju* (Korean vodka), and (more to the point) taste and buy traditional Korean liquors.

See sheets of *hanji* being manufactured in the **Jeonju Korean Paper Institute** (☎ 232 6591; admission free; ☯ 9am-5pm), housed in a gloriously atmospheric *hanok* down an alley. A slop of fibres in a big tank magically solidifies into paper.

The tiny but fascinating **Kkotsuki Gongbang** (Gyeonggiro; ☯ 10am-9pm Mon-Sat) is a workshop, where lessons are available in the art of making traditional Korean paper dolls. Feel free to pop in and watch.

Run by a third-generation Jeonju fan maker, the **Folding Fan Museum** (☎ 232 2008; admission free; ☯ 9am-9pm) has the fan-maker's father's tools on display along with antique fans. It takes 12 hours to complete one fan and the designs are burnt on by hand.

Gyeonggijeon (☎ 281 2790; Gyeonggiro; admission free; ☯ 9am-6pm) was originally constructed in 1410 but was reconstructed in 1614 and contains a portrait of Yi Seong-gye, the founder of the Joseon dynasty (1392–1910), whose family came from Jeonju. Portraits of six other Joseon monarchs, and palanquins, are also on show.

On the left are shrines, storehouses and guardrooms relating to the Confucian rituals that used to be held here. Treating ancestors with the utmost respect was a cornerstone of the Confucian philosophy that ruled Korea for centuries.

The stylish red-brick **Jeondong Catholic Church** (☎ 284 322; admission free) was built by French missionary Xavier Baudounet on the spot where Korean Catholics were executed in 1781 and 1801. Built between 1908 and 1914, the architecture is an outstanding fusion of

---

HYANGGYO & SEOWON

Hyanggyo were neighbourhood schools established by *yangban* (aristocrats) in the 1500s to prepare their sons for the *seowon* (Confucian academies), where the students took the all-important government service exams. The pupils studied Chinese characters and key Confucian texts. Over 600 *seowon* were spread across the country, making Korea more Confucian than China. In the 1860s Regent Heungseon Daewon-gun forced most of them to close as he reasserted the king's authority, but the buildings remain as symbols of Koreans' unwavering passion for education.

Asian, Byzantine and Romanesque styles. The elegant interior contains stained-glass windows portraying early martyrs.

Housing the artwork and art collection of a well-known 20th-century calligrapher, Song Sung-yong (pen name, Gangam), is **Gangam Calligraphy Museum** (☎ 285 7442; admission free; ☯ 10am-5pm Tue-Sun). The artist's response to the meaning and connotations of the words is expressed through the brush strokes.

Stroll around **Jeonju Hyanggyo** (☎ 288 4548; admission free; ☯ 10am-7pm), a well-preserved and very atmospheric Confucian shrine, school and dormitory complex that dates back to 1603 (see above).

Don't miss the lanterns, boxes, ties and clothing all made out of paper at the **Craft Treasures Centre** (☎ 285 4403; Gyeonggiro; admission free; ☯ 10am-7pm). The courtyard is pleasant for a rest and on the nearby hill is **Omokdae**, a pavilion where General Yi Seong-gye celebrated a victory over Japanese pirates in 1380, prior to his overthrow of the Goryeo dynasty. Cross the bridge to **Imokdae**, a monument to one of Yi Seong-gye's ancestors written by King Gojong.

Pungnammun, an impressive stone-and-wood gateway, is all that remains of Jeonju's fortress wall and four gateways. First built in 1398 but renovated many times since, it's a landmark that marks the beginning of the sprawling **Nambu Market**, where farmers' wives sell fresh produce direct to the public.

Just past the Traditional Culture Centre, go under the bridge to **Hanbyeokdang Pavilion**, on rocks overlooking the river, where herons, egrets and swallows can be seen in summer.

JUNGNIM ONCHEON 죽님온천

Soak and steam all night and day in Jeonju's best **hot-spring spa** (☎ 232 8832; admission W5000-7000; 🕑 24hr). A free shuttle bus (9.35am, 11.35am, 2.35pm and 4.35pm) leaves from outside the Jeonju Core Riviera Hotel (p290).

BICYCLE HIRE

Hire a bicycle from Jeonju Traditional Life Experience Park (right) for only W1000 a day. Why not cycle around the traffic-quiet Hanok Village, along the river and even further afield?

DEOKJIN PARK 덕진공원

Join Korean couples who hire paddleboats in this charming **park** (☎ 281 2436; admission free; 🕑 5am-11pm), in the north of the city, to view the lotus lilies, which are at their best in July.

Festivals & Events

The **Jeonju International Film Festival** (www.jiff.or.kr) is a nine-day event every April/May that focuses mainly on indie, digital and experimental movies. Around 200 films from 40 countries are shown in the Primus cinema multiplex and others nearby, and many have English dialogue or subtitles.

Sleeping

An ever-expanding galaxy of motels surrounds the bus terminals.

BUDGET

Munhwa Sauna Motel (☎ 251 5435; r W20,000; ☒) The best of the cheaper but unmodernised *yeogwan* (motel) is owned by Mr Kim who speaks some English. He also runs a sauna (W5000) in the same building. The modern motels are better but cost W10,000 extra.

Good Morning Motel (☎ 251 9948; r W30,000; ☒ 🖳) Despite an unimpressive exterior, this is a popular, no-fuss motel where the staff is helpful and the spacious rooms and bathrooms are modern and clean. Rooms vary so look at more than one – some have round, heated waterbeds, and all-body showers as well as baths, while rooms with a computer are W5000 extra.

Apeulleoseu Motel (☎ 273 4193; r W30,000; ☒) Stay here if you like 'love motel' ornate, as not only the furniture but even the lift design is fancy. Large French windows, round beds and all-body showers add to the overall designer effect.

Kkumui Gungjeon Motel (☎ 274 7373; r W35,000; ☒ 🖳) A new love motel that sets a new standard. Look round a number of rooms to choose which décor, bed shape and facilities you want. Electronic gear options include a giant TV, a smart computer, a DVD player and a bidet with as many dials and knobs as a pilot's cabin.

MIDRANGE

Mint Motel (☎ 271 3992; r W40,000, ☒ 🖳) Stay in this love-motel palace with spacious, fully equipped rooms if you fancy trying out a two-person Jacuzzi.

Seunggwangje (☎ 288 4566; r from W60,000) The best *hanok* stay as the small rooms have a TV, fridge and *yo* (padded quilt or mattress on the floor) as well as a tiny, modern en suite bathroom. The unique feature is that Seunggwangje is owned by English-speaking Lee Seok, a grandson of King Gojong, who lives in the adjoining *hanok*. If he is busy or away, Ms Lim Lee will look after you and she speaks some English. It's a special place down an alley with royal photographs on display. Breakfast is W5000.

Jeonju Traditional Life Experience Park (☎ 287 6300; www.jjhanok.com; r W60,000, r with en suite W80,000 & 90,000) Stay in tiny bare rooms and sleep on a *yo* in this newly built but traditional-style *hanok*. Prices include a Korean-style breakfast and free loan of a bicycle.

Jeonju Tourist Hotel (☎ 280 7700; r/ste W60,000/ 80,000; 🖳) This reasonably priced tourist hotel has a retro feel and the central location is close to Jeonju's main entertainment and shopping area. A sun umbrella and chairs brighten up the lobby, which has free internet access.

TOP END

Jeonju Core Riviera Hotel (☎ 232 7000; www.jeonjucore rivierahotel.co.kr; r/ste W170,000/330,000; ☒ 🖳) Ask for a room overlooking the *hanok* district in Jeonju's best hotel, which has spacious rooms and suites that feature natural wood décor, glass showers and a computer. Live music livens up the Windsor Bar (6pm to 2am; beers/ cocktails W5000/6600) at 10pm. There's also restaurants, a fitness club and a sauna.

Eating & Drinking

Gimbap Ma-eul (meals W2000-4000; 🕑 10am-9pm) A small, clean eatery that offers budget meals such as a range of *gimbap* (김밥) that includes cheese, tuna and salad.

Sambaekjip (meals W3500; 🕒 24hr) This 50-year-old restaurant specialises in *kongnamul gukbap* (콩나물국밥), a local Jeonju dish of rice, egg, bean sprout and seasoning cooked in a stone pot. It's said to be a hangover cure and comes with side dishes. To find the restaurant, walk down the road past Primus cinema and turn left.

Daho Teahouse (teas W4000; 🕒 11am-midnight) The best of the *hanok* teahouses is down an alleyway and has rustic, goblin-sized rooms overlooking an attractive garden where birds flit around. Listen to ethereal music as you sip the excellent teas such as *daechucha* (대추차; red date) and pink *omijacha* (오미자차; dried five-flavour berries).

Nadeulbeol (Hanok Village; meals W4000-8000; 🕒 10am-8pm) This small rustic restaurant serves up what many locals say is the most delicious *baekban* (백반; rice, fish and vegetable meal) in Jeonju.

Banya Dolsotbap (Maegok 1-gil; meals W6000-10,000; 🕒 11am-9.30pm) Hotpot rice is the speciality here with side dishes that include *deodeok* root, honey-coated potatoes, salad and soup. The ginseng version costs extra and *moju* (모주), a gingery alcoholic homebrew, is W1500. Service is off-hand but the food is good.

Hankookkwan (Girinno; meals W7000-10,000; 🕒 11am-9pm) A dozen cooks and a dozen waiting staff provide speedy service even at hectic times in this ever-popular restaurant that serves up classic Jeonju *bibimbap* (비빔밥). Order *dolsot bibimbap* (돌솥비빔밥) if you don't want raw meat. It comes with side dishes and tea, while the medicinal homebrew *moju* is W1000 a bowl.

Traditional Culture Centre (☎ 280 7000; meals W9000-30,000; 🕒 10am-9pm) Visit this stylish, up-market restaurant in a modernist building for Jeonju *bibimbap*, *galbi jeongsik* (갈비정식; ribs and side dishes) or a full-on *hanjeongsik* (한정식; banquet). Next door is a teashop and a hall that hosts traditional music and dance shows.

Shopping

Hanbok shops are at the far end of Jungangno, while the bustling Dongbu and Nambu Markets sell everything under the sun.

Ntepia (🕒 11am-11pm) A large fashion store in the youthful shopping precinct at Gaeksa, surrounded by beauty shops like The Face and Skin Food and Western restaurants such as Outback Steakhouse and Pizza Hut.

Lotte department store (🕒 10.30am-8pm) Has a cinema and is an 800m walk from the bus terminals

Core department store (🕒 10.30am-8pm) Next to the Jeonju Core Riviera Hotel; houses 300 fashion outlets on seven floors.

Getting There & Away
BUS

Destinations from the express bus terminal include:

Destination	Price (W)	Duration	Frequency
Daegu	10,800	3½hr	hourly
Daejeon	4500	1½hr	hourly
Gwangju	5300	1¼hr	every 30min
Seoul	8500	3hr	every 10min

Departures from the intercity bus terminal include:

Destination	Price (W)	Duration	Frequency
Buan	3700	1hr	5 daily
Daedunsan	4500	1¼hr	8 daily
Gochang	4900	1½hr	hourly
Gunsan	4000	1hr	every 15min
Gurye (Jirisan)	7500	2hr	hourly
Gyeokpo	6400	2hr	hourly
Jeong-eup	3000	1 hr	every 15min
Jinan	3300	50min	every 30min
Muju	7000	1½hr	hourly
Naesosa	6000	2hr	1 daily

TRAIN

There are KTX (Korea Train Express; W27,000, 2¼ hours, 19 daily), *Saemaul* (express; W22,700, three hours, four daily) and *Mugunghwa* (semi-express; W15,300, 3½ hours, 14 daily) trains to Yongsan station in Seoul, but KTX trains involve a change at Iksan. Trains also run south to Jeollanam-do.

Getting Around

Numerous buses (W850) run from near the bus terminals to downtown, while buses 105, 509 and others run to the train station. Taxis are plentiful and cheap (W1500 flag fall).

GEUMSANSA & MOAKSAN PROVINCIAL PARK
금산사, 모악산도립공원

This **park** (☎ 548 1734; adult/youth/child W2600/1700/1000; 🕒 8am-7pm), which contains Moaksan (794m), is only 40 minutes from Jeonju and is a popular destination for hikers at weekends. The main attraction is **Geumsansa**, a temple that dates back to AD 599. To stay in the temple (W40,000 including meals), contact the **information office** (☎ 5481330; ☉ 9am-6pm, closed 2 weekdays a week). The **Maitreya Hall** is special, a three-storey wooden structure built in 1635 that retains an air of antiquity. Inside is an impressive Mireuksa Buddha, the Buddha of the Future, behind which is a huge painting.

On the left is a museum and a hall, with carvings of 500 Buddha helpers who all look different. Near the entrance, sip soothing tea in the serene, Zen-style atmosphere of **Sanjang Dawon** (teas W6000).

Between 10 and 20 monks live here for a maximum period of five years. Monks now have a TV in their common room and to keep fit they play games of soccer and volleyball (or Ping-Pong if it's wet).

The usual climbing route up Moaksan goes past the temple, up Janggundae and along the ridge up to the peak. The hike is relatively easy and you can be up and down in three hours.

Overlooking the car park on the left is **Hwarim Hoegwan** (화림회관; meals W5000-20,000), a restaurant where you can sit inside or outside under the wisteria. Choose between local black pig, *tokkitang* (토끼탕; spicy rabbit soup) or roast *ori* (오리; duck).

Geumsansa and Moaksan are easily reached by bus from Jeonju. Local bus 79 (W1400, 45 minutes, every 15 minutes) can be picked up along Girinno, Jeonju's main street. Don't get on buses that go to the other end of Moaksan park; ask for Geumsansa.

DAEDUNSAN PROVINCIAL PARK
대둔산도립공원

Yet another of Korea's beautiful parks, **Daedunsan** (☎ 263 9949; adult/youth/child W1300/850/450; ☉ 8am-6pm) offers craggy peaks with spectacular views over the surrounding countryside. Although relatively small, it's one of Korea's most scenic mountain areas.

Aside from the superb views, the climb to the summit of Daedunsan (878m) along steep, stony tracks is an adventure in itself, as you cross over a 50m-long cable bridge stretched precariously between two rock pinnacles and then climb up a steep and long steel-cable stairway. Vertigo sufferers are advised to take the alternative route! For the less active, a five-minute **cable car ride**

(one way/return W3000/5000) saves you an hour of uphill hiking.

Daedunsan Tourist Hotel (☎ 263 1260; fax 263 8069; r W65,000; ☒ ☐) has an *oncheon* (hot spring bath) and a sauna (W3000) that is open to all, and is the perfect place to soak aching hiking muscles. Relax further, playing pool or four-ball in the bar (open 1pm to midnight) or sitting in an armchair with a view.

Many restaurants serve *sanchae bibimbap* (산채비빔밥; rice, egg, meat and mountain veggies) and the usual country-style food.

Daedunsan can be reached by bus from Jeonju (W4500, 70 minutes, six daily) or from Seodaejeon bus terminal in Daejeon (W2500, 40min, six daily).

MAISAN PROVINCIAL PARK
마이산도립공원

This is a must-see **park** (☎ 433 3313; adult/youth/child W2000/1500/900; ☉ sunrise-sunset). Maisan means 'Horse Ears Mountain', which refers to two extraordinary rocky peaks as they appear from the access town of Jinan. The east peak, **Sutmaisan**, is 678m while the west peak, **Ammaisan**, is slightly taller at 685m. Both ears are made of conglomerate rock, which is rare in Korea. Only Ammaisan can be scaled. It's a steep half-hour climb, but grinning grandmas make it to the top without any problem.

Tapsa (Pagoda Temple), at the base of the female ear, has a unique sculptural garden of 80 stone towers or pinnacles that were piled up by a Buddhist mystic, Yi Kapmyong (1860–1957). Up to 15m in height, they represent religious ideas about the universe and miraculously never seem to crumble, although no cement has been used. The diverse stone towers are an intriguing sight, evoking the atmosphere of a lost world.

Nearby is **Unsusa**, a temple with a Dan-gun shrine, a centuries-old pear tree, attractive gardens and, best of all, you are allowed to bang the big drum.

An easy 1½-hour, 1.7km hike with a splendid view at the top and ever-changing views of Ammaisan starts by Tapsa and takes you back to the car park at the entrance. In April the cherry trees around the nearby lake burst into blossom.

Frequent buses (W3300, 50 minutes, every 30 minutes) run along the scenic route from Jeonju to the small town of Jinan. From Jinan, buses (W850, five minutes, hourly) run to the park entrance.

DEOGYUSAN NATIONAL PARK
덕유산국립공원
Sights & Activities

In the northwest of this **park** (☎ 322 3174; adult/youth/child W3200/1200/600; ☼ sunrise-sunset) is **Jeoksang Sanseong**, a fortress that was rebuilt in the 17th century. Encircled by the 8km wall are the ruins of a Joseon-dynasty archive, a reservoir and An-guksa, a temple that was built in the 1860s. Buses only run along the main road to Gucheon-dong, so you must get off at the access road and walk (4km) or hitchhike.

Opened in 1990, **Muju Ski Resort** (☎ 322 9000; www.mujuresort.com) is one of Korea's top winter playgrounds, with 26 ski slopes that range between all skill levels. Snowboarding, sledding, night and mogul skiing and lessons in English are all available. The season runs from mid-December to April. The resort has top-notch facilities including an alpine-style village where you can shop, dine, dance, drink in a glass dome, play billiards, steam in a sauna or surf the net.

A few shops, restaurants and bars are open all year. The **gondola** (adult/child return W10,000/7000; ☼ 10am-4pm) to the top of **Seolcheonbong** (1520m) takes 15 minutes and also runs in the off-season. **Mountain bikes** (adult/child per hr W10,000/8000; ☼ 9am-7pm) can be hired to ride round a special track.

Further on from Muju Ski Resort is a tourist village at **Gucheon-dong**, the start of the park's best hike (1¾ hours, 6km) that follows the river and valley past 20 beauty spots to a small temple, **Baengnyeonsa**. Fairies are said to slide down rainbows to bathe in the pools, and the hike is enchanting at any time of the year. The trail continues past Baengnyeonsa for a strenuous, steep, 1½-hour ascent of **Hyangjeokbong** (1614m). Yew trees, azaleas and alpine flowers adorn the summit.

Sleeping

Accommodation is available in condos, or 2km up the access road in *minbak* (private homes with rooms for rent) and *pension*, which are connected to the ski slopes by free shuttle buses. The best policy is to buy a package deal that includes accommodation, ski hire, clothes hire, transport and lift passes.

JEOLLABUK-DO

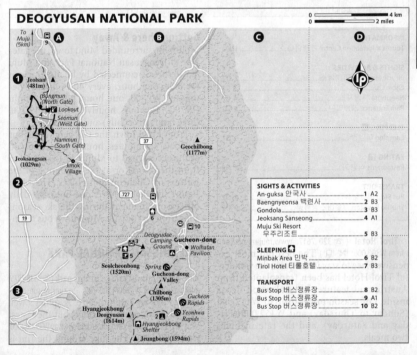

DEOGYUSAN NATIONAL PARK

0 — 4 km
0 — 2 miles

SIGHTS & ACTIVITIES	
An-guksa 안국사	1 A2
Baengnyeonsa 백련사	2 B3
Gondola	3 B3
Jeoksang Sanseong	4 A1
Muju Ski Resort 무주리조트	5 B3

SLEEPING	
Minbak Area 민박	6 B2
Tirol Hotel 티롤호텔	7 B3

TRANSPORT	
Bus Stop 버스정류장	8 B2
Bus Stop 버스정류장	9 A1
Bus Stop 버스정류장	10 B2

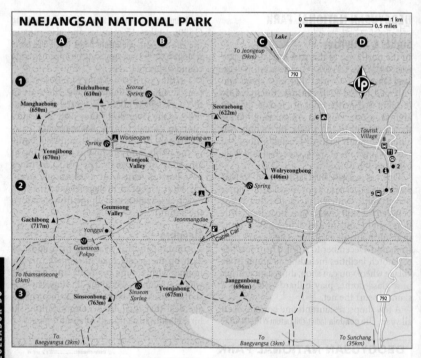

NAEJANGSAN NATIONAL PARK

Tirol Hotel (☎ 320 7617; www.mujuresort.com; r from W300,000; 🍴 💻) The best but most expensive place to stay in the park, the wonderful Tirol Hotel has been transplanted from Austria and features natural wood décor inside. Off-season prices drop to W112,000 (Sunday to Thursday) and W152,000 (Friday and Saturday), and the rate includes two meals.

Getting There & Away

Mountain-surrounded Muju town, the gateway to Deogyusan National Park and Muju Ski Resort, is connected by bus to Daejeon (W3800, one hour, every 40 minutes), Geumsan (W2300, one hour, hourly), Jeonju (W7000, 1½ hours, hourly), Seoul (W12,100, three hours, five daily) and other cities.

From Muju town, the Gucheon-dong bus (W3000, 45 minutes, hourly) can drop you at the access road to Muju Ski Resort (2km from the resort) or at the beginning of the fortress or Gucheon-dong hikes. The Muju Resort shuttle bus (free, one hour, six daily off-season, frequent during the ski season) runs from just outside Muju town bus terminal by the river.

NAEJANGSAN NATIONAL PARK
내장산국립공원

The mountainous ridge in this **park** (☎ 538 7875; adult/youth/child W3200/1300/700; ⏰ sunrise-sunset) is shaped like an amphitheatre. A spider's web of trails leads up to the ridge, but the fastest way up is by **cable car** (adult/child one way W3500/2000, return W4500/2000). The hike around the rim is strenuous, but with splendid views on a fine day. The trail is a roller-coaster ride, going up and down six main peaks and numerous small ones before you reach Seoraebong, from where you head back down to the access road.

There are metal ladders, bridges and railings to help you scramble over the rocky parts. Give yourself four hours to hike around the amphitheatre, with an hour for breaks and a picnic. If you find the hike too difficult, turn right at any time and follow one of the many trails back down to Naejangsa.

An easy and picturesque 2km walk from Naejangsa goes through Geumsong valley, which becomes a steep ravine before leading to a cave, a natural rock arch and a waterfall.

A tourist village clusters around the entrance, but it's not usually busy except in October. **Camping** (small/large tent W3000/6000) is available before the tourist village. A shuttle bus (W900, 9am to 6pm) runs between the ticket office and the cable car terminal, saving a 2km, 20-minute walk.

The **tourist information centre** (☎ 537 1330) has free internet access, and across the road is a **bicycle hire stall** (☎ 011-9449 4383; per hr W3000; 9am-6pm). Cycle up to the temple or back out of the park and around the nearby farms and villages.

Buses (W3000, one hour, every 15 minutes) run from Jeonju to Jeong·eup. From just outside the bus terminal on the left, local bus 171 (W1000, 30 minutes, every 20 minutes) runs to Naejangsan.

SEONUNSAN PROVINCIAL PARK
선운산도립공원

This pretty **park** (☎ 563 3450; adult/youth/child W2800/1800/1300; sunrise-sunset) has always been popular and has inspired poets such as Sa Chong-ju:

Every spring I go to Seonunsa
To see the camellia flowers
But this year they haven't bloomed yet
So I'm thinking about last year's visit
And the husky-voiced singing of a bar hostess.

Sights & Activities
A 20-minute walk along a rocky, tree-lined river brings you to **Seonunsa** and just behind the temple is a 500-year-old **camellia forest** that flowers around the end of April, although a few blooms linger into summer.

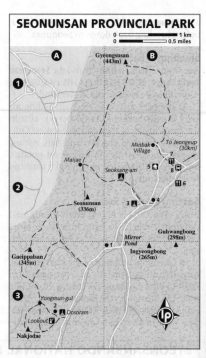

SIGHTS & ACTIVITIES
Garden 공원 **1** B3
Giant Buddha Rock Carving 마애불상 **2** A3
Seonunsa 선운사 **3** B2
Ticket Office 매표소 **4** B2

SLEEPING
Seonunsan Youth Hostel 선운산유스호스텔 **5** B2

EATING
Food Stalls 분식포장마차 **6** B2
Restaurants 식당가 **7** B2

TRANSPORT
Bus Stop 버스정류장 **8** B2

Another 35 minutes further on is Dosoram and just beyond is a giant **Buddha rock carving**. Folk art in style, it probably dates back to the Goryeo dynasty; the amazing image is carved into the cliff face and is 13m high. Despite centuries of erosion the Buddha is still an impressive sight, a testament to the faith of ancient times. On the right is a very narrow grotto, and next to it stairs lead up to a tiny shrine and a great view. From the Buddha, you can climb **Nakjodae** and carry on to **Gaeippalsan** and **Seonunsan,** with views of the West Sea, before heading back down to Seonunsa.

Sleeping & Eating

Accommodation is limited and the **Seonunsan Youth Hostel** (☎ 561 3333; fax 561 3448; r W40,000) can sometimes be booked out at weekends.

At the park entrance are stalls selling locally grown *bokbunja* (wild berry), also in the form of juice, *soju* and rice-cakes. Others sell barbecued chicken and fish, *norang goguma* (tasty strips of dried sweet potato), *muhwagwa* (tiny dried figs), gingko fruit and roast chestnuts.

Getting There & Away

Buses (W4000, 1½ hours, every 30 minutes) run from Jeonju to Gochang, from where buses (W1800, 20 minutes, hourly) run to Seonunsan.

In Gochang, walk out of the bus terminal, turn left and at the main crossroads turn right to visit Gochang Fortress, a 10-minute walk. On the right is the **Pansori Museum** (☎ 560 2761; adult/youth/child W800/500/free; ☻ 9am-6pm Tue-Sun), with memorabilia on this unique solo opera musical form. The well-preserved, ivy-covered, 1.6km-long, 15th-century **fortress wall** (admission free; ☻ 9am-7pm Mar-Oct, 9am-5pm Nov-Feb) surrounds buildings such as a three-cell prison. A local belief is that if a woman walks three times around the wall with a stone on her head in a leap month, then she will never become ill and will enter paradise.

BYEONSANBANDO NATIONAL PARK
변산반도국립공원

This coastal **park** (☎ 582 7808; adult/youth/child W3200/1300/700; ☻ sunrise-sunset) contains **Naesosa**, where the buildings look old, with lots of unpainted wood. Take a close look at the main hall, especially the lattice doors, the painting behind the Buddha statues, and the intricately carved and painted ceiling with musical instruments, flowers and dragons among the motifs.

Hike up the unpaved road to **Cheongneonam** (20 minutes) for sea views; another 15 minutes brings you to the ridge where you turn left for Gwaneumbong. From the peak follow the path, which goes up and down and over rocks for an hour until you reach **Jikso Pokpo,**

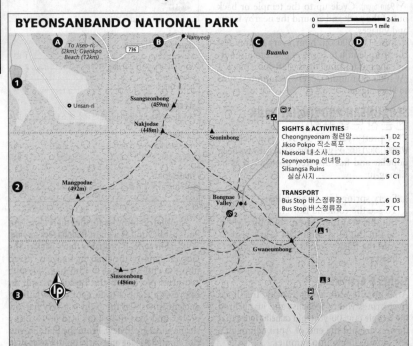

BYEONSANBANDO NATIONAL PARK

SIGHTS & ACTIVITIES	
Cheongnyeonam 청련암	1 D2
Jikso Pokpo 직소폭포	2 C2
Naesosa 내소사	3 D3
Seonyeotang 선녀탕	4 C2
Silsangsa Ruins 실상사지	5 C1

TRANSPORT	
Bus Stop 버스정류장	6 D3
Bus Stop 버스정류장	7 C1

a 30m-high waterfall with a large pool. Another pretty spot is **Seonyeotang** (Angel Pool). From there walk along the unpaved access road past the ruins of **Silsangsa**, destroyed during the Korean War. You may need to hitch a lift as buses are infrequent. For a more challenging hike head up **Nakjodae**, which is famous for its sunset views.

Beaches along the coast attract crowds in summer.

Gyeokpo beach has dramatic stratified cliffs and caves as well as seafood restaurants. The beach is safe for swimming but the sea disappears at low tide. Gyeokpo is also the starting point for ferries to **Wido**, a small island where every house in the little fishing village of Jinli is a *minbak*-cum-restaurant. The large sandy beach is a cool place to hang in summer, almost like being on a beach in Thailand.

Only one direct bus (W6000; two hours) runs from Jeonju to Naesosa. Otherwise take a bus from Jeonju to Buan (W3700, one hour, five daily) and then a local bus to Naesosa (W2000, one hour, every 30 minutes). Buses (W6400, two hours, hourly) also run from Jeonju to Gyeokpo.

Ferries (☎ 581 0023) go from Gyeokpo to Wido (W6500 one way, 40 minutes, three daily September to June, six daily July and August).

GUNSAN
pop 280,000

Gunsan is a major port and industrial city that has a US airbase nearby, but the only reason for visiting is to catch a ferry to Seonyudo, Eocheongdo or further afield to China.

SEONYUDO 선유도

A 43km ferry trip from Gunsan brings you to the relaxing and increasingly popular island of Seonyudo, situated amid 60 mostly uninhabited small islands. This is Korea's very own secret Polynesia. When the tide is in and the sun is out, the views are as beautiful as anywhere in the country. These days there are more bicycle-hire stalls than fishing boats; you can hire bicycles (per hour W3000) or a quad bike (per hour W20,000) to pedal or zip around laid-back fishing villages on

Seonyudo and the three islands that are linked to it by bridges. Six-person *bungbungka* (auto rickshaws; per hour W30,000) take pensioner parties on fun tours.

The main attraction is the 1.6km **beach**, a 10-minute walk from the ferry pier, on a spit of soft, golden sand with great island views on both sides. At the far end the adventurous should climb up rocky **Mangjubong.** Take the right turn towards Saeteo village and on your left are tracks leading through the grass up to some ropes that are fixed to the rock, which you can use to haul yourself up to a wooded gully. The view from the top is a wonderful panorama of islands.

Raw fish and squid dominate the restaurant scene, but you can find *baekban* (백반; rice, fish and vegetable meal) and *galbi* (갈비; beef ribs). Accommodation prices double in July and August. A friendly, weather-beaten owner welcomes guests to the clean and tidy rooms at **Jung-ang Minbak** (중앙민박; ☎ 465 3450; r W25,000 🅿). Next to the school, it has a distinctive rock-clad exterior.

The newer **Uri Park Minbak** (우리파크민박; ☎ 465 0657; r W30,000) has better views but *yo* mattresses rather than beds. The restaurant cooks up *galbi* if you're not a fish or seafood fan. Both are in the main fishing village, with its shops and restaurants, a 10-minute walk from the jetty and very near the beach.

Buses (W4000, one hour, every 15 minutes) leave from Jeonju for Gunsan. Ferries (adult/child one way W11,700/5500, 1½ hours, three or four daily) leave from the new **Yeonan Yeogaek** (Gunsan Coastal Ferry Terminal; 연안여객터미널; ☎ 467 6000), a 15-minute, W7500 taxi ride from Gunsan bus terminal.

EOCHEONGDO 어청도

Ferries leave from the Gunsan Coastal Ferry Terminal for nine other islands including **Eocheongdo** (adult/child one way W22,900/5750, one daily), 70km from Gunsan, which has *minbak* to stay in, varied bird habitats and a reputation for being one of the best places in Korea for bird-watching, with 228 recorded species including 24 rare ones. View www.birdskorea .org for more details.

Chungcheongnam-do
충청남도

Gongju and Buyeo in Chungcheongnam-do, commonly shortened to Chungnam, (www.chungnam.net), were once capitals of the ancient Baekje kingdom. The treasures found in King Muryeong's tomb make him Korea's Tutankhamen, and a rich heritage of ancient Baekje relics can be found in other tombs, fortresses and museums. The province could host a capital again, as the government is planning to relocate ministries to a new administrative city northwest of Daejeon to ease congestion in Seoul. The province's attractive west-coast beaches have become a popular summer playground for city folk cooped up in their high-rise apartments, and Daecheon beach hosts a merry mud festival in late July that is popular with foreigners.

Much of the region is still rural, with rice fields interspersed with vegetable plots and small orchards in the wide valleys between the forested hillsides. Unfortunately the national trend of growing crops under polythene mars the views.

Another feature is the quirky churches of all shapes and sizes that can be found in virtually every village as well as in every town and city neighbourhood. Haemi fortress encircles a prison where early Catholic converts were tortured and killed, as their beliefs undermined the strict Confucian apartheid-like hierarchy of aristocrats, peasants and slaves. Geumsan, south of Daejeon, is the Mecca for ginseng lovers with countless shops and stalls selling the medicinal root in every conceivable form.

HIGHLIGHTS

- Marvel at the 1500-year-old treasures from **King Muryeong's tomb** (p313) in Gongju
- Tour around the fortress, royal pond garden and tomb sites of Baekje's last capital, **Buyeo** (p316)
- Relax on **Daecheon beach** (p319) with its sandy beach, seafood eateries and mud therapies
- Relive the epic struggle against Japanese colonial rule at the **Independence Hall of Korea** (p322)
- Enjoy ginseng in all its healthy manifestations in Ginseng Town, **Geumsan** (p311)
- Offer a prayer for the early Catholic converts imprisoned and executed in **Haemi fortress** (p322)

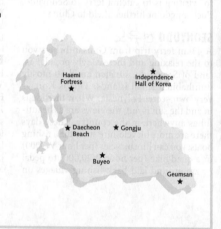

- Haemi Fortress ★
- Independence Hall of Korea ★
- Daecheon Beach ★
- Gongju ★
- Buyeo ★
- Geumsan ★

■ TELEPHONE CODE: 041	■ POPULATION: 1.9 MILLION	■ AREA: 8586 SQ KM

History

The province was the site of two Baekje kingdom capitals during the Three Kingdoms Period (57 BC–AD 668), Ungjin and Sabi. Ungjin (now called Gongju) became the second capital of the Baekje kingdom in AD 475 when the first capital at Hanseong (Seoul) was captured by Goguryeo troops. The astonishing tomb of King Muryeong, discovered near Gongju in 1971, with its treasure trove of nearly 3000 items, all over a thousand years old, reveal the outstanding craftsmanship and highly developed culture of the period.

In AD 538 the capital was forced to move south again, this time to Sabi (Buyeo), but it didn't last long before it was overwhelmed in AD 660 by the joint army of Shilla and China, and the Baekje kingdom disappeared forever.

National & Provincial Parks

On land, hike around temples and hermitages and up to the rocky peaks of Gyeryongsan National Park (p312). At sea, catch ferries around the islands, beaches and sunsets of the magnificent Taean Haean National Marine Park (p321).

Getting There & Around

Daejeon is less than an hour from Seoul on the new KTX train, but except for Boryeong and Cheonan other destinations are only served by buses.

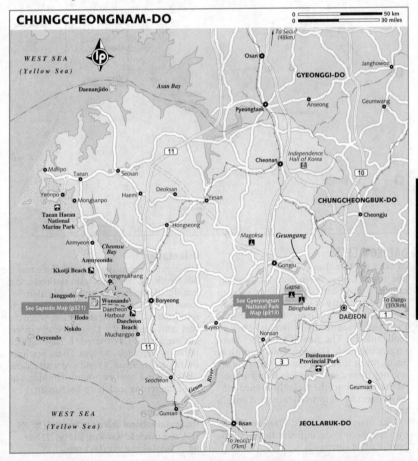

CHUNGCHEONGNAM-DO

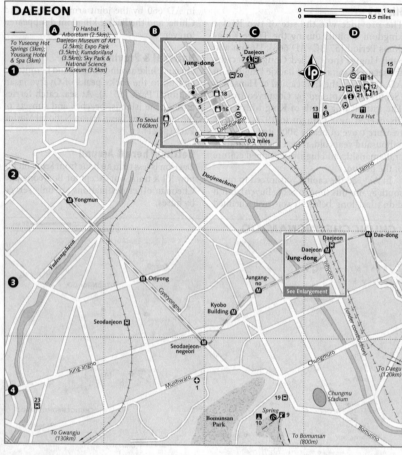

DAEJEON 대전

☏ 042 / pop 1.5 million

Daejeon is Korea's science and technology capital, a transport hub and the gateway to the ginseng centre of Geumsan and to hiking trails in nearby Gyeryongsan National Park and Daedunsan Provincial Park in Jeollabuk-do. The new KTX bullet-train service has made Daejeon, 160km south of Seoul, into a suburb of the capital, since the journey there now takes less than an hour. At the same time, the recently opened subway system has improved transport within the city.

Like other major cities, Daejeon has its own telephone code, different to that of the province that surrounds it.

Orientation

Daejeon is a confusing city with three major bus terminals, two main train stations and a handful of scattered shopping and entertainment areas. A cluster of shops and markets is in front of Daejeon train station, while the best motels are in the Dongdaejeon/express bus terminal area. To the west is Yuseong with its hot-spring hotels and spas. To the north are the remains of Expo '93 and a new arts plaza. The city is in a bowl, surrounded by hills. The most interesting walk is up Bomunsan.

Information

Chungnam National University Hospital (☏ 220 7114; www.cnuh.co.kr; Munhwaro) Take bus 223 from outside Dongdaejeon intercity bus terminal.

Post offices On Inhyoro and behind Dongdaejeon bus terminal.

SC (Jung·angno; ☼ ATM 7am-11pm) Exchanges foreign currency and has a global ATM.

Shinhan Bank (Dongseoro) Exchanges foreign currency.

Tourist information centre Outside express bus terminal (☎ 632 1388; www.metro.daejeon.kr) Inside train station (☎ 221 1905; ☼ 9am-6pm) .

Sights & Activities
EXPO PARK & AROUND 엑스포과학공원
The space-age pavilions of **Expo Park** (☎ 866 5114; www.expopark.co.kr; adult/youth/child W3000/2000/1000, Big Five Rides W9000/6000/5000; ☼ 9.30am-6pm Tue-Sun) are left over from the very successful Expo '93. Check to see which science pavilions and shows are still up and running.

To the right of Expo Park is **Sky Park** (☎ 861 0300; adult/child W15,000/12,000; ☼ 9.30am-7.30pm), where you can enjoy a 15-minute helium-balloon ride that rises 150m for the best view over the city.

Kumdoriland (☎ 863 2633; day pass adult/youth/child W20,000/18,000/14,000; ☼ 9.30am-7pm, open later in summer), on the left of Expo Park, is a fun amusement park with parades, acrobatic shows and enough thrill rides to keep youngsters screamingly happy for a couple of hours.

Connected by a pedestrian bridge to Expo Park, the **National Science Museum** (☎ 601 7894; www.science.go.kr; adult/child W1000/500; ☼ 9.30am-5.50pm Tue-Sun) was designed with children in mind. Exhibits range from the age of dinosaurs through to the digital era, and everyone should find something of interest.

From Expo Park stroll down to the river and turn left for a short walk before crossing over the new bridge. On the right is **Hanbat Arboretum** (admission free; ☼ 9am-6pm Oct-May, 9am-

9pm Jun-Sep), a tranquil, green oasis perfect for a picnic. Further on **Sinnara** (☎ 016-465 7858; per hr W3000-5000; ☼ 10am-midnight) rents out bicycles and funky-looking skateboards, scooters and trikes for exploring along the riverbank cycleways. On the right is **Daejeon Museum of Art** (대전시립미술관; ☎ 602 3200; admission fee varies; ☼ 10am-6pm Tue-Sun), which has ever-changing exhibitions and is the city's leading gallery.

Bus 103 (W1300, 35 minutes, every 15 minutes) leaves from outside the express bus terminal and Daejeon train station. Get off at the National Science Museum.

YUSEONG HOT SPRINGS 유성 온천
In the west of Daejeon is Yuseong, where 20 therapeutic *oncheon* (hot-spring baths) are fed from 350m underground. Rejuvenate tired limbs and stressed minds in the indoor hot pools of a range of hotels and spas. If you're not a hotel guest, you can still enjoy a hot (and cold) pool for under W5000 and stay as long as you like.

Yousung Spa (☎ 820 0100; adult/child W4500/2200; ☼ 5am-10pm) in Yousung Hotel is a top hot-spring spa. Women can enjoy either pine needle, mugwort or even coffee baths (they vary each day), while both the women's and men's sections feature a ginseng and green-tea bath plus hot and cold saunas. The men's section has an outdoor pool.

Take bus 102 (W1300, every 15 minutes) from outside the express bus terminal (one hour) or outside Daejeon train station (45 minutes).

BOMUNSAN 보문산
Daejeon is encircled by a ring of wooded hills that provide a green backdrop to the city. The

CHUNGCHEONGNAM-DO

most accessible is Bomunsan (457m) on the south side of the city. You can look around tiny Wongaksa and do a spot of bird watching on your way up past the **observation deck**, with panoramic views of the city, to **Bomun Sanseong**, a small fortress that encircles the summit.

To get there, catch bus 724 (W1300, 20 minutes, every 20 minutes) from outside the express bus terminal or Daejeon train station. The bus drops you near the tree-lined access road.

Tours

City tours (☎ 253 5960; tours W6000/10,000; 🕑 10am-5pm Tue-Sun) depart from the small ticket office on Jung-angno outside Dongbang Mart. The tours follow two different routes but both include the main sights.

Sleeping

Hundreds of comfortable, reasonably priced new motels cluster around the express and Dongdaejeon intercity bus terminals.

Jinju Park (진주파크; ☎ 624 4776; Yongjeon Gosok 1-gil; r W20,000; 🅿) For the budget-minded, this *yeogwan* (motel with small, well-equipped en suite) is near the bus terminals. The rooms are rather shabby, but are better than you would guess from the outside.

Coupleria Motel (☎ 637 9600; 21 Yongtam 3-gil; r W30,000; 🅿 🖳) A clean and comfortable motel where rooms are modern, spacious and have large TVs and natural wood decor, with both a bath and a shower. A room with a computer is W5000 extra.

Limousine Motel (☎ 621 1004; Yongtam 3-gil; r W40,000; 🅿 🖳) Opposite Coupleria, Limousine is new and flashy. Bathrooms come with large glass showers and a bath, and electronic gear includes computers and DVD players.

Yousung Hotel (유성호텔; ☎ 820 0100; www .yousunghotel.com; Yuseong; d, tw & ondol from W190,000; 🅿 🖳 ♨) Way out west, the comfortable rooms here have computers and are furnished with an occasional touch of flair. No one goes hungry, as buffet spreads are available at every meal. Hotel guests receive a 50% discount on the excellent spa (p309), but the swimming pool costs W7000.

Eating

Yeongsuni (meals W4000-9000; 🖐) A popular and famous sit-on-the-floor restaurant that specialises in budget cook-it-yourself *shabu kalguksu* (샤브칼국수): a first course of rather spicy mushroom vegetable soup with thin strips of meat and thick noodles is followed by rice, egg and garnish added to the remains of the soup. The seafood option is great too, as is the squid *pajeon* (green-onion pancake). Near the bus terminals, Yeongsuni is child-friendly and has an indoor play area.

Tesco Home Plus Food Court (meals W4000-10,000; 🕑 10am-9pm; 🖐) Above the supermarket is this fun food court with huge fusion food platters of curry rice, pasta and burger meat that can feed three people.

Pungnyeon Samgyetang (meals W8000; 🕑 9am-10.30pm) Drop into this large, unpretentious restaurant for its *samgyetang* (삼계탕; ginseng chicken) with lettuce and cucumber side dishes. It's within easy walking distance of the bus terminals and the manager is helpful.

Shopping

Shops in the **underground shopping arcade** that runs under Jung-angno from Daejeon train station sell mainly clothing and souvenirs. On the left is the sprawling **Jung-angno market**, which stocks everything from live eels to US$5 'Louis Vuitton' bags. Further along, every evening a tsunami of young people swirl around the pedestrianised shopping district near the **Milano 21** (Jung-angno; 🕑 11am-11pm) fashion store.

Getting There & Away
AIR

The nearest airport is Cheongju, 60km north of Daejeon in Chungcheongbuk-do, which is linked to Daejeon by bus (W3200, 45 minutes, five daily).

BUS

Daejeon has three bus terminals: the Seodaejeon (west) intercity bus terminal, the Dongdaejeon (east) intercity bus terminal and express bus terminal, which are side by side near the motels.

Buses depart the express bus terminal for the following destinations:

Destination	Price (W)	Duration	Frequency
Busan	12,700	3¼hr	hourly
Daegu	7400	2hr	every 30min
Gwangju	8,200	3hr	every 30min
Seoul	7000	2hr	every 10min

From Dongdaejeon intercity bus terminal, destinations include:

Destination	Price (W)	Duration	Frequency
Cheongju	3000	50min	every 15min
Geumsan	3000	1hr	every 20min
Gongju	3100	1hr	every 45min
Jeonju	4500	1½hr	every 30min
Taean	13,300	3½hr	every 30min

Departures from the Seodaejeon intercity bus terminal include:

Destination	Price (W)	Duration	Frequency
Boryeong	8600	3hr	every 15min
Buyeo	5000	1¼hr	every 20min
Daedunsan	2500	40min	6 daily
Gongju	3100	1hr	every 20min

TRAIN

Daejeon train station, in the centre of the city, serves the main line between Seoul and Busan, and all trains en route to either city stop there. Seodaejeon station, in the west of the city, serves the lines to Mokpo and Yeosu.

Superfast KTX trains (W19,500, 55 minutes, every 30 minutes), *Saemaul* trains (express, W13,900, 1¾ hours, hourly) and *Mugunghwa* trains (semi-express, W9300, two hours, every 40 minutes) run from Seoul station to Daejeon.

Getting Around

BUS

Bus 841 (W900, 20 minutes, every 15 minutes) links Seodaejeon bus terminal to Daejeon train station and the Dongdaejeon and express bus terminals. The useful bus 102 (W1300, every 15 minutes) links Dongdaejeon bus terminal to the Science Museum, Yuseong Hot Springs and Gyeryongsan National Park.

SUBWAY

Daejeon's new subway line (per trip W900) has 13 stations open, with another 10 to go, including one in Yuseong, the hot spring spa zone.

GEUMSAN 금산

pop 65,000

This market town (www.geumsan.chungnam .kr) is where 80% of the nation's *insam* (ginseng) is marketed. Leave the Geumsan bus terminal and turn left, walk for 10 minutes and turn right across a bridge along Bihoro/ Yakchoro.

On the left is **Matkkalbokjip** (맛깔복집; meals W10,000-15,000; ⊙ 11am-10pm), where two ladies serve up local ginseng specialities such as *insam twigim* (인삼튀김; ginseng tempura).

Walk on a few minutes more across a bridge and on the left is **Geumsan Insam & Herb Market** (금산인삼약령시장). The hundreds of shops and stalls display large glass jars containing weirdly shaped ginseng roots. Pomegranate liquor, mulberry candy, and sweet potato and prickly pear tea are also on sale.

The first shop on the corner is **Buheunggeon-jaedomaeyakeopsa** (부흥건재도매약업사; ⊙ 9am-6pm), which sells *insam* tea, deer antler velvet and *bureomcha*, a sweet tea made of nuts and beans.

Left of the shop is **Geumsan Wellbeing Sauna** (금산웰빙방가마사우나; ☎ 754 0020; W5000; ⊙ 24hr), which has a ginseng bath, a hot and ice-cold sauna, sleeping rooms, a PC *bang* (internet room), a *noraebang* (karaoke room; W500 a song), an exercise area and massages (W10,000).

Along the next road on the left, Insam Yakcho-gil is a stall on the right that serves *insam twigim* and bowls of *insam makgeolli*.

CHUNGCHEONGNAM-DO

KTX

Korea joined the elite club of countries with super fast trains in April 2004, following the successful development of its own sleek 300km/h KTX trains (http:ktx.korail.go.kr). Though based on the French TGV system, most of the 46 trains have been built in Korea. The sleek trains have over 900 seats and have already turned Daejeon into a suburb of Seoul, as it now takes less than an hour to travel between the two cities. It's faster to reach Seoul Station from Daejeon by KTX than from Olympic Park by subway.

The project is mega expensive but the peninsula will shrink further when the special KTX track is extended all the way down to Busan in the southeast and to Mokpo in the southwest. Carbon-dioxide emissions will also be reduced as trains are a greener transport system than cars and aircraft.

WONDER ROOT

Ginseng is a Korean health product that's in demand throughout the world. It's grown under black netting (to simulate its natural habitat under shady trees), and the root takes years to grow to its optimum size. Roots with unusual shapes can be worth a fortune, as is ginseng that has grown wild. The more mature red ginseng is always more expensive than the white. The plant has attractive red berries but they seem to have no use – only the root has commercial value. Numerous health benefits are claimed for ginseng, and it turns up in products as diverse as *soju,* rice wine, tea, candy, biscuits, coffee, noodles, body lotions and shampoo.

The market is larger on the second, seventh, 12th, 17th, 22nd and 27th days of every month.

Geumsan can be reached along a scenic route by bus from Daejeon (W3000, one hour, every 20 minutes) and from Muju (W2300, 35 minutes, hourly) in Jeollabuk-do. Buses also run to Daedunsan Provincial Park (W1600, 20 minutes, hourly).

GYERYONGSAN NATIONAL PARK
계룡산국립공원

The eastern entrance to **Gyeryongsan National Park** (☎ 825 3003; adult/youth/child W3200/1200/600; ☺ 6am-7pm) is 18km from Daejeon. The park contains two famous temples surrounded by forested hills, which give way to rocky cliffs towards the peaks. It's a small but pretty park – the name translates as Rooster Dragon Mountain because locals thought the mountain resembled a dragon with a rooster's head. **Donghaksa** (a nunnery) is 1km from the park entrance, and from there you can hike up to another temple, **Gyemyeongjeongsa**, and then on to Sambulbong and Gwaneumbong before returning to Donghaksa via **Eunseon Pokpo** (Eunseon Waterfall).

Gapsa, a temple at the park's western end, is best visited from Gongju and is a 20-minute walk from the bus stop. Look out for birds and butterflies on the way. The temple has a superb bell, crafted in 1584. **Yongmun Pokpo**, a 20-minute hike beyond the temple, is a small waterfall but sits in a very scenic location.

One recommended option from Gongju is to take a bus to Donghaksa at the eastern end of the park, hike to Gapsa (4.7km, four hours), and then take another bus back to Gongju.

Sleeping & Eating
The eastern park entrance (Donghaksa) has a line of duck restaurants. At the western park entrance (Gapsa) is the usual tourist village.

Gyeryong Youth Hostel (☎ 856 4666; Donghaksa; dm/f W10,900/40,000; ☒) Clean and pleasant en suite rooms, but guests sleep on a thin *yo* (mattress on the floor). Grab a bunch of *yo* for a more comfortable sleep.

Gyeryong Geurintel (☎ 825 8211; Donghaksa; r W40,000) Probably the best motel in Donghaksa tourist village, with rooms that have fancy furnishings, light decor and a glass, hi-tech shower. Fluorescent wallpaper brightens up the corridors.

Matjarang Tongnamujip (Gapsa; meals W5000-15,000) This is located at the far end of the restaurant area – look for a shady courtyard with a double watermill wheel. Try *dotori bindaetteok* (도토리 빈대떡; acorn pancake) and mountain vegetables, or *pyogobeoseot deopbap* (표고버섯 덮밥; mushrooms on rice with a banquet of side dishes).

Mushroom (Donghaksa; meals W6000-17,000) In this mushroom-shaped restaurant, dine on mushroom *ssambap* (버섯쌈밥; assorted ingredients with rice and leaves), *hanbang oribaeksuk* (한방 오리백숙; duck in medicinal soup), which serves two, or just sip Korean tea amid eclectic furnishings that include a rhino head and a knight on horseback.

The camping ground has only basic facilities but the low prices (W3000 to W5000) attract plenty of nature lovers in July and August.

Getting There & Away
Bus 102 (W1300, one hour, every 15 minutes) from outside Daejeon express bus terminal goes to the eastern end of the park.

From the Gongju local bus terminal, take a local bus (W950, 30 minutes, every 30 minutes) to Gapsa at the western park entrance, or to Donghaksa (W950, 30 minutes, six daily) at the eastern end.

GONGJU 공주
pop 140,000

Gongju became the second capital of the Baekje kingdom in AD 475 when the first

GYERYONGSAN NATIONAL PARK

capital at Hanseong (Seoul) was captured by
Goguryeo troops. Less than 70 years later,
in 538, the capital was forced to move south
again, this time to Sabi (Buyeo). The city is
most famous for King Muryeong's tomb and
its treasure trove of 2900 ancient artefacts.

Information
KB Bank (Ungjinno) A global ATM and foreign exchange.
Post office South of the market.
Tourist information centre (☎ 856 7700; ☑ 9am-
6pm Mar-Oct, 9am-5pm Nov-Feb) At the entrance to
Gongsanseong, the Baekje fortress.
Tourist information centre & craftshop (☎ 840
2548; ☑ 9am-6pm Mar-Oct, 9am-5pm Nov-Feb) At the
entrance to King Muryeong's tomb site.

Sights
GONGJU NATIONAL MUSEUM
공주국립박물관
This new **museum** (☎ 850 6300; adult/youth/child
W2000/1000/500; ☑ 9am-6pm Mar-Oct, 9am-5pm Nov-
Feb, closed Mon) exhibits the treasures discovered in King Muryeong's amazing tomb.
Videos with English subtitles show how the
tomb was made, and paint a vivid picture of
Baekje culture. Exquisite golden earrings,
Chinese porcelain, silver bowls and a unique
necklace of burnt wood and gold are on display. Upstairs unique Baekje jar coffins are
displayed.

On the right of the museum are Joseon-era
provincial government buildings, while on
the left are private tombs (visitors must keep
to the paths).

The museum is a 15-minute walk from the
royal tombs, or a W2500 taxi ride from the
fortress entrance.

TOMB OF KING MURYEONG 무령왕릉
Seven **Baekje tombs** (☎ 856 0331; adult/youth/child
W1500/1000/700; ☑ 9am-6pm), including King
Muryeong's, are clustered on a hillside near
Seongsan-ri. The burial chambers have all been
sealed to protect them, so you cannot look
inside. However the **Exhibition Hall** contains ac-
tual-size replicas of the tombs that you can go

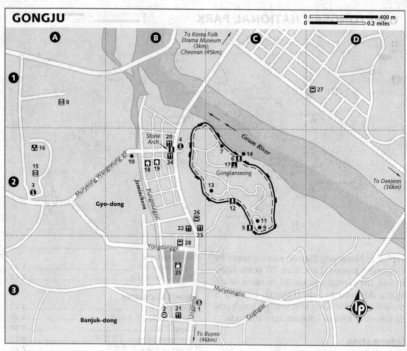

GONGJU

into. Sit down in King Muryeong's brick tomb, with its cleverly designed arched roof, and experience the special atmosphere of its lotus-flower pattern, symbols of Buddhist heaven. Another tomb has dragon, tiger, tortoise-snake animal and phoenix designs inside.

Bus 25 (W950, 10 minutes, every 15 minutes) runs from the local bus terminal to the tombs, or catch a taxi (W2000). Otherwise it's a 15-minute walk from the fortress entrance to the tombs.

GONGSANSEONG 공산성

This hilltop **fortress** (adult/youth/child W1200/800/600; ☒ 9am-6pm Mar-Oct, 9am-5pm Nov-Feb), floodlit at night, is crammed with Baekje and Joseon relics. The 2.6km wall that encircles the 110m summit of Gongsan was made of earth during the Baekje kingdom. The stone facing was added in the 17th century.

Ssangsujeong is a pavilion built where King Injo rested during his 10-day stay in the fortress to which he had fled to escape an insurrection. Nearby is an impressive stone-lined Baekje pond. An unusual **step well** is in front of the temple, **Yeong-eunsa**, which housed warrior monks who fought valiantly against the Japanese in the 1590s. Korean monks were pacifist except when their country was attacked. **Gongbungnu**, **Imnyugak** and **Gwangbongju** are all pavilions.

At the main entrance gate, a 10-minute **Changing of the Baekje Guard** takes place hourly between 2pm and 8pm on Saturday and Sunday in April, May, June, September and October. You can dress up as a Baekje warrior and try your hand at archery (W1000).

HWANGSAEBAWI 황새바위교성지
Walk up to this serene **hilltop park** (☎ 856 3923; Muryeong Wangneung-gil; admission free; ☼ 9am-5pm), which has a poignant monument and solemn memorial chapel. Three hundred Catholics from all social classes were executed on this spot, mostly in the 1860s, but now their spirits lie in peace, surrounded by birdsong.

Tours
A free day-long **bus tour** (☎ 856 7700) of all the sights of Gongju runs every Sunday from April to October, and departs from the fortress car park at 10am, returning at 6pm.

Festivals
Gongju's golden age is re-enacted and celebrated from 9 October to 12 October every odd-numbered year with a **Baekje-themed festival** of 100 events that includes a huge parade, dancing, music, games, sports and fireworks. The festival is held in nearby Buyeo in even-numbered years.

Every October a three-day **folk drama festival** takes place at the **Korea Folk Drama Museum** (공주민속극박물관; ☎ 855 4933; adult W2000; ☼ 10am-5pm Tue-Sun). International folk music, dance and drama continue all day from 10am. Take a taxi (W4000) to get there.

Sleeping
Minarijang (☎ 853 1130; Bldg 7, Minari 2-gil; r W25,000; ⊠ ⌨) One of a dozen budget *yeogwan* clustered opposite the fortress, this is clean, well-priced and has a smiling hostess. The big plus

is a computer in all the rooms, although bathrooms contain bowls rather than basins.

Ganseojang (☎ 853 8323; Pungmul Geori; r W25,000; ⊠ ⌨) In a quiet spot overlooking a stream, with flowers at the entrance and a homely feel, this *yeogwan* has a friendly owner who keeps the rooms spotless. A room with a computer costs W5000 extra.

Eating & Drinking
The Gongju area is famous for chestnuts and strawberries.

Han's Deli (meals W3000-5500; ☼ 10am-11pm) This is a bright and breezy eatery with music and a very youthful vibe that provides well-priced Italian/Korean meals and W1000 coffee in a fast-food ambience.

Yeonmun (meals W5000-8000) A brand new, all-white restaurant that serves two unusual and tasty dishes – *ochae bibimbap* (오채 비빔밥), which has no red-pepper sauce and is eaten wrapped in dried seaweed, and *bammukbap* (밤묵밥), thick strips of chestnut jelly in a soup with seaweed and a few pieces of *kimchi*. Both come with side dishes and tea.

Gomanaru (Ungjinno; meals W5000-15,000) Amid rustic decor, this charming and long-established restaurant opposite the fortress specialises in *ssambap* (쌈밥; side dishes) and *dolsotbap* (돌솥밥; stonepot rice with beans) served with excellent side dishes, tea and a *bulgogi* (불고기; slices of barbecue beef in a lettuce wrap) option. Try their delicious homebrew *gudeuraeteukju* (구드래특주).

Japanese Restaurant (Ungjinno; meals W6000-20,000; ☼ 11am-10pm) Eat in your own snug little Zen-style room in this cute fusion restaurant, and tuck into decent-sized and delicious *samchigu-i* (삼치구이; grilled fish) accompanied by 10 unusual side dishes including boiled peanuts, squid salad, *pajeon*, tiny snails and even *beondegi* (silkworm larvae).

There's a **Pizza Hut** (Ungjinno; meals W6000-28,000; ☼ 11.30am-10pm) if you're pining for pizza or pasta.

Shopping
Join the locals who still prefer to buy everything they need in the character-filled **Sanseong market**.

Getting There & Away
The intercity and express bus terminals are together north of the river, although most buses from Daejeon will drop you off

in the city centre. Departures from the terminals include the following:

Destination	Price (W)	Duration	Frequency
Boryeong	5400	1¾hr	every 30min
Buyeo	3100	45min	every 30min
Cheonan	3900	1hr	every 20min
Daejeon	3100	1hr	every 20min
Seoul	6300	2½hr	every 15min

Getting Around

Head to the local bus terminal to get around town or else just jump into an inexpensive taxi.

AROUND GONGJU

Magoksa (마곡사; adult/youth/child W2000/1500/1000; ⏱ 6am-6.30pm) is a remote and historical temple that nestles beside a river, 25km northwest of Gongju. It has largely escaped the mania for renovation and repainting, so some buildings retain an ancient look and atmosphere.

Cross the 'mind-washing bridge' to the main hall, **Daegwangbojeon**, which was last rebuilt in 1813 and has an intricately carved and decorated ceiling supported by immense beams and pillars. Behind the shrine is an unusual two-storey prayer hall, **Dae-ungbojeon**, constructed in 1651. Another delight is **Yeongsanjeon**, which contains hundreds of pint-sized, white-painted devotees, each of them slightly different.

Three circular **hiking trails** branch off from behind Magoksa. The longest trail (5km, 2½ hours) includes two peaks, **Nabalbong** (417m) and **Hwarinbong** (423m). The other trails are 2.5km and 4km long and should take 1½ hours and two hours respectively. The trails connect up with small hermitages scattered around the forested hillsides.

The usual tourist village includes food stalls offering roast pig, roast squid *sundae* (sausage) and roast chestnuts. Worth exploring is the **totem-pole park**, where hundreds of carved totem poles surround hobbit-style restaurants. Some pole carvings are traditional while others, like the soccer world cup and political sections, are more modern. Fertility symbols include giant penises and a fish with legs.

Chueogui Samhak (추억의삼학; meals W5000-20,000), housed in a mushroom-shaped castle, offers *sanchae bibimbap* (산채비빔밥; rice, egg, meat and mountain vegetables with a spoonful of hot sauce), *dotorimuk bindaetteok* (도토리 빈대떡; mung bean pancake and acorn jelly) and banquet meals, as well as *hanbang oribaeksuk* (한방 오리백숙; duck in medicinal soup). The burnt rice 'bowls' are a crispy rice snack called *nurungji* (누룽지). Gongju *Albam Insamsul* is rice wine flavoured with chestnut, ginseng and pine needles.

Bus 7 (W950, 50 minutes, every 40 minutes) runs from Gongju's local bus terminal to Magoksa, but the less-frequent bus 18 (W950, one hour) takes a more scenic route. The temple is a 20-minute walk from the bus stop in the tourist village.

BUYEO 부여
pop 95,000

Buyeo was the site of the Baekje kingdom's last capital, Sabi. The capital was moved there from Gongju in AD 538, and six kings ruled as the dynasty flourished until it was destroyed by the combined forces of Shilla and the Tang (of China) in AD 660. Today Buyeo is a quiet backwater surrounded by wooded hills and rice fields, with friendly and tradition-minded inhabitants. Baekje relics include a fortress, burial mounds just out of town, a reconstructed pond garden and a five-storey stone pagoda. Many other treasures are inside Buyeo National Museum. The Jung-ang Covered Market is a great place to barter and bargain for food, clothes, souvenirs and just about anything else.

Information

Hana Bank (cnr Wangungno & Sabiro) Foreign exchange.
Post office (Sabiro)
Tourist information centre (☎ 830 2523; www .buyeo.go.kr) Tourist information kiosks are outside Buyeo National Museum and inside Jeongnimsaji.

Sights
BUYEO NATIONAL MUSEUM
부여국립박물관

This **museum** (☎ 833 8562; adult/youth/child W1000/500/ free; ⏱ 9am-6pm Mar-Oct, 9am-5pm Nov-Feb, closed Mon) houses one of the best collections of Baekje artefacts. A wonderful 114kg incense burner with its unbelievably intricate and well-preserved metalwork and superb design is the outstanding item, but there is lots more to admire. Government records were kept on wooden strips, and other metalwork such as a small Buddhist halo are superb. Unusual items include a seven-pronged dagger, ornate tiles and a man's chamber pot shaped like a tiger.

GENERAL GYEBAEK'S LAST STAND

General Gyebaek won many battles, but in AD 660 when he learnt of the size of the advancing Shilla and Chinese armies, he knew it was the end. Not wanting his family to face the suffering and disgrace of becoming slaves, he killed his wife and children.

After this extreme act he marched out with his small army of 5000 men to confront an enemy whose troops outnumbered his by ten to one. The general and his brave soldiers repulsed four enemy attacks on the Plains of Hwansanbeol, but the fifth attack resulted in the death of General Gyebaek and all his soldiers. Their defeat meant the end of the Baekje kingdom, and 3000 court ladies are said to have thrown themselves off Busosan cliff rather than surrender.

A statue of the general on horseback is in central Buyeo, and by Gungnamji pond is a stirring memorial to his final battle. The general and his men represent the unflinching martial spirit of the ancient kingdom of Baekje.

BUSOSAN 부소산

This **park** (adult/youth/child W2000/1100/1000; ⏰ 7am-7pm Mar-Oct, 8am-5pm Nov-Feb) covers the forested hill of Busosan (106m), the fortress of the Baekje kings, and contains the remains of 2.4km of ancient earth walls. It also served as the palace garden, and makes for a lovely area to walk for an hour or so among its temple, pavilions and shrines, which reflect Baekje culture. Chipmunks, squirrels and birds have turned it into a nature reserve.

A soldier's thatched pit-house has been reconstructed, and Samchungsa shrine is dedicated to General Gyebaek (above) and two Baekje ministers whose invasion warnings to the last Baekje monarch, King Uija (r 641–660), were ignored.

A wide river, Baengmagang, protected the northern side of the fortress, and the cliff above it was where 3000 Baekje court ladies threw themselves off a large rock into the river. The rock was later named **Nakhwa·am**, 'falling flowers rock', in honour of those who chose death rather than dishonour. At the bottom of the cliff is a tiny temple, **Goransa**. Behind it is a spring that provided the favourite drinking water of Baekje kings, and nearby is a plant that only grows near the spring. Slaves had to pick a leaf and put it in the water to show that the water came from this spring.

From Goransaji, ferries (one way adult/child W2700/1500) run to Gudurae sculpture park. The boats run daily from sunrise to sunset and the 1½km trip only takes 10 minutes. From Gudurae park it's a 15-minute walk to the town centre past Buyeo's best restaurants.

JEONGNIMSAJI 정림사지

This small **temple site** (☎ 830 2532; adult/youth/child W1000/600/400; ⏰ 9am-6pm Mar-Oct, 9am-5pm Nov-Feb)

contains a five-storey Baekje stone pagoda that fits together like Lego and is one of the few that survived the sacking of the town. In the pavilion is a Goryeo dynasty Buddha so worn and weathered by age as to be hardly recognisable.

GUNGNAMJI POND & PAVILION 궁남지

A 15-minute walk past Jeongnimsaji is a reconstructed royal pleasure garden for the court ladies. A nature-viewing pavilion overlooks lily-filled ponds that are surrounded by willow trees, flowers and rice fields. Ducks, egrets and herons have moved in. On the left is an imposing memorial to the last battle of General Gyebaek and his 5000 soldiers.

BAEKJE ROYAL TOMBS 백제왕릉

These seven **royal tombs** (adult/youth/child W1000/600/400; ⏰ 8am-6pm Mar-Oct, 8am-5pm Nov-Feb), dating from 538 to 660, are on a hillside 3km from Buyeo along the road to Nonsan. It's not possible to enter them, but an **exhibition hall** has small-scale models of the tombs that have been excavated. One tomb has murals painted on the walls, but they are not very distinct.

The earth bank on the left is the remains of the city's outer defences, which once stretched for 8km and were wide enough to ride a horse along. Pheasants and chickens now wander where once Baekje soldiers marched.

To get there from the bus station or along Wangungno, hop on one of the local buses (W900, five minutes, every 30 minutes) to Nonsan (논산), or take a taxi (W4000).

BAEKJE HISTORICAL MUSEUM
백제역사재현단지

This brand new **museum** (☎ 830 3400; adult/youth/child W1500/1200/800; ⏰ 9am-6pm Mar-Oct, 9am-5pm Nov-

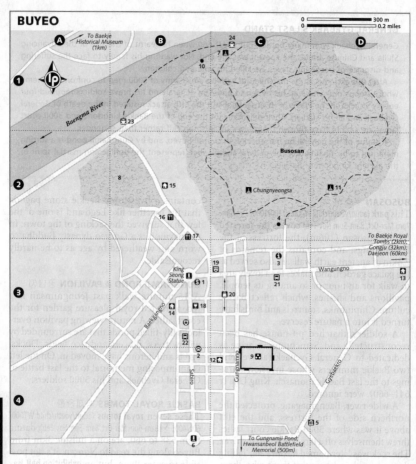

BUYEO

Feb) focuses on Baekje culture. It's a W5000 taxi ride over the river from the town centre.

Sleeping

Samjeong Buyeo Youth Hostel (☎ 835 3791; dm/f members W11,000/31,200, nonmembers W16,000/43,000; ✕ ⚐) The dorm rooms have two double bunks, en suite facilities and a less institutional feel than most other hostels. Family rooms are of motel standard and have twin beds and dark furniture.

Arirang Motel (☎ 832 5656; r W30,000; ✕ ⚏) Rooms in this central motel are smallish but stylish with an ultramodern shower and mood lighting in the bathroom. Rooms with a computer are the same price as those without.

Myeongseong Motel (☎ 833 8855; r W30,000; ✕) Rooms like No 315 are light and bright, while No 313 is the best *ondol* room in this very central but quiet motel with touches of class that include some fine artwork and photographs on the walls.

Myeongjin Motel (☎ 835 0371; r W30,000-40,000; ✕ ⚏) This stylish modern motel has a sauna (W3500) in the basement. The more expensive rooms are the best in town with a computer, armchairs and enough space to swing a cat.

Eating, Drinking & Entertainment

The road down to the river ferry is the best street for restaurants.

Mobeom Eumsikjeom (meals W5000-12,000; ✕ 11am-11pm) Order the W7000 *joseon wanggalbi*

(조선 왕갈비; royal *galbi*) in this popular and atmospheric *hanok* barbecue restaurant for some real meat and assorted side dishes washed down with *soju* (the local brew).

Gudurae Dolssambap (meals W5000-15,000; ☑ 9am-9pm) Always packed with locals, this is the place to come for Buyeo's best countryside-style cooking that includes *dolssambap* (돌쌈밥), *bibimbap* (비빔밥) and hotplate *bulgogi* (불고기) with an army of side dishes.

Bubble Castle (Sabiro; beer W2200; ☑ 4pm-2am) A convivial Western-style bar on the main street with a menu of fusion food that makes for a relaxing place to unwind after a hard day's sightseeing.

WOW Music Club (☎ 838 1818; Wangungno; per hr W12,000; ☑ 24hr) Sing your heart out in bungy-jumper Mr Kim's *noraebang*.

Getting There & Away

Many intercity buses depart from the Buyeo bus terminal:

Destination	Price (W)	Duration	Frequency
Boryeong	3700	1hr	hourly
Daejeon	5100	1hr	every 20min
Gongju	3100	45min	every 30min
Seoul	11,200	2¾hr	every 20min

BORYEONG 보령

pop 122,000

Boryeong is the gateway to Daecheon beach (10km away) and Daecheon harbour (a further 2km), from where ferries sail to a dozen rural islands. All the frequent buses that connect Boryeong bus terminal and train station continue on to Daecheon beach and continue on to the harbour.

The **tourist information centre** (☎ 932 2023; www.boryeong.chungnam.kr; ☑ 9am-6pm Mar-Oct, 9am-5pm Nov-Feb) is located inside Daecheon train station (despite the name it's in Boryeong, not Daecheon beach).

Getting There & Away

BUS
Departures from Boryeong include the:

Destination	Price (W)	Duration	Frequency
Buyeo	3700	1hr	hourly
Daejeon	8600	2½hr	hourly
Jeonju	7600	2½hr	3 daily
Seoul	8700	2½hr	every 30min

TRAIN
Saemaul (W15,700, 2½ hours, three a day) and *Mugunghwa* (W10,600, three hours, 13 a day) trains run between Daecheon station and Yongsan in Seoul.

DAECHEON BEACH 대천해수욕장

This is the best beach on the west coast; it's almost golden-coloured sand is kept cleaner than most. Although 3.5km long and up to 100m wide, the beach can still be crowded on summer weekends. The sea is shallow and calm, and in the evening everyone gathers on the beach to watch the sunset and let off fireworks.

Architecturally, Daecheon beach is the Las Vegas of Korea with amusement parks and row upon row of fancifully designed and named motels, some of which have luridly coloured plastic palm trees outside that light up at night. It's purely a tourist town with *noraebang*, bars, nightclubs, billiard halls,

CHUNGCHEONGNAM-DO

cafés and countless raw fish and seafood restaurants, but no banks.

Daecheon harbour, 2km away, is packed with fishing boats and is the ferry terminal for visiting the relaxing offshore islands, where the only residents are fisher folk. For less commercialised beaches, take a ferry to Sapsido or on to Anmyeondo.

The **tourist information centre** (☎ 931 4022; ☽ 8am-8pm) is in the Mud House (see below).

Activities

Water-skiing, canoeing, windsurfing, horse-and-carriage rides along the beach and speed-boat, banana-boat and jet-ski rides are all available in July and August.

Located on the beachfront just to the left of the access road, **Mud House** (보령 머드하우스; ☎ 931 4022; ☽ 8.30am-8pm) is a super new facility that offers a sauna, mud bath and aroma spa for a bargain W3000 for foreigners. Extras like massages and mud packs cost more. The local mud is full of health-giving minerals, and mud soaps and mud shampoos are on sale.

Sleeping

Daecheon beach has hundreds of large, modern motels with elevators and almost luxurious rooms. Prices start at W30,000 but usually increase on Friday and Saturday and in July and August.

Motel Coconuts (모텔코코넛스; ☎ 934 6595; r W30,000; ✖) This offers bland but neat and modern rooms, some with sea views, but the price doubles on Friday and Saturday.

Motel If (모텔이프; ☎ 931 5353; r W30,000-50,000; ✖) Next to Motel Coconuts, on the left of the access road, this stylish motel has cosy rooms with black–rafter ceilings and bare brick walls that are hidden away inside the modern exterior. Rooms like No 503 have great sea views and cost W40,000.

Eating

Seafood and raw fish restaurants stretch along the beachfront, many with aquariums of fish, eels, crabs and shellfish outside. A pile of *jogae modeumgui* (조개 모듬구이; mixed shellfish) is barbecued at your table for W30,000 (enough for three people). Raw fish like *ureok* (우럭) and *gwang·eo* (광어) is expensive, while octopus or eel are other options.

For fast food there's Lotteria or convenience stores.

Yeonggwang Sikdang (영광식당; Haesuyokjang 4-ro; meals W6000-30,000; ☽ 8.30am-10pm) Try the *saeugui* (새우구이): 28 large prawns for W30,000 cooked on salt on a hotplate at your table. Great taste and colour! It's the fourth building from the access road on the left.

Donguhoessenta (뉴동우회쎈타; meals W30,000; ☽ 24hr) On the beachfront, just to the right of the access road, is this typical restaurant where meals are meant for sharing: raw fish, eel, octopus or the more expensive but delicious *kkotge jjim* (꽃게찜; steamed blue crab).

Getting There & Away

Buses (standard/deluxe W930/1300, every 30 minutes) run from Boryeong terminal and Daecheon (Boryeong) train station to Daecheon beach (대천 해수욕장) and on to Daecheon harbour (대천항). Get off at the first stop in Daecheon beach for the Mud House and the main access road to the beach.

SAPSIDO 삽시도

This small relaxing island, 13km from Daecheon harbour, has few cars and three relatively unspoilt sandy beaches. It attracts so many visitors that it's become Minbak Island, with nearly every one of the several hundred households offering accommodation and meals. *Minbak* (private homes with rooms for rent) are sprinkled around the island but are concentrated around the two ferry jetties. Residents don't usually lock their houses or cars.

From Sulttung harbour walk for 15 minutes past the primary school to reach **Geomeol-neomeo beach,** with its fine stretch of sand between two rocky headlands, backed by sand dunes and fir trees. The only blots on the landscape are a few huts and the garbage that

---

MUD GLORIOUS MUD

The holiday atmosphere on Daecheon beach reaches a surreal climax during the week-long **Boryeong Mud Festival** (www.mudfestival.or.kr/english) held at the end of July. Foreigners flock to the mudsummer mudness, where you can tune into your inner child and enjoy mud *ssireum* (wrestling), a mud bath, a mud slide, mud football – and watch a mud parade and a Mr Mud and Ms Mud contest.

SAPSIDO

0 ——— 1 km
0 ——— 0.5 miles

Geomeolneomeo Beach

Sapsido Primary School

To Daecheon Harbour (13km)

Sulttong Harbour

Jinneomeo Beach

Keunsan

Mulmangteo

To Daecheon Harbour (14km)

Bamseom Beach

SLEEPING
Haedotneun Minbak 해돋는민박 1 B1

EATING
Eommason 엄마손 2 B1
Store 수퍼 3 B1

TRANSPORT
Bamseom Ferry Jetty 밤섬선착장 4 B2
Sulttong Ferry Jetty 술똥선착장 5 B1

the tide brings in. Except at high tide, you can walk left and clamber over the rocks to smaller **Jinneomeo beach**, which takes another 15 minutes. You might see terns, oyster catchers and cormorants. The walk back to Sulttong harbour takes another 15 minutes, past fishermen repairing their nets and squid (rather than washing) hanging out to dry. **Bamseom beach** is the largest and least developed.

Accommodation in *minbak* rooms or huts is more expensive than on the mainland, especially in summer. Almost up to motel standard, **Haedotneun** (☎ 935 1617; Sulttong Harbour; r W40,000), a red-brick *minbak*, has rooms with kitchen facilities. For dinner, order chicken or a fish meal or the excellent *doenjang jjigae* (된장찌개; locally caught crab and tofu).

You can dine alfresco and informally at **Eommason** (meals W1500-10,000; ⊗ 11am-9pm) on the harbour side, sitting on plastic stools at oil-drum tables. The menu covers *ramyeon* (라면; instant noodles), *kalguksu* (칼국수; thick noodles), shellfish soup and *pajeon* (파전).

For a snack or drink, pop into the store located in the owner's converted front room.

Getting There & Around

Ferries (☎ 1544 1114; adult/child W9200/4600) run from Daecheon harbour to Sapsido at 7.30am, 12.50pm and 4pm. They take an hour but can take longer if the ferry visits other islands first. At low tide the ferry goes to Bamseom jetty in the south, but at high tide it goes to Sulttong jetty in the north. The island has no buses, but someone might give you a lift or else it's a 40-minute walk from one end of the island to the other.

A ferry returns to Daecheon harbour at 5.30pm (check which jetty it leaves from!). Or you can catch the 8.10am ferry the next day to Yeongmukdang on the tip of Anmyeondo (below). Other ferries from Daecheon harbour run to Manmyeondo, Oeyeondo, Hojado and Wonsando (all adult W4200, child W2100) if you want to explore where few – if any – foreigners have ever ventured.

Buses for Daecheon beach all continue to the harbour.

TAEAN HAEAN NATIONAL MARINE PARK 태안해안국립공원

This beautiful **marine park** (☎ 672 9737; adult/youth/child W2000/1500/700; ⊗ sunrise-sunset) was established in 1978 and covers 329 sq km of land and sea. It includes 33 sandy beaches such as Kkotji, Mallipo, Yeonpo and Mongsanpo and about 130 islands and islets.

Anmyeondo 안면도
pop 13,000
The largest island (87 sq km) in the park has numerous beaches dotting its western coast. Ferries run from Daecheon harbour (W7000) and Sapsido (W7200), taking around 45 minutes to **Yeongmukhang** (영묵항). Once you disembark, you turn right and then fork left for the two-minute uphill walk to the bus stop. The rugged bus (W1500, one hour, hourly) goes on safari down narrow, sometimes gravel backcountry roads that wind between rice paddies and vegetable allotments to the island's main town, **Anmyeon** (안면). From here the best option is to take the bus (W950, 30 minutes, hourly) to **Kkotji beach** (꽃지해수욕장), which runs down the west coast past a line of sandy beaches. This attractive seaside area is being rapidly developed, creating a festive atmosphere in July and August.

From Anmyeon, buses run over the bridge to Taean (태안; W2100, 40 minutes, hourly) or further afield to Daejeon, Cheonan and Seoul.

CHUNGCHEONGNAM-DO

Taean 태안

pop 25,500

Taean is the gateway to the northern maritime park beaches. Buses from Taean include:

Destination	Price (W)	Duration	Frequency
Anmyeon	2100	40min	hourly
Cheonan	9200	3hr	every 20min
Daejeon	13,300	4hr	every 30min
Haemi	2400	50min	every 20min
Seoul	9600	2½hr	every 20min

Mallipo Beach 만리포

Gorgeous, golden Mallipo beach has a rocky headland on one side and a cute fishing harbour on the other. Eighteen kilometres from Taean, it's far less developed than Daecheon, but seafood restaurants, *minbak* and motels are beginning to sprout.

Just 2.5km up the road is the privately owned **Cheollipo Arboretum** (천리포수목원; ☎ 672 9310; guided tour W10,000; ◷ 9am-4.30pm Sat & Sun), founded by an American who loved Korea and trees equally. With 10,000 labelled trees and plants, tours take over an hour.

Local buses (W1400, 30 minutes, hourly) run from platform 11 at Taean bus terminal. Buses also connect Mallipo directly with Seoul (W8600, three hours, four daily) and Daejeon (W14,700, 4½ hours, two daily).

HAEMI 해미

pop 9600

This imposing **fortress** (☎ 660 2114; admission free; ◷ 6am-9pm), a five-minute walk from where buses drop passengers in the main street, was built in 1418 and served as a military headquarters until 1895. The walls are 1.8km long, 5m high and made with large stone blocks at the base and smaller ones at the top. Originally built to strengthen defences against marauding Japanese pirates, Joseon-era government offices and a guesthouse have been rebuilt inside. Steps lead up to a colourful hilltop pavilion, where silk-clad aristocrats used to compose nature poetry with a philosophical twist while listening to birdsong and admiring the view of distant misty mountains.

The fortress is a reminder of the dreadful persecution of early Christians by the Confucian Joseon kings – hundreds were executed here during the 1860s. The small prison has been rebuilt, complete with whipping frames, and outside is a gallows tree from whose branches the converts were tied by the hair to be tortured or killed.

Buses (W2400, 50 minutes, every 20 minutes) run from Haemi to Taean. Other buses run via Hongseong and Gongju to Daejeon (W10,900, 3½ hours, every 30 minutes).

CHEONAN 천안

pop 403,000

Cheonan is the gateway to a top museum, the Independence Hall of Korea, 14km east of the city.

Independence Hall of Korea 독립기념관

This major **museum** (☎ 560 0114; www.independence .or.kr; adult/youth/child W2000/1100/700; ◷ 9.30am-6pm Tue-Sun Mar-Oct, 9.30am-5pm Tue-Sun Nov-Feb) shines a light on Korea's plucky but doomed fight for independence against Japanese colonialism from the 1870s to 1945. Built on a grand scale with expansive plazas, 50m-high monuments, fountains and 800 Korean flags, it enjoys a parklike setting.

The seven exhibition halls contain some English-language descriptions and use historical photos, scale models, waxworks and relics to give a very detailed account of the pro-independence groups. They kept the spirit of a Korean identity flickering even during the darkest days of colonial oppression. But don't expect anything much on the numerous Korean collaborators or on the American and allied contribution to Korean independence.

Getting There & Away

Take subway Line 1 to Cheonan (W2300, 2½ hours, every 15 minutes) from Seoul (or Suwon). Turn left at the ticket barrier and left again to East Square. Straight ahead is the **tourist information centre** (☎ 521 2038).Turn right for the bus stop, where city buses (W900, 20 minutes, every 10 minutes), such as buses 413 and 490, run to the museum. They stop on the main road, a 15-minute walk from the exhibition halls. A taxi costs W15,000.

Cheonan intercity bus terminal is in the basement of Galleria department store, 150m from the express bus terminal, and is a W2500 taxi ride north of Cheonan train station. Bus destinations include Seoul (W4200, one hour, every 20 minutes); Daejeon (W3600, one hour, every 15 minutes); and Gongju (W3900, one hour, every 20 minutes).

Chungcheongbuk-do
충청북도

Chungbuk is the only province that has no coastline, but it makes up for it by being the country's lake district. A two-hour ferry ride along Chungju Lake zips past attractive cliffs that inspired Joseon-era artists and poets. Lakeside, Cheongnamdae is a holiday villa used by Korean presidents that is open to the public for most of the year. Another lakeside attraction is the resort town of Danyang, within walking distance of a huge limestone cave and a bus trip away from a national park and the unique Gu·insa temple complex.

You can stroll round the attractive spa resort of Suanbo Hot Springs in a matter of minutes, but after a therapeutic dip and massage, you can savour local specialities such as rabbit, duck and pheasant meals in the restaurants that make up most of the town. Just a couple of kilometres down the road is Korea's most modest ski resort, which lures beginners who don't want a crowded ski-resort feel.

No less than three national parks line the province's southwest border with Gyeongsang-buk-do: Songnisan, famous for its giant Buddha statue; Sobaeksan, popular in late spring when the mountain azaleas paint the hillsides purple; and Woraksan, where rare but shy goral antelopes roam freely.

The province produces apples, peaches and chestnuts and provides a weekend escape for city folk from Seoul and Daejeon.

HIGHLIGHTS

- Board a fast ferry on **Chungju Lake** (p328) for Korea's most scenic waterway trip
- Tour the presidential holiday villa and gardens at **Cheongnamdae** (p327)
- Relax in lakeside **Danyang** (p340) and visit limestone caves, temples and mountain summits
- Soak in **Suanbo Hot Springs** (p338), savour pheasant meals, and hike or ski
- Safari through **Woraksan National Park** (p339) looking out for goral antelopes
- Explore **Songnisan National Park** (p328) and admire Beopjusa and its huge Buddha

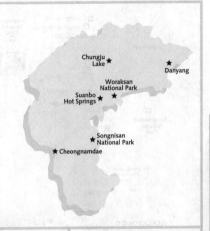

- TELEPHONE CODE: 043
- POPULATION: 1.5 MILLION
- AREA: 7432 SQ KM

History

The province was historically the southern boundary of the Goguryeo kingdom, and Suanbo Hot Springs has been providing therapeutic baths for a thousand years, but the province's main claim to historical fame is based on Heungdeoksa, a temple in Cheongju city that no longer exists, where the world's first book was printed using movable metal type (p325).

National & Provincial Parks

Don't miss the unique temple complex in the north of **Sobaeksan National Park** (p343) or the wonderful azalea blooms in May in the park's south. **Songnisan National Park** (p328) has a huge Buddha statue and peaks over 1000m,

while **Woraksan National Park** (p339) is home to a growing herd of goral antelopes.

Getting There & Around

The province is best reached and toured by bus, but don't miss the Chungju Lake boat trip.

CHEONGJU 청주

pop 579,000

Cheongju is the provincial capital and an education centre, but is easily confused with Chungju and Jeonju. It's the gateway to the presidential villa (Cheongnamdae) and Songnisan National Park. The city boasts some historical sites that include an easy-to-reach mountain fortress, as well as a popular pe-

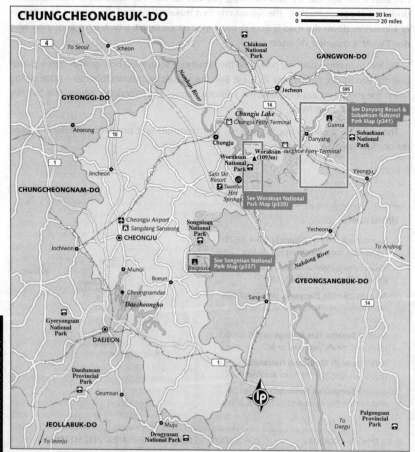

CHUNGCHEONGBUK-DO

destrianised shopping precinct and the lively Chungdae Jungmun student district.

Information

Hana Bank (Sajingno)
Post office (Seong·an·gil)
Shinhan Bank Near the express bus terminal.
Tourist information centre (☎ 233 8431; ♈ 8.30am-7pm) Outside the intercity bus terminal. Free internet access.

Sights

EARLY PRINTING MUSEUM 고인쇄박물관

A small but modern **museum** (☎ 269 0556; adult/youth/child W800/600/400; ♈ 9am-6pm Tue-Sun, 9am-5pm Nov-Feb) tells you everything about *Jikji*, a book of Buddhist sayings that is the oldest book in the world printed with movable metal type. Unfortunately the book is not here but in the National Library of France (it was purchased by a French official in 1853). The book was printed in 1377 at Heungdeoksa, a temple that used to stand to the right of the museum. Discipline was strict in those days – any mistake by a printer was punished by a flogging. On the left is **Uncheon Gong·won**, a small park with an artificial waterfall.

Take bus 831 from outside the express bus terminal or take any bus downtown, get off at the stadium stop and walk 15 minutes to the museum.

KOREAN CRAFT MUSEUM 한국공예관

Next to the Early Printing Museum, this **exhibition centre** (☎ 268 0255; admission free; ♈ 9am-7pm Tue-Sun) has three floors of imaginative modern ceramics and other craft by leading local artists.

HEUNGDEOK SEONGDANG
청주교회흥덕성당

This fortresslike **Catholic church** (Jijingno) incorporates many diverse elements in a unique design. Mass in English is held every Sunday at 5pm.

GOLDEN PAVILION 청 주종합운동장

The Daesun Jillihoe Buddhist sect (www.daesun.or.kr), founded by Gang Jeungsan (1871–1909), known as Sangje, has a striking five-storey golden pavilion on Sajikro, Cheongju's main street. Ask at the office and someone may be free to show you inside the pavilion, which contains an awesome golden statue of Sangje, with clouds and birds on his gown, that hardly fits inside. The rock garden outside is beautiful when the azaleas are in bloom.

YONGDUSAJI IRON FLAGPOLE
용두사지 철당간

Outside Cheongju department store is one of the oldest and tallest (13m) iron flag poles in Korea, made in AD 962 during the Goryeo dynasty. Originally 30 iron canisters high, it would have been placed outside a temple, where flags would have flown from it on special occasions such as Buddha's birthday.

JUNG·ANG PARK 중앙공원

A shady little historical park across the road from the flagpole contains pavilions, memorials, a 900-year-old tree and one of Heungseon Daewon·gun's anti-foreigner stone inscriptions that were erected throughout the country in the 1860s and 1870s. In those days Korea really was the Hermit Kingdom.

SANGDANG SANSEONG 상당 산성

This large mountain fortress is 4km northeast of Cheongju. Originally built in the 1590s and renovated in the 18th century, the walls stretch for 4.2km around wooded hillsides. Korea's many amazing mountain fortresses are an Asian treasure that should be more widely known. Burn calories and immerse yourself in the natural surroundings as you hike round this significant historical monument (1½ hours) before dining at an excellent country-style restaurant (p326).

Bus 862 (W850, 30 minutes, hourly) leaves from the stadium bus stop and goes all the way to the fortress. Buses 861 and 863 drop you 1km from the fortress.

Sleeping

The best motels are clustered around the bus terminals.

Plaza Motel (☎ 234 1400; r W30,000; ꊶ) Located off Gwagyeongno. Look for the castle turrets and alpine log-cabin entranceway in this clean and well-kept motel with rooms that include fancy headboards and a sofa. Hand the key to the jovial owners when you go out.

Sting Motel (☎ 235 6668; r W30,000; ꊶ 💻) This smart, high-rise castle motel, next door to Baekje Tourist Hotel, has light and airy rooms that are filled with facilities. The owner welcomes you with a smile. Rooms with a computer are W40,000.

CHEONGJU

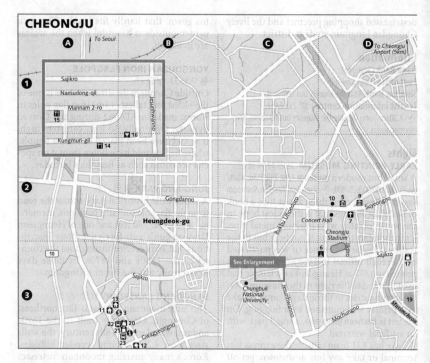

Baekje Tourist Hotel (☎ 236 7979; fax 236 0979; d/tw/ste W85,000/105,000/140,000; ☒ ☐) The ordinary rooms are uninspiring, but go for a suite for more space than nearby motels offer. Carpets need cleaning, but prices include breakfast and a computer in your room.

Eating & Entertainment
CHUNGDAE JUNGMUN

Restaurants and stalls in this entertainment zone outside Chungbuk University compete to offer the lowest prices. To visit Chungdae Jungmun, take any city bus (W850) to Sachang bus stop.

Gongpoui (Kungmuri-gil; meals W2500-4000; ☒ 10am-6am) A lively student hang-out that always provides a good deal, with self-serve greenery wraps and free *pajeon* (green-onion pancake) with the *samgyeopsal* (삼겹살; barbecued pork). Otherwise try *gochujang bulgogi* (고추장 불고기), which is pork, *ramyeon* (noodles) and sauce cooked in a foil tray – you mop up the sauce with a mixture of rice, lettuce and dried seaweed.

Yugane (Mannam 2-ro; meals W3000-6000; ☒ 9.30am-midnight) Another student cheapie that offers

simple *bokkeumbap* (볶음밥; fried rice) meals with chicken or seafood, cooked at your table in a big metal pan. Put in only half the sauce for a less spicy version. Self-serve coffee is free.

Pearl Jam (Kungmuri-gil; beer & whisky W4000; ☒ 6pm-late) This comfortable rock-music den hosts a local band, The Smokers, who play Western rock classics every Friday at 11pm. Saturday often features live music too.

SANGDANG SANSEONG

Sangdangjip (상당집; meals W5000-16,000) Opposite the bus stop, this restaurant makes its own tofu in a giant cauldron – try *dubujjim* (두부찜; steamed tofu) for something light, but the recommended meal is *hanbang ogolgye* (한방 오골계), locally sourced black chicken in a medicinal broth of bark, roots and cloves, and served with *bindaetteok* (mung bean pancake), rice and tasty side dishes.

Makgeolli (rice wine) is W1000 a bowl or W4000 a kettle. *Hanbang oribaeksuk* (한방 오리백숙; herbal duck soup) is also available. Buses (p325) run from the bus stop back to town until 9.50pm.

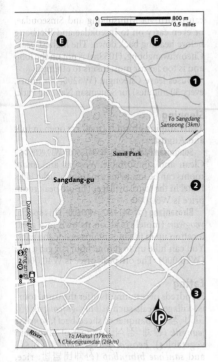

Shopping

Carrefour/Homever (Sajingno; ⏰ 10am-11pm), **Cheongju department store** (Seong-an-gil; ⏰ 10.30am-8pm) and the covered market are always buzzing with a cheerful crowd, as is the pedestrianised shopping street, Seong-an-gil.

Dream Plus (Fashion Ville) Next door to Lotte Mart, this high-rise fashion mall is packed with small stalls. A 24-hour sauna and spa is on the 3rd floor, a food court is on the 6th floor and cinemas are on the 8th floor.

Getting There & Away

AIR

Cheongju Airport has flights to Jejudo and China, with services to Japan in summer.

BUS

Departures from Cheongju express bus terminal include:

Destination	Price (W)	Duration	Frequency
Busan	14,200	4¼hr	9 daily
Daegu	10,000	2¾hr	hourly
Seoul	6500	1½hr	every 10min

Departures from the intercity terminal:

Destination	Price (W)	Duration	Frequency
Chuncheon	14,300	3½hr	hourly
Chungju	6400	1½hr	every 20min
Daejeon	3000	50min	every 15min
Danyang	12,500	3½hr	every 30min
Gyeongju	14,800	3hr	9 daily
Songnisan	6200	1¾hr	every 30min

CHEONGNAMDAE 청남대

The **holiday villa** (☎ 220 5677; http://cheongnamdae .com; adult/youth/child W5000/4000/3000; ⏰ 9am-6pm Tue-Sun) of South Korean presidents overlooks Daecheong Lake. It was built by President Chun Doo-hwan in 1983. The gardens and lakeside setting are beautiful, but the villa is surprisingly modest. President Chun enjoyed skating on the pond, while President Roh Tae-woo liked the five-hole golf course. Beef was served to all the employees whenever he had a good round. President Kim Young-sam disapproved of golf because of its association with corruption, and the golf course hasn't been used in recent years. President Kim Dae-jung planted the honeysuckle (the Korean word for it means 'overcoming hardship', which was his nickname) and built the thatched pavilion containing mementos from his hometown in Jeollanam-do. It's thanks to President Roh Moo-hyun that the residence was opened to the public in 2003. All of the villa and gardens are open to the public, and you can even peep into the presidential bedroom.

Getting There & Away

Take local bus 311 or 302 (W1250, 50 minutes, hourly) from outside Cheongju intercity bus terminal to Munui, 15km south of Cheongju. Walk out of Munui bus depot, turn left, and in a couple of minutes you reach the parking lot and ticket office for the shuttle buses (W2000 return, 15 minutes) to Cheongnamdae, which operate between 9am and 4.30pm.

SONGNISAN NATIONAL PARK
속리산국립공원

This **park** (☎ 542 5267; adult/youth/child W3800/1500/1200; ☼ 5am-8pm) covers one of central Korea's finest scenic areas with forested mountains and rocky granite outcrops. Its name means 'Remote from the Ordinary World Mountain', which refers to its famous temple Beopjusa. A **tourist information centre** (☎ 542 5267; ☼ 9am-6pm) is in the park's bus-terminal building.

The large temple complex of **Beopjusa** dates back to AD 553, but has often been rebuilt. **Dae·ungbojeon**, with its large golden Buddha statues, and **Palsangjeon**, a unique five-storeyed wooden pagoda, are outstanding features. The huge, 33m **bronze standing Buddha** weighs 160 tonnes and was completed in 1990 at a cost of US$4 million. **Ancient relics** include stone lanterns, an elegant Unified Shilla seated Buddha hewn out of rock, a massive bell and a giant iron cauldron, cast in AD 720, that was used to cook rice for the hundreds of monks who once lived at the temple.

Beyond the temple, **hiking trails** extend up to a series of 1000m-high peaks. A popular hike is the relatively easy climb up **Manjangdae** (1033m); back in 1464 King Sejo was carried up to the top in a palanquin. Using your own two feet, it's three hours up and two hours down. If you still have the energy, at the top you

can return via Munsubong and Sinseondae, or even carry on to Ipseokdae and Birobong before heading back down. The highest peak, Cheonhwangbong, (1058m) is not on the loop and is too far for most hikers to attempt.

Buses leave Cheongju (W6200, 1¾ hours, every 30 minutes) for Songnisan National Park.

Sleeping

Two camping grounds (free) are open in July and August.

Songnisan Park Hotel (☎ 542 3900; r W39,000; ☒) Clean and comfortable Western and *ondol* rooms can be found here in front of Lake Hills Hotel in the tourist village. The off-peak room price is W30,000.

Birosanjang (☎ 543 4782; r W60,000) This special *yeogwan* (motel) is all on its own in a great location up in the mountains inside the park. You can hike up to it (one hour) or get a taxi (W10,000). The off-peak price is W40,000.

Eating

Hundreds of restaurants offer the usual tourist-village meals such as *bulgogi jeongsik* (불고기 정식; banquet of sliced beef); *sanchae jeongsik* (산채 정식; banquet of mountain vegetables), *beoseot jeongsik* (버섯 정식) and *sanchae bibimbap* (산채비빔밥; rice, egg, meat and mountain vegetables). Snacks include rice crackers and pizza-sized slabs of toffee, sesame and nuts, but dentist bills could result. *Dongdongju* (rice wine) flavoured with red dates is served from big pots.

CHUNGJU 충주
pop 220,000

Chungju (www.chungju.chungbuk.kr) is the gateway to the Chungjuho (Chungju Lake) ferries, Woraksan National Park and Suanbo Hot Springs. Every autumn the World Martial Arts Festival (p337) hits town.

A **tourist information centre** (☎ 850 7329; ☼ 9am-6pm) is located inside the bus terminal.

Chungju Lake 충주호

The two-hour, 52km **boat ride** (☎ 851 5771; www .chungjuho.com; adult/child under 12 W18,000/9000) along the large artificial lake from Danyang to Chungju (or vice versa) is a highlight, with constantly changing scenery that on misty days looks like a sequence of Joseon-era landscape paintings.

(Continued on page 337)